Mending the Flag, Healing The World

Politics can be done differently, done better!

21/09/19

Andy

ANDY BILIK

tellwell 🪶

Tellwell Talent
www.tellwell.ca

ISBN
978-0-2288-1138-1 (Paperback)
978-0-2288-1139-8 (eBook)

For All the Children, and for Donna.

Acknowledgements

First and foremost, I would like to thank my brother, Alex, for pushing me to write this book. Around May 2017, I told Alex about some ideas I had to make things better for all of us in Canada. He said it sounded like a story that needed to be told. Since these ideas had been on my mind for about three years, I finally found the motivation to put pen to paper.

I would also like to thank my beautiful fiancé, Donna, who has been incredibly supportive and encouraging during the process of writing this book. Not only has she understood how I felt compelled to write this book, she has put up with me during my intermittent bouts of preoccupation with this project. Of course, my episodic distractions have typically occurred while Donna herself has been working hard almost every evening during the week. Fortunately, we have still been able to spend the time together that we needed to. As someone who attends church along with her daughter who has Williams Syndrome, I have long marvelled at Donna's solid work ethic: something she likely inherited from her parents. She is a wonderful spirit and has helped me to become a better person.

The moral support my parents gave me as I wrote this book deserves acknowledgement too. They had a difficult life abroad, but they are incredibly resilient; as a result, they have succeeded here in Canada. They purchased a home, raised my brother and me the best way they knew how, and contributed a lot more to this country than they ever asked of it. As a crane operator, my father had a hand in Toronto construction projects ranging from the depths of the subway system to the heights of the CN Tower. He should be a lot prouder of himself than he is.

I am also grateful to my friends. Although they did not have a direct impact on my writing this book, they have always been there for me. So, too, has the staff at the Sheraton Centre in Toronto and Coffee Culture in Whitby, where I have spent countless hours writing. Last, but not least, I would like to thank the good folks at Tellwell Publishing for making my vision for this book become a reality. I am particularly grateful to Jennifer, Caitlin, Von, and Ann Marie (what a fantastic editor) who have been great to deal with.

Jesus replied, "To be sure, Elijah comes and will restore all things."

—Matthew 17:11 (NIV)

TABLE OF CONTENTS

Introduction

RIGHT OR WRONG? Do you know the difference? The majority of us know what is right and wrong for ourselves as individuals. Most of us were raised well and have since let our own free will and life experiences guide us. However, I am wondering if many of you share a feeling with me, which often surfaces and manifests into a belief, that something is terribly wrong—no, strike that. Something is not terribly wrong, it is desperately wrong. And it has nothing to do with us as individuals, even considering our imperfections, and despite any and all life challenges we have had to, or will, face.

But just what is it that is so desperately wrong? The bonds that unite us as Canadians are dissolving. Our collective values, and the institutions we have created based on those values, form the 'glue' that holds Canada together. Therefore, when the government institutions that unite our country and reflect our collective values come unhinged, it significantly hampers us from reaching our potential: individually and collectively. Alarming? Absolutely. Surprised? You should not be …

After all, a recent survey of more than 33,000 people from 28 countries found that Canada ranked only ninth for average trust in institutions, including government. This survey, the 2018 Edelman Trust Barometer, conducted in the fall of 2017, determined that countries with a 'trust' index of 1–49 have a 'distrust' of institutions. While Canada's result of 49 was not the worst, the score indicates we do indeed feel something is wrong with our institutions.

Unsurprisingly, as I learned reading about this survey in a *Vancouver Sun* article, "false information or 'fake news' being used as a weapon is a concern for 65 per cent of Canadians, while the U.S. sits with Russia and China in the 71 to 75 per cent of people concerned . . . [and] Canadians' trust in journalists has risen 17 per cent since last year, with 43 per cent of respondents rating them as 'very/extremely credible.' "[1]

That reminds me, we should thank professional and reputable journalists, those honest folks with a solid track record in accurate and investigative news reporting. Such journalists are invaluable in informing us of what is really happening here in Canada and elsewhere. And Canadians agree. The Edelman survey advises: "Canadians have a renewed appetite for credible, authoritative voices."[2]

This book, in no small part, is a result of the efforts of credible journalists, who often reveal disturbing trends adversely impacting Canadians' quality of life. I suspect the efforts of journalists working in other democracies around the world would reveal similar disturbing trends in their own respective countries—perhaps especially in America, currently presided over by its controversial leader, Donald Trump.

I love my country: this heretofore ill-defined and diverse land known as Canada. It was not always the case, that I loved it so. When I graduated from university in the early 1990s, a fairly long and deep recession began to grip our nation. I found it difficult to obtain work of any kind and began to resent my country. Over time, during which I went abroad, where I did find work, and completed graduate school, which bought me some additional time to ride out the recession, I learned my resentment was ill-founded. I realized I bore some responsibility for the predicament I had found myself in the 1990s. We all mature over time and are refined by our personal experiences. And if we are curious and read a lot to satisfy that curiosity, this too can change our perspective: so, too, does considerable travel around the world. When we experience different and challenging environments, and bear witness to poverty, we gain a newfound respect for a blessed country such as Canada.

All the same, I have come to gradually understand, through my experiences both here, in Canada, and around the world, that we are increasingly facing significant problems that are not being resolved by governments. There seems to be a growing sense of helplessness around the world that things are not working as they should. Despite there being so many democratic regimes, they are not working the way we want them to for everyone's benefit. There appear to be more and more haves and have-nots and less in-betweens, mounting scandals, threats to the environment, giant waves of displaced people, climate change, conflicts and so on.

Governments seem overwhelmed and stumbling to get anything done, often crippled by internecine political infighting and the seemingly complex issues of the day. As political leaders come and go with the government of the day, nothing seems to change except the frustration and apathy of a public craving real leadership and problem solving. I firmly believe positive change can begin here in Canada. We can formulate the solutions so desperately needed both in our own country and around the world.

To say Canada is a land of plenty would be a gross understatement, owing not only to its massive expanse containing a wealth of beauty and resources, but also to its hugely talented and vibrant people. Canadians hail from all parts of the world. We reflect Earth's collective hopes and humanity in one colourful, aspiring place. Our place, Canada, is a collage of potential as varied in its hues of latent possibility and creativity as the raw landscape of the country itself—so wonderfully revealed in the famous paintings of the Group of Seven artists.

Of course, our centre, or rather those who first had their roots firmly planted here, are the Indigenous Peoples of Canada—themselves, a widely diverse group. Though much time has passed since 1867, when Canada became a country, they were here first. They suffered much at European hands. They deserve our respect, recognition and reasonable redress, for as the renowned early Canadian settler and author Susanna Moodie wrote, "It is a melancholy truth, and deeply to be lamented, that the vicinity of European settlers has always produced a very demoralising effect upon the Indians."[3]

We still have much to learn from the Indigenous Peoples. As you will see, this learning is important. It can paradoxically serve to unite Canadians of all walks of life, reflecting a shared identity. Perhaps ironically, it can even create a sense of nationhood in a world increasingly divided. I know you are probably thinking that many First Peoples do not identify as Canadians, and who am I to believe they, or even others, may. Absolutely true! However, despite all of our differences, we are all people at the end of the day who should love one another.

This book has been a journey of self-discovery for me. I believe it can be for you, too, regardless of your background (gender, race, religion, place of birth, etc.). Still, you should realize the importance of this book lies not in my attempt to inform you of our shared core Canadian identity, but of how that identity can help us solve significant and growing problems in this country in a meaningful, clear and transparent way. In this regard, we have a huge opportunity as Canadians to implement solutions to problems within our borders that are often similar to those problems found by people living in other democracies around the world, such as the United States and the United Kingdom.

Repairing the institutions that unite us and reflect our values is not a monumental task. In fact Canada can shine as a beacon for all democracies and international institutions plagued by the same problems. However, before we get into all the common problems we Canadians face, and the simple solutions that need to be implemented so we can productively move forward, we should understand who we are. Are you a member of Canada's First Nations or Indigenous Peoples, a post-World War II immigrant who passed through the gates of Pier 21 in Halifax? Perhaps you are a much more recent immigrant, fleeing the brutal Syrian conflict or struggles in war torn parts of Africa. You may be a woman or a man who has dreams of building a better life. Maybe you are fleeing alone from the sex trafficking trade, religious persecution, or child labour. Perhaps you are an investor looking to make an immediate contribution to Canada while bettering your own life and those around you. Regardless of your race, religion, gender, education, wealth/socioeconomic status, you are in Canada, and whether you were consciously aware of it as a citizen or not, we have a number of shared values.

It is time for Canadians to lead by example. It is time for Canada to invoke a new narrative, perhaps even a new slogan. We need to champion something different. Our friends to the south such as Barack Obama, stated, "Yes We Can" in the 2008 United States presidential campaign. Donald Trump's 2016 motto, "Make America Great Again," was possibly borrowed from Ronald Reagan's 1980 presidential campaign championing, "Let's Make America Great." Canadians are a practical people that tamed a huge wilderness. It is time we punched above our weight. It is time we showed ourselves and other democracies around the world "how" to be great again! That is what Susie and Frank on Main Street want to know. They aren't stupid, and they are probably tired of empty slogans without a clear roadmap to success.

We have to start getting things right and that means making good decisions. That is the fundamental challenge of our time. The price is too high, as you will see, to do nothing here in Canada to make things better, never mind around an increasingly polarized and at-risk world. We need to start improving the lives of Canadians. We need to show ourselves and the world that things can and will be a lot better. It is time to stop playing the blame game and to get to work. It is time to mend the flag to heal the world. Read on to see exactly how.

Chapter 1
Who am I?

Some people come in your life as blessings. Some come in your life as lessons.

—Mother Teresa

I am what I am. But I am nothing without the rest of you, which forms the whole. For your amusement, dear reader, I may as well tell you some things about me, your author. Not unlike many of you, I am a simple person with humble roots as the child of migrants to Canada. Interestingly I ended up, like the main character in *Forrest Gump*, to be the kind of person who observed unusual events and places due to happenstance or fate. But I will tell you a lot more involving how that came to pass later on.

My parents faced the horrors of World War II. As a child, my father witnessed people hanging from telephone poles in a way that reminded him of Christ's own tribulations, striking fear into all who bore witness to this evil. He also witnessed the strafing of partisan forces (our allies, likely) from enemy aircraft, although for children like my dad, it was often difficult to know who the enemy exactly was. Father observed even more death around him as he foraged through garbage to find something to eat, while fleeing his burning city—Kiev, the capitol of Ukraine—with his mother and grandmother to some unknown destination, anywhere that bore a semblance of safety. In this regard his experience was quite similar to the Syrian diaspora of refugees, currently fleeing for their lives from a homeland ravaged by war.

What my dad, Henry, witnessed as he fled his home, or what he thought of as home at the tender age of nine, was not nearly as bad as what he experienced at an even younger age. You see, despite respecting Ukrainians and other nationalities, my dad always considered himself Polish. This was mainly because his own parents had Polish roots and were Catholic. Historically, the borders of many countries such as Poland and Ukraine changed over the years. I never knew much about Poland when I was growing up, except that some former Catholic religious leader, named Pope John Paul II, came from there. Unfortunately, the grandfather I never knew—Basil, my dad's own father—was a victim of Joseph Stalin's Great Purge.

Academics, for the historical record, describe the Great Purge as a campaign of political terror and bloody oppression led by Stalin in the late 1930s. It is credibly estimated that about 750,000 people were executed during the Great Purge.[1] The purpose of this diabolical initiative was to eradicate any potential opponents of the dictator, including political and government leaders, the educated classes, military officers, and anyone else who might have been perceived as a threat.

For my dad, who was only about five years old at the time, the Purge began with a sharp and foreboding knock at the door of his family's apartment on Khreshchatyk Street in Kiev, in 1937. An officer of the NKVD (People's Commissariat for Internal Affairs)—forerunner to the infamous KGB (Committee for State Security)—had come to take his own father away. Grandfather Basil, a former Polish military officer, was either taken to be summarily shot or to be shipped off to one of the far-flung labour camps, in what Alexander Solzhenitsyn aptly and infamously called the Gulag Archipelago. How revealing when Solzhenitsyn wrote:

And everything which is by now comprised in the traditional, even literary, image of an arrest will pile up and take shape, not in your own disordered memory, but in what your family and your neighbors in your apartment remember: the sharp nighttime ring or rude knock at the door. [2]

Experts estimate that over a million people were sent to the Gulags. It would be a gross understatement to think that this trauma must have impacted my own father's perspective on life in many ways. Dad's perspective was further influenced by his birth on Ukrainian soil in 1932. Many well-reputed historians, such as Robert Conquest, have deemed the period of 1932 to 1933 "as a terror-famine inflicted on the collectivized peasants of the Ukraine." The Holodomor (death by hunger, in Ukrainian), "by the methods of setting for them grain quotas far above the possible, removing every handful of food, and preventing help from the outside . . . from reaching the starving," killed millions. [3]

Conquest's well-respected work, *The Harvest of Sorrow*, estimates that by the time Stalin "crushed" both "the peasantry of the USSR as a whole, and the Ukrainian nation," the death toll surpassed even the Holocaust perpetrated by Nazi Germany during World War II. Of Ukraine's "forty million inhabitants . . . [a] quarter of the rural population, men, women and children, lay dead or dying, the rest in various stages of debilitation."[4]

Pope Francis remembered the Holodomor, and on November 25, 2018, called it "a terrible famine instigated by the Soviet regime which caused millions of people to die." Of note, "the Vatican City State is one of 16 countries to consider Holodomor an act of genocide carried out by the Soviet government."[5] As I write this, I am beginning to understand why my dad always had a good appetite and placed emphasis on healthy food in our home being available at all times, regardless of how many mortgages were on that home. "When you're cold, don't expect sympathy from someone who's warm," quipped Solzhenitsyn in another of his works.[6]

Adding to my dad's burden of grief, in 1941, where he was about nine years old, he experienced yet another foreboding blow. It came in the form of another knock at the door: a prelude yet again to Henry's long escape to that still to be found sanctuary from what was likely Hell on Earth. This time the hand that came knocking was perfunctorily and dutifully German in nature. It was an emissary of Hitler's Third Reich in the form of a Nazi soldier, who forcibly proceeded to remove my father's only two siblings, his older brothers, from the apartment. Walter and Roman were brothers my dad would never come to know. They, along with countless others the Reich considered *Ostarbeiters* (foreign slave workers), were taken from their homes and forced into slave labour in Germany.

It was shortly thereafter that Henry, as a child, fled with his mother and grandmother from the only home he had ever known, soon watching the entire city of Kiev burn, as it had been set aflame by yet another malevolent invader of Europe's breadbasket.

Years later, around 1993 to 1994, when at the Minsk Linguistics University in Belarus as an exchange student and instructor from the University of Western Ontario (UWO), I searched for my missing relatives. Armed with an obscure letter from Lviv, Ukraine, supposedly written by one of my missing uncles in the early 1950s, and which my kind undergraduate Russian history professor at Trent University had translated for me into English, I crossed into Ukraine to find them. This was no simple task.

Firstly, it proved impossible to obtain a travel visa from the Ukrainian embassy in Minsk, owing to the bizarre fact that it repeatedly kept its doors locked to the public from one weekday to the next during normal business hours. Secondly, upon travelling by *Elektrichka*, a local train, from Minsk to the town of Baranavichy, near the Ukrainian border on the Byelorussian side, it also proved impossible to obtain a ticket for a train going to Lviv, in western

Ukraine. Apparently, and notwithstanding the lack of any other people in the train station, the tickets were sold out for the next train headed to Lviv.

Persistence being the mother of invention as it were, and since, as my high school Canadian history teacher, David Morrison, aptly stated upon sizing me up: "A little rebellion can be a good thing." (I am not sure if he was referring to the British Conquest of 1760 or my teenage character.) I came to understand the three options I faced: return to Minsk; cross on foot into Ukraine, near the Pripyat marshes and where the Chernobyl nuclear plant exploded less than ten years earlier; or pay the ticket-booth officer US $10 to board the train without a real ticket.

As you may have guessed, and to the shock of my parents when they learned of my penchant to take risks, I chose the last option. If you know much about post-Soviet society in the years immediately following the fall of the Berlin wall and dissolution of the USSR, you may have also guessed the train was almost empty when I boarded it. Apparently, the tickets being sold out was a bit of fake news given to both me and BBC, the nickname of my Byelorussian translator. (While I have been known to take risks at times, I also like to be prepared.)

I learned from the train conductor, as well as the two ladies of dubious repute partying with him in his cabin, Ukrainian border security guards would be stopping the train around midnight as it entered their country, to check passports and travel visas. This did seem to be a scary proposition in terms of what unknown punishment might be facing BBC and me if we were caught without proper travel documents.

With a positive attitude, largely fortified by two tumblers of vodka and another US $10 bank note for our patriotic conductor, BBC and I agreed to seek asylum in the conductor's own compartment. He assured us the border guards never checked that compartment. This proved to be correct information, despite also being an exercise in youthful foolish decision-making, and we made it to the Lviv train station a few hours later. To make a long and unfortunate story short, and as verified by the local municipal archives and Polish genealogical society (I believe that was the type of office we also visited), the address from which my missing uncles wrote from, never existed. Although certain street names had changed, reflective of shifting political power and what successive leaderships deemed as appropriate to erase from collective memory and culture, knowledgeable sources confirmed there never had been a Lingaura Street in Lviv, Lvov, or Lwow—as the city had been rebranded over the years.

Therefore, and as my previous professor at Trent University duly warned me, the obscure letter my uncles had sent to my grandmother in America so many years ago, was likely a rouse. It was the same rouse or wicked game inflicted by Stalin's henchmen on those living in the West who had family members still living in the former Soviet Union after World War II. In the case of former slave labourers, such as my uncles, or even POWs who had fought for the Russian motherland, Stalin's paranoia was such that they were all enemies of the people: their crime being that even living meagrely in involuntary servitude to, or as prisoner of, the Third Reich, they had been exposed to the West and its corrupt ways. By Stalin's thinking, anyone living outside the fold of his supposed communist utopia, as impoverished, barbaric and totalitarian as it was, must have been an enemy of the people. By extension, and for whatever twisted purpose it served Stalin's police state, any relatives of enemies of the people living abroad needed to be convinced to return to the USSR where everyone supposedly lived in paradise.

Luring such people back to Soviet territory after the war likely served at least two purposes. First, the propaganda—that post-war Soviet society was a wonderful place to live—would seem more plausible if people wanted to return to their families in the USSR rather than flee its borders. Second, anyone who knew what life in the USSR was really like could potentially work against the party from without. If they lured them back, they could be summarily shot or shipped off to one of the vast seas of gulags, just as their loved ones had been before them.

The letter writers, masquerading as loved ones, imploring expatriates to return home, were probably members of the state security apparatus. Of course, during the Cold War, Russia, under communist rule and largely influenced by the KGB and its predecessor organizations, had always excelled at masquerading. Its leadership continually excels today at disingenuously creating situations to 'deflect,' sowing division amongst others and confusing perceived opponents, all the while camouflaging its real goals and intentions. Then again, so do some leaders in the West; the difference is Russia has historically needed strong-armed leadership, be it under Czarist rule or that of Stalin and others.

Sadly, given the West's failure to do a better job of nurturing the seeds of democracy to grow worldwide after the collapse of the USSR, and the ensuing chaos, we can only conjecture what Russia's current objectives are under Putin. Certainly, when it annexed the Crimean Peninsula just a few years ago, Russia demonstrated that it wants to interfere yet again in Ukraine, adding to its troubled and tumultuous history. But I digress.

Upon learning the letter from my real uncles to their mother in America, where my grandmother and her own mother had settled, was probably a ploy, I checked into a rather basic hotel for one US dollar and BBC went his own way. I had the entire night to mull over how I would get back to Minsk, still without a visa. Fortunately, the next morning I was able to purchase a train ticket. However, without the assistance of an engaging conductor, there existed the strong possibility that I would face some difficulties at the border this time, trying to again get past the border guards. Improvisation seemed to be necessary. I cannot call it the foolhardiness of youth after all, when, as you can imagine, I was compelled to look for my missing relatives. Improvisation came in the form of desperately praying the guards would not check the washroom on the train where I intended to seek refuge and relieve myself of any panic or unforeseen physiological responses. Problematically, the bottom of the washroom door had several vents that would have made it easy for the guards to see my boots. A quick-thinking decision to stand on the toilet, together with blind luck, enabled me to be spirited back to Minsk without facing arrest like my grandfather did. If only he had been so lucky.

And my own father, in his youth, could only dream of far-flung places like Canada, where the rule of law, healthcare, personal safety, opportunity and democracy were better. The United States, despite all its current political malaise and challenges facing its machinery of government and collective values (I have been a student and teacher of American history), has typically been a steadfast ally and friend to Canada, as well as democracy. It too became a friend for my dad, when he, his mother and grandmother finally found sanctuary in the American zone of occupation in postwar Austria. It was there that my dad, in his later teens, on an American military base, ended up driving a US colonel around in a jeep and appreciating Western values. After all, the United States Forces in Austria (USFA) was "charged with the mission of re-establishing a free, independent and democratic Austria, possessing a sound economy capable of ensuring an adequate standard of living."[7]

Ultimately, while dad's mom and grandmother worked in the mess hall on the US base, making soup and such to feed the troops, the good colonel arranged for my dad to learn the construction trade. As dispossessed people with no desire to be repatriated to a totalitarian state, my dad, and what was left of his family, needed to find a home more permanent than the American base in Austria. The US was willing to take them, but with the outbreak of the Korean War in 1950, and his mother and grandmother imploring him not to be involved in yet more war, Dad agreed to stay behind in Austria to complete his tradesman's education. The last of his relatives then headed for Chicago as Dad, again, experienced loss.

A year or so later, but before the Korean War ended, my dad filed paperwork to go to Canada. Then, at the still young age of 22, although having had to grow up fast, Father boarded a ship, for which the Catholic Church had paid his passage, and traveled toward the unknown, like so many others before and after him. He had a mere five dollars in his pocket, hardly spoke English, and was entirely alone. It was no small wonder then, that despite not really having a penchant for alcohol, he drank a bit too much on board the ship, later and guiltily admitting to me that he had tossed a deck chair unceremoniously into the sea. Thankfully nobody had been sitting in it!

Like Hurricane Hazel, Henry landed in 1954. He arrived at Nova Scotia's port city of Halifax, passing through Pier 21, and finally being deposited in Hamilton, Ontario, by train. Not being one inclined to ever go on the dole, my dad looked up some old acquaintances he met in Austria, whom had also immigrated to Canada. They helped him find a place to live and he spent some time in Kitchener, Ontario.

Dad worked a number of odd jobs right away. He picked weeds, laboured for bricklayers, sold sausages and did other work to get by without asking for any financial help from Canada. A little while later he caught a break, obtaining a job as a crane operator in the construction industry. That was great since he had trained to do exactly that abroad, and now he would do so for the rest of his working life here in Canada, putting food on the table for me and the rest of our family, as well as paying his fair share of taxes to the government.

I believe my dad, in his later years, always felt a bit small or somewhat embarrassed because he spoke with a little bit of an accent, was 'blue collar' and did not possess much of a formal education. At the same time, I know now as I write these pages, that my father has accomplished much more than most anyone could, surviving tragedy and then going on to build something out of almost nothing. I also know that he embodies most of what Canada stands for—a place where hardworking people, from all kinds of backgrounds, including those backgrounds involving much hardship, can collectively build something good, each making a positive contribution that, inevitably, exceeds the sum total of the entire population's efforts. Dad always possessed that determined spirit of nation building. I should have told my father this a lot sooner.

My dad met my mother around 1961 through a mutual acquaintance. From my perspective, one of the main things they have in common, or at least still do after more than 50 years of marriage, is a tragic upbringing and a history of loss born of World War II. My mother had the misfortune of being born in 1941, in what was considered the Sudetenland, the area of Czechoslovakia that Hitler had invaded in 1938. With one of her parents being Czech, the other German, she had the further misfortune, in late 1945, of also being considered an enemy of the people—if a four-year-old can really be deemed such.

A lesser known fact of history is that history often operates according to what the great philosopher Voltaire once whimsically stated: "History is nothing but a pack of tricks that we play upon the dead." Another lesser known fact is that the victors of war, even when justified, cannot always claim to possess a higher moral ground in their perception of what is right versus what is wrong. For example, shortly after VE (Victory in Europe) Day on May 8, 1945, and the supposed cessation of hostilities, under what is commonly referred to as the Beneš Decrees, some 2.5 million Sudeten Germans and more than half a million ethnic Germans were expelled from Czechoslovakia. The expulsion is considered ethnic cleansing by a number of historians and legal scholars. "Even Czech historians say some 19,000 died in the process, 6,000 violently. Innocent Germans were randomly scalped or shot. Countless women were raped."[8]

For my four-year-old mother, expulsion, in practical terms, meant the loss of the home she knew in Czechoslovakia and the beginning of a new life in war-torn Germany, a foreign land to her. Of course, you can keep going back in time, peeling the onion so to speak, to see that borders have not been immutable, with governments and nation states coming and going like tides ebb and flow. Any innocent victims, subjected to the vagaries of these forces, have had to make do as best as possible.

Indeed, the maps of the world looked much different even before World War I, never mind after the global conflagration that ensued 20 or so years later. "Historians say many of the border changes—agreed upon after the war, were made for political rather than economic reasons, creating new problems, whose impact can be felt even today." Further, "after four years of carnage and more than 16 million dead soldiers and civilians, three empires that had lasted for centuries—Austro-Hungarian, Russian and Ottoman—gradually ceased to exist and many new nations emerged," says Mike Heffernan, professor of historical geography at the University of Nottingham.[9] Putting all of this into additional perspective, Margaret MacMillan, professor of international history at Oxford University opined:

> Suddenly people throughout the Middle East and the center of Europe found themselves living in a world where they didn't know what country they belonged to; it wasn't quite clear what the borders of those countries would be; a whole lot of small wars were breaking out between different national movements trying to grab territory, and so it was in fact a very difficult time for people.[10]

People experiencing difficult times seems to be a constant throughout the world's tumultuous history, with technology appearing to change much faster than people themselves. The challenging times ensuing after yet more border changes in the wake of World War II, revealed themselves to my mother, Christine, when her parents' marriage ended in a bitter divorce. She endured the hardships of living in a German orphanage for a few years, with even the nuns at the time being well schooled in dishing out cruelty. Ultimately, through upheaval, the division of lands and reconstitution of national identities usually translates into changes in family relationships, with devilishly spirited characters all too pleased at the entire process. There were more challenges for my mother ahead, just as there were for my father on his own path. However, she too reached out to Canada, also emigrating alone in 1961 and meeting my father shortly thereafter. My parents married in 1964, first settling in Guildwood, just a few train stops east of Toronto, Ontario.

I have an older brother, Alex, born in 1965. He is an awesome fellow, being both a mentor and a friend. As now, he was always there in a pinch, except when he wanted to barter for my portion of food at the dinner table. He must have inherited my father's larger-than-life appetite to devour any and all manner of sustenance confronting him. Gluttony can be a sin, but it is forgivable for sure. Born one morning during a snowstorm on the 333rd day of 1968, a leap year with 33 days remaining on my birthday, I am about three-and-a-half years younger than Alex. Guildwood was a predominantly white Anglo-Saxon neighbourhood in the late 1960s and early 1970s, with a flourishing artists' community radiating around the Guild Inn and its expansive gardens and woods. When my parents bought a house there soon after getting married, the area was sparsely populated and considered a suburb of Toronto.

In those days, there seemed to be a greater sense of community and purpose, reflective of Canada's generally strong democratic institutions, fit for the times. A stronger sense of democracy shared by Canadians just 15 or so years after the war may have also existed. You could leave your home or vehicle unlocked back then without much fear. Immigration continued apace as did the baby boom. At times our family bore the brunt of some racist comments, and so too did many Italians and other strangers from Europe—the Italians were 'Wops,' the Poles were 'Polacks,' etc., regardless of being fairly white-skinned. And since I learned from other kids that our family spoke 'horse-language,' whatever that is, English was always spoken at home and Alex and I never mastered any other languages growing up. However, we mastered the use of our fists to settle some neighbourhood disputes with a few resident bullies. Generally, I gave as good as I got, but grew more insular because of it.

On balance, looking back and despite some of the racism our family faced, it appeared to be a period of confidence and expansion for the country. Major construction projects appeared successively, providing my father with ample work. We were not wealthy by Canadian standards. However, having grown up in difficult times, I imagine my parents considered themselves well-off in Canada indeed. My mom worked locally for a brief period before deciding, largely out of necessity, to be a stay-at-home mom. This was customary at the time and Mother did not have any relatives to help with child rearing. To save money, she often would cut my brother's and my hair, recycle bits of soap, and ensure any leftover food, or clothing Alex grew out of, never went to waste. She rarely spent money on herself, and, since Father often worked six days a week, leaving the house around six in the morning and returning about seven each night, she did all the yard work and housework when we kids were small. Owing to my dad's general absence and the family's spending priorities, Alex and I never participated in extracurricular activities or went on a holiday outside of Ontario. But boy did we eat like kings!

Mom was an excellent, albeit almost too meticulous cook. Everything was homemade, rarely with any ingredients emanating from a tin can. Except during the winter months, every Sunday dinner consisted of the best cuts of steak available at the butcher's shop, fresh vegetables and giant baked potatoes overflowing with sour cream and green onions or chives. The desserts were also super-sized and delicious. As for the Sunday dinners in winter, there were always massive pot roasts, barely able to fit in the pot destined for the oven, with all the trimmings. Even during the week, the meals were huge and tasty. Holidays like Christmas, New Year's, etc., were absolute feasts! To this day, despite now being generally confined to a nursing home and suffering from the debilitating effects of Parkinson's, my dad's healthy appetite remains a constant reminder to me of his high regard for plentiful and hearty food. And who could blame him. As a kid born during Stalin's Terror-Famine and later foraging for food amidst garbage cans during the war, he knows what an empty stomach feels like.

Yet he also knows what it feels like to build something tangible, something that produces positive results for Canadians. Father was never a builder of institutions in the philosophical or theoretical sense, like America's Thomas Jefferson or James Madison, but he certainly was a builder of Canada in other ways. His contribution in building the infrastructure of our country remains today—the Toronto subway system, the CN Tower, and a myriad of unseen sewer and water mains supporting the foundation of many of our towns and cities. He was always of a practical bent and God knows we could use more builders like him today as our ageing infrastructure crumbles beneath the façade of greatness.

In the little spare time he did have, father taught my brother and I how to use a lot of different tools; how to change car axles and water pumps; how to bleed brakes; and how to swap an engine in my brother's first car, a VW Rabbit. We even learned how to use torches and strip cars (legally of course) for spare parts when we gave up our motorcycles for four-wheeled transportation. Dad was not so much book smart as street wise and mechanically inclined. He taught us how to think practically, how to play chess and cards, and somehow in between all that, managed to take us fishing a couple of times—although mom was at the campsite a lot more. Both my parents were honest and good citizens, but had some difficulty, in their own way, dealing with the ghosts of their past. That, in retrospect, is entirely understandable.

In 1978, we moved from our small bungalow in Guildwood to a larger home in the countryside, in a small village in Innisfil. The nearest large town was Barrie, Ontario, which has grown considerably since then. After graduating from a small elementary school in Innisfil, I attended high school in Barrie. Though fairly shy, I can tell you there was no greater feeling at times than passing the school bus on my motorcycle. Hanging out with my older brother and his friends also proved to be a lot of fun in the non-winter months. Alex had a motorcycle too.

Interestingly, my fairly quiet and somewhat socially awkward character notwithstanding—you know, like the leather-jacket clad fellow who starred in the movie *The Breakfast Club*, I became fond of history and excelled at public speaking in high school. Yeah, no fear! My Canadian history teacher, David Morrison, had a great impact on me. He looked beyond my leather jacket, work boots, long hair and motorcycle helmet, and cultivated my love of learning and interest in our history. This culminated in my receiving a $100 award from the Royal Canadian Legion at my high school graduation ceremony. It also served as an impetus for me to pursue studies in history at both Trent University and UWO in later years, almost accepting the opportunity to then pursue a PhD at the University of Alberta in 1995.

Beginning at the age of 15 or 16, during my spare time at high school or during the summer, I worked a number of jobs to save for a car, records for my Hi Fi and future university studies, to supplement what my parents could give me for post-secondary tuition costs. These jobs encompassed everything from bussing tables after school at Barrie Raceway (The horse track and my job prospects there ended up being flattened by the awful Barrie tornado in 1986. I recall being in Allandale Heights after it struck, volunteering to help look for anyone trapped, injured or killed), working at Solty's garden nursery in Cookstown, working in a few factories such as Kolmar of Canada, which used to make Close-Up toothpaste and Timotei shampoo, to performing security patrols inside the old Sterling Drug plant in Aurora and a number of other jobs. Alex and I developed a healthy work ethic and what Ralph Waldo Emerson plainly called *Self-Reliance*.

I acquired acute peritonitis, basically gangrene of one's internal organs—mine having arose from a ruptured appendix—as well as a strong case of pneumonia, during the Christmas holidays of 1986. I spent a few weeks in a Barrie hospital after being readmitted there, having been sent home just 12 hours earlier at three o'clock in the middle of the night when my appendix had actually burst. I spent another few weeks generally bedridden at home, a nurse visiting me daily to drain the cavity where the surgeon had made his incision to ensure I would carry on in this world for a while longer. Thankfully I had already accumulated enough Grade 13 credits to complete my high school education, having pursued a few while in Grade 12. This meant I finished high school early and did not lose a semester due to my illness. After recuperating at home a bit, I found that by the beginning of February 1987, I felt well enough to get a job. So, at around the same time, I obtained a full-time position working the night shift at a manufacturer of plastic plumbing and pipe fittings in Barrie, Ontario.

In that factory I usually worked six days a week, from about midnight until eight or so in the morning. Often, I would work 12-hour shifts to earn time-and-a-half pay after the first eight hours. My nocturnal job continued until September 1987, when I began my post-secondary studies in Peterborough at Trent University. My parents used to joke that when I returned home and exhausted in the morning, especially after the longer 12-hour shifts in the factory, and opened my mouth to say anything, they usually could smell plastic. Certainly, the PVC (polyvinyl chloride) fumes could leave their mark on you those days.

You can meet a lot of memorable characters working nights in a plant. I recall nicknames of co-workers, such as Tiny, a tall fellow who weighed several hundred pounds, Redbag, who sported a red mane that would rival any Englishman's, and Spider, whose wiry body was covered in a web of tattoos. If memory serves me correctly, one morning the police had to come looking for one of these persons of interest because they missed their court appearance for something. Anyway, you had to respect these fellows for busting their butt all night to make an honest living.

Having been cooped up in the confines of a noisy factory for the better part of seven months and armed with a healthy bank account, but still immature in my understanding of things, I proceeded to university. There I imbibed a little from the fountain of knowledge and way too much from the local bars at the time, including but by no means limited to, The Pig's Ear and The Red Dog, places suitable for animals and young undergraduates alike. My body, conditioned to staying up all night, often accepted the challenge of partying all night, or, occasionally, the challenge of writing an essay the night before it was due. Sometimes, during the non-winter months of the academic year, I would drive about in my 1973 customized VW Bug, shepherding my friends aimlessly along to wherever the night encouraged us to go.

Despite all the carousing about with my friends, I somehow managed to get all of my academic work done at Trent, obtaining suitably decent but not stellar grades, during my first two years of university. The subconscious influence of my parents' strong work ethic and values likely kept me on the right path at the time. By my third year of studies, that little voice we all have within us, prompted me even more to work a little harder. As a result, and despite taking on two part-time jobs during the school year—one in the university's audio-visual department, the other helping to run its film society—my marks improved to mainly A's and B pluses. I remained quite the procrastinator, leaving the completion of many assignments until the last minute. In one instance, I recall writing an entire essay of 5,000 words during a single day, with my friend Mark, dutifully typing it up as I dictated it to him during the night; his payoff being a full case of cold beer!

All told, I spent four years at Trent, matriculating with an Honours BA in History, minoring in Geography. I did not date much in my youth but had a steady girlfriend near the end of my studies at Trent. As a hobby, I also spun rock n' roll records on Saturdays at the campus radio station. My show, called *The Timeless Ebb*, reflected my belief that classic rock would always be around to enjoy.

Ironically, while not realizing it at the time in the factory I worked at before going to university, it is entirely possible that I would install many of the plastic pipe fittings I helped produce when I became a plumber's assistant for the Simcoe County Board of Education. This is the summer job position I held, from about 1989 through 1992, while I continued pursuing my studies at Trent, and later UWO. I did not think being a plumber's assistant could possibly be a fantastic job. I mean, would most of you? I remember being quite worried on my first day of work, almost dreading the prospect of just showing up. I conjured up all kinds of dramatic images in my head, such as how I was destined to unplug toilet after overflowing toilet, in dirty washroom after dirty washroom, in school, after school, where the kids had used the restrooms to conduct all manner of experiments outside of science class. Basically it seemed likely there would be shit to deal with on a daily basis; the stench of it all would likely also be much worse than that of plastic fumes arising from a moulding machine, whose hopper full of PVC pellets had somehow clogged and gotten much too hot to contain itself, virtually blowing its stack like some ill-tempered politician during *Question Period*. I could visualize an imperious boss and mean-spirited custodians ordering me around to mop-up all kinds of crap and given the over 100 public schools, it all appeared overwhelming indeed. But it wasn't …

As life seemingly, if not always, leads us down a path of irony, I loved my summer job. My boss, Marty, was one of the most decent, modest and down to earth human beings I had ever met. He had a larger than life sense of humour and was a great teacher, enabling me to learn how to gut an entire bathroom—later installing a new one; how to remove and replace huge steam valves; how to repair equipment in giant below-ground cisterns; how to cut out damaged or old leaky pipes of all sizes and configurations, installing new plumbing in its place; and how to do a ton of other repairs, which were as various as the summer was long. If you ever happen to read this book Marty, you may be surprised to learn that I have successfully installed a few bathrooms and done some plumbing repairs on my own over the years.

I became adept at not only looking professional by carrying a big torch on my shoulder and all kinds of power and manual tools, but also becoming almost a professional in using all those things to tackle any number of problems, some highly unique. I recall repairing existing plumbing in a couple of historical Ontario schools that had long ago used cast iron pipes and horse-hair-sealed joints, and how we removed asbestos wrapped piping using the correct abatement procedures.

Marty and I also worked on plumbing systems not visible to most people when they pass by or walk through a school. I remember crawling in the service tunnels of my old high school, fixing neoprene seals to address a leaky roof drain, checking the pH levels of water in schools, repairing chlorinator pumps and crisscrossing large distances that connected all the schools in Simcoe County, from Bradford to Wasaga Beach, from Aliston to Brechin, and so on.

In between all the plumbing jobs we had to do, Marty and I had to get supplies. Getting parts to do our work always proved to be a highlight of the day. Wholesalers like Westburne would sometimes host free barbeques where customers such as us would get free burgers, chips and pop. I often got to drive the school board's large cube van to Westburne or other suppliers, and it felt pretty cool to do that and load it up with stuff we would be using later on for one project or another. Another periodic highlight of the day was when we dropped by for lunch at Dino's Burger Pit if we were working in the area. Owned by Marty as a side-business and operated by his wife and the students she employed, this burger joint, located in Oro Township at the time, had a lot of tasty food, and my boss always let me eat for free. Like I said, I loved being a plumber's assistant!

Thinking of Marty, I am reminded also that a sense of humour goes a long way to get you through any rough patches. As Marty said one day, when we were repairing a large sewage pump in a nauseatingly confined space, "Just remember Andy, payday is on Wednesdays and the brown stuff always flows down!" I think he offered me a drag on his cigarette that time too for good reason.

I am doubly reminded that there is often a synchronicity to things. Like the old cliché goes—everything happens for a reason. My career path continued on a trajectory of problem solving, building on the skills my father, and then Marty taught me. By using a common sense and innovative approach to solving problems, I became more and more skilled at spotting clogs in systems. I understood increasingly the reasons behind major problems, even seemingly hidden problems responsible for the way our government works. Just as I probably made some of the pipe fittings in the factory that I would later use on the job to repair things with Marty, so too would I use my other experiences, both academic and practical, as building blocks of insight into how we might make Canada and the world a better place.

When I think of people like Marty or my father, I am regularly assured that most Canadians, given the opportunity, are hardworking. In my case, after completing my degree there just appeared to be no work for university graduates, not even at factories. I recall going everywhere to drop off resumes, seeing signs similar to the one posted at a shoe manufacturing plant in Newmarket at the time: "We are not accepting resumes at this time." This was during the deep and prolonged recession of the early 1990s here in Canada. It seemed impossible for those of us born immediately after the baby boom, the so-called Generation X'ers, to find employment. Similar to the job prospect challenges facing the current generation of millennials, we found there was a lack of opportunity to contribute to Canadian society, to feel part of something bigger.

These days it is a common viewpoint that young people should not expect much in the way of employment when they have a liberal arts degree and not much in terms of practical skills. Still, I was open to anything and had been honing my practical skills since the age of 15. Prior generations of liberal arts graduates were routinely offered entry-level positions in hiring organizations as well, because you had to start somewhere in terms of your career. Additionally, a university education usually helps one mature, developing transferable skills such as writing, communication, presentation, research, analytical and other 'soft' skills. That is of value to most businesses and innumerable other organizations today, not just IT skills, which also paradoxically requires some of the other transferable skills I mentioned. Obviously, a web page designer needs to understand how to read and write well.

Funny how an appreciation of history also gave me an insight into how many of the problems we face have developed over time, and under specific circumstances, even here in Canada. Our problems include a wide range of economic challenges and other issues that have put a strain on the services required by everyday Canadians, such as those with disabilities or other healthcare challenges; those facing unemployment; those without a home or food; those who cannot receive their duly promised pension or pay; and those confronting a host of other issues, many of which should never have materialized in the first place.

As a society, we face a panoply of serious problems. Our Indigenous Peoples alone lack adequate drinking water and housing in many of their communities. We are all facing environmental issues, as well as challenges associated with foreign policy and trade, military and defence, and the list goes on. Perhaps such problems could better be resolved by some liberal arts graduates instead of just those trained in economics. The economy is important for sure, but so too is the fabric of society and the well-being of our democracy. Everything is interrelated and connected, no different than the air we breathe.

Practically, the fact that my parents lived in a rural area did not help my chances to find gainful employment, especially over an hour's drive away from Toronto, a hub of potential job opportunities. Employers typically want their employees closer to work. Being so far away from larger cities made my job search all the more difficult. Pragmatism led me to Orleans, just outside of Ottawa, when I moved to my brother and sister-in-law's townhouse in 1991. With the nation in debt and the Chrétien government deciding to shed existing jobs in the Canadian Public service, never mind curbing most, if not all, of the hiring of younger people, while simultaneously raiding the Federal employee pension plan to the tune of $30 billion to pay off the national debt, Ottawa was not a pleasant experience for me. Truthfully, I became quite dejected, if not angry, especially after realizing even the army had no opportunities for people in my situation. Doing some renovation work for my brother, such as installing a bathroom, drywalling and painting the basement, kept me a little busy, but not busy enough.

After pounding the pavement and submitting about 200 resumes, I began to give up on finding work. Worse yet, I probably began to give up on myself. Unproductive hours turned into unproductive days. In turn, each day turned into a week, and every week a month, until time itself seemed to be a blurring of emptiness, with me being trapped by some intangible force of inertia. I remember watching that infamous scene, of Prime Minister Chrétien grabbing a protester, who had gotten in his way, by the neck and throttling the man on national television. At the time, I almost wished I could have done the same to Chrétien himself (not literally), demanding he wake up and do something for the growing class of unemployed youth in our country. I imagine unemployed millennials feel the same way now, only with a different prime minister in power.

After many months had elapsed, and with my shoe soles and hopes of employment growing ever thinner, I finally got a break at the military recruiting centre in Ottawa. The Air Force needed a few recruits for their Air Traffic Controller program, meaning if I passed a series of tests, I would be off to 'boot camp' in British Columbia. Amazingly, I passed the aptitude test and a medical exam at NDHQ (National Defence headquarters) in Ottawa. Thereafter I only had to pass an optometrist test. However, in the interim, I received a letter from UWO, accepting an application I had sent there earlier to pursue a master's degree in history, mainly out of interest, but also to escape the dismal job market. A lot of Gen X'ers like me opted to stay in school. Since the letter of acceptance also mentioned that I would be provided with a scholarship worth a few thousand dollars, along with a paid teaching assistant's position, I decided that the air traffic controller gig was not for me, my 20/20 vision notwithstanding.

My old boss, Marty, at the Simcoe County Board of Education advised that he could take me on again as a summer student before my graduate studies commenced in the fall 1992. That was great news, especially since that job paid about $12 an hour, almost $5 an hour more than the full-time job I finally landed in Ottawa. (I got a job with a contractor, processing the government's new goods and services tax, the GST, in Ottawa, around the same time UWO accepted me into their graduate studies program.) Interestingly I met a lot of laid-off former government employees at the GST processing centre. They took what they could get to put food on the table. If memory serves me correctly, the contractor's operation was located in the Novotel Hotel building near the Rideau Centre. Comically, I recall receiving one GST remittance form from a Canadian farmer, who symbolically had burned a corner of the document, writing a few expletives which formed his opinion of the government's new tax on the back of it. I cannot help but wonder how Quebec's dairy farmers are doing these days.

It was a good time to leave that low-paying job in Ottawa to perform more meaningful work with Marty and some of the other tradespeople I already knew. It was also nice to have something else to look forward to, such as perhaps becoming a teacher like the one who had influenced me so much in high school, or maybe working for the Canadian Foreign Service in some far-off exotic place. At the age of 22, I could still afford to dream and stumble a year here or there.

Teaching two classes of first-year students at UWO was fun. My students seemed to genuinely enjoy the classes as well, even the one or two mature students who were older than me. I should have applied myself a bit harder academically in my own courses but managed to pull off some respectable grades. Those marks would later garner me an acceptance letter from the University of Alberta to pursue a PhD in history, something I decided not to do. In retrospect, I believe my interest in academics began to waver when I found myself living in Minsk, under Europe's last dictator, Alexander Lukashenko, for almost a year.

The unusual circumstances that led me to move to the capitol of Belarus were precipitated by one of my graduate studies professors at UWO. He invited me to have dinner at his home one evening. The guest list included him, his wife, me and the Vice-Rector of the Minsk Linguistics University, Yuri Stulov. Professor Stulov had been visiting UWO at the time. Since one thing leads to another, the dinner conversation included me being invited to Minsk, to study the Russian language while teaching Canadian history/studies. Although I had never travelled outside of Canada up to then, let alone Ontario, except for my brother's wedding on Prince Edward Island (I was too busy to see much of the island), I readily accepted the opportunity to explore the unknown. Admittedly I did not fully grasp what would be in store for me at the time. On the other hand, I knew that Belarus lay on the border of Ukraine, where my missing uncles had presumably written from so long ago.

There are many things I could tell you about my ten months stay in Belarus during 1993 and 1994. I could tell you about all the good people I met, not only from that country, but also from the United States, the United Kingdom, Vietnam, Argentina, Morocco, Russia and Canada (we had students from different departments at UWO participating in our exchange program along with some from Sir Wilfrid Laurier University). I could tell you about the trips I made to most of the regional cities in Belarus, save for Gomel and Mogilev, which suffered radioactive contamination after the Chernobyl nuclear catastrophe in Ukraine. It was on the fateful day of April 26, 1986 that reactor number four exploded in what is commonly referred to as the Chernobyl incident. The accident released fallout equivalent to 200 times the combined impacts of the atomic bombs dropped on Nagasaki and Hiroshima.

Sadly, about 70 per cent of the radioactive fallout from Chernobyl blanketed Belarus. It covered almost a quarter of the country. The results? As Nigel Roberts wrote on the 30th anniversary of the Chernobyl incident, "Today, almost two million people continue to inhabit areas within Belarus that remain subject to radioactive contamination, largely from caesium-137."

In stark medical terms, "over 500,000 people in Belarus alone present thyroid problems to this day, resulting from absorption of radioactive iodine into the thyroid gland." Roberts notes, "Caesium-137 has a half-life of 30 years," meaning, "it will be another 30 years and another generation before it halves again" to its long drawn-out end. [11] Before that, it will continue to wreak havoc where it invisibly rests as a major threat to people's well-being.

I could tell you about the trips I made to Moscow. During one of them I observed the after effects of a failed attempt to overthrow then Russian President Boris Yeltsin. On October 4, 1993, a few weeks before my trip, Yeltsin ordered the storming of the Russian legislature by military force. The marks left on Russia's parliament building, also called the White House like in America, were clearly visible to me just a few weeks later. There were broken windows, charred and blackened around the frames, and other visible damage. The damage was not surprising, since the parliament building had been blasted by Russian tanks. Dozens of people were left dead. *The Atlantic* described the event as something that "brought Russia to the brink of civil war and resulted in the worst street violence in Moscow since the 1917 Bolshevik Revolution." The backdrop to this 'constitutional crisis' arose when Yeltsin's post-Soviet economic reforms became more unpopular. According to *The Atlantic*, "He found himself increasingly in conflict with the legislature, the Supreme Soviet, its speaker, Ruslan Khasbbulatov, and his own vice president, Aleksandr Rutskoi." Then, "with gridlock and confrontation paralyzing the country, Yeltsin on September 21, 1993, signed 'Decree No. 1400,' which dissolved the legislature and set elections for a new bicameral parliament for December." [12]

The rest is history. Members of the legislature barricaded themselves in the 'Bely Dom'—the White House—impeaching Yeltsin, as they did not believe he had the power to dissolve parliament according to the constitution. It was then, "in the early hours of October 4, Yeltsin reportedly ordered Defense Minister Pavel Grachev to have his troops shell and storm the White House." [13] I found it intriguing that Yeltsin, after winning another term as president in

1996, and having enabled the Russian oligarchs or super rich to pillage the Russian economy, ended up resigning at the end of 1999. He passed the torch of power to then Prime Minister Vladimir Putin, known to us for his even more militant and authoritarian ways. Putin's military involvement in Syria and Ukraine reflects this reality, as well as his iron-fisted control of domestic affairs in Russia.

During another trip to the Russian capitol, around New Years' Eve, my friends and I enjoyed copying what some local kids were doing on the steep banks by the Kremlin's wall. We went tobogganing on some large pieces of cardboard we found strewn about. I felt much safer than I had during my previous trip to Moscow, but that may have just been the feeling of ringing in the New Year in a strange land, fortified by its all too abundant vodka and cheers of 'Nasdrovya.'

On a trip to St. Petersburg, formerly called Leningrad, in honor of the founder of the Soviet Union, who has lain in state for decades in the Lenin Mausoleum on Red Square, I got to see some interesting sites. Although seeing Vladimir Lenin lying in a glass-covered case in Moscow with a disgustingly shrivelled and brown thumb did little for me—hey, I am not one to visit wax museums either—I found the historic sites in St. Petersburg to be spectacular. The Peter and Paul Fortress established by Peter the Great on a small island on the Neva River contained many tombs of Russia's famed Czars, like Peter himself, who had built the city initially named after him—and now again.

I also saw the prisons contained in the fortress, where prominent anarchists and others were imprisoned during Russia's tumultuous past. The fortress even featured a small space museum and the grounds of the entire island were pleasant to walk around. I had the opportunity to see the Czars' Winter Palace, better known as part of the buildings housing The Hermitage, ranked the world's second largest art museum. I must have spent eight hours in that place, which has over 1,000 rooms, and I still came out feeling that I had hardly seen anything in there due to the sheer size of the place.

Many tourists do not make it beyond Nevsky Prospekt, the main thoroughfare of St. Petersburg, much less make it to Pushkin, a suburb of St. Petersburg. Fortunately, I had the chance to stay a few nights in Pushkin. My accommodations were all previously arranged by Professor Stulov's office. This meant I could see the Czars' summer palace too, where the likes of Catherine the Great whiled away her summers.

The patriarch of the family I stayed with in Pushkin had been a member of a Russian Arctic naval expedition. He showed me fascinating slides of it all, including the submarine he had been on. I am not sure if Canada or NORAD (North American Aerospace Defense Command) had tracked this guy and his mode of transportation, but it sure looked like he had gotten around, perhaps beyond international waters. Then again, Russia is always doing one thing or another in the Arctic.

I could also tell you about all the parties and discos I went to in Minsk. I could tell you what my students and fellow teachers were like, about the host families I boarded with, or any other number of interesting things. But none of that would prove to be as relevant, to the core purpose of this book than to describe to you what it was like to live in Mr. Lukashenko's post-communist dictatorship. At the time, and even now given his tenure at the helm of an oppressive, albeit enduring regime, in Belarus, Mr. Lukashenko symbolizes the power of tyrannical and malevolent systems to persist in our modern and so-called progressive world. Unfortunately, his and other undemocratic societies of varying types remain: this, despite the seemingly best efforts of countries such as Canada, and global institutions, like the United Nations, that have traditionally stood for the rights of the individual and of democratic values.

Evidence of the USSR's command and control over the economy remained in Belarus when I arrived in Minsk in 1993. So, too, did the chaos ensuing from the collapse of the Soviet Union. It all merged together, forming some kind of nightmare for ordinary citizens who had to deal with the fallout of a near impossible and unplanned transition from Soviet-state to capitalist state.

It may not have been as immediately threatening as the Chernobyl incident, but it too wreaked havoc on Byelorussian society. I remember how people would read the famous newspaper *Pravda*, meaning 'Truth,' only to recycle it later, since toilet paper was in short supply. I recall lining up to purchase bread and giving up sugar and butter that were hard to come by. Seeing so many people struggle daily with the financial crisis, an authoritarian government and the generally dire circumstances, somehow transformed my interest in academics and history into sheer disillusionment with theory and formal education. It is only now, with the gift of hindsight and a modicum of wisdom that comes with age, I finally realize I experienced a personal transformation while living in Belarus. I have come to understand that I learned quite a lot on the streets of Minsk, perhaps just as much, if not more, than I learned in the classroom or from books.

There is an obvious value or need for any society to know their history. Its members should know where they came from and where they currently stand as a community. This may even be a precursor for any nation to know where it is headed: down a blind alley of confusion or a well-thought-out path that rewards all citizens. All the same, one begins to question the relevance of all the historical books, the theoretical arguments and the academic perspectives, vying for some type of intellectual supremacy in a cerebral arena of those 'in the know,' when one is dealing with history unfolding right in front of them. This line of thinking struck me in Belarus as I confronted 2,000 per cent annual hyperinflation and what that really means on the streets of Minsk. One starts to wonder, how did this all come to be? Perhaps, as Voltaire suggested, history merely is just a pack of tricks we play upon the dead.

Roaming the streets of Minsk during the early 1990s gave me a good appreciation of what it was like to live under a recently collapsed communist regime. Central to my streetwise learning was an evolving appreciation, fuelled by daily experience, that the former USSR's organizational structure—its systems, institutions and party apparatus—as well as its leadership personalities, created a society fraught with misery for those trapped within it. Simultaneously, that organizational design ensured senior government officials had the most to gain by maintaining it. They were the one per cent, or elites of the USSR, with only the façade of communist ideology pretending that equality prevailed throughout society.

For almost 75 years, since the Bolshevik Revolution of 1917, the USSR persisted. Like a stubborn weed, it clung to the vestiges of an impossible ideal, that those toiling the most would somehow benefit from the growth of an ever-burgeoning and rotting bureaucracy, known as the state, where few worked much themselves. The ideal proved to be rooted in fantasy. The USSR failed spectacularly, with the lifting of the 'Iron Curtain' unveiling what seven decades of decrepit institution building had wrought for the majority of its forlorn people: little in the way of progress.

The collapse of the Soviet Union has been debated by many historians and writers. Some attribute it to Mikhail Gorbachev's policies, such as allowing multiparty elections. Others believe US President Reagan's policies isolating the Soviet economy were instrumental. My personal view is that its institutions could not last. Their decay, amplified by an ever bloated and archaic bureaucracy, could no longer be hidden from the people. The Soviet system's true purpose—self-promotion, increasing power, wealth and stature of senior party officials at the expense of others—is not something that could be hidden forever. The very size of the ever-expanding bureaucracy, cracking under its own weight in an environment of increasing telecommunications and globalization, doomed it to fail. And once enough fissures and cracks opened up in the rotting edifice known as the USSR, enough light began to shine on its contemptible hypocrisy, its oppression of the masses, that the situation became transparent enough for citizens to demand change and threaten the toppling of the corrupt Soviet regime.

With a receptive leader in the form of Mikhail Gorbachev in power, advocating policies of *Glasnost* (openness) and *Perestroika* (restructuring), the frail structures and systems that enabled the USSR to exist at all, were finally broken on the back of the collapsing institution of communism itself. Gorbachev may likely not have intended the dissolution of the USSR. He inherited from his predecessors a stagnant economy and bloated bureaucracy to preside over. In the final analysis, none of that matters. The centre could not hold.

Unfortunately, as I will later discuss, the hopes and dreams of those living in the former USSR were wasted. If we are being honest with ourselves, this is at least partially due to the failure of the West to collectively support the establishment of real democracy in what was the Soviet Union. That may well yet go down as one of the greatest missed opportunities to move humanity forward in the twentieth century. We end up with the current and undesirable situation staring us straight in the face. The rise of Vladimir Putin as Russia's leader and resurgence of the command-and-control institutions that now let him and his cronies maintain their grip on power, just as they did for so many of the USSR's leaders, bears testament to the West's failure to support what might have been. Then again, with so many countries in the West unable to ensure real democracy is built and maintained in their own backyards, all of this should not have come as a surprise.

When I returned to Canada and completed my master's at UWO in 1995, the recession that had taken hold earlier appeared to be persisting. Newspaper articles at the time emphasized the hopelessness many young people continued to face. Feeling somewhat disillusioned with academics for reasons I already explained, and facing uncertain job prospects yet again, I did what many young adults did and still do in such circumstances. I returned to my parents and their supposedly empty nest. Not one to sit idly or go on the dole, and increasingly growing weary of looking for work in Canada, I decided to go abroad again. Despite being accepted into a doctoral studies program at the University of Alberta, no guarantees of funding were made and being an academic did not seem a good fit for me anymore. I wanted to see more of the world and what it really was like instead of reading and writing about places I had never been. As Saint Augustine once said, "The world is a book, and those who do not travel read only one page." Given my limited job prospects in Canada and my piqued interest in travel as a result of living in Belarus for almost a year, it seemed a no-brainer to pack my bags again. Being under 30 years old at the time also meant I probably had a few years more to burn before beginning to worry about my future in Canada.

At first, in 1995, I spent a few months teaching English in South Korea. It was interesting to see helicopter gunships periodically doing fly-bys to assure everyone ensconced south of the demilitarized zone that they were safe from the tyrannical regime north of it. As we all know today, North Korea remains one of the world's most dangerous countries. It has one of the world's largest armies and has long planned to increase its nuclear weapons capabilities. Whether or not ongoing international negotiations to reduce those capabilities are successful remains unclear. North Korea's current leader, Kim Jong Un, has continued to test the hermit kingdom's nuclear missile capabilities.

Although markedly different from Belarus, with a long-lasting family dynasty at its head since 1948, North Korea's regime shares some similarities with that of Alexander Lukashenko's, if not to a much more oppressive degree. Recent BBC (British Broadcasting Corporation) monitoring reports note: "Decades of [the] rigid state-controlled system have led to stagnation and the leadership dependent on the cult of personality." Disturbingly, "aid agencies have estimated that up to two million people have died since the mid-1990s because of acute food shortages caused by natural disasters and economic mismanagement." Even more alarming, "Amnesty International estimates that hundreds of thousands of people are held in detention facilities, in which it says that torture is rampant and execution commonplace." In the case of the Korean Peninsula, "Seoul's 'sunshine policy' towards the North aimed to encourage dialogue and aid." However, this policy "was dealt a blow in 2002 by Pyongyang's decision to reactivate a nuclear reactor and to expel international inspectors."[14] The sunshine policy necessarily ended when the South elected a new president. Sunny talk only gets you so far where bullies are concerned.

Having only lived in South Korea a few months, I did not come to understand that country very well. However, its success as a fairly young democracy is unquestionable. Economic progress since World War II has been admirable with companies such as Samsung, Hyundai, Kia, etc. being significant competitors in their respective markets, including here in Canada. Christian Caryl, in the article he penned for the *Washington Post* in March 2017, "South Korea shows the world how democracy is done," outlined how that country has "one of the world's most dynamic economies," which "continues to evolve and broaden its democratic institutions."[15] While North Korea presses ahead with its sabre rattling in the form of yet more missile tests to prove how mighty it's decaying regime is, the fledgling democracy to the south exercises its right to uphold its Constitution.

On March 10, 2017 the Constitutional Court of South Korea upheld President Park Guen-hye's impeachment after "revelations of corruption at the highest levels of political power." President Park was "accused of using her close friend, Choi Soon Sil, to funnel bribes to businessmen." Samsung Corporation's Vice Chairman, Lee Jae-yong was also on trial for corruption. The unanimous decision of eight court justices to remove the President was, as Mr. Caryl emphasizes, "especially remarkable when you consider that democracy is a mere 30 years old" in South Korea.[16] He notes that the president was removed from her position legally and without violence. Reading this article prompted me to understand the privileged one per cent may not always be able to dupe the rest of the people when proper checks and balances are in place within the system many feel powerless against elsewhere. As Professor Sung-Yoon Lee of the Fletcher School at Tufts University, whom Mr. Caryl cited, articulates in the case of Park and the Court's judgment: "It's significant because it really speaks to the deep problem of collusion between the government and big business . .

. the people in the country who have money and power feel they're above the law . . . it's a victory for the rule of law."[17]

In this regard, the South Koreans deserve our respect in maintaining democracy for their people. South Korea has a good relationship with Canada. It views Canada as a long-standing friend and supporter of its position vis-à-vis the North. As the ambassador to Canada proclaims on the South Korean embassy's website:

> Canadian missionaries were among the first to visit Korea in the 19th century and are recognized for their important contributions to the country's health, educational and democratic systems. Canada is also widely known to Koreans as a friend and ally whose soldiers stood shoulder-to-shoulder with them during the Korean War. Over 27,000 Canadian soldiers participated in the War—the third largest contingent among the United Nations armed forces. For this, Koreans are forever grateful.[18]

It remains to be seen how not only North Korean society evolves in the years to come, but even how Trump's presidency evolves to the south of our own border. That includes his overtures to the North and his praise of its dictator that has allowed so many people to suffer under his reign. Of his recent negotiations with Kim Jong Un, Trump had this absurdity to say, as reported on by Jessica Vomiero of *Global News*: "I was really being tough and so was he, and we would go back and forth. And then we fell in love. No, really. He wrote me beautiful letters." [19]

After working in Korea, I spent 1996 to 1998 working in the Czech Republic, mainly at a sprawling factory complex in Moravia that made automotive components for one of the Big Three car manufacturers. The Czech Republic, which is the western offshoot of what was once known as

Czechoslovakia, where my mother was born, became an independent state along with the Slovak Republic in 1993. In the wake of the dissolution of the Austro-Hungarian Empire, Czechoslovakia was one of the few democratic nations in Europe between the first and second world wars. At that time, it even bore some similarities to the Canada we know today. In addition to being a democratic republic, it was a multicultural state, welcoming many diverse people fleeing persecution of one sort or another. *Radio Praha* coverage in 2005 discussed Czechoslovakia as an "island of Democracy and Refuge between the wars."

> Between the wars, Czechoslovakia was—according to official documentation—host to tens of thousands of refugees. They arrived in waves, with the first and largest group, that of Russians and Ukrainians, arriving in the early 1920s. They fled the new Soviet regime, along with smaller groups of Byelorussians, Armenians, Kalmyks and others who found themselves on the losing side of the Bolshevik revolution.[20]

Of course, the tragedy of Western leadership in facing an increasingly emboldened Hitler, is that it allowed him to cement his power in countries such as Czechoslovakia. This occurred through policies of appeasement during the 1930s, championed by then UK Prime Minister Neville Chamberlain. Allowing an insecure bully to do as he pleased, resulted in countless, needless deaths during World War II, and the dislocation of so many others from what they called home. True, the culpability of the West is debatable when Germany itself bears so much of the blame. Despite the onerous terms Germans faced, in the form of crushing reparation payments demanded by the victors under the Treaty of Versailles ending World War I, there can be no excuse for the atrocities committed by Hitler and his overzealous followers. Nevertheless, when Germany annexed all of Czechoslovakia in March 1939, following its annexation of the Sudetenland in the fall of 1938, the West looked the other way.

Chamberlain gullibly believed he brought "peace with honor" to the UK by allowing Hitler to take over the Sudetenland, disregarding the Führer's increasingly bellicose ways. Hitler had already remilitarized the Rhineland and annexed Austria before marching into Czechoslovakia. Only a fool would believe his ambitions had already been satisfied with those moves. Yet it would only be on September 1, 1939, when Germany invaded Poland, that Chamberlain would request a British declaration of war against Germany. Thankfully for Britain, Winston Churchill became Prime Minister after Chamberlain resigned in 1940.

By early 1948, the Stalin regime meted out yet more unfortunate irony on Czechoslovakia's already war weary population. The Czechoslovakian government had expelled millions of Germans after Hitler's defeat, expropriating their property and ignoring not just the rights of the guilty, but also likely the innocent. However, so, too, did the Soviets usurp the rights of the Czechoslovakian victors by expropriating their property. And, "an attempt to change and humanize communist totality and to weaken ties to the Soviet Union failed when the Soviet army invaded the country in August 1968," the year I was born in Canada.[21]

The collapse of the USSR dramatically manifested itself during what is referred to as the Velvet Revolution in Czechoslovakia, a six-week period from November 17 to December 29, 1989. "Massive demonstrations of almost 750,000 people at Letna Park in Prague on November 25 and 26 and the general strike on the 27th were devastating for the communist regime." Representatives of the communist government were "forced to hold talks with the Civic Forum, which was led by still-dissident (soon to be President) Václav Havel," and the rest, as they say, is history.[22] When I found myself in the Czech Republic in 1996, around three years after it had become a newly independent state separate from Slovakia, the famed dissident and playwright

Václav Havel was still its President. He had held that position earlier, soon after communist rule ended, but the role had encompassed all of Czechoslovakia.

Despite some personal challenges when I arrived, I developed a high regard for the Czech people and the country itself. Both geographically and architecturally, save for the towering grey monolithic apartment buildings known as 'panalaks' built during the communist regime, the Czech Republic is a visually stunning country. It is blessed with lush and verdantly dark green forests, rolling hills and towering mountains, with fairy-tale-like cities and towns such as Czesky Krumlov. This UNESCO (United Nations Educational, Scientific and Cultural Organization) protected town, and so many other beautiful towns that dot the country from one end to another, are worth visiting. Remarkably, and I imagine in no small part due to its democratic tradition as well as the resiliency of the people themselves, the Czech Republic quickly adopted and cultivated democratic institutions after the fall of communism. This struck me. And just as it took me time to realize the oppressive structures and systems I bore witness to in Belarus enabled its dictator to maintain his grip on those struggling to escape it, so too do I now understand how admirable the work of leaders in countries such as the Czech Republic has largely been, to build something good anew.

In the article "Czechoslovakia after 25 Years: Democracy without Democrats," Jiří Pehe states Czechoslovakia, after the Velvet Revolution, was "just like the other states emerging from the era of communist dictatorships, with a centralized economy, no political pluralism and a civil society limited to a few dissident initiatives." Appropriately, he saw the new leadership being "faced with the tremendous task of creating the institutions of liberal democracy, a market economy, the rule of law and a civil society." Pehe painted a clear picture of the extraordinary hurdles confronting Czechoslovaks in the wake of them peacefully overthrowing their communist leadership in 1989. Curiously he found "the creation of a democratic political system being the easiest—in relative terms" of the transformational reforms pursued by Czechs and Slovaks during the first 25 years after the Velvet Revolution. This is principally because there were many democracies such as Canada that they could learn from and newly formed governments could embark on pursuing democratic initiatives, such as "introducing the necessary constitutional frameworks . . . through legislative measures or in some cases, government decrees." [23]

Pehe believed that the move from state-planned economies into market economies, the introduction of the rule of law and growth of a civil society, were incrementally more challenging. His argument was succinctly that "while creating a system of free and political institutions and processes could be in many ways directed from above, both the successful introduction of a market economy and the establishment of the rule of law required varying levels of engagements." Speaking of which, Pehe illustrated the levels of engagement in the eastern and western parts of what was once Czechoslovakia as being quite different. In contrast to the rising of "a pro-reform liberal/conservative grouping called the Civic Democratic Party" in the Czech lands, the Slovak political experience "ushered in nationalist groups, demanding autonomy or Independence for Slovakia." Ultimately, "the federal institutions were paralyzed as a result," with the incompatibility of the regions splintering off into the Czech and Slovak republics in 1993. [24]

Regardless of the division, Pehe concluded that "judged solely as an exercise in institutional transformation, the results have been spectacular. Arguably, never have so many countries burdened with backward and authoritarian political institutions changed so quickly into essentially modern democratic regimes with market economies and the rule of law." All the same, he pinned ongoing challenges facing the Czechs and Slovaks on their own internal and particular issues. In terms of internal strife, he mentioned "the high levels of corruption in both societies have to do with the fact that political parties are often controlled by behind-the-scenes economic interests." He indicated challenges associated with globalization, such as foreign capital inflows by multinational corporations and the declining role of traditional political parties, distort the democratic development of these states. [25]

Pehe avowed that other developed and democratic countries were "eager to assist with democracy building" in the new republics and "ushered them into supranational organizations like the European Union and NATO [North Atlantic Treaty Organization]." Here I take exception to his view, especially when he states that "both Western Europe and the United States engaged in a massive transfer of know-how." [26] This illusion presumes our modern-day democratic institutions, including our government structures here in Canada, are both well-designed and effective in carrying out their obligations to the people, when in fact they are not!

It has been said, with likely too much hubris, that the world, and presumably its developing democracies or those that strive to establish a democracy, needs more Canada. Possibly such a need can easily arise. But first we in Canada must mend our own institutions that we collectively expect to reflect our values and aspirations. Only then can our country exemplify what the world needs more of. Only then can our know-how help others improve their lives. Only then can we lead by example. We will be exploring just how Canada can lead the rest of the world in improving democracy and people's lives in real and meaningful ways. For the time being, I will continue discussing what I observed in the Czech Republic along with some other matters.

Many of the towns I visited in the Czech Republic were quite vibrant. The centre of each of them typically had a beautiful square with a perimeter of buildings occupied by a diverse array of bustling shops, restaurants and even clubs, their respective owners doing a brisk business, and the amply stocked shelves beckoning yet more patrons. Wine cellars, often doubling as discos, entombed underground in cavernous and dimly lit spaces, were a great place to unwind. I can remember as if it were just yesterday, the sounds of base guitars reverberating off the natural cave-like rocks and a parade of attractive couples enjoying the moment. They were the envy of all the single people who, thankfully, had the world-renowned Czech beer to comfort them in the absence of a lithesome dancing partner. The point being that a lot of people seemed genuinely happy, or at least content. This was the situation not just in the capitol city of Prague, but in a multitude of other Czech cities and towns that I visited while travelling across the land my mother came from so many years ago.

Even in that small town called Nový Jičín, where I lived for two years, seemingly in the middle of nowhere, the tree of democratic institution building appeared to be bearing fruit for many of its citizens. Nový Jičín is nestled in a picturesque region known as Moravia, once part of the Holy Roman Empire for some 800 years. During the time I lived there I observed there were hardly any foreigners living in the town. And this was not just a result of what came to be known as 'the flood of the century' in 1998, when it rained for so long that I almost began to build an ark like Noah did. Upon my arrival in 1996, I found that of the 25,000 or so inhabitants of Nový Jičín, there were only a handful of Americans amongst the Czech population. They mainly lived in some well-appointed townhouses outside the centre of town. Most, if not all of the Americans, worked at the large Autopal factory that Ford Motor Company bought in 1993. It manufactured automotive lighting and climate control products, and this is the same plant I worked at as an instructor.

A lot of foreign businesses engaged in significant capital investments in the Czech Republic after the Velvet Revolution. For example, between the ends of 1991 and 1995, Volkswagen, alone, invested $540 million, raising its stake in Škoda to 70 per cent. Its light vehicle production steadily increased to 348,168 units in 1997. VW's investment in lands Germany previously contested rose thereafter. "Between 1999 and 2001 VW: 1) invested an additional $300 million to construct a new assembly hall in Mlada Boleslav; 2) financed with Škoda revenues, the completion of a new $562 million … engine … gearbox capacity factory at the main complex; and 3) committed to significantly upgrade its Kvasiny operation." By May 2000, "VW purchased the Czech Government's remaining 30% interest in Škoda for approximately $310 million."[27]

As for Ford's operation in Nový Jičín, it had invested $140 million into modernizing the plant by 1999. The plant's turnover quadrupled in the last six of those years and wages were 2,000 crowns above the regional average by the end of the same period.[28] I can tell you, having had the pleasure of knowing and working with Autopal's local Director at the time, Ladislav Glogar—incidentally one of the most brilliant people I have ever met—that the Ford plant made a huge difference to the local economy. This became especially true after Philip Morris closed its tobacco manufacturing plant that had operated in Nový Jičín as well.

Mr. Glogar, though I never told him, is also one of the most enthusiastic and generally caring Czech citizens I have ever met. He is highly educated and, even having attended Duke University, always humble, often walking the shop floor to see how management could do things better. His best efforts were despite, as a Czech marketing executive at the plant humorously quipped to me one day, "the innumerable volumes comprising the Ford Production System resembling the communist regime's endless policies and procedures." All kidding aside, I was unsurprised to see these public comments made by Glogar in 1999: "What people noticed first was investment into the kind of things which no one thought worthwhile investing in before … Nice clean toilets, washrooms, restrooms and kitchenettes with fridges and microwave ovens."[29] He understood that all people like to be treated with dignity and fairness.

Glogar subsequently moved on to become Executive Director of the Moravian-Silesian Automotive Cluster, established to promote the region as a competitive and innovative sector for the automotive industry, encouraging innovation, etc. He continues to champion good jobs for ordinary people, and his passion to build something positive appears as strong as ever. We lost touch over the years, but I still recall his exceedingly down to earth character, his common sense and enthusiasm to make things better for others. I can still picture him in his office at Autopal in the late 1990s, and the maps of his country that hung there. I remember how he proudly told me of the history of Czechoslovakia before World War II and how devastating it had been when the West did not stand shoulder-to-shoulder with his people to prevent the Nazi occupation. Glogar is a true champion of democracy and a role model for others. He is exactly who you want at the head of an organization, automotive or otherwise, driving its purpose to succeed, not only as a business endeavour, but as a positive contribution to nation building.

Regrettably, due to the challenges posed by a form of globalization that is not entirely democratic or well thought out (we will visit this issue later on), as well as other challenges faced by Ford Motor Co. itself, the Autopal factory ended up being reorganized several times. First, Ford announced in 1997 that its large Automotive Products Operations Unit (APO) would be renamed Visteon. Since Autopal's Czech operations in Nový Jičín, as well as smaller plants in Rychvald and Hluk, were part of APO, they too would fall under the Visteon brand. Ford's rebranding initiative was "an attempt to increase non-Ford auto industry sales." [30]

At the time of this initiative, I witnessed Mr. Glogar's adept handling of the situation. He transformed Czech factory capabilities from just supplying parts to Ford assembly plants, such as those based in Germany, France, Spain and Belgium, to also having the capacity to supply Ford's competitors, like Škoda, in Europe. Glogar, being who he is, meant it was a foregone conclusion that the Czech operations would succeed, just as they had been able to rise above the constraints of Soviet industry practices.

Ultimately, and something that proved beyond Glogar's control, Visteon agreed to sell its automotive lighting business to India-based Varroc Group. The sale included the factory where Golgar had first sparked my interest in business as a means to help people improve their lives. As a resident of Oshawa, Ontario, where General Motors recently announced it is ceasing production at the local vehicle assembly plant at the end of 2019, it is an understatement to say the car business is a competitive one. That issue also goes well beyond NAFTA (North American Free Trade) negotiations and US President Trump's threats to the Canadian auto industry. But I digress. In addition to the handful of Americans living on the outskirts of Nový Jičín, there were a couple other Canadians, an Australian and a Frenchman. It is no lie that we, unlike the Americans, lived directly in town. Jacques, that moniker being a good indicator, was the Frenchman and a good soul. I will be forever grateful to him for letting me use his car and well-furnished apartment when my parents came to visit me in 1997.

Owing to the fact that my spartan accommodations in Nový Jičín merely consisted of one room in a small inn, where I shared the bathroom with whomever happened to be overnighting in another room down the hall, I did not have space myself to put up my parents. Nor did I have a vehicle to pick them up at the Prague railway station. They planned to arrive in Prague by train after spending some time in Germany where my mother had grown up. So, it was fantastically generous of Jacques to offer up his place and car, especially since my father was celebrating his retirement and 65th birthday at the time and had not been to Europe since he had left at the age of 22. Jacques would be out of the country when my parents arrived, and this too emphasized his trust in our friendship as well as French hospitality.

I had arranged for my parents and me to stay in some dormitory rooms at a university in Prague, my budget being limited. But I spared no cost in ensuring a gargantuan and fine variety of hors d'oeuvres, along with a bottle of champagne and other Czech delights, awaited them after a long overnight journey. My parents loved the time we spent in Prague, taking in all the usual and countless tourist sites the city had to offer. During their roughly one- to two-weeks' vacation in the Czech Republic, I showed my parents all over the country my mother was born in but never really knew. She found it quite a twist of fate that I had, by then, developed a rudimentary knowledge of the Czech language, while she could speak none. We visited several castles and many picturesque small towns, such as Štramberk in Moravia, where the crepes are to die for at the Hotel Gong. They also enjoyed seeing the Wallachian village in Rožnov.

We even ventured into Slovakia, visiting the High Tatra mountains. We took three cable cars up to the summit of Lomnicky peak, where my dad's broad grin made me feel great that I had arranged for my parents to see so many different things. Never mind that the apartment we stayed in Trenčín unexpectedly had no running water and we brushed our teeth by the side of the road using bottled water, we still had a wonderful time on a low budget. We also spent a day in Austria, eating lunch at the city hall in Vienna and walking a few of the streets of Linz, where Father lived when he worked at the US army base so many years ago. All in all, despite some challenges, the two years I spent in the Czech Republic were fairly enjoyable. Showing my parents around was one of the highlights of my stay there.

It was now 1998, I was nearing 30 years old and had not yet put down any roots in Canada. However, destiny, or perhaps some other unseen force, had enabled me to see where my parents had come from. My travels had also helped me develop a real-world and innate understanding of how different forms of government can either help or hinder the lives of those they seek to lead. Still, it would not be until many years later, when working for the government here in Canada, that I would be able to connect the dots and see what we, as a people, need to do to make things better for ourselves and perhaps others around the world. This is the amazing and transformative power of ideas.

The first President of post-Soviet Czechoslovakia, and later the Czech Republic, Václav Havel, recognized that pernicious structures detrimental to a society's well-being can be overthrown by ideas and ones determination to make things better. He stated, "I really do inhabit a system in which words are capable of shaking the entire structure of government, where words can prove mightier than 10 military divisions."[31] In our journey together in this book, I will explain what structures need to change in the Canadian government and governments around the world. Such changes could help prevent other businesses from shuttering their Canadian operations like GM has done. Canadians do not like to be betrayed.

For now, I feel it worthwhile to mention that Mr. Glogar, whom I spoke of earlier and admired greatly, aroused my curiosity in private sector business and in how it can make a significant contribution to employees and towns alike. At the time, this seemed more important to me and my self-perceived rudderless direction than the countless history books I read earlier in my life. So, I began to look homeward with a view of working in business.

Returning to Canada in late 1998, when the prolonged recession of the 1990s was at last abating, I finally obtained an entry-level position with an insurance company. By then, my brother Alex had worked in the insurance industry for many years as a commercial underwriter. Basically, his position required him to provide the insurance coverage that a business, such as a factory or plumbing company, would need to continue operating in the event of an insured loss. He underwrote the risk for an acceptable and hopefully profitable fee to the insurance company he worked for. Alex's success motivated me to explore pursuing a career in the same field. Frankly, I felt the need to work anywhere that allowed me to start a career in something and pay the bills.

For a few years I lived in a tiny attic in an old house in Toronto's Greek Town. My so-called apartment was not far from the Broadview Subway Station, which I walked to on weekdays to get to and from work using the metro. At one point in 1999, I found myself working full-time and taking three different business courses associated with my fledgling career. I attended each of these courses in a classroom setting on a different weeknight after working all day. As you can imagine, I did not have much of a social life in comparison to when I had lived abroad. Near the end of the year 2000, and after duly completing the 12 courses required to obtain a professional designation in the property and casualty (P&C) insurance industry, I obtained a junior commercial underwriting position with a company downtown in Toronto. It seemed I would be following in my older brother's footsteps after all.

Helped by my unofficial mentor at the new company, Kevin, a burly and straight-to-the-point kind of guy from Newfoundland, who became my friend for many years, I quickly excelled in my business-focused position. My success enabled me to soon begin underwriting some of the company's largest risks in another of its departments. So, in 2001, I found myself underwriting the insurance needs of pharmaceutical companies, including their clinical trials and other operations, some carried out internationally. I remained in the insurance industry for several years thereafter. At one point, I even worked as a broker covering most of the risk transfer needs (which is really what the property and casualty insurance business is all about—transferring insurable risks to insurance companies) of a diverse array of clients. These clients included municipalities, universities, vehicle manufacturers, giant utilities, oil and gas risks and so forth. It actually was kind of fascinating, although most people initially, and to a large degree incorrectly, would think that the insurance industry is a rather boring profession.

Once you start to think about all the natural catastrophes, such as the recent wildfires, the Alberta floods of 2013 and other disasters around the world, likely increasing due to climate change, you begin to grasp just how important the insurance business is. Organizations require insurance for a wide range of exposures. The coverage is not merely for their property and revenue generating capabilities, but also for liability exposures such as medical malpractice, construction defects, shipping of goods, pollution, any liability arising out of the products they may manufacture and/or distribute, the treatment of their employees, etc. Of course, you need insurance to drive your car on public roads too. Most people buy insurance for their home, especially if the bank that provided them with a mortgage demands this. Some organizations even purchase insurance against the peril of terrorism. One could write numerous books on the vital role of the insurance industry in our society. Suffice to say, here in Canada, the Fort McMurray disaster alone is the largest insured loss in Canadian history. It contributed to 2016 being the worst year on record for catastrophes sustained by Canada.

The President and CEO of the Insurance Bureau of Canada, Don Forgeron, notes the "Fort McMurray wildfires alone accounted for $3.7 billion of the $5.03 billion of Canada's catastrophic losses in 2016." Ominously, and contrary to US President Trump's views, Forgeron aptly opines that "in Canada and around the world, climate change is not a future threat but a present danger."[32] On a more positive note, considering its key importance to Canadians and our economy, Canadian P&C insurers paid out $32 billion, or the equivalent of 63 per cent, of their revenues in claims.[33] Also of importance, the P&C industry employed almost 125,000 people throughout Canada and had about $111 billion in invested assets here in 2016. Moreover, in 2015, it contributed $9 billion in taxes and levies.[34]

Many private-sector businesses, not-for-profit organizations (NGOs) and, sometimes, even various levels of government, have risk managers. These individuals have often come from the insurance industry. It is there that a lot of minds have been trained to think about a variety of exposures and how to manage them to prevent losses to life and property. Since irony has been a constant in my life, I ended up leaving the private sector late in 2005, concerned by a scandal embroiling my employer at the time. The scandal emanated from the United States where my employer was headquartered. I survived the two waves of cuts to that company's global staff but heeded the little voice in my head that guided me to move on. So, about 12 years ago, I found myself working for a behind-the-scenes government agency most Canadians have never heard of, the Office of the Superintendent of Financial Institutions (OSFI). The importance of this somewhat obscure yet venerable organization will be discussed in greater detail in Chapter 5, along with the tools the organization possesses that might help us mend our flag.

For now, it is enough to know that OSFI helped Canada avoid most of the tragedies associated with the global financial crisis we are only now, if at all, emerging from. I do not use the term tragedy loosely. It clearly was a tragedy to those who lost their homes and their livelihoods in America, Greece and elsewhere. And it certainly was a tragedy for those who took their own life because of it, perhaps leaving distraught family members behind. The roots of the financial crisis have been fiercely debated since that infamous day in September 2008, when the failure of Lehman Brothers in the United States almost cratered the entire international financial system. The near collapse of international insurance behemoth AIG stoked the fire even more. Credit became hard to come by and the efforts of various governments around the world to stimulate their economies has led to an ongoing debt crisis, as evidenced by global debt now reaching a record $247 trillion by March 2018. This is according to the Institute of International Finance, which notes that figure is up almost $150 trillion over the last 15 years. [35]

One view, while recognizing the crisis had "multiple causes," finds "the most obvious is the financiers themselves—especially the irrationally exuberant Anglo-Saxon sort, who claimed to have found a way to banish risk when in fact they had simply lost track of it." [36] By February 2011, the Financial Crisis Inquiry Commission, created to "examine the causes of the current financial and economic crisis in the United States," had released to "the President, the Congress and the American people the results of its examination and its conclusions as to the causes of the crisis." [37] At 688 pages, the document is quite a read. However, it likely does little to alleviate the pain of so many millions of Americans who, as the commission itself notes, "have lost their jobs and their homes." The "financial upheaval … wreaked havoc in communities and neighbourhoods across [the] country," and at the time of its publishing, the commission found that "nearly $11 trillion in household wealth had vanished, with retirement accounts and life savings swept away." [38]

It seems a gross understatement when the report claims that the impacts of the crisis are likely to be felt for a generation. This is especially so considering its authors' mission was to understand how America, by 2008, had to "choose between two stark and painful alternatives," to "either risk the total collapse of our financial system and economy or inject trillions of taxpayer dollars into the financial system and an array of companies, as millions of Americans still lost their jobs, their savings and their homes."[39] From my perspective as an ordinary citizen, I am appalled that the commission and the work of others really does nothing to hold anyone accountable for, as a Supertramp song is called, the "Crime of the Century." The financial crisis surely seems that.

The commission, in describing this crime of the century, tells the majority of us what we already knew. It opines that "it was the collapse of the housing bubble—fuelled by low interest rates, easy and available credit, scant regulation and toxic mortgages that was the spark that ignited a string of events, which will lead to a full-blown crisis in the fall of 2008."[40] Somehow, and surprisingly to bureaucrats and heads of financial institutions and other organizations around the globe, "trillions of dollars in risky mortgages had become embedded throughout the financial system, as mortgage-related securities were packaged, repackaged, and sold to investors around the world."[41] Inevitably, when everything collapsed, a lot of people seemed as confused as Winston Churchill trying to describe Russia in his renowned radio broadcast, claiming that country was "a riddle wrapped in a mystery, inside an enigma."

It is as if the purposeful creation of a bewilderingly complex financial system, with all of its unnecessarily complex products and technologies, and poorly organized and staffed oversight mechanisms, somehow caught the world off guard. Somehow, as the ballooning debt held by the financial sector soared from $3 trillion to $36 trillion, with financial sector profits constituting 27 per cent of all corporate profits in the US already by 2006[42], the world was surprised when the massive bubble popped. And pop it did, the savage reverberations being felt by everyone as described. The commission appropriately concluded that the crisis was avoidable. It ascertained "the crisis was the result of human action and inaction, not of Mother Nature or computer models gone haywire." Commission members determined that "the captains of finance and the Public stewards of our financial system ignored warnings and failed to question, understand, and manage evolving risks within our system essential to the well-being of the American public." Importantly however, they miss the basic rationale as to why that behaviour occurred, even when they state there "was pervasive permissiveness" with nobody seemingly taking responsibility for the mess.[43]

Here is the crux of all the problems we face collectively as human beings. Whether those problems entail financial calamities, unemployment, poor access to healthcare, environmental degradation and climate change, and so on, the key issue is the same. Our leaders here in Canada and around the world have failed to build democratic institutions and structures that effectively serve citizens responsibly. All of the problems confronting us are merely symptoms of the key issue that remains unaddressed: broken democracies do not work for people. There has been a great abdication of responsibility by government leaders everywhere. So, things do not work entirely right. The financial crisis that occurred, and the ramifications of it that persist, together form just one indicator of poor government.

As gravely outlined in a June 2016 article in the *New York Times*, Greece became the centre of the European debt crisis after Wall Street teetered in 2008. By early 2010, Greece was headed toward bankruptcy, threatening to ignite a new financial crisis. "To avert calamity, the so-called troika—the International Monetary Fund, the European Central Bank and the European commission—issued the first of two international bailouts for Greece, which would eventually total €240 billion." The Times article keeps it real in describing what happened to Greeks themselves. We should not lose sight of what the prolonged crisis has meant for people on the streets. "The economy has shrunk by a quarter in five years, and unemployment is about 25%." So, what about all the bailouts? Where did all the money go? It "mainly goes toward paying off Greece's international loans, rather than making its way into the economy."[44] It seems like a vicious feedback loop. The Greek economy needs to improve on the one hand, but mountains of accumulated debt remain. Successive austerity measures have done much harm to, rather than supporting, the recovery of consumer purchasing power.

Simon Kuper, in another June 2017 article, concludes the following: "The euro zone countries didn't want to decimate Greece, but they did not want to keep it in the euro while cutting Greek spending, and the consequence was economic decimation." A modern-day Greek tragedy is illustrated by Kuper as he finds the current generation facing major economic hardships. "A common wage for educated young Athenians is €500 a month, but some earn as little as €300, to work the longest hours in Europe." Moreover: "Real wages in Greece dropped 10 per cent from 2007 through 2015, worse than any other advanced country except Britain."[45] I could spend much time discussing all the suffering and devastation wrought by the global financial crisis. An entirely separate book could be written about it. And it is not just a Greek tragedy. Economic problems persist not only in Italy, Spain and the UK (especially given Brexit), but in other European countries as well as America and elsewhere around the globe. Real people's lives have been impacted. Some have lost their jobs and depleted their life's savings. Others have lost everything, including their home. Low interest rates, high national debts and structural problems in the broader global economy persist. Mismanagement of the economy in some countries has exacerbated this situation.

A backlash against globalization and more and more countries entering another period of isolationism are fuelling greater uncertainty for people and the international community. This in turn has given rise to a wave of populism and the election of various ultra-right-wing proponents, their success largely based on the politics of fear and blame. It is a volatile time to be living in. If you have children, you may be concerned about their future. If you are not, the lessons of history suggest you should be. I have seen enough of history myself to know this is not an exaggeration. On a more positive note, my work at OSFI—a government agency that helped Canada avoid the financial crisis—coupled with my travels, practical experience and study of history, have enabled me to see a way forward for Canada and the world. I am an ordinary person, but I have had an extraordinary vision. Perhaps, more than anything else, my belief in God and in the goodness of most people has compelled me to outline the way forward for us all. I hope it is a useful message. I hope it is a gift.

CHAPTER 2
WHO ARE WE?

The Canadian Identity, as it has come to be known, is as elusive
as the Sasquatch and Ogopogo … Canada resists any definition.
—Andrew Cohen

As I put pen to paper,

Canada, in 2017, has just celebrated its 150th year of nationhood. However, we are no closer to answering the key questions: What exactly does it mean to be Canadian, and what really is Canada itself? Instructively, these questions were already being raised by some individuals, including around 50 years ago when our country was about to celebrate its centenary, 100 years of Confederation. Just as it is a struggle today, likely to an even greater extent given our increasing diversity, so too was it decades ago to conclude who we really are. If collectively we are unable to define what we stand for, it makes it a challenge to foresee where we are going. What should the road ahead look like for us?

The predicament we find ourselves in is even greater considering our youthful complexion. Our history is fairly short. As noted by Brooke Jeffrey, a professor of political science at Concordia University, "It would take more than 100 years after Confederation for Canada to acquire its own version of even the most basic national symbols such as a flag (1965), an anthem (1980) and a coat of arms (1921)."[1] From my own research, I can tell you that much of Canadian history also often makes for some dry reading. It is a myriad of facts, dates, events of varying importance, all leading to something not readily grasped, much less understood by most of us. Jeffrey also finds in discussing Canada that "there was a distinct lack of heroic national figures."[2]

Writing in the November 1964 issue of the *Atlantic Monthly*, three years before our centenary celebration, John Conway insightfully stated, "A great many Canadians are not sure what we are supposed to be celebrating." He questioned, "Is it the foundation of a great bicultural nation united in a common purpose? A glance at the headlines of any newspaper from Halifax to Vancouver will show the absurdity of the idea. We cannot even decide on a national flag." Disturbingly, according to Conway, "In the absence of a unifying idea, the provinces tend to assert the identity which emerges from their own geography and circumstances. We have so far failed at Ottawa to agree about the nature of our country and its people."[3]

Conway discerned a fundamental reason as to why we Canadians, even after 100 years, have largely failed to succinctly describe our core values and key objectives as a people. He described us in 1964 as more "seriously divided than we have ever been."[4] Of course we did go on to decide on a national flag. However, the argument that we lack a unifying idea to cement our identity as Canadians does seem to have persisted for another 50 years, into 2017 and beyond. Even our current Prime Minister, Justin Trudeau, appears to subscribe to this view. As unfathomable as it may seem, our current leader could not even articulate who Canadians are in his own words. For Trudeau, "There is no core identity, no mainstream in Canada … There are shared values—openness, respect, compassion, willingness to work hard, to be there for each other, to search for equality and justice. Those qualities are what makes us the first post-national state."[5]

I do not believe this makes absolute sense. After all, we remain a nation, equipped with our own currency, borders, government institutions, such as healthcare and the Canada pension plan, military force (in need as it may be), laws, educational system and so on. As for the bit about our values, I do not presume to know what your or your family's values truly are, dear reader. Perhaps you are fairly conservative or liberal in nature. Maybe you believe in God or you do not. You may prefer a large family or no kids at all. Protection of the environment and climate change may be huge issues for you, or perhaps the plight of the poor, unless you believe everyone should pull themselves up by their own bootstraps. Maybe you would like to have marijuana legalized, maybe not, depending upon how much it is for fun and how much it is for medical usage. And so it goes, a multitude of beliefs and differences of opinion, reflecting a hugely diverse people known as Canadians, all with unique backgrounds and experiences—men and women, girls and boys, some fairer skinned than others, some born in Canada and some not, some indigenous to the land and some not.

Our shared land is an immense panoply of colourful tints and hues, mesmerizing textures of abundance, rugged carved-out basins bountifully filled with endless supplies of water, skyward reaching mountains and peaks yet to be scaled, fertile soils and lush forests, glistening masses of ice sheets, cities clinging for meaning to the south. It is all of this and more, congealing into a sum of individual parts that is somehow greater than the whole. What are we to make of it all? How can we possibly define Canada and any semblance of shared values between its monumentally diverse peoples living in such a diverse place? There has been so much debate about this, all of it missing the point, which I will get to soon in this chapter.

As recently as 2016, one of the four Ontario candidates vying for the leadership of that province's Conservative party made the mistake of basing her campaign somewhat on the notion that immigrants should be screened for "anti-Canadian values." Perhaps Kellie Leitch was mindful of many Canadians increasingly being wary of terrorists and other nefarious individuals seeking to undermine the rule of law upon entering Canada. Nobody wants anyone causing havoc or harm to ordinary law-abiding Canadians. Leitch likely had good intentions when she suggested that migrants to Canada should be screened for such things as "intolerance towards other religions, cultures and sexual orientation, violent and/or misogynist behaviour and/or a lack of acceptance of our Canadian tradition of personal economic freedom."[6] All the same, and not unexpectedly, as Canada is such a diverse society, her views became a sore point for many Canadians and probably cost her some points in her leadership bid, which she ultimately lost.

As questioned by Aaron Wherry in a September 2016 *CBC* Parliament Hill Bureau news piece, "Are we comfortable with the idea of regulating beliefs? Who defines the values and how they will be measured? How specific would we get?"[7] The idea of engaging in an exercise that seeks to ascertain one's values raises the spectre of George Orwell's *1984*, where 'Big Brother' watches us all and government invasiveness penetrates every private aspect of our lives: the result being some kind of dystopian future. Wherry also reasonably wonders about Canada's newcomers facing a values test. "How would we know they were telling the truth? Would we hook them up to a lie detector? Would we have public servants checking Twitter histories and Facebook profiles for evidence of intolerance or unacceptable views?"[8] In all likelihood, the latter question, which may be valid for those immigrants with documented identities, is best left to existing front-line immigration officers and their reasonable judgment. This is preferable to some nebulous and prescriptive values checklist, and yet more layers of bureaucracy in Ottawa, in the form of the 'values police.'

We need to trust in the good in most people, applying common sense when screening all immigrants, based on a wide array of useful information to minimize risks to Canadians and Canada. Most people know the difference between right and wrong, including our civil servants, especially those serving in the trenches who best know how to do their job.

Canada is a path with a definite end, despite all the differing opinions and nuances of perspective each of us has. Bemoaning our lack of identity 50 years ago, Conway wrote we "may be a confused people." Whereas "the American people carved out their national identity through an uprising against their British masters and entered into their legacy by a revolutionary act in 1776," here in Canada we "have so far failed to enter fully into our legacy." For Conway, this was "our one great, overarching problem as our Centennial [approached]." At the time, he argued that "on its solution everything else depends" because "we have failed to vest sovereignty where it properly belongs—in the Canadian people." By having "allowed it to remain in the British monarch," Conway proclaimed, "we have divided our country and inhibited our emotional and creative development as a people." His belief is that "a nation, like an individual, can achieve integrity and identity only out of its own experience and not derivatively from a parent."[9]

Admittedly, Britain plays a lot less of a role in our daily lives half a century after Conway was writing. We could opt to gently take the next step in nation building by removing the influence of the British monarchy, including all its symbolic trappings within our government and upon the nation. In doing so, it may well be time for a new constitutional conference that strengthens those institutions that bind us, simultaneously vesting sovereignty within our borders. I do agree with Conway, especially after half a century more, that it will be only "when we take the long-overdue step and transfer sovereignty to where it properly belongs," that "it will become clear that Canadians … have been and are engaged in a common enterprise which is a far greater concern than the separate concerns of each group." I also agree that "we must cease to live in a state of psychological and emotional dependence on a structure of symbols that no longer express our common experience."[10]

Where I differ in my view is that while it may be a good idea for us to finally break with our ever present parent, the UK, which is currently undergoing its own identity crisis as it grapples with Brexit and several interrelated problems, we must also engage in a kind of democratic restructuring to improve our situation. This is an internal and greater problem for Canadians. So yes, as Conway stated, there is indeed a "structure . . . that [can] no longer express our common experience,"[11] or, I daresay, expectations after another 50 years of nationhood. That of course has to do with our crumbling institutions, those institutions being what truly reflects our national identity. And it is here that we must turn our attention, knowing the real and main values we all share that has escaped Justin Trudeau, a core identity he says does not exist. As I emphasized at the beginning of this journey of discovery we are on together, I trust that you and most other Canadians know the difference between right and wrong. We all collectively want to do the right things, and our principal task at hand is to mend our government institutions that are not working for the majority of 'we' Canadians, our own 99 per cent here in Canada.

Our democratic institutions are of vital importance to our national identity. They are vital to our sense of self, belonging and well-being, as participants in something much greater than ourselves: the great and evolving experiment known as Canada. Professor Jeffrey recognized, in the absence of a long history of national symbols, heroic figures and events, etc., that our national identity became linked to those institutions we established. "For Canadians, government institutions and programs were substitutes for such symbols and became an integral part of national identity."[12] Supporting this view is that of Rudyard Griffiths, who Andrew Cohen mentions in his book, *The Unfinished Canadian, The People We Are*. Griffiths, cofounder and executive director of the Dominion Institute, an organization promoting the study of Canadian history, believed it was "institution and not the free play of ideas that Canadians came to rely upon in entrenching a common civic culture."[13]

Neither Jeffrey, Cohen or others, have been able to fully describe the Canadian identity by merely agreeing that it is visible in our democratic institutions, and leaving it at that; leaving us with the understanding that strong Canadian institutions make for a strong Canadian identity, a strong country. In trying to go beyond this, attempting to describe our collective values in detail, many writers, sociological researchers and the like, just end up going in circles. Some, like Cohen, after 200 or so pages, wind up discussing ambiguity and its power, seemingly running after an ever-disappearing horizon that leads to more questions than answers. "Canada, it has been said, is less a country than a question. What is it, anyway? What does it stand for . . . Is it French, English or both? Is it a multicultural mosaic? American or European? Free market or Social Democracy?"[14] And so it goes, nowhere. But *'Seek and ye shall find'* goes a well-repeated phrase in the bible. Maybe what so many have sought, to describe who Canadians are and what Canada is, has always been staring us right in the face, being right in front of our noses!

There is a Luke Bryan song entitled "Most People are Good," and he is on to something there. We need to let go of trying, in a telling way, to 'tell' our fellow citizens and outsiders what all our Canadian values are, when most people, in this great adventure, undertaking, and democratic experiment called Canada, already know the difference between right and wrong. Through the years, we have voted to develop and implement institutions that reflect this collective understanding of who we are, and what is right instead of wrong. Now it is time to restore and rebuild. It is time to strengthen or change those institutions that no longer work for us and a common good. In doing so, we will not only strengthen our democracy by doing what we believe is right and just, for rich and poor alike, creating a level playing field for all citizens across this great nation (not a post-nation to be absorbed by others calling the shots beyond our borders), we will also 'punch above our weight,' leading other democracies, by our example in deeds rather than empty talk and uninformed decision-making. In this way we will define the Canadian identity.

Acclaimed Ottawa-born writer, John Ralston Saul, also understood that "Canadians have a fairly solid sense of themselves." Put simply, "Whenever asked, whenever listened to, citizens express with some confidence what kind of education system they want, what kind of health care, what minimum standards of living, what approach to justice."[15] Although he does not go into detail about how to truly fix the system—the need to redesign it so informed decisions can be made with an understanding of all the risks concerning various issues, he does certainly see it is not working for some reason. He makes indirect and somewhat oblique references to structures and institutions that do not seem to work. So, while acknowledging that Canadians generally know what they want—I call that the shared value of knowing the difference between what's right and what's wrong, he laments, "Yet our structures of leadership seem unable to digest … expressions of fairness, inclusivity and effectiveness. Although entrusted with the mechanisms of power, those in charge seem to lack the self-confidence to listen. They seem paralyzed by the reality of their responsibility."[16]

Paralyzed is right, Mr. Saul! But it is by the very design of the government itself, a throwback from earlier and simpler times, wherein our leaders did not face the vast complexities and risks associated with a modern and ever interconnected and technologically advancing world. When Saul "takes a look" at how "my country functions," what he initially sees "is a largely failed elite," or as he elaborates, "people given responsibility and power in a multitude of ways by the citizenry and yet somehow unable to act."[17] Is it any wonder given the lack of a well-established risk-management function within an archaic government, especially when individuals are often inexperienced in the area of focus their departments are tasked with overseeing? I don't know about you, but I would rather try to take a hill in wartime knowing that those who gave the order included experienced generals, who at one point lived the life of a foot soldier in the trenches, rather than just administrators or bureaucrats with little or no knowledge of what a soldier does or needs to do.

Saul grasps at trying to understand the fundamental problem apparent for "the elite's" (maybe he means top bureaucrats') "lack of self-confidence and disturbing mediocrity." Considering there may be "all sorts of explanations," he muses some might be "the results of a bad quarter-century," while, obtusely, "others are the modern expression of problems that have been with us for centuries . . . one part of our collective unconscious, the negative part of that long sweep of our history running underground, then unexpectedly resurfacing with seemingly inexplicable force."[18] No, Mr. Saul, there is a clearer explanation. The system is designed or set-up to fail (as will be abundantly clear to you in the next few chapters). And things have only gotten worse since Saul wrote what I have referenced above, some ten years ago. This may seem ambiguous or somewhat confusing to you, but when you look hard enough, you can see there are clear and discernable reasons why government is 'paralyzed.'

Humorously, I found buried on page 209 of Saul's book, *A Fair Country: Telling Truths About Canada*, in a chapter called "Signs of Failure," his statement that there is "the absence of a sense of risk." He then intellectually ascribes "a mediocre managerial class" being responsible, or "at the core of our problems." In this context, he even goes beyond the realm of government, mentioning how private-business interests have made decisions, such as owners, whose "reward lies not in building wealth but in selling off the company."[19]

I would say that much of our nation's problems, including the selling off of our major companies and inability to innovate, has more to do with the poor design of our government institutions and bureaucracy than with private business decisions. Private business decisions can be made in the absence of an informed government that understands the associated ramifications, and whether or not the outcomes will be good for Canadians or pose risk to them instead.

Yes, Mr. Saul, I agree "it is frightening that Canada's economic policies are largely shaped from the ideas of Ministry of Finance economists." But that is how government has been designed and why, as you grumble, "no attempt has been made . . . to think about [their] assumptions."[20] And yes, as you aptly wrote, "More than half of our manufacturing is in foreign hands, while the United States, Japan, Germany, the United Kingdom, France, Italy, the Netherlands, Norway, Finland and Sweden have kept the outsiders down to

4 percent." Agreed that there is "nothing more fascinating than delusionary behaviour by public figures," as Saul sarcastically quips, inveighing against the elites he deems responsible for the decisions Canadians are left to deal with. [21] His disdain for what he sees as incompetent elites is palpable, such as when he compares finance ministry thinkers' assertions at times, akin to "dealing with the brain dead." [22]

I can be a bit of a sarcastic jerk myself. However, it is patently unfair to blame the problematic behaviour of those doing what the system expects of them, rather than blame the design of the system itself. It is the system which is responsible for the undesirable behaviour and lack of risk management in decision-making that gets Canada and Canadians nowhere.

At this point, it is useful to mention one of the best things about Saul's *A Fair Country*, while simultaneously curbing my own sarcasm. He does, to a degree, honor contributions of certain Indigenous Peoples in shaping a positive way to view things. This is not surprising given that the beginning of his book avows that "we are a Métis civilization," significantly shaped and influenced by Aboriginal ideas (I prefer the word Indigenous but will cite Saul's work accurately in his words). [23] Saul discusses this to a great extent, and one of my favourite parts is when he surfaces "the Aboriginal idea of society as a great circle." Saul regards that circle as "a mechanism of inclusion," and one that is presumably quite flexible since it, for example, "absorbs new members, adjusting as it does so." [24] The concept of the circle "explains how we function," how we are "living together on the land," and how we are "seeking balance" and "a broader harmony." [25] Saul sees this Aboriginal approach being "built upon a philosophy that has interdependence at its core." [26]

We can learn much from Indigenous Peoples, such as considering the interdependence of things and building government institutions that would recognize that interdependency to facilitate better outcomes in key decision-making. Seeking a 'broader harmony' and 'balance' between competing ideas and generating the best outcomes for Canadians also sound like worthy goals. It sounds like good risk management to me since consideration of a broader or greater whole, the entire circle of our citizenry rather than an elite few (i.e., all of society, not just the one per cent), will likely produce better results for everyone if that way of thinking is adopted on Parliament Hill. However, this practical approach to solving problems, including those faced by Indigenous Peoples themselves, is not Saul's main consideration. He does not see some Indigenous Peoples' way of thinking as a means to rebuild our broken institutions. This is especially because he has not understood that the poorly conceived design of our government system is creating the undesirable outcomes associated with the bad decision-making he takes issue with.

Rather, as Chelsey Vowel, a Métis herself notes in her ground-breaking book *Indigenous Writes: A Guide to First Nations, Métis & Inuit Issues in Canada*, Saul has simply "tried to whip together a cohesive Canadian identity . . . using the Métis as a synecdoche [a figure of speech in which a part is made to represent the whole, or vice versa] for a unique people (i.e. Canadian)." [27] In noting Saul's central argument, that "Canadian culture was less a result of English and French Enlightenment values, and more a result of interaction between English and French newcomers and First Nations," Vowel sees "the goal of this approach" being "to encourage Canadians to 'learn who they truly are' via reconnecting with their Indigenous roots—real or very much imagined." [28] On the positive side, Saul raised the issue of Indigenous Peoples in his book, trying to weave it into our national identity. However, Vowel reminds us, in sharp, honest focus, that Indigenous Peoples have been unfairly treated throughout Canada's history. She reveals the complexity of the various groups, at least those that can be defined, and how, in her words, "Every single one of us, Indigenous and non-Indigenous alike, has been fed a series of lies, half-truths and fantasies intended to create a cohesive national identity." [29]

Although I am not a member of Canada's Indigenous Peoples myself, I must admit that Vowel's logic appears to be based on solid reasoning. For how can we non-Indigenous Canadians share a sense of identity or values with those who are, without first dealing directly with the never-ending plight and ill-treatment of our Indigenous brothers and sisters? Where Saul missed the point entirely in his arguments and musings is when he failed to understand that our government has been a longstanding source of division. It has been responsible for Canadians historically lacking a sense of national identity. Sure, the early government forged a nation. But its leaders left the Indigenous Peoples out of it. By excluding them over and over again from deciding their own honourable and much deserved fate, they prevented Canadians of all walks of life and backgrounds from cultivating any shared values that could arise from a common sense of what's right and what's wrong. The result of this exclusionary circumstance in our history is the difference between what might have been—all Canadians being contributors and benefactors of a collective journey known as Canada—and the fait accompli that confronts us now. In present-day Canada, some people feel as outsiders, to be occasionally seen and rarely heard. There is nothing more divisive than exclusion. It is the fertile seedbed from which conflict and wars are ignited and evil flourishes.

Many other Canadians, in addition to the Indigenous Peoples, have been poorly served by our government. So too have people living around the world in many so-called democracies, where they feel helpless—the working poor; abandoned children; refugees, who were supposedly granted access to 'the system'; young people with grim job prospects; the battered and abused; the homeless we carefully tread around; those with special needs, such as the mentally challenged; and all too many 'others.' They are not 'the one per cent,' the most affluent we so often hear about, neither are the Indigenous Peoples of Canada, whom have been treated so poorly throughout history. Consider the following. When First Peoples lost much of their land in Canada, in the face of what can only be called European conquerors (Vowel labels them settlers), and ended up on reserves, they found that on these small parcels of land, with some of the roughly 2,300 current reserves being "postage stamp" in size, they did not even have any ownership rights.[30] Whereas "reserves account for only

0.28 per cent of all the land in Canada," less than one half of one percent, the *Indian Act* states "no Indian is lawfully in possession of land in a reserve."[31]

There is also a huge disparity between the services received by Canadians living on reserves compared to Canadians living anywhere else in Canada. As Vowel summarizes, "responsibility and funding for systems of education, healthcare, or social services, provincial infrastructure (water and waste management, roads and so on) are generally a provincial power." However, "Section 91 (24) of the Constitution states the federal government is responsible for 'Indians,' and Lands reserved for Indians." This means "the federal government must provide to 'Indians' the services normally provided by the provinces (education, healthcare, social services, and so on)."[32]

Perhaps one of the most egregious acts that has taken place here in Canada against Indigenous Peoples was the implementation of what infamously came to be known as the residential school system. Residential schools operated in Canada for more than 150 years. Their stated purpose, according to the Truth and Reconciliation Commission of Canada, was "to eliminate parental involvement in the spiritual, cultural and intellectual development of Aboriginal children."[33]

In *Indigenous Writes*, Vowel presents some startling numbers about the residential school system, which involved "150,000 children who attended and 6,000 children (at least) who died in the system." She notes "1996—the year the last school closed," and how "7,000 interviews with survivors" occurred, contributing to "6 volumes in the final Truth and Reconciliation Report."[34] Given these facts, it seems abysmally clear that we non-Indigenous people, and especially those colonial "settlers" as Vowel describes "the non-Indigenous people living in Canada who form the European-descended sociopolitical majority," cannot possibly share a Canadian identity.[35] Not when our Indigenous neighbours and supposed compatriots have been given the proverbial shaft. All the same, it is useful to discuss how both Indigenous and non-Indigenous people in Canada, including more recent immigrants from around the world, despite not sharing a common experience, generally share a similar sense of right and wrong, which paradoxically can lead to a greater sense of common identity.

That may sound somewhat confusing, so what do I mean? Well, if we all typically know the difference between right and wrong and want our society to move forward in an inclusive manner that addresses and meaningfully resolves injustices, including those injustices faced by Indigenous Peoples, this presumes we can collectively find solutions that have held all Canadians back for so long. The solutions are there for Canada and everyone within its borders, as you will see. And it is our shared responsibility to implement them because it is the right thing to do. The current problems confronting us all, Indigenous and non-Indigenous alike, are representative of something that is wrong and which cannot continue going unaddressed. I mentioned at the beginning of this journey that I trusted the majority of you, as individuals, know the difference between what is right and what is wrong. My job is not to tell you that.

Many Indigenous Peoples who have been wronged countless times have traditionally had a good sense of what is truly right versus the opposite. This can give us a better perspective of how Canadians may actually have shared values. Then, if we can act upon those values and show each other, Black or White, Indigenous or non-Indigenous, male or female, and so on—striving together to do right—then we can build a unified Canada that leads the world by example. That outcome would be of incredibly more value than just high-sounding words like 'The world needs more Canada.' Phrases such as this do little for many Canadians not being treated fairly by our government, let alone other countries looking to better their own situations.

If we look back in time, to the Haudenosaunee, a First Nations People of what is now the Niagara region, we see a forerunner of modern federal governments such as ours in the form of the Haudenosaunee Confederacy. In fact, it has been stated that "The Haudenosaunee Confederacy has been in place since time immemorial."[36] You may know of the Haudenosaunee by the name 'Iroquois.' What you may not know is 'Iroquois' is an exonym, a derogatory name given to them by the French, meaning 'black snakes.' The Confederacy (also known as the league of nations) originally comprised five sovereign nations: Kanienkahagen (Mohawk), Onayotekaono (Oneida), Onundagaono (Onondaga), Guyohkohnyoh (Cayuga), and Onondowahgah (Seneca). Later a sixth nation—Ska-Ruh-Reh (Tuscarora)—was added. [37]

Whereas many European societies and early settlers were most familiar with a ruling class, consisting of, as an author on Firstpeoplesvoices.com puts it, "Kings and Queens in their class system of higher and lower," the Confederacy "blended the sovereignty of their several nations into one government."[38] This early form of government appears similar to the US and Canadian constitutions. And so, "our forefathers, escaping oppression in their homeland, adopted this concept in creating the Constitution, and today we call this a federal system whereby states monitor their own affairs and the national government regulates all affairs in common."[39]

According to the official Haudenosaunee Confederacy website, the "Confederacy's constitution is believed to be a model for the American Constitution."[40] Yet the Confederacy's constitution has its own special characteristics which are admirable, especially considering the modern and challenging environment we live in today. "What makes it stand out as unique to other systems around the world is its blending of law and values." That is to say, "For the Haudenosaunee, law, society and nature are equal partners and each plays and important role."[41]

Although the rudimentary form of our Canadian government can be somewhat likened to the Haudenosaunee Confederacy's own, we have hung on, if not sadly clung to, the vestiges of colonial monarchy and some of its trappings. We have almost imprisoned ourselves, relying on an outdated and unhelpful way of thinking, not moving forward as a nation. Here, in Canada, we have provinces rather than states, but presumably our national government, based in Ottawa, manages all our common affairs. We do have a House of Commons where parliamentarians are expected to manage Canada. Interestingly, "The nations of the [Haudenosaunee] confederacy recognize themselves as Haudenosaunee from their own language meaning 'They made the house,' symbolizing all the nations coming together as one."[42]

What stands out for me the most as I embark on the journey of writing this book, is how much I have learned in the process. In no small measure, although I could learn so much more about them in many lifetimes, the Indigenous Peoples' way of thinking fascinates me. They seem to have a good handle on knowing the difference between right and wrong, not having aspired to build institutions that confuse and artificially distort that understanding, producing undesirable outcomes. They seem to have a lot of good values too. Consider that a core value in Haudenosaunee Confederacy decision-making is something called the 'Seventh Generation.' Of note, "the Seventh Generation value takes into consideration those who are not born but who will inherit the world."[43] Maybe if we all loved each other more, we could adopt this line of thinking instead of just "living in the now," as the fashionable saying goes. Appropriately, "In their decision making Chiefs consider how present day decisions will impact their descendants."[44]

Of course, there may have been conflicts between some Indigenous groups at times, reflecting a lack of perfect harmony within Indigenous societies themselves. However, we still see a useful way of thinking when we look at, for example, the Haudenosaunee. Apparently the Haudenosaunee Confederacy, which predated the Confederation of Canada (customarily known as the birth of our nation in 1867), "exhibited an advanced social organization requiring no written laws, no police, no jails, no lawsuits."[45] Yes, the complexities of the modern world and society requires us to have laws, police and so on. All the same, having an innate sense of the difference between right and wrong would get us all a lot further in advancing humanity with a lot less problems. Central to any democratically advanced society is its understanding and practice of doing what's right instead of what's wrong. That requires people to be truthful and to have a sense of honour, treating each other with respect instead of dealing in the realm of deceit, lies and half-truths.

Interestingly for the Haudenosaunee system, "honor and truthfulness were inner guides in their society," with "lying" in such nations "punishable by death."[46] Now, mind you, I still believe that most people, not just Indigenous Peoples, are good and know the difference between right and wrong. It is the government's traditional way of doing things that has gotten in the way of reflecting our shared values of doing what's right for everyone's sake. The government's way of doing things is not only undermining our individual desire to have things done right with positive outcomes but impeding the development of a shared Canadian core identity. Our federal government should be most concerned with ensuring our collective sense of doing what's right is reflected in our government institutions and government decision-making. In the words of Slow Turtle—John Peters, 67; Medicine Man of Mashpee, Wampanong Tribe:

> [In today's democratic societies] you've got a power structure here; you've got the pyramid type of government. For Native People of this land, our form of government was always in a Circle. There was never a hierarchy. Our traditional form of government is always in that circle where everyone contributes … part of the whole … we don't have that hierarchy and for that reason we don't have the competition and the jealousies that go with it … where you have a few people at the top who have it all, and the rest are always wanting."[47]

The Canadian writer, Mr. Saul, adopts and talks about the Indigenous Peoples' concept of the circle, but not in a way that can solve the problems confronting us and other democratic nations. Hierarchically organized government bureaucracies are what break the circle. These bureaucracies are ill-suited to empower front-line civil servants, those rank-and-file employees who usually know how to do their jobs better than anyone else. It is typically the executive ranks of the civil service, the masters of the bureaucracy, proliferating in number and level as they build their empires, who rarely contribute to the services Canadians on Main Street need. Many executives serve only to block those in the circle of government who have the real-world experience and know-how to do the right things.

The result is a negative feedback loop, where wrong decisions are often made for the wider public. I will elaborate on this sad state of affairs in later chapters. Slow Turtle has got it right though. The 'system' is an enabler of wrongs. It frequently encourages senior government bureaucrats to play their roles rather than performing the needed functions of those roles. A system that motivates empire building and wrong outcomes for the majority of us is one in desperate need of overhaul. For that system is also responsible for dividing us, for preventing our core Canadian identity to naturally emerge—our identity as a sovereign, mature, respectful and refreshingly new country that has finally recognized and welcomed First Peoples' views. Principal among those views is the concept of the circle, a concept that can unify Canada and all Canadians when we understand that we all want to do what is right and true. We should also keep the Haudenosaunee's Seventh Generation value in mind. After all, the future belongs to our children, and our hearts should cherish them accordingly.

It is only through the rebuilding and redesigning of the system that divides us that we can also start, as quickly as possible, to mitigate and address the adverse impacts being forced upon all Canadians. Our government institutions are no longer fit for purpose because the system encourages poor decision-making, which our journey together will reveal. Our civil servants are growing increasingly ill, something that is reflective of the broken system that is not built to encourage real achievements and a sense of belonging within all its ranks. Most people want to do the right things, but the system is also not built to engender mutual respect. Here again Slow Turtle has something to teach us:

> We had democracy here before the Europeans came, but we had spirituality in our democracy. We had respect for each other, respect for differences in other people's way of life. This is a partnership model of governance. White people don't allow for that in their system today.[48]

Slow Turtle is on to something here. I believe, unequivocally, that we all want respect. Most of us also want the system to work for everyone's benefit as much as possible. We are aware that problems seem increasingly daunting here in Canada and internationally. So, when Slow Turtle says we "have removed the spirit out of democracy, so it can't work right—because there's no respect,"[49] how can we possibly, and tangibly in a clear way for all to understand, put that spirit and respect back where it belongs? Fortunately, we can! We can do this quite easily, or at least more easily than you may suspect. And in doing so, we can lead, by example, other troubled democracies around the world to do the same.

We can fix that which is broken. We can make our system work. There is a way to mend our flag. And it has nothing to do with any specific political party or with radicalism. I would wager the vast majority of us have a sense of personal honour, guiding how we live on a day-to-day basis. Since we each share a sense of wanting to do what's right, then collectively, on a broader and national scale, doing what's right, honourable and correct for everyone becomes as self-evident as the need to fix a leaking pipe in our own home. As a Lakota elder said about his own tribe, "We believed in honor." Quite simply, "Our guide was inside—not outside. Honor was our guide. It was more important for us to know what was right then what was wrong."[50] The elder is oh so right!

So, I challenge you dear reader. I challenge you to read on and see the solutions we so desperately need to implement here and around the world. I trust, as did Eunice Baumann-Nelson, a Penobscot Indigenous woman whose work, *Profiles of Wisdom* was referenced by others in some of my research as saying, "Self-judgment constitutes a stronger check on wrongdoing than does the judgment of others." For when you possess "your source of morality within you—arising out of an inner perception of what is wrong or shameful, [then] you are your own judge."[51] Now, if you agree with my premise that most people are fairly decent and want to do the right thing for themselves, their families, their neighbours, their immediate communities and their country at large, does this by extension mean that our politicians of various party affiliations are somehow different than the rest of us?

We do keep hearing scandal after scandal at the federal and provincial levels of government. Are our leaders and politicians generally in some separate category of citizenry, or are they human beings who do not know the difference between right and wrong? Is this why they have constantly made poor decisions, which have had terrible consequences for many of us in our daily lives?

Certainly, as we will see in Chapter 3, the evidence of a broken government making our lives less positive than they could be is overwhelming. All the same, research indicates that our senior government representatives typically want to do the right thing. This speaks to politicians actually sharing our own values and even our core identity. It truly speaks to them believing in representative democracy upon entering into politics, a profession filled with minefields. How do we know this? Beyond giving our politicians the benefit of the doubt and blindly trusting in the good in most people, authors Allison Loat and Michael MacMillan have done an excellent job revealing who many of our politicians really are. In their unique book *Tragedy in the Commons: Former Members of Parliament Speak Out About Canada's Failing Democracy,* Loat and MacMillan have taken a fairly intensive look at the views of a large group of former Members of Parliament (MPs). Published just a few years ago in 2014, *Tragedy* grabbed my attention because its authors interviewed a diverse group of men and women across Canada who had previously served as MPs in the national government. These individuals had varying careers and tenures as politicians and, on balance, represented all five of Canada's political parties sitting in the Parliament from 2004 to 2011.

Loat and MacMillan wrote, "We believe this to be the first large-scale systematic series of exit interviews with former Members of Parliament in Canada or, for that matter, anywhere in the world."[52] The authors took the unique approach of interviewing so many erstwhile MPs because they wanted to better understand why so many of us Canadians were so apathetic, increasingly disengaged and/or plain fed up, with how our national government was running the country. Apparently, there is a "growing sense among Canadians that the country's politics are not working quite as they should." Specifically:

> For well over a generation, in election after election, voter turnout has declined, and millions of dollars of government and political party advertising have done little to arrest the decline. Political party membership is rare to non-existent in most parts of the country, and many who do join . . . become disillusioned and cynical . . . public opinion research commissioned by Samara in 2012 revealed that only 55 percent of Canadians were satisfied with the state of their democracy.[53]

Loat and MacMillan genuinely appear to want to fix things as they explore in their discussion with so many MPs why things are the way they are. Their logic and approach appear sound. It arguably could be duplicated in other democratic countries where people seem increasingly frustrated at the erosion of representative government that works to serve people's interests at large. For when they raise questions, such as "So who is best positioned to solve this problem?" and "who is most responsible for and often takes much of the blame for our lamentable state of affairs?" they naturally received a seemingly obvious answer: "Members of Parliament."[54] After all, such folks should be in the know and ought to best understand, from their experience, what needs to be done to make things better. They ought to know how to improve the broader public's perception of our government, and more importantly, how to find solutions to make government work properly.

Sadly, yet I must confess unsurprisingly, despite the authors' admirable work, they admitted, "These exit interviews didn't offer up all the solutions that we hoped to find for what ails Canadian democracy."[55] On the surface, the revelation that so many generally well-educated and presumably talented and experienced men and women cannot make things better for regular folks on Main Street seems incredibly disappointing. Indeed, there were "more than four thousand pages of transcripts from [their] eighty interviews with MPs from across the political spectrum and every province."[56] Woefully, in reference to how MPs spend a lot of time and effort "acting as customer service representatives for the federal bureaucracy," *Tragedy* concluded that "the impact of their efforts was more like plugging a single leak when the entire plumbing needs repair."[57] Having been a plumber's assistant myself, that view certainly resonates with me. So, too, do a few good ideas Loat and MacMillan raise near the end of their book about how to improve our democracy.

While falling short of tackling the elephant in the room, so to speak, which is indeed the whole plumbing system that needs an overhaul, their ideas are good, nonetheless. We will discuss them in greater detail later along with what we really need to do to make things better for Canadians of all walks of life. For now, let's focus on one of the truly wonderful discoveries outlined very well by *Tragedy*: how its authors' razor-sharp research found the majority of MPs they had discussions with are fairly decent people who want to do the right thing. Perhaps even the shrewd Lakota elder, who believed "our guide was inside—not outside" and that "HONOR was our guide," may have even found the majority of MPs interviewed also thought it "important . . . to know what was right, then what was wrong."

A common theme observed in *Tragedy* was that although representing a hugely diverse group of people, the MPs all viewed themselves as not being politicians. According to Loat and MacMillan, "Many articulated opposition to the political establishment as an important reason why they entered politics in the first place." Curiously, even upon successfully being voted into Parliament and taking up their new duties, "many MPs continued to identify themselves as outsiders."[58] Even more intriguing, *Tragedy* not only reveals that a lot of MPs, by nature, appear to be against the existing system, or status quo per se, but that they entered Canadian politics to effect positive change. A majority of those MPs who agreed to be interviewed said they "saw a system that didn't reflect them or what they viewed as important."[59] They appear to have felt the way I do when I decided to write this book—that something is desperately wrong and broken. Underscoring this, *Tragedy's* authors found that "some [MPs] believed the political system was moving in the wrong direction: that the link between government and citizens was broken, and prime ministers, red or blue, acted too frequently beyond accountability."[60]

In this regard, I found a certain synchronicity with my research for this book. The more I conducted my investigation, the more I saw that many authors writing about the Canadian government found a broken system. You will see ample evidence of this as you read on. In *Tragedy* we also see much of this despair, such as when its authors cite a famous Canadian journalist:

"PEOPLE OFTEN ASK: How can we reform politics?" asked columnist Andrew Coyne at the start of the 41st Parliament. "And the answer is: we can't. There are very few institutional changes that would do any good, and whatever would has no chance of being enacted. We're not going to change politics until we change the culture." Coyne concludes his thoughts fatalistically: "And we're not going to change the culture."[61]

The authors of *Tragedy* "hope Coyne is wrong" offering a few useful suggestions as to what can be done now, which we will certainly explore. Nonetheless, I beg to differ when they say "institutional or constitutional reforms . . . would likely take years."[62] It does not have to when one understands that all of those MPs who wanted to buck the system, for that certainly appears to be a major finding in *Tragedy*, already revealed to its authors what the major problem is, along with the desperately needed solution. OK, so maybe all those MPs did not verbally tell the writers of *Tragedy* how to fix our broken democracy and re-engage all of us voters. However, if the majority of Members felt "they were most proud of the things they'd achieved by working entrepreneurially, outside the traditional lines of power,"[63] as *Tragedy* states, it stands to reason the design of our government institutions is providing the wrong outcomes. If our highest elected officials must work outside the system to get anything done, we have some serious work to do to make things better.

There is also an urgency to make things better. The individuals running our country are afraid to do their jobs, to represent our true interests and to make the right decisions at the right time for Canada and Canadians. In the words of former Conservative MP Inky Mark:

> "They're scared—they're scared of the leader, scared of the caucus officers," he said, referring to the MPs in party leadership positions, such as the whip. "They are scared; they are just bullied. . . . Do you know what they're afraid of? They are afraid of not climbing the ladder. They are afraid of not getting the plum jobs."[64]

This all speaks to human nature and how people tend to act a certain way when the system they operate within is broken and encourages the wrong

outcomes, not only for MPs themselves, but for those constituents they purportedly represent. While not a behavioural psychologist, I will sensibly be
discussing how our system is built to fail us all, including those decent and
well-intentioned politicians of various party leanings who genuinely want to
make things better. The fact of the matter is that we have an opportunity to
lead by example here. Of course, just because we are Canadian does not mean
we have a monopoly on possessing good and better values, some inherent claim
to a moral superiority over other democratic nations that are struggling with
problems similar to our own. Those problems include increased polarization
between rich and poor, environmental degradation, decaying infrastructure
in dire need of repair, inequality between men and women, ongoing scandals
within government itself, and ever-growing voter apathy in the face of successive
political administrations' inability to deal with all of the foregoing and so much
more, as you will see readily enough.

If you perform an Internet web search on Canadian values, you are
bound to find the typical results, that Canadians are generally champions
of equality, freedom and peace among people. We appreciate and respect
cultural differences between people as well as the rule of law, which applies to
everyone. But a lot of other democratic nations champion the same ideas. Are
we all so very different from say Australians, Americans, New Zealanders and
the British? What about other Europeans, such as Germans, French, Italians,
Swedes and so on? How about those living in Southeast Asia and Africa? Are
there not individuals residing in all these places that share some fundamental
values and beliefs with other members of humanity, including us Canadians,
who mostly came from such places? Think about it! Maybe we all are not as
different as we have been led to believe and do not require walls to be built
between us. Nevertheless, some authors have gone to great lengths to portray
us as being very different from others residing in democracies elsewhere,
especially America.

One author's work that received a lot of attention is *Fire and Ice*, written by Michael Adams. In that book he seeks to prove Canadians have very different values than Americans. Likewise, he argues that we are not becoming more like our US neighbours in our thinking. I do not fully buy Adams' argument, much less his "story of social change in North America based on three snapshot surveys in the United States and Canada over the past decade" (*Fire and Ice* was written in 2003).[65] It may well be that we exhibit certain traits that markedly differ from Americans, as Adams finds using such things as his many social values maps, trying to place each populous generally within the box it needs to go, or as he calls them—Quadrants. He utilizes Environics surveys and a listing of 100 social values in Canada and the United States. It's all pretty heavy stuff, especially his roughly 60 pages of appendices, from A through G.

Frankly, I am not sure I understand all of it. Then again, Adams implies he may be susceptible to his own bias when he writes, "As a sociologist I am in a long-term, sometimes stormy, often rewarding relationship with generalization."[66] It does seem rather extreme to use the trends observed in his sociological data and research to make sweeping generalizations about Americans, such as:

> This pattern of social change suggests . . . many Americans are shutting themselves off from the world around them, becoming increasingly resigned to living in a competitive jungle where ostentatious consumption and personal thrills rule, and where there is little concern for the natural environment or for those whose American Dreams have turned into nightmares.[67]

Returning to the boxes Adams' research, for better or worse, attempts to place Americans and Canadians in, he has this crucially to say, or ahem, conclude:

[I]n terms of . . .the four quadrants, the difference between
the two societies' social values are plain. Canadians are
far better represented than Americans in the Idealism and
Autonomy quadrant, and far less present in the more nihilistic
Exclusion and Intensity quadrant . . . to the extent that they
reside in the upper quadrants, Canadians tend to fall on the
right side of the map—the Fulfillment end of the Survival
versus Fulfillment axis.[68]

Perhaps even more interesting, Adams finds "it is clear from [his]
research that Canada and the United States are socio-culturally distinct and
will remain so for many years to come—perhaps indefinitely." He believes
"historical, geographic, and institutional differences between the two countries
have placed Canada on a separate footing."[69] Some would argue this is a type
of clairvoyance since our neighbour to the south has indeed elected Donald
Trump, who may be a good candidate in representing the Exclusion and
Intensity leanings of Americans that are increasingly on that trajectory of thinking. Trump's election in 2016 just took over a dozen years after Adams' book
was published, placing his research perhaps in a credible light. Nevertheless, you
will see in Chapter 3 of my own book that the institutional differences between
Canada and America are actually lessening. This is extremely important because
while there are some differences in our respective democratic institutions,
both are under attack and becoming increasingly dysfunctional. Both are not
working for Americans and Canadians alike.

As our own institutions crumble, so to do the unifying values of
Canadians, which I contest are not so dissimilar from other citizens of the
world living in modern democracies elsewhere. We all want to do what's right.
It may be that our American allies are further down the road of institutional
decay, precipitated by the stronger toehold the polarizing elites have secured for
themselves in Washington DC and various state capitals. But make no mistake

as you read Chapter 3, our own futures are on a slippery slope as the institutions that bind us together and our shared identity become increasingly unhinged. You will see, unequivocally, that in the context of present-day Canada, Adams is completely incorrect in his earlier assertions that:

> Canadian democracy . . . is more democratic than the US system if judged on the basis of predictable policy outcomes. . . . The Canadian system of government, I would claim, does a better job of reflecting the considered judgment of the people and therefore keeping them engaged in the political process than does that of the United States.[70]

You are wrong, Mr. Adams. We are not so different. We, too, are shaped by our institutions, impacted by their relative health or mounting despair. Our national identity is inextricably tied to the well-being and effectiveness of our institutions, no different than nations elsewhere. That is why it is wrong to assert that we are somehow better than Americans. We are certainly not worse. But to extrapolate from a variety of data that our values are so very different, when each country's citizens are at different stages in dealing with the decay of their democratic institutions, misses the point entirely. When people are scared, afraid democracy is not working for them, afraid they are being left behind, their opinions can become darker by degrees. Democracy around the world is imperilled, by degrees, and that is likely what is shaping people's differences from country to country, also by degrees. There may be differences in our institutions and with certain beliefs, such as Americans sacred holding of their Second Amendment, the right to bear arms. Still, we all want our institutions to work the way they were designed to. We generally want the economy to work for everyone as well. And after all, even the Occupy Movement began in America, reflecting certain desires for fairness in that country. It is now our opportunity to lead by example.

I am not pro-American, and this book is mainly about Canada. However, I find it rather distasteful when Adams also states this about our American neighbours:

> Unlike Canadians, Americans are increasingly isolated from the poor, from immigrants, from 'the other.' This is both caused by and exacerbates Americans' fear of strangers and in turn their sense of estrangement from the larger society. . . . Americans pursue heaven on earth by fleeing their cities in search of bucolic bliss. Canadians, on the other hand, prefer to congregate in their cities."[71]

What absolute nonsense and jingoism. Maybe Americans feel they have to get away to places that are safe and working for their community, just like we are doing more and more. Maybe they are pretty decent people who want their government to do the right thing, just like we need to do. It is dangerous to throw stones in glass houses. Our values, just as those in other democracies, are at risk. We will never begin to solve problems that are global in nature until we fix our own problems, leading by example. Adams concludes that Canadians' sense of autonomy matters most to them. That won't matter at all if our institutions continue to falter, putting all Canadians and the country at even greater risk of being incapacitated, unable to move forward at all as a people with shared values.

There may even be a danger championing the Canadian identity as a multicultural one when the people who believe and respect our institutions are generally the same anyway. Does it matter what they look like or where they are from if they generally share in the belief that we need healthy and strong democratic institutions to reflect who we Canadians are? The dangerous paradox of multiculturalism is described well indeed by Andrew Cohen:

It is seen as a means to a unified society of universal values but an end in itself. The danger is that ethnic nationalism will trump civic nationalism, instead of the other way around. In the absence of competing visions of ourselves, multiculturalism is defining Canada.[72]

Maybe there would be a lot less problems in every country around the world and between countries themselves if we could all do a better job ensuring government decisions reflected our collective and innate desire to do the right thing instead of the wrong thing. Imagine if we could readily solve a huge and seemingly overwhelming number of problems in our own backyard. Imagine if we demanded major reforms that were clearly laid out for us to grasp, that could be as easily understood by most everyone as how to fix a leaky pipe in their house, with the instructions unambiguously listed for all to see. This is not as far-fetched as it may seem. There is a way to easily make things better for you, me and our families. All that is required is that you read on with an open mind. For within Canada, with all its diversity, lies the answer to many problems, not only facing Canadians, but other democracies around the world. There are answers to problems besetting Trump's America, a post-Brexit UK, or elsewhere in other countries. There are even answers to problems confronting international organizations that cannot seem to get anything done.

It's time for us Canadians and our country to punch above our weight, to show the rest of the world how to make things right in an era where most leaders, including our own, have talked a good game, often just focusing on their image and their political party's image, without implementing solutions to problems that desperately need fixing. Let's take a closer look at why the status quo is no longer tenable, why things need to change. There is too much being done wrong. We need to make it right.

CHAPTER 3
BETRAYAL

When the people fear the government, there is tyranny. When the government fears the people, there is liberty.

—Thomas Jefferson

This is a great country—Canada. Our young nation is still one of the best places in the world to live, especially considering the war, famine, poverty and oppression that continue to ravage far too many places on this earth. But we all face numerous, almost insurmountable challenges, not the least of which is global warming and climate change. We cannot afford to be complacent about the fact that we currently seem to be faring better than many other countries. There is simply too much to be done to fix everything that is going wrong here, and in other countries, for us to be lulled into a false sense of security.

While the truth of what is actually happening may weigh heavily upon us, it is only by willingly looking at that truth, honestly and openly, that we can possibly move forward to a significantly better and more productive Canada. Otherwise, the enormous and troubling state of affairs we are now all in will continue to grow, making it increasingly improbable to realize our potential. My intent here is not to paint a hopelessly negative picture of Canada or to make you, the reader, feel lousy and depressed. My hope is that by shedding light on what is going wrong in Canada, we can all begin to understand the urgent action required to swiftly begin making things right, not only for our own country but, through our example, for countries where the urgency is even greater.

The truth is . . . we and our country have been betrayed—perhaps not intentionally but that is of little consequence. Many of our government institutions, departments, agencies and organizations meant to serve Canadians and strengthen our democracy, are under attack. Such is our betrayal. The attack at times is direct. It is a response to some irrational and political ideology. In other instances, it arises out of sheer neglect or because various leaders are pursuing their own agendas to obtain more financial gain or stature amongst their colleagues and others.

This betrayal grows deeper still, an enlarged wound that grows apace where the tipping point between life and prosperity for all, rather than just plain struggle, is not so easily defined. The betrayal we face is not always visible, often masked by soundbites in the news and carefully crafted images conjured up by political theatre. Some Canadians, such as the Indigenous or First Peoples of Canada, as well as other groups of people in different so-called democracies, have been betrayed more than others. As a result, the majority of us are suffering to varying degrees due to the adversity we each face from the betrayal we continue to endure.

Still, in order to move forward as Canadians and fix what is in dire need of repair, we must make an honest effort to reveal that which has gone wrong and continues to go wrong around us. I will not be covering everything that may be adversely affecting you, your family and friends in Canada. But I hope the sheer volume of examples I raise will provide you with ample evidence that it is time to make things right. And doing so requires your participation because, while exercising your democratic right to vote today may not make much of a difference, it could soon if enough Canadians demand the changes they deserve.

In his pocket-sized and fairly short book *On Tyranny*, Yale history professor Timothy Snyder cleverly warns Americans to heed 20 lessons from the 20th century. These lessons are just as applicable to Canada, the UK and elsewhere. And Snyder's second lesson may perhaps be the most important one—*Defend Institutions*. He writes, "We tend to assume that institutions will automatically maintain themselves against even the most direct attacks." Snyder uses an extreme example, stating, "This was the very mistake that some German Jews made about Hitler and the Nazis after they had formed a government."[1] Other examples could certainly be used, and we have seen how Putin uses organizational design to actually maintain his iron grip of power. We have also seen how the president of Turkey, Recep Tayyip Erdoğan, centralized that country's government for his own advantage, all the while creating havoc for ordinary Turks.

As Adnan Khan recently wrote in an opinion piece for *Maclean's*, Erdoğan "now governs over an increasingly divided nation, with an economy in the throes of an inflation and foreign-debt crisis…" For Khan, Erdoğan is "democratic in name but more aligned with a view that power is dictated rather than debated…"[2] Remember the case of Jamal Khashoggi and his gruesome murder in October 2018? He was "the dissident journalist who was lured into the Saudi consulate in Istanbul, strangled to death and then dismembered."[3] For existing democracies that need to defend institutions, "the mistake is to assume that rulers who came to power through institutions cannot change or destroy those very institutions."[4] Democracy everywhere is a fragile thing. We need to protect those institutions meant to reflect democratic values. We need our government institutions to work effectively and efficiently so that they operate to do that which is right instead of so very wrong.

I recall a long time ago hearing there are three kinds of people in the world. The first kind of person sits in an easy chair, reading newspaper stories about some terrible events, thinking it is too bad people are suffering. The second kind of person also sits in an easy chair reading terrible stories, but they take it a step further, actually wishing they could do something to make the lives of those suffering better or perhaps to prevent such events from happening again. However, even this kind of person feels they cannot make a difference in our modern and complicated world because they believe some problems just cannot be solved, or that it is up to others, such as elected officials, to do that. The third kind of person is rarer. They not only read about the same terrible events and wish they could do something about it, but they actually decide to get out of their comfort zone—that easy chair—and really do something about it.

Maybe most of us like the nice feeling of that easy chair. Yet, I have a feeling a lot more of us would be willing to get out of our easy chair and tackle seemingly unsolvable problems if we knew there were clear and workable solutions for them. We would not likely sit in our easy chair knowing a water leak in our house was doing damage and costing our family money. We would not idly sit by while that leak did so much damage it would destroy the quality of life in our home we were used to. We would be apt to repair it as soon as possible to improve our own and our family's situation.

Well, our nation may be a lot bigger than our own comfortable residence, but this home we all share, called Canada, has some serious plumbing issues. And all those leaky pipes, while seemingly far away in places such as on Parliament Hill in Ottawa, or in various provincial legislatures, are nonetheless also costing us dearly. They are eroding our quality of life in a meaningful and downright nasty way. They are also costing us, as taxpayers, a lot of money.

Our Payroll System

Let's start with one of our leakiest pipes—the dysfunctional mess known as our federal government. In no particular order of importance, I will discuss some of its unmitigated disasters adversely impacting you, your family and your neighbours. The cost of it all in terms of wasted money, resources and time, not to mention the missed opportunities for Canadians to improve their standard of living, is absolutely unacceptable. Many of you have undoubtedly heard of the colossal waste associated with 'Phoenix,' a supposedly modern high-tech payroll system, touted as the best replacement for all the disparate systems previously used by various federal government departments in Canada. It would be a gross understatement to say the Phoenix system has not been working properly. According to a recent Senate finance committee report, it "is on track to cost Canadians $2.2 billion in unplanned costs by 2023."[5] Apparently we, here and now in a first world country, cannot even make payroll for our federal employees. This is something our forefathers in the era of the horse and buggy could do regularly. I guess it is just too complicated.

We have been hearing regularly in the weekly papers about tens of thousands of federal government employees who have not been receiving their appropriate pay. Many of these thousands of employees have not been paid at all and have gone into substantial personal debt, with some even facing foreclosures on their homes. You can imagine the immense physical stress such individuals are under as they fall increasingly behind on their financial obligations, including to their children. The case of Jacqueline Cordova, as reported on by the *CBC* in June 2017, is instructive. Ms. Cordova had no income for more than nine months and, upon missing a payment tied to her mortgage, she faced foreclosure. Twenty-seven-year-old Jimena, Cordova's daughter, was forced to take time off from her post-secondary studies to help out her mother by working three jobs to improve their income situation.[6]

If this is not appalling enough, the mother, who required leave for eye surgery, also did not automatically receive her record of employment that would qualify her for sick pay while on leave from her job with the Defence Department at CFB (Canadian Forces Base) Edmonton. Thankfully, after *CBC's* "Go Public" made inquiries, Cordova's bank notified her it would agree to refinance her rather than foreclose on her home.[7] This is just one of the many ways the Phoenix disaster is impacting Canadians who continue to face the wrath of technology run amok like one sees in *The Terminator* movie series. By late November 2017, after Canada's Auditor General (AG), Michael Ferguson, released a report damning the government of its handling of the Phoenix pay system implementation, the damage inflicted upon the public service and taxpayers had been done. We all bore the brunt of the negative fallout arising from yet another absurd decision emanating from our broken government in Ottawa.

The AG's report only reviewed the implementation phase beginning in February 2016. Per a report from *The Star*, the AG found it will take years and cost over $540 million to repair the botched system involving a backlog of more than $500 million in pay arrears, impacting over 150,000 federal government employees.[8] Curiously, I have yet to see any major public reports concerning those who have been collectively overpaid to the tune of hundreds of millions of dollars. What and where are the account numbers involving the overpayments and who exactly are the people and faces behind these accounts? I hope recipients of overpayments are all good and honest individuals, but we know there can always be some bad apples. Are any recipients higher government officials working on Phoenix itself or closely allied to those working on the project? Perhaps account holders are on contract from the third-party service providers working on this great and innovative new system? Or maybe the individuals receiving overpayments have family members working for the high-tech geniuses working on this modern marvel that attempts to pay employees, which is oh so difficult!

Who even knows, if at all, just how much in dollar figures are the larger overpayments being made to various account holders? It is all so very damn complex, or meant to be so. I really have no answers, being an outsider like you. There are so many questions yet so little public information. We do know from the AG that, as of April 2017, "51 per cent of federal employees were getting paid too much or too little."[9] We also know from yet another *CBC News* piece, this one from January 2018, that as of June 2017, about 59,000 federal employees had received overpayments according to the November 2017 AG's report. The AG also concluded in his report that as of June 30, 2017, the amount the government owed to its federal employees was $228 million versus overpayments of $295 million.[10]

The January *CBC* story also highlighted how unbelievably wrong things are going for some honest individuals who have been overpaid and wanting to make things right. Jerome Marty, a former scientist employed by Fisheries and Oceans Canada, left his job in 2016 but continued to receive payments via the Phoenix system. By his own reckoning, which I trust is sound since he is a scientist, rocket or otherwise, Mr. Marty owed around $25,000 of accumulated overpayments. However, when he was finally able to get through to the typically jammed Phoenix call centre, they did not believe he actually owed anything.[11] Maybe they thought he had merely 'Gone Fishing' and was still around. In Marty's own words dealing with the call centre:

> The person looked into my file and revealed to me that I didn't have any amounts due to the government . . . As far as I'm concerned that's absolutely incorrect . . . After spending so much time and energy, I will never walk away, because I find it's part of being a good citizen and being honest . . . There is also the implication in terms of pension, RSP, my own pension plan.[12]

What a debacle! Fortunately Mr. Marty knows the difference between right and wrong. One can only wonder at the possibility of other individuals out there who may not and if there is another zero after $25,000 owed. Hopefully such individuals are still in the country with our tax dollars. I am not sure we will find them though. Even if you have little sympathy for civil servants unable to get appropriately paid for months and months, by the end of this book, you may have more empathy for the bulk of them who really want to do a good job. And after all, aren't people entitled to be paid for doing their jobs? How would you feel? Never mind the fact that, had the Canadian government not spent well over half a billion dollars (and growing) on a payroll system that does not work, it could have better spent that money elsewhere. It could have provided additional funds to subsidize housing for the poor, improve healthcare services, lower tuition costs for students, purchase modern equipment for our military forces, etc.

According to a May 2017 article by the *National Post*, "Liberals will spend $142 million over two years to hire 200 temporary workers on top of the 300 hired to date to deal with the problems wrought by Phoenix."[13] And, *CBC News* reported on February 27, 2018 "the Phoenix fix was approaching $1B and that the federal government is finally looking at 'scrapping the system.' "[14]

It definitely has been hard to track all the evolving and opaque scandals. How would Shakespeare have responded to all the confusion costing Canadians so much? Perhaps by remarking as he did in Act II, Scene 3 of *Macbeth*, "Confusion now hath made its masterpiece." And it is precisely within massive chaos and confusion that fraud and deceit is perpetrated easily, just as in the global financial crisis some ten years ago.

As *CBC News* reported, Canada's 2018–19 budget "calls for an additional $431 million to address problems created by Phoenix . . . in addition to the $460 million already committed to both implement the pay system and resolve subsequent problems." Additionally, "the budget also earmarks $16 million to begin the process of replacing the troubled system."[15]

Our Indigenous Peoples

Perhaps our leaders could have even spent some of that wasted money to ensure our Indigenous Peoples have access to safe drinking water, a basic human right. Indigenous Peoples, our fellow citizens of a distinctive heritage, deserve to be treated with dignity and respect. We only need to read about the tragedies involving unsafe drinking water on reserves, such as those surfaced by the *Globe and Mail* recently, to grasp how well our national government is doing at ensuring First Nations People have access to safe and clean water. Per the *Globe's* research, which began in the summer of 2016, "one-third of First Nations had systems that were at medium or high risk of providing unsafe water according to [Indigenous and Northern Affairs Canada] INAC's assessment criteria." Apparently, there are "numerous examples of failed water treatment plants, water towers and other infrastructure."[16] Worse yet, this is what Vowel has to say in *Indigenous Writes*. When Bill S-11, the *Safe Water for First Nations Act* was passed into law in 2013, "no regulations were ever drafted or implemented under the Harper government, and the situation remains as dire as ever as one can tell by the stories that come out of First Nations' communities."[17]

We could discus many national tragedies involving Canada's Indigenous Peoples, such as the travesty of the residential school system where thousands of children died of abuse, or the more recent horrors of all the missing Indigenous women and girls. The abuse concerning the erstwhile residential school system is well documented, especially in the voluminous reports generated by the Truth and Reconciliation Commission of Canada. We already know from Vowel's *Indigenous Writes* that there were "6,000 children (at least) who died in the system."

In terms of missing Indigenous women and the violence perpetrated against them, a January 2019 *CBC News* article summarizes some disturbing statistics concerning this ongoing issue, and the Canadians involved. "A 2017 report from Statistics Canada showed Indigenous women are six times more likely to be victims of homicide than non-Indigenous women."[18] Breaking down the numbers further, but always keeping in mind that they involve real human beings, our fellow citizens, we learn this. "An RCMP report in 2014 found 1,181 police-recorded incidents of Indigenous female homicides between 1980 and 2012, and missing Indigenous females dating back to 1951." Results indicate that "Indigenous women and girls" are "over-represented among missing and murdered women in Canada."[19] You may have already heard that a national inquiry is looking into the circumstances involving why there have been, and continues to be, so many incidents of missing and murdered Indigenous women. The inquiry was initiated in 2016 and the report is supposed to be completed soon. Its purpose is "to examine the disproportionate numbers and investigate how such cases are handled."[20]

Yet as Muriel Stanley Venne, "a member of [the] National Aboriginal Advisory Committee" and "founder of the Institute for the Advancement of Aboriginal Women, based in Edmonton," believes, and whom CBC cites, the national inquiry report may not produce all the answers we need. For Venne, "a lack of information around what drives killers to prey on Indigenous women will leave that final document lacking key answers…"[21] Hopefully the report will be of some value to Indigenous and non-Indigenous Canadians alike, in concluding upon how we can significantly reduce the violence facing the descendants of First Peoples. This is especially important given the suicide crisis facing some Indigenous communities, and how such a crisis may have potentially been avoided. How so?

In another January 2019 news item, this one featured in *The Chronicle Herald*, we learn that "Months before Eskasoni declared its second suicide crisis in a decade, an independent audit showed Indigenous Services Canada was failing First Nations communities."[22] Specifically, the audit "concluded that Indigenous Services Canada did not satisfactorily measure or report on Canada's progress in closing the socio-economic gaps between on-reserve First Nations people and other Canadians…" Moreover, "the Auditor General of Canada report released last spring [2018]…concluded that the department's use of data to improve education programs was inadequate."[23] If this is indeed true, and I have no reason to doubt Andrew Rankin's journalism, we need those in charge of the government department concerned to be better schooled themselves, perhaps becoming more well-versed in the Haudenosaunee core value known as the Seventh Generation. After all, as we learned, it avers that Chiefs should "consider how present day decisions will impact their descendants." The only difference being that our government Chiefs are likely poor students. According to Rankin, earlier in January 2019, "Leroy Denny, chief of Nova Scotia's largest Mi'kmaq community, declared a mental health crisis in his community after a rash of suicides there."[24] Rankin also cites Dalhousie University's Wayne MacKay, a law professor, who "says the situation in Eskasoni reflects a country-wide crisis facing First Nations."[25] Truth and reconciliation does not seem to be working, not in deeds anyway. At least that is my opinion.

Emphasizing the importance of their core value, the Seventh Generation, as well as the obvious notion that some First Peoples feel they are being unfairly treated, is a comment made by one protester at a recent town hall in Kamloops, BC. In that early January 2019 town hall, where Prime Minister Justin Trudeau spoke to many First Peoples, angry and upset about the recent arrests of some pipeline protesters, "a man who identified himself as Will George stood up and began to yell that the prime minister had lied about wanting reconciliation with First Nations." Apparently, and as carried by Toronto's *City News*, "George said 'You're a liar and a weak leader. What do you tell your children?'"[26] During the same town hall, another upset participant raised the issue of the Canadian government not having the right to build a pipeline across First Peoples territory. "A man who identified himself as Arnie Jack from the Shuswap Nation said Canada does not have a deed to its territory and has no right to build the Trans Mountain pipeline expansion through its lands." As well, "Jack described the arrests in northern B.C. as a 'national disgrace.'"[27] Clearly some Indigenous Peoples may be feeling betrayed by Canada's leadership and the decisions that leadership has been making. This has likely gone on for years. As for the pipeline issue, we will elaborate on that later.

Did you know that, while eight per cent of all Canadians four years old and younger identify as First Nations, Métis or Inuit, they comprise more than half the pre-schoolers in foster care.[28] We will discuss more about the plight of our Indigenous Peoples and what more we can learn from them later in the book (Please do not mistake my brevity here as an intention to gloss over serious issues, all deserving our government's attention and action, rather than its nice-sounding words to address them.).

Our Military

Since I hopefully have the attention of a diverse group of readers fed up with bad decision-making by governments, let's examine many more examples of how Canadians of all walks of life are being adversely impacted by their own government. It is a kind of tyranny. If you believe our military is being suitably run, so that Canada has some degree of defence capability and can make a meaningful contribution to NATO, the UN (United Nations) and peaceful institutions around the world, consider the following: our Royal Canadian Navy has endured continuous setbacks to modernize its depleted and aging fleet. As dismally portrayed in an opinion piece by Senator Colin Kenny, also past Chair of Canada's Senate Committee on National Security and Defence, things are looking pretty bleak for our dedicated sailors. Kenny puts it succinctly when he states, "The Navy is unable to do what the government needs it to do." That encompasses "protecting our exports, preventing smuggling, providing humanitarian and disaster relief, enforcing domestic laws, projecting force and supporting our allies."[29] Sounds pretty important. Obviously you, I and all Canadians should expect our navy to be able to perform its core functions, just like the federal payroll centre, Veterans Affairs, Immigration and other critical departments that exist to serve Canadians. Too bad our government cannot meet our expectations and remains unaccountable year after unaccountable year.

Over three years ago our naval fleet found itself without any refueling supply ships, which are vital to ensuring the rest of our ships can sail to wherever they need to go to do what they need to do. The last two of our refueling ships were lost in 2014: the HMCS *Protecteur* by fire and the HMCS *Preserver* by rust. As Kenny found early in November 2017, Vancouver based Seaspan, was still waiting for a contract to build two joint support ships and faced timing, cost and compliance issues. Briefly, Seaspan would only be able to start on the supply ships after 2023 because of other construction commitments to the Coast Guard. So the navy will not get its first refueling ship until 2026, the second in 2028. The government has allocated $2.6 billion for these new ships but the watchdog Parliamentary Budget Office (PBO) indicated costs could end up being as much as $4.13 billion. According to Kenny, Seaspan is also using a 26-year-old German design that does not meet NATO interoperability standards at this time. He wonders, "Why so old?" [30]

Our navy's position is even more dire, so please pay attention. Previously, in August 2015, the government at the time did accept a proposal from a Quebec shipyard, Davie, to provide the navy with a supply ship called the MV *Asterix*, which the government would lease. That ship apparently met all the requirements, including NATO's. [31] Intriguingly, upon the Liberals' ascension to power in November 2015, a few months after the Davie naval project was announced by the Conservatives, the leader of Irving, another Canadian shipbuilder, sent a letter to several cabinet ministers objecting at not being given a chance to bid on the Davie contract. As Andrew Coyne wrote in a January 2018 article for the *National Post*, "The Irving family is very rich, very powerful, and very close to several prominent Liberals." Here's the catch as Coyne wrote. Coinciding with the Irving letter being received, a cabinet committee recommended putting a hold on the Davie contract, at least for a couple of months. Then, only after the news was leaked, maybe because some navy officials feared they would be without refueling ships even longer, and "amid the ensuing uproar in Quebec," did the Liberal government allow the Davie contract to progress. [32]

More intriguingly, Vice Chief of Defence Staff, Vice-Admiral Mark Norman, was removed from command on January 9, 2017. He was apparently not told why. This led to much speculation and likely tarnished his reputation. It has been longer than a year since he lost his command, and to date, he has not been charged with anything. Confused? Coyne views Mark Norman's treatment "disturbing enough were there not a strong whiff of politics surrounding the whole affair." Coyne states, "So far as the case against Norman has been made out—in the RCMP's application for a warrant to search his home—it is that he is supposed to have leaked confidential cabinet discussions to a private defense contractor, which were then leaked to the press." It remains uncertain whether or not Vice-Admiral Norman was the one who leaked information about potential and further delays for our navy's desperately needed refueling ships. Still, as Coyne astutely points out in two entirely reasonable arguments: "No one has alleged that Norman had any motive but to prevent yet another procurement decision from being consumed by politics," and "Charge Norman or clear him, but present the evidence against him and be damned." [33]

The renowned Canadian historian, J. L. Granatstein, raises a good question for Canadians in his January 2018 special piece carried by the *Globe and Mail*. Poignantly, it is headlined, "If we can't defend ourselves, are we truly sovereign?" Granatstein, like most of us, is not a warmonger. He talks about how our government "claims to protect Canada and Canadians" but "does not do that job in a credible fashion." Regarding the shipbuilding procurement issue we already touched upon, he finds it "a fiasco, producing very little at a huge cost." He notes that our replacement frigate ships are decades away from materializing. Worse yet for our northern residents, arctic patrol vessels will be "unable to go into the Arctic in winter."

As for the Royal Canadian Air Force, most of us already know that our ancient CF-18 fighters have long been obsolete and in urgent need of replacement. Granatstein finds our military air capability to be "in even worse shape" than our navy, our sea capabilities already "reduced to an ineffective constabulary."[34]

Apart from the Conservatives' F-35 replacement jet procurement nightmare I will touch on in Chapter 5, not only have the Liberals abandoned the plan to buy these newer jets, they intend to purchase used Australian F-18s instead. According to Granatstein's analysis, that means Canada will be without any newer, more capable jets until the mid-2020s at the earliest.[35] I guess we will not have proper jets and ships for quite a while, something that likely does not motivate those serving in our navy and air force very much (not to mention motivating anyone new to enlist), especially if their own equipment puts them at risk while trying to do their jobs. Columnist Andrew Coyne sums up the absurdity of the fighter jet debacle alone nicely:

> ". . . to meet an urgent 'capability gap' . . . the federal government is kicking the competition to produce a replacement jet that it promised two years ago. A winner will be chosen no sooner than 2022 . . . The planes will be deliverable in 2025 . . . as an interim measure, it will upgrade its current fleet of 30-year-old CF-18 Hornets with 18 virtually identical second-hand Australian F-18 Hornets of the same age. This follows its decision to cancel . . . [buying] the same number of new F-18 Super Hornets from Boeing, in retaliation for Boeing's invocation of U.S. trade remedy laws against Canada's subsidies to Bombardier."[36]

What a train wreck for our patriotic citizens who want to serve their country. It is like asking someone to play hockey with a ski pole instead of a hockey stick and snowshoes instead of skates. Simply un-Canadian. And I have not even mentioned our army capabilities yet. Even just scratching the surface, Granatstein paints a bleak picture here too. "The Canadian Army is tiny, its three brigades [understaffed] and ill-equipped."[37] Canada once touted itself as a large contributor to international peacekeeping efforts, our soldiers known for their blue helmets, harkening back to the days of Lester B. Pearson. Now, as Granatstein observes, "only one brigade is deployable abroad, and the Army reserve can handle only one emergency at a time."[38] As for the army's equipment, our dedicated service personnel are faring not much better on the ground than those in the air or at sea. Our troops appear to be increasingly at risk, operating with obsolete and insufficient equipment to protect Canadians and maintain our once proud reputation as a respected member of the international peacekeeping community.

Nonsensically, and "on the drawing board for more than a decade, new trucks are only coming into service; the Army's armoured vehicles are being slowly upgraded, its tanks are obsolescent and the defence systems to protect troops in action are almost completely absent."[39] So states Granatstein, a very credible source and great Canadian.

Our Veterans

Compounding the miserable state of affairs regarding our military equipment, which likely can contribute to putting those who honourably serve our country in harm's way, is the manner our veterans have been treated upon leaving the military. It appears that thousands of veterans, of all race, gender and creed, are waiting an unreasonably long time, in some cases months and even years, to obtain their rightful pensions and benefits upon being discharged from their duties. It sounds like another backlog akin to Phoenix.

As reported on by the *Globe and Mail* in July 2017, one veteran who had to wait more than six months for his initial pension cheque is a lead plaintiff of a proposed class action suit against the federal government. The suit accuses the government of breaching its responsibilities to former members of the military as they relate to retirement benefits owed.[40] According to the *Globe*, the lawsuit claims "Discharged members are humiliated . . . and are not permitted to transition to civilian life with dignity."[41] Of course, aside from the ludicrous fact that the government attracted a class-action lawsuit because it did not pay former military personnel retirement benefits owed, who knows in such and similar cases how much we taxpayers can be on the hook for more given the egregious wrongs being committed by the federal government of Canada.

One sad example of far too many is the case of Tricia Beauchamp. As documented by *CBC News* reporter Murray Brewster early in 2017, Ms. Beauchamp, a retired sergeant and former member of the Canadian Air Force's logistics branch, waited more than five months for her military pension and severance. During that period, she was evicted from her home close to Ottawa. Brewster outlines a very difficult time in Beauchamp's life. A single mother who survived two onslaughts of cancer, including one which necessitated 26 radiation treatments, Beauchamp was medically discharged from the air force in the summer of 2016. By November 2016, with insufficient income, she was evicted from her home. Despite finally obtaining her severance and pension just prior to Christmas, Beauchamp's Veterans Affairs disability and other medical benefits still had not been processed at the time *CBC* published Brewster's news item. She is not alone. *CBC* reported in the fall of 2016 that Veterans Affairs was dealing with a backlog of more than 11,500 disability claims, indicative of why people like Beauchamp were getting the shaft.[42]

This situation is also disturbingly similar to the Phoenix payroll system debacle in its unacceptable treatment of ordinary, hardworking Canadians. As Gary Walbourne, Canada's military ombudsman exasperatingly mentioned in referring to Beauchamp's situation, "How do you expect the mother, a veteran who has served the country, to raise children on a baby bonus check? That's absolutely ludicrous."[43] According to my research, things are not only going poorly for injured veterans when they want to collect their generally modest pension and benefits, but even for those decent Canadians who want to help them. Published in a fall 2017 article carried by the *National Post*, David Pugilese wrote about how one proponent of veterans' improved treatment actually had his job offer rescinded by the Canadian military. Disgustingly, it appears the veterans' advocate lost the opportunity to make things better for veterans because "he wrote to Prime Minister Justin Trudeau to complain that injured military personnel, including a soldier who died, weren't being treated properly."[44]

As is the case in most situations, Master Warrant Officer Barry Westholm, the job applicant who lost his chance to help veterans struggling with their disabilities, was one of the soldiers closer to our troops in the trench; he was someone with a better understanding of what injured military personnel face upon medical discharge. Before resigning in 2013 "to protest the poor state of affairs in the unit that is supposed to take care of injured troops," Westholm held the title of Sergeant Major in Joint Personnel Support. Commendably, as Pugilese summarizes, when Westholm in June 2017 was offered a position to "turn around" the unit, he replied to its deputy commander that "he would work for free since he felt an obligation to help the injured." So when precisely was the job offer revoked? Only "two months later because Westholm sent emails to Trudeau, Defence Minister Harjit Sajjan and Chief of the Defence Staff Gen. Jon Vance outlining how the current system failed military personnel, including Pte. Leah Greene. And who can blame Westholm when, as Pugilese pens, he "emailed Trudeau on July 22 to complain that Greene, who suffered a spinal injury during her military service that left her partially paralyzed, had run into roadblocks trying to get help from the Canadian forces and government."[45]

And what of Greene, another faceless Canadian had it not been for Westholm's obvious concern and one journalist's article? She needed and deserved some help from our government. Helping her would have been the right thing to do. Well, sadly, after years of "dealing with bureaucratic red tape, chronic pain and mental issues," she "died July 26," just days after Westholm wrote to Trudeau. Unbelievably, in the wake of Greene's death, when Westholm sent more emails to various high officials asking why the system failed her and "highlighting problems both with the JSPU and Veterans Affairs" in her case, the deputy commander of the JSPU, who had first offered Westholm a job with his organization, had this to say: "You have repeatedly made slanderous, inappropriate and ill-informed statements about the JSPU and its personnel to our CDS, MND, PM and many others," concluding he "wouldn't be a good fit."[46]

Westholm, who doesn't strike me as being a fool, has discerned a huge problem concerning human nature and what really strikes our government as being important, something we will be examining in greater detail in Chapter 6. In his own words, "They don't seem to want to hear about where the problems are and how they can be fixed . . . The focus is more on optics, making sure no one in the leadership is embarrassed."[47] Perhaps, as we learned from the Penobscot Native earlier, a healthy dose of embarrassment would be a good thing for our leadership. Most citizens know the difference between right and wrong. But let's move on.

Our Handling of the Omar Khadr Case

Another great travesty concerning the treatment of our military personnel is the way both Conservative and Liberal governments have botched up the case of Omar Khadr. As you likely are aware, when Khadr, a Canadian citizen born here in 1986, was just 15 years old, he was embroiled in a shoot-out at what was believed to be an al-Qaeda compound nestled in Afghanistan. Apparently Khadr had been taken to Afghanistan by his father, who was affiliated with al-Qaeda and other terrorist groups. It was in that hornet's nest—Afghanistan, as the Russians came to know it in their long war there, that Khadr was captured by American soldiers after a heated battle between them and the Taliban. That battle cost Christopher Speer, a US Army Sergeant 1st Class and medic, his life. Layne Morris, another US Sergeant, lost one of his eyes. Khadr allegedly lobbed the grenade that caused Speer's death, and was soon shipped off to that infamous American base known as Guantanamo Bay in Cuba.[48]

Being the youngest detainee on the American base did not curry Khadr any favour or sympathy with the US forces there. In 2003 he was interrogated for his war crimes. In 2010, Khadr pleaded guilty to murder and other charges. Sentencing was for eight years in addition to time he had already served. In 2012, he was back in Canada to serve the rest of his sentence. By May 2015, after 13 years of incarceration, he was out and back on the streets, pending appeal of his earlier admission of guilt, which he said was made under duress. Interestingly during the same year Khadr made his guilty plea, in 2010, the Supreme Court of Canada ruled that Canadian intelligence officials obtained evidence from Khadr under 'oppressive circumstances.' This, as Rob Gillies wrote in a story published by *Global News*, "included sleep deprivation, during interrogations at Guantanamo Bay in 2003." That evidence was subsequently shared with US officials.[49]

Recently, the current Liberal government under Trudeau decided to settle a $20 million lawsuit that Khadr's lawyers had brought forth earlier, for wrongful imprisonment, to the tune of $10.5 million and an apology.[50] Khadr's lawyers argued our government had "violated international law by not protecting its own citizen and conspired with the U.S. in its abuse of Khadr," who had spent ten years in Guantanamo.[51] Many Canadians were outraged that our tax dollars were going to support what many people see as a terrorist who killed a soldier doing his job to protect others. As reported on in July 2017 by the *Globe and Mail*, "Seven in 10 oppose the settlement, according to an Angus Reid Poll." The government had a different take on things.

The Liberals, as the *Globe's* John Ibbitson wrote, "kept changing their story." Firstly, "previous governments had violated Mr. Khadr's Charter rights and this government was simply doing right by him, Justin Trudeau maintained." Indeed, the history of the supposed complexity behind Khadr's case seems to have involved former governments, both Liberal and Conservative. Secondly, "when that didn't fly, the Prime Minister insisted that the government was saving the taxpayer money by settling for a smaller amount now, instead of a larger amount later."[52]

All of this smacks again of yet more government bungling with ordinary Canadians losing out on many fronts. It all boils down to this. It has cost Canadian taxpayers over $10 million to pay off someone, whether guilty or not, who killed an American soldier and severely injured another. Successive Canadian governments somehow found themselves in violation of a minor's *Charter* rights, having been outside the parameters of the law by allowing, what many call a 'child soldier' to languish in the abyss of Guantanamo Bay. It sounds like something right out of *Homeland Season 6*! Whether you are on Khadr's side or not, it is clear the situation should never have gotten as far as it did. What the hell were our leaders thinking? How could it have all gone so legally wrong that we had to pay Khadr all those tax dollars while short-changing our vets and not supplying our soldiers with the equipment they need? What a bloody mess!

Oh, and the widow of the US soldier killed, along with the soldier who lost an eye, filed a wrongful death and injury lawsuit against Khadr himself in 2014, fearing he might get a big payout from Canada when his lawyers filed their own case. A US judge granted $134.2 million in damages in 2015.[53] Legal representatives reportedly then, around the summer of 2017, filed a case in Canada to go after Khadr's payout—his newly taxpayer-lined pockets. Again, what a bloody mess for everyone concerned, especially the family of the late Christopher Speer.

Our Foreign Aid

And while we are on the topic of messes and Afghanistan, we should not forget about the Canadian government's botched handling of a project known as Promoting Women's Political Participation in Afghanistan (PWPPA). Per an August 2018 *CBC News* article, this initiative "was approved by the Conservative government of Stephen Harper in 2013, and delivered between May 2014 and July 2016." However, according to an independent evaluation of Canada's efforts to help [Afghan] women have a voice in their country's politics, the project did not deliver much in the way of solid results. With respect to the $5.6 million in project costs, "most of the money went to the salaries and benefits of . . . workers and consultants delivering the project, with little committed to field activities directly benefiting Afghan women."[54]

We taxpayers must have a lot of money to burn when it comes to Afghanistan. We have paid off Khadr and funded projects on the ground in Afghanistan that have not yielded the results most Canadians would likely expect. The *CBC* article noted that Canada has committed more than $2 billion in aid to Afghanistan. Many Canadians take it for granted that our aid has substantially helped the war-torn country. But has it? *CBC* cites Nipa Banerjee, senior fellow of international development at the University of Ottawa, who reveals taxpayers may have a less than full grasp of how useful our aid has been. In Banerjee's view, "Monitoring is hardly done," and "substantial analysis is hardly ever done."[55] This raises a necessary question. If Canadians spend billions of dollars on aid to other countries, what is the point if we really don't have a sensible understanding of the outcomes and benefits achieved? Heaven forbid the aid cheques are generated by the Phoenix system! Our soldiers have worked hard in Afghanistan. Their legacy merits our government properly handling the Afghanistan file. Then again, they should also equip our soldiers properly and ensure our veterans live in dignity, receiving the pension and benefits they not only deserve, but have earned.

Our International Relations

How is it even possible that, during Justin Trudeau's recent February 2018 state visit to India, a former member of an illegal Sikh separatist group convicted of murder, named Jaspal Atwal, attended at least one event related to the Trudeau visit? During that event, Atwal was pictured with our Prime Minister's wife and Canadian Minister of Infrastructure and Communities, Amarjeet Sohi. Atwal was also invited to dine with Justin Trudeau at a formal event hosted by the Canadian High Commission in Delhi, but that invitation was later rescinded.[56] I wonder just how much it cost taxpayers to send Trudeau, his wife and delegates, to India where they could sabotage the good relationship we have with India and to have Canada and Canadians ridiculed as imbecilic all around the world! We know better. Too bad our government does not. I will not write at length about our faltering international relations of late. We have enough domestic problems to worry about, never mind problems involving the Chinese, Saudis and so on.

Our Immigration Programs

Negative consequences arising from poor federal government decision-making are also impacting some of the most vulnerable new Canadians: refugees from war-torn countries such as Syria and Iraq. The bad decisions being made are creating havoc outside the Trudeau Liberals' own government-sponsored refugee program, with the parallel private-sponsored refugee applications running into serious trouble. Trudeau's administration does not have a monopoly on bad decision-making. However, we live in the present rather than the past or the future, and, as of the summer of 2017, "Trudeau's political decisions may be putting lives at risk." At the time, there were close to 45,000 refugees sponsored by churches and community groups waiting to gain entry into Canada. These refugees, who have a Canadian sponsor willing to assist them in settling into Canada and finding jobs, are not a sizable group of extremists and terrorists. As Candice Malcolm writes, they are "often Christians being persecuted in places like Iraq and Syria. And while the Liberal government is processing government-sponsored refugees on average in 15 months, the average wait time for higher risk privately sponsored applications is 56 months.[57]

Startlingly, as we usually portray ourselves as a country helping those in need—again, Canadians like to do the right thing—the "Trudeau government has admitted many of the government-sponsored refugees were not [at] risk." Rather, they "were living in safe apartments away from the war zone before being flown to Canada."[58] Perhaps someone somewhere in our government knows why there is such urgency to bring foreigners to Canada who are living in safe areas instead of those facing imminent peril. And whether you agree with immigration from the war-torn Middle East or not, the government has not fully set out what it initially promised to do here. A goal under the Liberals was to "eliminate the backlog of privately sponsored Syrian refugees by '2016 or early 2017.' Instead, the backlog has proliferated."[59]

Our Tax Collection Agency

So far we have seen massive backlogs and associated waste concerning our national government's ability to pay its employees properly, pay ex-military service personnel what they are owed, and tackle all the reasonable needs of our indigenous Peoples, such as ensuring they have safe drinking water and fixing all the deficient water treatment plants. We have also seen the government's inability to deal with the mounting equipment and personnel needs of the military to protect Canada and its people. And we have seen a tremendous backlog of at-risk, privately-sponsored refugees mushroom. If you have any doubt that this is indeed a disturbing trend and indicates Canada's federal government is broken, something that negatively impacts you, me and our families, read on.

Recently, senior executives at the Canada Revenue Agency (CRA) have been pocketing higher bonuses, what is commonly referred to as performance pay, than their counterparts in other federal departments. For example, as documented in the late January 2018 article by *CBC* reporter Elizabeth Thompson, "At the CRA, performance pay is in addition to base salaries that are between $152,800 and $202,500 for employees in the EX-4 and EX-5 classification. In 2016/17, the CRA officials pocketed an average of more than $29,000" in performance pay. Looking at the year before that, for which data was also available to the *CBC*, CRA's top executives pocketed an average of $35,000 of at risk pay in 2015–16 versus the top average of $18,000 in the rest of the public service. CRA top executives also took home the biggest performance bonuses in relation to other lower level employees in their agency.[60]

On the surface this may appear reasonable. When executives and other employees usually have to meet certain performance expectations, it stands to reason they could qualify for a bonus. Having had the opportunity to work for the federal government at OSFI, I myself, while never having once applied for a position above the manager level despite the opportunity to do so, know that performance appraisals are done annually. You have to meet or exceed expectations to qualify for performance pay, a bonus. But how can CRA executives be deemed to have met or exceeded expectations when fulfilment of some of the department's core work seems to have lagged so badly? Critics have cited a few examples of this.

Perhaps first and foremost, there is what Thompson calls the "damning auditor general's report that found the agency couldn't handle high call volumes, often didn't answer the phone and gave taxpayers incorrect information 30 per cent of the time."[61] Since that sounds like yet more backlog and incompetence making the quality of our lives less enjoyable and more costly in terms of wasted tax dollars (by the agency responsible for collecting those dollars, no less), I did a little more research. As reported on by the Ottawa Bureau of *The Star*, with reference to work done by the *Canadian Press*, "The auditor general also found that the Canada Revenue Agency has tried to gloss over the problem and make its performance 'look better than it really is' in public reports, in part by failing to account for the millions of unanswered calls"[62] If you happen to be one of those millions impacted, perhaps calling with important tax questions regarding your private life and income, or maybe your business, you likely already know just how ludicrous the situation has become.

AG findings have indeed been shocking, pointing to an unacceptable backlog of calls. "From March 2016 to March 2017, individuals and businesses made more than 53.5 million phone calls to CRA's call centres. However, over half, about 29 million were 'blocked' and therefore not answered by either an agent or automated self-service system."[63] The latter I presume is of the type you must navigate, a labyrinth of options requiring you to stay on the line for a wearisomely protracted period of time. I am not sure but can imagine. It all makes me wonder if any of the calls that went unanswered were from federal employees too. They may have been calling about their incorrect Phoenix paycheque and taxes due, thereby getting whacked multiple times by our broken government institutions that don't serve our needs. Obviously, as the AG found, "taxpayers need timely access to accurate information to help them prepare their tax returns and to ensure that their benefits are correct."[64] As we will be reviewing in further detail later, one also wonders how good a job all the CRA officials are doing when Canada seems to be lagging in its pursuit of tax evaders. This has been well documented and is yet another blemish on our government's ability to distinguish between doing what's right instead of what's wrong. Unlike the majority of us, Ottawa too often turns a blind eye to wrongdoing.

Just like myself, you are probably aware of someone's son or daughter at college or university being audited by the CRA. Or maybe it's someone living on a scant pension income, in a nursing home, that you know has been audited. Those individuals are just getting by. Nothing like the CRA having its priorities straight when it goes after the big fish who are tax evaders. In one of the most outrageous examples of an abuse of power by our government, inflicting harm upon the very citizenry it exists to serve and benefit, we find the CRA doing again what's wrong rather than what's right. Considering its voracious appetite to collect more of our tax dollars on behalf of the government, the following situation involving the CRA is absolutely flabbergasting. It should raise the ire of every Canadian who wants our government institutions to function properly, with integrity and generally beyond reproach.

The very headline, "CRA slammed for 'reprehensible and malicious' prosecution of B.C. couple," yet again reveals all that is wrong with our failing institutions that no longer bind together Canadians and what they stand for. We need healing and we need it fast. That loaded headline, the opening to a March 2018 *CBC* report by Jason Proctor, outlines how Robert Punnet, a British Columbia Supreme Court judge, " 'slammed' the CRA for ruining the reputations of Tony and Helen Samaroo, 'through malicious prosecution of tax evasion.' " The judge ordered the CRA to pay the Samaroos almost $1.7 million in damages for what appears to be its mishandling of their case and the Nanaimo couple's mistreatment. A whopping $750,000 of the award was for punitive damages, $300,000 for aggravated damages and almost $348,000 to cover off the Samaroos' legal bills to defend themselves against their provincial trial, ending in their acquittal. [65]

If we take a high-level view just of this specific situation, employing a rare resource known as common sense, we can conclude the following: our tax dollars employed certain staff at the CRA to have, as Judge Punnet described, "a government agency maliciously [use] the criminal justice system to pursue the plaintiffs, and its wrongful conduct continued into the criminal trial itself." The judge, who also noted "the CRA was seeking substantial terms of imprisonment and significant penalties," suggested "an unfortunate culture [exists] within the CRA" as shown by the twisted comments in an email exchange by employees dealing with the file that read: "Front page of

Wednesday's Nanaimo Daily News. I can't wait to read the edition after the guilty verdict" and "Doesn't a guilty verdict call for a guillotine?"[66]

Justice Punnet's careful review of the matter found fault with a CRA investigator involved in charging the Samaroos for tax evasion. That investigator provided "incomplete and erroneous information." Moreover, "he wrote the Prosecution Report as an advocate, not an investigator." Punnet also wrote of the investigator, "His clear intent was to see that criminal charges were laid. The presumption of innocence appeared to be meaningless to him. The manner in which he approached the evidence was not objective."[67] Therefore, on the one hand, we have paid CRA staff with public funds to conduct what looks like something that ended up to be a frivolous and malicious investigation of some innocent Canadians. Secondly, we will end up using even more Canadian public taxpayer money to fund the almost $2 million in damages awarded to the Samaroos.

But let's not lose sight of the even more tragic outcome of this: the adverse impact on Tony and Helen Samaroo themselves. The quality of their lives has suffered immeasurably from yet another fiasco involving our dysfunctional government institutions. As *CBC News* reported on the impact of the case on the Samaroos, "The couple no longer live together and Tony Samaroo said he drinks and smokes more, claiming he 'lost his spirit and his strength' dealing with the charges." As for Helen Samaroo, "she felt others looked at her with suspicion, claiming she had a breakdown after the acquittal." The Samaroos' daughter, Tricia Miller, even "stopped using the surname Samaroo because of its association with the criminal charges."[68]

As for the big fish who may not be paying their fair share of taxes, CRA employees feel they cannot always catch the tax cheats. In August 2018, *CBC News* reporter Dan Beeby outlined how a PIPSC (Professional Institute of the Public Service of Canada) union sponsored survey of more than 1,700 auditors and other tax professionals working for CRA found that "Nine out of 10 surveyed agreed with the following statement: 'It is easier for corporations and wealthy individuals to evade and/or avoid tax responsibilities than for average Canadians.' " The article goes on to describe how "the poll report . . . argues that the computer algorithms used to replace laid-off CRA workers have unfairly focused the agency's efforts on small fry."[69]

And if we go back a few years and look at a *CBC* March 2016 report, it had this to say at the time: "The Canada Revenue Agency offered amnesty to multi-millionaire clients caught using what's been called an offshore tax 'sham' on the Isle of Man—a reprieve that was supposed to remain secret and out of the public eye."[70] Apparently this involved some KPMG clients. I guess Canadians like the Samaroos are the big fish on CRA's radar. Big business may be too much of an influence on government and the effectiveness of our supposed democracy. Restoration efforts are desperately needed everywhere. One almost has to make a whip to chase the moneychangers out of the temple of democracy, the legislature.

Our Export Development Agency

Have you ever heard of Export Development Canada (EDC)? It is a multibillion-dollar Canadian government agency which, according to a news story published by the *Globe and Mail*, is "the second- or third-largest export development bank in the world." Journalist Richard Poplak also describes it as "an entirely opaque megalith of money that has no master," which probably explains why he further claims that "when parliamentarians do the math, they'll find that [EDC] is the vast Death Star in the middle of the Canadian economy, lending money to companies that have behaved poorly abroad." We will delve into those loaded comments shortly. As we do, please remember that EDC offers loans or credit that is guaranteed by Canada's taxpayers. Please also remember that, as Poplak wrote, most of "its loans and financial instruments have benefitted the extractive sector—the oil, gas and mining sector."[71]

Illustrative of this is the fact that "in 2014 alone, EDC provided a staggering $28 billion-worth of financial instruments for the extractive sector."[72] I am unaware if the majority of Canadians, including those concerned about the future of their children and the damaging effects of climate change, support the EDC's activities. One problem is that it appears challenging to know what those activities really are. Poplak noted that "oversight is not just scant, it's non-existent" at the EDC. Apparently, there is an "exemption in the Export Development Act—the piece of legislation under which the agency is mandated—that treats as confidential any information pertaining to clients."[73] Somehow this kind of thing all reminds me about the Panama and Paradise Papers and a lack of transparency about high-flyers duping we commoners so badly. The Panama Papers involved the leaking of 11.5 million documents, revealing how the super-rich around the globe use shell companies and other schemes to evade paying their share of taxes. The Paradise Papers, involved an additional leaking of almost 13.5 million confidential documents, also revealing how the wealthy elite use offshore tax havens and such to game the system. We must be a gullible lot, we supporters of some kind of grand illusion commonly referred to as democracy.

Before I forget to tell you, and since I raised the ugly spectre of leaked documents such as the Panama Papers which revealed a bunch of off-shore tax evasion, EDC has recently found itself embroiled in a potential scandal involving leaked information. Poplak reported on this succinctly: "In December 2014, according to a massive cache of emails and documents initially leaked to South Africa's *Daily Maverick and amaBhungane* news outlets, a company called Westdawn Investments, owned by the infamous South African/Indian Gupta brothers, concluded a deal to purchase a spanking new Bombardier Global 6000 luxury jet."[74] You have probably heard of Bombardier. It is the Quebec based Canadian industrial icon that seemed to take forever to send Toronto its new streetcars, only then reportedly recalling a lot of them for welding repairs. Anyway, Poplak's news piece, which appears reliable, raises more than a few concerns about the Bombardier jet deal.

He says this of the Guptas: "The brothers are closely associated with former South African president Jacob Zuma, and were deeply embedded in a systemic decade-long looting effort, allegedly siphoning off hundreds of millions of dollars from state-owned companies." Interestingly, we find that "Bombardier, which has faced bribery allegations in South Africa and Sweden (to name only two examples), was hoping to secure a piece of a US$1.2 billion locomotive contract, of which the Gupta brothers served as gatekeepers." I wonder if those trains will arrive on time if Bombardier gets the deal? Did they? Here's the thing though, as so unpalatably but eloquently put by Poplak: "When Bombardier cast about for a financial partner in order to close the sale, they approached the one lender on the planet that would hold its nose and hand over tens of millions of dollars to a family that was world-famous for its political connections. Enter Export Development Canada."[75] Just another mess that Ottawa needs to deal with. Something that even the Washington Press reported on while Canada seems to somehow think that America has a monopoly dealing with nasty problems.

It could be worse however. Much worse. Writing in an opinion piece for South Africa's *IOL* in October 2018, Siyabonga Hadebe paints a bleak picture of 'state capture' concerning that country. He states that "in the middle of what was thought to be an onslaught on the Gupta family last year," the prestigious global auditing, tax and advisory firm, "KPMG, inexplicably agreed to 'die for other people's sins.'" Apparently, "KPMG withdrew some of its findings pertaining to its investigative report on the South African Revenue Service (SARS) 'rogue spy unit.'" According to Hadebe, who appears to have a wry sense of humour, "the company agreed to be hanged [on] the cross like Jesus in an attempt to clear corporate SA of a bad image which is beset with deep-rooted corruption and also with serious dealings resembling those of the underworld of professional criminals." Ultimately, "by retracting the SARS report, the audit firm had done a public penance for exposing the rogue unit."[76] My, my, it could well be that democracy in South Africa requires some restoration, lest the hopes and dreams of such people as the late Nelson Mandela are dashed.

Our Environment

One of the greatest risks facing not only Canadians, but the entire world, is that controversial subject known as climate change. (I will discuss the topic a bit more in Chapter 8.) Whether or not you agree that extreme weather phenomena are occurring more frequently, resulting in ever-growing human suffering and property damage, as well as what may be irreparable damage to our shared environment, you probably would agree that it is important to have sound information to determine the truth. The truth is important, even if it is as "inconvenient" as Al Gore suggested in his poignant documentary on climate change. We expect our government to make informed decisions for the benefit of all Canadians. But when it comes to understanding our immediate environment and mitigating any unnecessary risks, here too we see problems emanating from our public leaders. They again appear to stumble just as badly as in the areas of their responsibility covered earlier.

As worrisomely detailed in a *Globe and Mail* feature article published in June 2017, major threats are facing our water supply. These threats go well beyond what our Indigenous Peoples face, not because the seriousness of unsafe drinking water issues they confront should be minimized, but due to the widespread degradation of Canadian waters which can pose problems for even more communities across the land. Our government should have responded immediately to concerns about the quality of drinking water available to our Indigenous Peoples. Simultaneously, our government should have strived to ensure all watersheds within our borders (where we have control over them) were appropriately protected. However, as often seems to be the case, the government has been remiss in dealing with the backlog of issues threatening our environment. It is no different than its performance dealing with the backlog of obsolete military equipment our service personnel have faced. As Canadians, we need protection on all fronts, including the environment we and our children need to sustain us and the country.

Case in point. According to the first national assessment of Canada's freshwater ecosystem in decades, "Each of the country's 25 major watersheds is facing multiple environmental threats." However, "the data required to track changes and guide policy makers are surprisingly inaccessible or non-existent."[77] What does this mean in real terms for Canadians who pride themselves on doing the right thing and residing in one of the best, if not amongst the leading, countries in the world? Well, as the *Globe* outlines, "the assessment finds that the data are deficient in 110 out of the 167 sub-watersheds to perform a baseline picture of ecosystem health, including in some relatively populated areas where freshwater is essential to communities, such as in southern Manitoba, Nova scotia's Annapolis Valley or the Bruce."[78] In other words, it's hard to get a clear picture of how healthy Canada's freshwater supply is for human consumption and the sustainability of the overall environment.

It may be hard for Canadians to imagine that our water resources are threatened, especially since we are blessed with almost 20 per cent of the entire world's freshwater resources. Those resources include water contained in our lakes, underground aquifers and glaciers. We are only one country out of almost 200 on the planet, and we have a mere population of just over 36 million compared to the earth's total population of over 7 billion people. So most people may automatically think there is nothing to worry about in relation to our freshwater supplies. Yet, as the *Globe* reported, there is a "glaring absence of a standardized national water-monitoring program in a federal system where water has traditionally been regarded as a provincial or local matter." According to David Schindler, cited by the *Globe* as one of Canada's most respected freshwater scientists and professor emeritus at the University of Alberta: "If things continue as they are, he said, freshwater ecosystems are likely to face unprecedented change while Canadians are left in the dark about what is happening to their country's most important resource."[79]

Scientists generally like to base their good decision-making on sound research, observable facts, data, solid documentation, reason, logic and so forth. They are mindful that their work should be credible, their positions and reputations unassailable. It therefore came as no surprise to me when I learned that more than 500 scientists and doctors from across Canada signed a letter in February 2018, addressed to Prime Minister Trudeau, requesting him to consider changing the *Canadian Environmental Protection Act* (CEPA). Those changes would place responsibilities on companies to demonstrate their products are safe prior to being sold on the market. As reported on, the letter indicated "Canada has a serious pollution problem that is a threat to both human health and the quality of our environment."[80]

Many of you may be shocked to learn that, as in the case of our freshwater supply, Canada has patchy and inconsistent standards regarding the air we breathe and pollution we are therefore exposed to. Various provinces appear to have some standards but there are no set standards at the federal level for all Canadians to ensure they are not breathing harmful contaminants. As journalist Mia Rabson wrote, "[the signatories to the letter] want national, enforceable, air quality standards." They believe Canada "is the only industrialized country in the world without legally binding, and enforceable, air quality standards."[81] If only our parliamentarians were better informed, grasping the relative threats facing our environment, maybe they would be more receptive to fact-based concerns rather than merely political or ideological concerns.

Things have gotten so bad regarding the breakdown in trust between the government and the governed, that even during times of crisis, where you would expect people to pull together, there is division. We can see this in relation to another environmental problem, the tragic 2018 British Columbian wildfires. By the end of August, the amount of land ravaged by wildfires in

BC had already broken the previous record in 2017. Strikingly, and as reported by the *CBC News*, there have been protests by citizens in BC regarding how the 2018 fires have been battled by those in charge of fighting them. During a weekend in August, "some residents of Burns Lake staged a protest in an attempt to prevent firefighting resources from leaving town." According to the *CBC*, these "protests are just the latest in a series of disagreements over wildfire management, from initial concerns that insufficient resources were given to stop the fires earlier to residents defying evacuation orders."[82]

Obviously tensions would run high when you have a record-setting wildfire season and people facing the loss of their livelihood and homes. Still, *CBC* reports John Rustad, MLA for Nechako Lakes and former parliamentary secretary for forestry, expressing much concern about the declining trust between residents and those responsible for fighting the fires: "There needs to be a serious review, perhaps a royal commission on how the province fights fires to be able to rebuild the trust but more importantly . . . be able to have a better response."[83] Whatever the reason for the instances of broken trust, residents probably want to know what information government officials are basing their decisions on when it comes to fighting that which imperils their quality of life—in this case, the wildfires. They probably want that information on a timely basis, just as you would in the same situation. One thing is for sure, the concerns likely have more to do with management than front-line firefighters busting their butts and putting their lives on the line for Canadians. They deserve our thanks, just like our service personnel in the trenches of the military.

Our Intergovernmental Relations

The lack of an informed federal government, something that would serve to strengthen good decision-making capacity and national unity, contributes not only to threats to our environment, but even to disputes between the provinces and territories and Ottawa. You probably heard about what appears to be an unprecedented row between Alberta and British Columbia. It arose from the federal government's approval of the Kinder Morgan Trans Mountain pipeline. The pipeline has also been an issue for indigenous Peoples, as described. After BC decided to try and block the pipeline, with that province's Premier, John Horgan, citing environmental concerns, the province of Alberta then banned wine from British Columbia and ceased electricity negotiations. And we thought our only trade disputes were with the US Trump administration as regards to NAFTA![84] The repercussions of this interprovincial squabble, wherein the federal government already approved a pipeline plan that a sizable province is against, are likely far reaching.

As the President and CEO of the Canadian Chamber of Commerce, Perrin Beatty, stated in February 2018, "We're sending a message to the rest of the world that this may not be a good place to invest."[85] The divisiveness between the provinces also points to a lack of leadership in Ottawa, just as it does over environmental concerns regarding our freshwater resources. In a sense, the issue is not so much about whether or not the pipeline is built, but why did an approval of it by the federal government occur without seemingly addressing the concerns of British Columbia in a proactive, transparent and meaningful way. Our Indigenous Peoples' voice and any concerns they may have should also have been properly addressed. Is it any wonder we are hearing about the current federal government introducing a new regulatory regime now? Of course, this public position shows others you may be doing something when all the while it may be more fence sitting. According to GMP FirstEnergy, a major investment bank to the energy sector, and cited in Bloomberg News: "A lack of hard timelines and a regulatory process that has been subject to dithering and near endless legal challenges will become the major stumbling block for domestic and international investor confidence in the Canadian energy sector."[86]

The poor handling of the country's environmental assets and issues obviously may have detrimental effects on the health of Canadians. Compounding the problem is the division sown between Canadians living in different parts of the country. Unfortunately, when it is not readily apparent if good and well-informed decisions have been made for everyone living in Canada, and when mitigation of risks to those not benefitting from a decision is absent, division between people is the result. As Perrin Beatty directly questioned, "We have to decide at this point in Canada, whether we are one country or 13?"[87] Friends, I will discuss the Constitution later. Let's return to our examples of our betrayal.

Our Retirement Savings and Benefits

This is not entirely a federal issue as, for example, some retirement savings plans are provincially regulated. Nevertheless, all of the following discussion is instructive when it comes to bad government decision-making with respect to our retirement savings and benefits.

If you are one of the thousands of hardworking Canadians entitled to a pension from Nortel or Sears Canada, you don't need me to tell you that you took a massive financial hit when those companies went bankrupt and therefore reneged on their promises to provide you with decent retirement benefits. Perhaps you worked for a different company that went belly-up. As Sears is one of the latest and most prominent insolvencies to grace Canadian news headlines, it is instructive to use it as a recent example of how the government is doing at protecting Canadians' retirement savings and benefits. It appears, when companies are not ensuring their profits support pension liabilities at reasonable levels, the government is doing a lot less than it could. And by reasonable, I mean fair and from a common sense and democratic perspective; democratic in that shareholders don't end up with the lion's share of profits when a business is a profitable going concern, while employees' rights are dispensed with as if we are living in the dark ages of feudal landlords and indentured servants!

As summarized by business reporter Francine Kopun early in 2018, "The Sears Canada failure once again exposed problems with defined benefit pensions, pension regulations and weaknesses in the federal acts governing bankruptcies and creditor protection applications that could affect more Canadians if fixes aren't made."[88] It has almost been ten years since Nortel imploded, leaving 20,000 employees wondering what their pensions would look like. Nobody usually wants to work in their twilight years after busting their chops throughout an entire working lifetime. Yet since the Nortel failure, nothing appears to have been done to protect Canadians from similar situations such as the one that has now unfolded at Sears. Generally, as Michael Campbell, vice-president of Nortel Retirees and former employees Protection Canada (NRPC), as well as court-appointed representative for the Nortel Companies' Creditors Arrangement Act (CCAA) legal proceeding remarked: "The legal and regulatory backdrop has not changed one whit."[89]

And who can expect retired pensioners to go looking for work, especially if they have health issues and/or must compete against younger job applicants who need work themselves. Indeed, young Canadians need work, too, in their important earning years—important because they, too, must save for retirement in an increasingly expensive environment, such as Vancouver or Toronto, where the cost of living has been ballooning. As for pensioners living in those cities whose employers have reneged on their promises, God knows how they can make ends meet. According to Campbell, "We had pensioners at Nortel . . . when their pensions were cut 50 per cent . . . moving in with each other, they were selling their homes . . . so they could survive." He wonders, rightly so, "if one day you woke up and you had a 50 per cent salary cut overnight. What would you do"?[90] It seems rather wrong, whether lawful or not, when looking at the Sears situation, that its controlling shareholder was able to divest the business of many of its core assets, all the while paying huge dividends to shareholders in a time of general market constraint, while simultaneously unfunded-pension-plan liabilities hit the stratosphere.

As Kopun revealed in her article, Edward Lampert, a hedge-fund manager, became the controlling shareholder of Sears Canada when, in 2005, he acquired control of Sears Roebuck in the US. Of interest, and perhaps similar to what a modern day Gordon Gekko from the original *Wall Street* movie would do, Sears Canada began to find itself being stripped of valuable assets under its new owner. Meanwhile, the pension plan racked up massive liabilities. "From December 9, 2005 to December 9, 2013, Sears Canada paid shareholders $3.4 billion in dividends." These were funded by the sale of some of the company's most profitable assets, such as Sears Credit and Financial Services operations, which sold for $2.4 billion in 2005. The leases of key flagship stores in Toronto, Calgary and Vancouver were also sold.[91] Unsurprisingly, we see that in the aftermath of such moves, the company became increasingly unprofitable.

Certainly its business model may have been questionable, such as what appeared to be a weaker online consumer platform during an age of increasing online retail sales. Still, one wonders how the business could succeed when major assets were being sold off. Also, it seems difficult to reconcile these two stark facts. While operating income fell every year after 2007, turning into losses in 2011 that deepened annually, the average dividend yield for Sears' shareholders was 17.8 per cent. Not to mention the fact that the average dividend yield for companies listed on the TSX during the same period was a mere three per cent.[92] I do not know about you, but it seems patently unfair to me that pensioners, such as in the case of Sears and Nortel, are so low on the pecking order of creditors when their employer goes bust. Usually employees must make mandatory contributions to their employer's pension plan and are unable to influence the plan's financial viability. Ironically, members of the Sears Canada Retiree Group (SCRG) began expressing concern to various officials about their Sears Canada pension plan as long ago as 2009. They were not fools. Like most of us, they knew the difference between right and wrong. Spokesperson Ken Eady put their efforts this way: "We knew then that it was wrong. If the Ontario government had taken action in 2014 or 2015, we wouldn't be here, the pension plan would have been wound up, the deficit issue would have been addressed."[93]

By late June of last year, the proverbial end so to speak, the deficit in Sears Canada's pension plan was over $250 million. The shareholders did well. Legislation allowed shareholders to receive huge dividends while pensioners appear to have lost much of what they thought they had, including their own money put into the plan. The pension income they must do without also means that 16,000 Sears Canada pensioners will not be spending what they thought they had earned to support their families and local communities. Family members and local businesses will likely feel the pinch, placing even more reliance on other supports and stretching our collective tax-dollar waste even further.

People have also had their benefits attacked on other fronts where they have contributed some of their own earnings in support of Canada's national Employment Insurance (EI) plan. In principle, EI is generally designed to provide regular benefits to those who have lost their jobs through no fault of their own (such as layoffs, shortages of work, etc.). EI provides unemployment, maternity and certain parental and sick leave benefits. It can also provide certain job-search and (re)training benefits. The benefits are financed by employee and employer premiums. You likely know, from your regular pay stubs, or when you complete your income tax return annually here in Canada, that EI premiums are deducted from your earnings on a regular basis. That is based on a formula for insurable earnings. The point being that if you are generally employed to work, you are paying into a plan that is supposed to protect you for certain types of job loss. Yet here too we see some bad outcomes for Canadians arising from poor decision-making in Ottawa.

According to Les Whittington, by 2012, the EI program was already far from the reach of many laid-off employees given that the rising percentage of part-time and temp jobs made it even more difficult for Canadian workers to successfully qualify for EI benefits. Also, Whittington writes, "a study of the EI system released in 2014 found that complaints from EI claimants about long waiting times for a decision on their claims exploded in recent years."[94] The figures are telling in terms of the number of people being affected. Maybe you were one of them or know of someone who was. "Nationally, these complaints shot up to 10,000 in 2013 from 444 in 2007."[95] Of course, this is not surprising given the other examples of outrageous government backlogs we looked at earlier. And once again, IT (Information Technology) solutions appear to have exacerbated the problem rather than being a panacea for incompetent decision-making to begin with.

The government at the time "moved to hire 400 people on two-year contracts after the surge in complaints caused by a bungled attempt to automate the handling of [EI] claims."[96] By now you may have caught on that the implementation of various IT projects by the federal government have gone incredibly wrong and are costing Canadian taxpayers a lot of aggravation as well as money. Be it botched IT projects in the form of Shared Services, the Phoenix payroll system, EI payments, etc., the unacceptably disappointing, costly and downright absurd results are always the same. We will absolutely get to the reasons behind all of this and why it actually benefits certain interests to implement such projects in the first place. We will also get to the basic and common sense solutions required to STOP THIS AND OTHER NONSENSE FROM GOING ON. However, I may still need to convince you even more about all the things going wrong that need to be made right because the status quo is not doing you, your family, friends, neighbours and Canadians across the country any good. Continuing with the EI story . . .

Unsurprisingly, in February 2018, 200 Canadians protested outside a Service Canada office in Tracadie, New Brunswick, against, as *CBC* reported, what is being called a 'black hole' for seasonal workers trying to survive on EI. Apparently, it is because of a gradual dip in unemployment between January and August of 2017 in the Restigouche-Albert economic area, that the government made adjustments to the formula calculating EI benefits. In short, the number of qualifying weeks that benefits are available to applicants went down. The direct result being that residents of the Restigouche-Albert area say their EI benefits are running out before their seasonal jobs, in industries such as blueberries, tourism and fishing, commence again. Issues seem to go well beyond Restigouche-Albert. A spokesperson for the Action Committee on Employment Insurance for Seasonal Workers was referenced as stating that "the protest was done in solidarity, with people in Eastern Quebec and the Magdalen Islands, who are also struggling with the changes."[97]

My own research indicates that changes in the EI formula in different regions of the country may cause disparities between recipients and reflect unrealistic estimates of EI benefits being made by the government. For example. According to a January 2018 article in the *Globe and Mail*, a Liberal program to give extra EI benefits to workers in 12 regions "hit hard by a drop in energy prices will end up costing almost $2 billion, more than double the original estimates."[98] Certainly there is nothing wrong with providing EI benefits to those who need them. However, one wonders if some are getting less than what they should in comparison to others, such as those who protested in Tracadie. Even more worrisome, for those recipients of benefits in the energy-rich western parts of Canada, the government seems to have been way off base in estimating the needs of the unemployed there to begin with. As stated by Frances Wodley, an economics professor at Carleton University, and referenced by the *Globe* article: "They [the government] failed to estimate just how hard it was going to be for people to get work . . . I'm kind of surprised that mistake was made."[99]

Given all the bungling outlined in this chapter, I cannot say that I am surprised. In fact, another research professor at Carleton, Andrew Jackson, wrote in a *Globe and Mail* opinion piece during late October, 2017: "There is a need for much closer consultation with labour, employers and community-based organizations on wider reforms needed to make the program more inclusive for those who need the most support."[100] EI is obviously important to all Canadians who can face job loss at any time during their working lives. You or someone you know has probably relied on the vital program that provides some modest income security, often during a stressful, albeit temporary, period of unemployment—when bills must be paid and mouths must be fed. EI's importance is emphasized by the fact that "in 2015–16, 1.9 million new claims were made, and total income benefits paid amounted to $17.7 billion."[101]

Distressingly for Canadians, especially considering all the wasted tax dollars on such fiascos as Shared Services and Phoenix, the federal government raided earlier surpluses generated by the EI program, just as it did to the pension plan for federal civil servants, to pay down the federal deficit. In this regard, members who contributed to a mandatory plan found themselves getting much less than what they thought they were originally paying for. As Jackson summarizes:

> The Liberal federal government made deep cuts to regular unemployment benefits in the mid-1990s, raising entrance requirements in terms of the number of hours worked to qualify, cutting the duration of benefits and freezing the maximum weekly benefit for more than a decade. Some $60 billion of surplus premiums were used to reduce the federal deficit as the proportion of the unemployed eligible to collect benefits fell to less than four in 10.[102]

But friends, the story gets even uglier. Something that happened about a decade ago is indicative of all that is wrong with our broken institutions and the ongoing betrayal we face by our, too often, self-serving leaders. Granted, in the case we are about to cover, the ineptitude and waste reaches grandiose proportions. Admittedly it does not approach anywhere near the scale of the Phoenix fiasco, but it does concern EI and is absolutely ridiculous. In 2008, the Conservative Harper government created another bureaucratic organization contributing to the alphabet soup of government agencies and departments whose tentacles run so broad and so deep that it bewilders one to grasp the purpose of such a confusing hodgepodge. Since I am just an ordinary citizen with maybe a little more curiosity than some other folks, far be it from me to think the wall of confusion is deliberate, but you will soon see why it may just be that. At any rate, Harper's newly minted agency was The Canada Employment Insurance Financing Board (CEIFB).

Problematically, there never appeared a reason for this agency to be set up in the first place, to spend millions of tax dollars on physical assets and personnel where none were required at all. As outlined by *CBC's* National Affairs Specialist Greg Weston back in 2012, four years after the establishment of the agency was announced: "So far [CEIFB] has spent over $3.3 million for new offices, computers and furniture, well-paid executives and staff, travel budgets, expense accounts, board meetings, and lots of pricey consultants. All that's missing is a reason for it to exist at all." [103] So here's the thing, and keep in mind all the hardworking Canadians who have had their EI benefits, or access to EI, cut, with EI calculations at times not reflecting the reality faced by the unemployed on the ground.

As Weston observed, the CEIFB was created to fulfil a few objectives. Firstly, it was to set the annual EI premium rates that determine how much, in contributions, working Canadians and their employers pay into the EI plan. Secondly, the agency was tasked to invest any surplus EI funds. Lastly, the CEIFB had the responsibility of managing a presumed contingency fund of $2 billion, which the Conservatives promised to create. The results of the objectives assigned to the CEIFB by 2012? Well, "all three years the board has been in existence, the Harper government has simply capped EI rates." Therefore, the rate-setting agency never set a single rate during that time. Once the rates were capped, meaning there were no premium increases to support the plan in line with any wage increases or other factors, the EI plan also ran deficits. At the time of Weston's article, those deficits totalled about $9 billion. [104]

Amazingly, as we know, when EI was running a surplus, the government, just like with the federal public service employee pension plan, raided it to pay down the national debt. Much of that debt had been fuelled by uniformed decision-making. Too bad those surpluses were not saved for harder times—when unemployment insurance benefits are in demand or pension deficits need to be funded—such as in the wake of the 2008 financial crisis. And what of the contingency fund by 2012? Since the government never set up that fund, there was nothing for the CEIFB to administer. To sum up, the agency did nothing for three years. Or as Toronto lawyer and Chair of the CEIFB, David Brown, put it, "We haven't had to do so nearly as much as our original mandate intended us to do." [105] Yet as Weston reported, the agency was indeed busy, spending a lot of our money on the bureaucrats who were not doing much at all!

For 2012, "its published budget [included] giving everyone raises, and moving the entire agency into new offices—all at an expected cost of $1.8 million." Further breaking down the costs for 2012, three years after it was established, Weston found this: "Compensation costs include stipends and expenses for the seven appointed board members, and $244,000 for a couple of executives. The agency's executive director, retired senior public servant Phil Clarke, is being paid about $150,000 a year to work part time." Even more absurd. "The budget provides another $200,000 to pay an investment manager if the agency ever has any money to invest. Another $300,000 is budgeted for 'additional' corporate services such as IT." You get the idea! And "with two full-time employees on the payroll [in 2012], the entire agency was to move out of its former offices into larger space in a different building to 'improve the corporate culture.' " [106]

So what was the core of CEIFB's purpose when you look at the reality of the situation versus the marketing of an illusion? Weston sums it up perfectly: "Aside from spending money, what the agency seems to do best is create bureaucratic plans and policies for itself."[107] The organization was inevitably dissolved in 2013, about five years after its creation. We often hear about the need to vigorously investigate and prosecute those who may have defrauded the EI system, by claiming benefits while they are working and receiving wages 'under the table' as they say. We hear about the need to go after the little guy who may be cheating the system, not just in terms of EI but perhaps the tax system. Honestly, how can the government justify going after the little guy when, as we have observed, the government does not have their own house in order. That borders on fraud itself: the fraud of pretending our democracy works for the people. Most assuredly, it is also the betrayal of Canadian values, of the national identity of wanting to do what's right. There are so many people, both living and dead, who have participated in this betrayal. Surely they will be judged, including by the light of truth.

So where have EI claimants ended up now in early 2018? If you want to look at the real dollars the average Canadian on EI receives, things are fairly bleak for those in financial need. Jackson finds "the average claimant gets a weekly benefit of $446 for twenty weeks, just under a maximum weekly benefit of $553."[108] Considering most Canadians are living paycheque to paycheque, especially if they live in one of Canada's urban areas that have seen exorbitant rises in housing costs, such as in Toronto or Vancouver, it seems inconceivable that EI provides the financial support required by many Canadians who may actually qualify for the benefit. Jackson views the current EI amounts available as "a limited social safety net for a world of work in which job loss is likely to become an even more frequent occurrence, often leading to workers taking new jobs at much lower wages."[109]

Our Youth

If you are a younger Canadian, you are probably aware, or will soon become aware of the daunting challenges you face. Successive governments have allowed intergenerational inequality to spiral out of control. We often hear about racial or gender inequality, discrimination of many kinds, and these are serious issues. The 'Me Too' movement seems to have garnered much attention on female sexual harassment issues of late, with harassment cases front and centre in the daily news. However, another of the most prominent challenges of our time, intergenerational inequality, involves inequality between all races and sexes, and is rarely talked about.

Writing in an August 2017 article published by the *Wall Street Journal*, Simon Nixon captures the unfairness unleashed by the 2008 financial crisis on youth: "In the early stages of the global financial crisis, policy makers assumed that the shock to the global economy would soon pass." What happened? "Instead, the greatest legacy of the past 10 years has been a dramatic rise in intergenerational inequality."[110] As something that occurred previously for Generation X in the 1990s, and arising from a lack of job opportunities in a challenging economy, today's millennials are also increasingly found dwelling in their parents' basement. There, they idle away in a Canada that more and more seems a less inclusive and equal place for its aspiring youth.

Tuition costs continue their inexorable assent to some point that will soon shut out those with less financial means to pursue postsecondary education. And that education is required for most of today's jobs in our growing service-oriented and knowledge-based economy. It has even come to pass that with an explosion in housing costs in several of Canada's major urban centres, coupled with the meteoric rise of postsecondary tuition costs, many students in this country are struggling to eat. For example, "the 2016 study Hungry for Knowledge, by The Meal Exchange, found that nearly two-in-five post-secondary students in Canada experience some degree of 'food insecurity.'

" At Ryerson University, where food bank usage is on the rise, students are looking to help each other out in the face of mounting educational and basic living costs. Students, whose tuition ranges from $7,000 to $11,000, are voting on a proposed $2.50 annual levy on full-time student tuition that would go directly towards the food bank. [111]

Instructively, and pointing toward the unaffordability of basic costs for many students just scraping by, Ryerson is not the only post-secondary school in and around Toronto where the future leaders of our country are in need. Shamefully, as *CBC News* published, the University of Toronto, York University, George Brown, Humber and Seneca colleges all have food banks. [112] Who can deny that the health of our cities is deteriorating, with all layers of government allowing the situation to fester? *CBC's* Trevor Dunn writes that "the irony in asking students who can't afford to pay more tuition in order to fund the food bank isn't lost on staff." [113] Then again, successive governments do not appear to understand the folly that results from poor decision-making. The fact that the government must write off upwards of $200 million in student loan payments in arrears merely reinforces that higher tuition costs don't solve overall cost pressures for post-secondary students. Indeed, as *Global News* revealed, the government's inability to collect some $203.5 million in debts from 34,240 students will be the third time in four years it has had to write off outstanding loans. [114] Student groups have repeatedly asked the government to make higher education more affordable. That common sense request, especially given our increasing knowledge-based economy and the demand for an educated workforce to build anew this country, seems to be falling on deaf ears.

As alluded to earlier, housing costs have become a huge drain on pocketbooks and the government at all levels appears to have done little for those in the greatest need of shelter. We will discuss yet more bungling in this critical area momentarily. Younger Canadians will likely not have the pensions and other employee benefits that most preceding generations, such as the baby boomers did. It has gotten to the point that we have different generations of Canadians, working side by side in the same organization, such as the federal public service or at General Motors, receiving a different amount of total compensation. This is because younger people are working under different compensation and benefit schemes, and even have to retire later, such as in the public service, due to more restrictive provisions in their employment contracts.

Younger people typically require more education, technical savvy and experience than those Canadians hired ahead of them, just to land the job. Yet those older Canadians working alongside them will likely retire earlier and with more benefits than their younger counterparts. Again, this is a huge issue that is gender and race neutral in its adverse impacts and challenges to Canada's youth. The government appears to be doing little here. Negative consequences arising out of poor decision-making or inaction appear to continue unabated.

Our Middle Class

The disparity between wealthy and poor Canadians also appears to continue unabated, with all levels of government appearing to do little. This is a national catastrophe of sorts for Canadians. The lack of a national housing strategy, especially when housing costs were permitted to balloon so much over the past few years, with Canadian household indebtedness reaching all-time highs, reflects yet more bungling at the highest levels of government—if not simply an abyss of obliviousness.

Governments should serve the people's interest at large. That has been a traditional expectation of a sound democracy, its solid foundation being a healthy and strong middle class, underpinning nationwide prosperity. In stark contrast, the reality for most Canadians is that our environment has deteriorated. We have a dying middle class, despite our good-looking poster boy, Justin Trudeau's, self-portrayal as a defender of the middle class. What did he say in his speech about the middle class on May 4, 2015, as found on the Liberal party's website? "We need middle-class Canadians to have money in their pockets to save, invest, and grow the economy."[115] Of course, Trudeau is not the only Canadian leader who has not perceived what is really wrong in our society. Successive governments of all political stripes and all levels (city, municipal, provincial, federal) have not always governed in Canadians' best interest. Perhaps they truly wanted to but just did not know how. Regardless of their intentions, the dismal result is now highlighted so disappointingly by a team of researchers led by University of Toronto professor David Hulchanski.

As documented by reporter Daniel Tencer, the team's recent work found that "all four of Canada's largest metro areas—Toronto, Montréal, Vancouver and Calgary—are seeing their middle-income neighbourhoods disappear, replaced by increasingly segregated high-income and low-income neighbourhoods."[116] The alarming transition from healthy cities across Canada, filled with thriving, sizable and contributing middle-class segments, to dys-functional 'us and them' type urban blemishes on our supposedly fair country took only a few decades to occur. The research team's data indicates that "in 1980, 60 per cent of census tracts in Toronto were middle-income areas; by 2015, only 28 per cent were middle income." Concurrently during this period, the gap between haves and have nots grew enormously. "Wealthy areas rose from 12 per cent to 21per cent of all tracts, while low income areas exploded from 28 per cent to 51 per cent."[117]

If you reside in Toronto, you would likely be unsurprised to learn that its widening gap between rich and poor is the greatest of the four cities. Researchers pinpointed four broader causes for the increasing disparity between what appears to be the more polarized classes and the smaller middle-class: a changing labour market; an unaffordable housing market; taxes and transfers; and discrimination. With regard to the first reason—a changing labour market—Hulchanski was cited: "You have a job market that isn't paying middle-class wages anymore." With respect to the second reason—an unaffordable housing market—and clearly that is the case if you live in more expensive cities, such as Toronto or Vancouver, "The cost of housing is not going down in real terms, whereas the incomes of many people have stagnated or gone down." The third cause—taxes and transfers—which interestingly may not be so obvious, but credibly supported by the researchers' data and findings, arises from actions beginning almost 30 years ago. In the 1990s, there were major cuts to social spending, with successive waves of tax cuts following that time. All of these policies benefitted high-income earners as they "helped redistribute income to the upper end," says Hulchanski. The last reason—discrimination—is a cause of the growing gulf between the wealthy and poor because the burgeoning numbers of visible minorities are finding it difficult to obtain and advance in their jobs.[118]

Aggressive cuts to social spending under Liberal Prime Minister Chrétien and corporate tax cuts under Conservative Prime Minister Stephen Harper have been blamed. Hulchanski points to the broader lack of appropriate government decision-making as a major issue causing the negative situation we now face in our largest cities when he opines: "We did it to us, in the way we govern ourselves, starting in the 1990s."[119] Certainly the housing situation seems dire. If we look at the situation in Canada's largest city alone, data recently released from the Toronto Community Housing Corporation (TCHC) indicates that "one half of its buildings could be deemed 'critical' five years from now if new funding isn't provided."[120] In case you did not know already, TCHC is the largest residential landlord in Canada, with 110,000 tenants spread over more than 2,100 buildings, representing $9 billion in public assets.[121]

Imagine what it is like for those law abiding Canadians, our fellow citizens, who live in some of the subsidized units that are crumbling. Buildings infested with cockroaches and rats, buildings without working air conditioning, plumbing or appliances and so on. Never mind the gangs of criminals, drugs and prostitutes who are making the lives of decent citizens a virtual living hell. By way of example, consider Teresa da Silva's situation. As written about in a February 2018 report by the *Toronto Sun*: "In a recent interview Miss da

Silva, a tenant at 155 Sherbourne St., lamented how officials have turned a blind eye to the many crack dealers and prostitutes who frequent her building while recently spending $197,000 to decorate offices at the location."[122] Residents of subsidized housing may be recent immigrants trying to land their first job, refugees Canada decided to bring here, Canadians who merely are down on their luck and looking to be a productive member of society again. Is it reasonable to expect such people will escape poverty and become contributing members of our society (many already work and pay their fair share of taxes) when they must deal with the added psychological challenges of trying to cope with their crumbling living accommodations, especially if there are children in the household?

I am not some bleeding-heart left-wing zealot, but it strikes me as preposterous and patently unfair that in such a rich city as Toronto, in one of the best countries in the world to live in, that so many people have to live in such humiliating conditions. "Data provided by TCHC shows many of its 364 buildings will need more and more costly repairs while 30 are already in serious disrepair." Even more threatening to those who require subsidized housing in an era of skyrocketing house and rent prices, TCHC "has already closed hundreds of units in 2017 and warns it will have to shutter up to 1,000 by the end of next year without more funding."[123] Thus far, at the time of writing this book, there has been no announcement by the federal government that it will help those in need across Canada by funding subsidized housing where it is desperately needed. Toronto's mayor, John Tory, has been pushing to obtain about $800 million from the Ontario government.[124] But the problem is not all about money. There is also the issue of poor management.

Our Other Levels of Government

We have covered a lot of negative issues Canadians face, arising from the federal government and how it operates. Disappointingly, other levels of government across Canada are also culpable, and there is much room for improvement. It is beyond the scope of this book to cover all the provincial and territorial government decisions, or indecisions, that have also produced undesirable outcomes for Canadians, deepening our betrayal. It is similarly beyond the scope of this book to do the same for regional, municipal and city/town governments. However, a few additional and brief examples are useful. We can then discern that, where they exist, these problems compound the adverse impacts Canadians are already facing as they grapple with the negative fallout and inept decision-making on Parliament Hill. It is like a 'force multiplier' whereby when more than one level of government is making misinformed and wrong decisions, the blow to us is all the more severe in terms of wasted tax dollars, resources and opportunities to make everyone's lives better. We exponentially wither in our own capabilities as a nation, drowning in the pool of foolishness we have allowed to overtake the antiquated structural plumbing of our failing democracy.

I will stick to problems mainly concerning Ontario, of which the disaster of TCHC is but one example, as this is the province where I grew up and am therefore most familiar with. This chapter only has so much room for me to create a vivid picture for you, the reader, to see how much is going wrong. People in Canada's other provinces face issues that are similar to Ontario's. Hopefully I am getting your attention, especially if you have children and are worried about their future here in Canada.

Here is a brief overview of the waves upon waves of foolishness pelting households across the province. The epicentre of the incessant storm is what we have come to call the 'Wynne government.' If ever there was a test of tolerance and endurance, then Ontarians, reeling from the effects of the provincial Liberals under Kathleen Wynne, would surely have been tested severely. Not that I have much in the way of positive commentary for the Conservative party, led by Doug Ford, that recently assumed power in Ontario. The Conservatives' election win is largely a reflection of another round of voter dissatisfaction with what was the prevailing party of the day.

The same to and fro occurs at the federal level. Here we have the Liberals and Conservatives usually dominating. In America, they have Republicans and Democrats. But the changing of the guard does not usually mean a change in how government functions. So it makes no difference if the pendulum swings left or right with the perception of the electorate, except that virulent forces in the extreme of either direction can capitalize on the opportunity. In doing so, they can take an upset and ill-informed electorate in directions that electorate never intended to go when they cast their ballot. That is the danger.

This may happen in Canada. We have already seen Doug Ford in Ontario politics maneuvering where he sees an opening. Then there is the case of Maxime Bernier at the federal level, creating the right-wing People's Party of Canada. Of course, our usual experience has been similar to that of many other countries when mainstream political parties switch to and fro from positions of power. The name of the party in power changes but misinformed and misguided decision-making continues, only now couched in a different vernacular and reasoning. But it's all theatre, a play on words and optics management, with no substantive progress on the issues of the day. The recent Ontario provincial election was a good example of this theatre.

In the case of the Conservatives, we have already witnessed the epic soap opera involving its erstwhile but recent leader, Patrick Brown. In January 2018, Brown reportedly resigned following accusations of sexual misconduct. Significantly, the Ontario Conservative Party found itself in turmoil after Brown's departure. Yet, less than two weeks into March 2018, the party had elected a new leader to tackle the careening Liberal Wynne government. Just who could this distinguished, knowledgeable, experienced, insightful and Churchill-like statesperson be? None other than Doug Ford. After all, he used to be a Toronto city councillor—you know—the city with the widening gap between haves and have-nots. And to quote some *Thompson Reuters* reports, "Fifty-three-year-old Ford is the brother of late Rob Ford, the former mayor of Toronto who gained global notoriety for admitting to smoking crack cocaine while in office."[125] Enough said. Such is the state of Ontario politics and the Conservative party. But let's return to reviewing some of the real and tangible issues that have been impacting Ontarians. Those issues that further reduce Ontarians' quality of life are of far greater importance than the less scientific and corrosive practice known as the art of politics.

By April 2017, as described in an article *Toronto Sun* published that same month, TCHC had gone through four CEOs who had "left (or been forced to leave) the scandal-plagued organization since March 2011." *Sun* reporter Sue-Ann Levy also wrote: "In the two years since the Mayor's Task Force on Community Housing delivered its sharply worded rebuke of the way the corporation manages its offices, little has improved."[126] Highlights from the 2015 task force's report appear to imply that the publicly funded TCHC is significantly mismanaged. It appears to be yet another broken government institution that is not improving people's lives and is not spending taxpayer's money the way it should.

The issues outlined by the task force sound all too familiar where modern government is concerned: "a lack of respect and responsiveness towards tenants; secrecy and a lack of transparency; an inability to aggressively evict drug-dealing thugs who have infiltrated several TCHC buildings and are intimidating law-abiding tenants; a long list of financial and management issues that include a deficit of $107 million on a Regent Park revitalization that is not even half done, the need for a $31 million bailout this year to balance the books, recent arrears that ballooned to $12.8 million at the end of 2016 compared to $6.9 million five years ago, an inability to turn around vacant units in a timely manner [and] resulting in 3,540 vacant units, an increasing repair backlog despite efforts to tackle it coupled with a refusal to sell off vacant stand-alone homes in a more aggressive manner."[127]

Some of the mismanagement even appears to have contributed to a loss of life. If that is not a negative consequence arising from the betrayal of our institutions meant to protect and safeguard our values, I don't know what is. We all know it is simply wrong when a publicly funded organization such as the TCHC is charged under the Ontario Fire Protection and Prevention Act. That "followed a tragic February 2016 blaze at a Malvern seniors' building that left four people dead and another 15 residents hospitalized."[128] This stirs up memories of that terrible conflagration involving the Grenfell Tower in London, UK, during the summer of 2017. That fire caused 72 deaths in a largely working-class housing complex. The poorest of humanity seems to always face the cruelest of realities.

Fast-forwarding to February 2018, we see another scathing report being produced about certain practices at the TCHC. This time, new city Ombudsperson Susan Opler's 65-page report found the housing organization had a "broken and downright arbitrary internal transfer system." In another alarming piece written by *Sun* reporter Sue-Ann Levy, we learn that Opler's report, which focused on 'priority transfers'—meaning when tenants wish to move due to safety and security reasons, found a priority transfer waiting list of 1,413 tenants. Of those on the list, 55 per cent have been waiting for a transfer more than five years and 76 per cent have been waiting for more than two years.[129]

You can get a better sense of why people are applying to move from one unit to another by understanding Opler's report was prompted by the case of two tenants. The first instance involved a young mother who had applied for a priority transfer twice, each time being denied. This, "after witnessing a violent crime outside her home, escaping to a shelter, and coming back to find a loaded gun in her child's dresser drawer." In the second instance, a family was denied a similar transfer "after two shots were fired into their living room and their teenagers were assaulted enroute home from school." According to Opler's report, the "requirements for a transfer are 'unclear' and the decisions 'inconsistent and contradictory.' "[130] This again speaks to the government's inability to manage its responsibilities and the institutions we rely on generally, as well as more massive failings at TCHC specifically, to the point of almost indifference to those who are most vulnerable in our society.

To top things off at TCHC, it seems that some of its own employees are afraid to work for what appears to be a dysfunctional organization. According to a January 2018 *Toronto Star* article written by Jennifer Pagliaro, "One current manager and five former employees who spoke to the Star described a corporation plagued by a 'culture of fear' that has left employees feeling bullied, harassed and terrified amid a slew of recent firings." Things have gotten so bad that TCHC's former general counsel, Mark Johnson, filed a wrongful dismissal case against the corporation. As well, "a letter sent on December 21, 2017 from the law firm Rubin Thomlinson LLP to the [city's] ombudsman confirmed it had been retained to conduct an investigation into the housing corporation's 'human resources practices.' "[131]

If you are less than fortunate enough to gain entry into one of TCHC's crumbling rat-traps, you may find yourself on the streets of Toronto, in the dead of winter perhaps. There you will endure what is known as Toronto's homeless-shelter crisis. It, too, is another example, but at city-government level, of poor decision-making that impacts the most vulnerable in our society. In a January 2018 *Metro News* opinion piece, Matt Elliott writes again, as he did about five years prior, of the misguided policies concerning homeless shelters and the fallout in Toronto. In February 2013, he found the city's shelter system operating nightly at around 95 per cent of capacity. This was well above Toronto's target of 90 per cent. The consequences were naturally that "shelter workers, volunteers and activists on the street were reporting homeless people were being turned away and forced to sleep on the streets." At the time, Elliott goes on to mention that "calls to open the armouries or use city-owned buildings like Metro Hall as warming centres weren't answered."[132] Rob Ford, then mayor, may have been otherwise indisposed, perhaps dealing with his own unfortunate personal issues and demons that do not bear repeating here. I am not sure if his brother Doug, a former Toronto city councillor and now Premier of Ontario, will improve things for Toronto's vulnerable. But clearly Mayor Rob Ford's successor, John Tory, has done little to improve the shelter crisis.

As Elliott states, the 2018 shelter crisis "is almost a carbon copy" of 2013. "Same bitter cold. Same 95-per-cent capacity reported in the shelter system most nights. Similar slow response from politicians." Elliott does credit Tory for reversing his decision not to vote to have the Moss Park armoury opened, which subsequently accommodated those on the street. He also credits him for opening warming centres at a community centre in Regent Park and Metro Hall itself. Nonetheless, Elliott justifiably finds "the suggestion that this crisis is surprising or unprecedented" to be "frustrating."[133] Admittedly, other levels of government could kick in some funding and resources to support Toronto—especially if the city demonstrates some much-needed common sense in running organizations like TCHC. Still, as Elliott points out, "The reason it's so hard to get out of this hole is because [the] city has spent so many years digging it." Indeed, regardless of their political leanings, "Toronto's last two mayors have spent eight years—including [2018]—calling for budget freezes or budget cuts."[134]

You know what the right thing would have been, for any municipality or city in this situation, don't you? Rather than have fellow Canadians down on their luck or mentally ill, dying in the street, maybe we could be doing a lot better, so they do not end up there to begin with. Surely it does not take a rocket scientist to understand what Elliott is saying: "A municipal government devoted to a long-term fix and to supporting vulnerable people would make those investments before the need reached a breaking point."[135] I am not sure about you, but the TCHC and shelter crisis (only two examples of so many) are not the kind of situation I would expect within city government. Be it the Ringling Brothers or any other brothers who have politically influenced

Toronto, this is not the circus and clowning around people want in Toronto, or elsewhere in Canada for that matter.

Lorrie Goldstein, in a June 2017 opinion piece brazenly headlined: "Wynne's Ontario? Oh are we ducked!" sarcastically quipped about the after effects of enduring 14 years of Liberal Ontario government under Premier Dalton McGuinty and then Premier Kathleen Wynne. Following, are examples excerpted from that article:

> "The Cancelled Gas plants Experience: Spend a delightful hour with Ontario premier Kathleen Wynne and former premier Dalton McGuinty, learning how to build two gas plants for the price of four. Cost: $2.6 billion . . .; The Hydro Bill Shell Game Tent: Bring in your outrageously high monthly electricity bill and the Ontario government will help you pay for it by loaning you your money, with interest. Plus, you'll get a free can of cat food for dinner! Cost: $21 billion . . .; The Smart Meter, Stupid Liberal Double or Nothing Booth: Place your bets as you watch how Ontario spent $2 billion on a $1 billion plan to install smart hydro meters in homes and businesses across the province. Cost: $2 billion . . .; The eHealth Information Superhighway Highway: Watch, from the safety of our glassed-in viewing area as Ontario's health care bureaucrats reveal how they met the challenge of spending $1 billion on not creating a workable system of electronic computer medical records for Ontario patients. Cost: $1 billion.; The Orange Helicopter Thrill Ride: Finally, end your day by taking the whole family on an exciting aerial tour of all our exhibits on executive helicopters that were supposed to be used for transporting air ambulance patients across Ontario, except they either had no place to put the

patients, or made it almost impossible for paramedics to perform CPR. Cost: still under investigation."[136]

I have included these examples, not because I have it in for Wynne and the government she led, but for the sake of brevity and because Goldstein really does an excellent job briefly listing the mind-boggling costs to Ontarians for yet another dysfunctional level of government It really is all the same, broken government, at all levels, everywhere in our country: our institutions no longer work for us to strengthen our democracy. They do the opposite, and the waste is both shameful and destructive to our and our nation's well-being. We are increasingly betrayed by our own leaders, well-intentioned as they may have been.

Goldstein's examples, save his sarcasm, point to provincial government waste in the magnitude of tens of billions of taxpayer dollars. The litany of undesirable outcomes that led to this also points to even more misguided and uninformed decision-making in government. The only difference being that here we see it at the provincial rather than federal level. A double whammy for Ontario, and leading to the election of someone, who like many who have led government in modern times, may not know how to effectively address the issues. Again, the changing of the guard at election time really changes nothing at all. Voting for a candidate is just the backlash of an angry citizenry with nowhere else to credibly turn. It sounds like an American or British story but it is our own, too. Again, we could discuss other regions of Canada or levels of government and likely discover the same alarming scandals and abuse of public trust. We could also view the same disturbing trends in other countries that are supposed to be democratic and working for the wider good of their citizens. There is only so much room in this chapter, but clearly there are disturbing trends that reveal the need for democratic renewal in this country.

Imagine how much better use those wasted tens of billions of dollars could be put to in Ontario. Crumbling housing for the less fortunate could be fixed, schools repaired, the healthcare system improved with reduced wait times, tuition costs reduced and so on. The real lives of Ontarians could be improved, perhaps even saved, if not for the wrong decisions being made by those, time and again, leading a government that serves its own interests rather than ours. Is it any surprise at all that Ontario, which contains Canada's largest city and the bulk of its population, beat out all other jurisdictions by winning the latest 'Teddy' award? If you do not already know this, the honorary recipients of a Teddy are distinguished by their success in wasting taxpayers' dollars. The recent Wynne government's plan to lower electric bills for Ontarians that appears, in reality, to do well beyond the reverse, garnered Ontario the discreditable award.

The former provincial Liberal's plan, as *Radio Canada International* reported to the world, involves Ontario Power Generation (OPG) borrowing money to keep hydro rates relatively flat until 2021. But then rates will increase a sizable 6.8 per cent every year until 2027 to pay back the borrowed money plus interest. According to *Radio Canada* "Ontario's Auditor General concluded that the plan would ultimately end up costing taxpayers an additional $39 billion ($18 billion in borrowed funds, plus $21 billion in interest costs)."[137] So it looks like Goldstein's comments, sarcastic or not, are based on fact. Undoubtedly, young Ontarians will be paying for the sins of current and past governments that are betraying them and their sacred future trust repeatedly. Oh, and in case you are also wondering who topped the overall list of the 2017 Teddy awards, you could probably guess, if you did not already know, it was the feds.

Yep. The federal government genius (no doubt it was a committee of geniuses) whose brainwave it was to create a temporary skating rink on the lawn outside the parliament buildings in Ottawa merited the top Teddy award. Apparently the rink would only last a few months before it melted and cost taxpayers $8.2 million to build. To boot, as the CTF (Canada Tax Foundation) noted, "the expensive taxpayer funded rink is located only a couple of blocks from the famous Rideau Canal, billed as the largest outdoor rink in Canada and possibly the world."[138] I don't know about you, but my view is that any top bureaucrat who can justify the insanity of building that white elephant of a rink is likely skating on thin ice indeed.

As I put ink to paper here, I just read another disturbing article in the *Globe and Mail* by Andre Picard. In that piece, headlined "Ontario is courting a home-care fiasco," we learn that in the fall of 2017, the Ontario Wynne government was establishing a new institution, Personal Support Services Ontario (PSSO). The PSSO's raison d'être seems to be to recruit, train and employ personal-support workers (PSWs) to provide the home care certain individuals require. However, we also learn that "a coalition of 11 not-for-profit home-care providers who, between them, provide 95 per cent of home care services in the province, allege that the move 'will have dire consequences for patients and their families, for service providers and their employees and for the home care and health care system at large.'"[139] The coalition group appear to have begun a lawsuit against the government's PSSO plan. Picard goes as far as to say that "The agencies that provide home care were gobsmacked, and now they've taken legal action to prevent the government from following through on PSSO."[140]

Picard writes that according to leaked government documents, the lawsuit also alleges that "by the time that PSSO is fully operational in 2021, it will provide about 40 per cent of home-care services." He talks about how renowned organizations such as the Victorian Order of Nurses, almost a Canadian institution, and Saint Elizabeth Health Care could be devastated along with other agencies. He also mentions that "while patients are frustrated by lack of availability of home care, there is no issue with the quality of care these agencies provide." So what was behind the rationale to create yet one more bureaucratic initiative, following so many other misguided initiatives undertaken by the Liberal government of the day? The lawsuit says the Liberals are creating the agency as a political gift to SEIU (Service Employees International Union) healthcare, a major donor, to enable it to hire more union members.

Another union, OPSEU (Ontario Public Service Employees Union), has alleged the same thing. [141] There appears to be two rather sensible conclusions made in the lawsuit, too, as summarized by Picard:

> 1) if PSSO has a monopoly on training workers and becomes the central employer for PSWs, the supply of workers for other providers will dry up and wages will be driven up; and 2) home care is provided by teams of nurses and PSWs (and other specialists), and if PSWs work for one agency and nurses for another, it will be more difficult, not easier, to coordinate the provision of care. [142]

I have found many of Picard's articles on health care rooted in common sense. His reporting on home care, as well as what I will discuss shortly, hospital overcrowding and the reasons behind the long waiting lists to get care, etc., resonate with me. My parents are in their twilight years and have been experiencing what it is like to be 'in the system' so to speak. My father is in the nursing home wing of one Ontario facility, with my mother in that same facility's independent living wing. Previously they were living together in what is known as the assisted care division of that long-term care facility. To make a long story short, my parents generally have nothing but positive things to say about the front line and hardworking PSWs, nurses, etc., who are doing their best to provide the care required for seniors who need a wide array of assistance in an institutional environment. However, my parents, my brother and myself, have witnessed firsthand just how difficult it can be to navigate the labyrinth of bureaucracy that comprises access to long-term solutions for the elderly—such as access to appropriate accommodations or medical assistance in those accommodations. Therefore I completely agree with Picard when he says, in relation to the new PSSO bureaucracy, "It's time to let the good providers we have innovate and expand, not to burden patients with more red tape and shackles."[143]

I recall my dad having to be physically separated from my mother for several months after he had hip surgery. My parents have been married over 50 years. However, dad was unable to return to the same facility as my mom because the prior gate keepers of access to long-term care, the fully government-funded Community Care Access Centres (CCAC), did not deem it important for such a long-married and elderly couple to remain together. The fact that my father was just recovering from surgery and depended on my mother for companionship (he has Parkinson's), made the situation all the more distasteful. The absurdity of it all was reflected by my brother and me buying our elderly mother, who suffers from her own health issues, taxi chits as a Christmas gift so she could visit our father residing a few kilometers away. I wonder how much my parents paid in mandatory taxes, including any health taxes, over their roughly 60 years in Canada. All to receive this treatment from the CCAC bureaucracy!

The CCACs, those fully funded agencies spread across Ontario and responsible for home-care, became another scandal-plagued pariah. They became discredited after a number of *Toronto Star* news reports "revealed lavish salary increases for CCAC executives and huge administrative costs." Of course, simultaneously "the CCAC bosses were ordering services to patients halted or cut to reduce costs and wage freezes on front-line workers."[144] Again, it is the lower-level or front-line staff who actually provide the core service to seniors like my parents. Conversely, it is the often swelling ranks of senior public servants who only put up bureaucratic roadblocks that get in the way of retired Canadians trying to enjoy their final years.

Unsurprisingly in 2014, Ontario Auditor General Bonnie Lysyk found that barely 62 cents of every $1 CCACs received went toward face-to-face patient care. Instead, more than $900 million was spent on administration.[145] So what did the Liberal stewards of Ontario's government do in the face of all his? Well, through 2017 reforms under *The Patients First Act* (PFA—which sounds really good) legislation, they shuttered the CCACs, transferring most of their employees to another bureaucracy, the 14 Local Health Integration Networks (LHINs). [146] The LHINs were in charge of overall healthcare planning and coordinating same in their respective regions of Ontario. I hope I have not lost you! So you have a situation wherein the CCACs are rolled into another bureaucracy, which perhaps means less bureaucracy. The move was marketed by the government as a decision that would improve the lives of those needing homecare. But not so.

Most of the CCAC employees remained in the newly bloated LHINs with little in the way of savings for Ontarians. On the service side, this is what some medical professionals, such as Darren Cargill, MD, a palliative care physician in Windsor believe (and who I tend to take seriously since he comments directly from the trenches):

> "The government argues this is about frontline care, but the reality is that LHINs don't provide frontline care—doctors, nurses, PSWs and others do. The struggles my patients have in accessing adequate home care, mental health care or even a MRI can't be fixed by more administration or more power to the minister and LHIN CEO. Government, LHINs and front line doctors must work together with patients to address the challenges with our health care system." [147]

Of course the negative consequences have been devastating for Ontarians, just as have the skyrocketing and clearly unsustainable electricity costs. And not only do we suffer from a lack of adequate services, which in the case of healthcare can put real lives at risk, we are constantly paying more and more for the massive waste in tax dollars and resources, both of which are preciously earned and foolishly spent. In January 2017, Picard reported on how most provinces have already moved away from having regional health units to a more centralized approach in managing their provincial health needs. To wit, Saskatchewan recently announced it will scrap its 12 health regions to create a single authority. Picard further elaborates that "Prince Edward Island, Nova Scotia and Alberta all have a single administrative body for health care; British Columbia has gone from 20 regions to five, Manitoba from 11 to 5, New Brunswick from eight to five . . . holdouts are Quebec, which has 18 regional health and social-services agencies, and Ontario, which has 14 Local health integrated networks (and 76 sub LHINs)."[148]

So many provinces are opting for centrally managed health networks while others like Ontario continue to support a more regionalized structure, ostensibly that better serves local communities. Structurally, in either case, none of this matters if the required services are not delivered to patients effectively and efficiently. Obviously administration could be organized to get in the way of, rather than better facilitate, the delivery of healthcare services. That problem confronts both centralized and regional models. If we take a high-level view, we can see that uninformed and poor decision-making continues to occur around the crucial healthcare needs of Canadians, including how to organize the Ontario system. It may interest Windsor palliative care specialist, Dr. Cargill, referenced earlier, to know what Picard laments. Picard's view, using our provincial healthcare system in former Premier Wynne's Ontario as an example, is that "the most remarkable aspect about the radical changes that provinces have implemented is that they are evidence-free and there have been virtually no follow-up studies to examine whether there have been benefits, financial or otherwise."[149]

Again, we could be talking about the farce known as the provincial Liberals' handling of the electricity file, the cancelled gas plants that cost Ontarians more than $2.4 billion, etc. That goes for this comment made by Picard as well. "Too often, it is change for the sake of change—or to give the illusion of reform—and it amounts to little more than shifting the position of the deck chairs on a listing ship."[150] Well said. All of the changes being made, such as centralizing or decentralizing bureaucracies, renaming them, creating new ones, or rolling them into one another, is really just more optics management. Remember, misinformed and misguided decision-making is usually the art of politics these days. Whether this erodes the public trust or not does not seem to matter. It is all, as the popular TV show about an aspiring politician Kevin Spacey portrayed for a while, a *House of Cards*. Or you could view it as a shell game. Only instead of a peanut, the government must hide its problems to always ensure it looks good. Rebranding of the CCACs or other failing organizations, in efforts to make it look like you are really doing something constructive, is always easier than tackling root problems themselves where governments are concerned.

Our Infrastructure

The mess we face does not just concern the erosion of the government institutions that are supposed to reflect our values and contribute to our well-being. It also concerns the actual physical destruction of our past. They say it helps you to know who you are when you know where you have come from. But the neglect of so many of Canada's landmarks, historic and cultural buildings, results in a situation whereby we are not sure what Canada represents. Is it then surprising we have struggled for so long to form a national identity? To feel that we belong to something bigger than ourselves? The physical destruction of what Canada was, along with the slow destruction of its democratic institutions, the very fabric that holds the country together, is a national disgrace. All that has been achieved, even the mistakes that have been made, must be made visible. We must learn and grow as a unified people. That is impossible when so much is left to wither and die in the mess created by successive governments.

Andrew Cohen wrote informatively in *The Unfinished Canadian*, that "saving Canada's forts, churches, ancestral homes and factories, as the auditor general has recommended, should be another priority." [151] With palpable dejectedness as well as eloquent succinctness, ruing the lack of leadership and vision for nation building and greatness across the land, Cohen writes: "You see it in the lethargy of a municipal government that has allowed a city core to rot. And in the somnolence of a federal government . . . [that] cannot itself find the ambition to build institutions worthy of a country of this size and stature." [152]

Our Healthcare System

The current situation is not only untenable, it is unhealthy. But then again, so too is the Canadian healthcare system at the national level (we already discussed healthcare problems in Ontario). Our lives and those of our loved ones are actually at greater risk because of more senseless decisions made in Ottawa that, paradoxically, have caused the healthcare system to ail itself! In *Dismantling Canada: Stephen Harper's New Conservative Agenda* (mind you successive governments have been dismantling, if not ruining our institutions with their uninformed decision-making), professor Brooke Jeffrey paints a dark picture of our healthcare system. "In the 2012 budget, the federal government . . . reduced funding for Health Canada by more than $200 million and cut the budget at the Public Health Agency by $68 million and the Institute of Health Research by $45 million." [153] These are obviously not small figures. Yet they pale in comparison to the ballooning shortfall that came with removing the mechanism of equalization payments that ensured our national and universal healthcare system was on a sure footing.

Regardless of the wealth of the Canadian province or territory you live in relative to others, Canadians reasonably expect adequate healthcare under the universal system. Consider that Tommy Douglas, a key figure in creating Canada's universal healthcare system, was chosen by popular acclaim as the most important or influential Canadian. This happened when a *CBC* television series that aired in 2004, invited viewers to choose who they thought was the greatest Canadian ever. In *The Unfinished Canadian, The People We Are*, Andrew Cohen quoted the now famous George Stroumboulopoulos, the broadcaster who nominated Tommy, saying, "Tommy's values became Canadian values."[154] Although that may be a stretch, the remark certainly reflected that we know it is right to ensure the health of our country and its people. A strong publicly funded healthcare system has always been an important national institution for most Canadians who are not members of the one per cent but that of the 99 per cent. However, as we learn in *Dismantling Canada*:

> In the 2014 budget, Harper followed through on the plan
> to eliminate the equalization portion of health-care transfers
> in favour of the per-capita transfer—once more benefitting
> only Alberta, and leaving have-not provinces with an
> insurmountable gap of $16.5 billion over the next five years.[155]

Tommy is probably turning in his grave given the betrayal of what he so proudly tried to build. If we look at the current state of Canada's healthcare system, you know things are far from firing on all cylinders. Across the land, Canadians are forever lined up in what seems to be ever-growing queues, trying to get prompt medical attention for either themselves or their loved ones. Too often, it is an exercise in futility. In fact, as the Associate Director of the Fraser Institute's Centre for Health Policy Studies indicated in a December 2017 *Maclean's* opinion piece, the average wait times for proper medical attention have reached all-time highs, hitting 20 weeks for treatment by a specialist (across 12 medical specialties) upon referral from a general practitioner. This was the situation facing Canadians in 2016. The record wait times are more than double the 9.3-week waiting period measured by the Fraser Institute's annual survey in 1993.[156] Regional disparities also appear to be stark, chipping away at Tommy Douglas' dream of universal healthcare for all Canadians. For example, while Quebec broke the 20-week mark for the first time since 2003, patients in New Brunswick have to wait 41.7 weeks, or almost a full year, to get treatment. [157]

The Fraser Institute is often perceived as a somewhat partisan organization. However, a recent Commonwealth Fund International Health Policy Survey (the Canadian Institute for Health Information (CIHI) and the Canadian Institute of Health Research (CIHR) are the national Canadian co-partners of this annual survey) also paints a distressing picture. Per the CIHI's website, the Commonwealth Fund's 2016 international survey "shows that Canadians continue to report some of the longest wait times for doctors, specialists and emergency department visits compared with citizens in peer countries." [158] Here are a few of the gloomy findings revealed by the international survey:

Less than half (43%) of Canadians get a same- or next-day appointment with their family doctor or at their regular place of care . . . compared with top performing countries like New Zealand (76%) and the Netherlands (77%); access to after-hours care is also more difficult in Canada than most other countries with only 1 in 3 (34%) patients able to receive [it] . . . without going to the emergency department; Canadians visit emergency departments more often than people in other countries, and have the longest reported waits there as well. More than 40% of Canadians said that the last time they visited an emergency department, it was for a condition they could have been treated by their regular provider; Canadians also report the longest wait times for specialists, with more than half (56%) waiting longer than

4 weeks to see a specialist, compared with the international average of 36%. [159]

Journalist Andre Picard, a Public Health Reporter for the *Globe and Mail*, has recently written quite a bit on the challenges we ordinary Canadians have been facing with our once, much admired, but now crumbling healthcare system. This institution needs to be triaged for sure before things get much worse. Picard views the problem arising from clogs in the system. So yet again we see the need for a good plumber. According to Picard, the real challenge is not waiting times. He probably would agree they are just symptoms of the central problem plaguing our dysfunctional healthcare system. He sees the 'fundamental' challenges being: "To provide the right care at the right place at the right time at an affordable price (to individuals and society)." [160] The current system is unsustainable, but we continue to throw good money after bad, putting resources where they are not actually needed. We keep treating the symptoms of the real disease without addressing the disease itself, head on. It is almost as if this is an indication of the dystopian future we are all headed for.

Both in a February 2017 and a late November 2017 article, Picard emphasized the insanity of this approach. In the first piece, he wrote, "Long-term care and nursing home beds are full. Home care hours are limited. As a result, thousands of patients who no longer need care can't leave hospital, a reality so common we have an Orwellian term for it—alternate level of care." [161] In his second article, Picard mentioned that, "in Ontario alone, there are almost 4,000 'alternate level of care' (ALC) patients (7,500 Canada-wide), an Orwellian euphemism used to describe people who have been discharged but continue to live in hospitals because they have nowhere else to go, for lack of long-term-care beds and home-care spots." [162] For Canadians paying into the system, the outcome of such a situation is less than palatable. "Because these patients are not discharged and beds are scarce, elective surgeries are cancelled, and those waiting for admission spend days on a gurney in the ER." [163]

This seems ridiculous, if not intolerable. But that is modern government for you. To think that in Canada, a first-world country, that people cannot get adequate medical care—in still another backlogged system that is costing us all a fortune—it is unacceptable!

I can only imagine what the hardworking medical staff toiling away in the trenches, such as devoted nurses, orderlies, therapists and doctors, etc., think of their officials responsible for the system. CIHI work reveals that that "patients are often left to navigate the complex system on their own, and too often fall between the cracks." It also find that "Canada relies more on doctors to provide care than any other country." This, as Picard writes, simply means "we underuse nurse practitioners, occupational therapists and the like." [164] On the surface, it looks as if some governments are trying to meaningfully address the problem. As Picard wrote in November 2017, the Ontario government recently announced "it will spend $100 million to add almost 2,000 temporary beds to deal with Ontario's so-called overcrowding crisis." [165] Unfortunately, this is just more of the same, dealing with symptoms rather than root causes.

Of course the optics of such announcements may look good for leaders of the day; they appear to be doing something but are actually continuing to dither when it comes to generating the real changes needed to benefit the healthcare system and those Canadians who rely on it. Sensibly, albeit perhaps counterintuitively, Picard writes: "The problem won't disappear by simply adding more beds . . . We won't solve our chronic hospital overcrowding problem until we come to grips with the fact that it is a system-wide structural problem of which hospital misuse is only one element." Perceptively noting that "the ER overcrowding problem won't be solved in the ER, nor will the hospital overcrowding problem be solved in the hospital," he again avowed: "It's about treating the right patients in the right place at the right time." [166] Unfortunately, it appears his words of wisdom are falling upon deaf ears.

This is but one more backlog, and not just in Ontario, in addition to so many other outrageous ones caused by misguided government decision-making.

The only difference, other than perhaps that faced by our ill-equipped military when they must perform dangerous missions, is that the real well-being and real lives of Canadians are at risk. So much could be written about our healthcare system problems, as well as other issues that have been covered in this chapter, along with even other issues that have not been raised. Only recently *CBC News* reported on how "millions of Canadians rely on surgically implanted medical devices," but "many of those devices are approved for use in Canada with scant scientific evidence to show they are safe and effective." This according to "a new *CBC/Radio-Canada/Toronto Star* investigation."[167]

To wrap-up our discussion on our government betraying us by not making good and informed decisions regarding Tommy Douglas' dreams, we should raise the spectre of our exploding opioid crisis in Canada. By mid-December 2017, Dr. Theresa Tam, Canada's chief public health officer, said, based on available data at the time that "the number of overdose deaths are on pace to surpass 4,000 by the end of the year, far above last year's tally of 2,861 opioid-related fatalities." In discussing the national fentanyl crisis, she also indicated that "it could hit all other areas of Canada and that's why it's so concerning."[168]

Many of you have heard about what appears to be an epidemic of deaths related to fentanyl. Some of it is illegal and users of this opioid, whether they realize that is what they are taking or not, may not get a second chance, it is so deadly. In other cases, there is substance abuse related to doctors and pharmacists over-prescribing fentanyl. At any rate, and not unlike our dysfunctional healthcare system when it comes to managing the overcrowded hospitals, clogs in the system that is supposed to treat opioid patients appropriately and on a timely basis, etc., have also emerged. Dr. Tam agrees that people need to work together to solve such a system-wide issue. Her common sense opinion that would resonate well with most Canadians is that "as we move into 2018, we really need the whole of Canada to be prepared."[169]

Our Access to Information

Journalist John Ibbitson artfully contrasted the Omar Khadr debacle, which I wrote of earlier, with that of former Prime Minister Harper's census scandal, both highly offensive to Canadians, albeit different in nature. The census scandal of course is another example of stupid decision-making in government that negatively impacts all of us. After all, when the Conservatives did away with the mandatory long-form census in 2010, they were effectively ensuring the government would have even less credible data to base good decisions on in the future. This makes things even worse for Canadians, reducing our quality of life yet again and wasting even more of our hard-earned tax dollars. It seems even normally quiet Canadians got riled over the absurdity of it all, especially in the shadow of Munir Sheikh, the well-respected head of Statistics Canada, resigning in protest.

As Ibbitson stated, "The story dominated for weeks. Municipal and provincial governments, academics, pundits—everyone with an interest in knowing the state of the Canadian population protested that gutting the census was an act of political vandalism."[170] I would add the phrase 'of our institutions that bind us together and define our values' at the end of that! Speaking of the vandalism of our institutions that bind the nation and Canadians together, the Prime Minister's Office (PMO), arguably the most important institution that represents Canada, both here and abroad, appears to be producing unbelievable gaffs itself. This further erodes our trust, creating negative outcomes for the country and its reputation abroad.

Of course, if any Canadians are even bold enough to check if the government is actually listening to us, trying to solve the problems that confront us and the country in a meaningful way, they are greeted by a wall. That wall is designed to keep any government outsiders just that, 'outside' the system and generally in the dark. What better way to ensure the citizens of the nation generally trust in what you are doing then to prevent any information indicating otherwise from leaking out. Even to get the information I needed to put this book together, I have had to rely mainly on the important work of many credible journalists, researchers, authors, government workers, etc., as well as my own work experience as a civil servant in Canada.

In his book *Spinning History: A Witness to Harpers Canada and 21st Century Choices*, Les Whittington wrote forlornly about how Canada's ATIP (Access to Information Program—a barometer of how transparent a nation's government is to those over which it governs) compares poorly with other democracies. "Canada's Access to Information program, regularly cited as one of the least open and least efficient in the democratic world gets combed through as a last resort for non-classified information that should be open to the public."[171] Similarly, in his own book *Dismantling Canada*, Jeffrey outlines a bleak picture of our government's transparency. Credibly, he cited former Information Commissioner Robert Marleau's 2009 annual report. "Too often, responses to access requests are late, incomplete, or overly censored. Too often, access is denied to hide wrongdoing or to protect officials from embarrassment, rather than to serve a legitimate confidentiality requirement."[172]

Marleau resigned from government shortly after his report was released. In today's modern, complex, globally integrated and increasingly risky world, we need our government to make informed, risk-based and credible decisions. Those decisions must benefit Canadians. We need the government to do what's right instead of increasingly the opposite, so painfully illustrated above. A lack of transparency resulting from several issues such as a poor ATIP system, has enabled successive governments—with perhaps Harper's command-and-control government being the poster child in Canada—to hide what is really going on. All the poor decision-making based on wrong assumptions, erroneous facts, personal gain, competing and dated ideologies, and above all, optics management; that is the real fake news. And it is not just eating away at the fabric of Canadian society and its democratic institutions. This is happening all over the world in once healthier democracies that functioned somewhat better in less complex times. The irony is that we have the ability to generate and access more information than at any other time in history.

Rather than cultivating the garden of democracy itself, so that it thrives for future generations, politicians of all backgrounds and party memberships are cultivating their own images and that of their respective groups. It is all about saying the 'right' thing, telling the citizenry what they want to hear, no matter that real issues are ignored or wrong decisions are made to the detriment of Canada and its people. This is the calamity of modern politics and serves to explain why the needed work is often not done at all or done the wrong way. We are then left with more weeds impeding the blossoming of our democracy, instead of thriving institutions that reflect our values of doing the right thing, at the right time and in the right place. Politics has often been called the art of decision-making, but it needs to be so much more in the 21st century. It needs to be responsible to the people, transparently informing the constituents of our democracy why certain decisions are being made and how those decisions will benefit the country as a whole. We need less art and pageantry in our government's decision-making. Instead we need more risk-based and wise decision-making grounded in good information that will generate the right outcomes.

Just as when US President Ronald Reagan told former Soviet leader and General Secretary, Mikhail Gorbachev, to "tear down this wall," during his famous speech at the Brandenburg gate in Berlin in June 1987, we must tear down the wall that shields our government from being accountable to the voting public. You could even argue that our national security is already at stake when our government is set up to endanger our well-being, and even its own. The wall, of which ATIP is just one piece, has too long been obstructing our path to the truth. It has been obstructing our ability to discern just what facts and information the government is using to base its significant decisions on. Those decisions of course, be they involving the CRA, the military, EI benefits, IT projects, the environment, etc., affect us all.

Our government cloaks itself behind a wall of opaqueness and non-transparent decision-making in many ways. In February 2013, the Information Commissioner of Canada, Suzanne Legault, received a formal request from the Environmental Law Centre at the University of Victoria and the non-profit Democracy Watch. That request, as Jeffrey wrote, was "to investigate what they termed the 'systemic' efforts of the federal government to obstruct access to information and to limit its researchers."[173] Maybe Legault's predecessor, Marleau, would have agreed. Interestingly, during March 2018, *CBC News* reported on the results of Legault's investigation, arising from the Environmental Law Centre's formal request. According to the *CBC*, "It took five years, but the results…were released and the verdict is in: the Harper government did muzzle scientists."[174] In one case, "Two University of Alberta scientists were given a script telling them how to answer media questions about their own research that found evidence of air and water pollution from Alberta's oilsands." In a different case, "it took 11 government employees and 50 emails to decide how to answer a reporter's request to interview a Canadian government scientist who was part of a NASA team studying regional snowfall patterns."[175]

Turning to another sorry situation involving an independent commissioner of the Government of Canada, the Public Sector Integrity Commissioner, we see more problems. The Integrity Commissioner's office is supposed to bring some semblance of accountability and transparency to the operation of our national government by shedding light on any wrongdoing. I suspect that would include any outrageous decisions made by government officials not adhering to their respective department's mandate. For example, you would expect those responsible for maliciously charging innocent Canadians with tax evasion, creating a federal employee payroll system that does not work and damages the broader public service, allowing a convicted murderer to be linked to a state visit by our Prime Minister and so on, would presumably, and at least occasionally, be investigated for some kind of wrongdoing! And since the Integrity Commissioner's job, ostensibly, is to protect whistleblowers and investigate complaints within the various departments and agencies of the federal public service, you would think their office would be somewhat busy. Think again!

In *Dismantling Canada*, Jeffrey observes that "Commissioner Ouimet abruptly resigned shortly before a scathing report by the Auditor General. That unflattering report indicated that, while 228 cases were filed with the Commissioner's office, just seven were actually investigated." Moreover: "Of those seven, five were closed with no finding of wrongdoing and the other two were still being investigated at the time of Ouimet's resignation." Even more startling: "Evidence also emerged that Ouimet had often communicated directly with several cabinet ministers and officials in the Privy Council Office, despite her position as an independent officer of Parliament."[176] So much for bringing transparency of what's happening in government to an ever confused if not outright duped Canadian public. That is not to say we are not faring better than our American neighbours down south under the Trump Administration. But you get the picture.

In the final analysis, we are faced with repeated blundering by governments of all political leanings. Their obvious misguided and misinformed decision-making is hidden behind nice-sounding departments like the Office of the Integrity Commissioner or Information Commissioner. Those offices are just more layers of bureaucracy that do not appear to work optimally in the interest of Canadians. They, too, along with a less than desirable ATIP system, perpetuate the status quo, further enabling the deterioration of the institutions that should unite us. We are rendered impotent as a people, unable to achieve that which we are capable of. We can never lead by example if we cannot be empowered to lead ourselves. This is the issue of our time, central to all democratic nations that are also seemingly unable to pull themselves out of the various quagmires they are sinking into.

I have always agreed that example is more powerful than precept. However, when I pick up the newspaper or turn on the evening news, in a moment of curiosity, to see if commentators (there do not appear to be many real, professional journalists left on TV) are talking yet again about Donald Trump's latest tweets—whether or not the Russians are colluding with, and hacking into the White House, or who and what now is being blamed for Brexit or other problems plaguing various countries—I am simply reminded of this. No nation around this great and suffering earth can claim moral superiority over other nations. No nation is leading other nations by example. No self-proclaimed democratic nation really has its own house in order.

The world continues to repeat the mistakes of the past. It attempts to build walls, be they physical ones such as Trump aspires to create, or hidden ones designed to obscure and twist truths. This is not new. We had the Berlin wall and the propaganda emanating from the Soviet Union during the Cold War. We also had many countries entering a period of isolationism prior to World War II, in the aftermath of the Great Depression. Now too, many countries are embarking on this road, turning inward, away from 'the other,' as they seek to implement trade barriers such as tariffs. Growing right-wing rhetoric, grounded less in facts and sound information, echoes dangerously from the past. It is leading civilization perilously again to its ruin, fortified by a newly installed and growing cadre of extreme right-wing leaders, most with healthy egos and few with solutions to restore the health of society and the environment itself. These leaders are false prophets who will only repeat the sins of the past. Beware of what they offer and the falsehoods they speak. Beware also of left-wing activists with right-wing bank accounts who do little, but say much.

We appear to be reducing ourselves to the lowest common denominator, fraying at the edges, embracing infantile behaviour rather than growth. Here in Canada, our government's infantile behaviour is perhaps most pronounced in that perennial sandbox known as the House of Commons, particularly during what is commonly known as Question Period. Whittington describes the puerile behaviour of what should be our much esteemed and professional

Members of Parliament (MPs) best: "Since 2006, Question Period, in the House of Commons has degenerated into a demeaning, juvenile exchange of insults and recriminations."[177] Considering Question Period is meant to keep the Canadian public informed as to what their taxpayer-funded government is doing, presumably in our interest, it is nothing short of ridiculous to learn that "in recent years any semblance of meaningful debate has largely disappeared in 45 minutes of partisan wrangling."[178]

Yet it is not only the circus of Question Period and the disingenuous operations of less than independent or effective Information and Integrity Commissioners that eats away at the fabric of our democracy, preventing good decision-making. Our leaders' desire, or permissiveness, to hoodwink and confuse the public further enables the erosion of our democratic institutions. All of this guarantees voters end up duped into believing good decisions are being made on their behalf by a less than sincere government of the day.

One way the government shoves new laws and measures down our throats, whether they are beneficial or not to the nation, is by employing what is called omnibus budget legislation. As Whittington writes of Prime Minister Harper's use of the technique, it is "a budget bill of 400 or more pages into which are crammed dozens of pieces of legislation . . . using huge omnibus bills allowed the government to quietly bring in all kinds of measures—in one piece of votable legislation."[179] Returning to Jeffrey's opinion, which seems unassailable good sense, "with little or no access to accurate information or informed policy debate, the public has been successfully misled or kept in the dark."[180]

I believe good decisions result from careful analysis and deliberation of pertinent facts and data. They also arise out of thoughtful debate, transparent to the public, and above all, a genuine interest in the overall well-being of those impacted by the decisions being made. If you agree, then usage of omnibus legislation is just another nail in the coffin of democracy. Or, as Whittington concludes of the Harper government's adoption of the omnibus tactic—mind you it is the same result in any government: "This had the effect of reducing the amount of attention the media and the public paid to any single measure in the massive, legalese-filled bill." [181]

Post-Harper we see that in relation to the dreaded omnibus legislation, it matters little that the Liberals now preside over the federal government in Ottawa. In a June 2017 *Globe and Mail* piece discussing Bill C-44, Finance Minister Bill Morneau's omnibus budget bill, we find even a Liberal senator questioning the Liberal government's own use of the legislative tactic. Liberal Senate leader Joseph Day warned this: "The bill contains provisions that quietly—one might even say stealthily—remove Parliament's oversight of government finances, and increase the power of the executive—of the cabinet." [182] Beware of any government in power that uses ghostly stealth to elicit change.

Of note, Bill C-44 included legislation creating Canada's new infrastructure bank, which has been quite controversial, even viewed as another layer of unnecessary bureaucracy. The omnibus legislation contained increases in taxes for Canadians as well as other significant measures. Another Liberal senator, Terry Mercer, who used to be National Director of the Liberal Party of Canada, had this to say in reference to tax increases on beer and liquor. "If you're going to increase tax, have the guts to stand up in front of the House of Commons yearly and increase the tax instead of hiding behind this sneaky way of increasing taxes." [183] By now if you are like most Canadians and decent people around the globe, you have a pretty good idea that some things have been going terribly wrong in this country. Our federal government is not always doing what it needs to do for you, your family and Canada. The waste is both colossal in scale and tragedy.

Our Democratic Restoration

You may wish to throw up your hands in exasperation, wondering what the point of all this negativity is. Similarly, you may ask what the point of raising these issues is if things have and will always be this way. True, it is not like we are living in the UK and have to deal with Brexit. Nor are we living in the US where we must deal with Trump and all the monumental, unforeseen, and yet to be discovered, implications that go along with such things. Sure, since what seems to be time immemorial, democracy has wrestled with its challenges. It is not perfect, or as Winston Churchill said in reference to democracy on November 11, 1947, "Indeed it has been said that democracy is the worst form of Government except for all those other forms that have been tried from time to time."

Stop right there! What if I told you, especially after surfacing so many huge problems in this chapter, that those problems can substantially be resolved? Not only that, they can pretty much be avoided in future! Finally, in achieving this, we can become a model of success for other countries. And if you believe in the goodness of most people, that they actually want to do the right thing, then perhaps even problems that are international in scale—such as climate change, poverty, and maybe even the refugee crisis and other seemingly intractable problems—can be confronted in a more realistic and solution-oriented way than they are now. Too fanciful and idealistic? Churchill also said that day in 1947, "No one pretends that democracy is perfect or all-wise." But why can't we strive to approach that state rather than continuing to stray so far away from it? The good news is we can!

We will be exploring how to curb the undesirable behaviour that has contributed to the erosion of the public institutions that are supposed to bind Canadians together. Thankfully, we are not in as dark a place as some other nations that claim they are modern democracies. But we have a lot of restoration work to do before we lead the modern world by example. As you will see, the restoration needs are structural and psychological in nature. They must take place here in Canada, where our flag requires mending, as well as elsewhere, before the world can be healed.

Chapter 4
Mending the Flag

Every problem has in it the seeds of its own solution.

—Norman Vincent Peale

Three Key Problems Requiring Our Attention

Earlier in our journey of self-discovery, we learned who we Canadians collectively are, our unique individual lives and experiences all contributing to a greater definition of what Canada is. Thus far, our sojourn has also traversed a great divide, the gap metaphorically being as expansive as our great land shines from sea to shining sea. This gap is the widening chasm that exists between our collective expectations of a reasonably well-functioning government bureaucracy, regardless of the political leanings of the party in power at any given time, and the stark reality of what increasingly confronts us. We face a broken and dysfunctional government machinery that is a betrayal of who we Canadians are and what Canada needs to be.

Successive governments, as well-intended as they may have been, have shirked their responsibility. In doing so, they have allowed the rot to set into our government institutions and systems, the very foundation of our parliamentary democracy. And the scaffolding erected outside our House of Commons on Parliament Hill to repair the façade does little to address the real needs hidden below the surface of what we Canadians actually see. It is clear we need more than optics management. We require more than the appearance of construction crews repairing the outer veneer of our government, more than photo ops, 'selfies' and vacuous speeches made by inexperienced leaders and non-doers telling us that all is well when it really is not.

The disingenuous words and actions of our leaders needs to stop. We can and must do better. The legacy of our Canadian taxpayers, who have worked so hard; our forefathers, who toiled so much; our war veterans, who have given so much; our Indigenous Peoples, who have sacrificed so much; and so many others, demands it. We can no longer afford to betray our history and ourselves, imperfect as our history and we are. We must recognize our mistakes, learning from them, to mend the flag.

It has often been said the world needs more Canada. But this nationalist hubris needs to be quelled, silenced until such time as we generally begin to get our own affairs in order. For only when Canadians unite, showing the world we can fix our own problems, can we truly say with confidence and honestly earned pride, that the world needs more Canada. Fortunately there actually is a clear and sensible way forward to mend our fraying institutions, the structural fabric of our democracy that bonds us together. Much work needs to be done though. And a lot of it will not be immediately visible for all to see. However just as my old boss, Marty the plumber, or my father, Henry, the hoisting engineer, both knew, properly maintaining the hidden infrastructure we take for granted is what keeps things running smoothly.

We expect water to be readily available when we open a tap. Similarly, we expect a light to shine brightly and effortlessly, at the flick of a switch. We do not give much thought as to how these plumbing and electrical systems work. And because they are everywhere, it is easy to think designing, building and maintaining them is easy. We just expect them to be there, in good working order, when we need them. The same can be said of our democratic institutions. But hopefully I have provided you with enough evidence to conclude, as I have, that the hidden infrastructure that is supposed to support democracy is in need of immediate repair.

To begin the required repairs to our democracy here in Canada, we must identify the problems impeding our ability to move forward as a country. Of course, we also have to care about the damage caused by those problems to begin with. That is why I took great effort to reveal to you, through much research, how all of us, from all walks of life, are being adversely impacted in our day-to-day lives by ineffectual government. This is happening regardless of the figurehead and party in charge. How could it be any different, considering so many leaders have repeatedly failed to identify the problems leading to each government's poor results to begin with? So what are the issues preventing our democracy from working effectively to produce the positive outcomes we Canadians rightly expect? It all boils down to three key problems:

1) Poorly designed organizational structures within government;
2) Wrongly motivated individuals (highly correlated with the first point); and
3) Ineffective oversight of all levels of government (unaccountability).

The problems are really quite simple. They only seem complex because they are buried beneath the façade of government, much like the plumbing system so vital to make our taps run is buried behind the walls or underground. The seriousness of these three problems, especially when they act in combination with one another, will become much more evident in the next three chapters. For now, when you stop and really think about it, these three key problems not only impact Canadians from all walks of life, but reflect a greater malaise affecting people around the world. They have significantly contributed, if not led, to war, famine, impoverishment, and disparities among citizens and among nations. In all likelihood, these key problems also reflect the seething, albeit heretofore ill-defined, anger undulating beneath the social fabric of modern democracies.

Populist Angst

The term 'populism' is increasingly being used to describe what lies behind the recent successes that many right-wing politicians have had in winning elections, leading their respective nations in new and more divisive directions. Consider the case of Donald Trump as an example. The leaders of Hungary (Viktor Mihály Orbán) and Turkey (Recep Tayyip Erdoğan) are but two additional examples of many. Brexit has also been viewed as a kind of populist movement. But what is populism?

Almost flexibly, "The term populism can designate either democratic or authoritarian movements."[1] On the positive side, it seeks to represent the interest of the people. Therefore, "In its most democratic form," it "seeks to defend the interest and maximize the power of ordinary citizens, through reform rather than revolution."[2] I recall studying populism at UWO and remember that the movement's roots stretch fairly far back in American history. I do not remember it being an authoritarian movement. And apparently, "In the United States," it was "the Populist Movement, which gave rise to the Populist, or People's, Party in 1892."[3] Perhaps Canadian politician, Maxime Bernier, based his new party's name, The People's Party of Canada, on America's old 'People's Party.' I am not really sure. What I am sure of, is that we must be wary of any political leaders that may take misinformed voters down dangerous and authoritarian paths, all the while saying they are a champion of the people. We have seen the dismal results produced by the Trump administration.

In a March 2018 *BBC* News piece authored by David Molloy, we learn that "Experts point to both societal changes like multiculturalism and globalism, and more concrete crises as behind the rise of populist parties in

Europe."[4] We further learn that, "In political science, populism is the idea that society is separated into two groups at odds with one another – 'the pure people' and 'the corrupt elite', according to Cas Mudde, author of Populism: A Very Short Introduction."[5] I am not going to dwell at length on the term, populism, below. However, it is instructive to outline, along with a few other things, some of the populist angst that has been developing. This angst serves to emphasize why many people, misinformed and misguided as they may be (the reasons for this are explained later), have felt it necessary to express their angst by voting for politicians that promise to address their concerns, even if that proves something those politicians do not know how to do.

Many democracies are increasingly caught up in a wave of protests, pullback from seemingly disreputable international organizations, populist angst and, I dare say, growing extremist tendencies. Consider the 'Occupy' movement. On the surface it appears to be some kind of rudderless global protest that has no clear direction or spokesperson. It is the same movement that proclaims "we are the 99%" yet has no clear agenda, leadership, objectives or solutions to solve the world's current and growing inequalities. Spontaneously, beginning in September 2011 when a small group of protesters occupied Zuccotti Park in Manhattan, the Occupy movement swelled beyond the United States into an international movement. Its rallying cry or "point of unity" according to *Washington Post* reporter Heather Gautney: "We are the 99% that will no longer tolerate the greed and corruption of the 1%—an obvious reference to the well-known, yet still appalling statistic that the top 1 percent of households in America own somewhere between 30 to 40 percent of all privately held wealth. And counting."[6]

Indeed. If we jump ahead six years, to 2017, even the highly esteemed American tycoon and investment guru, Warren Buffet, acknowledges the increasing polarization between the haves and have-nots. "The real problem, in my view, is the prosperity has been unbelievable for the extremely rich people," he told *PBS Newshour* in June. According to Buffett, "If you go to

1982, when *Forbes* put on their first 400 list, those people had $93 billion. Now they have $2.4 trillion, [a multiple of] 25 for one."[7] In other words, and most startlingly, as referenced by Jason Le Miere writing for *Newsweek* in June 2017: "Since the 1980s, the richest 1 percent of Americans have seen their share of total income roughly double, to 20 percent. Meanwhile, the bottom 50 percent have seen their share decline in a big way, to 12 percent from 20 percent." Le Miere aptly writes that "inequality in America is now even more pronounced than in China."[8]

On the positive side, the Occupy movement drew attention to the ever-widening gap between the growing rich and the rest of us growing poorer. It did so not only in America, but around the world, as evidenced by the protests that took place on October 15, 2011 in almost 1,000 cities in 82 countries. Significantly, it also focused our attention on how the political process involving the workings of supposedly democratic governments can be adversely influenced by the wealthy, usually for their benefit. This is because the wealthy often control the purse strings (do I really need to talk about the Trump family and big business as an example!), currying favour with the political leadership. In this regard, the movement connected big business as a way to control government, ultimately reflecting the idea that government no longer represents the collective will of the people. Is this any surprise considering the long shadow of the financial crisis? People perceived the system did not work when it enabled the privatization of profits, but socialization of losses, in those countries that experienced taxpayer bailouts of financial institutions that were 'too big to fail.'

And yet people lost their jobs and homes with little help from unsympathetic governments who preferred to bail out their cronies. Not only that, many countries impacted by the 2008 financial crisis implemented a series of austerity measures that just made things worse for people on Main Street. As with other betrayals of the people, the proximate cause of all this misery for ordinary people was poor decision-making by big business and governments alike. In some cases it smacked of purposeful self-aggrandizement of wealth by an elite few, all at the expense of ordinary and decent people: the 99 per cent. As noted in a *Washington Post* article, published in October 2011, "The failure of representative democracy in the United States is perhaps one of the most serious problems of our time, and the Occupy movement is a symptom of this crisis of legitimacy." Moreover, "the people no longer trust their leaders and are even starting to indict the system itself."[9] Such lines of thinking are undoubtedly not confined to America. For as illustrated by the Arab Spring and countless other ongoing protests around the globe, people are not happy with the status quo.

Sadly, while Occupy focused the world's attention on growing inequality and the lack of truly democratic governments working for their respective citizens, it did not meaningfully address the three key problems I mentioned above. These issues have increasingly plagued Canada and the world: namely ineffective organizational structures and wrongly motivated people within government, and ineffective oversight of government. Ironically, but sadly expected when I researched the issue, the Occupy movement was never appropriately organized or governed to enable it to produce the desired solutions required: a reversal in the growth of inequality and lack of representative democracy around the world. This failure of imagination represents a loss of time for humanity to right its careening path forward into darkness. The world continues to cry out for leadership where there is none, including here in Canada, and certainly to our south. We can see the continued lack of leadership in France, with its 'yellow vests' protest. Just like Occupy, "the 'yellow vests' have no single leader, but many protesters manning roadblocks across the country," and in December 2018, "voiced the demand for a new system of government by referendum." Apparently they wish, "the right to hold referendums on new legislation that would overrule parliamentary votes, in what they claim would be a 'more direct' form of democracy."[10] The wellspring of protests occurring in many European countries in late 2018 requires our immediate attention; they are leading to violence and conflict at times. This is not the answer.

Writing in a June 2015 issue of *The Atlantic*, Michael Levitin puts the predictable stumbling block for grassroots movements, such as Occupy, best: "Occupy was at its core, a movement constrained by its own contradictions: filled with leaders who declared themselves leaderless, governed by a consensus-based structure that failed to reach consensus, and seeking to transform politics while refusing to become political."[11] Apparently, as outlined in the *Washington Post*, Occupy and similar groups "want to avoid replicating the authoritarian structures of the institutions they are opposing."[12] The failure of all the good intentions, associated with a multitude of people collaborating to try and make the world a better place, is both predictable and understandable. If the United Nations has a less than impeccable history of actually getting things done (its inability to resolve the Syrian refugee crisis is but one example of far too many), weighed down by its own ineffective organizational structures and governance, how could we ever expect such a geographically, culturally, educationally and otherwise diverse group such as Occupy—unorganized at that—to put forth concrete solutions to solve global inequality.

To be fair, and especially if you believe in the good that resides in most people, the members of Occupy are likely decent people. They are just tired of the status quo and of being disenfranchised by their leaders. They want to make things better and to participate in a society meant to support everyone, not just the elites, whatever their political ilk. Additionally, we should acknowledge not only Occupy's success in focusing our collective consciousness on the difference between right and wrong, but also on some of the movement's lesser known successes. For instance, in my home province of Ontario, the unpopular Liberal Wynne government passed legislation to increase the provincial minimum wage to $15 an hour. This push may have been linked to Occupy's earlier protests that "motivated fast-food workers in New York City to walk off the job in November 2012, sparking a national worker-led movement to increase the minimum wage to $15 an hour." The fact that several US states and cities responded to the challenge to raise base pay for workers by doing exactly that, is testament to Occupy's efforts. [13] This is not to say I am an overall fan of the erstwhile Liberal Wynne government. Nor does it suggest I believe the concerns of small business should have been ignored if they thought the wage increases may have hurt them. Tax breaks or other concessions could have been considered. Still, who can make a reasonable argument that low-income earners do not deserve a mere $15 an hour in exchange for their labour? It borders on the absurd.

Occupy also added greater impetus to the environmental movement. As reported on by the *Chicago Tribune*, it was apparently "inspired by the idea that a small handful of elites were using their power to accumulate wealth at the expense of the many, said Guido Girgenti, an organizer with the group 350. org." Furthermore, "Occupy, Girgenti said, helped jumpstart 'a new kind of climate movement' that questions the power of the fossil fuel industry." [14] For young people increasingly burdened by swelling student loans and debt, Occupy also had some success influencing change. "Occupy offshoot movements like Strike Debt, Rolling Jubilee, and Debt Collective are tackling America's $1.3 trillion college-debt conundrum by buying back student debt for pennies on the dollar and forgiving it." [15] As well, Occupy has influenced politicians to call for the lessening of wealthy elites influencing the political process. In the US, "presidential candidates from Clinton to Republican Senator Lindsey Graham [have called] for a new era of campaign-finance reform to remove big money from electoral politics." [16]

Here in Canada so too has a light been shining on the influence of the super-rich on our political landscape. The effects of Occupy, as well as general discontent, have likely been a motivating factor. Published in 2016, the book *Income Inequality: The Canadian Story*, with contributions from almost 30 economists and experts, concludes the following about the very wealthy: "With their increased relative income comes an increased ability to influence policy through lobbying and other means." Therefore, "the troubling implication is a future in which an increasing disaffected majority suffers from policies made by, and for the few."[17] That doesn't sound like a vibrant democracy to me.

Despite the successes outlined above, Occupy and other movements have failed to address the three central problems I raised earlier. Interestingly, during a recent British Columbian election campaign, the Liberals raked in more than $12 million in 2016. Swanky 'cash-for-access dinners' with the premier costing $10,000 a plate helped with the funding.[18] It becomes very clear just who can do the influencing when one considers that between 1982 and 2010, the bottom 90 per cent of Canadians counted a total growth in family income of two per cent versus a 75 per cent increase in income for the top 10 per cent.[19] According to Andrew Heisz, Assistant Director of the Income Statistics Division at Statistics Canada, "the share of market income earned by the top 1% percent in Canada is now larger than in any decade since the Great Depression in the 1930s."[20]

Worse yet, and glaringly, a recent *Oxfam Briefing Paper* released in January 2017 paints a dire picture of democracies worldwide failing to provide for the needs of people. Using data collected from the *Forbes* Billionaires list and the *Credit Suisse Global Wealth Data Book* (2016), Oxfam shockingly finds the following: collectively the richest eight individuals have a net wealth of $426 billion, which is the same as the net wealth of the bottom half of humanity.[21] One view may be that the elite octet, along with the other super-rich have worked much harder than the rest of us to amass their wealth and power. If we subscribe to this perspective, we likely would say that the one per cent all deserve to be at the top and we common folk are just too envious and plain lazy to make it big like they have. If we only worked a bit harder, or were a bit smarter, we too could reap the immense rewards that are available to all. What rubbish! It's like the Horatio Alger myth that members of an impoverished youth can easily pull themselves up by their own bootstraps, to enter the higher classes through sheer hard work and determination.

Simply put, it is not easy out there. It is not easy for indebted millennials, especially when Oxfam has determined this: "One third of the world's billionaire wealth is derived from inherited wealth, while 43% has some presumption of links to cronyism."[22] Cronyism equates to the influence of the super-rich, or giant corporations, exerting their power to ensure the system remains organized to benefit them rather than everyone as a whole, regardless of their work ethic or political leanings.

Speaking of cronyism and work ethic, does the world really need politicians like President Trump? His blatant nepotism is exhibited by his administration having appointed his daughter Ivanka and her husband Jared Kushner as special advisors on all things. What exactly qualifies these unelected individuals? Maybe it's the fact they have accumulated so much in the way of earthly treasures, being good apprentices that emulate the president instead of any spiritual father. God only knows how many treasures they have accumulated in heaven.

Americans were fed up with the status quo. They wanted to see things change. And when the Republican presidential candidate, Trump, had such a catchy slogan—"Make America Great Again"—it was almost a foregone conclusion the United States, under his leadership, would be headed in a new direction. But what exactly is the plan to make America great again? In Canada we currently have Justin Trudeau carrying on the family tradition of leading this country. Recent news also indicates that former Prime Minister Mulroney's daughter, Caroline, is now involved in politics as a member of Ontario's provincial government led by Doug Ford's Conservatives. Of course, the US and Canada are not North Korea. However, it is instructive to see how family political dynasties carry on across the globe, almost like the royal family in the UK, and regardless of the calibre of the personalities involved.

It is a misguided conception to believe that multinational corporations are working to improve those societies they operate in. The facts point otherwise. They point toward large transnational corporate behemoths having a salacious and unending appetite to pursue profits at the expense of others. A mature capitalist society should consider that big business must not only profit from its efforts, but so too should those contributing labour, material and other resources to the success of business ventures. The success of any business and that of a nation and its people need not be mutually exclusive things in a democracy. This is not communism or socialism. It is just common sense to ensure the economy is working reasonably well for everyone and for democracy. A thriving society is one that has capitalist structures benefitting private business as well as the democratic institutions which support the operations of that business. There is no reason private enterprises cannot make profits in Canada. It is simply a question of the degree to which profits end up in the hands of those running the business, be those hands located in Canada or elsewhere, such as in China.

Nobody wants trade wars. It is all about what is fair and reasonable according to the citizens of any country. It should be up to them and what they believe is right. The will of the people must always take precedence over the will of an individual, no matter how wealthy and well-connected that individual may be. That is fundamental to a healthy democracy. It is all about knowing the difference between what is right and wrong, and acting accordingly. History is replete with examples of big business suffering when citizens find they have become disenfranchised from 'the system.' It is a slippery slope to go down a road that leads to such dead ends for both private business and citizen alike—as communism, fascism and other totalitarian regimes. Often these roads lead to war, whether civil war, such as in the immediate period known as *war communism* after the Russian Revolution, or between neighbouring countries. War between nations is often sparked by one or more countries looking to blame others for their own internal problems. Mismanagement of the country's affairs is usually a prominent feature of those nations casting aspersions and taking up arms against others. It is also usually a prominent characteristic of a divided nation that will not last.

Nobody benefits from embarking down a path of national division, whereby polarized groups of citizens either benefit or suffer under the supposedly democratic government in power. And regardless of the soundbites and optics management used to cultivate an image that it actually cares about everyone it governs over, a mismanaged government that produces little in the way of good results for citizens, is destined to fail. Modern democracy in the United States, in the United Kingdom, here in Canada and elsewhere, has become an ugly aberration. This is being amply revealed by all the adverse consequences we are experiencing. Doubtful? Read Chapter 3 again.

Let's explore the reality of how our world is organized a little more for the benefit of the few instead of the many. Rather than actual countries, most of the world's richest entities, in terms of monetary value, are now corporations operating transnationally. As referenced in the Oxfam report, "The world's 10 biggest corporations—a list that includes Walmart, Shell and Apple—have a combined revenue greater than the government reserves of 180 'poorest' countries combined, in a list which includes Ireland, Indonesia, Israel, Columbia, Greece, South Africa, Iraq and Vietnam." [23] Wealthy corporations have exerted tremendous influence on governments to ensure the system works mainly for them and their rich executives. They have lobbied and financially backed certain political candidates accordingly. The Oxfam report sheds light on many examples, revealing a lack of conscience and shame amongst those with an insatiable appetite for yet more earthly treasures. "Alphabet, the parent company of Google, has become one of the biggest lobbyists in Washington and is in constant negotiations in Europe over anti-trust rules and tax." [24] Without any sense of right and wrong or shame, "billionaires in Brazil lobby to reduce taxes, and in São Paulo would prefer to use helicopters to get to work, flying over the traffic jams and broken infrastructure below." [25]

An increasingly polarized US is inexorably moving toward some type of national crisis. Truly, I tell you. It has lost most of its credibility in the international community. The super-rich and corporations continue to wield immense political influence there, not just in Russia where the oligarchs continue to bleed the people dry. Lobbying in Washington, "pharmaceutical companies spent more than $240 million in 2015."[26] Oxfam also finds that "the Koch brothers, two of the richest men in the world, have had a huge influence over conservative politics in the US, supporting many influential think tanks and the Tea Party movement, and contributing heavily to discrediting the case for action on climate change."[27] Closer to home here in Canada, the Ontario MP for Barrie-Springwater-Oro-Medonte, found that on June 28, 2017, lobbyists from the big banks lobbied the head of the government agency OSFI (Office of the Superintendent of Financial Institutions), Jeremy Rudin, to limit their competition.

Broadly, and according to an analysis by *CBC News*, "Canada's big banks and the association that represents them have lobbied government officials hundreds of times since the last election—including the watchdogs charged with policing them and members of the parliamentary committee now examining their [sales] practices."[28] Wealthy corporations and the super-rich are not just making more money than ever and exerting influence over governments around the world, they are systematically avoiding taxes to support the societies which they themselves derive benefits from, and where decent law-abiding citizens pay their fair share. Is it any wonder there are long lineups to get beds in our hospitals and long-term care facilities, decaying infrastructure all around us, army bases and schools that are falling apart, increasing child poverty, etc.?

Again, refer to Chapter 3 to remind yourself how you are being negatively impacted by a long litany of issues, resulting from your government's bad decision-making. And if the government is designed to support the top one per cent instead of you and your family, those making a positive contribution to the coffers of the very government working against the middle and lower classes, isn't it time to strengthen democracy instead of continually weakening it? If capitalism is to benefit everyone on a level playing field, the immoral cheat-the-system attitude needs to stop. So, too, must stop the corrosion of the institutions that once bound us all together. The design of 'the system' is not fostering the belief that hard-working individuals can typically get ahead. For our system is more and more impeding our ability to realize our dreams, to have a fair shot at making a positive contribution to our collective good, to exemplify the true merits of fair capitalism through our efforts. A fair capitalist system would reinforce our democratic institutions and belief in democracy rather than destroying them. We will be discussing what to do about the ineffective organizational structures and people in our government, along with the ineffective oversight of government, in the next few chapters.

Let us now examine more how a minority of people are cheating the system around the world, leaving the majority of people to suffer unfairly. 'Snow washing' continues apace. So what exactly is snow washing? As a *Toronto Star/ CBC-Radio-Canada* investigation recently outlined, it is when our country's seemingly prudent reputation and sound economy is utilized to make suspect transactions seem legitimate. You may recall I raised the issue of the Panama Papers in Chapter 3. Well, according to an internal memo from Mossack Fonseca, the legal firm at the epicentre of the scandal, "Canada is a good place to create tax-planning structures to minimize taxes like interest, dividends, capital gains, retirement income and rental income." [29]

Successive Canadian governments have made it simpler than ever for criminals and tax cheats to transfer money in and out of Canada by signing tax agreements with 115 countries—the most in the world. [30] If one connects the dots, our government seems immorally complicit in enabling the rich to avoid ponying up their share of taxes. Perhaps all that lobbying and cronyism pays off for the one per cent instead of folks on Main Street, who dutifully pay taxes to support our crumbling infrastructure. Ordinary Canadians are paying their taxes while desperately needed government revenues are being siphoned off by tax-cheating parasites. Those parasites do not play by the same set of rules and are sucking our public resources dry. The International Consortium of Investigative Journalists (ICIJ) obtained documents indicating

Mossack Fonseca actively marketed Canada as a tax haven, establishing shell companies here to evade taxes. [31]

Robert Cribb and Marco Chown Oved's January 2017 piece on all this also references Zürich-based independent tax consultant, Mark Morris, specializing in international tax agreements. He believes "Canada is a horrible tax haven. Everybody is now switched over from using [British Virgin Islands—BVI] companies to Cayman companies to Canadian [Limited Partnerships]. It's like the ultimate tax haven entity in the world." [32] Consider Barbados as just one example. When Canada signed a treaty with Barbados, it then "effectively encouraged Canadian businesses" to channel their international profits through that low-tax island. Later on, in 2009, Canada began signing tax treaties with other jurisdictions, such as BVI and Luxembourg, "offering" businesses "the same tax-free benefits" through those treaties. [33] With poor design and weak controls, this is just one more example of how we are failing to put Main Street first rather than the interests of nefarious cheats and wealthy schemers.

The Star/CBC-Radio-Canada investigation also discussed, among a host of issues, that the names listed on public registries have nothing to do with the companies' real owners, meaning Canada has done nothing to register the real 'beneficial owners.' Mr. Cribb and Oved's article additionally quotes Chris Mathers, a former RCMP officer, who also participated in money laundering busts as an undercover agent. With concern, he remarked, "If you launder money in Canada and get caught, FINTRAC [Financial Transactions and Reports Analysis Centre of Canada] suspends your golf membership. No one goes to jail in Canada for even the most significant financial crimes." [34] Indeed, in another article published by the *CBC* in June 2017, we learn of Canada's poor record in revealing who the real or beneficial owners are of suspected tax-haven corporations. Apparently when Britain's Chancellor of the Exchequer wrote to our Finance Minister, Bill Morneau, in December 2016, looking for Canada's support in exchanges of so-called "beneficial ownership" information, we did not have much of a response. Our disorganized and unaccountable government was on full display for the Chancellor when Minister Morneau responded to him disappointingly in a letter dated February 8, 2017. In that letter, which has some redacted/blacked out information, our Finance Minister stated:

> As you are aware, jurisdiction over corporate law is shared between federal, provincial and territorial governments in Canada, and trusts fall under provincial and territorial law . . . We are working with provincial and territorial counterparts to overcome some of these challenges in addressing beneficial ownership transparency.[35]

The problem with optics management is that, just as in the case of many photo-ops and brief soundbites in the media, it does little to effect real positive change in our lives. We are constantly impacted by an incessant barrage of negative outcomes arising from a poorly designed government that no longer serves its constituents. In the developing world most people would like to lift themselves out of poverty. It is a human travesty that $100 billion is lost annually to tax dodging. Of course, as logically summed up by Oxfam, it is "the poorest" individuals who bear the heaviest losses "as they are most reliant on the public services that these foregone billions could have provided."[36] Is this the kind of modern aberration of capitalism we want, no matter what political party we support? How can we consider the world to have evolved to a better stage when those at the top continue to cheat those who are less fortunate? Is this the spiritually correct and democratic thing to do? A few bad apples can ruin things for everyone.

Appallingly in 1990, the G-20 average statutory corporate tax rate was 40 per cent. In 2015 it was just 28.7 per cent. It seems to be a race to the lowest common denominator. By way of example, during 2014, in competition for Samsung's investment, Indonesia offered a corporate-income-tax exemption for

10 years, while Vietnam offered 15 years. [37] Can we not come up with a better idea to woo investment in countries by multinationals who seem to be racing to invest in those countries they can contribute the least to, all the while selling their wares to the local population which lets them profit even more?

An apolitical common-sense solution would be to apply a greater sales tax to those corporations selling their stuff to local consumers, when they do not have a significant local operational presence (no plants, offices, warehouses etc.) in comparison to their competitors who do have that visibility. If a foreign chocolate manufacturer closes all of its plants in Canada, why should they profit as much as Purdys, Rocky Mountain or other chocolate manufacturers who actually have a presence here? The foreign seller of chocolate could still profit, just not as much in the absence of making a greater contribution to Canada.

If this line of thinking were applied globally, maybe there would be more local manufacturers, local jobs, local consumers, and a lot less poverty. And it doesn't have to be rocket science. Thresholds could be set for local content required in goods and services that qualifies for any corporate tax credits, up to reasonable maximums. Right-minded people can figure a way to make fair and free trade work. Anyway, we should refocus our discussion on the bigger problems at hand, and for which solutions will be presented.

Closing our discussion on tax evasion, the infamous leak of the Paradise Papers, which followed the leaking of the Panama Papers, revealed several prominent Canadians were utilizing offshore tax havens. "According to reports by *CBC/Radio Canada* and the *Toronto Star*," there were even some high-level politicians using offshore tax schemes. "More than 3,000 Canadian entities and individuals, including three former prime ministers and key Liberal Party fundraisers, are named in the Paradise Papers, a leak of millions of records from offshore law firm Appleby and the corporate registries of 19 tax havens…" To put it succinctly, many high-profile individuals around the world appear to have been using offshore tax havens. "Former Canadian prime ministers Jean Chretien, Paul Martin and Brian Mulroney are among the most high-profile individuals named in the document release, revealing the offshore interests and activities of 'more than 120 politicians and world leaders' . . . according to the ICIJ."[38]

In terms of American leadership, "the leaked documents also show that U.S. President Donald Trump's commerce secretary, Wilbur Ross, is doing business with Vladimir Putin's son-in-law through a shipping venture in Russia."[39] Hmmm . . . Too bad all the lost tax revenues are not helping all the neighbours of the well-heeled. Their earthly treasures grow apace while so many people go wanting in undemocratic societies. Insightfully the Oxfam report stated, "If the well-being of all and the survival of the planet are to be the primary aims of the economy rather than a hoped-for by-product of free markets, then we need to explicitly design our economies to achieve these things."[40] Its authors believe we need a human economy that works for everyone. Following are a few, of several, goals they deem as 'essential ingredients' for this human economy:

> National governments accountable to the 99% and playing a more international role in their economies to make them fairer and more accountable; national governments [that] cooperate to effectively fix global problems such as tax dodging, climate change and other environmental harm; businesses designed in ways that increase prosperity for all, and contribute to a sustainable future; progress measured by what actually matters, not just by GDP. This would include women's underpaid care, and the impact of our economies on the planet.[41]

The above are all laudable objectives, and I really enjoyed reading the well-written Oxfam report. However, whereas Oxfam believes we must "design our economies to achieve" benefits for everyone and the planet itself, we likely have to start by redesigning our broken government structures and institutions, so they are fit for their intended purpose. We must adjust the taps in the waterworks of our democracy so the benefits of the system flow to all who support its cause. As I have been demonstrating, governments around the world are broken. Therefore they are currently incapable of implementing the changes we so desperately need to create a human economy. It is of critical importance for a country, such as Canada, to take the lead and implement the required solutions. Only then can we achieve positive change in the real world, not just the economy. I am in full agreement with Oxfam that "governments must work for the 99%." I also completely agree that it is advisable "to restore a positive, proactive role for government," and "at the same time require a resurgence of genuine democracy and the protection of public space."[42]

But is government currently the most efficient and effective provider of many public services, or is it really its own worst enemy? We disappointingly saw in the prior chapter that there are countless examples of all levels of the Canadian government failing the public they were created to serve. The fact of the matter is our government is dysfunctional. It is not set up to make good and informed decisions. Therefore it often works against those it purportedly works for, regardless of the party in power. This problem, which is eating away at so-called democratic countries around the world, is exacerbated by the one per cent (or thereabouts) that prefers the status quo—that prefers to increasingly exert its influence and avoid paying its share of taxes. What can we do about it?

When leaders around the globe do not seem to have any solid answers to deal with growing and monumental problems, let alone the house of cards they represent, something is terribly wrong. We need to fix this. Fortunately and with the right spirit in mind, we substantially can. First, we have to become plumbers, recognizing that the democratic system often does not work for people because it is full of clogs. The proverbial toilet is plugged because the structural piping underneath it, not readily seen, has a flawed design. And we, dear reader, are dealing with all the shitty fallout. South of the border, President Trump talked about "draining the swamp," meaning he is not entirely misguided. It is no different than anyone who wishes to be first among others but will end up last. Trump was on to something when he perceived a swamp. The flawed design of government is that quagmire. However he seems to be at a loss in terms of how to make America great again.

Apart from recognizing the ineffectual design of our government, we need to understand human nature and that wrongly motivated leaders, all the way up to the Prime Minister and their Cabinet members, can turn well-designed democratic structures into bad ones. It is no different than the characters in Star Wars where the characters' spirits are either aligned with the forces of good or the forces of darkness. The force of light is with you when you know the right thing to do and you do it. The last thing required to restore our democracy is to implement mechanisms that drive accountability in government. Those mechanisms are currently lacking. For clarity, let me highlight again the three main issues preventing us from collectively moving forward—the obstacles we can and must overcome to show the world why it really needs more Canada:

1) Poorly designed organization structures within government;
2) Wrongly motivated individuals working therein; and
3) Ineffective oversight of government.

By simply observing the latest news, one can see that different groups of people are blaming other groups of people for all the problems they may be experiencing. Around the world, and perhaps most dramatically in the US, we have race pitted against race, religion against religion, neighbour against neighbour and so on. There are protesters clashing with counter protesters. And even those who are so angry physically attack their own history, denying it most emphatically by attempting to tear down statues of once respected people (even if not fully deserving of such respect now given changing attitudes). It is as if there must be someone else to blame for all of our ever-growing troubles, a focal point for the resentment, pent-up wrath and non-understanding. In the UK, Brexit arguably is another manifestation of a need to focus blame on others (the rest of Europe) for the collective misfortunes of Brits themselves. As a Canadian, I am seeing the seeds of a more divisive society taking root. There is increasingly a need to blame others and deny, rather than learn from, our history—warts and all.

Just recently we have heard calls for the name of our first Prime Minister, Sir John A Macdonald, to be removed from our schools or in other public places. This follows the Trudeau government's decision to rename the Langevin Block, the building which houses the Prime Minister's Office as well as offices of the Privy Council. Hector Langevin was one of Canada's founding fathers. However, because he was associated with the design of Canada's erstwhile residential school system, a dark page in our history, the Liberals thought it appropriate to remove his name from the building. It should be noted that the residential school system was where the children of Canada's Indigenous Peoples were sent after being forcibly removed from their families. Also, it was in residential schools that many Indigenous children were subsequently abused, physically and otherwise.

Of course abuse should never be condoned, let alone celebrated, and Canada must do better with concrete and immediate action to address the genuine and long overdue concerns of our Indigenous Peoples, we must move forward rather than backward. But rather than denying our past, we must acknowledge it fully. By celebrating our past successes, we reinforce the importance of replicating and building on those types of actions. And by realizing our past mistakes, we reinforce the importance of not replicating them and of doing better in the future. A good counsellor or psychologist would tell you the same thing. Our Indigenous Peoples have a lot to offer here. For example, their concept of society as a great circle can teach us to be more inclusive.

Recall, as we learned in Chapter 2, that our Indigenous Peoples' philosophy of interdependence can help us do things in a better way. Revamping our government institutions to recognize interdependency can facilitate better outcomes in key decision-making.

Canada is not immune to the global trend we are witnessing: the trend of increasing divisiveness, both between countries and within a country's own borders. In a June 2017 article, Stephanie Levitz states it appears "Northern populism" may be growing here too, potentially sprouting yet more extremism and divisiveness as it has in other democratic nations. Although we defined the term at length above, Ms. Levitz views 'populism' as a term usually used to describe the political movement that led to outsider Donald Trump's rise to the US presidency. She notes it has also been used to describe Britain's startling referendum results leading to Brexit: Britain leaving the EU.[43]

In a *Canadian Press/EKOS Politics* survey, "29% of those surveyed think their lives will improve over the next five years, 35% think [things] will stay the same and 33% think [things] will get worse." Unsurprisingly, 25 per cent of those who believe they have fallen behind over the last five years support populism.[44] Also, and not totally unlike what is happening in other Western democratic countries, the highly educated appear to be more against populism than those without a university degree. Perhaps that is because those with a degree should have a better chance of benefitting from the current system, although as outlined clearly above, the one per cent of income earners continue to reap more and more benefits than anyone else, be they highly educated or not. The poll found 42 per cent of those possessing a university degree think populism is a bad thing versus only 26 per cent and 30 per cent, respectively, of people with a high school diploma or a community college education. The poll claims "we have effectively divided ourselves into two Canadas."[45]

Personally I subscribe to Albert Einstein's view that "education is what remains after one has forgotten what one has learned in school." When I reflect back on my learning, I learned just as much from Marty the plumber, my parents, and Mr. Glogar at that car-parts factory in Moravia, as I did from my university professors. Sometimes (not always, mind you, as I have met a lot of down-to-earth and practical professors while at university), academics can have their heads way up in the clouds or the comfortable confines of those ivory towers that are often divorced from the reality most people face in the real world. I am reminded of that novel by David Lodge entitled *Nice Work*, about a factory executive whose practical ideology clashes with that of the theories of a university instructor he meets.

At any rate, it was with some disgust that I read that populism has to somehow be a bad thing because many less-educated people support it. Really? Certainly I am not a Trump supporter. Nor do I support the more local Canadian political views of the physically attractive, yet misguided, Faith Goldy. She is the university educated extreme alt-right individual who has been a political commentator, including for far-right wing media organizations. Apparently Goldy is also a Christian, raised Catholic. Yet as all Catholics, Christians, Muslims, Buddhists and other spiritual people know, all that glitters is not gold. Pope Francis spoke out against something called 'clericalism.'

Pope Francis discerned what clericalism is in his August 2018 Letter to the People of God. He sagely equated it to abuse of power by stating, "To say no to abuse is to say an emphatic no to all forms of clericalism."[46] Doris, Keiser, a theologian at the University of Alberta's St. Joseph's College, said this of clericalism. "It is inattention to the dynamics of power, or equally abuse of the dynamics of power, within the Church."[47] Hmmm….her words seem appropriate for both Church and state. In government, Canadians also suffer much from the dynamics of clericalism. Church and state each have honorable objectives, but perhaps the administrative workings of both institutions must be restored for future generations of people to benefit from them. We don't have clerics in government, but we do have certain types of bureaucrats that must be considered on our journey towards mending flags to heal the world. We will be doing that in some other chapters of this book. People guided by the right spirit should always speak out against forces that sow division and conflict rather than the opposite and a clear, understandable, loving and constructive path forward. Shall we not love our neighbour second only to loving our maker? Problems can be resolved when people look hard enough to do just that.

Leaders around the world and here in Canada need to wake up. They need to understand that the status quo is not working for huge chunks of the populace, rather than laying blame on the people for rightly clamouring for positive change. I mentioned previously that there is a growing tendency for individuals and groups to blame others for their seemingly ever growing problems. This can breed the wrong type of populism. It can lead to extremism and the rise of demagogues, such as before World War II. However, when I cast a wary eye across the globe, I also see that most leaders do not know what to do to make things better for the people they lead. So we continue to play the blame game instead of cultivating a better populism.

Flawed Arguments Blaming Voters

The absurd rationale, according to researchers at the University of Leicester, as to why Britons decided to leave the European Union, illustrates just how alive and well the blame game is. Once again blaming the supposedly uneducated for a debacle created by leaders who cannot see past their own highbrow noses, British university researchers pinned Brexit on commoners, instead of the educated class that allowed dysfunctional government to persist. It was that government in the first place which enabled the decline of the UK and the ongoing status quo rejected by ordinary Britons. And yet for academics, the results of the British June 2016 referendum, where 52 per cent of people voted in favour versus 48 per cent against to leave the EU, would have been much different if only three per cent more Brits had gone to university. This is because the university researchers determined that whether people had gone to university or pursued higher education was the "predominant factor" in how they voted.[48] However this misses the point entirely. The focus should be on how an unwelcome divisiveness was sown by the government. That is the key issue, in the UK and elsewhere in Europe and America, not the voters' level of formal education. A higher level of discernment is required to see through the optics management, not necessarily a cleric's higher education.

It grieves me to learn that some Ivy League professors in modern day America have begun to blame others for the failings of democracy. They do so from the comforts of their ivory towers, spreading misguided notions. They are likely good people, but have just fallen victim, along with so many others, to the blame game. It is always easier to find fault with someone else even when you are a high-browed intellectual. It is much easier than seeking that elusive 'something' that is creating all the problems around you. In 2016, Princeton University published a book emblazoned with the title *Against Democracy*. Authored by distinguished professor Jason Brennan, it argues that certain segments of the population should not have the right to vote. Yes, you read that correctly. And while the book is written from an academic perspective in America, it may as well be about democratic systems floundering globally.

Near the beginning of *Against Democracy*, Brennan openly proclaims: "Here I'll contend that if the facts turn out the right way, some people ought not have the right to vote, or ought to have weaker voting rights than others."[49] Brennan believes that because so many people are misinformed about politics and significant issues generally, especially if they are uneducated and democracy in turn fails to educate them, then they should participate less in democracy. He further proclaims, "We should hope for even less participation, not more."[50] He elaborates, "I contend that for most [of] us, political liberty and participation are, on the whole, harmful." And if that is not controversial enough, he states "we would be better off—and others would be to—if we stayed out of politics."[51] Apparently, in Brennan's eyes, we are all pretty stupid voters. We are too misinformed about politics and the complexity of issues to contribute to a workable and effective democracy.

I hate to go on quoting him, but Brennan's material in *Against Democracy* makes for better entertainment than watching Alec Baldwin masquerade as US President Trump on *Saturday Night Live* or watching Canadian reruns of the SCTV troupe—John Candy, Eugene Levy, Catherine O'Hara, etc. On regular people, whom he appears to blame for the poor results democracy is producing, Brennan has this to say: "They tend to be ignorant and irrational about politics."[52] His fellow, yet lesser educated Americans are, presumably, just as responsible for the demise of American democracy as are the uneducated Brits who voted for Brexit—or so some academics would have you believe. "The median voter is ignorant."[53] That is Brennan's conclusion. So I guess we are all to blame, whether we are ordinary folks in America, Britain, here in Canada, or residing in other teetering democracies.

We do not know what is right because most of us are actually wrong according to the professor. "Many citizens are wrong; they know less than nothing."[54] Now, if you read Chapter 2, you know I take an opposing view. I believe we actually know what is right. There is just something getting in our way of making democracy work better for us all. But let's continue learning what the book-smart people have to say before we delve more into that. Professor Brennan continues his argument by stating that "not only do citizens lack understanding; it's not clear that many of them could acquire that understanding."[55] Everybody off-campus seems to be pretty stupid. We are not sharp enough to even size up presidential candidates like Donald Trump in contemporary America. Apparently only those who can grasp economics have enough brain cells to be a capably informed voter. For "unless someone understands basic economics, they are usually not in a position to evaluate different presidential candidates."[56]

I do not know about you, but this smacks of elitism to me. It is true that democracy in its current form in Canada, and likely around the world, does not generally produce desired outcomes for the citizens it claims to serve. However, to blame the average voter for that is a hollow argument. It is also horribly unfair. To put forth the idea that the broader public is too ignorant to make good decisions and must understand economics is, quite frankly, downright shameful. Think of it this way. If Susie the waitress is busting her chops all day serving customer after customer in the restaurant, does that mean she is an ignorant person incapable of being a good voter in a democratic election? This despite her coming from a less wealthy family that nonetheless raised her well? This despite her being a God-fearing, decent, honest and hard-working taxpayer who is, in turn raising her own kids well? Is it reasonable for anyone to say she cannot make good decisions, to blame her and others like her because democracy is not working well?

After all, she is not a professor or economist, both of whom cannot possibly be ignorant compared to her! Hah, how ridiculous! Is Frank, busting his ass in a manufacturing plant in what's left of Rust Belt America, also to blame for the travails of a broken democracy that leaves so many of its citizens wanting? He cannot possibly know how to vote in his and the country's general interest. Hah, again! University professors of Brennan's ilk would have you believe this is likely the case. He states, "I could write an entire book just documenting how little voters know."[57] He even refers to another professor, Bryan Caplan at Virginia's George Mason University, in *Against Democracy*. Maybe Caplan is Brennan's erudite latte drinking buddy on campus, where they discuss how so many people off-campus are dumber than a doornail when it comes to politics and understanding the issues they and the country face. Regardless, what I do know is that Brennan quotes Caplan's *The Myth of the Rational Voter* to support some of his own elitist views.

So when it states in *The Myth* that Caplan said, "What voters don't know would fill a university library,"[58] we see a certain like mindedness in these gentlemen and scholars, these scribes. Of course, I could not help but read Caplan's book, written almost 10 years earlier than Brennan's. In *The Myth* we see yet more elitist thinking. It paints typical voters as irrational in their beliefs, which impedes good economic decisions. I can almost imagine Brennan nodding his head in affirmation, agreeing with Caplan over steaming lattes, as to how democracy fails. In *The Myth*, Caplan writes "this book develops an alternative story of how democracy fails. The central idea is that voters are worse than ignorant; they are, in a word, *irrational*, and vote accordingly."[59] One wonders if Professor Caplan would deem our fictitious every-day hard-working citizens, Susie and Frank, as being totally unequipped to have valid views about politics and issues that may be impacting their ordinary lives and those of their fellow citizens. Remember, they are likely ignorant in that regard. Or, as the economics professor is more equipped to pontificate: "The naïve view of democracy, which paints it as a public forum for solving social problems, ignores more than a few frictions."

Caplan maintains "it overlooks the big story . . . when voters talk about solving social problems, [the] priority is to boost their self-worth by casting the workaday shackles of objectivity."[60] Perhaps, with a string of letters behind his name that reflects his higher education, Caplan is not weighed down or shackled by a lack of insight about politics and the social problems we all face. Hey, even the George Mason University website indicates *The Myth* was named 'best political book this year' by the *New York Times* upon its release. And after all, the author is an economist, who has drank from the fountain of education instead of the local pubs that hapless Susie and Frank may be envisioned as frequenting on Main Street. Nonetheless, he and his colleagues such as Brennan, are intoxicated by their own hubris, a pride that pretends to know what is right instead of every-day regular folks on the street knowing it.

Although Brennan and Caplan agree on voters being ignorant on matters of politics and major issues, they differ in their solutions to those problems. Caplan, who wrote his book first, appears to believe that free markets should drive society more than democracy (and presumably government institutions and systems that underpin democracy), which is failing. There are a lot of dazzling graphs, tables and such in Caplan's book, and I must admit they are intimidating. They mainly support his argument that voters do not know a lot about pertinent issues. In the end, he sees that as fuelling the demise of democracy in America, and likely around the world. He finds that "objections are not strong enough to reverse the conclusion that the public's economic beliefs are riddled with large systemic errors."[61] At the end of the day, he is not happy with democracy and its current form. And, as one would naturally expect of an economist, he ends up desiring broader market forces to play a more important role in our society.

That could obviously lead to even further polarization in society, with the wealthy 0.5 per cent on one end of the spectrum rather than one per cent, versus the rest of us. For Caplan, it leads to this observation: "No matter how well you think markets work, it makes sense to rely on markets *more* when you grow more pessimistic about democracy." His position is that "economists should be more pro-market than they already are." They "should embrace the free market in spite of its defects because it still outshines the democratic alternative."[62] I dare venture to guess that Professor Caplan would have us all support unfettered markets no matter the consequences, be there still more inequalities between poor and rich, more environmental degradation in a world faced with increasing natural catastrophes, less democratic rights, and so forth. It is all the common voter's problem anyway. They are so blind in their common thinking in comparison to the economists. In Caplan's words, "The real problem is not that greed blinds economists but that anti-market bias blinds the public."[63]

Buried on page 197 of his book is an even more startling solution that Caplan raises to get rid of troublesome and ordinary voters like Susie and Frank. His ivory tower idea to strengthen society is to weaken the very democracy that he sees threatened by its own larger constituency—which I suppose means he views ordinary people and their right to vote, irrationally as he sees it, as being obstacles to free markets reigning supreme. His view: "A more palatable way to raise the economic literacy of the median voter is by giving *extra* votes to individuals or groups with greater economic literacy."[64] Professor Brennan takes this unpalatable, I say, view disturbingly further down a dark path. He advocates what is called 'epistocracy' as a solution to failing democracies; these failures again driven by incompetent voters.

He notes in *Against Democracy*, "Epistocracy means the rule of the knowledgeable."[65] Or, as he further expounds, "A political system is epistocratic to the extent it distributes political power in proportion to the knowledge or competence, as a matter of law or policy."[66] Brennan explores several different forms of epistocracy and what they might look like in his book. He admits to some of the challenges that such political systems may face, including what he deems "the demographic objection." That objection being how some groups of people are already disadvantaged in that "political knowledge is not evenly dispersed among all demographic groups." He states that "whites on average know more than blacks . . . men know more than women . . . high income people know more than the poor." Therefore, "In general people who are already advantaged are much better informed than the disadvantaged."[67]

Nevertheless, he still believes we should continue to experiment with epistocracy. He seems to live in a kind of isolated fear on campus, although his fear is ironically akin to that of ordinary people who sense that democracy is not working well for them these days. Is it any wonder they vote for those who tell them what they want to hear instead of how to meaningfully restore and improve democracy? Highly educated people in terms of formal education, like Professor Brennan, seem to fear their fellow citizens, blaming them for their own and their country's circumstances. He expresses his own fears best so we must cite his own words, couched in blame, again:

> Most of my fellow citizens are incompetent, ignorant,
> irrational, and morally unreasonable about politics. Despite
> that they hold political power over me . . . They wield their

power in ways that they cannot justify, and impose policies on me that they would not support if they were informed or processed political information in a rational way. [68]

Fear is a powerful and dangerous thing. It gives rise to bad decisions or well-intended decisions that have unintended consequences. History is riddled with examples of this, many of them dastardly and horrific, reflecting the darker side of the human character. It has often been said that supposedly knowledgeable and smart people have lead nations into war and butchery. The professor's fears lead him to his own seemingly inescapable argument. "The only reason to put up with democracy, I will argue IS if we cannot find a way to make epistocracy work better."[69] Cloaked in fear of his fellow Americans, Brennan ends his book with two sentences that evokes both the blame and divisiveness we see so much of in contemporary America. "My fellow citizens exercise power over me in risky and incompetent ways. This makes them my civic enemies."[70]

Although I vehemently disagree with this perspective and Caplan's notion that voters are to blame for the sad state of democracy generally, in America—the professors would probably say here in Canada or elsewhere too, I concur with some of their other views. And I actually support university environments where the free exchange of ideas is usually encouraged. For example. I completely agree with Brennan that "institutions that help us live together in peace and prosperity are good. Institutions that, compared to the alternative, hinder us in doing so give us little reason to support them, regardless of what they symbolize."[71] Of course I would agree with this line of thinking. I believe our institutions need to be healed and made effective as the principal means of ensuring democracy works for and serves citizens well. It is no different than Pope Francis likely bearing witness to the Catholic Church's need for healing, to ensure the 'Word' serves parishioners well.

And I absolutely agree with Brennan that "citizens have at least a pre-sumptive right to have a competent decision-making body . . . They ought not be subject to incompetently or capriciously made high-stakes political decisions."[72] I do fully disagree that voters like Susie and Frank are to blame and that only economists or other ill-defined competent people should have a greater say in politics than they do, through exercising a right to vote or by other means. I also fully disagree with Brennan that, regarding ordinary citizens, including all disadvantaged people, "unless they have tremendous social scientific knowledge, they are unlikely to know how to vote for politicians or policies that will produce . . . favoured outcomes."[73] Lastly, I disagree with Caplan's sweeping statements that "voter ignorance is a product of natural human selfishness . . . It is hard to see how initiative . . . or any of the popular ways to 'fix democracy' strengthen voters' incentive to inform themselves."[74] Gentlemen, and others who subscribe to their well-intended but erroneous views, you are greatly mistaken. There is a way to restore all things. That is the message of this book.

Ivy League professors such as Christopher H. Achen and Larry M. Bartels, at Princeton and Vanderbilt University, respectively, are also wrong. They, too disturbingly point toward Main Street folks being ill-equipped to understand the issues of the day that can make democracy strong again. In their 2016 book *Democracy for Realists—Why Elections Do Not Produce Responsive Government*, these professors state that "America is a democracy, but it is not very democratic."[75] They understood the blame game is always prominent, opining for example, that "when collective misfortune strikes a society, someone must be blamed,"[76] but fall victim to blaming people themselves. In over 300 pages of detailed discussion in the book, also replete with many graphs and tables, they take great pains to prove that people vote according to their identity. In what they refer to as "the *group theory* of democracy," they view "citizens first and foremost as members of social groups, with . . . special identities and group attachments figuring crucially in their political loyalties and behaviour."[77]

Their argument is that "voters, even the most informed voters, typically make choices not on the basis of policy preference or ideology but on the basis of who they are—their social identities."[78] From heaps of social scientific research, and believe me they pile it on, Achen and Bartels argue that "even in the context of hot-button issues like race and abortion, it appears that most people make their party choices based on who they are rather than on what they think."[79] They fail to imagine that most people know the difference between right and wrong and can indeed make informed decisions that benefit themselves and their fellow citizens, be they American or others. Instead, they rail against what they call "folk theory of democracy," which presumes that ordinary voters like you, me and others, can meaningfully vote in democratic elections exercising good sense. They do not believe voters can influence the direction of government in the right way. Their academic view concerning "most residents of democratic countries" is as follows: "mostly, they identify with ethnic, racial, occupational, religious, or other sorts of groups, and often—whether through group ties or hereditary loyalties—with a political party."[80]

There are shades of the voter ignorance argument in this book too. It helps support the central premise in *Democracy for Realists* that we vote based on the groups we identify with. For example. The authors suggest that "Elite culture is usually (though not always) less susceptible to nutty or dangerous visions."[81] I take that to mean the elites, whether in ivory towers or in the confines of their own gilded business communities, have a greater monopoly on knowing the difference between right and wrong—or at least they are supposed to in terms of the direction of representative government. And of course Achen and Bartels believe that "real voters often have only a vague understanding of the connection (if any) between incumbent politicians' actions and their own wellbeing."[82]

This sounds a little like a rehashing of the ignorant voter argument for sure. What is doubly concerning is that all these professors expect ordinary voters like you and me to somehow have an innate ability to know what all the issues facing government are and then vote accordingly. Is that reasonable? It is as if our very consciousness should be pre-populated with infinite understanding and wisdom regarding matters that concern the democratic country we live in. Presumably that consciousness must be omniscient, all-seeing and all-knowing at all times, including during times of great change such as here and now. How could it be otherwise when Achen and Bartels raise these assumptions regarding traditional democracy—or what they again label the 'folk theory' of democracy?

> Can ordinary people, busy with their lives and with no firsthand experience of policy-making or public administration do what the theory expects them to do? Can they formulate policy preferences, assess where candidates stand on the issues, set aside cognitive biases and group prejudices, and choose a candidate . . .?[83]

As you may have guessed, these ivy-league scribes also find us dwelling in the realm of ignorance, maybe even indifference, when it comes to politics and democracy. Their proof appears spurious to me though. Especially when they observe that "numerous studies have demonstrated that most residents of democratic countries have little interest in politics and do not follow news of public affairs beyond browsing the headlines."[84] This is all too general and dismissive of the real reasons why our traditional democracy is not working. Their argument just doles out more blame on residents of democracies, we simpletons. "They do not know the details of even salient policy debates, they do not have a firm understanding of what the political parties stand for, and they often vote for parties whose long-standing issue positions are at odds with their own."[85] I love how Achen and Bartels employ usage of the word 'they.' After all, the problem must be an 'us' and 'them' thing when you argue that "party and group loyalties are the primary drivers of vote choices."

The Ignorance of Government

Ironically, while spending a lot of ink to get to that point, professors Achen and Bartels are as mistaken as professors Brennan and Caplan, and probably so many more academics and students they have influenced in their scholarly works. All of these like-minded academics never considered that the voters are not the problem. Voters, including well-intended professors at times, by far possess the necessary street smarts and practicality to do the right thing. They can distinguish between that which is right and that which is wrong. Therefore, they can act in their own and their communities' best interest. The only thing that has been overlooked is that it is not the job of ordinary voters on Main Street to run the country and possess the exact same knowledge, insights, vision and so on, as those who collectively should—namely members of the legislature. They, including the Prime Minister, are our elected representatives.

Rather than being 'apart' from 'us,' Members of Parliament should be 'a part' of 'us,' the body politic. It is no different than a Church requiring all of its members to be part of the body of Christ. No individual within the body should stand apart from it, lest they succumb to or fuel the pernicious effects of 'clericalism' as defined by Pope Francis. Notice also how extremist Muslim groups have corrupted the Muslim faith and its spiritual guidance. In fact many faiths have parallel teachings to kindle the spiritual goodness in people. Each of us has a soul to be opened by degrees. For example, as George Wolfe mentions in *Parallel Teachings in Hinduism and Christianity*. some "research has revealed that the five great world religions share numerous themes and symbols which, when viewed cross-culturally, demonstrate the world religions are much more closely allied than orthodox or fundamentalist Christian views would have us believe."[86] And are not many fundamentalists extremists? Hmmm . . .

In his comparative study, Wolfe reveals a staggering similarity in some of the parallel teachings concerning Hindu scriptures and those contained in the Bible. This is despite the undeniable truth that the Hindu scriptures he cites "predate the Christian New Testament by 500 years."[87] Here is just one example:

> "I am the origin of the whole world and also its dissolution . . . I am the beginning, the middle, and the end of all things" (Lord Krishna in the Bhagavad Gita, 7:6, 10:20).

> "I am the Alpha and the Omega, the first and the last, the beginning and the end" (Jesus in the book of Revelation, 22:13).[88]

Of course Wolfe finds some differences in the teachings. By way of example, "unlike in Hinduism, they are given expression through the life and teaching of a single individual who in Christianity is said to be Jesus Christ, the incarnate Lord."[89] Importantly, in the final analysis though, Wolfe opines that "connections with Hinduism and Buddhism should be viewed as adding to the power and universality of the gospel message."[90]

Returning to our discussion of the body politic and democracy, if Members of Parliament (MPs) are to be part of 'us,' they need to understand the issues in the Canadian communities they have been sent to/elected from. They need to represent those communities in Canada's House of Commons. In turn, they need to understand the risks facing all communities across the nation, be empowered to do their part in managing the country and, perhaps most importantly, they must be well-equipped to keep their own constituents informed on the issues that should be of greatest importance to them and their communities. In short, for government to get a good sense of the 'us' that makes up Canada, it needs to be less ignorant, less incompetent and less subject to ideological group-think in what they are doing. That requires knowing the difference between what is right and what is wrong, like most voters do already.

My father helped to build this country, asking little of Canada in return. The completed construction sites reflecting his hard work are testimony to that. He, like most of you, has earned his right to vote. If he is ignorant of politics and issues, as some academics would have us believe, it is only because the government and opposition candidates have not kept him informed on the priority issues facing Canada and his community. He needs that information to exercise his vote responsibly, knowing also how each political party would tackle the associated problems and risks arising from the issues. My father knows the difference between right and wrong. He knows government has not been working as hard as it should to build this country up because its leaders are not motivated to do what is right, too often building themselves up instead. The system is broken. Therefore democracy is broken, in Canada and around the world. It suffers from its own form of clericalism, where too many ministers, rather than clerics, work to build themselves up outside the body politic, thereby eroding democracy further.

To put it bluntly, government does not work properly. That is the 'something' we should be blaming for our daily challenges. It is what shackles Canada from achieving its latent potential and greatness. It is what has restrained us from reflecting the ingenuity and resourcefulness of such a blessed people and land for far too long. Government failings can be seen in the tyranny of our legislature. The MPs, through largely no fault of their own—for they too are not to blame—cannot perform the jobs we have elected them to do. And even if they were the most rational and competent of Canadians, the disastrous outcomes we witnessed in Chapter 3 would still be the same. The current system of our imaginary democracy guarantees this, just as it does in struggling democracies across the globe such as modern day America, preordained by the design of its flawed democracy to deal with the monumental problems it faces now.

And when legislatures do not work the way they should, danger abounds for ordinary, mostly good, decent, honest, hardworking citizens who actually know what's right versus what's wrong. That is the genius of the citizenry rather than its ignorance. Individuals work for themselves and their families. They reasonably expect the government system to work. It has been said by many scholars throughout the decades that have passed since it was first published, that the greatest book ever written about democracy is *Democracy in America* by Alexis de Tocqueville. I am what I am. So I decided to read it. All 700 pages or so of that cinder block! I would be lying if I did not tell you that it makes for some really dry reading. The sheer length of it is intimidating. It is typically written in scholarly prose and seems endless in documented observations of democracy, especially in America versus the aristocratic system of Europe Tocqueville was born into. He lived a short life, from 1805 to 1859. But it was precisely during that time, in 1831, that young Tocqueville journeyed to a fledgling America, to study its prisons.

To make a long story short (no pun intended), Tocqueville far surpassed that objective. His immense observations led to a broader understanding of American democracy and society in relation to European aristocracy. He documented his thoughts and conclusions in his seminal work, *Democracy in America*, first published in 1835. Unsurprisingly, in the 2000 edition I borrowed from the library, the introduction written by the editors and translators had this to say of Tocqueville's work: It "is at once the best book ever written on democracy and the best book ever written on America."[91] Therefore, I knew I might be able to glean some useful insights from it regarding democracy generally as I related it to Canada. One does not have to possess a string of letters behind their name to do some reading, even heavy reading, and some thoughtful observing. It is like Marilyn vos Savant, who incidentally was listed under the category of 'Highest IQ' in the *Guiness Book of World* Records a few decades ago, once remarked, "To acquire knowledge, one must study; but to acquire wisdom, one must observe."

Maybe this has already proven my case—that ordinary people are not so ignorant—but we should continue our journey. So you see, that while necessary, universities do not have a monopoly on wisdom. Many citizens are already wise enough, through first-hand experiences and observations, to know when something is wrong with democracy. I know, get to the point. OK. Tocqueville, having travelled extensively, including in America, was a keen observer. He viewed the legislature as being at the heart of democracy, vital to the well-being of the people and, one can reasonably conclude, to the health of nations themselves. "Democracies are naturally brought to concentrate the whole social force in the hands of the legislative body. The latter being the power that emanates most directly from the people."[92] Tocqueville viewed US President Thomas Jefferson as the greatest proponent of democracy. In his own words, "I consider him to be the most powerful apostle that democracy has ever had."[93]

Of course, Jefferson was not only the principal author of the *Declaration of Independence* and a two-term US president (1801–09) but a slave owner. That has to be his greatest failing. However, we can still learn from his glaring mistakes as well as achievements. Tocqueville quotes Jefferson in his book as well as writing of his prescience in forecasting a daunting future that may well face America now. Revealing one of President Jefferson's greatest concerns regarding democracy, Tocqueville notes, "The tyranny of the legislature is the most formidable dread at present, and will be for long years. That of the executive will come in its turn, but it will be at a remote period."[94] Jefferson may as well have been commenting about democracy in modern-day Canada or other countries than America. He knew that it is not so much a tyranny of incompetent and politically ignorant voters that should be feared, but a tyranny of the legislature.

We have observed that tyranny, the betrayal taking root in our own country—Canada—in the preceding chapter. The voter is not to blame for that tyranny. It is how our system of government is designed that fuels how we betray ourselves and others. As I have mentioned repeatedly, Canadians generally know the difference between right and wrong, just as others around the globe do. It is only the unrelenting and mounting confusion that emanates from government, mainly from the parliamentary legislature (House of Commons in Canada) that is the centre of democratic incompetence, which leaves voters in the lurch. It leaves us wondering how we, or apparently incompetent parliamentarians, can effect positive change at all.

The irony of Achen and Bartels' *Democracy for Realists* is that they come close to discerning this issue but nevertheless missed it completely. They skirt the most important issue confronting democracy, and quite likely humanity, when they mention "the problem is not that voters are necessarily irrational, but that most voters have very little real information, even about crucially important aspects of national political life."[95] Exactly, and while their book focuses mostly on Americans, you will see it is the same problem facing Canadians. Skating around the key issue again, the professors opine: "Academic theorists of democracy . . . have often seemed unimpressed by mere electoral democracy, and thus uninterested in the pressing question of institutional design and legitimacy raised by analyses like ours."[96]

If only they probed deeper into the design of democracy, they would see the very structure of democratic government itself is to blame for its failings. This is the important debate, not voters exercising their vote based on social identities. And of course voters would because that may very well be the most they have to go on in their busy lives. Especially when the MPs they send to work in the legislature are not able to do their jobs! What is the point of writing a book that is several hundred pages long on democracy, a book supposedly for realists, when you cannot identify the greatest problem confronting it? And if academics who wrote that book also cannot present clear and concrete solutions to resolve the problems afflicting democracy, why bother writing it at all? The last page of *Democracy for Realists* has its authors admitting that "our approach raises a host of problems and questions for which political scientists—ourselves very much included—have no real answers."[97]

Think of it this way. John Dewey, renowned for his writings on the subject of education, had this to say in his book *Democracy and Education*: "When I hear a noise and run and get water and put out a blaze, I respond intelligently; the sound meant fire, and fire meant need of being extinguished."[98] Basically Dewey is saying people know what to do and how to react in certain situations for obvious reasons. This is based on people's knowledge, experience and education; call it what you will. However, he also says this about more ambiguous situations. "When things have a meaning for us, we *mean* (intend, propose) what we do: when they do not, we act blindly, unconsciously, unintelligently."[99] I believe Main Street voters know how to put out fires, but they should not be expected to restructure our broken government or 'the system' when that is the principal job of those sitting in government themselves. It is primarily the job of our reigning Prime Minister to ensure MPs are doing their job as well.

We can therefore and logically conclude that it is our system, or government, that is incompetent, not most voters. This situation is likely the greatest problem all democracies face. By extension, it is the greatest issue humanity faces at the outset of the 21st century. It is the reason why things do not seem to work. It is why there is war, famine, a refugee crisis, environmental degradation, and perhaps even more concerning, climate change. The earth's global problems continue to largely go unaddressed because individual nations cannot address problems in their own backyard. National governments cannot organize themselves properly to resolve issues in a manner that effectively meets the spiritual needs of their voters, their sense of right versus wrong. Until they largely do, international problems will continue to grow without being appropriately addressed in a sensible manner. Here, in Canada, since the government is doing little to ameliorate the situation for Canadians facing an onslaught of foolish decisions, I will lay out the urgent solutions required to mend the flag in the next three chapters. We must no longer be refrained from reaching our collective potential. It is our birthright, regardless of our race, colour, gender or creed.

The Need for *Democratic Restructuralism*

In *Against Democracy* professor Brennan correctly thought a new form of government is required. He seemed to come down on the side favouring epistocracy. I am in favour of what I call *Democratic Restructuralism*. I believe democracy can work if it treats all voters fairly, giving them, if they so choose, a say in it. While writing over 175 years ago, Tocqueville even then perceived the huge importance that design plays in government. He substituted the word 'form' for the word 'design' and emphasized how it is not considered enough by many people in understanding how their day-to-day lives can be impacted by it. His perceptiveness should duly be regarded, even almost two centuries later (although we should substitute the word 'people' for 'men' in his writings). "The inconvenience that men in democracies find in forms is, however what renders them so useful to freedom, their principal merit being to serve as a barrier between strong and weak, he who governs and he who is governed."[100]

While not being a professional academic, I take it he means this. The overall design of government institutions and structures that a nation adopts, can significantly influence the degree of equality that will exist between citizens of that nation. Tocqueville's wise counsel, derived from astute observation, is just as valuable today as it was in the 1830s. "Men who live in democratic centuries do not readily comprehend the utility of forms; they feel an instinctive disdain for them."[101] Certainly discussing the design or form of government that best suits democracies to be effective may not be something people are interested in when they usually socialize. And it probably is not something people initially think of when considering politics in their everyday lives. It's just not that sexy in comparison to some titillating soundbites or scandals in the news involving politicians. Yet it is here, within the architect's realm of structures and forms, that we can find both the problems and solutions involving modern day democracy in Canada and internationally. For as the American religious leader Norman Vincent Peale intimated, every problem contains its own solution.

Referring again to the appropriateness of Tocqueville's thoughts in the present century, consider those buried on page 669 of *Democracy in America*, "the smallest questions of forms have acquired an importance in our day that they had not had up to now. Several of the greatest interests of humanity are linked to them."[102] Absolutely! I am beginning to like this Frenchman's thinking. The fact that his parents were imprisoned during what is known as the Reign of Terror during the French Revolution tells me that Tocqueville was no snob either, despite being born into aristocracy. One can only conjecture if those tragic circumstances influenced his desire to visit America's prisons. There he observed the treatment of inmates firsthand as he increasingly weighed the meaning of liberty, equality, rights, democracy, etc., as so prodigiously revealed in his writings on those subjects. Whatever his motives so long ago, Tocqueville knew the design of government, its organizational structure, was tied to many of humanity's greatest interests.

Interestingly, not unlike Brennan and Caplan, Tocqueville appeared to struggle in finding a government system that worked more equitably for the people, not just the elites: "A political form that equally favors the development and prosperity of all the classes of which society is composed has not been discovered up to now."[103] If he were alive today, Tocqueville might even emphasize this observation more about ruling elites and their business cronies—the proverbial one per cent we hear so much about—than he did long ago considering the aristocracy. "It is not that they see the suffering of the poor man without pity, but they cannot feel his miseries . . . they therefore take them to be satisfied and expect nothing more from the government." Or, as Tocqueville succinctly articulated the case, "Aristocracy considers maintaining more than perfecting."[104] That could well be the outcome of Brennan's so-called epistocrats as well. They do indeed rhyme and seem to fit well, aristocracy and epistocracy, and probably would benefit their leaders and elitist friends most.

In *Against Democracy* Brennan did admit that "epistocracy is inherently elitist the way that plumbing or medical licensing schemes are inherently elitist."[105] Hmmm, my boss Marty never struck me as an elitist! Brennan also said of democracy that "voters remain ignorant and irrational because democracy incentivizes them to remain ignorant and irrational."[106] It looks like Tocqueville and Brennan have something in common. They both did not think about plumbing long enough to come up with a better democratic system less prone to clogs, leaks, and countless other practical issues in need of repair. I can be more forgiving of Tocqueville because he was a product of the 19th century, a time of less complexity in terms of globalization, technology and so on. Brennan does however legitimately raise a challenge I intend to meet head on: "Ideally someone who advances the education argument would supply us with specific proposals about just what forms of participation are supposed to enable and educate."[107] Well then, my general premise has always been that voters, such as Susie and Frank or a competent plumber, know what's right and what's wrong.

We talked of blame earlier. This is a wrongminded thinking that leads to the politics of division and conflict. Blame prolongs existing problems and breeds new ones, while misguided leaders flail about in the ever-growing quagmires enveloping their nations. They know not what to do, only whom to blame and what sounds good to say. Around the world, and here in Canada too, people need to start blaming something else, rather than someone else, for the mounting problems they face. That something is the poorly designed structures of our government, namely the bureaucracy which really does not change no matter how you vote, and the poor oversight of that bureaucracy in place. Ironically, the ill-design of our government bureaucracy often manifests itself in the swelling ranks of the civil service taking stress or other mental leave.

The system is not only driving us all crazy, turning us all on each other as we play the blame game, but even making innocent bureaucrats themselves sick.

The important thing to remember is that we can unify all Canadians by coming together to rebuild the systems and structures that divide us. We can build something better to unify us and our national spirit. This does not require heaps of consultation papers and study after study. Nor does it require wheelbarrow after wheelbarrow of taxpayers' money to implement new technologies. It does require clarity of purpose, common sense and somewhat of a nonpartisan or apolitical attitude. Above all, it requires knowing the difference between right and wrong on a very basic spiritual level. We need not define that because if you do not automatically know it, regardless of your politics, then you should not be reading this book. You may as well join the Donald Trump brigade and start building a wall. I hope Maxime Bernier and Faith Goldy will not be there cementing this attitude. They should know better.

But if, like me, you believe in the goodness of most people, it really is a 'no brainer' to start making things better. As I stated at the outset of this book, I am not here to explain the difference between right and wrong. You know what it is, just like Slow Turtle of his people does, and Pope Francis or other spiritual people do. Reflecting on the Occupy movement again, and how people supporting it must have felt something about democracy was wrong, we can discern this. Although Occupy could be ignored due to its lack of direction, it would be foolish to ignore it altogether. It and similar grassroots movements, such as 'Black Lives Matter' and our Canadian homegrown 'Idle No More' movement, painfully reflect a deeper angst among groups of people feeling disenfranchised or excluded from modern society. Illustrative of this is the Black Lives Matter website, affirming that "we've committed to struggling together and to imagining and creating a world free of anti-Blackness, where every Black person has the social, economic, and political power to thrive."[108]

Here in Canada, which incidentally has chapters of the Black Lives Matter organization, we also see that the Idle No More movement has a website affirming the rights of Indigenous Peoples. That movement "seeks to assert Indigenous inherent rights to sovereignty and reinstitute traditional laws and Nation to Nation Treaties by protecting the lands and waters from corporate destruction."[109] Idle No More has specific requests and many seem reasonable to me, a non-Indigenous person. For example, they even wish to "deepen democracy in Canada through practices such as proportional representation and consultation on all legislation concerning collective rights and environmental protections, and include legislation which restricts corporate interests."[110] Why this cannot be explored, especially on the limited lands Indigenous Peoples have a legal right to, is beyond me. Most Canadians, knowing the difference between right and wrong, probably share that feeling.

The grassroots movements the world is witnessing are like the canary in the coal mine, warning us all not to repeat the sins of the past. It does not bode well for humanity to provide fertile ground for extremists and demagogues to grow in popularity, asserting more and more power, as they feed off the bitter resentments of people increasingly feeling there is no hope for a better future. We must collectively address why so many people are feeling disenfranchised, disempowered, disrespected and disgusted by repeated and deepening scandals within governments that are supposed to protect the public good. Is it such a far-fetched idea that, regardless of all the technological innovations we humans have made over the past century, including in the area of developing the Internet that is supposed to bring communities together, that another Stalin, Hitler, Idi Amin, Bashar al-Assad, etc., could not ascend to a position of power, anywhere?

Perhaps you should pick up a newspaper, and I do not mean a tabloid, and begin to understand how many ultra-right wing folks are assuming prominent leadership positions around the world. They are well-organized and well-financed. They are also adept at playing the blame game. So please read on to learn how we can stop that dark hour which is fast approaching. Our collective spirit needs to shine a light on the righteous path toward a better future. This is what it means to be Canadian.

Chapter 5
Fixing the Plumbing

Good Design stands out, Great Design fits in.

—M. Cobanli

Understanding Good Organizational Design

I bet all of us at one time or another, or far too many times than we care to count, have felt like a mouse navigating a never-ending maze in search of the elusive cheese, when trying to obtain service from a government institution. This is not generally the fault of mainly well-intended and largely hardworking rank-and-file civil servants. They similarly suffer outside of their workplace when dealing with the government. Many Canadians have been adversely impacted by such things as following voice prompts that lead to nowhere, or being put on hold or even disconnected when trying to get government services; being added to endless waiting lists to obtain a spot in a nursing home, subsidized housing, or specialized medical treatment, etc.; trying to get paid by that ill-conceived and God-forsaken federal payroll system known as Phoenix; foregoing normal use of their household appliances, heat and air conditioning, in the desperate hope that their Ontario electric bill will not be higher yet again than the prior month's bill; and so many other issues that were outlined in Chapter 3.

Certainly we are blessed with living in a first world country, but things do seem to be increasingly amiss. Of course our government institutions could be a lot worse. They could be designed to deliberately oppress and control us, as was the case under the former USSR and other totalitarian states. In those regimes, the slightest misstep by a citizen could be met with severe consequences. The point being that the way governments and their institutions are designed has a direct bearing on our collective well-being, and likely the planet's. So if the mouse had a direct and unobstructed path to get to the cheese, it would get there a heck of a lot faster and more efficiently.

We observed in Chapter 1 that the former USSR collapsed under its own weight. The less than agile bulk of communism reflected a bloated party system wherein those who were higher up the pecking order of the communist hierarchy, often displayed an avaricious tendency, accumulating as much wealth, perks and privileges as they could. Unfortunately, human nature being what it is, some people, regardless of the political system they live under (e.g. communism, fascism and even modern democracies), usually wish to get ahead at the expense of others. Getting ahead in a fair way and playing by the rules everyone is subject to is not necessarily a bad thing. Everyone should be able to profit when there is a level playing field and they possess more talent or just simply work harder than others. The problem is when hypocrisy, cheating, lying and breaking the law, or clearly not abiding by the spirit of the law, becomes the creed one lives by.

Regardless of our colour, professed religion, gender and political ideology, that creed has too often reared its ugly head throughout human history. Let's turn our thoughts to the former Soviet Union for a moment again. It provides a perfect example of a political system designed to oppress most people, while a select few benefit at their expense. The propaganda of the former USSR, meted out to ordinary people within the confines of its physical borders, as well as externally for all the world to dubiously accept, was that we were all supposed to believe the Soviet Union was a worker's paradise. The common people had freed themselves from their capitalist-leaning masters, and were now all sharing equally in the immense wealth abundantly provided by the motherland. Really?

Although this book is mainly about Canada, we should understand the reality of how the USSR was organized; its government institutions and structures were designed for the benefit of the higher echelons of the communist party, rather than ordinary people themselves. This is important to understand because it underscores the importance of strengthening the democratic institutions that bind us all as Canadians. It can be a slippery slope downward to end up in a society whose leadership uses design to control, oppress and feed off of its young, leaving them nothing for the future.

Democratic Restructuralism is where we need to focus our efforts if we are to evolve and mature as a people. Before we begin to look at the flawed design of our own democratic institutions and structures in need of this new philosophy, we should first gain an appreciation of what constitutes good design. Good design is something you often can tell when you see, feel, operate, etc., physical objects. You know what clothes, electronic devices, cars, homes and such that you like. We typically attribute better quality to good and useful design. Sometimes there is an 'X Factor' or perhaps a certain styling that appeals to you.

What is often overlooked is that the way something is designed, typically determines how it behaves. This is clearly illustrated by Lex Sisney in *The 5 Classic Mistakes in Organizational Structure: Or how to Design Your Organization the Right Way*, as follows:

'Why does a rocket behave the way it does and how is it different from a parachute that behaves the way it does? . . . Well, duh they're designed differently. One is designed to go fast and far and the other is designed to cause drag and slow an object in motion. Because they're designed differently, they behave differently.' . . . How something is designed controls how it behaves. [1]

The Sisney article cleverly links the concept of how design affects behaviour in concluding that "how your organization is designed determines how it performs." [2] No wonder the former USSR collapsed under its own weight. Although the discussion does not mention government and has a rather business flavour to it, the argument "if you want to improve organizational performance, you'll need to change the organizational design" [3] is definitely applicable to government. Having worked for OSFI, Canada's national regulator of financial institutions, for a dozen years or so, I speak from experience. But hold that thought for a minute. There are some common sense oriented and useful points made in *The 5 Classic Mistakes*. As form follows function, something many of us have heard when considering design, Sisney reasons the design of something should support its purpose. Of course, as he clearly points out, "if the organization has a flawed design, it simply won't perform well." [4] Imagine if we substituted the word 'government' for 'organization' in that last sentence. "If the [government] has a flawed design, it simply won't perform well."

Earlier we saw how people have been blaming each other for the problems they face, how even nation has turned against nation. The attacks are sometimes violent. Recent and deadly violence at an August 2017 white nationalist rally in Charlottesville, Virginia, revealed that plainly. It was there that Heather Heyer died, a victim of America's increasing division. The US has traditionally been a steadfast friend, and not only to Canada. But we need to guard against replicating the environment of divisiveness sadly taking root to the south of us, lest the seeds of blame blow across our borders. Faith Goldy's alt-right antics in Toronto should be taken seriously, much like the growth of clericalism in religious quarters.

It is imperative we Canadians begin to lead by example, by attacking the 'something' that is wrong, namely the flawed design of government. We must do this instead of maintaining the status quo, which risks our citizens attacking each other, either verbally or physically. Attacking is not our way, although we are all prone to misguided anger. Fortunately, most of us already know the difference between right and wrong. We just need to focus on restructuring the poor design responsible for so many of the problems we face. That is an initial step, pulling up the weeds that have overgrown the garden, pursuing the *Democratic Restructuralism* necessary to redesign our government institutions. This is our principal task at hand, to ensure democracy works better for everyone, including the civil servants who want to do right by us, performing work that actually matters.

According to Sisney, organizations (or for our purposes here—governments) are shaped by three things that control how they behave:

1) **The function it performs**, or the core areas or activities in which the organization must engage to accomplish its strategy;

2) **The location of each function** . . . in the organizational structure and how it interacts with other functions; and

3) **The authority of each function within its domain** or each function's ability to make decisions . . . and to perform its activities without unnecessary encumbrance."[5]

Logically, as mentioned by Sisney, a sound organizational structure "will make it unarguably clear what each function (and ultimately each person) is accountable for." Additionally, "the design must both support the current . . . strategy and allow the organization to adapt to changing market conditions . . ."[6] Sisney warns us of the calamity that occurs when organizational (think 'government' again) structures get misaligned with the environment they operate in. He talks about old power structures hanging on and not adapting to new conditions. He finds that inertia is the most common reason, among several, as to why organizational structures get misaligned. Specifically, "the [government—I couldn't resist putting the word right in here!] gets stuck in an old way of doing things and has trouble breaking free of the past."[7] And what of the voters view on Main Street when we continue to exchange the word 'government' for 'company' or 'organization' in Sisney's analysis? Well, "from an outsider's perspective, it may be hard to figure out how and why the [government] looks and acts the way it does."[8]

That would certainly be the view of most Canadians! More concerning, "and yet from the inside, we grow used to things over time and question them less."[9] For Sisney, there are numerous ways to discern an organization is improperly designed. Applied to government and the results it has been generating, we can clearly see things must be out of sync. Certainly they are relative to what our democratic values demand of government.

Apparently there are five signs of structure done wrong and having a negative impact on performance. For Canadians, the impact of government decision-making is on our day-to-day lives. Considering how important government performance really is, in view of how extensively it touches upon our lives (public health and safety, taxation, the legal system, immigration, the economy, etc.), we can no longer afford its structures to be wrong. So what are the five signs or mistakes indicating that design is hindering performance?

"Mistake #1: The strategy changes but the structure does not;

Mistake #2: Functions focused on effectiveness report to functions focused on efficiency;

Mistake #3: Functions focused on long-range development report to functions focused on short-range results;

Mistake #4: Not balancing the need for autonomy vs. the need for control; [and]

Mistake #5: Having the wrong people in the right functions."[10]

As a Canadian citizen who was born and lived here most of my life, as well as having been a government employee in the federal public service for the better part of 12 years, I am well positioned to comment on these five mistakes as they relate to Canada's public service. Having been a student of history and raised with a practical nature also gives me some insight. Then again, when you really think about it, you do not need to be a rocket scientist to see how our government is not set up to be effective, to make informed decisions that benefit us all. This is the tragedy of modern democracy around the world. It is also why we have long been betrayed here in Canada as painfully discussed in Chapter 3. Let's explore this a bit more. However, please note that we discuss Mistake No. 5, having the wrong people in the right positions, at length in Chapter 6. That has a lot to do with motivation, not just an obvious lack of experience, knowledge or suitable disposition. That is my view, anyway.

Regarding Mistake No. 1, it is a huge one we need to spend much time investigating. As for Sisney's Mistake No. 2, we will not spend much time focusing on it in this chapter. It is straightforward enough to understand that functions focused on effectiveness (such as oversight mechanisms responsible for driving accountability—like internal audit) should not report to functions focused on efficiency. Of course, the unique nature of government does require that Parliament is kept well-informed as to how effective its oversight functions are. We will be discussing how to ensure our government is kept more accountable in Chapter 7. We will spend some time on Mistake No's. 3 and 4 in this chapter, raising them when necessary and appropriate.

Looking again Sisney's five classic mistakes, the first can easily be related to government. The structure of our government has been fairly static over the years while strategies have needed to change. This situation is mainly responsible for many of the problems we face today. The other four mistakes Sisney raises all appear to relate to overall structural inadequacies anyway.

We often vote for fresh leadership or the perception of it. When some well-groomed candidate says all the things we want to hear, albeit in brief soundbites that are catchy and in fashion, many of us gravitate toward the attractive promise of change even though no credible plan has been established to effect real and positive change that will improve our lives. This happens because we want to believe the new candidate has a new vision and strategy to change the status quo and make things better. Yet even if there genuinely is a new strategy, the old plumbing, or rather the government bureaucracy, stays the same. We take it for granted, just as citizens in other democracies do, that we have the right organizational structure in government at all times. But Canada's government has largely remained stuck in the past when it comes to organizational structure. Apart from implementing the *Charter of Rights and Freedoms* in 1982, the government has not really changed, while the complexity of the world around us has evolved.

We still have, as Andrew Cohen describes in *The Unfinished Canadian*, remained anchored to our past. We still have "a governor general. The Supreme Court. A prime minister and Cabinet. The House of Commons and the Senate." In the final analysis, "powers and roles have changed, but institutionally Canada hasn't."[11] And is it any wonder that the institutions meant to bind Canadians together are coming unhinged? Or that the very structure of our government and the democracy it is meant to underpin, are becoming antiquated relics? Cohen did not connect the dots. But what he said about 150 pages earlier in his book, before mentioning that Canada has not institutionally changed, points to a museum-like obsolescence regarding old government structures not suitable for modern times. In his own words: "Until the Canadian Museum of Civilization reorganizes and reorients itself, a visitor can come away without a clear sense of the great events and great people of this country's past. It is staggering really."[12] Indeed it is, Mr. Cohen. Canada, and not just its prominent museum (although I am disposed to like the one in Québec City more—even though I am not Québécois), is in dire need of a makeover.

We need to redesign our government. Does it not then make perfect sense to engage in *Democratic Restructuralism*? After all, like Cohen said 11 years ago when he wrote his book, "In 2007, Canada remains much as it was in 1867."[13] No wonder Ottawa did not seem to celebrate so much on the nation's 150th birthday last year. Unlike Canadian Pamela Anderson, Canada is simply too old and tired in its ways to get up and show the world it has some good moves and rhythm to lead on the international dance floor. We have remained rooted in the past despite the world having changed constantly around us. Sure there may be new Cabinet members or ministers at the highest echelons of the government after an election. They may even have some new strategies. However, the old bureaucracy that impacts our day-to-day lives so much generally remains the same. Or as Sisney clarifies in discussing Mistake No. 1, "A new strategy is created but the old hierarchy remains embedded in the so-called 'new structure.' "[14]

It is like people trying to move on after a breakup of a serious relationship or some other trauma. They may have a new strategy for their life, entering into new relationships and circumstances. However until they come to terms with any issues or fears stemming from problematic earlier relationships, their existing personal makeup/structure may impede them from happily moving forward. So, just as the composition of an individual—mind, body and spirit—is important to the success of a relationship, so too is the structure of government important to the success of its leadership. Each must be fit for purpose at all times so the health and well-being of individuals and the greater body politic is assured. At this point of our journey, and before we look at some of the other mistakes Sisney raised and how our government is making them too, it is useful for me to comment on my current employer, OSFI.

The vast majority of OSFI's front-line staff are very dedicated, results-oriented people. They are motivated by good intentions to fulfil OSFI's core mandate as the federal regulator of financial institutions in Canada, ensuring those institutions are in sound financial condition and meeting OSFI requirements. The regulator generally did a great job helping to ensure Canada's financial institutions, and by extension the wider public, remained largely unscathed from the 2008 financial crisis. That is not to say we were not impacted by what happened elsewhere, especially in our modern and technologically advanced and interconnected world. Nor is it to say that OSFI's actions were the only factors that contributed to the 2013 World Economic Forum conclusion: "For the sixth year in a row Canada's banks have been ranked the world's soundest," albeit "tied with banks in New Zealand."[15] Even now, Canada continues to have one of the strongest banking systems in the world, although we have slipped out of the top spot. Still, and especially having been there, I believe OSFI had a positive and material impact in ensuring we did not suffer the same ravages of the financial crisis as say Greece, America, etc.

The risk-management framework used by OSFI is one of the reasons the organization was so successful in assessing and mitigating risks during and immediately after the financial crisis. It really is a common sense methodology, in which well-intended, experienced and knowledgeable people can make informed decisions to improve organizational performance. That has been my experience applying the framework to institutions, both small and gigantic. From a high level, the framework looks at a financial institution's significant activities, the basic or inherent risks associated with those activities, and what management and associated oversight mechanisms do to mitigate and improve those risks. It also considers the impact an organization's earnings, or revenue streams and capital levels, have in offsetting its overall risks, as well as identifying any potentially future adverse risks. In business terms that just means you have enough money and other assets to pay for bad events if and when they occur.

OSFI's teams, when they have an opportunity to go on site to the financial institutions they regulate, assess the relevant risks. They collaborate to make sensible risk-based recommendations to management and the institution's board of directors. The objective is to make the regulated organization safer for Canadians and customers, which as often has been my experience, actually makes them more profitable. Simply put, if you run your organization effectively, having designed it to manage risks well, you succeed more than your competitors who may not.

During the financial crisis, and as reported on in many media articles at the time, the superintendent who was then in charge of OSFI, Julie Dickson, received much praise as to how she handled a multitude of issues associated with that crisis. A 2009 *Globe and Mail Report on Business* magazine feature on Ms. Dickson commented on her abilities thus: "When talking about her strengths, more than one associate refers to Dickson's common sense, and her ability to listen to a problem and identify key issues. 'Julie is very tough—she's got a very strong backbone,' says Palmer, the former OSFI head."[16] Speaking as an insider, I can tell you the vast majority of my colleagues and I had a lot of respect for Julie. She tackled issues and generally ran our government agency from a practical rather than political or theoretical standpoint.

When one considers all the fast-developing, complex, and often international issues Ms. Dickson had to juggle in real time during the crisis, she can very easily be forgiven for increasing resources as deemed necessary. One can similarly overlook the creation of a variety of specialized groups within the agency, each with its own management structures. Front-line employees are increasingly asked to do more as senior ranks grow apace, much in the wake of Ms. Dickson's departure and that of the financial crisis itself. The financial regulator has roughly doubled its staff count since the crisis. Even its number of assistant superintendents has grown. Make no mistake, OSFI is a venerable organization with an incredibly effective framework to both assess and manage risks. That is something it continues to do. It just might be suffering a little from some of *The 5 Classic Mistakes* outlined by Sisney as it grows horizontally and vertically.

In reality, and across the globe where modern government organizations are concerned, many nonunionized staff are playing a vital role rather than performing one. Although not as extreme, this idea conjures up images of the old USSR, where senior party members let everything go mismanaged. But all the while they were solidifying their positions of power and attendant perks. They were pretending to be valuable comrades and party officials, much more so than those oppressed below them who lived in fear of their bosses purging them. In the former Soviet Union, there were even 'show trials,' where anyone who dared to speak out against the corrupt regime found themselves the subject of fake news in a courtroom stacked against them. Show trials, where one's life may be at risk, are the ugliest form of optics management. Even the biblical Son of God knows that.

I assure you I am not an extreme left-wing proponent by any means. I abhor all forms of extremism. Some of the worst are those leftists with right-wing bank accounts, not just members of the alt-right. And I am sure there are some bad apples in many unions, just as there are in the executive ranks of government. The point is we must beware of optics management, which usually emanates from the ranks of nonunionized members of government running their departments. Optics management is always crucial for bloated bureaucracies, whether they be here in Canada or elsewhere. The use of spin and propaganda is not confined to dictators and undemocratic regimes. Representatives of all forms of government can use this messaging to hide the truth of ineffective government services from citizens.

It all comes down to human nature, which we will explore in detail in the next chapter. The ego is a fragile thing. We all like to feel important, aside from whether or not any glorified feelings of self-importance are warranted or not. Is it any wonder that certain opportunists in government will jump at the chance to add more and more positions within their erroneously perceived fiefdoms? Within such empires, they clamour for higher and higher sounding titles, while actually doing very little to execute on the mandate the public expects them to. Truly, it is a form of government clericalism that needs to be uprooted. Expanding upon Pope Francis' concerns about clericalism in the Catholic Church, the Archbishop of Brisbane and President of the Australian Catholic Bishops Conference, Mark Coleridge, had this to say:

> There will also have to be a change in the culture associated with the Catholic priesthood . . . Part of that change will involve proper professional supervision for the sake of greater accountability . . . a greater sharing of responsibility with laypeople—which in turn requires a reconsideration of our structures of decision-making. [17]

The good Archbishop may as well have been speaking of self-important government officials working for themselves instead of the body politic. Church and state may need to be separated, but they do indeed share some similarities. One can likely find the same forms of clericalism in other religious orders. By necessity, a restoration of things is certainly required within the structures of government and likely church organizations as well. That is no heresy, just a stark truth leading to a more divine design, both earthly and spiritual. I hope Slow Turtle would agree.

And when the average passerby on the street takes it for granted that what needs to be done is actually getting done, especially when the work may be complex with even its own jargon of acronyms and terminology, so much the better to pull the wool over their eyes. Unfortunately, that unconscionable line of thinking in not confined to misguided government officials, or a select group of wayward priests. We saw the spider's web of complexity draped over the global financial crisis, manifesting itself as an impenetrable shroud of grey. Within that web of deceit, any loose end that initially appeared to lead to any accountability, usually led nowhere. And the multitude of personal tragedies that unraveled around the world, belied a crime of the century that went unpunished.

Many government organizations are now pursuing major technological changes rather than structural ones. It remains to be seen if those changes will yield much better results than technology initiatives rolled out previously, such as the Phoenix payroll system here in Canada. But I digress. I firmly believe that OSFI's Risk-Management Framework is an excellent tool to assess any organization's risks such that good and informed decisions can be made to lower those risks. The framework points to any entity's organizational chart as a good way to identify its key activities (including where they take place and who is involved) and oversight mechanisms that manage those activities. A key oversight mechanism many large organizations should have is an independent risk-management function. It should be of great concern to Canadians that our federal government has no independent Chief Risk Officer (CRO) ensconced in Ottawa! Many of our government's large and important departments also do not have an independent CRO.

Since the Canadian federal government has no CRO, and considering how often the leadership of our government changes—such as recently from the Conservatives led by Stephen Harper to the Liberals led by Justin Trudeau—is this why not a lot changes in government even when the party in power has changed? Hmmm . . . Certainly each political party has a different political platform to attract voters. But the outdated structure of our government never substantially changes with the changing of the guard or its leaders and MPs. And if there is no CRO to brief the highest levels of our government and MPs on the issues of the day, the leading risks that need to be managed, how can any leader, regardless of their political leanings or good intentions, make informed and appropriate decisions for Canadians? Tragically they cannot. The flock or citizenry is only left with a shepherd in name only. Their path can then easily go astray, led incorrectly by a few wayward guides. Misguided shepherds can take us down wrong paths, steering us too far to the right, or too far to the left. They know not what they do. And individuals suffer regardless of the extreme and thoughtless direction the country may take. It is hard to forgive, but forgive we must to move forward.

Is it any wonder, as we read in Chapter 2, that the MPs we elect to represent our communities in the federal legislature—our local shepherds—also cannot do their jobs? Recall how *Tragedy in the Commons* found that, after assuming their role in Parliament, "many MPs continued to identify themselves as outsiders." Recall that a majority of the MPs that were interviewed "saw a system that didn't reflect them or what they viewed as important." Recall that "some MPs believed . . . the link between government and citizens was broken, and prime ministers . . . acted too frequently beyond accountability." Think of the huge ramifications when you let these thoughts enter the forefront of your consciousness. The design of our government is such that the prime minister and his executive team (cabinet, ministers, etc.) cannot make fully informed decisions. The Roman Curia, or administrative institutions of the Holy See that conduct the affairs of the Catholic Church, but in less visible manner than its spiritual guide, the Pope, could similarly be afflicted. That is why Francis has been attempting to effect positive change. Spiritual health requires good design to prevent abuse, no less than the institutions of democracy. Restoration of all things is possible through good or divine design.

In this fast-paced, globalized, interconnected, increasingly complex and ever-changing world, the antiquated organizational structures of governments around the world will not do. They make it next to impossible for world leaders to reliably make fully informed and risk-based decisions. And yet we need them to. For good decision-making enables people to effectively and positively address issues. Good decisions advance the human race forward.

It is therefore imperative that we fix the plumbing so to speak; restructuring of democratic institutions must take place. *Democratic Restructuralism* is required in countries, such as our own, suffering so woefully from a lack of representative government. It must also take place in international organizations such as the United Nations and World Trade Organization, etc., which are also dysfunctional. The world is changing rapidly. Strategies to deal with the issues of the day need to alter and be reflected in good public-policy making for voters. Our government must be nimble, but its organizational design is not fit for that purpose. That is the glaring mistake setting Canada up for failure, just like other democracies around the world.

Here Canada has an opportunity, not only to define who we collectively are and what we stand for, but also to lead by example through a redesigning of our ailing democratic institutions and structures. These institutions and structures have been attacked and undermined far too long, including by former Conservative Prime Minister Stephen Harper. He solidified his own power and that of the Privy Council Office at the expense of the people's power, the legislature. Economists like Harper, no less than the professors of economics we discussed earlier, always seem to think they know better when in fact they do not. They see everything through a singular and myopic lens of business interests and economics, ignoring the country's other needs, dismissing the collective wisdom and spirit of its people. These thinkers, as well-intended as they may be, are misguided in their focus on economics as the main driving force of democracy. And they are powerful.

This is exemplified by Harper, now heading as Chairman, the International Democratic Union (IDU). According to its website, the IDU's founding members include former UK Prime Minister Margaret Thatcher and then US Vice-President George Bush Sr. "Formed in 1983, the IDU provides a forum in which Parties holding similar beliefs can come together and exchange views on matters of policy and organisational interest."[18] It looks like a well-oiled machine with not only Harper at the helm, but with its Deputy Chairman, another well-known Canadian Conservative, Tony Clement. The objective of this machine is that "the IDU plays an essential role in enabling like-minded, centre-right parties to share experiences in order to achieve electoral success."[19]

The misguided beliefs of those focusing mainly on economics as the great lever of democracy are also exemplified in Harper's new book, *Right Here, Right Now: Politics and Leadership in the Age of Disruption*. Perhaps it is an advertisement for the collective wisdom of the over 80 members of the IDU, including the Conservative Party of Canada. We will be investigating a few of Harper's views in *Right Here, Right Now*, shortly.

It will only be when Canada embarks on a path of *Democratic Restructuralism*, showing the world that there can indeed be representative government, that democracy will be restored. The economic argument is not nearly enough to renew democracy. How could it be when the design of our democracy does not facilitate good government decision-making when it comes to the economy or other important areas of the public space (the environment, arts and culture, military defence, education, healthcare, justice, Indigenous Peoples rights, etc.)? People are not just economic units; nor is the earth merely one to be used up and extinguished. We can only become a beacon of light and hope for other nations when that which has been taken from us has been returned, democracy. We must reclaim that which is right and true—a government that works for all people rather than just the one per cent—a government that makes the right decisions for our collective good.

I believe in the goodness of most people: that they largely know the difference between right and wrong and have good values. When you embrace this idea and that good design of government will lead to better decisions being made by our elected officials, then you realize people can make a real difference in improving their own lives. Canada can lead here, in a meaningful way. If people on Main Street can see positive changes impacting their and their children's day-to-day lives, then we can realistically envision a world where even repressive and undemocratic regimes can be faced with a popular movement seeking to take back what is rightfully theirs. Is that wishful thinking? Maybe. But I think it is fair to say that people everywhere want a government that nurtures their well-being instead of one that defiles it.

But consider how poorly many, if not most, so-called democracies around the world are leading by example. We live in a time when cell phones and the Internet, both revolutions in communications, have arguably made the world much smaller and information sharing all that much easier. Yet the polarization of society in the West has continued unabated as described. And our tragedy is that we continue to blame others (someone) for our problems, rather than the obsolete and ineffective design of our government (something). Perhaps if we build government right, we could even envision a day when our planet and all of its international organizations are working for a common good. Imagine the power of our collective spirit and will, fuelling good decision-making by governments both locally and internationally.

To dispel any remaining doubt you may have, even after reading Chapter 3, that our daily lives are being negatively impacted by poor government decision-making, let's take a look at what Kevin Page, Canada's first Parliamentary Budget Officer, had to say. In his damning book *Unaccountable: Truth and Lies on Parliament Hill*, Mr. Page reveals how former Prime Minister Harper did not appear to want the Parliamentary Budget Office (PBO) to succeed. Born in Canada but descended from Polish and Czechoslovak roots, with even some ancestry on his mother's side extending to the soil of Ukraine, I found myself identifying personally and somewhat philosophically with Page. In *Unaccountable*, he traces how Stephen Harper of the Conservatives rose to power in the wake of the prior Liberal government's 'sponsorship scandal,' having promised to establish an independent budget authority. Without going into too much detail, the sponsorship scandal involved the Liberals being accused of fiscal irresponsibility and being unaccountable to Canadians.

Mr. Page describes how the PBO was "proposed by Harper to over-come lack of transparency and accountability of Parliament Hill" and how the PBO's head "was to be responsible for forecasting the cost of purchases resulting from specific policies."[20] Basically the PBO was to "forecast real costs so that decision makers could make informed decisions."[21] Unfortunately for Page, the PBO may have been, as his first chapter is entitled, "Set Up to Fail." Apparently, "the PBO had been designed to 'kick the tires' on a business case before public money is ever spent."[22] However, the way the PBO was structured ended up hindering its effectiveness from the get go. In this sense, we see the PBO suffering from the same malaise as our and other governments' broadly, poor design. Just like the Phoenix payroll system! Amusingly, as it is better to laugh than cry about the obviously absurd structure of the PBO, its leader: "would be positioned as a mid-level bureaucrat instead of at the senior levels of government; would stay on the job at the leisure of the prime minister and could be fired at his discretion; was not created as an officer of Parliament but rather as an officer of the Library of Parliament . . . Making the PBO an officer of Parliament would have meant that the chosen person would then be responsible to Parliament for scrutinizing both the legislative mandate and the administration of taxpayer monies . . . The new reporting structure made little sense; PBO offices . . . Initially . . . were scattered across different parts of the Library of Parliament, making it a clumsy operation on all fronts, disruptive and designed . . . to make life as complicated as possible for the PBO team."[23]

Whether or not the motivation behind this absurdity was deliberate or not is debatable. It may well be that there were good intentions behind the incompetent design. We do not know for sure, which ties into Sisney's Mistake No. 4: "Balancing the need for autonomy versus the need for control." Page discusses the Harper Government and its notorious command-and-control way of doing things. I am not sure if the IDU is run the same way, so it can carry out its economic agenda globally under the guise of democracy. But for Page, Harper's approach (I might conjecture his unabashed clericalism) may have been a kind of deterrent to the effective functioning of an independent and healthy PBO, one that could challenge the fiscal assumptions and basis for government spending.

Be it the muzzling of our scientists, emasculation of data emanating from Statistics Canada, weakening of our ability to safeguard the environment, or the general disempowering of our public service, one does not have to do much research to discern there was a pretty significant consensus that Harper liked to do things his way as Prime Minister. His style did not embody consulting with or tapping the wider bureaucracy for feedback, much less guidance. And if he were leading this country or the free world via the IDU, *Right Here, Right Now*, as his book is called, we would probably be on the receiving end of yet more command-and-control style politics that do little to mend that which is broken, that which requires restoration.

Harper personally visited the White House in Washington DC during July 2018. It is unclear whether he availed himself of the opportunity to visit the National Geographic Museum while in that beautiful city, but when I was there in July 2018, I did. It was my specific intention to see the exhibit called the *Tomb of Christ*, a virtual reality experience to visit Jerusalem's Church of the Holy Sepulchre in the wake of its own desperately needed restoration. And I am so glad I went. The exhibit was both spectacular and informative as to how democracy can be designed to work better as we seek to restore it. You see the church, located in Jerusalem and where Jesus is thought to have been crucified, provides a good lesson in how diverse people can come together to solve problems. There are six Christian groups vying for room within the Holy site: the Ethiopian, Armenian, Greek Orthodox, Syrian and Franciscan priests. Only the Armenians, Greek Orthodox and Franciscan groups are charged with taking care of the 'Aedicule,' the Tomb of Jesus. Yet these three groups "have set aside their differences for a task all can agree is of critical importance: restoring the crumbling structure of Jesus's tomb."[24]

As well, the other groups "co-exist with the help of small compromises." Interestingly, "the keys to the church are in the hands of two of Jerusalem's most prominent Palestinian families who open and close its heavy doors each day."[25] All of this emphasizes that people with differing views can come together and, in the right spirit, collectively do the right thing. They can restore that which requires mending and do exactly that in a democratic way. The various sects still have their own part of the church and abide by a lot of strict rules. Nevertheless, when important decisions need to be made, these groups are able to make good ones. That is what our political parties need to do. They need to come together and restore that which is broken, our democratic institutions and the processes and structures that are meant to support them. Oh, and yes, I did visit the Capitol building in DC. That seemed important as well.

In fairness to former Prime Minister Harper, he does raise some valid points in *Right Here, Right Now*, although they are fairly obvious ones. He notes in the context of US politics and the Trump phenomenon that "voters were understandably dissatisfied with the status quo."[26] He deems the recent waves of populism impacting many countries such as America as being understandable, cautioning that such public sentiments deserve serious attention. The discontent reflects portions of society that are not doing well in the face of globalization and policies that only benefit certain segments of that society. He states, "We can keep trying to convince people that they misunderstand their own lives, or we can try to understand what they are saying. Then we can decide what to do about it."[27]

But Harper ignores the valuable lessons you can glean from visiting the *Tomb of Christ* exhibit: that democracy must rest with its curators, those best positioned to restore it. The legislature must be made whole again, reflecting the spiritual needs of the body politic, its sense of what is right. In turn, the legislature must reflect the political will of the people by making decisions and implementing policies they desire and benefit from. It should be no different in any church, Catholic or otherwise. It's Curia, or administrative organs, must also be restored to make decisions and implement policies that the greater body desires and benefits from. Anything short of that can breed clericalism and its ugly offshoots, including abuse that may go undetected. The seeds of abuse and scandal must not be permitted to germinate below that which is easily visible, in Church or state. On each rock, the foundations for church and democratic nations, one must easily find good design. This has always been intended by the creators of each.

Harper is correct in opining thus: "There is one thing I know for sure: in this age of widespread disruption in the United States and other Western societies, we do require some new approach."[28] He is doubly correct in raising this salient point. "The world simply does not agree on how to balance equality against opportunity, economic security against innovation, health and environment risks against social and cultural mores, let alone how to choose basic governance models."[29] However, he is incorrect, if not blatantly deceitful, in arguing that his band of Conservatives are best positioned to resolve these issues. If anything, Harper has been part of the problem. His track record speaks to this. The poor decisions mentioned in Chapter 3 along with his penchant to control things as he sees fit is not a restorative approach. His blueprint for success is a false path that does not lead one to address the elephant, as invisible as it is, in the room—the problematic design of government which too often results in poor decision-making for citizens. As a trained economist, Harper simply cannot seek and find anything beyond economics and policy making as being fundamentally responsible for the waves of populism he is worried about. That, of course, is to be expected.

Therefore, when Harper says something like—"A poorly designed immigration system can have negative effects on labour markets"[30]—that too is to be expected. To him, everything must be in stark economic terms. That is the gospel he preaches, a message of how everything comes down to economics. It is like an ultra-right-wing evangelical missionary cultivating a false prophecy; that when people are not faring that well, it all comes down to poor economic policies impacting them. Sounds a bit like the Trump presidency, supported as it is by the spiritually misled who are too fearful to see the truth that tests them. False prophets bearing blueprints for humanity's success would never dream of probing further beyond that which is immediately visible. They would never dare say the design of government itself is the problem, not the economy! Ironically, Harper does write that "policies have to be changed, and, sometimes even institutions themselves." [31] But would he ever admit to his own sins in government, some of which caused mayhem and tumult for government institutions and civil servants alike, and the Canadians who depend on them to work properly? Probably not as he had the opportunity *Right Here, Right Now* to do so but chose otherwise. There is no 'mea culpa' in his musings.

So what solutions does Harper have for people who are hurting around the world? He sees a flexible Conservatism as the way forward. Having missed seeing the fundamental and apolitical structural design issue, all the mistakes incorporated in how government has organized itself, he champions 'the Right' instead of what is actually right! I generally consider myself to be apolitical when it comes to the work of political parties and their candidates. Therefore, and so as not to appear biased, I found it useful to examine what others beyond Page thought of Harper's leadership style as Prime Minister. The exercise proved instructive. Not inasmuch as what it revealed specifically about Stephen Harper the man, but what it revealed so profoundly about the design of our government; how it enables certain behaviour and resulting outcomes to occur.

Our Over-centralized Government

In *Democracy Rising*, Bill Freeman opines that "the Stephen Harper government was the most centralized in recent memory." [32]

That may be so. But the anachronistic design of the federal government served as an enabler, facilitating the centrifugal forces that allowed Harper to put his thumb on so much that affects Canadians' daily lives. However it could be any Prime Minister doing that. Any Prime Minister, that is, who did not run on a campaign to reorganize government so that better decisions can be made for the country and its people. Canada has yet to elect such a Prime Minister. As Freeman wrote, "The over-centralization of government has created serious problems because it shifts power to bureaucrats and politicians remote from communities."[33] And when the power of the legislature is considerably weakened at the expense of an overly-centralized government situated so remotely from the people, the people and their vote come to mean very little indeed. That is a crucial problem for Canada and other countries. The voices of duly elected representatives of the people are increasingly silenced, deemed perhaps too ignorant and incompetent to be heard. Still, the spirit of Alexi de Tocqueville, so far ahead of his time, mockingly whispers to those clever economists labelling voters as being hopelessly ignorant: "There is a point at which the legislator is obliged to rely on the good sense and virtue of citizens."[34]

For me, that sentence goes to the heart of the matter. Canadians are sensible enough to vote for what is right and true rather than what is wrong and cloaked in fake news. The problem is that the present system does not allow the MPs we send to Ottawa to do their job. This situation nullifies our vote, which ultimately carries little to no weight in a democracy controlled by a much too powerful PMO. We need the legislature to work properly on behalf of voters. The bully pulpit in the form of a much too controlling PMO is not an institution that can take the place of the electorate's collective sensibilities. The spirit of Tocqueville echoes across the centuries. "There is no country where the law can foresee everything and where institution will take the place of reason and mores [meaning morality]."[35] Paradoxically, an outwardly strong Prime Minister may seem like a good thing to the public, especially during the honeymoon period following an election. A good-looking and politically correct individual, saying all the right things to the people, will only carry them so far though. This is because you cannot fool all of the people all of the time, as President Abraham Lincoln said.

When what is hidden beneath the immediate surface does not work, whether it be the corroded plumbing or government infrastructure, the image of the strong leader inevitably collapses under its own weight. That is what led to the implosion of the USSR. Or, as Whittington argues in *Spinning History*, the judiciary rather than an inviolate legislature becomes the only opposing force to the executive prerogatives of the PMO. "Not surprisingly, in a parliamentary system lacking checks and balances on the prime minister's nearly absolute power, the courts had by 2014 emerged as a kind of default opposition and perhaps most effective limitation on the Conservative's legislative ambitions."[36] Again, it is really not so much of an issue about who is in power, although that has a bearing as we will see in the next chapter.

The real issue is that until we democratically restructure our government, we could end up continually relying on dubious court decisions (where judges are politically appointed by the Governor in Council—the Prime Minister and Cabinet), such as challenges to the 1982 *Charter of Rights and Freedoms*, to deal with the iniquities emanating from a far too incompetent and ignorant PMO—to the degree it cannot make informed decisions for those who rightfully deserve that public service. There are other sources pointing, if not explicitly, to the nonsensical design of our federal government. The current leader of Canada's Green Party, Elizabeth May, had this to say in an essay on Westminster parliamentary democracy, "The growth in the power of political parties has steadily reduced the scope of action of individual members of Parliament . . . The General drift has been toward centralizing the powers of the executive (prime minister and Privy Council) at the expense of the legislature."[37]

In his own book, Brent Rathgeber, a former Conservative MP who also resigned from the Conservative caucus in 2013, similarly remarked on the diminishing role of Parliament. He viewed the fulcrum of power residing in the legislature, tilting more toward the dysfunction of a too centralized PMO. "At the federal level, consolidation of power, first in the Cabinet and more recently in the Prime Minister's Office, has not only led to a diminished role for Parliament in both the budgetary and legislative processes, but also to the predictable growth in government's size and expense."[38] No small wonder we learn that, whereas "originally the Canadian Cabinet consisted of twelve ministers," it has "ballooned since then." In terms of size, "Brian Mulroney had the largest cabinet with forty ministers."[39] Rathgeber logically states that "it is the hard-fought-for principle of responsible government that guarantees that it is the elected assemblies that control the executive branch of government and not the other way around."[40] Then again, as Sisney emphasized, it is a structural mistake not to balance the need for autonomy versus the need for control.

Too bad our military veterans, who fought hard to maintain our democratic system and responsible government, are getting such a raw deal when it comes to collecting their pensions. If anyone has served their country well, offering the ultimate sacrifice to safeguard our liberty and freedom, it is our veterans. They deserve our respect, not blatant disregard, and so too do the voters. Rathgeber correctly notes that "Canadians do not directly elect their governments, we elect our legislatures." Moreover, "if the government is not accountable to the elected parliament, that government, by definition, is unaccountable."[41] I would also deem it incompetent, regardless if an economist leads the government or not. If the highest elected official in the country, the Prime Minister, cannot be democratic—cannot see what needs to be done—what gives them the right to hold power in the first place?

When you consider all the things going wrong and so much that can be right-sided, it is time to get on with *Democratic Restructuralism* as soon as practicable. As it is, the fundamental challenge to our increasingly elusive democracy, articulated quite well by Rathgeber, is "given the increased size of the cabinet, the reliance on committees attended by senior public servants has facilitated the transfer of power from the cabinet to the Privy Council Office and the Prime Minister's Office."[42] Underscoring how our vote matters increasingly less, except perhaps for the optics of it meaning something, is the disturbing situation of a transfer of public power to the PMO and its unelected administrative personnel staff. The legislature, viewed so vitally by Tocqueville, has been bypassed and left to wither and die. Therefore the people's voice, that of Canadians who themselves know what is right, in stark contrast to an elitist and misinformed PMO, has been left to die as well.

According to Rathgeber, "The growing trend is to have policies, priorities, legislative initiatives, and even budgetary plans developed in the Prime Minister's office and by its unelected staffers."[43] In *Tragedy in the Commons*, Loat and MacMillan cited Gordon Robertson, former Clerk of the Privy Council, when discussing the overwhelming power of the PMO. "With the lack of checks and balances, the prime minister in Canada is perhaps the most unchecked head of government among the democracies."[44] Returning to Kevin Page's views, as Canada's first Parliamentary Budget Officer, he had this to say in bearing the brunt of Harper's hugely centralized government in Ottawa:

> The government consistently attempted to discredit people who stood in opposition on the Hill or dared to disagree with its programs or policies. It did a lot of 'spinning' in order to secure votes, and personal attacks were not outside the boundaries. It was the Conservative modus operandi and became an undeniable pattern over time.[45]

In any event, I believe it would be a bit unfair to characterize the Harper Conservatives as having a monopoly on 'spin,' not that Page goes as far as to say that. Harper's successor, Justin Trudeau, and the Liberals he leads, are playing pretty much the same game. They, just as other governments around the world, have created a whole cottage industry around optics management and the need to look good. They are always interested in saying the right and politically correct things, all condensed in the briefest of soundbites. This masks the less visible and gigantic problem that lurks beneath their triteness, the fact that they are not making informed decisions and substantially improving the lives of Canadians in a meaningful way. But as long as it looks like they are, that suits Prime Ministers of all stripes just fine.

We will also see in the next chapter that it was Pierre Elliott Trudeau, Justin Trudeau's father and a former Prime Minister himself, who is credited with first having begun to centralize power in the PMO. So we should be careful to solely blame Harper for operating a command-and-control style of government when he merely took up the torch, perhaps succeeding more than his predecessors. So much for balancing the need for autonomy versus the need for control! In *Unaccountable*, Page describes the tension between the PBO and the larger government. He saw it especially building when he and his PBO colleagues published analysis contrary to that of the government's own. One example he mentions is the PBO's review of how Canada's then called Department of Indian Affairs and Northern Development decided on funding. Page's team "found that there was no model to follow" since "it appeared that the people in charge of distributing funding were simply throwing darts at an imaginary target. It made no sense."

Unaccountable documents how the PBO's own report revealed an "annual shortfall of $100 million to $200 million for educational funding in Aboriginal communities."[46] The PBO's work here helped in motivating the government to provide additional funding later. Although Page uses other examples to highlight the PBO's value in producing transparent and relevant reports based on real data and information rather than spin, it is the F-35 Fighter Jet controversy that he sees as illustrating the PBO's vital role in Ottawa. He viewed this issue as a defining moment. As most Canadians know, and as outlined in Chapter 3, many of our military branches are in desperate need of new equipment. Whether it be search and rescue helicopters to replace our obsolete and unreliable fleet of Sea Kings that came into service in the 1960s, new war ships to restore our almost non-existent navy, or modern fighter jets to replace our aging squadron of F-18s, Canada requires a proper defence capability.

According to Page, the Harper government's Minister of Defence "attempted to take manipulation to a whole new level." The government was not being entirely transparent with Parliament, and by extension Canadians, during its bid to purchase dozens of F-35 jets to upgrade our air force capabilities. Apparently, in the fall of 2010, the federal government "was prepared to spend billions of taxpayer dollars on a fleet of fighter planes, but all it could muster was a one-page summary for members of Parliament with literally no supporting documentation."[47] The work of the PBO, as reflected by a report it released less than a year later, stood in stark contrast to that of the government's. Without going into too much detail, the PBO "estimated that the F-35s would cost billions of dollars more than the government had projected in its one-page document."[48]

Adding fuel to the fire, the Auditor General's report on the F-35 procurement process, released in April 2012, "indicated that the Harper government had in its possession numbers for the F-35 life cycle costs that were even larger than those . . . predicted at the PBO."[49] All of the tension between the Conservative government and the PBO, which often seemed at odds with each other, appears to have surfaced publicly for all Canadians to see during a public-accounts committee meeting in May 2012. In the ensuing media spotlight, just moments after the PBO presented its own findings on the F-35 jet controversy, Page was confronted by reporter Julie Van Dusen, who posed this direct question: "Are you suggesting that the government wanted Canadians to think that these planes would cost a lot less money?" Page's response, "Yes."[50]

When the Harper government announced initiatives concerning public service compensation and a National Shipbuilding Procurement Strategy involving our naval defence and Coast Guard capabilities, the PBO again had to shed light on the real cost of such programs. Of course, they involved tens of billions of dollars of public monies. Page argues that, once again, "if not for the work of the PBO, our members of Parliament and all Canadians would not have received any information on how these expenditures were going to be managed by the government." Critically, he further avers that "if our democratic Parliament had been functioning as intended, you would have received information from your government first and the PBO second . . . You got information from the PBO only. That should concern you greatly."[51] Hey, and you know what? He's right! Which means Harper's government acted wrongly back then, just as a similar one would act wrongly right now and right here in Canada. Our government does too many things backwards because its leaders have been thinking and doing things backwards, not the right way.

Throughout *Unaccountable*, Page hammers home that our government is not transparent. His book reflects that politics and hidden agendas seem the order of the day rather than government decisions being made for the benefit of us all collectively. Credible data to support informed decision-making seems to have gone the way of the dodo bird. Having worked for government, I tend to agree good decisions are not always made for the public by a broken public service. Sure we live in one of the best countries in the world, maybe even the best one, but it is a slippery slope to ending up lacking representative government. You will know you have arrived at that undesirable end when your country is divided with people blaming each other for their problems rather than the real culprit— poorly designed government institutions and organizations that no longer serve our individual and shared needs.

Page appropriately views us all being "disconnected from our Parliament." He insightfully states an ugly truth that I believe is impacting all so-called democracies, but to varying degrees. "We have lost trust in our political leaders and public servants."[52] Much of Page's concern is based on his direct experience as a senior public official, especially under the tightly controlled Harper regime. He nonetheless and astutely finds that the reason "real debate with analysis on Parliament Hill is virtually dead" is because "successive Liberal and Conservative governments have made this happen while the vast majority of the public service have silently stood by and watched."[53]

Right again! Moreover, Page writes, "The public service in Canada needs an overhaul. Normal isn't good enough."[54] Absolutely. The optics management game of effective government has gone on long enough. Just like Leonardo DiCaprio's character in *Catch Me if You Can* repeated, after watching black and white reruns of *Perry Mason* in preparation for his masquerading as a lawyer, "I concur."

Better yet, Page claims *"the public service has stopped showing its work. Its capacity to fulfill its duties has been so severely eroded as to make the public service virtually impotent."*[55] Page is onto something here that I unequivocally agree with. Yes, I am not a high government official like he was. But I have studied enough history, lived in enough places, and worked long enough as a mid-level bureaucrat (not wishing to clamour for more status that does not lead to good results) in God's country to know he is absolutely right. He is also right that "the context of renewal" in our public service can begin with a focus on values and ethics, but I do not believe we really need a code of conduct for that like he kind of does. As I mentioned at the beginning of this book, I believe most of us, including public servants, know the difference between right and wrong. We do not need me or some code to clarify who we are and what is right and lawful. Now, while I enjoyed reading *Unaccountable* and identify with Page's work ethic, integrity, and family history, I also vehemently disagree when he laments this: "If only we could institutionalize trust, but alas, that is impossible."[56] No, it is not! I will explain that a little later on.

Yes, "public servants must share accountability with elected representatives as the caretakers of institutions" as Page points out. And true, this is not generally happening. However, that has more to do with poor generals than with poor troops. I will get to that too. And, yes, Mr. Page, "The stakes are high." Yes, "Our institutions have been degraded."[58] You've got me. And agreed, just as he mentions in his epilogue, "There is a growing democratic deficit, an erosion of trust in our institutions."[59] But no, I am not convinced that a new government needs to reconstitute the PBO in exactly the way Page champions. Although a PBO is still required, it should be only in the manner I will discuss in Chapter 7.

We should credit Page with shedding much needed light on how our government institutions have become unhinged from the reality of what we expect from them. We certainly need our officials to be transparent and make informed decisions. Page and his colleagues likely did an amazing job in doggedly pursuing the truth and publishing highly important and meaningful information for all Canadians to see. Their efforts helped to ensure the public was not duped by any hidden agendas and personal motives of the Conservative government at the time, right then and there! Hidden agendas and motives are offensive and distasteful, and quite frankly, undemocratic. They potentially arise from over-centralized governments who are not managing risks, but often creating them.

I would even love to have a drink with Mr. Page, as we probably have a lot in common. My belief is just that we need to go way beyond considering that we require a PBO when the entire design of the government is in dire need of what I earlier called *Democratic Restructuralism*. Redesigning government, transforming it, much like an individual can transform their mind to overcome personal defects in their outlook, is the way to institutionalize trust. Remember, "how something is designed controls how it behaves." So institutionalizing or restoring trust, be it in Church or in state, is not impossible. And even Page himself admits, although it is 50 or so pages into his book, "Soon after I became the PBO, I began to notice some strange behavior." He elaborates: "The press was being shut out, the civil service was fearful, and simultaneously the government was trying to muzzle the PBO . . . It was a concerted effort at a centralization of power and information, the likes of which I had never seen in all my years on the Hill."[60] But that is how the system was designed!

Certainly Harper may have had a reputation, even a natural disposition, for being a bit of a control freak. Yet as we observed previously Harper and no single political party has a monopoly in behaving badly. Significant, and at times monumental, problems continue to go unaddressed in a meaningful way here in Canada and around the world. It is the very organizational design of government that serves as an enabler of this. Therefore we need to seriously repair and adjust the system, to ensure undesirable behaviours are no longer the result of our, as Page puts it, 'virtually impotent' public service. Of course, in redesigning our government, we must avoid the five mistakes Sisney refers to. Those mistakes corrupt good design, motivating undesirable behaviours and outcomes in government decision-making. It is that simple.

It also bears repeating, in case you missed the reference earlier, what Page said about the dysfunction in our major institution known as Parliament: "If our democratic Parliament had been functioning as intended, you would have received information from your government first . . . you got information from the PBO only." That, dear reader, tells us that something is desperately wrong with the plumbing. It tells us the government is not behaving in the best interest of Canadians, whatever their background, by performing its duties and making sound decisions based on credible information. The fact that any decisions made are not transparent to parliamentarians (regardless of their political affiliation) and ordinary Canadians is also concerning. This is an indicator that the issues of the day are not being tackled appropriately. It is as if there is some huge leak in the waterworks below ground. And instead of the plumbers fixing the leak, they pretend they know what they are doing, telling those being impacted by the leak, who incidentally are paying them to repair it, that everything is fine—that they need not worry about it. Meanwhile, everyone will be drowning in short order.

Regardless of the fake news and optics management to convince us otherwise, the outcome remains the same. The leak remains below our immediate view, eroding our democracy. Though largely arising from neglect, from not doing what is spiritually right, it remains a form of abuse, given all the adverse results. And where the media have lauded Prime Ministers, Presidents and clerics alike, not based on the fruits of those leaders' work but merely on perceptions of it, they too are culpable. Fortunately, we still have enough credible investigative journalists left who have painted a vivid picture of what is really happening. Without having a real and credible plan to do so, US President Trump said Americans needed to *"Drain the Swamp"* ahead of his election victory. That makes him a poser in the plumbing community where practical hands-on and skilled repairs actually stop leaks.

The Urgent Need for Better Risk Management

We also need to restore the plumbing in our government quickly. We cannot afford to lose more time as people suffer. Former Prime Minister Harper would have us believe that an approach of "incrementalism proved to be the best method of evaluating the effects of policy reform and of building political support for further change."[61] We have no more time to doddle, Mr. Harper! We cannot afford more fiascos and taxpayer waste, emanating from Conservative, Liberal or other misguided governments. Not in the here and now. Unbelievably, in the chapter "Rediscovering Conservatism" in his latest book, Harper also tells us "by any measure, we left the country in good shape."[62] What? He should read chapter 3 of this book over and over again until he repents for the error in his thinking. But I am not sure he can, repent that is. In his own words, Harper states that "my economic conservatism was a conversion early in my adult life as a witness to the failures of Keynesian intervention."[63]

Maybe it is time to bear witness for what is right and true beyond economics. For spiritual people, God's economy is one that is humble. One that serves others instead of oneself. One that does not bear false witness through fake news and other deceit. Maybe we could accomplish a lot more good if we harnessed the power of everyone in Canada, not just the elites who want us to bend toward their will alone. Harper admirably states that we must "adapt conservatism to the practical concerns, interests and aspirations of working-and-middle-class people." True. But based on his track record, I disagree that "conservatives" are currently "well placed to respond to populism."[64] A new approach, incorporating *Democratic Restructuralism* is required, that can be judged by the fruit it bears. So, then. What do we do to expedite repairs? How would a modern day Elijah initiate real *Democratic Restructuralism* to restore all things in our democracy, much as spiritual leaders might restore cracks in the *Tomb of Christ* or an institution that underpins their religion?

Well, if you excuse my boldness (not meant to be overly 'invasive' beyond the body politic), here we can look at OSFI's purpose. Kevin Page even said in *Unaccountable* that former OSFI Superintendent "Julie Dickson and her predecessor, Nick Le Pan, are also recognized worldwide for their superior work . . . their leadership helped ensure we did not have a financial meltdown in 2008."[65] And it does not matter if OSFI is now functioning perfectly or not, as all government organizations may be in need of the proverbial 'Maytag Man' (or Woman) to pay them a visit. The important thing to understand is that there is one OSFI guiding principle that helped Canadians ride out the financial crisis much better than most other countries—even if it is not explicitly stated. We need proper risk management to properly solve our problems, especially those that are complex and changing. But what does this really mean in simple terms? What does it look like in plain speak? How does it help us and our families in our day-to-day lives, where we face more and more challenges?

Well, think of it this way. From a common-sense perspective, the major decisions our political leaders are required to make for our benefit, regardless of the party they represent, need to be based on credible information and sound analysis, taking into consideration all the risks and impacts that may arise from what they choose to do. It then makes perfect sense that government should be organized to do just that! Just as any religious or spiritual institutions should be organized to cultivate the right messages they seek to spread, the right spirit to invoke. Doing otherwise merely undermines the credibility of the message and the intended results. At times, the results may even be wrong, corrupting the body. We all need effective leaders, not ones that only sow disbelief in institutions, perhaps even anger toward them and unintended consequences. We all need to mend and heal in this regard: local communities and nations first, then the entire world, led by positive example. It is the only way forward.

Unfortunately for us, constituents of government, the state is not currently organized to produce effective democracy. That is the reason government does not work and why, in no small measure, history is replete with extremists and evil results. We did it to ourselves. Our free will has been the great enabler in our tragedies, just as it has been in our lives as individuals, myself included. Our elected officials are often unable to debate meaningful issues in the House of Commons, provincial legislative assemblies, etc. because the bureaucracy is set up to fail in so many ways. This means the right decisions often do not get made. Issues do not get raised at the right time, if at all, when they are in desperate need of attention and management by our elected officials. How so?

It goes without saying that Canada, not unlike other modern democracies, faces complex, global and often interrelated issues, such as those associated with the broader economy and international trade (think of the recent NAFTA talks and globalization); the environment (think of climate change); inequality (think of how tough things may be for the next generation); healthcare (think of the aging population); technological innovation (think of the ramifications of the Internet and cell phones), security (think of terrorism and global security issues); and immigration (think of all the displaced people and the impacts on other countries). All of these issues, and more, may have positive as well as negative impacts on people, depending on where you reside and what the obviously numerous risks to you are, etc.

Basic risk management teaches us the following regarding how to manage risks well and properly. You have to first identify the risks, then develop solutions to deal with them, then select the best methods to do just that, then implement those methods, and then finally monitor the situation afterwards—taking action as sensibly required. It is the job of our government to ensure they are tackling the issues that impact Canadians in a positive way.

That means they need to be identifying and managing applicable risks to Canadians so they can make good decisions for all of us. In the absence of the government being designed to have an effective and efficient means of managing the risks Canadians face, it will continue to make bad or wrong decisions for the country and its citizens. Ultimately this would mean Canadians, as individuals and a people, would never be able to maximize our potential. It means that Canada would never be the best country it could be, never mind leading the world by example.

Our greatness can shine if we set ourselves up for success. It will only be then that we can show others around the world, instead of telling them, what needs to be done to achieve a better world for everyone and our shared habitat, the earth. So let's cut to the chase. Who and where is Canada's CRO, again the Chief Risk Officer? For that matter, who and where are all the CROs in the various ministries, departments and agencies within all levels of government, federal, provincial and municipal? If there typically is not a CRO in those organizational structures, how possibly can our leaders in government make informed decisions based on reliable data and relevant debate? Just believing something is right, whether you are Faith Goldy on the far right, or Kathleen Wynne on the left, does not make it so. The government, no matter its political leanings, is far too ignorant in its design for its own good. Its existing structure incorporates the errors outlined in Sisney's *5 Classic Mistakes*.

Do we just base our votes on the soundbites, optics management and spin provided by ill-informed politicians and political parties? Is this the kind of democracy we want? One ruled by clerics of misinformed opinion rather than ministers of truth and reason, guided by scientific facts as well as that 'inner' and spiritual sense of what is right? Should we not require, if not demand, our political leaders have knowledgeable perspectives arising from a well-organized and functional bureaucracy that provides them with information regarding the 'real issues' of the day and their related risks? How can we even know what our government's priorities should be, or that of the political party we most identify with, if they themselves do not know what the bigger risks for Canadians are? And how can our political leaders deal with the risks we face, if they do not even know what those risks are to begin with? So many questions!

Our Historical Dilemma

To address this mess in a constructive way, we should first understand how this illogical state of affairs came to be, how it is that our democracy really does not work for the people. It is then we can truly grasp that something is indeed amiss, that something—not someone—really is to blame for a lot of the problems we face. We need to stop attacking each other, our history and our neighbours. Let's start to understand what's wrong. Let's begin to consider our historical dilemma.

OK, so Canada is a country. For better or worse (I subscribe to the former view because I think this country can move forward and benefit everyone, even those who lost so much earlier and deserve a fair deal), Canada exists. As many of us should know, Canada first came into being when Queen Victoria gave royal assent to *The British North America Act*, later named the *Constitution Act*, with it coming into force by royal proclamation on July 1, 1867. That is why we celebrate Canada's birthday every July 1st. The birth of Canada, referred to as Confederation, was really the uniting of Ontario, Quebec, Nova Scotia and New Brunswick. Other provinces and territories that make up present day Canada joined later. The *Constitution Act,* its amendments, and the *Constitution Act 1982*, as also amended since its enactment, forms the fundamental design of Canada. For the sake of simplicity, we will just call all of the legal bedrock forming Canada, the *Constitution*. I know it can be confusing. Suffice is to say that, right from the beginning, the *Constitution* outlined a fairly basic organizational design for our nation. As you might expect, there certainly was no provision for a CRO, be they the leader of the country or a separate person.

We all know that the British monarch has been a mainstay of Canada, as reflected over time on our currency/coinage, postage stamps and such. The *Constitution* actually stipulates "the Executive Government and Authority of and over Canada is hereby declared to continue and be vested in the Queen."[66] It is not my intention to describe all of the *Constitution,* especially since I am just a layperson who has read it from that perspective. Still, it is instructive to generally understand the early basic design of Canada, to grasp how our government was organized historically. Yes, it is a bit of a snooze fest to read through the *Constitution*. Being ever-curious, I nonetheless read it to try and learn who manages all the risks facing Canadians. I could not discover that but did learn some interesting things.

I learned "there shall be a Council to aid and advise in the Government of Canada; and the Persons who are to be members . . . chosen and summoned . . . to be styled The Queen's Privy Council for Canada."[67] Since that sounds pretty important, we will be looking at the Privy Council in greater detail later. The *Constitution* also describes how "all Powers, Authorities," and such within the government are to work. Fundamentally, "there shall be One Parliament for Canada, consisting of the Queen, and Upper House styled the Senate, and the House of Commons."[68] The *Constitution* goes on in great detail to describe the composition of the Senate and the House, including the qualifications required to be a member of one of those bodies. It also outlines the representation allowed by each province or region of the country. A lot of procedures are described, along with the importance of the Governors or Lieutenant Governors of the provinces and what powers they have. Before you yawn—there were no suggestions for those folks to have any CROs either. For example:

> The Executive Council of Ontario and of Quebec should
> be composed of such Persons as the Lieutenant Governor
> from Time to Time thinks Fit, and in the first instance
> of the following officers, namely—the Attorney General,

the Secretary and Registrar of the Province, the Treasurer
of the Province, the Commissioner of Crown Lands, and
the Commissioner of Agriculture and Public Works, with
in Quebec the Speaker of the Legislative Council and
the Solicitor.[69]

Hmmm . . . There is a section on page 26, entitled "Distribution
of Legislative Powers." Yet even reading that, I could not find the CRO, or
a description of a similarly designated person responsible for risk management.
Presumably the legislature is supposed to manage the risks which Canada faces,
advising the Prime Minister and other government officials accordingly on
what exposures the nation faces and how to deal with them. Perhaps that was
somewhat easier in simpler times. At any rate, this section of the *Constitution*
just says the following: "It shall be lawful for the Queen, by and with the
Advice and Consent of the Senate and House of Commons, to make Laws
for the Peace, Order, and good Government of Canada, in relation to all
Matters not . . . assigned exclusively to the Legislatures of the Provinces."[70]
The section on parliamentary powers does elaborate on what the feds are
responsible for though.

In fact, on pages 26–28, there is an itemized list of several dozen
areas for which the Parliament of Canada has Legislative Authority over. Such
exciting things include the public debt (we all know it seems to keep going up
too), Regulation of Trade and Commerce, Unemployment Insurance, Taxation
(taxes also seem to always be increasing), the Postal Service (not sure if our
senior citizens' mailboxes have all been taken away yet), Defence (got any F-35
Jets by the way?), Salaries and Allowance of Civil and other Officers of the
Government (although the Phoenix system cannot seem to pay anyone properly), Currency and Coinage, Banking, Bankruptcy and Insolvency, Indians,
and Lands reserved for the Indians (the phrase Indigenous Peoples hopefully
has been substituted somewhere), Marriage and Divorce, Naturalization and

Aliens (I take that to mean immigration), The Establishment, Maintenance, and Management of Penitentiaries, and a bunch of other areas—none of which has the term 'risk management' in them.

Similarly (mainly on pages 28–29), there is a list of items for which the Provincial Legislatures have exclusive powers over. But it too makes no reference explicitly to risk management in any of those areas. One ends up confused as to where risk management might begin and end in this country. Adding to the confusion is the fact that provincial or regional responsibilities appear to somewhat duplicate federal responsibilities. There is Direct taxation within the province (yes, ever-mounting provincial taxes), the borrowing of money (you guessed it, more debt!), Public and Reformatory Prisons (those must be different than federal penitentiaries), Hospitals, Asylums, Charities, and Eleemosynary (remember that word when you play Scrabble!) Institutions— other than Marine Hospitals, Shop, Saloon, Tavern, Auctioneer, and other Licenses (I guess that will have to include 'weed' in Ontario soon, too), The Solemnization of Marriage, some Property and Civil Rights, generation and production of electrical energy (oh crap, that is how we got into that electricity mess in Ontario), and a big one here—Education with lots of subclasses. What a nightmare, except for the lawyers who designed this mess and are likely extra billing to work with this complexity at Susie and Frank's expense on Main Street.

And I just glossed over the federal and provincial powers, but you get the idea. Other sections of the *Constitution* deal with the appointment of judges, some specifics concerning Revenues, Debts, assets and taxation, certain Miscellaneous Provisions and the Admission of Other Colonies. I really do not know why some items are capitalized and others are not. Then again, I am not a lawyer—just a guy from Main Street with a knack for spotting faulty plumbing. Taken as a whole, none of the areas of our Constitution speak to who is responsible for managing Canada's risks, be they risks at the federal, provincial or other regional levels. Furthermore, none of the areas state how the leaders of the country can make informed decisions in Parliament or the respective provincial legislatures, etc. One begins to see why the status quo prevails and poor decisions happen all too often, regardless of the colour of the Prime Minister's tie and the appeal of the parties' vacuous campaign slogans.

Admittedly, the world and Canada was a lot less complex around 1867. There were no advanced technologies, such as cars, airplanes, advanced military-industrial complexes, weapons of mass destruction, televisions, computers, GPS devices, smart phones, etc. There were no increasing catastrophic events arising from climate change and terrorism. There was a lot less pollution, and life was likely a lot simpler. The institutions of government were a lot simpler too. That is not to say there were not huge problems to deal with back then. Daily existence would have been a challenge, reflected in the lower life-expectancy rates. Canadian author Susanna Moodie probably said it best in her renowned book *Roughing It in the Bush*: "The unpeopled wastes of Canada must present the same aspect to the new settler that the world did to our first parents after their expulsion from the Garden of Eden; all the sin which could defile the spot, or haunt it with the association of departed evil, is concentrated in their own persons."[71] Then again, "few educated persons, accustomed to the refinements and luxuries of European society, ever willingly relinquish those advantages, and place themselves beyond the protective influence of the wise and revered institutions of their native land."[72] The irony is, they must do so now as we have outgrown the simplicity of some of those institutions that bars our progress toward the garden of democracy.

But even then, as the very idea of Canada was taking shape, a more modern approach to risk management would have benefitted people. The immediate concerns of roughing it in the bush so to speak, obviously would have precluded that. So, too, would feelings of moral superiority on one side of history, as is so often the case. Still, we are left with the historical reality that our Indigenous Peoples could have been treated better. Unfortunately their plight occurred before civil rights movements gained traction around the world.

When Diefenbaker went on to become Prime Minister of Canada in 1958, he continued to be a proponent of civil rights. Ultimately, Diefenbaker's work culminated in "an ordinary act of parliament which would not become lost in controversy over amending the constitution."[73] Of course, under Prime Minister Pierre Elliott Trudeau, the act "would be transmuted into the more comprehensive *Canadian Charter of Rights and Freedoms*."[74] But while civil rights are important for everyone, we need mechanisms to safeguard them. Neither Diefenbaker nor Trudeau advocated for a system of government that embedded informed decision-making within the bureaucracy, let alone the restrictions on monopoly that Thomas Jefferson wanted in the US *Bill of Rights*.

Curiously, in the 1950s, Pierre Trudeau did begin to question government institutions and their workings, "notably the governments in Quebec City and Ottawa". Apparently, "he considered the provincial administration corrupt, autocratic, and socially regressive." He believed the federal government "ignored the French fact even when Louis-Stephen St.-Laurent was prime minister, too casually embraced the American approach to the Cold War, and too often ignored the constitution."[75] Perhaps a bureaucracy being run by the right people at the right time, and equipped to make informed decisions, may have been helpful to the government of the day. Neither Trudeau prime ministers, father or son, have embraced the spirit of democracy that could have bound either of them to their electorate and its wishes. The right institutional mechanisms in government were lacking; they could not discern the will of the body politic to make informed decisions for its common good, including for Indigenous Peoples.

If we look back even earlier at some of Canada's Prime Ministers, before Diefenbaker and Trudeau senior, we can see some of the benefits of trying to make good and informed decisions for Canadians. The views of Prime Minister William Lyon Mackenzie King are instructive here, even though he too did not have or implement a formal risk-management system within government to facilitate informed decision-making. King first took office to lead the country in 1921. For him, "leadership did not mean imposing policies or adopting ones because they were popular." Rather, "it meant a cautious and incremental approach: discussion in cabinet and caucus . . . with the leader ensuring that all points of view were presented and that a consensus would be reached."[76] Sounds like a good basis for risk management to me. It also sounds a bit like former Prime Minister Stephen Harper's view in *Right Here, Right Now*, but it is not. And not just because King was a Liberal versus Harper being a Conservative. So much for originality in Harper's book. Remember, Harper also found 'incrementalism' the 'best method.' But as my own research painfully illustrates, he is no consensus builder like King may have wanted to be. Regardless, we urgently need *Democratic Restructuralism*, not incrementalism, be it Liberal or Conservative incrementalism!

When we look again at the *Constitution Act*, promulgated in 1982, it, too, is entirely deficient in providing for a CRO in the organizational structure of our government, even at the federal level. Of course the *Charter* outlines the fundamental rights we Canadians have. It just does not state how the risks and issues around those rights should be managed to guarantee them outside of the court system. There is description of our democratic, mobility, legal, and minority language education rights. The later does not apply specifically to Indigenous Peoples, just those whose first language is English or French. However, there is also a brief section on the "Rights of the Aboriginal Peoples of Canada," recognizing and affirming their existing treaty rights.[77] Another section discusses "Equalization and Regional Disparities," averring that the government is "committed to the principle of making equalization payments to ensure that provincial governments have sufficient revenues to provide reasonably comparable levels of public services at reasonably comparable levels of taxation."[78]

It all sounds great, but there is still nothing around how those risks are to be managed in a reasonable fashion. The *Charter* portion of our *Constitution* and its championing of the many rights most (I am not convinced the Indigenous Peoples have been treated fairly) of us appear to have is likely well-intended. However, in the absence of there being a CRO and, for that matter, appropriately placed risk-management staff throughout all areas of government reporting up to that CRO, I fail to see how the government can make good decisions to guarantee good intentions. A CRO needs an effective and efficient organizational structure to ensure they can adequately brief our leaders and elected officials on the priority issues and risks that should be addressed for Canadians. Without that, Canadians will never know that our *Charter* ideals and rights are being upheld. Consider the following points stated in the Charter: "Everyone has the right to life, liberty, and security of the person and the right not to be deprived thereof except in accordance with the principles of fundamental justice."[79] But how so? Where is the straightforward and easily discernable mechanism within the structural design of our government that ensures this?

Is there security for our fellow Canadians on First Nations reserves when there is dirty and toxic water, and inadequate housing and social supports? Is there security for our fellow Canadians who serve in our decrepit military, when some of our used submarines are catching fire and other key equipment is obsolete and perhaps unsafe? What of our fellow Canadians reportedly living in areas of severe environmental degradation, such as Indigenous Peoples in Grassy Narrows? How about the tens of thousands of our fellow Canadians employed by the federal government who cannot even get paid properly? Is this security of the person in modern-day Canada? Why aren't these risks being managed with appropriate briefings to our leaders so they can prioritize issues and make informed decisions for our collective good? Where will future generations of Canadians, our children, be without a government that can manage risks to them effectively?

The *Charter* eloquently states that "every individual is equal before and under the law and has the right to the equal protection and equal benefit of the law without discrimination . . . based on race, national or ethnic origin, colour, religion, sex, age or mental or physical disability."[80] Fantastic. But again, without a risk-management mechanism embedded in a well-designed, transparent and streamlined government organizational structure, how do we even know if everyone is being treated equally under the law and not disadvantaged by 'the system,' by a bureaucracy that no longer works? By now you are probably thinking that there surely must be a government-wide risk-management function somewhere in the plumbing of our public institutions. You may even be thinking that provision for this vital piping network likely exists outside the *Constitution,* in the broader plumbing of the federal government. Think again!

Our Epicentre of Problems Revealed

Earlier, I raised the spectre of the Queen's Privy Council as sounding quite important, namely because the *Constitution* deemed it having responsibility to 'aid and advise in the Government of Canada.' So let's take a closer look at the almost 1,000 people-staffed Privy Council. A great place to start is the Council's own organizational chart. For as I have learned at OSFI, that document is a key resource to use in determining any business or operation's key or significant activities. As is the case in the structural design of most government organizations, the Council's organization chart (at March 2017) is convoluted. The head of the Council, Michael Wernick, who has the esteemed title, Clerk of the Privy Council and Secretary to the Cabinet, has ten people reporting directly to him. Such employees include his Chief of Staff. There are also several individuals reporting to Wernick who have Deputy Secretary or Assistant Secretary as part of their respective titles.

One direct report is a Deputy Secretary to the Cabinet, Results and Delivery, whatever that means. Another is Deputy Secretary to the Cabinet, Governance. However, while there is both an Assistant Secretary to the Cabinet, Machinery of Government (a good name for our overly complex and increasingly opaque and impersonal government), and Assistant Secretary, Parliamentary Affairs, there still does not seem to be anyone clearly charged with briefing the Prime Minister and our senior leaders on the top risks facing the country and its people. One is left incredulous, if not stupefied, when confronted by the awful truth. On a colossal scale that defies all common sense, our government has been set up to fail. It is, quite simply, irresponsible. There appears to be no area of our government that methodically identifies, assesses, and prioritizes the issues of the day, based on developing a risk profile of the country (the lay of the land if you will) and a means of managing the applicable risks associated with each issue. As such, with no risk-management mechanism in the organs of our government to guide them, political parties have developed their platforms by blindly throwing darts at voters to see what sticks.

That is why there are so many attack ads on television during election campaigns and the issues of the day seem more salacious and titillating than relevant for Susie and Frank on Main Street. Politics has become theatre, a dull soap opera of optics management. It has no substance other than betrayal of the people it claims to serve. There is less and less clear and coherent debate in Parliament. Meaningful issues and risks are left unaddressed because they are not even surfaced. And that sad reality has not just taken root here, but in democracies around the world—perhaps most pronounced in America. The clerics win. We lose as they minister to more nonsense like incrementalism. The planet loses. Unless we choose a better path forward.

Back to the Privy Council Office (PCO). The Assistant Secretary to the Cabinet, Intergovernmental Affairs, also does not appear to be receiving reports on the issues of the day facing government and the attendant risks that should be addressed on a priority basis. In the final analysis, the PCO has no methodology to advise Parliament and its members on the issues and risks they need to manage. Therefore, it does not really add much value to Canadians who need to make informed voting decisions themselves, and not just on which Prime Minister might look better shirtless. We all know the emperor has no clothes anyway. On its website, the PCO claims to be "the hub of non-partisan, public service support to the Prime Minister and Cabinet and its decision-making structures." Apparently, under the leadership of its head, "the PCO helps the Government implement its vision and respond effectively and quickly to issues facing the government and the country."[81] Really? How so?

If there is not, or no need for, a CRO and a streamlined way to evaluate and report on risks and how they are being mitigated for Canadians, how is the PCO able to realistically function and achieve its claims? Is the lack of true risk management across the entire government, and the resulting poor and largely uninformed decision-making, so woefully apparent in Chapter 3, reflective of a poorly conceived PCO? Quite likely. The PCO is supposed to have three main roles: 1) Advisor to the Prime Minister; 2) Secretary to the Cabinet; and 3) Public Service Leadership. In the first instance, it supposedly "brings together quality, objective policy advice and information to support the Prime Minister and Cabinet."[82] The PCO website states this is accomplished by getting "non-partisan advice and information from across the Public Service; consultation and collaboration with international and domestic sources inside and outside government (including the provinces and territories); information on the priorities of Canadians."[83]

None of this speaks to a truly embedded risk-management framework in the plumbing of the broader government, with risk-based priorities (i.e., issues that need to be addressed and proposed solutions from the various ministries within government, etc.) flowing up through the PCO to the PM and Cabinet. So, I really do not get it. And, regardless of any optics management to the contrary, we have learned from Kevin Page in *Unaccountable*, together with the travesties summarized previously, the current system is not working. On a national level, this situation appears to point to deficiencies within the PCO.

In terms of being Secretary to the Cabinet, the PCO's role is to "facilitate the smooth, efficient and effective functioning of Cabinet and the Government of Canada on a day-to-day basis."[84] And if we ask how that exactly is done, it is seemingly by doing such things as follows: "management of the Cabinet's decision-making system; coordination of departmental policy proposals to Cabinet (with supporting policy analysis); scheduling and support services for meetings of Cabinet and Cabinet Committees; advancing the Government's agenda across the federal departments and agencies and with external stakeholders; advice on government structure and organization; preparation of Orders-in-Council and other statutory instruments to give effect to Government decisions; administrative services to the Prime Minister's Office, PCO Ministers and, in some cases, to Commissions of Inquiry."[85]

Here, again, we see no mention of regularly providing the Prime Minister, Cabinet, or Parliament, with a listing of the issues of the day, or risk-based priorities that require appropriate decision-making by government, derived from a network of risk-management systems and personnel spread across the federal government. Logically, if there is no enterprise-wide (the business of government) risk-management framework or system in government, the PCO cannot possibly give the best advice on government structures and organization. As we will see shortly, existing government organization structures are overly complex, non-transparent, largely self-serving due to human nature, and generally designed to fail in meeting the needs of Canadians.

Certainly the PCO may be there to advance the government of the day's agenda. But it likely is not doing that in a non-partisan way. It cannot, if it is not transparently providing the government with routine risk reports emanating from the government's own various ministries and agencies to facilitate risk-based decision-making, regardless if those reports would support the Prime Minister's agenda or not. I purposefully used the phrase 'not transparently' because, short of there being a national security issue, I believe the PCO should not only be providing the PM and Cabinet with risk-based reports on the issues of the day across all the key government ministries and such, but also providing leaders of the opposition and other MPs, and even the media, with that information as well. The general public should also have access to information impacting their daily lives. Every Canadians' eligible vote would matter a heck of a lot more if they could better discuss the information politicians are basing their views and decisions on. We are all tired of political spin and disingenuous arguments leading Canada nowhere. I will explain how to introduce greater transparency and accountability in government in Chapter 7.

Creating the vital and independent position of CRO within the PCO, as well as establishing independent positions for his or her direct reports within the key ministries and departments of the federal bureaucracy, would meaningfully change the way Canada does business for Canadians. Imagine it, nonpartisan directors of risk management, strategically placed in core government ministries dealing with finance, justice, health, Indigenous Peoples' affairs, etc., all reporting upwards on the real issues of the day impacting Canadians. Imagine a real nonpartisan Risk Management Office (RMO), housed inside the PCO or elsewhere that makes sense, prioritizing the risks that need to be addressed by Parliament. Imagine the RMO providing the legislature, the voice of the people, with all the information it needs to make good decisions. The permanent bureaucracy can generally manage itself, routinely reporting to ministers as necessary. However, an independent RMO needs to assure parliamentarians that the issues and risks facing each government ministry and department are being effectively and efficiently managed.

This is the *Democratic Restructuralism* we require. It would reengage a largely disengaged and indifferent electorate. One that is sick and tired of soundbites and politicians seeking power for their own benefit and that of their cronies, the one per cent. It would also reengage the civil service. In February 2016, the *Ottawa Citizen* reported on Canada's Treasury Board President, Scott Brison, and his push to hire a lot more millennials to transform the federal public service. According to Brison, "The next 'golden age' of Canada's public service will be led by millennials."[86] He seems to think the bureaucracy will change if a significant cohort of millennials joins its ranks. The *Citizen* reported that "he is turning to millennials, who are generally seen to have the skills and attitude to drive that transformation, which Brison argues could create a better workplace for all public servants."[87] Certainly there are talented and skilled individuals in any age group of Canadians.

However, if we consider the mental-illness rates and other problems within the civil service, I doubt the culture will magically transform by adding younger and more technologically savvy bureaucrats to its ranks. What is needed is a government system that actually works. Redesigning it to do just that is what is required, not targeting certain age groups to join the currently dysfunctional system that does anything but consistently produce good results for its employees and the Canadian public. This brings us to the PCO's supposedly third main role, Public Service Leadership. The PCO says it "ensures that Canada and Canadians are served by a quality public service—that delivers advice and services in a professional manner, and strives to meet the highest standards of accountability, transparency and efficiency."[88] In the words of a tech-savvy Internet generation used to email and text messaging, LMAOL. Really! Once again, please refer to Chapter 3 for the truth.

The leadership of governments around the world, including Canada, are more focused on managing their own reputation in the media, through optics management, rather than rolling up their sleeves and doing the hard work of managing the affairs of their country. This optics management is the real 'fake news' that Donald Trump always rails against, but without a true understanding of what is really going on. You do not have to look far to see the government is often engaged in optics management instead of doing what is right. Let's look at a few examples. Perhaps it is best to start with discussing the blame game I mentioned earlier. You may recall that people are often blaming *someone* else for their problems rather than *something* else. Ironically you can even see this at play in the PM's own office and that of the PCO. The Langevin Block, which was the name of the building that housed the Prime Minister's Office (PMO) as well as the PCO until June 2017, had to be erased from history by the Trudeau government. That is because Hector-Louis

Langevin, one of our Fathers of Confederation, and for whom the building was named, has suddenly fallen victim to the blame game.

Instead of tackling the real and desperate situation facing our Indigenous Peoples, such as the fact that more than half the pre-schoolers in foster care are First Nations, Métis or Inuit, the government opted to play the optics management game. It needed to appear to be doing something concrete to improve things for Indigenous Peoples while actually doing very little. Interestingly, as is often the case, it even was unfair for the Trudeau Liberals to blame Langevin for being the culprit behind the residential school system: never mind that it is better to discuss and learn from the mistakes of our history, rather than ripping it apart, treating it as Voltaire quipped—like "a pack of tricks we play upon the dead."

University of Guelph's Professor Matthew Hayday, who specializes in Canadian history, says Langevin might not even have been responsible for the injustice of the residential school system imposed upon First Peoples. This is documented in an article by Naomi Lakritz, published by the *Calgary Herald*. According to Hayday, Langevin "wasn't even" what was called the "Indian Affairs Minister" at the time, but underlings always make useful scapegoats. "The title" apparently "belonged to Sir John A. Macdonald." Worse yet, "Langevin also argued for leniency for Louis Riel."[89]

As Lakritz writes, in addition to pointing out all of this, "The fact that we can acknowledge past wrongs is something to celebrate on Canada's 150th birthday. Acknowledgement and recognition lead to insight, understanding and wisdom."[90] Quoting Hayday's comments on activehistory.ca, Lakritz aptly shows that Voltaire's quip is alive and well, part of the optics management game in Ottawa and other government capitols around the world: "in the absence of more compelling evidence, what (Langevin) appears to be is a dutiful minister carrying out the will of the minister actually responsible for this dossier, insofar as it touched his ministry."[91] It is the height of supreme trickery that the presiding government changed the name of the building it occupies. This chess move led Canadians to believe real change for the better is taking place for Canada's Indigenous Peoples. Yet it is the less prominently visible organizational structure, the plumbing behind the façade of what was the Langevin Block —the Machinery of Government—as the PCO calls one of its departments, that is really responsible for the growing problems plaguing all Canadians: Indigenous and non-Indigenous alike.

We did not need to change the name of the Langevin Block. We needed to change the misguided way its occupants continue to do things. For those dated, obsolete and primitive ways of government are producing undesirable behaviours and outcomes. Reading this, the PCO would likely say it is already implementing cutting-edge risk management within the government and knows what it is doing. And certainly we can see some examples of efforts in this regard. Back in March 2000, a Report of the Assistant Deputy Minister (ADM) Working Group on Risk Management, examined *Risk Management for Canada and Canadians*. The *Preface* to the ADM's 2000 paper, written by Mel Cappe, Clerk of the Privy Council at the time, logically stated the following: "Unpredictability exists whenever and wherever decisions are made, whether of an administrative, operational, regulatory, scientific or policy nature."[92]

Cappe sensibly concluded that "success in managing risk should result in improvements in the quality of government services and the effectiveness of public policy, for Canadians." He suggested that because of this and a few other factors—"risk management merits a strong policy, research and development capacity within the Government of Canada."[93] In case you missed it, this means that at the beginning of the new millennium, in 2000, when the ADM produced its paper, the Clerk of the PCO was telling us Canada's national government needed to be developed so it could be more effective and improve its services to you, me and other Canadians. Therefore, for almost 150 years, since Canada was established, that has not been happening! I dare say this is largely the case in other democratic nations and the main reason democracy is failing around, in what Cappe viewed in 2000, "an increasingly complex and ever-changing environment."[94] Cappe's *Preface* also indicated that the ADM's work on looking at risk management "complements noteworthy efforts that are underway within Departments and Agencies."[95] Hmmm . . .

I do not believe we have seen much progress on this. We have yet to see Enterprise-Wide Risk Management take shape in our national government, evidenced by the appointment of a CRO and the formation of a RMO carrying out this important oversight function. Interestingly, per comments made by Ruth Dantzer (Chair of the ADM), the working group noted that "early in the process, it became evident that approaches to risk management used in Departments and Agencies have developed at different rates and in different direction." Such was the situation almost two decades ago. This is why the Chair stated that the ADM's "primary objective was to identify common elements that are applicable across the Government of Canada."[96] Those common elements were, as the paper discussed, the initial step in creating a risk-management framework for the broader government. Page 11 of the paper further noted that Treasury Board Secretariat (TBS) "is developing a risk management framework for government-wide use."[97]

Apparently, a *Panel Report on Modernizing Comptrollership*, "mandated the [TBS] to create a more systematic and integrated approach to risk management across the government."[98] The ADM paper stated that "the Privy Council Office should work with the Treasury Board Secretariat to ensure that risk communication and consultation practices are integrated into the Government of Canada's Communication Policy."[99] Yet, there is no specific consideration on the need to develop a uniform, effective and efficient risk-management function so that our elected MPs can be empowered to make good decisions in Parliament for the Canadian public. There is no discussion of how MPs should receive pertinent risk-management reports, spanning the government's operations, so they can do just that. In reality, we actually saw the Harper government's command-and-control approach doing almost the very opposite. That government appeared to curb the free flow of information, muzzling people that should otherwise be empowered to do their jobs and speak freely on the issues of the day, backed by sound and credible information.

So what progress has been made in developing and implementing an Enterprise-Wide Risk-Management function here in Canada since the ADM paper's release almost 20 years ago? Not a lot if you search the Government of Canada website and Google for updates. We still do not appear to have a RMO, or its equivalent, overseeing the wider federal bureaucracy. And there clearly is no CRO position within the PMO, PCO, or elsewhere in the Ottawa bubble. Parliament continues to be a weak institution which does not have the ability to make risk-based decisions using credible information and timely reports on a variety of issues. We still do not know what the top risks facing Canadians and the nation are, let alone how they are being managed, if at all. The TBS, which appears to have its own problems as you will see in Chapter 7, does have a Risk-Management Framework posted on its website. It is a document you can read in less than 10 minutes. We can see how the buck is passed to the heads of the sprawling federal bureaucracy in that "the Framework reaffirms Deputy Head responsibility in the effective management of their organizations in all areas of work, including risk management and describes the expectations for an effective risk management practice."[100]

We can doubly see that there have been a few iterations or changes regarding the most recent framework, effective late August 2010. For example, the almost decade-old framework "will be supported by learning resources, which will replace the Treasury Board *Integrated Risk Management Framework* (2001) and the *Integrated Risk Management Implementation Guide* (2004)."[101] Since the framework is principles based, and relies on Deputy Heads to implement those principles, with a little guidance, TBS does not appear to be doing a lot in overseeing risk management as a separate and centralized function. It therefore is not making our MPs more effective in their roles. Rather, "the Treasury Board and the Secretariat provide guidance, tools and expertise to support departments and agencies in implementing a risk-informed approach to management."[102] So who is coordinating risk management for the Government of Canada? The departments and agencies are left to their own devices without a coordinating and independent body. It does seem so and goes a long way to explaining the terrible results Canadians have faced in government decision-making, as depicted in Chapter 3.

Further analysis of TBS's role in government-wide risk management reveals that it "also monitors and assesses departmental and agency performance on risk management through such means as the Management Accountability Framework and reviews of internal and external audits."[103] But again, who is performing an independent government-wide risk-management function and motivating parliamentarians to base their work in the House of Commons on pertinent reports and reviews? Where is the Enterprise-Wide Risk-Management function? Nowhere! In fact, TBS has been deficient in performing its more established financial oversight function, as well as its auditing function, which you will plainly see in Chapter 7. And if TBS is the management arm of the government of the day, which we will also see, it remains unclear how Canadians can be assured it is not politically motivated in its efforts. Those efforts, it claims, include "performing a leadership role by sharing information and fostering good practices on risk-informed approaches."[104]

There is no way of knowing if TBS may be more interested in achieving some shorter term goals in favour of the presiding government's objectives instead of ensuring longer-term results are good for Canadians. This situation reflects two of Sisney's mistakes in organizational design that may be hindering TBS's performance. Functions focused on long-range development (risk management—which TBS has not even developed or centralized well) report to functions focused on short-range results (the reigning government). As well, functions focused on effectiveness (again less than ideal risk-management efforts within a non-independent TBS) report to functions focused on efficiency (again the presiding government). So, although TBS may have some 'risk-informed approaches,' we need to arrive at some kind of final destination.

That should be *Democratic Restructuralism* whereby a more independent risk-management-oversight body ensures that risks are being managed well, in a uniform manner, reporting to Parliament accordingly.

I suspect most of the federal government's departments do not have a formal risk management unit and independent CRO. Why would they if there is no independent CRO at the highest levels of government, in the PCO or elsewhere! That is why it appears we have been betrayed by such abysmal results radiating from Ottawa. We have no independent assurance that all of Canada's government operations are operating as required by the voters. This is not to say that many departments are not doing a lot of good work for and on behalf of Canadians. For instance, the Government of Canada's *Treasury Risk Management Framework* appears fairly comprehensive. It is 42 pages in length and "provides information on the risk-management framework within which the government's liquid financial assets and marketable debt are managed."[105] The governance structure over that esoteric activity includes a risk committee and other committees, as well as a Financial Risk Office. The types of public reports available are discussed, along with how that drives transparency and accountability.

It also appears that Global Affairs Canada, formerly Foreign Affairs, Trade and Development Canada, "follows a five-step risk management cycle for development projects based on the department's Integrated Risk Management Policy, Treasury Board Secretariat guidance and international risk management standards (ISO 31000)."[106] We probably could find some other examples where specific federal departments and agencies, etc. are doing some good work. Again, what appears to be lacking is more uniformity around the risk-management process. This requires a coordinating and independent body to provide the right oversight and reporting to parliamentarians, as well as Canadians where possible. We need a common sense structure and process that supports good and informed decision-making in the legislature, not a piecemeal approach that merely presupposes there is a robust mechanism in place to manage the nation's affairs.

Looking more closely at TBS, we find it acts as the government's management board. This is according to a January 2018 *Cabinet Committee Mandate and Membership* government document, which also states this of the Treasury Board (TB): It "provides oversight of the government's financial management and spending as well as oversight on human resources issues." It "is the employer for the public service, and establishes policies and common standards for administrative, personnel, financial and organizational practices across government."[107] TBS also implemented, in 2003, something known as the Management Accountability Framework (MAF). TBS champions the MAF as "a framework for management excellence," noting that it is "accompanied by an annual assessment of management practices and performance in most departments and agencies." Additionally, "the MAF is a key tool of oversight that is used by [TBS] to help ensure that federal departments and agencies are well managed, accountable and that resources are allocated to achieve results."[108]

Perhaps it could be argued that the MAF is TBS's own type of risk-management framework, used to assess the organizations comprising the federal government. This would be in contrast to its Risk-Management Framework that we discussed above, something that the various government departments and agencies are to use in guiding them to manage their own risks. But this does not seem to be exactly the case when one digs deeper into the public information available. And boy, do I like to seek and find! For example, it appears that the federal government, with the aid of Goss Gilroy Inc., carried out an evaluation of the MAF between November 2016 and May 2017. This is according to TBS's own website, which also states the following in relation to the results of the evaluation—something that emphasizes to me that the MAF has more to do with compliance and general performance of government departments than actual and formalized risk-management oversight: "The evaluation found that TBS should continue the annual MAF assessment of policy compliance and management performance of selected federal organizations." As well: "The government-wide information obtained through the MAF is important for helping TBS understand strengths and gaps in compliance with Treasury Board policy instruments."[109] Apart from this, the review noted that some areas of the federal government questioned the utility of the MAF: "The perceived relevance and usefulness of the MAF varies by audience, with some organization and deputy heads finding limitations in the degree to which MAF can inform organizational management practices."[110] Even more problematically, though (unsurprisingly) I could not find it stated explicitly on the TBS website, MAF, for all its benefits in terms of compliance and such, is not an independent review to start with. The Management Accountability Framework is carried out by TBS, which is an arm of the ruling government itself. So we still have a situation where there is no overall and independent risk-management function in the federal government. That speaks to Sinsney's writings on *The 5 Classic Mistakes*, or certainly a few of the mistakes he discussed.

When you read Chapter 7, you will ascertain that much more needs to be done to ensure our government, funded by our tax dollars, is accountable to the electorate. If we leave the TBS for now though, searching for a risk-management function elsewhere and higher up the food chain of Canada's national government, we still find it absent from the structure of our democracy. Let's take another look at the PCO in what was the Langevin Block. There we find, according to a voluminous document (over 100 pages) entitled *Open and Accountable Government—2015*, signed by Prime Minister Justin Trudeau, that the PCO "is the Cabinet's Secretariat and administers the Cabinet decision-making process on behalf of the Prime Minister."[111] Bingo! The *Open and Accountable Government* guide was actually "prepared by the Machinery of Government Secretariat in the Privy Council Office."[112] Hmmm . . . *Welcome to the Machine* as the Pink Floyd song goes, housed within the Privy that may need some good flushing out of what ails us. The PCO appears to be the epicentre of our problems.

We should look much closer at the PCO guide signed by Trudeau junior, especially because it "sets out the duties and responsibilities of the Prime Minister and Ministers, and outlines key principles of responsible government in Canada."[113] Where better to search for an independent risk-management function and responsibility—responsibility being so ephemeral in any bureaucracy. In the guide, we ignorant voters can enlighten ourselves. We only have to seek and then find out good stuff. We learn that "the work of the Prime Minister and Cabinet is supported by a number of central agencies."[114] Those are our impersonal sounding Machinery of Government and the rest of the PCO, the Department of Finance and TBS. We already know that TBS is the administrative body of the Treasury Board, the latter being a committee of the Queen's Privy Council for Canada. We begin to discern the influence of the PCO is fairly weighty as a centralized agency in our constitutional monarchy. In fact, we see in Annex G of the guide that the PCO "provides the Prime Minister with comprehensive information and analysis on contemplated policies and priorities."[115]

We also learn that the TBS "has a central oversight role to play in government-wide management practices and ensuring value for money."[116] Of note, the guide also states the PCO "includes current and former Ministers as well as a small number of individuals holding honorary positions or who are sworn in to occupy particular offices."[117] But how do those ministers and so on make risk-based decisions? How do they, without assurance from an independent-risk-management oversight body, ensuring they are getting the right information at the right time, and understand how policies and priorities are being managed according to the risks they constitute? And how are we to know the leaders of the official opposition in Parliament are similarly receiving the information they need to do their jobs? Near its beginning, the guide avers that "Parliament is both the legislative branch and the pre-eminent institution of democratic accountability."[118] Yet how can its members do their jobs without the necessary information? Are they just to trust the PCO that the government in power is acting honourably, in the interests of Canadians and the spirit of democracy?

If we dig a little deeper, like my father used to for a living, we can ascertain what Cabinet is supposed to be doing in our federal government. I would like to think that the highest echelon of our government, along with the Prime Minister of the day, are managing the risks facing Canada and Canadians. Chief among those risks is the demise of democracy here and around the world due to lack of informed and risk-based decision-making to improve people's live. I would similarly like to think that Cabinet and the PM are doing the right things instead of just saying the right or politically correct things. Give me a hardnosed, hard-liquor drinking, and cigar-smoking doer like Winston Churchill any day over some mealy-mouthed and pandering fool. If former US President Ronald Reagan were here, he might revert to his quip, "Trust but verify," regarding this situation.

Annex D of the 2015 guide signed by Trudeau claims "the Cabinet is the political forum where Ministers reach a consensus and decide on issues." It is a domain where "considerations must necessarily reflect the views and concerns expressed by Canadians, caucus colleagues and other parliamentarians." Of course, as the guide obviously notes, "decision making is led by the Prime Minister."[119] I still do not see where the enterprise or government-wide risk management is though. There is an admission in the guide that "Cabinet business is extensive"—no doubt, and that "consensus at times is difficult to achieve," especially given "the limited time available to Ministers and the importance of clear decision to government." Apparently "Deputy ministers are expected to ensure . . . that coordination across portfolios is pursued, so that other Ministers are prepared for Cabinet discussion and government decisions are coherent and aligned with overall objectives."[120]

Well that sounds like it should be up to another sensibly structured body, huh? Sounds like those folks, deputy ministers, are pretty busy! Reflecting that is another comment in the guide, stating they are also "accountable to the Treasury Board and the Clerk of the Privy Council for the overall management capacity and performance of the department." This, ostensibly, is why it states in the same paragraph of the guide that "deputy ministers are required to implement the [TBS] Management Accountability Framework."[121]

In case you are wondering, no, I still have not found who or what independently structured organization is ensuring those deputy ministers are doing what they need to, or whether or not those executives believe they are. I have only found evidence of *The 5 Classic Mistakes* in the design of government. So I am at a loss to explain to you how your vote matters. I am at a loss to explain how elected MPs can expect that risks are both understood and well-managed within their respective departments. Ergo, I am at a loss to explain how MPs can make informed decisions. I can only reveal to you why it is that so many bad decisions and results are emanating from Ottawa, why we have all been betrayed. Our leaders do not understand how to design good and real democratic government. They have faith they are doing the right thing when they just say the right thing. The fruit they bear tells us a different story about their faith. For that, we all remain in an endless purgatory, waiting for something good to happen, when we have yet to do it ourselves, earning a salvation that must be deserving.

I really do not see how the PCO, TB and TBS are constructed to facilitate good decision-making in government. The consequences of that are shamefully summarized in Chapter 3. Since I am a glutton for punishment, let's give our search for risk management one final kick at the can as they say. Let's do that before we bring out the sledgehammer that drives home our point on the need for *Democratic Restructuralism* of our government institutions.

I downloaded what is branded the *PCO Department Plan for 2017–18*. It does appear important, even bearing the copyright, "Her Majesty the Queen in Right of Canada, 2017." This plan is about 40 pages long and the first page bears the "Prime Minister's Message," meaning Justin Trudeau's, not Winston Churchill's. Trudeau assures us that "in the pages of this report," we "will see what the [PCO] plans to do in the coming year," meaning "how it intends to coordinate the implementation of the Government's ambitious agenda to help grow the middle class, strengthen diversity and give more Canadians the opportunity to succeed."[122] Strong words, eh?

Trudeau also states the PCO "will continue to make the Government of Canada more open and transparent."[123] Inside the heart of the 2017–18 Plan however, there is nothing that convinces the reader how, or even if it can, achieve this. Nothing advises us how good decisions will be made. It is as if it will magically happen because the government said so. It is no different than a pharaoh of Egypt saying, "So let it be written, so let it be done." There is no mention of creating an independent risk-management function to safeguard Canadians' trust in how our government operates. Senate reform? Well, we all know how that went, and you will see my take on that in the next chapter. The PCO's plans sound and look admirable. It "will coordinate consultations and provide professional and non-partisan advice to," among other things, "advance the development and implementation of the Government's agenda and priorities," Those priorities include "a clean environment and strong economy" and, of course, "growth for the middle class" plus the "open and transparent government" mentioned earlier.[124]

We learn also that PCO's plans will "support senior leaders and advancing the renewal of the Public Service." It will additionally "promote a healthy work environment."[125] And yet, as former Conservative MP Brent Rathgeber wrote, the PCO has historically been long on fluff and short on actual implementation of practical measures to achieve this. There can be no 'golden age' of the public service, as Treasury Board's Scott Brison has called for, when, for example, and as Rathgeber discussed, "In 2013, the Clerk of the Privy Council Office released his plan to renew and reinvigorate the federal public service. It was largely fluff, addressing citizen engagement and smart use of new technologies. But nothing in the plan addresses the degree of independence that the federal bureaucracy once enjoyed."[126]

Returning to our discussion of the PCO's 2017–18 Plan, it is nice and fluffy too. Under the category, "Strengthen internal management practices," it states the "PCO will provide coordination, advice and support to: Continue to enhance security and efficiency of information management and technology and physical infrastructure; and Deliver timely services by improving tools and processes."[127] Boy, that all sounds great. Awesome optics management. Too bad the results do not match the claims. Phoenix and other doomed technology projects speak to the failure to adequately launch all of these lofty plans. The missing 'how to' aspect in the PCO's Departmental Plan also probably, and in no small part, reflects that failure. It was the same with Obama and Trump's slogans, different as they were, in America. Included in the PCO's "Raison d'être," are comments that it "coordinates responses to issues facing the Government and the country," and that it "supports the effective operation of Cabinet."[128] I just don't buy it.

The PCO cannot possibly work without proper and independent oversight of the day-to-day workings of government. We have witnessed that in the adverse outcomes Canadians face, regularly emanating from a broken and dysfunctional government. It is not merely that we have a lot of bad people in government. People are generally good and want to do the right thing, even in the PCO. It is only that the machinery of government does not work properly. The system is built to largely fail in our modern and increasingly complex environment. The system of government must be democratically restored. Its ecosystem, which principally involves people rather than machines (technology only amplifies the underlying design and people processes it should support), must be made healthy, productive and useful to Canadians.

The Privy Council Office's 2017–18 plan does state that "there are emerging domestic and global economic and political trends that demand fast-paced responses to emerging issues with precision and thoroughness." Absolutely! Moreover, "PCO must be able to provide timely advice, and respond effectively and quickly to issues and policy challenges facing the Government and the country as they evolve."[129] Sounds perfectly reasonable! But here is the thing my friends. How? That is the crucial problem in need of a solution. PCO's plan includes details on the "key risks" it faces. They are things that could affect its "ability to achieve—our plans and results."[130] Unfortunately, the plan does not list and prioritize all the risks the government and our country are confronted by. At this point, I dare say it stands to reason that the erosion of our democracy should be top of mind. Talk about an irony. It speaks to the desperate need for Canada to devise a way of ensuring our duly elected Members of Parliament are able to make risk-based and informed decisions for the good people of this great nation, the one we call home.

On the restoration of democracy, everything else depends. The means to harness every Canadian's inner sense of what is right instead of wrong, their spirit, must be restored. The resulting common good must be reflected in our system of government, our body politic. This is the Holy Grail of democracy that must be attained if we are to lead by example. If we wish others to voluntarily adopt their faith in a system, such as democracy, we must be persuasive and lead by example. It will not do to adopt the approach of a self-serving cleric, a wolf in sheep's clothing. We need confirmation that everything is working as it should.

A final word on PCO's current plan. Contained within it is a Departmental Spending Trend Graph. It indicates that PCO is spending about $182 million and $155 million in fiscal years 2017–18 and 2018–19, respectively.[131] Planned headcount for the overall department is reducing from 1,046 in the 2017–18 period, to 1,022 in 2018–19, which probably explains a bit of the decrease in year-over-year planned budget.[132] Nevertheless, given the deficiencies of not having a solid risk-management plan to achieve desired results, are Canadians getting the bang for the buck in funding the current machinery of government? We likely need a better system. We will now expand on the solution to getting more desirable results for our hard-earned tax dollars. This solution not only obtains better results to improve 'all' Canadians' lives, it will, by extension, improve the culture of the Canadian public service and shine as an example to other countries, in terms of how to improve democracy.

Regardless of the efforts of existing leadership structures within TBS, PCO its master, or even Cabinet and all the way up to the Prime Minister's Office, existing risk-management capabilities in the federal government are insufficient. They are unable to allow parliamentarians and the highest levels of our government's leadership to do their jobs. Any optics management initiative duping voters into thinking otherwise is massively outweighed by the evidence that we are in dire need of a CRO in government. That CRO is required to facilitate informed and better decision-making in government, not the muzzling of it. The evidence for this need is overwhelming. One could document an almost unending litany of examples, but due to limitations concerning the desired length of this book, here are just a few beyond what was laid out in Chapter 3.

Earlier we discussed Kevin Page's experience at the PBO and how that oversight body may have been 'set up to fail.' Coincidentally, the *Ottawa Citizen* published a lengthy piece by James Bagnall late last year entitled *Built to Fail: Politics sabotaged Shared Services before the department got off the ground.* That article traces the development of the ill-conceived and multi-billion dollar boondoggle (for taxpayers) called Shared Services. This organization was to centralize, modernize, and I have come to sadly—if not jokingly believe— weaponize the government against itself. Indeed. When career bureaucrat Liseanne Forand became its first president in August 2011, her mandate was, as Bagnall puts it, "breathtaking in its scope and complexity."[133] Examples of the mammoth scale of her responsibilities are as follows: in dealing with "about one-third of the federal government's $5-billion-a-year technology services budget . . . she was to simultaneously streamline and modernize the government's electronic backbone, and keep the old gear running." Her job also meant that "more than 500 data centers were to be decommissioned, to be replaced by a mere handful." As well, "fifty telecommunications networks connecting 3,500 federal buildings were to be upgraded."[134]

Just as Page's PBO faced nonsensical obstacles, so, too apparently did Forand's Shared Services. On her first day, "she had no office and the paperwork had been approved for just 1,200 of an eventual 6,000 employees."[135] However, it was only that same day that then Public Services minister, Rona Ambrose, and Treasury Board president, Tony Clement [now Harper's deputy at the International Democratic Union, unless he gets dismissed or resigns due to recent scandals], publicly announced new measures that will improve the efficiency of information technology services. The birth of Shared Services was, according to Ambrose, to "generate 'substantial savings' through economies of scale." Bagnall writes that "it was up to Forand to flesh out a strategy that had little substance at launch."[136] Astoundingly, Prime Minister Harper, on advice of the PCO, was already preparing government spending reductions that would, as Bagnall reports, "hobble Shared Services before it could even get going."[137] Maybe this is an example of Harper's incremental approach to solving our problems, which actually doesn't. So how was the new department hobbled? It went like this . . .

One of the deputy secretaries of the 950 employees at PCO, Daniel Jean (who reported directly to the head of the PCO at the time), was tasked with conducting a 'comprehensive review' on government spending on administration and overhead expenses.[138] Strikingly, this was not done in a transparent manner for the voters and likely Parliament itself to debate the findings. Apparently this is "typical PCO modus operandi."[139] Ultimately, just before the spending cuts, most of the Canadian government's departments were obligated to shift their IT groups and budgets, about 40 per cent on average to Shared Services, including some departments that were reluctant to do so, such as Canada Revenue Agency (CRA) and Department of National

Defence (DND). According to Bagnall, "the move would not be subject to scrutiny by Parliament" when Shared Services was created in the fall of 2011. [140] Worse yet, there does not seem to have been any common-sense-oriented risk management over this project. As we will see later, that circumstance is something the ill-fated Phoenix project has in common with Shared Services. Not that a lack of appropriate stewardship in managing risks is limited to IT projects in government. The disease is rampant in the bureaucracy.

Is it any wonder, given the lack of a national CRO properly placed within government, and the absence of a network of risk-management personnel embedded throughout government organizations reporting up to a CRO, that risks go unaddressed? I for one am not surprised that Shared Services and Phoenix have failed so abysmally. The risks associated with these projects were not adequately identified and managed. In all likelihood, this situation is persisting. As Bagnall indicated, "Cabinet—and to some extent the PCO—failed to account for the complexity." [141] Also, and something which plagues many executive ranks within a disturbingly high number of government departments, including its highest positions of leadership, a lot of the senior bureaucrats at Shared Services did not possess an IT background. Bagnall notes, "Most of the responsible bureaucrats were not trained in IT, yet were tasked with remaking the country's electronic infrastructure." Additionally, "Many also lacked experience in project management with a heavy IT component." [142] Exacerbating this already dire situation, it was only about two months after Shared Services was created, that its funding was cut.

When it was initially formed, Shared Services had been allocated roughly $1.5 billion for an annual base budget. However, shortly thereafter, Treasury Board wanted the fledgling and poorly conceived operation to cut that amount in phases over the next three years, by $150 million, to help reduce the government's national deficit. [143] One could go on and on at length about the Shared Services debacle, quoting a multitude of sources, such as those discussing the poorly handled consolidation of the federal government's email system. In the end though, from a common-sense perspective, especially considering how the organization did not have the budget and appropriate personnel to effectively operate, there was a colossal failure of risk management. The organizational structure of the government seems built to fail. And the failure of hugely important and expensive (to taxpayers) projects are symptoms of this malaise that destroys our democracy. It is the same disease eating away at the fabric of America and the European Union, fuelling Brexit and other divisions across the globe.

High-tech IT implementation plans are all well and good. They are likely needed to keep things going and to get things done. It is also reasonable to expect that government must attract tech-savvy millennials to the public service by offering modern tools for such new blood to work with. However, politicians playing the 'hipster' in Ottawa by having a bunch of media photo-ops and taking selfies does little to cure the real structural problems government faces. It is like deciding to install a turbo charger on a rusted out hulk of a car. If that vehicle has a wheezing engine that has not been properly maintained by qualified mechanics, who actually know how to do the required work to keep the fundamental parts of the motor running in top shape, what is the point of tacking on the turbo? Slapping it on and installing the latest tuning software will achieve very little in improving the performance of a tired-out clunker. It would be better to restore the car first, and probably a lot cheaper. We should apply that understanding in our approach to restoring government, so our democracy actually works for citizens.

Consider the unacceptably absurd costs of the Phoenix system, another unwanted IT child conceived by a dysfunctional public service that did not know what it was doing. The poorly thought-out design of our current government that does not include a risk-management function, is one reason for this. Another is that some misguided and egotistical politicians calling the shots, rather than qualified and empowered civil servants, have forced their inept ideas on the rest of us. Bagnall is absolutely right in pointing out that Shared

Services and Phoenix have something in common: "a botched introduction caused, it appears, by deep flaws in how government operates." He notes that "cabinet ministers and bureaucrats underestimated complexity and risk."[144] Again, is that any wonder, just as other departments have in relation to the host of issues I summarized in Chapter 3? When there is no system to identify, assess, prioritize and manage risks and complexity within government, the results are unsurprising. We only end up with mass confusion and piles of wasted taxpayer money when the right hand does not know what the left one is doing.

We also end up with the pendulum of our politics swinging from extreme right to extreme left. This is because voters prefer to blame political parties and their respective ideology for any problems they face—it's those damn lefties in striped socks, not us; or it's those right-wing fanatics who are responsible, not us! We end up blaming our perceived enemies, rather than the real one. And as for the real enemy, it is the one within. It is that 'something' wrong inside government that does not reflect our real spiritual desires, the prevailing desire to do right by each other. It never was a case of us versus them. If you fell for that beguiling message, sown by so many of its protagonists on the extreme right or left of our political theatre, then please begin to look behind the curtain of staged events. The truth is there. It is also within ourselves. Sometimes we battle our own enemy within, our own personal defects. We must always chose the righteous path. Sometimes, as the great writer W. Somerset Maugham opined, "The path to salvation is as narrow and difficult to walk as a razor's edge," but walk it we all must. We should do so without blame.

I was unsurprised to learn from the media that, in the case of some former top leadership at Shared Services, they were not impressed with how things work in government. To quote Bagnall's lengthy article again: "Privately, with colleagues, they have expressed frustration with the slow pace of getting things done in government, often related to multiple tiers of oversight by Treasury Board, Public Services, the PCO and other departments affected by Shared Services' plan."[145] That statement reminds me a lot of my time living in Belarus, shortly after the collapse of the USSR. The bureaucratic nightmare of communism and its impacts on the general population were still visible. So, too, were the impacts of the Soviet regime's successor in Belarus, the dictatorship of Alexander Lukashenko. His strong arm continues to flex its long-term authority over the land he rules.

The world's modern democracies are by no means the equivalent of Stalin's USSR. But make no mistake, their bureaucracies are not operating the right way for any of us, including civil servants employed within them. Back to the Phoenix system plaguing federal employees here in Canada, and just to make it crystal clear that it, too, was set up to fail because the risks were never managed from the get go. As we all know from legions of media reports, the federal payroll system was originally to cost $310 million and was advertised by the Stephen Harper Conservatives as a way, just like Shared Services, to save taxpayers' money. Implementation of Phoenix was to save taxpayers $70 million a year by centralizing all the different payroll functions that existed throughout all the government departments across the country.[146]

Of course, there seemed to be a political imperative here that superseded the practical one, and not only because risk management was absent from the decision-making process to centralize the payment system. As we all know, the Conservatives did away with the long-gun registry based in Miramichi, New Brunswick, costing 200 jobs there. They did this before subsequently announcing, in 2010, that the new centralized federal payroll system would move to Miramichi, which now houses the infamous, and apparently almost useless, Phoenix payroll system. Under the old system, some 2,000 or so payroll or compensation advisors, working in more than 100 departments across Canada, handled the pay for Canadian federal employees.[147] Generally, these folks were experienced and knew what they were doing, including with respect to complex payroll situations, including various types of leaves, overtime, shift work, applicable retroactive pay, acting pay, reimbursement for government business expenses, and so on.

All told, they handled about nine billion transactions, worth about $17 billion a year, for 300,000 employees in 110 departments. [148] Yet, in October 2016, when almost 1,000 payroll advisors handling those tasks received notice they were losing their current jobs due to the consolidation and transfer of work to Miramichi, that was the beginning of the end of any perceived efficiency in carrying out the rightful and proper compensation of our federal employees. Being paid accurately, I dare say, actually motivates federal employees to do a good job themselves, which requires discretionary effort given the demand for civil servants to possess the right skills, knowledge and experience in our increasingly complex world (approve clinical trials and drugs at Health Canada, perform risk assessments of financial institutions at OSFI, service and operate military equipment at DND, and a host of other vital services valuable to national security and the welfare of Canadians).

As mentioned by Rick Gibbons in an October 2017 article published by the *Ottawa Sun*, obviously "downsizing hundreds of pay experts across the country in order to relocate a new federal payment centre equipped with inexperienced staff and untested software in Miramichi was ripe for failure and . . . no other community with little resident technical expertise and virtually no institutional memory would have fared any better." [149] It does sound like the wrong kind of *Democratic Restructuralism* we need. It sounds like blind decision-making, something we can no longer tolerate *Right Here, Right Now* Mr. Harper. Our faith must be right and true, not resting just on people's economic well-being and an egotistical form of clericalism, but the well-being of the entire body politic: its spiritual, environmental and cultural well-being; the well-being of its access to healthcare, judicial and defence capabilities; and most of all, the well-being of its inherent democratic rights.

Compounding matters that set Phoenix up for failure were two other key issues. Each of them illustrates what appears to be a complete absence of risk management within government to support informed decision-making. As one former compensation manager referenced by Gibbons opined, "The system had not been fully tested prior to implementation." And "yet, by this time government departments had retired or reassigned compensation advisors so the expertise in Ottawa had diminished completely." Secondly, when a backlog of outstanding transactions began mounting, many of which were more complex cases requiring human rather than machine decision-making, the government still demanded Phoenix continue to handle the pay of additional departments. In the words of the former compensation manager, "The government insisted they had to meet the targets and the workload became overwhelming."[150]

Of note, IBM started work on the new pay system back in 2011. The rollout first impacted 34 federal departments in February 2016, with another 67 departments using it the following April.[151] As in the case of Shared Services, this too points to a serious management issue in Ottawa: the lack of the bureaucracy being designed to manage risks. Indeed, as the Auditor General (AG) stated in the House of Commons when presenting his report on the Phoenix nightmare: "They didn't understand the size of the problem."[152] The absurdity of uninformed decision-making in Ottawa reflects, not only the grave inadequacy of the design of our modern democratic institutions to facilitate appropriate outcomes for citizens, but a misplaced belief that technology is a panacea for our government's inefficiency. The very idea that technology is always the answer, when complex and unique situations are more easily handled by people in a more cost effective manner, is glaringly questionable. It reminds me of all the financial models, the 'black boxes' created by IT and actuarial 'quants,' that failed so miserably in their algorithms in predicting the financial crisis. Welcome to the machine, indeed.

AG Michael Ferguson's report indicates that "Phoenix was designed to include almost 200 custom programs to handle the 80,000 different pay rules inside the federal government." However, "it took Public Services and Procurement Canada more than year to determine that it needed to analyze the 200 programs in order to fix Phoenix, and by June 2017, it had looked at only six of them." [153] All the while there were countless media reports of many of the 300,000 strong federal employees being underpaid, overpaid, or not paid at all, including single parents, students and others who need to make ends meet. One can only marvel at the government's tenacity in insisting that the clearly unworkable pay system continue to be used, even after more than 18 months of its apocalyptic use. The fact that the Senate is looking to adopt a different payroll system than Phoenix just adds insult to injury. Certainly, we cannot have our politically appointed and largely well-heeled senators having their pay screwed up. Our government's tolerance for such a debacle only extends to the rank-and-file members of the bureaucracy. They, of course, are the ones who actually provide day-to-day services to taxpayers instead of generating scandal after scandal in the upper chamber.

The Phoenix disaster also reveals how the blame-others approach is always present in government and its politics. Rather than fixing the plumbing that led to the payroll disaster, which points directly to the PCO and the lack of a well-organized and independent risk-management system within government, our amateur leaders chose to castigate each other and play the blame game. Everything comes down to optics management instead of doing what is right, which would unify Canada. That is the problem with politicians here and around the world. Rather than performing their roles, they are all playing them. Performing a role takes vision, commitment, a proactive mindset and, most importantly, hard work. Playing a role more closely aligns to what Donald Trump laments so much south of the border, 'fake news.' The only trouble is he is part of the problem. Although he aptly surfaces the issue of fake news most citizens of democracy are only peripherally aware of, he masters it for his own use. And that, of course, is not the Good News we need, the restoration we require.

We are increasingly at the mercy of optics management: being fed information to reinforce the image our leaders wish to cultivate for themselves and their political parties. Their message tell us that everything is alright when it is not. Sometimes their message takes the form of entertainment as well as misinformation. Whether it is a background story of the types of socks our Prime Minister is wearing or the vacuous tweets of the leader of the free world down South, the truth and important issues of the day, become increasingly elusive. We are left just feeling that something is wrong, but we cannot exactly put our finger on it. We need to start telling the truth. We need to rebuild our government institutions that are wreaking havoc on the very people they are charged with helping and benefitting. Before our flag frays even more, symbolically reflecting Canada's deepening fragmentation, we need to elect a leadership that performs its role rather than plays it. Only then can our collective and desperately required task of *Democratic Restructuralism* begin to take shape. Only then can we have representative government for everyone, despite race, colour, creed, religion, gender and area of residence, including Quebec. We all need a voice and mechanism to solve the mounting problems we face as Canadians. The restoration of all things is possible when we unite in the spirit of doing what is right.

Abraham Lincoln once famously said, "You cannot fool all the people all the time." With this in mind, and understanding that most Canadians know the difference between right and wrong, we all need to wake up from our long slumber. It has been far too long that we have been fooled by those playing the optics-management game in the affairs of our nation, not theirs. All is not well with that which has traditionally bound us (save for some who deserve genuine redress for past mistakes) as Canadians during simpler times. Our democracy and its institutions are coming unglued and negatively impacting us and our families. Many government institutions and projects are set up for failure before they are implemented, with the PCO failing to do what it claims to do: "coordinate responses to issues facing the Government and the country." That means, Whittington argued in *Spinning History*, "the clerk of the privy council, the most senior public servant, needs to do more to protect the integrity of the 250,000-strong federal public service, which is paid for by Canadians to serve Canadians as an institution meant to function independently of the political aims and promotional activities of the ruling party."[154]

Of course, we should not blame the PCO and its head, Michael Wernick, for the predicament that organization finds itself in. The PCO is likely unable to mandate the changes needed, either because its masters do not want those changes, or because they are oblivious to the changes required. A Prime Minister and Parliament interested in making government really work for all Canadians has to restructure its operations, avoiding Sisney's fundamental mistakes in organizational design at the outset of that restructuring. We need democratic forms or structures to follow functions that are democratic themselves. Sisney would argue that the 'design' must suit the 'purpose' in organizational structures. That is why the universe contains so much order.

Applying Enterprise Risk Management in Government

So, what exactly is Enterprise Risk Management (ERM)? The reputable Committee of Sponsoring Organizations of the Treadway Commission, or COSO, defines it as follows:

> A process, effected by an entity's board of directors, management, and other personnel, applied in strategy setting and across the enterprise, designed to identify potential events that may affect the entity, and manage risk to be within its risk appetite, to provide reasonable assurance regarding the achievement of entity objectives.[155]

Quite a mouthful. But if we read this over again, substituting the word 'government' for that of 'entity,' we can discern how critical ERM is to a properly functioning and 21st century government dealing with all the growing and complex risks impacting Canadians and others globally. In simpler terms, the International Standard Organization (ISO) defines risk management as being "coordinated activities to direct and control an organization with regard to risk." [156] Obviously we need an independent function in the government's plumbing to perform this hugely important task; a job that can and must be designed to inform parliamentarians on the issues of the day so they can make good decisions for Canada and all Canadians. This is the right thing to do. So, too, is recognition that it is not just significant economic risks that should be known, assessed and managed. Our souls are not mere economic units waiting to prosper financially from available supply and demand. Our fulfilment must come from greater abundance than that only found in capital markets.

Major risks to Canadians' health and well-being must also be understood, prioritized, and effectively dealt with. Although there are interrelationships between many risks and issues, non-economic risks associated with climate change and environmental degradation must be tackled. A balanced approach is required that manifests the will and spirit of all Canadians, not just the one per cent or a few politicians and their cronies. We may not like the current leader of America, but a July 2016 memorandum issued by the Office of Management and Budget (OMB) within the Executive Office of the President of the United States during the Obama administration, is highly noteworthy. The *Memorandum to the Heads of Executive Departments and Agencies,* sent by OMB Director Sharon Donovan, discusses *OMB Circular No. A-123, Management's Responsibility for Enterprise Risk Management and Internal Control* (the Circular)—attached to Donovan's note. Yeah, I know this is kind of esoteric stuff, but bear with me as we get to its importance.

According to Donovan, "The policy changes in this Circular modernize existing efforts by requiring agencies to implement . . . [ERM] capability coordinated with the strategic planning and strategic review process established by [the Government Performance and Results Act Modernization Act] and the internal control processes required by [the Federal Managers' Financial Integrity Act] and General Accountability Office (GAO)'s Green Book." [157] It is a lot to swallow for sure, but it all points to the Obama administration's perceived need to have, as Donovan wrote, an "integrated government structure" to "improve mission delivery, reduce costs, and focus corrective actions towards key risks."[158] The Circular itself mentions that the US "Federal Government's core governance processes are defined by [OMB] budget guidance."[159] The Office of Management and Budget sounds similar to Canada's Treasury Board. The Circular itself is about 50-pages long. Interestingly, its introduction states that "leading international standard setters in the fields of risk management and internal control including both . . . [COSO] and the [ISO] incorporate internal control as part of the larger risk management process."[160]

The Circular covers a lot of ground. Of the seven key sections discussed, Section II "defines management's responsibilities for ERM, and includes requirements for identifying and managing risks." Also, and "most importantly, it encourages agencies to establish a Risk Management Council . . . develop 'Risk Profiles' which identify risks arising from mission and mission-support operations, and consider those risks as part of the annual strategic review process."[161] Section II of the Circular finds that "some agency governance structures are beginning to include a Chief Risk Officer (CRO), or equivalent function who champions agency-wide efforts to manage risk within the Agency and advises senior leaders on the strategically-aligned portfolio view of risks at the Agency."[162] Section II includes deliverables and due dates, such as agencies being required to develop their initial Risk Profiles by June 2, 2017. That all makes sense. However, and similar to Canada's own TBS, it is US government agencies' own "Management" that "is responsible for Enterprise Risk Management systems."[163] Or, as stated again in Section V, "Correcting Internal Control Deficiencies," "identifying and understanding of the root cause of control deficiencies is management's responsibility."[164]

The United States GAO appears to do a lot of good work, as we will see in Chapter 7. It may oversee American agencies' progress implementing ERM per the OMB's Circular. We do not want to spend a lot of time reviewing the

American government's recent attempts to embed an ERM program within its government. Still, we should understand, especially given all the debacles under the Trump administration, that our southern neighbours are also likely far from having a functional and consistent government-wide risk-management system. Certainly, and just like Canada's own TBS, there is not an independent risk-management function that has its own employees embedded within the various US government agencies. We will also see later in this book, that some distinguished and experienced Americans, who have been members of Congress, view that hallowed US institution to be dysfunctional and broken. Sound familiar? Therefore it seems logical, and surely when you turn on the US news, fake or otherwise, to conclude that sensible risk-based decision-making is not occurring in an empowered and effective Congress.

When we saw children being torn from their parents at the American border and separated for prolonged periods of time, and all the ensuing protests about how heinous, obscene, and un-American this situation was, it pointed to poor decision-making by the US government. It does not matter, and please understand that I am an admirer of much of America's rich and vibrant history that positioned that country as a role model for others, whether you are for more US immigration or not, as an American citizen. The implementation of a misguided policy that resulted in families being separated at the border, including babies from their mothers, reflects a gigantic failure in risk management. I severely doubt the failure of sound and risk-based decision-making like that reflects the will of the American people. It is likely just the will of American's bully pulpit, in the form of Donald Trump, who may or may not know that the devil is always in the details where management is concerned.

Again, we have our own problems here in Canada. Everywhere you look democracy has become an abstract perversion of what it originally was intended to be. Something good and right for people. So what do we do to make things work better, to metaphorically mend the flag? Earlier, I intimated that the PMO and PCO need to be democratically restructured. Not merely, and quite possibly, unfairly, by renaming the moniker of what once was the Langevin Block, where those offices reside, but more importantly by reconfiguring how the highest levels of our government actually operate. The erstwhile Langevin Block must contain an independent Risk Management Office (RMO) headed by an independent CRO. That would be of much greater value to Canadians, Indigenous and non-Indigenous alike, than the optics management of blaming others for the sins of the past, than changing names to suit image makers that are inauthentic in their approach to making amends. It would be of greater importance than politically appointed Senators who may not be required to begin with if our MPs in the House of Commons could effectively perform their roles. More on the Senate in the next chapter.

MPs should be doing real work, getting briefed routinely on the risks facing the government's various departments meant to serve Canadians, through the RMO. We likely would attract many more talented Canadians to run as candidates in our federal elections if everyone knew our Parliament was designed to empower MPs to make a real difference in the lives of ordinary Canadians. Having the RMO facilitate good decision-making by parliamentarians, as well as transparent and accountable government, is apt to generate interest among a multitude of Canadians looking to help make meaningful and positive changes in their communities. It would not matter if you are black, white, Indigenous, woman or man, etc. The work you would do in the legislature in relation to the information and data you receive, would be visible for all Canadians to see. The potential of this *Democratic Restructuralism* is hugely transformational. It can result in Canadians doing the right thing in terms of public policy and improving the quality of life for everyone. Our votes will begin to really matter as we shape the future of our great nation based on credible information and policies most Canadians want. Political parties would still be there to give their views, but those views would be based significantly less on optics management and fake news.

When political parties must tell us 'how' they credibly intend to implement certain political platforms and what sound information (provided by the RMO) underpins their policies, along with the expected results, we will harness the kind of civic and voter engagement our democracy requires to thrive. That is truly restorative. It is a process that would utilize the collective will and sense of right versus wrong within each of us. Susie and Frank on Main Street would likely feel they can make a difference by voting. Of this, I am sure. And, as in the case of ordinary MPs, the Prime Minister similarly needs to be briefed regularly by the RMO on the risks facing the nation. During election campaigns, each candidate running for Prime Minister should also tell Canadians how they would manage the nation's top risks. That is more important than whether or not your mother or father used to be an important politician, isn't it? How ignorant it would be for a self-entitled person to think otherwise.

The non-partisan CRO should be elected by Canadians for a set term, ideally one that overlaps that of elected MPs and the Prime Minister. The less influence the better. The CRO should be independent of the PCO and PMO. The RMO should report to both MPs comprising the government of the day, as well as to members of the opposition parties. All elected officials must be accorded the respect of being able to establish informed opinions from which to base their decisions and voting in the House of Commons. The RMO should also provide its independent reports to the permanent bureaucracy's department heads. Where Canada's national security may be at risk, government debates in the House, Cabinet or elsewhere, could occur on a need-to-know basis, with the RMO providing relevant and risk-based information to pertinent MPs and the PM accordingly. Information concerning sensitive issues, such as national security, could likewise be vetted before being made public, through the media or the RMO's website.

The RMO must contain an adequate number of suitably experienced and knowledgeable staff working independently in the diverse organizations of the government. As Sisney discerned in *The 5 Classic Mistakes*, it is not conducive to good organizational design 'Having the wrong people in the right functions.' Having worked for Canada's federal regulator of financial institutions, I can tell you we expect those institutions (many of which generate billions of dollars of income vital to our economy) to have common-sense-oriented processes and structures to manage the complex and emerging risks they face. It should be no different for the regulator, or the rest of government, which bears further scrutiny. This is why Caroline Cerruti and John Palmer, the latter being one of OSFI's most previously esteemed superintendents, had this to say in a report: "There is a need for sufficient numbers of trained and experienced supervisors to conduct a robust and extensive supervisory programme that includes monitoring of the financial system and intensive onsite supervision of financial institutions." Drum roll please . . . "It is important to have a critical mass of staff members who have worked at middle and senior levels of financial institutions, including risk management functions or with equivalent experience."[165]

Common sense! Why should it be any different for government? A newly formed and useful RMO would ensure it isn't! The RMO must also have a sufficient number of support and administrative staff. This is to ensure the work of the CRO and their delegates throughout the federal government is effective, with appropriate reporting to Parliament and its members accordingly. Of course, risk managers or designates of the CRO need to be appointed within the various departments and agencies of the government, where one would expect that to be wise. These individuals can be senior civil servants who are not elected officials but report to the CRO to maintain their independence from the numerous government operations they would be embedded within. Their salary should be paid directly from the RMO.

There would be tension created when independent risk managers from outside a government department are performing ongoing assessments of that very department, reporting to their handler, an independently elected and apolitical CRO. You may wonder if that tension would compromise the very functioning of that department. Not really. The risk reports generated by the RMO's risk managers would be shared with each department's head. And they would have the opportunity to respond to any recommendations regarding issues and attendant risks that may require their attention. It is important there be no misunderstanding. However, the evidence must always be viewed as the basis for truth. Any risk-based recommendations made by independent RMO personnel would be ranked by importance (risk to Canadians), prioritized and presented to department heads so they can implement, where required, appropriate action plans with suitable deadlines for follow-up by the RMO.

Hypothetically, if the case were such that the government department responsible for implementing the ludicrous Phoenix project—Public Services and Procurement Canada (talk about an oxymoron)—were held accountable by the RMO for attempting to implement a new payroll system, without having first properly considered how to manage all the risks, taxpayers likely would not be on the hook now for the wasted billions of dollars producing nothing—nothing but chaos for federal employees and those who foot the bill. Obviously the RMO must be involved in any major change initiatives within government. Risks need to be identified, evaluated and managed early on from a common-sense perspective. This also means RMO staff should be suitably experienced and knowledgeable about the area they are assessing. We do not want a journalist assessing IT risks for example. Unless they wish to spread fake news.

Of course, if the government department responsible for implementing Phoenix told our hypothetical RMO that they knew better and had already assessed all the risks associated with the project, they should have that right. But they should also have the credible proof. A suitably designed appeal committee with the RMO, transparent in its hearings to MPs and the public, could serve as a forum for relevant debate surrounding any appeals by department heads. The important thing is that no major project is launched before major and applicable risks are considered. That, in simple terms, is good management. It is also the right thing to do. Think of a public company's board of directors. They, too, are supposed to be independent of the company's management, although a few members of management often may sit on the board, but hopefully not enough to compromise its independence and objectivity. Where a public company has a CRO, that individual usually has an office within the organization and is paid from its revenues. But the CRO is still ideally independent from management and its compensation incentives. The prudent and useful layer of risk management makes for a better run and more profitable company. That has been my experience at OSFI anyway.

In performing a more independent risk assessment of the company, essentially developing and monitoring the company's risk profile, the CRO can provide valuable insights in its reports to the president, CEO, and board, as applicable. The CRO can advise on matters concerning the well-being of the company. It can report on significant current and potential exposures threatening the company's viability as a going concerning. Management can then make better and more informed decisions to ensure the company remains competitive and profitable. If we consider our Prime Minister as CEO of Canada, and the legislature akin to a Board of Directors, the CRO, supported by what should be a properly designed RMO, can facilitate better decision-making in Parliament. It is Parliament that is the centre of democracy, its preeminent institution. And while government should not just be concerned solely with profits (revenues from taxpayers) and being economically competitive, it too, must make good decisions for participative democracy to be a going concern. The voice of each citizen must be heard and respected by government, just as the voice of each customer must be heard in private business. Doing the opposite only puts an end to the government or business of the day.

Upon an effective risk-management framework being developed by the RMO, it should be implemented and applied in a consistent manner across the national government's operations. The idea is to facilitate a consistent approach in developing a uniform understanding of where material risks exist within the entire government. It is just like being a plumber. You need to know how to build a simplified waterworks and get rid of the clogs. Right now our politics is based too much on the art of decision-making, and all the fake news and optics management that goes with that. But we need the 'Good News' instead. It, of course and quite literally, is the credible and spiritual truth that paradoxically accompanies the science of decision-making. We must be motivated to obtain the truth when pursuing it and striving for positive outcomes. Rathgeber opined that "the system, by design, encourages and promotes sycophancy."[166] That is not how to arrive at good decision-making for customers or citizens. We need to restructure the plumbing to promote good work and culture in government. Establishment of an effective RMO is a linchpin in achieving that.

I agree with Rathgeber that "how a legislature functions is much more relevant to responsible government than how it is chosen."[167] That is why I am not too bothered by specific electoral process reforms such as how local candidates running to represent their political parties are chosen. Certainly I agree with arguments made by Loat and MacMillan that "the nomination process should be a chance to closely explore and debate issues that are important to the community that the candidates hope to serve in Ottawa."[168] I also agree that, among other factors they mention, there should be "fewer parachuted-in candidates. More transparency from the central party and local associations on how nominations are run, and how citizens can participate . . . clear processes . . . explaining how to become a candidate."[169] However, creation of the RMO can address all of this, and so much more, for the right and best candidates to end up in Parliament making the best risk-based decisions for their respective communities.

The RMO could additionally ensure that freshly minted MPs receive the initial and consistent orientation they require to perform their roles. MPs need to be on-boarded effectively, understanding their roles and responsibilities. In the same vein, the RMO could ensure that members serve on various parliamentary committees based on the suitability of their specific knowledge and experience. We saw in *Tragedy in the Commons* that things like this were areas of concern for many MPs. Therefore, not only should the RMO itself be structured appropriately to avoid Sisney's five mistakes in organizational design, but so, too, should parliamentary committees and any other mechanism that supports good decision-making in the legislature. In this regard, the RMO should be involved to optimize good results. A useful example of another mechanism that should support good decision-making in Parliament would be Question Period. Recently, it has been pejoratively described as a kindergarten where disempowered MPs engage in personal attacks on each other; a behaviour that is unworthy of supposedly distinguished parliamentarians.

A more productive Question Period, which would inform Canadians on the issues that matter to them, would have meaningful topics and discussion. It would have the proper background information available, suitable time allotted for the debating of opposing views, and the most subject-expert MPs available to present those views in support of specific issues. One can easily envision the RMO quarterbacking all of this equally for all MPs, regardless of their political party affiliation. That would ensure the debate starts on an equal footing with informed perspectives. Ideology may be important, but so too is evidence-based decision-making that reflects the will of the people. And when there are numerous issues confronting the nation, why not even have additional Question Periods as may be necessary? That, of course, would be common sense. The need for devolution of power from the PMO and PCO looks obvious to me. Considering, as Michael Harris wrote in *Party of One*, "in May 2014, a new poll done by Forum Research found that the Prime Minister's Office was one of the least trusted branches of the federal government, rivalled only by the Senate,"[170] how could it not be?

In terms of the application of a well-thought-out risk-management framework applied by the RMO, the framework would ascertain the activities of each government department. It would determine what services those departments provide to Canadians and each of the risks associated with the delivery of such services. In turn, the RMO would evaluate how those risks are being managed and mitigated by departments and their senior officials. It would assess whether or not the structure of each department makes sense, along with the number and title of the civil servants working there, such that departmental mandates are being effectively delivered for Canadians. One never knows if there are too many cooks in the kitchen. Front-line workers can easily be disempowered or muzzled by wrongly motivated executives who focus those workers on politically or otherwise wrongly motivated tasks and results. A lot of that may have nothing to do with a department's core mandate, thus creating more havoc for taxpayers.

Independent RMO staff must be on hand to see if government departments are sufficiently focused on the right results and the right outcomes for Canadians rather than on too many useless processes and projects that do not add value—that old game of form over substance. Independent risk managers strategically placed within the network of government operations must satisfy themselves that the performance-management system (employees' bonus payments and opportunities for advancement) in those operations is aligned with the results sought under each department's mandate. They must conclude upon who is doing the real work versus projects that just look and sound good to pad the bonuses of those prone to gaming the system. RMO staff must also assess if the department they are assigned to is adequately funded, too much or too little, and the ramifications of those circumstances. A good and independent risk manager, trained to work with an effective and easily understood risk-management framework that is consistently used throughout the government, will be able to figure this and more out. They would report accordingly to the CRO, to Parliamentarians and, where possible, to the public.

If RMO personnel are located within a large ministry or department that deals with complex work and issues (e.g., the Ministry of Defence or Health Canada), they should be supported by a few more staff where this makes sense and can be justified by the CRO. The RMO can further be structured to provide each risk manager and analyst with the training they need to carry out their duties, namely performing a risk assessment of the respective departments they are embedded within. The apolitical RMO would also vet the qualifications and experience of each risk manager to ensure they are qualified, in terms of knowledge and experience, in the area for which they are being tasked to identify and evaluate pertinent risks. This, as we learned from similar comments made by OSFI's former superintendent, John Palmer, is because knowing and applying a certain risk-management framework is not enough to be successful in the role of department risk manager. So, if a RMO employee is performing their work at Heath Canada, they should have some mid- to senior-level experience (ideally as much as possible) working in the medical field in Canada, supported by formal education as a medical professional (e.g., a doctor or scientist in the health field). Background checks to verify this would also be useful given all of the embarrassing moments Canada has faced lately.

The RMO would be publicly funded with, hopefully, the ongoing savings from an abolished Senate. If we cannot abolish the Senate (with the basis for doing so outlined in the next chapter), we may need to reconstitute the Senate as the RMO, and abolish most of what the PCO does in what was the Langevin Block. Something needs to substantially change in the design of our government to democratically restructure it beyond changing names of buildings or departments.

We should also not forget about the need for risk-based decision-making in all levels of government, not just at the federal level. I have focused the discussion here and elsewhere in this book on our federal government, in no small part because it must lead by example, setting the tone from the top. Interrelationships between the various levels of government cannot be ignored, as they are important to ensure local issues are getting the attention they deserve, especially where the actions of the national government have a bearing. Remember the importance of interdependency as reflected in the Indigenous Peoples' philosophy of 'the circle.' Maybe if we had a well-designed system in place to encourage good decision-making, we would not have had the intergovernmental squabbling over the Kinder-Morgan pipeline.

We also know that Canada's *Constitution Act* of 1867 referred to the division of responsibilities and legislative powers between our provinces and the federal government. We alluded to some of those jurisdictional differences earlier. It would be useful to explore how to establish RMOs similar to that of the federal government's within all the provinces and territories, facilitating better results and outcomes for Canadians living across the country, where the region of their residence is also impacting the quality of their lives. There must be a way to expedite creation of RMOs within the provinces and territories beyond, say, Section 91 of the *Constitution Act*. This section gives broader powers to our national government to establish legislation ensuring "Peace, Order and good Government of Canada, in relation to all Matters not coming within the classes of subjects by the Act assigned exclusively to the Legislatures of the Provinces."[171]

I am not a lawyer and do not wish to dwell on how to create more local RMOs, be they provincial, territorial, or even municipal level RMOs. There surely must be a way to do it quickly upon the federal government designing its own RMO. Poor decision-making is clearly a threat to our nation's "Peace, Order and good Government" that needs addressing one way or another. Imagine, if you will, each province and territory being able to prioritize and manage its own risks in the interest of their residents. And where the federal government's own operations have a bearing on those more local risks, imagine representatives of each region's own RMO interacting with the federal RMO to prioritize and resolve those risks accordingly. This process could be duplicated for municipal RMOs (such as the city of Toronto) that similarly could interact with their provincial or territorial RMO. Imagine common sense being applied to arrive at effective decision-making in government. That is how politics can become less the art of decision-making and involve more of the science of decision-making. We need less art in decision and deal-making between all areas of the body politic and more truth. Enough of the fake news already. It is time to seek and find something more conducive to our well-being. The body must be restored.

So you see, *Democratic Restructuralism* is possible at all levels of government. Like dominoes, the concept of knowing how to design an effective and efficient system to facilitate good risk-based decision-making for voters, can trickle all the way down to Susie and Frank on Main Street. We have heard about trickle-down economic theories. It may be high time to introduce trickle-down risk management that reflects the will of the people on Main Street. Since Main Street is usually a two-way thoroughfare, we also need to respect which risks are most important to Susie and Frank, meaning we also need to consider trickle-up approaches in managing risk. Community feedback in risk management is important. And that importance, a public trust, should be reflected during elections, when Susie and Frank cast their votes for the party they feel is managing the country's affairs best. When the voice of Main Street can better pierce the Ottawa bubble and reach the highest levels of power, we can proudly say we have restored our democracy, taking back that which is rightfully ours. This is how to restore the body politic that has been perverted by a form of state clericalism.

We will continue to focus our discussion on the federal government in the next two chapters. But please remember, all of this book's discussion on the concept of *Democratic Restructuralism*, on how to design a better government that restores our democracy, by harnessing our collective spirit to do the right thing, can be applied elsewhere. It can be applied in municipal or regional governments. It can even be applied in other countries, in international organizations (Chapter 8 speaks to this), and even in religious organizations where more earthly institutional practices and structures have become somewhat questionable. The restoration of all things is possible, to a degree, if you believe it so; if you have faith in the power of the collective will of the people and their spiritual desire to do good works. And why not? What else can move us forward? Everyone has been waiting for something or someone to fix things, to perform a miracle. Maybe we all need to take the first step ourselves to show we are deserving of something better. Are we worthy?

We can choose the fake or the 'Good News.' It is up to us, and within us as individuals, to make the right choice. That is our responsibility to the next generation. Since most of us already know the difference between right and wrong already, it is just a matter of doing what needs to be done after we have seen how. Perhaps Britons should reconsider Brexit and convince themselves and all Europeans to pursue *Democratic Restructuralism* instead.

The status quo is an untenable situation when it comes to how existing governments operate. Here, in Canada, the erosion of democracy continues, with poor results reflective of a poorly designed system. The more we permit the existing situation to go on, the more prolonged and greater will our problems and suffering grow. You have seen a few of the egregious failures presented earlier. Many projects like Phoenix and Shared Services appear to have been set-up for failure from the get go. The right infrastructure to facilitate empowered and informed MPs in the House of Commons, where the right decisions need to be made, instead of wrong ones being made elsewhere, such as in the PCO, is desperately lacking.

Is it any wonder that a 2011 Auditor General's report, which examined the military Reserve Force Pension Plan, "found that it had been implemented without adequate planning," something which "created significant backlog?"[172] Is it any wonder, as a self-labeled First Nations person wrote in the *Times Colonist* in 2017, that current Prime Minister Trudeau "is still talking about no drinking water, no proper housing, no transportation to reduce the risk of more men and women going missing or being murdered, discriminatory funding for social programs, education and health, and prisons over-represented with First Nations for misdemeanors due to the lack of legal representation?"[173]

The same First Nations person who submitted these credible views, Jo-Anne Berezanski of North Saanich, hit the nail on the head with this comment: "Perhaps if [Trudeau] were serious about fixing the relations between First Nations and government, industry and the citizens of Canada, he would stop talking and start doing."[174] Of course, it is not Trudeau himself who is to blame. It is a system not designed to generate the outcomes most Canadians want that is responsible for our collective predicament. This sad fact is applicable to Indigenous and non-Indigenous Canadians alike. And the longer this goes on, the more divided we are likely to be as a people who should love one another instead of blaming each other for all that is wrong in our lives.

We need the RMO and we need it soon. We require it to do something better for us all. Its capabilities to mend our broken institutions are preferable to all the useless photo-ops and optics management we are continually bombarded with from the existing system of government. Too many officials are serving themselves instead of the people. Justin Trudeau has attempted to make things better and perhaps these attempts are genuine. However, and by way of example, he appears to have much more work to do in achieving what he set out for the Minister of Indigenous and Northern Affairs (INAC) to accomplish in their *Mandate Letter*. Therein, Trudeau wrote, "It is my expectation that we will deliver real results and professional government to Canadians,"[175] and laid out an ambitious list of priorities for the minister to tackle. And yet, after his signature was barley cold on that *Mandate Letter*, the Trudeau government announced in August 2017, that the Ministry of Indigenous and Northern Affairs would be divided into two departments—Crown-Indigenous Relations and Northern Affairs Canada, and Indigenous Services Canada. On the surface this is a bit confusing, especially since the INAC website, as of July 3, 2018, states "this transformation will take time and include engagement with Indigenous peoples and others."[176]

In an August 2017 *CBC News* article, John Tasker wrote about the splitting of INAC. Apparently, "some experts warn fundamental reforms of this sort could actually lead to more headaches." Citing Christopher Alcantara, an Indigenous-settler relations expert at Western University, the CBC piece documents that "it's going to complicate decision-making because you now have two ministries competing for resources around the cabinet table." Alcantara also sensibly stated that, "instead of an integrated process, you're going to have silos, little empires that guard their resources . . . I worry about the lack of coordination."[177] So do I, considering there is no RMO yet. I also question whether or not this is real, informed and meaningful change for Indigenous Peoples or more optics management meant to just look like it. Tasker's article additionally cites Ryerson University's Hayden King, a professor of Indigenous governance. According to King, "the last thing Indigenous Peoples want is another layer of bureaucracy and twice as much obfuscation."[178] Well put.

King's comment that "if this restructuring is going to be successful the culture in the bureaucracy needs to be addressed" is also highly perceptive.[179] But to change that culture, we also require the RMO, as Chapter 6 and 7 will demonstrate. For now, let's hope the splitting of INAC into two other ministries, is not another initiative designed to fail from its inception, like so many others outlined in Chapter 3. There are too many 'crises by design' at all levels of government.

A crisis by design is how Matt Elliot described the shelter crisis in Toronto in early 2018. From a common-sense perspective, he stated this about the city's homeless people struggling to obtain the basic necessities of life: "A municipal government devoted to a long-term fix and to supporting vulnerable people would make those investments before the need reached a breaking point."[180] If you are a Torontonian or just visiting this supposedly great city, remember that when you pass a homeless person slumped over on the street. What does your sense of right and wrong tell you?

Should there be a well-designed RMO at the municipal level, coordinating with both an Ontario provincial RMO, and possibly a federal RMO, to resolve homelessness as much as possible? If Toronto's population were just

100 people, would you not wish to help the starving and homeless, regardless of your political party affiliation? The reality is that Canada contains tens of millions of people, with Toronto itself populated by a few million people. It would be refreshing to have Canadian politicians rolling up their sleeves and doing what is right. Thus far our political leaders, as well as their counterparts around the world, have failed to come up with real-world solutions to real-world problems. That is why our government must be first to undertake *Democratic Restructuralism*.

We cannot keep falling victim to optics management and sly theatrics conducted by deceitful characters of ill repute. This only leads us all into darkness, where we resort to blaming one another for our problems. It would be refreshing to see Canada lead by example in this fallen world where a more divine design is required to improve our lot. Let's get on with it. Let's restore our democracy so it is representative of our collective will and spirit. Others, including our children, are waiting in the wings for us to take action. We cannot wait much longer to repair that which needs mending. The democratic institutions meant to bind us together must be restored. Your vote should matter in this regard, just like right-minded politicians should. Which brings us to the next chapter . . .

Chapter 6
Minding the Plumbers

That to expect bad people not to injure others is crazy. It's to ask
the impossible, And to let them behave like that to other people
but expect them to exempt you is arrogant—the act of a tyrant.
—Marcus Aurelius, Meditations

Addressing Human Nature

Physically incorporating a risk-management system within the machinery of
government, with common-sense reporting to our elected officials through
a nonpartisan Chief Risk Officer based in the Privy Council Office will
go a long way to improving our day-to-day lives. Effective, risk-based decision-making will be encouraged. And while I believe people generally know
right from wrong and want to do the right thing, I also realize we all have
our dark side. No matter how good any of us really are, or may seem to be,
we can be susceptible to corruption, prone to self-aggrandizement, desirous of
more and more material goods, hungry for power, and so on. It is our human
condition, the good and the bad attributes, that have both driven us so often

to glory and tremendous feats of accomplishments, and despairingly to conflict and destruction, to a fall from grace.

As we have seen, no country, government and, I daresay, identifiable group is totally innocent. No race, colour, creed or religion is justly able to claim some moral superiority over anyone else. And no matter what political system or 'ism' people are governed under, be it Communism, Fascism, Maoism, Nationalism, Socialism, or even the 'isms' within our supposedly modern democracies, such as Republicanism to the South or Conservatism, Liberalism, etc. here in the Great White North, people are people. So, if we do not keep in mind the darker side of human nature, *Democratic Restructuralism* could fail to produce the desired outcomes. We need to manage the risks associated with those few bad apples who may try to subvert a well-designed system for their own nefarious purposes.

To demonstrate, let's explore what happens when government officials look after their own skins rather than that of the broader public. Consider again the Soviet Union. Having lived there shortly after its collapse, I can assure you it was never the worker's paradise it claimed to be. But let me document some of the research done by others in this sphere. Dissident Milovan Djilas, a long-time communist and confidant of Yugoslavian leader (or rather oppressor) Tito, wrote a book called *The New Class* some time ago. In that book, and according to a *Los Angeles Times* editorial, Djilas wrote about the new ruling class being a self-aggrandizing oligarchy made up of the communist political and managerial elite. According to Djilas, "despite all the talk of creating an egalitarian, classless society—communists are no different from other people when it comes to feathering their own nests."[1]

Presumably the revolutionaries who sought to overthrow the capitalist exploiting classes in the name of creating a so-called egalitarian society, merely created a more effective way of funneling power and wealth to the one per cent or so. After all, if you did not go along with what the government wanted you to do in the Soviet Union, there were always the labour camps, or the

Lubyanka, that infamous KGB prison in Moscow. In the USSR there existed the 'Nomenklatura,' perhaps the epitome, if not a leading example, of how a bureaucracy can be organizationally designed to reward those who serve it for their masters' gain. And the headmasters, such as Stalin and Brezhnev, knew how to motivate the darker side of human nature to ensure the system was designed to keep everyone in line, using a carrot (perks) and stick (threat of force) approach.

The Nomenklatura were those Communist Party members appointed to influential positions within the bureaucracy of the Soviet Union and other Eastern Bloc countries. They basically ran everything for the henchmen at the top of the pecking order. Members of the Nomenklatura had special holiday retreats, access to special medical facilities and, as the *Times* editorial references as being most resented by ordinary Russians, access to special stores that sold imported and Soviet-made merchandise not available in the regular stores. Many of these bureaucrats or administrators also had cars and chauffeurs. [2]

Of course, the offspring of such enablers of the system also benefitted from perpetuating an organizational structure that oppressed the masses. This ensured a future supply of yes men and women to sustain the status quo, regardless of what is right and wrong, in what former US President Ronald Reagan aptly described as 'an evil empire' in his famous speech of 1983. Since Nomenklatura children had an inside track on admission to the top universities, which usually meant they later obtained better jobs and positions in the system with its attendant perks, here too was another way to harness human nature. Financial gains, family gains . . . why not play along! Don't worry about those lining up for bread and on a long waiting list for an apartment. Who are they to you? There is no God anyway, only the great leader!

According to Dr. Kelly Hignett, Senior Lecturer in History at Leeds Beckett University, "In postwar Eastern Europe . . . Possession of a party card opened the door to numerous 'perks,' including the allocation of a superior standard of accommodation, access to special shops . . . and holidays in special health resorts." To put the motivation in clear terms, "the higher up the power structure you climbed, the more levels of privilege reached ridiculous proportions."[3] To supplement their salaries lower on the bureaucratic food chain, the smaller-sized Nomenklatura could get a little more for themselves by abusing their positions further. Basic income could be supplemented through corruption in the form of bribery.[4] That reminds me of the time I had to pay US $10 to get a seat without a ticket on a supposedly full train crossing from southern Belarus into Ukraine in 1994. Inevitably, I found that very train was near empty, contrary to what the person at the ticket office in the train station, who wished to line their pockets with hard currency from several customers, had advised. Ahhh, human nature. One does not have to be Sigmund Freud to be schooled in it.

If we turn to Poland and Boleslaw Bierut, the leader of the Polish Workers Party from 1948 until his passing in 1956, we see something similar. Jozef Swiatlo, a high-ranking Polish security officer who defected in 1953, had the following to say: "Bierut's living quarters comprised no less than ten lavishly and luxuriously furnished palaces . . . all fitted out with legendary magnificence."[5] And, looking at communist East Germany, "the SED leadership approved the building of a luxurious 'secure living zone' for the party leadership near Wandlitz." It "consisted of 23 luxury detached family houses; a clubhouse with private cinema; a gourmet restaurant; a shop stocking a selection of luxury Western goods; a market garden; a health centre; a shooting range; a swimming pool; a sports field and several tennis courts."[6] Understandably, it is best to hide such opulence from the regular folks, since this type of lifestyle can compete with that of leading capitalists, though occurring within the workers' paradise. "The area surrounding the complex was officially designated as a protected area for 'game research,' decreed off-limits to all ordinary Germans, and troops were stationed to guard the entrance."[7] No doubt they could practice on the shooting range in anticipation of dealing with any of the riffraff.

Unsurprisingly, SED leader Walter Ulbricht "not only enjoyed the comforts of a magnificent 25 room house" at the complex, "but also had a holiday home specially built on the small Baltic island of Vilm, which was subsequently deleted from the maps to avoid unwanted attention!"[8] There are so many examples of the leaders of oppressive regimes, and their minions, living in the lap of luxury while the broader population suffers. We talked a little of North Korea earlier and there are more examples all over the world, such as Idi Amin's Uganda, Poll Pot's Cambodia, and Bashar al-Assad's Syria. I have no desire to minimize the extreme corruption that has or is still occurring in those and other quarters, but discussion of all that would require another book. And perhaps drawing examples from the former USSR is easier for me because I have seen the remnants of that system, with even the last dictator of Europe, in Belarus, borrowing from its playbook.

Some examples from the old Soviet Union have also received a lot of media attention. Many of us have, for example, heard about Nicolae Ceaușescu and the obscenely lavish lifestyle he and his family lead while most Romanians languished in almost incomprehensible despair. "During his time as leader (1965 to 1989), Ceaușescu owned over 15 luxury palaces around Romania, including . . . the Primaverii Palace in Bucharest," featuring "rooms filled with priceless silk, porcelain, marble, silverware, chandeliers and carpets." More shockingly, "Ceaușescu's pet dog, Corbu, . . . was often driven through Bucharest in a limousine accompanied by his own motorcade." Corbu, was also a leader in the Romanian Army since he was awarded the rank of Colonel.[9]

Elsewhere in Europe, under the dictatorships of Adolf Hitler and Benito Mussolini, you saw those itinerant leaders of Germany and Italy, respectively, also amassing great wealth at the expense of ordinary citizens. Of course, optics management, just as it did in the former communist USSR, told any people suffering under fascism a different story. You likely do not need me to tell you about fascist Italy and Germany and how their megalomaniac leaders pursued their own agendas. Suffice to say that in a 2002 *New York*

Times article referencing a German TV documentary by Ingo Helm, we learn that Hitler "liked money, both for the luxuries it bought him and the loyalty it ensured, and he amassed a lot of it."[10] In this view, the Führer knew how to harness the darker side of people's nature, motivating their actions by dishing out wealth and power to those who carried out his purpose. Hitler was adept at using optics management and the blame game to point to those within Germany (such as the Jews) as well as outside of it (such as those living in lands he attacked), as being responsible for all of Germany's ills.

On Blame and the Equal Distribution of Bad Apples

Blame has been around for millennia and speaks to a human failing as timeless as humanity itself. It is alive and well now as we have seen, with nation still pitted against nation. Those wrongly motivated often use the tool of blame to manipulate circumstances in their favour, thereby achieving sinister objectives. We saw Adolf Hitler consolidate his power after the German Parliament building, the Reichstag, was set aflame on February 27, 1933. As mentioned in the March 6, 1933 issue of *Time*, and reiterated by Lily Rothman in a 2015 *Time* article, " 'The arson came amid a campaign of unparalleled violence and bitterness' by then Chancellor Adolf Hitler, in advance of an approaching German election." In the aftermath of the fire which destroyed the Parliament building, "an unemployed Dutch bricklayer linked to the Communist Party was tried and executed for the crime the following year." Rothman states however, that "even then *Time* questioned whether the Nazis who held him responsible were also the ones who paid him to set the fire." The rest is history, as they say. "By April [1933], Nazis were using the threat of another fire to ensure passage of the Enabling Act, which solidified Hitler's place as dictatorial leader for years to come." Curiously, the bricklayer's trial was found to be "a miscarriage of justice" by a West Berlin court in 1981.[11]

But is there really anything new under the sun when it comes to human behaviour and wrong-minded individuals' capacity to blame in instances where power and wealth may be gained or worrisomely lost? It all reminds me of Tacitus, whom encyclopedia Britannica names, "in full," as "Publius Cornelius Tacitus, or Gaius Cornelius Tacitus [born 56 A.D. – died 120 A.D.]." Interestingly he is deemed to have been, not only a "Roman orator and public official," but "probably the greatest historian and one of the greatest prose Stylists who wrote in the Latin language."[12] Buried in one of Tacitus' famous works *Annals* which concerns the Roman Empire around 14 to 68 A.D., we find more blame about a fire, the only difference being this one occurred in Rome when Nero was Roman Emperor. Funny how Hitler adopted, for his own malevolent purposes, so much of ancient Rome's stylized pageantry. We can see his adoption of certain Roman symbols in moulding his vision for Nazi Germany: the pomp and circumstance of parades and elite military units, such as the SS, akin to the Praetorian Guard of the Imperial Roman army; the grandiose plans to redesign Berlin, turning it into a sparkling Germania, capital of a new Reich to last 1,000 years; the one armed salutes; the ornamentation of banners and standards emblazoned with symbols of expansionist power, carried by fiercely dressed units.

It is ironic that Tacitus wrote about what is considered the most thorough description of Germania (a Roman term) back around 98 A.D. More ironic is that Hitler adopted Emperor Nero's blame game tactics. For in A.D. 64, when what is known as the Great Fire of Rome occurred, causing much destruction to that city, some argued Nero started the blaze. We do find in Tacitus's *Annals*, written almost 2 millennia ago, the following passage:

> But all human efforts, all the lavish gifts of the Emperor,
> and the propitiations of the gods, did not banish the sinister
> belief that the conflagration was the result of an order.
> Consequently, to get rid of the report, Nero fastened the

guilt and inflicted the most exquisite tortures on a class hated for their abominations, called Christians by the populace. Christos, from whom the name had its origin, suffered the extreme penalty during the reign of Tiberius at the hands of one of our procurators, Pontius Pilotus . . . an immense multitude was convicted, not so much of the crime of firing the city, as of hatred against mankind . . . Covered with the skins of beasts, they were torn by dogs and perished, or were nailed to crosses, or were doomed to the flames and burnt, to serve as a nightly illumination, when daylight had expired."[13]

We also find in background information concerning the Great Fire of Rome, in a PBS episode of *Secrets of the Dead*, that "there was no end to Nero's ambition." Apparently, "one of his grandest plans was to tear down a third of Rome so that he could build an elaborate series of palaces that would be known as Neropolis."[14] Sounds like an earlier version of Hitler's Germania! But when the Roman Senate objected to the scheme, we coincidentally, if not conveniently, find Rome soon to be mostly a scorched remainder of what once was a bustling city of 2 million. The PBS episode notes that after the fire burned for many days, with Nero "miles away in the cooler resort of Antium," the city was devastated. In mathematical terms, "10 of Rome's 14 districts were in ruin," reflecting the horror that "two thirds of Rome had been destroyed." Imagine the human suffering and carnage. PBS also aptly notes that "history has blamed Nero for the disaster, implying that he started the fire so that he could bypass the Senate and rebuild Rome to his liking." According to PBS, "the Domus Aurea, Nero's majestic series of villas and pavilions . . . was built in the wake of the fire."[15] The Domus Aurea (Latin 'Golden House') appears to be an expansively landscaped palace and perhaps Hitler's Germania would have had something like it too.

We saw above, in the writings of the great historian Tacitus, known for his detailed and scrupulous account of history, that Nero blamed the Christians for the fire. In the end, both Nero and Hitler committed suicide, which also reflects what may have been a combination of similar fates bitterly intertwined in the miseries of their own history. Their history culminated with a final reckoning of facts containing truths rather than fake news, optics management and deceit which were anchored in the worst kind of personal motivation—evil. Inevitably, the heavens offered their final judgments to those consumed by their own tortuous and wrong-minded motivations, a revelation to any who dared to follow in the footsteps of Nero and Hitler.

None of this is to say, in the instance of Hitler's rise to power for example, that Article 231 of the *Treaty of Versailles*, known as the 'War Guilt Clause,' was not overly punitive in blaming Germany for World War I and facilitating an environment where onerous reparation payments for that war were required of the German people. This unfortunate circumstance provided the seedbed for someone like Hitler to flourish, much like it does for other unsavoury and duplicitous characters to rise to power now. That is no excuse for what subsequently happened in World War II, and all the atrocities associated with that hellish conflict. It is merely another revelation of how one bad decision can contribute to the power of other bad decisions, leading to disaster. Hitler, who did no service to Germany, merely used and manipulated the opportunities he saw, taking control of the German government. He pillaged the German treasury and that of other countries, all the while nourishing a darker side of the human condition that has yet, and hopefully never again, to be surpassed by some other butcher of men, women and children, save for possibly Russia's Joseph Stalin in terms of numbers.

Such is the shame humanity bears, as it continues to allow pockets of barbarism, famine, pestilence and war to flourish, such as in Syria and Africa, with snail-paced and ineffective institutions like the United Nations conducting more optics management than dealing with real issues that need immediate attention on the ground. Hitler organized the system around him for his benefit. According to Helm's German documentary, he "spent millions, in lavish gifts and payments, to buy the loyalty of politicians and businessmen and to keep them dependent on him."[16] We hear quite a bit in the news now about tax dodgers, most recently in the newly released 'Paradise Papers,' and just prior to that, the 'Panama Papers.' However, tax evasion pursued by the super elites comprising the one per cent or so of the population, was a game played long before our own narcissistic super-rich decided to influence, create, manipulate, capitalize on, etc., a set of complex rules, mainly written for their benefit by themselves or those motivated to do their bidding. The rules of the age old game are often one-sided, so the playing field is to the advantage of the one per cent and to the disadvantage of ordinary people. Therefore, "in the development of his summer home at Obersalzberg, above Berchtesgarden in Bavaria, or in the development of his own art collection, Hitler freely used state funds. Nor did he pay taxes on his income or his property, meaning that there was no overall accounting of his worth."[17]

The culpability of big business, not just higher ranking soldiers within the design of the fascist system, also served to enable Hitler to maintain his malevolent grip on Germany. This reveals how powerful business leaders and individuals may work for their own gain, regardless of their actions being immoral or not and what the general population may consider right and just, versus wrong and dangerous, as afraid as the ordinary public may be to speak up. By way of example, when we look at Hitler, "He wasn't simply created by big business." Mr. Helm is cited as stating in the *NY Times* article that, "once he was in power, big business was opportunistic, contributing large sums to what was known as the Adolph Hitler Donation of German Industry." To put it into greater perspective, Hitler received around 700 million reichsmarks, or the equivalent of well over $3 billion, over the span of his becoming chancellor until his death in 1945.[18] Certainly, Hitler is an extreme example of the absolute corruption of an individual for what obviously must be self-serving purposes. Yet, history is replete with examples of leaders sucking the life blood out of their nations for their own benefit. It would also seem that such poor examples of humanity can be found across the globe, with factors such as race, colour, gender and the like being no common denominator as a predictor of behaviour. While not as strong in number or force as good people, bad apples are distributed equally across the earth.

In his November 2017 "Opinion Piece" published on *NewZimbabwe. com*, Tawanda Majoni astutely remarked that many authoritarian leaders "start off on a promising note . . . as darlings of the people." But what happens to these people, once they are in power for some time? Or do they change their nature at all to begin with? "From Hitler to Pol Pot. From Ferdinand Marcos to Haile Mengistu Mariam. From Charles Taylor to Muammar Gaddafi . . . they got so drunk with their popularity they turn themselves into demigods." Centring on President Robert Mugabe at the time, Majoni wrote that "almost everything about Zimbabwean national and party governance revolves around the sole whim of Mugabe."[19] That sounds like what we were talking about earlier, that how you design something, in this case the Zimbabwean government, affects the way it behaves. According to Majoni, Mugabe "is the president, commander in chief of the defence forces, head of government, chancellor of state universities, appointer (and disappointer) of all key positions, first secretary, president, head of the Zanu PF politburo and all that you can imagine relating to power."[20]

Interestingly, albeit unsurprisingly, we also again see an individual like Mugabe using optics management and the law to fulfill his own power-hungry agenda. Majoni puts it best: "When he wants things done his way, he uses the façade of the law, constitution and popular participation, but that does not remove the fact that he is a dictator."[21] There is some humour in Majoni's comparison of Mugabe and Ferdinand Marcos, Philippine President from 1965 to 1986. On the serious side, and not unlike other leaders letting the darker side of human nature fuel their actions, "they and their families became synonymous with corruption, reportedly amassing personal fortunes and regularly getting accused of abusing their power to create personal wealth."[22] Specifically concerning their wives, which displayed political power grabbing aspirations of their own, is where we find some dark comedy: Imelda Marcos being elected as a congresswoman four times in the Philippines' House of Representatives after the death of her husband, Ferdinand; Grace Mugabe looking to become Zanu PF Vice-President at the ruling party's congress in December, 2017. Majoni amusingly, if not dishearteningly, shows us in terms of their avariciousness, the one per cent are both colour and gender neutral. "As Imelda Marcos became infamous for owning thousands of handbags and pairs of shoes, Grace has been grabbing the headlines for multi-million finger rings and reports of insane accumulation of real property outside the country, in addition to shady transfers of mega-bucks to safe offshore accounts."[23] That makes for a good segue for us to get back into exploring how sound the world's leading democratic systems are. All this discussion about shady transfers of piles of cash to offshore accounts . . .

There are a lot of corrupt people and oppressive regimes. So, what of our modern democracies, and what appears to be quite a slippery slope, despite the differences in democratic versus authoritarian government structures? Even here in Canada, as in the US and many other democracies, the avaricious or darker side of human nature is alive and well and serving itself rather than others. Granted, we are not all living in some totalitarian state where we risk being sent off to a labour camp or summarily shot. That would be the case if we did not go along with things in a system that nefariously benefits a smaller portion of the population pulling the strings of us puppets. All the same, as Western society further polarizes, with the true purpose of our democratic institutions being eroded more and more, and with the one per cent controlling more power and wealth, we too may be in danger of slipping into an abyss. This abyss is being gradually created by 'the haves', whose increasing sense of self entitlement stands ready to push the have-nots to the brink even more.

Do I sound too extreme in my views, too conspiratorial in my thinking? It could never happen here, right, that our democratic institutions and structures slowly but inevitably become so transformed that they no longer serve the original purpose for which they were intended? Think again. We factually talked about the ever increasing wealth and power of the elite earlier. What of our top leaders today as I write these words? Are they truly and altruistically motivated to improve your and your family's day-to-day lives, toiling dutifully away in their offices accordingly? Or is the darker side of human nature taking root here, just as it does elsewhere, notwithstanding that some other places allow more obscene accumulations of wealth and power through sheer force than creative confusion and optics management?

It is my contention that we need to design a better government, not only structurally, considering the purpose of each function within government, but also psychologically, anticipating the motivation of the bureaucracy and individuals operating within it. That is because I, just as you, generally know the difference between right and wrong. And for *Democratic Restructuralism* to be successful, we will need to have the right people in the right jobs at the right time. Civil servants must also possess the right motivation to empower them as well as keep them honest. It is not all just about having the right plumbing in government. The right organizational structure in government alone will not produce an effective and efficient public service.

On Motivation: How Individuals can influence Design

Motivation. So much of human behaviour revolves around it. When we open our eyes in the morning after awakening, a multitude of competing motivations leads us to make a similar multitude of decisions throughout the day; all of those decisions reflect our behaviour, the choices we make. We make a cup of coffee for ourselves right away because we desperately crave it like a drug. Hopefully it is our only dependency before meeting the challenges of the day. And since it is the small things that exponentially matter and show you care, we dutifully get our significant other their morning fix too, having already committed to memory how much cream and sugar they prefer. We decided to memorize a lot of things about that special person because they motivated us to do so, making us feel special in turn by doing what they do for us.

Our next decision may be to wake up the kids, if we have any—it was a big decision to have them in the first place, unprotected sexual motivation or other reasons notwithstanding—initiating a host of other successive decisions based on a ton of other motivations. We need to wear this outfit to school 'Junior.' Eat this, it's good for you. Hmmm, what should we put in your backpack for lunch? Time to brush your teeth. Did we check your homework? Am I or your mom taking you to a hockey practice after school before the bus comes? You get the idea. We also have to get ourselves ready for work. That routine also encompasses an array of different motivations. Is there a formal meeting today? Should I wear the black or navy outfit? What can I do to stand out from the others so my boss sees how hard I am working? Gee, that individual in accounting, Terry, is really cute. I would like to ask them out but feel way too loyal to my spouse. There is no way I would ever be unfaithful . . . unless they started to pay less attention to me and behaved differently. Maybe I need to lose that extra 10 pounds I am packing on. Do I need to get gas today so I can pick up Junior, or do I just get the items on the grocery list and clean that dirty basement tonight like I promised? I better call dad in the nursing home. He misses me . . .

I am sure most of you can relate to the above. Our daily routines will be as varied as our individual selves and the reasons we do what we do. Most of us are pretty decent folks who want to make the right decisions for ourselves and the people we care about. But occasionally we may slip and, for the churchgoing, seek forgiveness for our sins in various quarters. On balance however, we would like to think that most people, like ourselves, are trying to do the right thing, at home, at work, in the community, and so on. Unfortunately, there are always a few bad apples. Also, many of us can slip and respond to the wrong kinds of motivation when it feeds our ego and does not seem to hurt anyone else (Maybe I'll just flirt with Terry. There's no harm in that.). That can be a problem, especially in government organizations and institutions where the bureaucracy, and the bureaucrats working within them, are often stereotyped as inefficient, left-leaning, lazy, union-loving types who will do the least work required to scrape by and live off the public purse. You know, like a leech. The motivation is all about what you can suck out of the system on the backs of others, not what you can contribute to the rest of Canada and Canadians. But is that really so?

Earlier we discussed how the way organizations are designed controls the behaviour of those working within them, so we know the motivations of those working within government are influenced by the design of government itself. We also know that design improvements can be made to better ascertain and manage risks facing Canadians so that better decisions impacting us all can be made by our leaders. However, we must be wary of the darker side of human nature. For just as the design of organizational structures within government influences the behaviour of those operating in them so, too, can the bureaucrats working within government influence the organizational design for their own benefit.

We covered a lot of ground previously in this chapter, discussing how the wrong motivation of various tyrants can create government power structures that are designed so that they and their cronies are the ones who benefit the most, at the expense of others. Returning to the epicentre of what once was known as the Soviet Union, we see the leader of modern day Russia, Vladimir Putin, organizing the administrative structures around him mostly for his own benefit. He has fashioned the bureaucracy around him such that he can maintain his long-established iron grip on the country and on Russians themselves. In a foreboding article written in 2016 by Andrei Soldatov, an investigative journalist, we learn that Putin has been busy resurrecting and redesigning government structures to serve his purposes, perhaps as well as they may have served such erstwhile dictators as Joseph Stalin. Soldatov, who is also cofounder of *Agentura.Ru*, a Russian information hub on intelligence agencies, grimly raises the spectre of Putin's true motivation: "The president, himself a former KGB officer, was too taken by KGB myths about the role of the Cheka [forerunner to the KGB] in Russian society to be satisfied with the FSB [federal security service] being a mere security organ."[24] In fact, to solidify its burgeoning influence within the state apparatus, Putin expanded the breadth and depth of the FSB's reach. Therefore, "the president began using the FSB as his main recruitment base for filling key positions in government and state controlled business; its agents were expected to define and personify the ideology of the new Russia."[25]

Over time, Putin embarked on a number of other initiatives to strengthen his position and focus control under him. He launched the Investigative Committee, described by Soldatov as "a sort of Russian FBI . . . conducting the most sensitive investigations, from the murder of Kremlin critics like Anna Politkovskaya and Boris Nemtsov to prosecuting political activists." Similarly, Putin embarked on "an expansion of the Internal Troops—Army units charged with operating within the country—and the launch of a new Department to Counter Extremism."[26] One wonders if some of the extremists are those who oppose Putin and his personal control over Russia. If you believe not, there is always his Czar-like and almost ancient Roman-styled Praetorian Guard to protect the Emperor and his empire to consider. "Putin created the National Guard, which is a massive and armed-to-the-teeth military force tasked with fighting internal dissent."[27]

By the fall of 2016, Putin appeared to be consolidating his administrative structures even more, specifically the security apparatus that serves to protect and ensconce the long-serving leader in the Kremlin. As Soldatov describes, news broke out in 2016 that Putin was "planning a major overhaul of the country's security services . . . to merge the Foreign Intelligence Service, or SVR, with the Federal Security service, or FSB, which keeps an eye on domestic affairs." The newly amalgamated organization was to be called the Ministry of State Security.[28] Connecting the dots, Soldatov raises the spectre of the malevolence of the KGB, its long history of repressing anyone who might speak out against the Soviet regime and the cronies who ran things mainly for their own benefit. Recall the wrong motivations of cronies like Ceaușescu, their common desire to amass more and more wealth and power, enjoying all the trappings that come with these things, despite so many of the masses, the 99 per cent, suffering in the totalitarian state. Soldatov notes that The Ministry of State Security "was the name given to the most powerful and feared of Joseph Stalin's secret services, from 1943 to 1953." More worrisome for the people of Russia as well as threats to world peace is the melding of Russia's foreign and domestic intelligence services. "In all but name, we are seeing a resurrection of the Committee for State Security—otherwise known as the KGB."[29] That is not the resurrection the world needs.

Clearly Putin knows how to design organizational structures around him to serve his own interests, thereby shaping not only his, but other Russians' realities, out of his own wrong-headed motivations, to acquire more personal wealth, status and power. It is a playbook the world has seen all too often, the outcomes of which always cause more suffering, damage, and violence than good. We should also not forget the purpose of the KGB's design. Soldatov writes, "Its primary task was protecting the regime. Its activities included hunting down spies and dissidents and supervising media, sports, and even the church. It ran operations both inside and outside the country, but in both spheres the main task was always to protect the interests of whoever currently resided in the Kremlin."[30] For someone like Putin, it comes almost as being natural to realize his motivations, his ambitions, through actively designing the institutions and bureaucratic web around him. In 1998, Boris Yeltsin, the President of Russia at the time, appointed Putin as chief of the FSB. That was a good fit for someone who worked for the Soviet KGB in East Germany when the USSR still existed.

By March 2000, Putin would be President. Yet, it is not only through the shaping of present-day Russia's security and political apparatus that Putin is able to advance his own, rather than ordinary Russians' interests. Although state-security organizations certainly could be of help in silencing dissidents and opposition forces ahead of the 2018 Russian presidential election, Putin's grand design included other factors to assure his fourth-term presidential campaign win. As Ingo Mannteufel wrote in a March 2018 opinion piece carried by *Deutsche Welle*, Putin garnered over 70 per cent of the votes in the 2018 Russian election because he already guaranteed that result in advance by laying the groundwork for his continued Caesar-like reign.[31] China's leader, Xi Jinping, knows the value of doing just that as well. The Chinese legislature recently approved his reappointment as President without any limitations on the number of terms he can serve.

According to Mannteufel, Putin "is popular because the Kremlin has for years blocked other politicians from developing their own public profiles in the centrally controlled media."[32] That statement reminds me of Joseph Goebbels, Hitler's Minister of Propaganda, who masterfully controlled and manipulated the German media to portray Hitler as the only possible and true leader, or Führer, of Germany. Never mind the road to ruin that Hitler led Germany down, fuelled by his messianic delusions of grandeur. While Putin is no Hitler (although the chess game being played in Syria is of concern), and Russia and Germany fought a gruelling battle that cost millions of lives in World War II, it bears repeating that Stalin's tactics killed and starved millions of people before that war, especially in Ukraine, where Putin recently annexed the Crimean peninsula in early 2014. Putin remains a highly relevant example today, of a contemporary individual adept at building an architecture around themselves to obtain and hold onto that which they crave most, power and wealth.

Mannteufel wrote about the huge influence of the media to shape people's views of the truth, which for the likes of Putin and similar characters, perhaps even for some leaders of powerful democracies, is something malleable rather than absolute. "The president's power rests not only on state repression, but also on the media's portrayal of him as Russia's only conceivable leader. No political competition."[33]

Often times the organizational structures built around wrongly-motivated leaders are purposefully built to be opaque and confusing, engineered to deceive and distract from a reality that is difficult to discern. Nobody can even clearly pinpoint Putin's real wealth in concrete terms. The Kremlin claims he lives in a modestly sized apartment and earns less than $150,000 a year. Others, such as Stanislav Belkovsky, estimate the Russian President's wealth to be $70 billion. And Bill Browder, a hedge-fund manager and vociferous critic of Putin, believes it to be closer to $200 billion, more than what Amazon's Jeff Bezos has amassed.[34] According to *Business Insider*, Putin's true personal wealth remains an enigma because of the purposeful obscurity that shrouds his assets in secrecy. "The 2015 Panama Papers revealed that Putin may obscure and bolster his fortune through proxies."[35] It goes without saying that many super rich oligarchs have been, and continue to be, close to Putin. His strong power base of political cronies and ability to hold wealth out of immediate sight act as a shield, cloaking his true motivation.

I recall obtaining a letter of acceptance to the University of Alberta to pursue doctoral studies in Russian history under the supervision of Professor David Marples. He is a well-respected historian, but I passed up the opportunity, deciding to live abroad longer. Coincidentally, I came across one of his articles published in a recent issue of the *Edmonton Journal*. Marples, in questioning why Putin even bothered to hold presidential elections in 2018, "in a state that has become increasingly belligerent and authoritarian," concludes ominously with this: "The answer is that elections are a necessary ritual to create an appearance of legality."[36] One could also argue that Putin's desire to obscure the amount of his real wealth is a necessary ritual, to create an appearance of legality around the collusion of his and his cronies siphoning off billions of dollars of Russia's wealth to serve his own motivations. Optics management has many uses, and can be facilitated through the design and control of government institutions and organizations. Public institutions can purposefully be designed to act as levers of power for those wishing to fulfil their own ambitions, all too often for the wrong reasons. And when things start to go south for the masses at large, it is often useful for the self-serving regime to manufacture hostile foreign enemies threatening the country's well-being, just as Hitler did before and North Korea's leader does now.

For Russians, Marples describes clearly the real reasons behind an argument designed to conjure up the image of enemies encircling the motherland. The element of "suspicion and fear of outside enemies is hardly new to Russians; it was a feature of Soviet foreign-policy thinking. Putin has re-cultivated it through social media and television, perhaps in part to detract from the struggles of the economy and the evident failures of once-successful oil and gas industries that he has brought under state control."[37] Here in Canada, we citizens are not faced with living in an environment akin to modern-day Russia. The media is not centrally controlled in Ottawa. Political opposition has not all but been eliminated. We are not residing in an increasingly militarized and police state under a repressive regime that seeks mainly to serve itself and a select wealthy group of oligarch-type cronies. Our Prime Minister cannot be at the helm of a one-party ship forever, all the while siphoning off Canada's wealth. Nevertheless, the case of Russia and Putin is certainly instructive. In it, we see that an individual's motivation, all the way up to the level of President, can manipulate the administrative structures and political apparatus around them to suit their nefarious purposes.

Earlier I stated that Putin is no Hitler. And he certainly is no Stalin. But he still operates as the master of an increasingly repressive machine right now in what should be a more progressive and 21st century world. He enduringly and purposefully stands as the head of state of the earth's largest country. His sabre rattling at the edge of the Baltics and other bordering nations, not to mention incursion into Ukraine's Crimea region, along with artful distractions and tactical moves of disingenuousness as he captures that which he covets beyond such trickery, should serve as a warning to all democratic nations, as fragile as they may be. People have not changed. Technology has. Yet even in that sphere, we see Mr. Putin attempting to successfully manipulate the outcome of elections, such as the latest presidential one in America.

We must be cognizant of the enemy within, such as those deliberately hacking into our obviously less than impenetrable computer and IT systems, as well as the more clear external dangers that may take the shape of hostile nations building up mass infantry and armoured units, nuclear first strike capabilities, and so on. Perhaps even more importantly, we must come to terms with the immediate need to strengthen our own democratic institutions and structures as described in the preceding chapter. We must also guard against them being compromised by any individuals who are motivated by their own ambitions and goals other than the well-being of the government administration that is supposed to serve all Canadians. This is what good risk management is about. Our government must provide it. Again, we are not living under Putin's thumb or some other repressive regime (sadly there are several examples as you well know), but it is a slippery slope to end up in a less than desirable democracy that increasingly appears to serve the needs of a select group of elites, the one per cent, rather than the citizenry at large. In the prologue to his work *On Tyranny*, Professor Snyder cautions our neighbours to the South:

> We might be tempted to think that our democratic heritage
> automatically protects us . . . This is a misguided reflex . . .
> Americans today are no wiser than the Europeans who saw
> democracy yield to fascism, Nazism, or communism in the

twentieth century. Our one advantage is that we might learn from the experience. Now is a good time to do so.[38]

True, we Canadians are not living in the politically corrosive atmosphere of Donald Trump's America, but one fanned by the uncontrollable wildfires in British Columbia, fuelled in no small part by the obvious climate change Trump denies. But know this, as Snyder warned. When it suits the leadership of the day, "sometimes institutions are deprived of vitality and function . . . of what they once were, so that they gird the new order rather than resisting it."[39] This can be done slowly and subtly so it largely goes unnoticed, like the neglectful or perhaps even purposeful mismanagement of some Canadian institutions as we saw in Chapter 3. In the extreme, where malevolent forces are clearly at work, this is what the Nazis called Gleichschaltung. Of course the personal ambitions of an individual, such as one's desire for a promotion, decent salary, etc., does not have to be mutually exclusive or at odds with the health of the organization that individual works for. Similarly, a civil servant's personal motivations do not have to be diametrically opposed to the effectiveness and efficiency of the government institution he or she serves. The key is to understand that while most Canadians and others around the world are good and decent people who know the difference between right and wrong, we need to ensure the well-being of government institutions is not compromised by any bad apples or those who may stop doing the right things for the wrong reasons.

I know. You are wondering what on earth I am talking about and how on earth do you do that? Okay, I don't blame you. Again, it is all about managing applicable risks. This is where we need to further explore how even a well-designed Canadian government bureaucracy can be compromised or even destroyed by certain people working in 'the system.' And we are not talking about Russian spies here, which would likely mean the right employee background checks have not been done, but something that should be much more obvious. Once we understand how the integrity of our government institutions and their design can be compromised, as you will see, we will be better able to outline how to stop this from happening in the first place. Arguably, as so clearly and dismally summarized in Chapter 3, many of our important Canadian democratic institutions that define who we are have already been compromised. They do not work properly. Therefore our democracy does not and cannot work properly. I imagine this is mostly attributable to some bureaucrats having the wrong motivation and wreaking havoc on the very institutions they were originally tasked to serve. Let's examine this further so we can put an end to it. Because if we do not, we will just be wasting our time trying to engage in *Democratic Restructuralism* solely through good physical design of the bureaucratic apparatus.

They say knowledge is gleaned from formal education but true wisdom is obtained through observation. So let's get wise and ensure our undertaking of *Democratic Restructuralism* is not jeopardized by those working against its pursuit, those who can destroy good design. We already know the motivation of those working within an organization is influenced by the design of that organization. We saw that organizations and people behave a certain way based on what motivates them to perform or not. You know, a performance bonus can motivate an employee to go the extra mile, just like your love for a spouse or family member can motivate you to get them that cup of coffee in the morning. Generally, a well-designed organization that empowers and motivates front-line staff to be effective in their roles, using their knowledge, experience and so forth to make a positive contribution to the efforts of something greater than themselves, likely will produce the right outcomes for everyone concerned. The only problem is that those who design an organization a certain way have their own motives for doing so. This can be dangerous to the health of an organization as well as that of its employees who mainly wish to do the right thing. Where government organizations are concerned, this is especially problematic given that their raison d'être is to serve the public.

I have observed through my research and first-hand experience that some people, whether they realize it or not, have the wrong motivations in mind when they are working in government. And yet, it is precisely in government, where the right motivations are what is really needed to provide desired results for the public. The psychology behind this manifests itself in many ways and, from a common-sense perspective, is the main reason government institutions here and around the democratic world have unraveled and do not work for the people, the 99 per cent. Therefore, whereas the physical design of our government institutions is very important when it comes to the *Democratic Restructuralism*, we also need, in no small part, an understanding of what motivates people working in government itself. The fact that Canadians significantly distrust their institutions, a finding of the 2018 Edelman Trust Barometer discussed earlier in this book, stands in stark contrast to one of its other findings—the credibility of not only journalists, but other authority figures has risen amongst those surveyed.

In fact, "The 'most-broken' institution is government, according to 46 per cent of respondents" to the Edelman survey.[40] In all likelihood, Canadians are not generally aware of how badly our institutions are failing due to their antiquated design, as well as the few bad apples with the wrong motivation operating within them, because they do not have the time to compile and configure all the facts and data that speak to the undesirable trend of our government institutions becoming increasingly ineffective. They do feel that these institutions cannot be entirely trusted, but seem nonetheless to trust the majority of civil servants working within the system. This is a predictable outcome.

As mentioned before, most people, including government employees are decent people who want to do the right thing. They are our friends, family members and neighbours. Given how bad things are going in certain other democratic countries and how unscathed Canada came out of the 2008 financial crisis, we probably feel the average government official is doing the best they can. All the same, we need to guard against the few bad apples and any other civil servants being influenced by the wrong motivations, which can result in the rejigging of the design of our government institutions for the purposes of a select few bureaucrats. Ironically, we can learn not only from First or Indigenous Peoples, an understanding that we need to honestly do the right thing, but also from the collective of our American brothers and sisters. Yes, Americans appear to be more divided than ever; however, if we reach beyond that tumult, into some of the richer rather than darker periods of American history, we can learn of the necessity and advantages of organizing our own government to 'stand on guard' against those that would usurp it for their own personal gain. Once again, that speaks to good risk management.

Learning from America's Forefathers

Long before Canada became the country we know today, long before our own *Constitution* and *Charter of Rights and Freedoms* existed, some brilliant, yet imperfect Americans (especially imperfect given their lack of consideration for Indigenous Peoples at the time, something Canada's own history suffers from), weighed how best to structure their own *Constitution* and government institutions. This was to ensure any individuals succumbing to the darker side of human nature would not pose a grave threat to their fledgling democracy. The insightful brilliance of America's forefathers appears in the early writings of what is known as *The Federalist Papers*, published in the newspapers of New York State. In the wake of America's Constitutional Convention in 1787, and the vigorous debate that ensued, *The Federalist Papers* discussed the US *Constitution* and rationale for its structure. Figuring prominently as authors of the *Papers*, and the *Constitution* itself, were renowned American intellects such as James Madison, Alexander Hamilton and John Jay. Madison would become America's fourth president as well as one of its founding fathers.

The most important issue of the *Federalist* was No. 51, in which Madison describes the philosophy behind the US *Constitution*.[41] And I found a passage contained within No. 51 to be of paramount importance. It reflects a deep understanding of the need to remain vigilant as some individuals may co-opt the design of government for their own desires. This understanding remains just as important today for modern democracies as it did in 18th century America. For while technological change continues apace, humans have not really changed that much. Perhaps we should even read more books, for in the beginning we had the printed 'word' rather than online blogs and Trump tweets to improve ourselves. Here are Madison's important words:

> But what is government itself, but the greatest of all reflections on human nature? . . . In framing a government which is to be administered by men [people] over men [people], the great difficulty lies in this: you must first enable the government to control the governed; and in the next place oblige it to control itself.[42]

Sounds like good risk management to me. This line of thinking by Madison also goes to the heart of American history because it is fundamental to the US *Constitution*. According to researcher Tom Byrnes, "This passage is the most famous in all of the Federalist Papers. It contains the basic philosophy behind the constitution . . . a philosophy of human nature."[43] Unfortunately, regardless of his individual genius, Madison was a product of his time, and his own nature had some glaring shortcomings that would become a permanent stain on American history. Apart from indifference to the plight of Indigenous Peoples, there was the institution of slavery, a stain which seeped through America's tapestry of largely positive accomplishments, blemishing the fabric of so many ideals championed by that country's founders. Indeed, as a journalism professor at New York University wrote recently in the *Washington Post*, when reviewing a book by another professor, Harvard's Noah Feldman, and entitled *The Three Lives of James Madison*, Madison tragically helped ensure slavery would exist in the US longer than it may have otherwise.

The contradiction lies in this according to Pamela Newkirk: "While drafting the *Constitution*, James Madison strove to ensure the protection of minority rights but also proposed that a slave be counted as three-fifths a person," the result being that "the contradiction, etched into the Constitution, would come to define Madison and a nation irreconcilably founded both on slavery and the ideals of liberty and justice."[44] Again, Madison was a product of his environment, 18th century America, before the *Emancipation Proclamation* and more recent civil liberty movements. He intuitively and probably knew that slavery was wrong, once indicating that he "thought it wrong to admit in the Constitution the idea that there could be property in men." Professor Feldman is cited as arguing that some of the drafters of the American Constitution were ashamed of their association with slavery, especially since other countries had already started to shun that institution. The catch being "they just did not feel sufficiently ashamed to do anything about it, at least not while their livelihoods and those of their families depended on the labour of enslaved persons."[45]

It may well be that things would have been different if the wider American public were more progressive in their notions of equality between people, women included. Perhaps then, as contemporaries of Madison and other drafters of the US Constitution, they would have shamed the founding fathers into doing the right thing. It is not so much that Madison or the other writers of the Constitution are to blame, just as Canada's own founding father, Hector Langevin, should not be solely blamed for the residential school system, as the obvious fact that the society of this time bears collective blame along with these individuals. The collective deficiency in the thinking of the time goes back to what the Penobscot Native we referenced earlier said. When you possess "your source of morality within you—arising out of an inner perception of what is wrong or shameful, you are your own judge." Or as Slow Turtle, the

Medicine Man we also referenced earlier believes, we largely have removed the spirituality from our democracy, the respect for each other, no matter who they are or where they come from. Without a righteous spirit, we are just hollow people, the decaying exterior husk of what should be torchbearers of a bright and prosperous future.

We still have much to learn from Madison, that overall in its breadth and depth, the structure of government is a reflection of human nature. Before delving into the utility of that, we should acknowledge this. Maybe what was lacking in his and his contemporaries thinking at the time was the spirituality piece. That aspect is also vital in ensuring the right things are done by democratic governments around the world, vital in a world where most people are decent and believe in fairness and justice. As we have just marked the 50th anniversary of Martin Luther King's passing, it is useful to quote a few excerpts from a speech he gave in Memphis, Tennessee, the day before he was unforgivably assassinated. In those excerpts, we see Reverend King's spiritual exhortations being as insightful, of value, and plain right for today's democracies in peril as they were 50 years ago. Maybe more so in America and elsewhere, but here too in Canada, considering the problems already outlined before, we should take heed of Doctor King's wisdom and spiritual guidance. His comments do seem applicable in many countries, by degrees, if we take stock of the global situation and our own:

> The nation is sick. Trouble is in the land; confusion all around
> . . . I know, somehow, that only when it is dark enough can
> you see the stars. And I see God working in this . . . in a way
> that [people] in some strange way, are responding . . . And
> another reason that I'm happy to live in this period is that
> we have been forced to a point where we are going to have to
> grapple with the problems that [people] have been trying to
> grapple with through history, but the demands didn't force

them to do it. Survival demands that we grapple with them
. . . It's alright to talk about streets flowing with milk and
honey, but God has commanded us to be concerned about
the slums down here, and [the] children who can't eat three
square meals a day.[46]

This speaks to some good motivation we need for our government to
work, the necessity of informed decision-making rooted in the good values most
of us possess. Turning our minds back to Madison, let's see how he counselled
people to be mindful of those with the wrong motivations, his personal failings
representing much of society at the time notwithstanding. Madison may have
even been a good steward to prevent the financial crisis from gripping modern
America. With his keen perceptiveness and understanding that organizations
need to control themselves through proper structures that keep wrong-minded
people at bay, he would be well-poised to make government work more for the
majority than a self-entitled minority. Elaborating on the need to keep wrongly
motivated people from accumulating too much power in government, Madison
wrote: "But the great security against a gradual concentration of the several
powers in the same department consists in giving to those who administer
each department the necessary constitutional means and personal motives to
resist encroachment of others."[47] Some good risk management advice again!

Basically, as Byrnes interpreted, this "statement goes to the heart of the
philosophy behind the Constitution."[48] Madison wanted to ensure that each
branch of the US government (i.e. Executive, Congress and Judicial) had the
motivation to keep a check on the others because any increase in the power of
one branch would be to the detriment of the others and of democracy. Byrnes
describes the effectiveness of the original design this way: "Thus, acting in its
own self-interest, each branch tries to curb any attempt by the other branches
to increase their power."[49] Madison himself clarifies this reasoning further in
No. 51: "the constant aim is to divide and arrange the several offices in such

a manner as that each may be a check on the other that the private interest of every individual may be a sentinel over the public right." Byrnes comprehends that passage from Madison's No. 51 in clever terms as follows: "Public rights are protected from an abusive government because of the check and balance system. The system is based on the understanding that individuals in government would seek their own self-interest, but in doing so would check [face may be a better word] the self-interest of others."[50]

So, if we are thinking of the American government or other democracies such as ours here in Canada, Madison believes it is hugely important that we ensure key departments and agencies of the government cannot grow at the expense of others, and that we be mindful of the darker side of human nature that can work toward that insidious end. Madison put it plainly this way: "Ambition must be made to counter ambition. The interest of the man must be connected with the constitutional rights of the place."[51] Of course, this should apply to women as well.

In all likelihood, Alexis de Tocqueville, whom we discussed before, saw the shrewdness belying Madison's genius when he wrote about the utility of the checks and balances in the early American system of democracy. He noted in *Democracy in America* that the ambitions of certain careerists in specific government positions can grow immensely, paralleling the power emanating from the government itself. For as the state's power grows, so too does the ambition of such individuals. "The ambition of particular persons increases with the power of the state; the force of parties."[52]

Zeroing in on the effectiveness of the design to curb the power of the legislature's impact on the executive branch, Tocqueville opined as follows: "The action of the legislature on the executive power can be direct," and "America took care that it not be."[53] Yet, since we already know he viewed the legislature as sacrosanct, a place where power is most directly reflective of the people's wishes, Tocqueville also deemed that body as an effective means to block the unbridled ambitions of, in the example of America, a president motivated by his own intentions. Whether or not he had someone like the current President, Donald Trump in mind, Tocqueville's thinking in regards to the role of the US President seems to be on solid ground indeed. "In everything essential that he does, he is directly or indirectly subject to the legislature; where he is entirely independent of it, he can do almost nothing." The brilliant conclusion that accommodates such thinking? "It is therefore his weakness, and not his force, that permits him to live in opposition to the legislative power."[54]

I am not convinced that President Trump and like-minded politicians are really committed to the constitutional rights of the various government institutions they are supposed to work alongside, much less understand the good intentions such perceptive American forefathers like Madison had in creating the *Constitution*. What I am convinced of is the value of we Canadians understanding what Madison cautioned—be wary of human nature and what motivates some people—bad behaviour—when you design the structures of your government. Madison may have liked our Canadian anthem, perhaps nodding approvingly from the heavens at the part that goes, "Oh Canada, we stand on guard for thee." Does this all really matter to modern day Canadians? Consider the following real world examples that I have observed, and the attendant risks that must be managed well.

Wrongminded Motivations that can Impact Government

In Canada, as in other democracies, it is not just the poorly thought-out design of government organizations that leads to problems. It is often the nonunionized management or executives within the public service that create the seedbed for poor decision-making to thrive, blossoming into all the disastrous results we read about in Chapter 3, such as the Phoenix payroll fiasco, messed up healthcare system, and so on. How so when we usually hear about problems stemming mainly from lazy union types who reflect the bureaucracy at large? Well, it goes like this. Although a manager or executive may possibly have been a member of the union immediately before climbing up the bureaucratic ladder and getting their latest non-union position within the pecking order of the organization, the changes he or she can make in terms of organizational impact shifts dramatically outside the realm of unionized employees. In real terms, the higher up the bureaucratic food chain the non-union employee climbs within the government organization, the more he or she can affect change. Too often the changes are undesirable for the rank-and-file employees as well as all Canadians.

Directors, Assistant Directors, Managing Directors, Senior Directors (there are so many proliferating senior titles in Canada's government these days) and upwards, all the way up perhaps to Deputy and full ministers themselves when they decide to tinker in their respective fiefdoms, may have a natural tendency to increase their status by doing the wrong things. In fact, this can happen in the Prime Minister's office (PMO) itself. In other democratic countries the same thing likely afflicts the upper ranks of their respective bureaucracies. Their wrongheaded motivations can be to:

1) increase the number of staff directly reporting to them, thereby increasing the size of their respective department and power base;

2) create a new division or silos of responsibility within their department, often under the guise of some kind of required specialization, regardless of it being necessary or not;

3) develop new and important sounding initiatives and projects, many of which are expensive 'frills' and based on a slick presentation of how urgently they are required, when the reality is they will be a burden to the organization, impeding its ability to perform core functions related to its mandate;

4) recycle prior initiatives and projects by repackaging them with a new name, revamped processes and technical jargon (changing the format

of documents and templates that adds no real value), and the degree of complexity to obfuscate the real intentions behind this all; and

5) support or oppose the political ideology of their masters who appointed them, regardless of that ideology being rational and in the best interest of the public at large (such as firing a whole lot of compensation advisors who capably ensured federal government employees were being paid properly and on time—only to replace them with that godforsaken Phoenix payroll system that does not work—despite the over $1 billion and counting costs to Canadian taxpayers).

This list is by no means an exhaustive one, but you can see that the leadership within bureaucratic institutions may not always be motivated by doing what's right. The intentions behind their bad motivations may be purposeful, for personal gain. Conversely, they may merely be fuelled by inexperience and lack of informed awareness in decision-making. In the case of the former, senior officials may be looking to increase their chances of promotion and higher performance pay/bonuses by appearing to effect positive change within the bureaucracy. Yet as we know, appearances can be deceiving. These officials could also be bullies, just looking to get their way by cracking a few skulls, the fallout being in their department or externally amongst members of the broader public. In the case of the latter, non-union government officials and ministers, too often than not, have hardly any industry or real-world experience in the field over which their department is supposed to serve the public. It has been my personal experience, and through observation as well as employment in the federal public service, that those running government institutions far too regularly promote loyal and obsequious individuals into roles they are not qualified to perform.

For example, and no personal slight is intended, is a journalist readily equipped and capable of running an already sprawling and ill-designed federal Public Works department? That absurdly designed department is organized to have wide ranging, complex, and disparate responsibilities, the direct result being that, together, the operating divisions do not appear to fit well. Indeed, if a child were playing a matching game, like the one where you are supposed to flip over a pair of cards amongst dozens placed face down in front of you, determining if they are similar enough to go together or not, that child would probably never dream of constituting our Public Works department the way it is now. They likely would spend the allowance given to them by their parents in a much wiser manner than the taxpayer dollars wasted by Public Works in its ludicrous procurement processes too. Even highly qualified individuals having the motivation to do a good job would find it overly challenging, to say the least, to run a white elephant like the Canadian Public Works department. The absence of there being an independent risk-management head in each of its divisions does little to help matters as we have seen. When you add ill-experienced and unknowledgeable administrators to the mix, you end up with a recipe for disaster. And it is not just the Phoenix payroll system or never-ending procurement processes that yield no desperately needed equipment for our military personnel that are problems.

Another federal government department led by too inexperienced, unskilled and unknowledgeable senior civil servants is Shared Services, which also fell within the purview of Public Works along with other incongruous responsibilities. It, too, has been a costly waste of resources for taxpayers. The negative outcomes are sadly predictable. And regardless of senior government officials' intentions being self-serving or innocently misguided, the results are the same. Canadians are all too often adversely impacted, including the mental health of our hard-working rank-and-file civil servants. You end up with uninformed and misguided decision-making that has terrible consequences for the pocket books and overall quality of life of Canadians. Certainly the leadership of any government department should have fairly good people skills, what are commonly called 'soft skills' to help generate the right outcomes for the public. But when you do not know what you are doing because you lack the overall experience, education and understanding of the risks associated with your department's work (scientific, financial, environmental, information technology, healthcare, etc.), all the good intentions in the world are not likely to compensate for your lack of credibility amongst the staff you oversee; nor are they likely to compensate for the unforeseen consequences of any poor, uninformed and wrong-headed decisions that are made.

It also bears noting that when management lacks credibility with the staff they are supposed to be leading because of the bad decisions they are making, all the good front-line employees begin to lose their motivation to try and do the right thing themselves. It is a vicious circle. If you doubt this view, consider the recent results of an Environics Research Poll conducted in 2017 for the Professional Institute of the Public Service of Canada (PIPSC)—the Union comprised of scientists and other government professionals, outside of the non-unionized and swelling executive cadre within the federal public service. The poll, done also in the wake of the former Harper government and its growing reputation for 'muzzling' scientists in the public service, an indication of less evidence-based decision-making in Ottawa, revealed little progress being made under the Trudeau Liberals now in power. As reported by Mike De Souza in early 2018, "Things continue as if there had never been an election." Additionally, "while the numbers show progress, respondents said that many of their managers haven't fully accepted and implemented evidence-based decision making and better practices."[55] More poignantly, "There is too much politics affecting decision making and research direction," said just one respondent referenced by several in De Souza's analysis of the PIPSC report.[56]

The corrosive influence of ill-informed politics is also alive and well in President Trump's America. You can see it in what could be interpreted as the muzzling of scientists within the United States Geological Survey (USGS). A recent *Los Angeles Times* article notes the USGS is America's "leading scientific agency on natural resources and natural hazards . . . and studies risks such as rising sea levels caused by climate change." The June 2018 *Times* article summarizes how "a new directive from the Trump administration instructs federal scientists with [USGS] to get approval from its parent agency before agreeing to most interview requests from reporters, according to employees and emails from officials with the Department of the Interior and USGS." Cutting to the chase, the *Times* reported that "current and former federal employees suggested the new protocols are an unwieldly attempt to control the voices of workers in the Department of Interior, which employs some 70,000 people, including thousands of scientists at the top of their fields."[57]

A former chief scientist of the USGS earthquake hazards team, William Ellsworth, who currently serves as a professor of geophysics at Stanford University, is cited by the *Times* in this regard: "This is really quite troubling . . . In the 44 years I was with the agency, I was never required to go through anyone for authorization to speak with a reporter." Funny too how, as the *Times* also mentions, that "the Center for Investigative Reporting wrote about the deletion of every mention of humans causing climate change in a draft report for the National Park Service; the reference was later restored."[58] Restoration is always good. Perhaps the Trump administration, much like the prior Harper administration here in Canada, wishes to test the limits of democracy. Regardless, the limits of democracy should not be restricted to politically motivated decisions and business decisions where the economy is concerned, and perhaps the personal gains of a select few pushing such decisions. Its limits must include all segments and facets of society, including important scientific or other information that is germane to good decision-making for all stakeholders in society.

Back here in Canada, illustrative of the continuing lack of risk-based decision-making within the broader bureaucracy, the PIPSC report stated this, among other disturbing points:

- "In 2013, 86 per cent said they felt they couldn't share concerns about health, safety or the environment without censorship or retaliation. In 2017, 73 per cent felt they were not free to raise these concerns."
- "In 2013, 71 per cent of respondents said that Canada's policies, laws and programs were compromised by political interference. In 2017, 40 per cent felt this way."
- "In 2013, 48 per cent of respondents were aware of cases in which their department or agency had suppressed or declined to release information, leading to incomplete, inaccurate, or misleading impressions by the public, regulated industry, the media and/or government officials. In 2017, 29 per cent of respondents were aware of these types of cases."[59]

From these survey results alone, we see that many unionized civil servants are under the thumb of their handlers, department executives in charge of things who obviously have the wrong motivations themselves, or forced onto them by even higher ups such as ministers or the PMO. Emphasizing that a good portion of the civil service is under the thumb of their masters rather than Canadian voters are the results of the 2017 Public Service Employee Survey, made public in early 2018. The survey canvassed a wide spectrum of Canada's federal government employees, garnering responses from 174,544 employees in 86 federal departments.[60] As reported by the *Hill Times*, the results point to a relevant portion of the workforce being harried, if not downright bullied. A statistically significant "18 per cent of the public servants said they've been victims of harassment on the job in the preceding two years." Further, the disturbing result "was only one percentage point lower than those who answered affirmatively in 2014."[61] We can only wonder if the over one-third of the public service who did not respond to the survey also represents victims of the abuse who thought completion of the survey would be pointless in achieving positive change.

To give you a flavour of only a few of the federal departments that are not satisfied with their organization, here are some of the numbers arising from the survey: forty per cent of the Canada Border Services Agency (CBSA) employees were unsatisfied, followed by Correctional Services Canada (CSC) and Shared Services Canada, each with a 33 per cent unsatisfied result. Additionally, when asked if their workplace was psychologically healthy, CSC and CBSA staff responded the most negatively, with a 53 per cent and 43 per cent disagreement rate respectively. Alarmingly, 34 per cent of CSC survey respondents, 26 per cent of CBSA, 25 per cent of the Office of the Information Commissioner, and 22 per cent each of Indigenous and Northern Affairs and the Transportation Safety Board, indicated they had been victims of harassment on the job over the last two years.[62] There are other departments with similarly disturbing results, but you get the picture. We could presuppose that the survey respondents, all roughly 175,000 of them, are riddled with left-wing, lazy union types that are a bunch of whiners, apt to complain about just anything. This would live up to the existing stereotype. However it does seem unlikely. There may be some bad apples but we have seen (and will see much more), counterintuitively, the motivations of the non-union civil service leadership being questionable.

One can easily make the argument that poor motivation in the leadership of the permanent bureaucracy also creates a partisan civil service that does not make good decisions in government. According to Donald Savoie, "a professor and expert on Canada's public service," our rank-and-file government employees need to be non-partisan. He believes "a new government that comes in has . . . minimum knowledge." Therefore, "it's important to have a public service that can speak to them without fear or favour."[63] Apparently, as *CBC News* reported in late 2015, "the so-called 'creeping politicization' of the public service dates as far back as the 1970s, under Liberal governments, but the Harper administration has come under special criticism from some scholars."[64] And if decisions are made based on the political ideology of the day rather than informed understanding (of facts and the will of the people) at the highest levels of government departments, no wonder the permanent bureaucracy has been politicized. Dumbed down may be a better term!

Leadership's ill-informed decisions often results in the broader bureaucracy being asked to do the wrong things. This produces the wrong outcomes for the public intimated earlier, such as the debacle known as the Phoenix compensation system. It also creates stress and reinforces bad behaviours amongst otherwise well-intentioned rank-and-file government employees. Again, leaders may be purposeful in asking subordinates to pursue the wrong results so those leaders can gain financially or status-wise via promotions or feed their self-importance in pursuing pet projects that add no value to the organization, or merely satisfy their own masters who are wrongly motivated themselves. Or leaders may be oblivious as to having the wrong intentions to begin with, unaware of the competence and experience levels required to make good decisions, which they do not possess themselves, having been promoted mainly because they talked a good game.

Since we mentioned the Phoenix system again, is it any wonder that a 2018 PSAC survey also found "more than three-quarters of the respondents said Phoenix problems have negatively affected their mental health"?[65] It should be obvious to all of us that many public-sector members reeling from Phoenix, feeling harassed and in a psychologically unhealthy environment where decisions are not always made in the public interest, are not likely being motivated to serve Canadians well. If it does not piss you off, it should. Especially since the rot at the root of our decaying institutions, and by extension our democracy, reaches all the way to Parliament, the apex of our government's power structure. There can be many cases in which various government department heads wish to suppress any information that may point to problems in their immediate sphere of influence, but further analysis suggests wrong motivations reach all the way to the top of our government. Again, in some instances, people simply do not know what they are doing.

Looking unbiasedly at the current Canadian Prime Minister, Justin Trudeau, Jordan Press finds that a recent federal ethics report tells us much about how the Prime Minister views his job. As some Canadians may know, our ethics Commissioner, Mary Dawson, investigated the PM for violations of the *Conflict of interest Act* after he and his family holidayed on the Aga Khan's private island. Apart from concluding that the PM violated some section of the act, Dawson curiously documented how Trudeau views meetings. Since his meeting with the Aga Khan may be viewed as a conflict of interest because the Canadian government has provided millions of dollars of grants to that billionaire's philanthropically deemed causes, as Press wrote, "Dawson described how Trudeau sees meetings as a way 'to further develop a relationship between the individual and Canada', and his role in those meetings 'as ceremonial in nature.' "[66] Trudeau must be one of those warm and fuzzy type leaders who focuses on soft skills himself since Dawson recounted that "the meetings he (Trudeau) attends as prime minister are not business meetings." Strikingly, Dawson continues, "Rather they are high-level meetings centred on relationship building and ensuring that all parties are moving together."[67]

I am all for being nice myself and collaborating with others. However, of crucial importance is how Trudeau's approach actually creates the wrong motivation for other senior bureaucrats working in government, reinforcing poor decision-making and handling of the public purse for we Canadians, who deserve better. Very perceptively, Press cites Alex Marland, a political science professor at Memorial University, in assessing the results of Trudeau's behaviour: "A hands-off prime minister allows some ministers to become more powerful than others, and also gives more power to political staffers in the Prime Minister's Office."[68]

We have observed in the preceding chapter how the PMO has become the epicentre of our national government's dysfunction. Changing its name from the Langevin Block only served as window dressing or optics management. The tactic disingenuously condemned Hector Langevin as being solely responsible for all the ongoing costly and disturbing trends in government, such as the horrific residential school system discussed earlier, rather than the current and some previous occupants of what was the Langevin Block.

Maybe Trudeau wants to mend relations with our Indigenous Peoples, even to the extent of conducting meetings that are 'ceremonial in nature.' But Indigenous Peoples and the rest of Canadians still need concrete solutions to problems that are way past the point of requiring more ceremonial treatment, such as yet more fruitless study and discussion rather than real common sense, fair and risk-based decisions that benefit our First Peoples. In elaborating further on the power concentration leading to the PMO, the erstwhile Langevin Block, Marland stated this: "The power doesn't vanish . . . it just diffuses to different places, including unelected and largely unaccountable staffers."[69] Another professor cited by Press, Kathy Brock at Queen's University, alludes to how wrong motivations are cultivated through the diffusion of power. "The Power has also diffused to the senior civil servants checking and coordinating policy across departments." More specifically she summarizes: "Diffusion weakens the lines of accountability because no one person or minister can be held responsible for a policy or program." Even worse, "this can lead a prime minister to become more detached from how policies are being written and implemented."[70] Brock seems to be a pretty sharp professor, as is reporter Jordan Press who quotes her in his piece.

Instead of the optics management or warm and fuzzy stuff, which basically entails politicians and senior government officials telling most people what they want to hear and carefully cultivating the image of capable leader, the real business of government is hard work. It is heavy lifting. We do not currently have many leaders like America's James Madison doing the real work, designing an effective government that guards against wrong motivation. We see lots of talk, the ceremony of real government instead of the practice of real and responsible government. Brock is suitably referenced stating this: "A lot of government work is tough slogging. It's getting down into the details and ensuring things work out and that's where [Trudeau] could run into problems as we saw with the China trip [no free trade talks that were expected took shape]."[71] We certainly have seen a lot of that, whether in Trudeau's poorly thought out trip to India, wherein he and Canada were linked to supporting those convicted of attempted murder as discussed, or the lacklustre China trip mentioned. Again, he is not to blame. Nobody is. The system does not work. It cannot harness the sincerity, compassion and kindness that resides in the hearts of most of us. It is not designed to reflect the free will of Canadians. This problem plagues all nations that could be great kingdoms of democracy, a New Jerusalem if you will. Restoring the kingdom of democracy is more important than moving state capitols about. Consider that Jerusalem is an earthly place in name only.

Press sees missteps being made, noting "those kinds of missteps are the consequences of being more focused on image politics and leaving the details to others."[72] For me, the bigger issue is not having the right structure in government to begin with. We need *Democratic Restructuralism* in the physical design of our government to begin with, as outlined in the last chapter. Another bigger issue is not considering human nature the way the great American thinker and principal framer of the US *Constitution*, James Madison, did in fundamentally designing American government. Our journey in embarking on *Democratic Restructuralism* must, to achieve its primary goal in improving the quality of life for all Canadians, learn from his wisdom. The failure of today's American government leaders to have learned from their predecessors that the fundamental underpinnings of democracy must be preserved, if not strengthened, should not preclude Canadians from carrying the torch of right-minded thinking forward. Let's reflect, as fairly as possible, on the current American experience under President Trump's leadership. The wrong motivation being created will likely result in yet more dysfunctional government and negative consequences for the good people of America who have long been our friends and allies, even our moral compass at times.

The world knows that Mr. Trump had little in the way of any government experience, logically leading to a lack of awareness and understanding of how to achieve real positive change in the American bureaucracy, leading to improved results for Americans. His wealth, ties to big business, and flagrant nepotism likely has done little to engage and ameliorate the lives of the 99 per cent, a large portion of whom may have ironically voted him into power due to their justifiably being fed up with the status quo. Tragically, not only may Trump's motivation be in the wrong place, but he is probably creating even more wrong-minded motivations in the US. How could it be otherwise when the following reports surfaced in March 2018? According to a *Washington Post* investigation, the American Presidential Personnel Office (PPO), the office responsible for vetting new appointments in the Trump administration, suffers itself from staff shortages and inexperienced personnel.[73] According to the *Hill.com*, the PPO "is responsible for vetting thousands of political appointees across the Trump administration." That equates to "about 4,000 jobs, about 1,600 of which require Senate approval."[74] And while most of you do not need me to tell you about all the comings and goings of senior officials within the Trump government, here is a recap for those unaware of the facts.

The front entrance to the White House has become a veritable revolving door with more than two dozen senior Trump officials passing through to what is likely greener pastures. In less than two years of the Trump presidency, just a few of the high-ranking individuals who were motivated to leave—being told the equivalent of "You're fired" or voluntarily departing—included: the Secretary of State, the Secretary of Veterans Affairs, the Secretary of Health and Human Services, both the White House Chief of Staff and the Deputy Chief of Staff, the White House Press Secretary and an Assistant Press Secretary, both the FBI's Director and Deputy Director, an acting Attorney General, several senior National Security officials, a Homeland Security adviser, the head of the Consumer Financial Protection Bureau, the White House Chief Strategist, a few Directors of Communications, and so on.[75]

By mid-November 2018, Jonathan Bernstein in an opinion piece carried by *Bloomberg* posed this question: "How chaotic are things now?" It seems self-evident actually. He notes, "There's no nominee to replace Attorney General Jeff Sessions, who was fired a week ago, and the acting [AG] is under fire from multiple directions." But there is more chaos. "There's also no nominee to replace United Nations Ambassador Nikki Haley, who announced her resignation back on Oct. 9." Bernstein states, "Nor is there one for the Environmental Protection Agency." Pouring on even more chaos, we learn that "the administration lost its deputy national security adviser—the third person to hold that critical post over the 22 months Donald Trump has been in office."[76] Nothing like creating even more risks for a confused and divided electorate! Just what is the goal of the Trump administration?

Then there were all the endless tweets and controversy surrounding this ongoing mayhem, with all the speculation and distraction sending the very structure of the nation, and those civil servants who otherwise want to do the right thing, into a tailspin, a growing abyss of self-doubt, questioning just what the point of it all is—especially when those running things cannot lead by example. Here, we see American institutions being co-opted and certainly compromised, by a senior administration that is not cultivating the right thinking, the right motivation, the right mindset within the trenches of a civil service that should serve the public good.

How could anyone take the current US administration seriously, including those in other nations, be they friend or foe? Think of the implications if you dare. They likely paint a bleak future if things are not right-sided. Along with the endless tweets are the titillating distractions associated with Trump Senior himself: the former stripper and pornographic actress, Stormy Daniels', salacious accusations; or all the lurid football locker talk from someone who should know better. It speaks to a nation guided by a supremely uninformed and ill-experienced leader, basking in the shadow of a wave of resentment that propelled him to the shores of the White House; that resentment being against the status quo that did nothing to improve the average American's lot in life. In turn, the unpalatable circumstances of the Democrats' status quo approach, emanating from more and more misguided and poor decisions that never considered the overall risks mounting for Main Street America, like in Flint, Michigan, served as a precursor for that which has arisen. The promise of *"Yes We Can"* becoming the empty rhetoric of an administration that did not know 'how,' like so many before it and yet to come, in all too many decaying democracies around the world. Now, the powerful yet wrongly minded only add to the mountain of chaos and dysfunction that was once considered a proud model of democracy, so carefully devised by the likes of Madison and spiritually envisioned by the likes of Martin Luther King.

The Hill reported that the PPO is "operating with about 30 staff members, about a third of the numbers utilized by previous administrations." That could be a reflection of greater efficiency you may think. However, "many of those staff members are friends and relatives of top officials, including . . . where one senior official had four members of his family receive appointments to the office."[77] What kind of motivation does this produce in government? Surely not the right ones which Madison, minus his stance on minorities such as Blacks or disenfranchised women and Indigenous Peoples, correctly understood—that "ambition must be made to counteract ambition."

Within the inexperienced and understaffed PPO, there also are some questionable figures in terms of their genuine interest to support the civic good by making reasonable decisions regarding senior appointments. Included in the staff of the PPO are two senior employees, "a lance corporal in the Marine Corps Reserves with previous arrests for assault and disorderly conduct, as well as a college dropout with drunk driving arrests."[78] One can only speculate about the motivations of such people themselves, aside from the more concerning notion as to the impact they are having in supporting an office tasked with vetting other US government administration appointments. It is like a domino effect whereby existing US institutions can be compromised by senior officials who may not be qualified, let alone interested, in strengthening the institutions of democracy, guided by the right balance of education, experience, insight and wisdom—to do right.

In the PPO, "most staffers now working in the office are in their mid-20s, the investigation found, and frequently come to the PPO from previous work on the Trump campaign, with little professional experience."[79] America! Your Forefathers, First Peoples and Spiritual Leaders—the Entire World—needs you to do better! We need you to check the wrong ambitions. We know you can! You've done it before!

Admittedly, Canadians including myself, should not be perceived to be casting any stones in the proverbial glass house. While not as extreme in terms of the US case, our own structures and systems of government are being hampered in their effectiveness by those possessing the wrong motivations. I alluded to this earlier, describing how some of our senior officials may purposefully or unknowingly go about their jobs, work that impacts us all, with the wrong motives in mind.

Problematically, the issue, while not that severe in its outward appearance to Canadians as the similar issue is to Americans, is also present in the highest echelons of our own national government. That is our own glass House. A Commons for the people in name only. It is built not only with an inadequate structural design that cannot withstand the weight of responsibility, but also filled with a leadership not capably motivated to weather the coming storms. Let they without sin among them, let they cast the first stone toward the other ailing democracies.

It may surprise you to learn that our government-employed scientists and other fact-based researchers are not the only ones who may be muzzled and limited in acting on Canadians' behalf. MPs we elect and gullibly assume represent our community's interest on Parliament Hill, are prevented from doing just that. In a spring of 2008 issue of the *Canadian Parliamentary Review*, Evan Sotiropoulos talks about how our government is not working the way it should. It does seem that the wrong motivations are being cultivated beyond the borders of America. "Today, most people do not elect specialists but instead, send generalists to Ottawa without the proper skill set and experience to fulfil the duties of a parliamentarian." Compounding this problem is the fact that MPs generally are not in their roles for a long time, which Sotiropoulos sees as something that "prevents the development of institutional memory."[80]

Sotiropoulos also raises Norman Ward's argument from decades ago, which exemplifies how deeply rooted our own revolving door is on Parliament Hill. That "most members of Parliament, far from being legislators who enact laws with a competence born of experience, are mere transients."[81] Sure, our revolving door may not be the whirling blur that Trump's White House entryway is, but it, too, is generating the wrong motivations to make things right in our own democracy. To put it succinctly, how can we expect our own significantly unqualified, uninformed and short in tenure MPs to do a good job leading the country, or make valid and rational opposing arguments to the party that does, in the House of Commons? How can the bureaucracy within all the institutions and organizations that make up the federal government be sufficiently motivated to do what is best, what is right, when their leaders, MPs, cannot?

Ironically, the ballooning government over the long span of Canadian history may often have served only to balloon our government's incapability to get anything done. Writing 10 years ago, Sotiropoulos already saw the ballooning effect was pretty big indeed: "In the middle of the 20th century, the federal ministry consisted of about 20 individuals; in recent times, Messrs. Mulroney, Chrétien and Martin have led ministries double that size."[82] Of course, Harper's command-and-control approach changed little, if anything at all. Logically then, "The growth in the number of cabinet posts has meant a corresponding increase in the federal bureaucracy."[83]

It is true that we live in a much more complex world that may require larger governments to cope with that reality, along with the fact that our population has grown over the years. Still, the complexity of our world, or at least that on Parliament Hill in Ottawa, may have a lot to do with the self-inflicted complexity that goes along with the bloated, opaque spider's web of government departments and agencies that do, as we saw, work less and less for the majority of Canadians. How can the exponential growth of the government administration make any sense at all, even where it likely would be warranted, when elected MPs may not know what they are doing to begin with?

Sotiropoulos understood "the need for long serving members able to competently hold the government to account."[84] Designing government institutions and structures to enable elected MPs to make risk-based decisions is one thing, such as having them provided with sufficient reports from a Chief Risk Officer. Yet when they are not provided with the right motivation to begin with, that may not matter anyway as meaningful debate and the integrity of good organizational design in government may be consequently swept aside. We are not in Trump's America. However, looking back to 2008, it was not just scientists and other researchers in government trying to work for the public good who were being muzzled. "Liberal party regimes—including the three under Chrétien's—would regularly muzzle backbenchers by declaring various non-money bills matters of confidence," wrote Sotiropoulos. He found that "customarily, cabinet solidarity and party discipline are integral parts of our Westminster-style parliamentary democracy."[85] Of course, things just got tougher under Harper and his unprecedented and tightly controlled PMO.

On Senate Reform

Sotiropoulos found a solution to the problem in—drum roll please—you guessed it, that oh so boring and long drawn-out discussion on Senate reform. Basically, he believes that an elected Senate in Canada would be a panacea to offset the "inexperience of most MPs" and "their numerous other commitments associated with public life." He rightly argues MPs' issues mean "the House of Commons will continually be unable to check the concentration of power in Canadian politics."[86] However, he never attempts to explore how to create a functioning House of Commons where qualified and informed MPs, whom Canadians have sent there, can actually do a better job. It is as if he has given up on that thoughtful journey before ever even embarking upon it. This is unabashedly why his article, which contains a lot of valuable insight, is boldly entitled *A Reformed Senate as a Check on Prime Ministerial Power*. I do not dispute that if we kept the Senate it would make sense for our senators to be elected by the good people of Canada, just as MPs themselves are. We do not need politically appointed senators doing the bidding of their puppet masters, being wrongly motivated to produce even more disastrous results for Canadians. Giving more power to the Senate seems to merely bypass, if not fully ignore, what MPs need to be motivated to do in the first place—their jobs.

Somehow Sotiropoulos just wants the evisceration of the lower chamber of our bicameral parliamentary system, the House of Commons, to be offset by an elected and somehow better informed upper chamber, the Senate. I would therefore ask: Why do a well-functioning, responsible and accountable House and Senate have to be mutually exclusive to begin with? Hold that thought. Why have a Senate at all if we have an effective House doing what voters want them to in Ottawa? Why not better design and strengthen our democratic institutions by ensuring our MPs in the House are provided with the necessary risk-based information to make good and informed decisions for all Canadians? I raised that issue in the previous chapter.

Sotiropoulos described how the Canadian Senate, even before the recent scandals, was pretty much a symbol of grand impotence: "Although the upper house regularly recommends technical improvements to bills, it is unable to veto misguided legislation from an unflinching House since the Senate operates in a political vacuum and habitually defers to the elected chamber."[87] I say again, why not better design the House so its occupants can do the jobs we reasonably expect of them? After all, we do foot the bill; and that bill is mighty large for we taxpayers when it comes to Senate tomfoolery.

Canadian readers may recall the widely reported Senate expense scandal. It started near the end of 2012 and involved such personalities as Mike Duffy, Patrick Brazeau (who also reportedly worked as a manager at the Bare Fax, a strip club in Ottawa, while suspended from the senate—but I am not sure if Stormy Daniels ever performed there or for President Trump in the US), Pamela Wallin and Mac Harb. Apparently these esteemed senators claimed questionable living costs that did not really qualify as living expenses reimbursable by the Senate. To make a long, costly and sordid story short, the Senate hired an external and reputable auditing firm to provide it with an independent report examining the dubious expense claims. By November 2013, Senators Duffy, Wallin and Brazeau found themselves suspended without pay. Criminal charges were laid against Brazeau, Duffy and Harb, but those charges really ended up leading nowhere. Duffy was acquitted and charges against the others were withdrawn. You also likely heard about Duffy butting heads with the PMO due to the following curious situation—I do wonder about the motivation of some senior government officials here, along with the design of the politically appointed Senate and its policies and procedures, or lack thereof.

In March 2013, prior to the auditing firm finishing its work, Duffy repaid $90,172 for the questionable living expenses he had claimed. However, Canadians learned from the media shortly after, in May 2013, that this money originated from a personal cheque provided by the PMO's Chief of Staff, Nigel Wright.[88] I could go on, but I imagine you have heard enough. Aside from the disrepute brought upon the Senate, which I am not sure really does that much constructive work for Canadians and democracy in the first place, the whole debacle has cost taxpayers a small fortune. The Auditor General ended up reviewing expense claims made by over 100 other Senators and erstwhile politicians holding the sinecure, finding in a 2015 report that 30 such officials made inappropriate claims.[89] Adding to the AG's costly investigation was obviously the accounting firm Deloitte's expenses, as well as the ongoing salaries and expenses of unelected Senators and their staff, which may be a constitutional necessity but highly unnecessary in modern-day Canada. The further costs associated with the upkeep of the higher red chamber, which no longer reflects good design, let alone decision-making within its walls, is both a waste of money and a drag on our democracy.

After Duffy's acquittal in the spring of 2016, he launched a lawsuit against the Senate and Attorney General for almost $8 million, which, if he is successful, might cost us even more. Hey, at least it is costing us less than Phoenix which is also paying civil servants more than they should receive in some instances, while shorting so many others. Oh look, there you have it again, all the way up to the PMO in the case of the Senate scandal, unsavoury motives and a suspect design that yields nothing but trouble for Canada and Canadians. Shame!

In any case, the motivations of the current Senate are questionable as it stands, with Senators being political appointees rather than a bastion of representative government; the House, we have aptly described, riddled with too many inexperienced MPs not receiving the necessary information and guidance they need to make the right decisions for Canadians and the country. Receiving the right and timely risk-based information from the various departments and agencies that make up the federal government would go a long way in acting as a compensating mechanism for inexperienced MPs. In the final analysis, whether they are experienced in government operations or not, what use can they be in either case if they do not receive the correct information at the right time to make the right decisions?

Amusingly, Sotiropoulos invoked the *Federalist Papers* just as this book did earlier, but he stopped short of trying to grasp that the "ambition must be made to counter ambition" in all chambers of government. He only commented that "the authors of *The Federalist Papers*, for example argued in favour of a senate, consistent with the Madisonian notion of checks and balances."[90] I don't know about you, but I would like to have my cake and eat it too. It is not enough to raise a bunch of issues that "stressed the need for Senate reform to fill the Parliamentary void."[91] We need to mend the flag that flies above both government chambers. To do that, we should do something counterintuitive: abolish the Senate altogether. In *Dismantling Canada*, Brooke Jeffrey noted that our Senate has often been perceived as undemocratic. He stated that "the Reform/Alliance Party described it as illegitimate since it was 'unelected, unrepresentative and ineffective.' "[92] Harper may have stacked it with his political appointees, yet arguably so have other parties. And there is no need to duplicate the work of qualified, informed and elected MPs making the right decisions for Canadians, by asking another chamber of duplicate bureaucrats to do the very same thing.

By abolishing the Senate, what can we do with the taxpayers' money we save from the salaries going to all the political appointees, their perks and pensions, their staff, etc.? We will use those funds in a more productive and effective way. We will utilize them to pay for the costs of the new RMO, thereby promoting risk-based decision-making in Parliament, the dissemination of much more useful information to voters, all of which should, ultimately, save us even more money in the long run. The additional waste associated with yet more betrayal of our values and collective wishes will most assuredly be avoided when the Senate is abolished.

Oh, and in case you are wondering if it is difficult to get rid of the Senate, it is not impossible. According to a May 2013 *Maclean's* magazine article, instructively headed "How to abolish the Senate of Canada," Nick Taylor-Vaisey outlined what we need to do. We can abolish the Senate "either by a constitutional amendment backed by at least seven provinces representing 50 per cent of the population, or one with unanimous provincial consent." At the time of the article's writing, Taylor-Vaisey commented that "experts are split on which amending formula applies."[93] Fast-forwarding a few years, the Harper government requested the Supreme Court look at the issue. As another subsequent *Maclean's* piece noted in April 2014, Harper had proposed to impose term limits on senators and create a "consultative election" process to choose nominees. Yet, it was the Supreme Court's unanimous decision, as reported by *Maclean's*, that "such reforms would require constitutional amendments, approved by at least seven provinces representing 50 per cent of the population." This apparently would be "a route fraught with political landmines which Harper had hoped to avoid."[94]

For our purposes, abolishing the Senate so we can spend taxpayers' money more wisely on a RMO, Canada's highest court ruled that "getting rid of the chamber altogether would require the unanimous consent of all 10 provinces." Part of the rationale arises from the court's view that "the Senate is one of Canada's foundational political institutions"; that "it lies at the heart of the agreement that gave birth to the Canadian federation."[95] I get it, and the fact that, as *Maclean's* states, "the Fathers of Confederation deliberately chose an appointed chamber, which was supposed to be independent, free of partisanship and able to apply 'sober second thought' to legislation."[96] But they lived in simpler times, and we have outgrown the antiquated design of the Senate. We can turn, too, to our Fathers of Confederation, or the Fathers of the US *Constitution*, or to Fathers (and Mothers alike) elsewhere now, learning and adopting valuable teachings. Yet we must cast aside that which no longer works, where even if our ancestors were alive today, they would approve of a more beneficial way of interpreting broader messages and intentions, learning from us, their children, in turn.

If, for example, we are mature enough now to understand that the residential school system imposed by our forefathers on First Peoples was, in hindsight, obviously wrong, why not have the maturity to also view some of their other designs as being outdated in their thinking? We need not give up the ghost, Holy or otherwise, in being flexible here. It is just a case of connecting with our inner spirituality and doing what is right and good for everyone, while not denouncing outright our history and embracing rigid interpretations that limits the potential of our democracy and its participants. Sins of the past must be forgiven, especially those that are institutional in design. Church, state or other, we must learn, adopting that which is good, correcting that which is wrong for our times, moving forward to embrace everyone along the way who, quite simply, wants to be on the journey of personal and collective growth. To do the opposite will only engender anger and misunderstanding, the division so prominent in church, state and society now. Our children will never forgive us if we continue down that path now. It is not the righteous one. It is not one of restoration, hope, and spiritual renewal that heals rather than destroys.

Personally, given what the credible and diverse research contained in this book reveals, as well as what the Senate scandal itself revealed, I see no logical reason why all the provinces could not agree to abolish the Senate. If the good Canadians in each province are presented with the facts, that the anachronism known as our Senate no longer works as intended, consists of unelected officials and is a complete waste of taxpayers' dollars, why would they not all vote to abolish this useless appendage so representative of our broken democracy! Again, the money and effort would be better applied in establishing and maintaining a RMO as described in the preceding chapter. And if we cannot get rid of the Senate, perhaps there is a way to transform it into the RMO. Surely we can overcome the constraints of what we created over 150 years ago so we can achieve our potential now. Anyway, it is in the interest of the provinces to have the Senate abolished so they can have their own risks suitably addressed by the MPs they elect. It is in all Canadians' interest to eliminate that which serves no purpose.

The Diminished Role of Parliament

Let's start to examine the broad characteristics of an effective and well-functioning public service. In issue No. 122 produced by the Mowat Centre—Ontario's Voice on Public Policy, and released in June 2016, we find this topic on the cover: "Creating a High-Performing Canadian Civil Service Against a Backdrop of Disruptive Change." What a mouthful to repeat! Incidentally, the Mowat Centre is housed at the School of Public Policy & Governance at the University of Toronto. Anyway, in its roughly 36 pages of commentary on how to improve the Canadian public service, the Mowat article proposes some reforms that likely would lead to positive change. The status quo appears undesirable because "failure to sufficiently modernize has slowly eroded the civil services' ability to meet the needs of Canadians."[97] Humorously, and I would rather be laughing than crying, the author of the Mowat article, Mark D. Jarvis, states this at the outset of his piece: "It is worth noting that the civil service does not work for the public."[98] Certainly we saw that already in chapter 3. The lack of the correct motivation, behaviour and organizational design in our leadership is also helping to ensure the bureaucracy does not work for us. One can only agree with Mr. Jarvis that "the civil service is purposefully under the political control of the government of the day through a hierarchical structure, with authority delegated from ministers down the departmental chain." The result is that "this establishes the democratic control . . . with ministers—as the heads of government departments—ultimately accountable to Parliament and voters."[99]

But is that not the problem to begin with—political control rather than risk-based reporting from an empowered and untethered civil service, with adequate Madison-like checks and balances therein, leading naturally to informed decision-making in and by Parliament? It seems clear what is impeding the ultimate accountability of MPs to Parliament and voters: too much political control. That control does not facilitate the right motivations and resulting outcomes for Canadians. But I digress again. We do not see a lot of specific answers with concrete solutions in the Mowat report as to how to really improve the civil service in short order. We do see, however, the six characteristics it identifies as a prerequisite for a high-performing civil service, namely: "innovation, transparency, accountability, collaboration, evidence-informed analysis and public and political commitment."[100] It all sounds good but, given its roughly three dozen pages, we are short on the 'how' aspect. If you think about the well-meaning and common-sense characteristics though, it once again all boils down to good design and good people having the right motives.

Good design would principally be concerned with innovation, but good people can be innovative themselves. Transparency and Accountability are mainly all about good design, which we will see even more of in the next chapter, as well as people with good intentions being motivated to act accordingly. We begin to see that even collaboration and commitment to the public relies not just on the right motivation of the right people wanting to do the right things, but also the right organizational design in government to facilitate just that, holding people accountable. The notions of good physical design and good motivations are inextricably intertwined, each dependent on the other to maintain their respective integrity when people are working in organizations. I learned this myself when attempting to neatly separate a discussion of the physical aspects of good organizational design from a discussion of human nature and how the wrong motivations of some people can mess up well-designed institutions. It proved to be a difficult task to compartmentalize the two issues because they are so hugely interrelated. In that regard, this and the preceding chapters may contain some of my research and writing that could just as easily have been in one chapter versus the other. I purposefully decided to leave things as they are for a few reasons. Firstly, I did not want a really long chapter that comingles a discussion of certain aspects of people's motivation working within government, with a discussion of how organizational design may impact that very motivation. That could become messy indeed, overly disjointed, confusing and unclear. Secondly, in attempting to isolate each topic, as imperfectly as each chapter does that in its current form, it became an easier task to discern the concrete solutions we need to make things right—how to metaphorically *'Mend the Flag'* by embarking on *Democratic Restructuralism*.

Grasping the issue of poor organizational design and how it can influence the behaviour of those employed as civil servants, which in turn can lead to some of the bad results experienced by the public, gets us thinking about the need to restructure our democratic institutions from a physical perspective. It is like an architect considering how to design a house. How many bathrooms and bedrooms do I need? Where am I going to park my car? Does the house need to be downtown or in the suburb? Will a bungalow be sufficient for our needs or do we require a two-storey home? Do we need a solid fence and a backyard deck or do we believe in open borders and a front porch where both make it easier to get to know those in the community? And so it goes.

The point is that a home's architectural design can reflect the residents' needs, attitudes and behaviours in the home. We have seen that redesigning Parliament, and how the larger House of Commons operates, can also lead to improved behaviours and outcomes—more effective results for Canadians. That hopefully gets us intellectually thinking about the possibilities and benefits of physically redesigning our government, shedding the old and antiquated design features that no longer serve our needs in a modern, sophisticated, talented, more complex, and immeasurably diverse Canada.

Grasping the issue of how wrongly motivated individuals working within government can upend any good design in a manner that mainly, if not solely, benefits them, is also useful. That is the principal concern of this chapter. We need to preserve the integrity of what we have built, changing the design only when, in a tangible and meaningful way, that improves the quality of our lives. We do not need our teenage kids throwing a party in our house and trashing what we have worked so hard to build for the family as a whole. Similarly, we do not need the innocently misguided and misinformed, or willfully wrong-minded disrupters who pursue their own nefarious goals, undermining and corrupting what should be an effective House of Commons. The House must be an inviolate and sacrosanct structure that preserves the family of citizens and its collective good will. Spiritually, the House must be filled with rightly motivated MPs able to engage in meaningful debate and able to make informed decisions on behalf of its citizens. The role of MPs is to lead, as a Father or Mother leads a child down paths yet to be discovered; the Prime Minister, serving as the voice of the people rather than only their own interests. This is all entirely doable and underpins the *Democratic Restructuralism* we require to move forward together.

It matters not who we are, black, white, red, brown, male, female, young, old, whatever sexual orientation (typically a private matter anyway), wherever you legally came from, and so on. That is not the point. What matters is that we, in spirit, are doing the right thing as much as possible in harmony with others doing the same. And as I wrote near the beginning of this journey, you do not need me to tell you what that is. You know, deep within your inner self, what the truth is, what the difference is between right and wrong. And when our vote can finally mean something, we will prove this to others as we put in place a government that leads by example, building that which we so desperately need. I told my son, Ryan, that life is a lot like Lego. Everything is in the design and the joyful spirit of the players involved when it comes to creating something with a strong foundation. It is no different on Parliament Hill. We need a strong foundation to start with there too.

It is near impossible for our more than 300 MPs to even get out of the starting gate and attempt, with the right motivation, to work on behalf of Canadians when they themselves are not prepared for the absurdity that greets them. The absurdity is one that perpetuates the status quo of a less than democratic PMO calling all the shots, with the façade of Parliament serving as a backdrop of make-believe theatre. In that theatre, over which our fraying flag flies less and less proudly, MPs are only able to play their role rather than perform it. As a consequence, the public is duped into believing that elected parliamentarians can actually make a substantial difference in our day-to-day lives. It is all too Shakespearean a tragedy. Which reminds me of that book we referred to earlier, *Tragedy in the Commons*! In it we learn that freshly minted MPs receive virtually no guidance upon entering the hallowed halls of Parliament we send them to. "The new parliamentarians' adjustment to public life was made more difficult by the dearth of structured orientation to help them acclimatize to their new roles."[101] Authors Loat and McMillan observed that "most of the MPs we interviewed felt that orientation was nowhere near sufficient." Quoting a Winnipeg area Liberal MP, Reg Alcock, initially elected in 1993, "There's no orientation. There is no training. There is nothing on how to be effective."[102]

Similarly, Randy White, one of the first new group of Reform MPs, told the authors of *Tragedy* this: "Fifty-one of us went and didn't know a damned thing about the House of Commons . . . [We were like] deer in the headlights."[103] Imagine it if you will. You likely received some training and/or certification to do your job, especially if it requires licensing and other professional standards, such as being an electrician, mechanic, hygienist, teacher, insurance broker, pilot, and so forth. But to go and run the country's affairs and represent the public (even if that is not the case, it is what we rightly expect), you are flying by the seat of your own pants, on a wing and a prayer. Or, in the words of former Saskatchewan Liberal MP Gary Merasty, as documented in *Tragedy*, "I didn't have a clear idea of what type of person I should hire to run my office. What are their day-to-day tasks?"[104] That tells us a lot about how prepared our MPs are to do some meaningful work. It also tells us why they start receiving the wrong motivation to make them successful as soon as they land in Ottawa.

Another Liberal MP, Paul Szabo, was also quoted as saying to Merasty, "Nobody will coach you" and "everyone is clawing up."[105] Adding to the difficulties and wrong motivation received by MPs in Parliament is the apparent lack of a uniform and collective understanding of what their responsibilities were. Imagine if your doctor did not know what they were supposed to do in the operating room when they got there. Imagine if your pilot and co-pilot in the cockpit with their hands on the controls were unsure of their responsibilities to you and the other passengers. Talk about a recipe for disaster! When Loat and MacMillan interviewed all those MPs for their book, reviewing "what they believed they'd been sent to Ottawa to do," they were "taken aback by the variety of their answers."[106] The authors' logical conclusion was as follows, pointing yet again to the wrong motivations being cultivated in parliament and the withering of our democracy where informed decision-making is rarely nurtured:

> These wide divergences pointed to an absence of any formal job description or definition of a MPs responsibilities. And the lack of any direction from parties, which typically exercise far more control over their members, made us wonder whether the higher-ups in the parties cared what the MPs were doing, as long as they showed up [for] votes in the House of Commons. As long as they didn't cause trouble, the MPs were largely left to fend for themselves.[107]

I interpret the notion of trouble mentioned above to encompass the independent and common-sense thinking we actually need in the House instead of the wrongly motivated drones, marching to the beat of a party ideological drum. Of course, MPs who are not sure what their job entails may easily be motivated by their 'handlers' to play a role rather than perform it. You may believe I am being a bit too harsh here. So perhaps we should reference some other researchers and their sources in case I am mistaken.

In *Spinning History*, Whittington refers to Brent Rathgeber, an Alberta MP who resigned from the Conservative caucus in June 2013: "PMO staffers 'half my age' expected Tory MPs to communicate and vote like 'trained seals,' he complained."[108] That does seem to smack of our elected officials being motivated to play a role, effectively being dumbed down rather than being permitted to seriously perform any parliamentary duties, as unclear as those may be. Rathgeber's comments appear to point all the way to the PMO as the epicentre of wrong-headed motivations of a seismic proportion emanating from our federal government. "I do believe the PMO has too much power, that they don't properly respect the legislation, and, most importantly, there is not a proper degree of separation between the legislative and the executive."[109]

In fact, Rathgeber went on to write his own book, aptly called *Irresponsible Government: The Decline of Parliamentary Democracy in Canada*, and published in 2014. While taking a different approach in his work, the former Conservative MP does claim that "all levels of government" suffer from the same thing. His view is that "the people's elected representatives have failed miserably in their constitutional duty to hold government to account."[110] His own good intentions seemed at odds with the motives of the Harper government's own, the command-and-control style of the PMO, and the mounting debacles emanating from it that we already discussed. Rathgeber's values, which so often fuel ones motivation, obviously misaligned with those of his masters. His only choice apparently was to resign. This seems clear when he dejectedly writes, "Values that brought me into the conservative family— government accountability, transparency, and respect for taxpayers—had all either disappeared from the government of the day's playbook, or had been so seriously compromised, sacrificed at the altar of electoral expediency, as to become unrecognizable."[111] Sinful for sure!

We also can glean insight from Rathgeber's firsthand experience as a MP in the command-and-control system, wherein our elected senior parliamentarians are increasingly motivated to follow instructions from the PMO instead of thinking for themselves and their constituents. The very idea of a MP making a meaningful contribution to Canada, by voting on the issues of the day after reviewing relevant information to support that vote, seems to be next to impossible. One begins to question why we Canadians even bother to vote ourselves when exercising that democratic right really changes nothing in Ottawa except the figurehead of a wrongly motivated and broken system. Does it really matter if Justin Trudeau is taking selfies there or another figurehead is? Either way, none of them possesses the insightful motivation to do the right thing—make Canada democratic again.

Have any of us heard any of our recent Prime Ministers talking about anything remotely related to *Democratic Restructuralism*? Of course not. That would mean giving up power, control, and the optics management that goes along with promoting yourself rather than the capability of other elected officials. It would mean being motivated to do the right thing and motivating other elected officials to do that as well, be they in your party or the opposition parties. It would mean championing and developing an environment of risk-based decision-making. It would mean doing some heavy lifting and hard work as Prime Minister for Canadians, not just photo ops and saying what is politically correct that hopefully offends nobody else. Where is such an individual? Does he or she need to be a relative of a former Prime Minister like Justin Trudeau or Caroline Mulroney, somebody with connections to the one per cent rather than the 99 per cent? Is that what qualifies one to lead a country: photo ops, connections and saying the right thing instead of doing it? If it is, that explains why democracy must be controlled from an increasingly powerful PMO who can motivate others to produce the desired outcomes for the few who benefit by perpetuating that system. Those folks are obviously the political and business elites who are motivated themselves to gain the most.

Rathgeber reflects this concern in *Irresponsible Government*. "Any Ottawa insider will verify that almost nothing goes on in the parliamentary precinct without the Prime Minister's Office's knowledge, consent, and, increasingly frequent direction."[112] If you believe in common sense, which I believe most of you do, it stands to reason that one office calling most of the shots in our government, the PMO, can easily motivate, if not absolutely preordain, the results it alone seeks to achieve. Those results may obviously not be in our collective interest as Canadians. With MPs powerless to influence desired outcomes for the country based on meaningful debate and the ability to make informed decisions when they vote, we are left with the illusion of living in a democratic nation rather than actually living in one. That, I am afraid, puts us squarely on the path that America may be further down. It is not the road to demanding major changes in a system that does not work for the people. Rather, it is the road to electing a demagogue that has told us what we want to hear, that others must be blamed for the problem instead of the system itself. Here you have the seeds of divisiveness that, once planted, grow into predictable conflicts and even hatred of others as well as truth.

The only alternative to heading in the wrong direction is to change course and aim correctly. Our goal should be *Democratic Restructuralism*, reflective of spiritual renewal. Earlier we talked about shame being a powerful thing. Penobscot Native Eunice Bauman-Nelson had said that "you are your own judge" when you possess that "inner perception of what is wrong or shameful." Rathgeber appears to know what is right—and I would be happy to have a beer with him accordingly—"I am ashamed to disclose that your elected MP is frequently so disengaged that he is not only reliant on his party whip for his voting instructions, but quite possibly will also need to be coached by mates only slightly more engaged in the process."[113] All of this sounds terribly depressing. This wrong motivation leads us in the wrong direction as a country during a time of increasing risks. The complexity and demands of the world places more strain on Canada, necessitating the need for good decision-making by our government. Yet what is the motivation for we Canadians to bother voting at all? We have got to elect a party and Prime Minister that changes the PMO. We need to change before it is too late. If Canada can lead the world in creating a re-invigorated and newly structured democratic system that facilitates risk-based decision-making, there is the possibility that even the most daunting of global problems could then be solved.

Preserving the status quo around the globe and here in Canada simply will not do. Concentrating power at the apex of our national government, in the PMO, amongst a few unqualified and wrongly motivated individuals will not get us to where we need to go. The right vision and motivation are needed to facilitate the right collaboration and informed decision-making amongst qualified and experienced individuals we send to Ottawa. Leaving things as they are will be foolish, if not absolutely dangerous. Consider Rathgeber's greatest concern. He does not talk about wrongly motivated government leaders directly, but the implication of what he says shows us their clearly adverse impact nonetheless:

> It is the increasing influence of the Prime Minister's generally, and, within the PMO, the relative growth and influence of Issues Management at the expense of Policy, plus Communication Branch's tendency to communicate (spin), frequently with little or no regard for reality, that are the sources of my greatest concern regarding the operation of the executive branch of government.[114]

Disturbingly, the PMO produces not only the wrong motivations within members of the House of Commons, but almost purposefully, within the mindsets of the unelected and inexperienced administrative staff it hires to do the party's bidding as well.

Rathgeber put it this way: "I have witnessed young seemingly normal and well-adjusted college graduates enter the PMO and, within six months, morph into arrogant, self-absorbed zealots, with an inflated sense of importance and ability."[115] You get a real sense of the PMO creating wrong-minded party staffers when he further writes that "the socialization and indoctrination effects of the PMO sub-culture cannot be overstated."[116] These days and around the world, there is mounting intolerance of individuals who bully others, cowering them into submission to do their bidding. We see the outcry in the international media, fuelled by such things as the 'Me too Movement' where women are fed up with being abused. This is not to say that there may not exist fraudulent claims of abuse, however where there is smoke, such as in Hollywood and the recent brouhaha involving all those sexual harassment and abuse claims, there surely is fire. We also see the growing intolerance over bullying in our schoolyards, reflected by movements in support of wearing a pink ribbon, or special anti-bullying days with parents and children alike asked to show their support by having kids arrive in certain coloured shirts. It may not be too far-fetched to even envisage movements such as 'Idle No More,' 'Black Lives Matter,' and 'Occupy,' as protests against being bullied.

Groups of individuals who feel disenfranchised, disillusioned, and disengaged from the broader society in which they live, are also a dangerous thing. Near the beginning of *Democracy Rising*, Freeman warns of the growing dissatisfaction amongst ordinary people around the world. "People are not happy with the cozy relationships their governments have with the elites." Additionally, "they want something done about the way governments are run, or there is going to be hell to pay."[117] All of this appears neutral where specific political parties are concerned. "There is deep dissatisfaction among the followers of the left, right and centre, and it goes through all parts of the developed world, Canada included."[118] Bullying at the summit of power in Ottawa is also palpable in Jeffrey's book, *Dismantling Canada*, when he flatly states the following: "Fear is their primary weapon, and their success has been little short of astounding."[119]

Unabashedly opining on how that fear and wrongheaded motivation reached gargantuan proportions as the PMO expanded under Harper, Jeffrey also stated this at the outset of his book: "His Government's suppression of dissent, iron-fisted control over information, disregard for parliamentary procedure and judicial rulings, and determination to ignore scientific evidence, contradict virtually all established norms of political behaviour in this country."[120] You can get a good sense of the madness by observing what goes on in what is known as Question Period. In Chapter 4, we observed how Question Period makes a mockery of Canadian democracy inasmuch as the MPs attending this publicly televised sitting of parliamentarians are not sufficiently motivated to engage in meaningful debate. Instead, political opportunists use their brief time in the limelight to lambaste one another, further eroding our confidence in any government to work for Canadians. It is like all the negative attack ads you also see on TV before an election. They are typically meant to undermine the credibility of a perceived opponent instead of outlining the aggressor's sensible position on significant issues facing Canadians, if indeed they have such a position. *Tragedy* quotes the eloquence of Paul Wells, describing the rot of Question Period in a *Maclean's* magazine column, as "where everything we hate converges every day. The half-truths, the conflicted fury, the mayfly attention span, the ritual humiliation of the thoughtful or eccentric. And above all, the waste: of time, energy, hope."[121]

Unremarkably, we read in *Tragedy* that "Question Period is broken," according to Wells.[122] Yet in an essay aptly headlined *How to Fix Question Period: Ideas for Reform*, Michael Cooper puts forward several ideas on how to motivate better results in the sandbox of childish parliamentarian antics. He must see the Speaker of the House almost as headmaster of the private school of buffoonery, thinking that individual should "exercise authority—basically getting members to behave."[123] He also feels it necessary to increase the 15 seconds of fame, so to speak (no pun intended), each MP has to ask something hopefully of relevance in Question Period. I suppose that only matters in case anyone from Main Street is actually watching the snooze-fest. Most people know it is a circus and would rather tune in to other soap operas. Cooper also deems it useful that the government begin "re-evaluating the 35 second allotment for members to pose questions."[124] I am wondering if perhaps they need one or two minutes instead, but would that really matter at all when MPs are not even routinely receiving the information they need to add value in deliberating the issues of the day? Which of them, if any, even knows what issues should be a priority to discuss in the absence of a straightforward, efficient and transparent process that would facilitate that?

The situation is so overwhelmingly absurd that Cooper even felt the need to recommend putting an end to clapping and restricting the use of lists, of those members that are only allowed to ask questions, as good ideas. [125] The fact that this even needs to be written points to the asinine motivations behind party leaders often instigating MPs to attack one another's credibility instead of the real problems Canadians face daily. But how could they do otherwise than perform staged acts when everything is designed to be about image and optics management? That precipitates the negative results for Canadians, a simple matter of cause and effect, perpetuated by the wrongly motivated architects of that asinine structural deformity known as Parliament. Cooper makes what is likely his most useful point when he states there should be "specific question periods," [126] ostensibly to tackle larger issues that should be considered by MPs. That certainly appears to make perfect sense, but again only if MPs attending such question periods are qualified and experienced to deal with the specific issues being discussed, and have already been provided with risk-based reports that are germane to the discussion.

One could envision several question periods during the week discussing specific issues where certain MPs, including within the opposition and governing parties themselves, are able to pose questions relevant to Canadians on a regular basis, with them being competently addressed in kind to keep interested and engaged voters informed. That would make Question Period valuable to MPs and viewers alike. It would motivate the right decisions to be made. The rest, such as rules around clapping and other procedural decorum, is just putting the cart before the horse stuff and window dressing. Worryingly, it also appears that those who are not amply motivated to march in lockstep with the PMO, regardless if that office does not know what it is doing, are met with bully tactics that would make the likes of James Madison, Martin Luther King, and many wise Indigenous leaders cringe. Those distasteful tactics run the gamut of public discrediting and humiliation, as well as outright dismissal, of those who may disagree with questionable decisions coming from the PMO to shutting Parliament down completely—effectively ensuring MPs all keep quiet in the House of Commons—by what is known as proroguing.

We have already seen the tragic case of Mark Norman and how he lost his position as one of the leaders of the Canadian Navy, possibly for the wrong reasons. That was under the junior Trudeau government. As for Harper, he mastered handling those who could think for themselves. Brooke Jeffrey described this succinctly. "The Harper government has not hesitated to dismiss public servants who run afoul of the government agenda, often vilifying them before and after their dismissal in a concentrated attempt to paint the individuals as both incompetent and unstable."[127] My friends, having worked in government, I am not surprised. While I have not been the victim of such reprehensible bad behaviour, I have researched enough to understand that much lambasting and vilification, of those who merely want to do the right thing, has taken place at the hands of those leaders who do not. Jeffrey gives some specific examples in *Dismantling Canada*, of the more egregious cases of crucifying individuals who are not toting the party line. "Among the most blatant cases was Linda Keen, a former senior bureaucrat and the Chair of the Canadian Nuclear Safety Commission, whose decision to shut down the Chalk River nuclear plant over safety concerns led to her dismissal in 2006."[128]

Having the power to get rid of government officials who are causing trouble by doing their jobs for Canadians is a natural outcome; one of wrongly motivated people accumulating more and more power to carry out an almost personal rather than responsible and informed national agenda. Here we see powerful individuals yet again influencing the design of government, so other government officials, including elected MPs, behave the way those powerful individuals want. As Elizabeth May, head of the Green Party of Canada, wrote in her essay on *Westminster Parliamentary Democracy*, relating it to Canada's democracy and where we find ourselves now: "as each prime minister assumed power each consolidated and expanded the powers of the prime minister they replaced."[129] That does sound like a Shakespearean tragedy of power hungry politicians motivated by personal ambition rather than the public good, with all the unwanted ramifications resounding in a hollow House of Commons that accomplishes very little indeed. Our politicians possess that Shakespearean tragic characteristic so well put in *Macbeth*, Act 1, Scene VIII. In that scene, the protagonist, Macbeth, rationalizes his intent to murder King Duncan to satisfy his own goals. "I have no spur. To prick the sides of my intent, but only vaulting ambition, which o'er leaps itself. And falls on the other."

Certainly many of our politicians possess an ambition larger than life. It is reflected in selfies and self-promotion rather than a desperately needed, almost Winston Churchill-like, statesmanship to make things right. May notes, "Mulroney's PMO was larger than Trudeau's; Chretien's once again . . . as the power of the PMO grew, the role of the backbencher shrank."[130] And just who is the PMO motivated to serve? It is not a far stretch to claim, as Freeman does in *Democracy Rising*, that "governments . . . have chosen to support the corporate business elite over the people."[131] We clearly have seen ample proof, including references from his book, in the preceding discussion. May is referenced again in Whittington's *Spinning History*. You may not agree with the Green Party's policies, but you should listen to May when she says what follows, especially when your vote really does not help MPs do the jobs you expect of them, and when your tax dollars are going down the drain in an ever poorly motivated PMO. It might not garner the entertainment news and spectacle of the Trump White House, but it is damaging all the same: "About $10 million a year disappears into the PMO with zero accountability. The guys in short pants who run around bullying MPs, muzzling scientists and harassing civil servants report to one boss."[132]

I tend to agree, despite some exceptions as to the cause and effect, that rank-and-file civil servants have too often been cowed into doing the wrong thing. In this regard, the PMO itself is largely responsible for creating a dysfunctional and ailing public service. Concordia University's Professor

Jeffrey aptly outlined in his research how the wrong motivations in this nation's leadership have debilitated our once proud public service:

> Not surprisingly, with the government's obvious lack of interest in expert opinion and evidence, not only our government scientists, but public servants involved in policy-making across the federal government, began to experience serious morale problems. Long-term disability leave increased dramatically, leading the Global Business and Economic Roundtable in Mental Health to declare there was a 'mental health crisis' in the federal public service. [133]

The irony is that during the early days of Justin Trudeau's reign, his administration proclaimed that our country was embarking on a "golden age" of public service. Of course the facts, as facts rather than fake news inevitably speak for themselves, show the opposite is happening. Jason Kirby, in an article published by *Maclean's* in January 2017, summarizes how public-sector workers in this country took a record number of sick days during 2016. According to Statistics Canada, "the average public sector worker missed 13.5 days of work," being "the most ever." This is in stark contrast to the "8.3 days for workers in the private sector." Kirby raises the obvious question: "So just why do public-sector workers take so many more sick days than their private-sector counterparts?" He attempts to find a reasonable answer in reviewing a 2013 StatsCan study which concluded this: "As much as 80% of the sick-leave gap is the result of the makeup of government resources." The composition reflecting civil servants that "are generally older," with "more females than males," and an employee base that "is [mostly] unionized." Apparently, all of this leads to a certain conclusion: "those groups tend to take more time off." [134]

I am not sure I buy it. The bully pulpit of the PMO logically reverber-ates across government operations, like dominoes cascading across the expanse they cover, impacting MPs, senior officials, and downwards through the chain of bureaucracy, reaching down into the trenches occupied by front-line troops providing government services, motivating wrong behaviours and outcomes for Canadians. This, too, is likely why so many civil servants are taking more and more sick-leave, or at least is a significant contributor to the leave numbers. Quite simply, maybe more and more civil servants are increasingly pissed off, sick of the highest levels of government not doing the right thing, making poor decisions and asking those below them to do that very same thing, when most of them want to make a positive contribution to Canada and do what is right. The fact that so many public servants must deal with the Phoenix debacle and cannot get paid properly after more than two years of dealing with that nonsensical automated payroll system does not help matters.

Admittedly there are some unionized government employees who fit the stereotype. There are underperformers who are lazy and not pulling their weight, bringing others down. They too can possess the wrong motivations and not want to make a positive contribution to their department and Canadians. However, it has been my personal experience that most unionized employees actually want to do a good job. They want to carry out their department's mandate and serve their country well. The problem is less qualified and experienced non-unionized government employees are not doing the same thing. They do not lead by example and cultivate wrong behaviours, leading to poor results. Again, this goes all the way up to the PMO, which should be setting a responsible tone from the top. That of course requires doing more real work. It also requires the government of the day, regardless of political affiliation—which does not really matter if Liberals and Conservatives do the same thing alike—to work for all Canadians. Unfortunately, as Freeman laments in *Democracy Rising*, "Corporate handouts, campaign donations, tax concessions, and the sheltering of money offshore illustrate how the wealthy elite of this country have reaped the benefits of our democratic system."[135]

If that is the real motivation behind what the PMO does, not just a lack of understanding on how to motivate others to make informed decisions that produce desired results, then we have bigger problems than I suspect. Imagine if you will, the waste of time, money, valuable resources, etc., when the PMO is given so much power that its occupants can even make elected opposition leaders redundant, unnecessary. The power imbalance, wherein the House of Commons has virtually been emasculated at the expense of an all too powerful PMO, means the opposition appears in name only, rather than in its usefulness or performance within the House of Commons. The wrong motives within the PMO leads to a situation where opposition MPs need not even exist. Jeffrey comments that Harper, for example, "was able to push through legislation without even attempting consultation or consideration for the opinions of the opposition parties."[136] In this circumstance we see that it is not just the governing party MPs who are motivated to keep their mouths shut but also elected members of the opposition in the House. Your tax dollars at work— Not!

Time and again we see the urgent need for voters to demand the *Democratic Restructuralism* required to restore an effective democracy in this country. Things have gotten so bad that we even see the PMO having the power to disrupt the good work of our journalists, motivating an outcome whereby the citizens of Canada are left in the dark about the federal government's decisions that impact our lives. Credible and professional investigative journalism is a key linchpin in the foundation of any workable democracy. It is absolutely unacceptable that journalists are prevented from doing their necessary work to inform Canadians about real rather than fake news. We often hear jeers involving Donald Trump and all the so-called fake news emanating from the White House. Many Canadians also joke about the American president, routinely in coffee shops, such as Tim Horton's, from sea to shining sea, doing their best to outdo Alec Baldwin's parodies on Saturday Night Live. Again, we really should not be casting stones in glass houses.

Not to centre on the Harper government, but it appears to have excelled in its attempts to control the messaging going out to the Canadian public, effectively creating the news regardless of its integrity. The fact that this also enabled the Conservatives to present themselves in the best image, regardless of that image's integrity, was an added bonus. Professor Jeffrey writes that "externally, it has reduced the free flow of information by limiting media access to politicians and bureaucrats . . . marginalizing political opponents through misleading advertising campaigns . . . mounted an unprecedented advertising campaign to disseminate its own message in as positive a light as possible."[137] In *Unaccountable*, Kevin Page also discusses the PMO's control of the media, stating that "little information was being made available to anyone, let alone the press."[138] Optics management portrayed the Prime Minister as a real leader, despite so little being meaningfully done for Canada and Canadians.

If only the government did the work required of it. Perhaps then there would be nothing to hide, unless it involved the security of the country. To sum up, we should be careful of mocking the US President when we have our own fake news as a developing story. The problems all point to a dysfunctional PMO and its self-serving motivations. Whittington said this of it in *Spinning History*. "The conservative media-shaped national image was only one of the roles of the PMO, which was also responsible for managing the government through the Privy Council Office, keeping MPs from running amok and implementing policy."[139] I am not sure what the House of Commons is really for these days, other than for presenting the façade of democracy. The much revered American President, John F. Kennedy, famously remarked to Americans that they should "ask not what your country can do for you—ask what you can do for your country."

On one level that makes good Yankee sense. The citizenry at large should definitely try to contribute to a greater good, a better environment for themselves and their loved ones. People need to be active, where possible, in ensuring democracy thrives. They need to be respectful of each other and the nation's institutions, lest they decay in effectiveness or fall prey to the unsavoury motivations of powerful egos with self-serving agendas. Nevertheless, on another level, JFK's catchy exhortation fails to consider that governments should also do right and work for citizens. It is patently unreasonable to expect elected officials, such as MPs here in Canada, as well as the Prime Minister, not to be working on behalf of all Canadians. After all, is that not the reason they took the job in the first place? Hopefully it is not for other reasons involving personal gain or to peddle the influence of business elites and lobbyists to the detriment of the nation and its latent potential.

Whittington seems to agree with those who wrote *Tragedy* when he states, "Party leaders need to address a situation where backbench members of Parliament often complain they are treated little better then puppets—expected to trumpet the government line as passed down by the PMO and otherwise keep their mouth shut."[140] In another book that he, along with other MPs, edited and which several MPs contributed as essayists, Michael Chong wrote in his own essay about the 'diminished role' of our MPs. Here once more we can discern how the design of government can negatively influence the behaviour of even what should be independent thinking parliamentarians. We also can see how leaders with the wrong motivation, and their obsequious unelected staff, namely the PMO, are able to detrimentally affect the design of what should be democratic institutions that are impervious to harm. Chong summarizes how we got here: "Rule changes within the House of Commons, changes in election laws and the increasing power of political parties have all contributed to the diminished role of the MP and the increased power of party leaders, particularly the prime minister."[141]

One of the great Canadian modern-day ironies is that the current reigning Prime Minister, Justin Trudeau, who was elected while portraying himself as a safer character than Harper, is the son of former Prime Minister Pierre Trudeau, who substantially increased the power of the PMO. The general public is apt to believe that Liberals are more likely to be progressive, however it was Trudeau senior's Liberal government that sought much centralized power to begin with. Yes, my friends, the elder Trudeau established the power structure where his son reigns from, the same seat of power that enabled Harper and others to keep doing the wrong things. I love historians and *Tragedy* refers to one by the name of Alan Levine, who mentions inescapably for our boxing and shirtless junior Trudeau this: "Pierre Trudeau and his key advisors are generally held responsible for inaugurating the ever-expanding and centralizing power of the PMO."[142]

Perhaps just as concerning is the distasteful situation involving the composition of parliamentary committees, where members at times have virtually no clue about the issues they are deliberating upon. The late MP Andy Scott, a Liberal from New Brunswick, was asked to serve on a committee he admitted to being ill-suited for. According to *Tragedy*, Scott's government expertise centred on literacy and skills training, but, shortly after landing in Ottawa, he found himself on the health committee. He was surprised to learn this, as he told Loat and MacMillan, because he was not knowledgeable about healthcare! "'I should be on the human resources committee', Scott insisted, to no avail . . . 'I was baffled that it didn't seem to matter.' "[143] I wonder if the relaxing of Canada's recreational marijuana laws was backed by input from informed government officials; informed in the sense that they were aware as to what the ramifications are for Canadians using the drug for non-medical purposes. Then again, what better way to keep voters ignorant than to have them high and oblivious to the ineptitude of government. Another Liberal MP, Andrew Telegdi, was put on the public accounts committee despite having his heart elsewhere. "I was not keen on being on public accounts . . . I couldn't get myself changed."[144] To top off the insanity as outlined in *Tragedy*, we learn of these other circumstances:

He ended up becoming the committee vice-chair . . . Despite
its topic, the public accounts committee had only two
chartered accountants among its members, one of whom was
Liberal MP Alex Shepherd . . . [who] voted against the wishes
of the party leadership on gun registry legislation, and as
punishment, according to Telegdi, the party higher-ups took
him out of public accounts—leaving only one accountant on
the committee. [145]

Talk about wrong motivation with serious repercussions. According
to *Tragedy*, " 'It didn't make any sense,' said Telegdi, who believed the move
'weakened the committee.' " [146] In his essay *Rebalancing Power in Ottawa:
Committee Reform*, Chong goes to great lengths in describing the composition of committees, what they do, and what are the challenges and problems
involved with them. His analysis is quite informative and in building up to
his argument that parliamentary committees require some key reforms, he
paints a bleak picture of how even committees have been motivated to be
ineffective. In relation to standing committees, which as Chong describes, can
for example oversee specific government departments or issues pertinent to the
entire government, he reveals a great divide between theory and practice. "In
theory, standing committees have immense powers to hold the government to
account, such as right to call witnesses, demand evidence and issue reports."
However, "in practice, they often do not exercise these rights for the reason
that party leaders exert substantial control over the chairs and membership
of those committees." [147]

The thumbprint of the PMO is visible again in quashing MPs' effectiveness, and by extension that of the committees they serve on, under a majority
government. Chong lays out the threat to democracy presented by leaders motivated to take control of what should be independent parliamentary committees
plainly: "In a majority Parliament, at least six of ten members of a standing

committee are appointed through the party by the Prime Minister. This means that part of the executive branch of government, the Prime Minister's office (PMO) effectively controls a standing committee of the legislative branch." Yet as Chong decisively comments, "This is at complete odds with the fundamental role of a committee of the legislature, which is to hold the executive branch of government to account."[148] To curb the unwanted motivation and control of that very executive branch over the legislative one, Chong makes some seemingly good suggestions. Examples include the following: "A reform that would go a long way toward rebalancing Power between party leaders and MPs would be to remove the power of party leaders, including the prime minister, to decide the membership of committees."[149]

Chong believes the adoption of such techniques as using secret ballots to elect chairs and potentially other members of committees makes good sense too. This is really about some specific committee organizational design features to motivate better behaviour and committee results. On the immediate surface, such ideas look very useful. Chong describes the practical utility of having a secret ballot committee membership process this way. It "would allow committees greater autonomy to amend legislation, review spending and hold the government to account." Another design suggestion he has, is "reducing the number of committees," which "would make more effective use of MPs time."[150] Again, these are great and specific ideas to motivate better outcomes that would support what was outlined in my prior chapters more focused on organizational design and its influence on desired behaviours. But the key problem remains. If committees are not being routinely provided with relevant data and information from the government departments related to the specific issues they are reviewing and working on, how can they even make risk-based decisions?

Having competent, capable, independent and unduly influenced committee members is one thing. Having them mandatorily provided with the necessary documents and risk-based analysis to make informed decisions on behalf of the Canadian electorate is quite another. We require government leaders, beginning with an insightful, knowledgeable, engaged and, most importantly, rightly motivated and caring Prime Minister, to set the entire government up for success.

Tragedy outlines the horrendous results for us and our country by posing two questions that have obvious answers: "If parliamentarians do not have a shared conception of a MPs job description, how are Canadians to know what MPs are supposed to be doing in office? And if citizens don't know what to expect from our elected officials, should we be surprised when they believe MPs don't deliver?"[151] You may be inclined to think MPs leading various government ministries know what their role is supposed to be because that is outlined in their *Mandate Letter*. Such letters, written on the letterhead of the PMO, are presumably meant to define the role and responsibilities—effectively the mandate—of the specific MP leading a specific government ministry. Each *Mandate Letter* provided to a MP is signed by the Prime Minister. Unfortunately, these letters also fall short of providing the correct motivation to ministers.

Let's take a closer look at the *Mandate Letter* Justin Trudeau gave to his first Minister of Democratic Institutions, Maryam Monsef, dated November 12, 2015. At about four single-paced pages in length, it is long on verbosity and short on providing the necessary impetus to effect the meaningful change Canadians expect to strengthen our democracy. But maybe Trudeau was never motivated to implement real reforms, only to just create the sense that he was going to during his election campaign. Curiously, it was Paul Martin who established, during his tenure as Prime Minister (2003–06), the position of Minister Responsible for Democratic Reform (previously called Minister for Democratic Renewal). This was to address the perceived 'democratic deficit' at the time. Justin Trudeau's government then rebranded the position again as Minister of Democratic Institutions, which is good optics management, making it seem like something substantially might change to mend our broken institutions. If it sounds like déjà vu and a shell game that accomplishes very little to you, then you are not as dumb as so many politicians would like you to be.

It would serve all Canadians well to remember that Trudeau campaigned on a promise of electoral reform. His campaign also championed the slogan 'Sunny Ways,' essentially recycling the same phrase that a previous Prime Minister, Sir Wilfrid Laurier, used in the late 1800s. So much for originality and new ideas to tackle our modern-day problems. It is akin to the uninspiring banality of President Trump borrowing Reagan's slogan about making America great, which I wrote of earlier. Anyway, as reported by the *National Post*, both during Trudeau's election campaign and after he won the election, "Trudeau repeatedly stated 2015 would mark the last federal election to use the first-past-the-post voting system."[152] That system, currently used in Canada, means the candidate with the most votes during an election in their riding (voting district) becomes a MP representing that riding. Many MPs are elected with less than 50 per cent of the popular vote in their riding. One way to avoid this situation is to have proportional representation in Parliament with MPs being elected based on how much of the popular vote they and their party receives. Much has been said about this, but if politicians cannot make informed decisions once they arrive in Ottawa, it does not really matter how they get there to begin with. This has escaped Trudeau and his sunny ways. Plus he has not budged much in terms of implementing electoral reform.

Looking at the few specifics in the 2015 *Mandate Letter* addressed to Ms. Monsef, we find her central motivation: "As Minister of Democratic Institutions, your overarching goal will be to strengthen the openness and fairness of Canada's public institutions. You will lead on electoral and Senate reforms to restore Canadians' trust and participation in our democratic processes."[153] Really? Of course there is no leadership or vision on exactly how to do that. There is also no mention of the crucial necessity of addressing the unmitigated structural risks our democracy has been straining under. Then again, the PMO motivates the wrong outcomes anyway as we have seen. More importantly, Trudeau and his first Minister of Democratic Institutions failed in carrying out the overarching goal stated in the *Mandate Letter*. That equates to Trudeau, like so many others who came before him, breaking his election promises to Canadians. I could have discussed this as yet another betrayal in Chapter 3, but it seems to make more sense here, where sunny ways are eclipsed by the stark reality of yet more wasted tax dollars and a failure to restructure our democracy so that it is fit for purpose. How so?

Shortly after Ms. Monsef was appointed minister late in 2015, she set about executing her marching orders, to come up with the electoral reforms Trudeau had promised to Canadians. However, as is often the case after much dithering, or to be politically correct from an optics management per-spective—after over a year of much studying—the Minister of Democratic Institutions had little to show Canadian voters. That is, unless you consider the waste of around $4.1 million of our tax dollars to dawdle about as being constructive. According to a *National Post* report, while a spokesman for the Privy Council Office (Raymond Rivet) could not confirm the total costs for the fiscal year, it did appear substantial at the time the *Post* published its article in February 2017. Thus "ministerial travel, committee work, MP town halls and 'communications activities' add up to about $4.1 million." In fairness, Minister Monsef's office did produce a "300-plus page report in December [2016] that recommended the government hold a referendum on whether to adopt a proportional representation system."[154]

In the end though, as Monsef had begun messaging, Canadians had "no consensus" regarding electoral reform. That "despite a majority supporting proportional representation at the committee's events."[155] No doubt Canadians are supposed to come up with all the solutions that the Prime Minister and his ministers should, supporting President Kennedy's contention that voters should not be asking what their country can do for them. I really doubt that is entirely reasonable, especially in the case of electoral and Senate reforms or other complex government matters our leaders should be well-versed in. Are they not the caretakers of democracy? I suppose they cannot make the necessary decisions because they are not provided with the necessary risk assessments that tell them people around the world are fed up with democracies that do not work for everyone. The people want change. A shame we are not listened to by wrongly motivated leaders.

Trudeau's 2015 *Mandate Letter* to Monsef is flagrantly disingenuous. In it he passionately states that "if we are to tackle the real challenges we face as a country—from a struggling middle class to the threat of climate change—Canadians need to have faith in their government's honesty and willingness to listen."[156] That sounds laudable and nice, but who cares when the leadership has no systemic way of making risk-based decisions to deal with the issues of the day, like those contributing to a weakening middle-class and climate change. How can they even begin to identify solutions when they have no way of pinpointing and prioritizing the risks, the problems that must be addressed? The answer is they cannot, and we end up with more of the waste laid bare in Chapter 3 or told we ordinary citizens must tell the government what to do. That, is just ridiculous! But so, too, is this: at the beginning of February 2017, Trudeau issued some revised *Mandate Letters* for a bunch of newly minted ministers, including one Karina Gould. She had just replaced Ms. Monsef as Minister of Democratic Institutions and found herself with some new motivations.

Specifically, Ms. Gould's revised *Mandate Letter* instructed that "changing the electoral system will not be in your mandate."[157] So much for Trudeau's election promises yet again. Like many of his predecessor's, Conservatives and Liberals alike, he is one that is big on lofty sounding words and short on deeds that support election promises. There is an Alpha, but no Omega, a beginning, but no end in terms of deeds. Or, as British Columbian MP Nathan Cullen of the New Democratic Party quipped somewhat bellicosely, "Rather than keep his word to the millions of Canadians who voted for him and the hundreds of thousands of Canadians who engaged in good faith with Mister Trudeau over the question of how to strengthen and broaden our democracy, Mister Trudeau chose today instead to spit in their face."[158] At the end of the day we are left again with the empty platitudes and spin that accompanies 'sunny ways' instead of the strengthening of our democratic institutions, including through possible electoral, or at least Senate reforms.

In his 2017 *Mandate Letter* to the Minister of Democratic Institutions, Trudeau said, "Sunshine is the best disinfectant to concerns about our political process."[159] I for one do not know what that means and would wager you do not either. As someone known to tinker on old engines to ensure they run properly, and someone also known to do a little gardening to cultivate the right backyard atmosphere, I daresay we need more than sunshine to deal with the real threats to democracy that Canadians are faced with. We need the bright light of undeniable truth to shine upon and expose our poorly designed government institutions. No more fake news; we need the good news, the truth. Then we need to apply some common sense and elbow grease and begin the process of *Democratic Restructuralism* forthwith!

Returning to the idea of fake news we hear so much about in the US, I found it interesting when *Tragedy* briefly mentioned that the "confusion among role definitions makes it difficult for the media who observe Parliament to report to Canadians how effectively the country is being governed."[160] As I wrote earlier, I am thankful to print media and the largely positive job journalists do reporting on so many significant and newsworthy events that affect us and others around the world. In compiling many credible, diverse, significant, and generally well-written articles about what our government has been doing, as plainly revealed in Chapter 3, we see that our leaders have been fairly ineffective at governing this once admirable nation. That is the great betrayal of Canada, unintended or not, arising from the highest quarters of government that motivates MPs in a way that does not allow them to perform to the best of their abilities. This situation stagnates MPs' personal growth as well as Canada's.

It is unsurprising to also learn from *Tragedy* that the authors' "interviews reflect that little substantive policy discussion actually does take place in those hallowed chambers"—referring to the House of Commons.[161] Even where MPs may be getting more work done and finding themselves to be of value outside the House, in any or a number of parliamentary committees, we repeatedly see the wrong motivations at play. The interviews conducted by Loat and MacMillan stated, "The majority of our interviewees emphasized that some of the best and most productive work on Parliament Hill took place in committees, as well as in the off-the-record, closed-door gatherings of MPs known as caucuses." Apparently it has been "in committees and caucuses that MPs could collaborate, debating and advancing policy, and bringing local issues to the national stage." *Tragedy* cites Liberal MP for St. Catharines Walt Lastewka, as a proponent of committee work. "Committee is where the work gets done," he said.[162]

Loat and MacMillan also quote Ontario Liberal MP Pat O'Brien as another supporter who also stressed the importance of committees. "The majority of work in Ottawa is done in committees. A lot of people don't realize that."[163] Then there were references to other parties' MPs sharing this view. British Columbian Conservative Werner Schmidt is cited stating, "We dealt with real issues, very substantial issues, and we came to grips with some real problems." He puts it succinctly when he avers, "The real work of parliament is done in committees."[164] Another former Conservative Alberta member, Dale Johnston, is referenced as opining: "Committees are good because there's a genuine desire to get things done."[165] All of this sounds very positive, and I have no doubt that a lot of good work has been done in those venues. However, there remains a lot of wrong motivations permeating even the atmosphere of committees, setting them up to fail from the get-go. Where they have succeeded at all despite this is a testament to the good work MPs can produce when not being bullied into submission by a powerful PMO.

So what are some of the forces impeding committees to do their very best and to be even more effective? First, there is the obvious fact the committees are not being routinely provided with risk-based reports from the various government departments and agencies that may have a bearing on a committee's work. We saw in the preceding chapter how our government has not been designed to embed enterprise-wide risk management within the span of its operations, thereby limiting the information and data that can be given to MPs. Committee work then falsely assumes that the operations of government, as if by magic, are running smoothly, when in fact the opposite is true. That means their work may have been jeopardized right from the start, as the committee may have never had all the information it needs, or the fruits of its labour may never be implemented correctly. This logic is inescapable.

In this chapter we have witnessed the corrosive power of wrongly motivated leaders, and how their attempts to deliberately weaken the institutions that bind us and this country together, have been all too successful. We have seen how MPs are ill-prepared to assume their parliamentary duties as soon as they arrive in Ottawa. This is not through any fault of their own, but because the system is not organized to produce the right results and supports our MPs need. We have seen how MPs do not receive the information they require—in a systematic (prioritizing the issues of the day), logical and routine manner—to make informed and risk-based decisions that benefit Canadians. We have seen how they are made fearful so they will toe the party line, however wrongheaded and misinformed the implications of doing so are. We have seen the absurdity of Question Period, an exercise in futility where our tragic heroes, the MPs we duly elect to represent us in the House of Commons, perform staged acts like an organ grinder's monkey, begging for something that is far too elusive—the respect that goes with dancing to their own tune rather than that of PMO handlers.

What would Shakespeare say of our actors in Question Period? Perhaps he would reiterate that "life's but a walking shadow, a poor player that struts and frets his hour upon the stage and is heard no more." Or maybe he would revise that hour to the 35 second allotment. Surely then we would have "a tale told by an idiot, full of sound and fury signifying nothing." We have seen how the good work of parliamentary committees is hampered by the illogical appointing of committee members unqualified for their roles and in the removal of members who may, in fact, actually be qualified. We have seen how committee outcomes may be predetermined by the self-serving motivations of the PMO in a majority government. We have seen how an increasingly powerful PMO can manipulate the messaging that goes out to the media, again motivating a less than democratic atmosphere to cloud and obfuscate the torrential storm of incompetence we face. This is our long monsoon season, our reality. That climate must change, as it must in other governments around the world facing similar political and spiritual problems, before the earth's climate can be improved.

We have observed how the undesirable motives of some government leaders can be curbed. For example, a Senate riddled with unelected members who do not seem to do a lot of risk-based work that benefits the country more than themselves, can be abolished. This, in the short term, would save Canadians a lot of money and ensure our government is not wrongly motivated and influenced by any individuals holding patronage positions that are doing little to improve the lives of average Canadians, let alone democracy. Well-intentioned individuals such as Michael Chong have revealed how parliamentary committees can be better organized to facilitate better outcomes for Canadians. Other well-meaning MPs such as Michael Cooper have reflected on how parliamentary discussion and decorum in Question Period can be improved to make those sessions of more use to Canadians. On balance however, none of these examples are strong enough, even if implemented together, or with other similar efforts, to meaningfully change the wrong-minded motivations radiating from an undemocratic PMO. The existing PMO is a centre of unchecked power that must be held to account.

Ensuring Our Government Leaders Have the Right Motivations

Physically redesigning the organizational structure of the federal government such that it incorporates an independent office of the CRO, which in turn has independent senior risk managers within the broader government departments directly reporting to that CRO, is a good first step in beginning the process of *Democratic Restructuralism*. We have outlined that in the last chapter as it would facilitate better behaviours and outcomes in government. However, we also have to ensure as we embark on the path of *Democratic Restructuralism*, that wrongly motivated politicians or senior unelected officials cannot, without informed debate and decision-making, change a newly formed and more effective design of government. Several things, heavily interrelated with the physical design aspects of the federal government, are therefore required to achieve this goal.

Although the government of the day sitting in power must still have the prerogative and legal ability to pass legislation and generally make decisions, it must do so in a way that motivates the best outcomes for Canadians. This means the independent Risk Management Office (RMO) led by the CRO (as we discussed previously), must be in charge of providing the right orientation to new MPs as they begin their new careers. Or perhaps the Governor General could lead that initiative. Our duly elected officials sent to represent our interests on Parliament Hill must be provided with the appropriate training and tools to ensure they will be successful in their new roles. Think of it as boot camp or basic training before they defend the interests of democracy in the field. The RMO could inform new MPs about where to find their office, the supply room and washrooms in Ottawa, as well as other obvious matters they should not have to ask about like:

- What is my role in Ottawa and the House of Commons, etc.?
- What are the general procedures and processes I must adhere to as a MP, such as in claiming expenses, ensuring I am not in a conflict of interest position, ensuring my staff has had appropriate background checks, creating a harassment-free workplace that promotes diversity while respecting merit and ability, and so on?
- How do I raise issues on behalf of my constituents?
- How can I serve on a parliamentary committee that uses my knowledge, experience and skill, so I can serve Canadians better in government decisions and policymaking?
- How do I routinely obtain, along with my fellow MPs, risk and issues reports from the independent RMO so that sitting government and opposition MPs can engage in meaningful debate and informed decision-making (voting in the house by way of example)?
- How do I know, ranked by priority, what the greatest risks are to each of Canada's provinces, and collectively to the country—and how should I as an MPs go about my work accordingly?
- How do I know the risks facing the country and Canadians are being managed effectively, with appropriate funding and resources in place?
- How can I be sure government departments and agencies are being held to account for the services they are providing in relation to the tax dollars spent?
- When will I be able to ask questions in the House of Commons or committee sessions, so that Canadians know what MPs are doing and how we are moving Canada forward?

This is by no means an exhaustive list of questions MPs may have before coming to grips with what it means to be an MP. But from the few examples listed, we begin to clearly see the value a well-functioning and effective RMO could have in motivating MPs to do the right things on Parliament Hill.

Imagine a straightforward and common-sense onboarding program run by the RMO, a few weeks in duration and that inspires and builds confidence amongst MPs, regardless of their party affiliation. MPs who know their role individually, as well as collectively, who know their rights and responsibilities, who know they can make informed decisions on behalf of their constituents, etc., are likely to be highly motivated and effective representatives of all Canadians. This is the positive real-world impact *Democratic Restructuralism* can have on the culture of the public service and all Canadians. Think of it as the renewal we need to build a leading and respected nation, blessed with so many resources, people included, that finally achieves its identity in the community of nations that desperately needs new leadership. Canada is a young member of the world community. However the message we reveal to the community of nations, as we pursue *Democratic Restructuralism*, is the wisdom that the old world spread throughout the globe should warmly receive. Light and goodness can prevail over the encroaching darkness that confronts all peoples. We need our New Jerusalem.

President Trump can try to make America great again. We need to *Make Canada and democracy right again*. We can heal and repair our broken and dysfunctional government institutions. We can mend the flag! An effective and independent RMO with a capable CRO at the tiller, can do so much good in comparison to a costly and ineffective Senate. A RMO can motivate the right course of actions and decisions instead of the wrong ones. It would also curb the power of that all too egocentric and wrongly motivated PMO. Certainly we need a strong Prime Minister to represent and guide the government. But we also need the prime minister to be hard-working, informed and rightly motivated do the job they were elected to do. We need this rather than a leader jet setting around for nothing that benefits Canadians. The humility of Pope Francis, Mahatma Gandhi and some other spiritual leaders is instructive. There is no use making an entire nation of people cower before an altar of poor decision-making that reflects the unraveling of what should be a mature and vibrant democracy.

With an adequately staffed RMO that is effective in having its qualified, experienced, and uniformly trained representatives performing independent risk assessments throughout the government's operations (applying a consistent framework and methodology to ascertain and evaluate pertinent risks, making recommendations on how to mitigate them to MPs accordingly), Prime Ministers and MPs could all get their own hands dirty rather than slinging mud at each other. Wouldn't it be nice for a change to have a Prime Minister and MPs pouring over informative reports telling them about the internal and external risks confronting Canada? Wouldn't it be refreshing to see our elected officials hard at work performing their roles instead of playing them, guiding the government in sensible decision-making that supports an informed party platform it ran upon? This is preferable to the current havoc arising from foolish decisions based on less than credible information.

If an independent RMO provides the exact same reports to all MPs, including those of the opposition, the Prime Minister and the presiding government could easily be held to account. We need not suffer more from a leader's "vaulting ambition" in a Shakespearean tragedy. Ambition can be made to check ambition, as Madison urged. A well-intentioned and rightly motivated Prime Minister will want to do the right thing. They will possess a moral compass that aligns with the Canadian values and identity we have spoken of. They should have an innate sense of what is right and what is wrong. We need leaders to possess that honor which the Lakota elder spoke of in discussing his tribe: "Our guide was inside—not outside. Honor was our guide. It was more important for us to know what was right." We need the spirit within people to be awakened, for each individual Canadian contributes to the overall soul and health of our democracy, our body politic. As Slow Turtle explained, "We have removed the spirit out of democracy, so it can't work right—because there is no respect." With MPs being bullied and not provided the information they need to make sound decisions, including risk-based ones for disenfranchised groups such as our Indigenous Peoples, there clearly is no respect: not in Parliament or for democracy itself!

These are the wrong motivations. I recall watching a brief video entitled *If the World Were 100 People* accessible on the TedEd website. In that video, the world's population of about 7.6 billion people is reduced to a mere 100. However, in doing so, the smaller population still reflected, by percentage, a number of disturbing truths regarding humanity on earth: 14 could not read and write; 1 person would control 50 per cent of all the money; 15 people would be malnourished and 1 individual would be starving; and 23 people would have no shelter, etc. The video ends with these words: "If the world were 100 people . . . Would we all fight harder for Equality?"[166] We require our leaders and especially our Prime Minister to fight for what is right. And that goes beyond fighting in the boxing ring like Trudeau or pursuing martial and other arts like Vladimir Putin. We need the heads of government to lead by example, motivating other government officials to champion democracy and the equality that it claims to embrace. Remember what Martin Luther King said: "It's alright to talk about 'streets flowing with milk and honey,' " which sure sounds like today's optics management and fake news, "but God has commanded us to be concerned about the slums down here, and [the] children who can't keep three square meals a day."

If there were 99 people standing in front of you and 16 could not get those square meals, would you be motivated to help them? Well, we know we have students increasingly using food banks at post-secondary institutions in Canada and that there is a shelter crisis in places like Toronto. Maybe we need our Canadian government leaders to be motivated to help those people rather than wasting billions of dollars on dumb decisions, so abhorrently outlined previously. With so many tax dollars going down the proverbial drain, we need not be a left-wing zealot to wish to make better use of those hard-earned dollars by actually helping others in need. Whichever political party is motivated to do the right thing—to make intelligent, risk-based decisions, backed by credible information for all current and future Canadians—they will have my vote. I might even run to represent that party if the good people of this country willed it and demanded *Democratic Restructuralism*.

Regrettably, until such time as we Canadians realize our vote really is not changing anything, we are in for more of the same in Ottawa; more of the political art of decision-making, the optics management, theatre and fake news that goes along with all that, rather than real and informed decision-making that benefits Canada and reflects the collective values of Canadians. Surely we can do better, even if it means holding a Constitutional convention to build a better Canada, respecting our heritage for better or worse, the contribution of all provinces and territories, the Indigenous or First Peoples of the land, and quite simply, doing more that is right for all Canadians.

By now you likely have a pretty good idea that the motivations and ambitions of government leaders, and especially the PMO, can have an exceedingly large impact on the design of government itself, how its various departments and agencies operate, and the results Canadians face. It is no different in America, the UK, Australia, and other challenged democracies around the world. Organizational design impacts the behaviour of those working in the bureaucracy and the results they achieve. Conversely, the purposeful or innocently misguided motivations of those leading an organization, such as the PMO in the Canadian government, can influence the design and attendant behaviours of the wider bureaucracy, and the results it achieves. Whether or not those outcomes are good or bad for you and me, our families, neighbours, and Canadians from coast to coast, depends on how set up for success government is rather than a predetermined failure.

Summing It Up (Our Need for Creative Solutions)

Referring back to the Mowat report, I really like thinking about the characteristic of evidence-informed analysis. We already talked about how to design our public institutions so that risk-based decision-making can occur. This would be done through a network of independent risk-management professionals keeping check, as Madison would likely approve, on the bureaucracy, while reporting on the issues of the day (and data/information behind them) for MPs to deliberate upon—then making wise and informed decisions for the public good within their respective ministries. Abolishing the Senate and reconstituting the PMO, such that a good portion of it is staffed by an independent risk-management department (the RMO), headed by a CRO with designates throughout the various federal government departments and agencies is the way to go. It is the way to achieve and advance, not only the evidence-informed analysis Jarvis briefly covers, but good decision-making for the country. Why pay political appointees in the Senate who we never sent there? Why not use public funds for something much more useful for all of us, something that can obviously improve the quality of our lives and prevent all the waste summarized previously?

Jarvis proves my case himself during his barely four page general discussion on the need for the public service to possess the characteristic of evidence-informed analysis. Referencing other credible sources, he briefly mentions two things: "Canada's record of using evidence on the effectiveness of programs and policies and departmental performance in allocating resources is substantial" and "critics have noted a number of limitations including too much focus on activities and outputs instead of outcomes, a lack of appropriate data and a lack of independent analysis."[167] Sounds pretty brutal, like there is a lot of process and not much in the way of results. Jarvis outlines some additional concerns but most of you already knew that we have muzzled our scientists and others, thereby muzzling the truth. When there is no truth, bad decisions are made based on fake news and lies. Things basically do not work the way they should with dumb decisions being made not only in Canada, but in other so-called democracies around the world. You do not have to look far.

We no longer live in a day and age where washing out the liar's mouth with soap and water is tolerated; nor do I advocate this. But we do need to clean our House so to speak, to facilitate the *Democratic Restructuralism* we need, to get rid of the lies, unintended or not, dragging this and other countries down all the rabbit holes leading to confusion and the unravelling of democracy. Jarvis, in outlining how we can move forward, is bang on when he remarks, "While evidence is never perfect, more can be done to centralize its role in decision making."[168] However he skates around finding a workable solution by just looking at how other departments, such as some that already exist in the US, can provide independent evaluation of what the federal government is doing. He wonders if the PBO (recall we discussed it and Kevin page's own book, *Unaccountable*) or some other 'parliamentary office' could be created "to assess the impact of policies and programs."[169] Then, in weighing the possibility of having "evaluation . . . remain the sole responsibility of government," he states it "could be centralized within a single agency (e.g. Treasury Board Secretariat) or other body to provide greater independence from those directly responsible for the delivery of policies and programs."[170] These ruminations avoid tackling the issues and the need for risk-based decision-making in our government head-on.

We do not have the luxury of yet more time to waste by duplicating the work that should be done by government in the first place. We do not need a Senate duplicating the work of what should be an effective House of Commons. Nor do we need the PBO—as much as I got to like Kevin Page through reading his book *Unaccountable*— duplicating the work of, what should be, an effective Canadian Finance, or other ministries, involved in budgeting and planning for large expenditures to provide deliverables that Canadians can actually benefit from, rather than suffer from. And we certainly do not need yet another government department duplicating all the work done elsewhere just to evaluate it (recall the PBO conducted its own financial analysis such as in the procurement process of the F-35 jets) and whether the right decisions were made. We need one government that works for Canadians. We do require appropriate oversight of that government. I summarize what that, including an effective PBO, should look like in the next chapter.

We Canadians are increasingly becoming creatures of the city, living in a more urbanized country that almost clings to our southern neighbour, if not in admiration, then by necessity. With that comes the unique challenges and problems of the modern world, such as affordable housing, the need for good jobs in the digital age and so on. But the status quo, like that old and comfortable leather jacket, needs to be shed. It is time for us to return to the roots of Canada, that vast and beautiful wilderness. Our wilderness can be demanding at times, a harsh environment calling for creative solutions to survive. The good Reverend Martin Luther King stated that "only when it is dark enough can you see the stars." He is of course, alluding to tough and difficult times for Blacks in America. But perhaps, I would like to think, he was also hinting at a need for creative solutions, something which can also benefit us here during these times. It goes without saying if we take his comments literally, then there is enough untamed wilderness still in Canada that could allow us to indeed see a bright and shining path forward, out of our long night of darkness.

Let's set the clock back and try to redesign this great country. It is time to be creative and start fresh with that keen inner intuition of knowing what is right, as we restructure a workable democracy. It may sound somewhat atavistic, but we need to be brave and confident in going down a new path that reaches back to go forward. The famous actor Alan Alda may be best known for his role in the American sitcom MASH. He played the character Hawkeye Pierce, serving as a doctor in Korea at an American medical base, called the 4077th. While helping to bring much laughter to American viewers via their television sets from the early 1970s to early 1980s, and later through reruns of the MASH series, Alda seems to have also been a pretty sharp and serious thinking guy. I stumbled upon this quote from him which would serve us well in our journey to mend the flag: "The creative is the place where no one else has ever been. You have to leave the city of your comfort and go into the wilderness of your intuition."

I have actually taken Alda's advice as I near completion of this book. You see I have two small children, Ryan and Maya, whose future also depends on Canada being run properly. I want our democracy to work for them and for all Canadians. So it seems sensible for me to go into the wilderness a little, leaving the city where we reside, and taking our 44-year-old VW camper dubbed the 'Mystery Machine' by the Scooby-do loving kids, down the Trans-Canada Highway to the Rocky Mountains. This well-planned trip will inevitably yield many surprises, however it should also produce some desired results. I am hoping the adventure, including half-a-dozen nights camping under the stars as part of the varied accommodations, is going to be loads of fun for the kids and their old man. We are bound to learn more about Canada just by watching it pass by through the van's windows. I am also hoping that some voice-activated typing software I intend to purchase, will enable me to get a somewhat presentable manuscript version of this book written slowly each night during the trip—when the little ones are sleeping.

Having a beer in one hand and a nice campfire might help with the tedious process of converting so many months of my chicken scratch into a typed work. Hey, even the great novelist James Joyce, reputedly preferred to handwrite his work before having it typed up. Maybe he was more interested in seeing the quality of his words materialize instead of the speed at which they appeared. So please cut me some slack on how I go about creating my own book and on the mode of my slow transportation across this wilderness known as Canada. I need to roam about this vast land, this wilderness, thinking about how our democracy must change such that we can feel free—free that is, not only on vacation, but free as equal individuals capable of solving problems together and moving Canada forward every day. What was it that Tocqueville said around page 300 in his cinderblock about democracy?

> If people whose social state is democratic could remain free only when they inhabit a wilderness, one would have to despair of the future lot of the human species, for men [and women] are advancing rapidly toward democracy and the wildernesses are filling up. [171]

Chapter 7
Making it Work

It is wrong and immoral to seek to escape the consequences of one's acts.

—Mahatma Gandhi

As demonstrated in the last chapter and stated so sensibly by Lex Sisney in *The 5 Classic Mistakes,* "Your structure is only as good as the people operating within it and how well they are motivated to do their jobs."[1] So, to avoid Sisney's Mistake No. 5: "having the wrong people in the right functions," where, as we also saw in the last chapter, the darker side of human nature can easily assert itself, we must redesign our civil service, government institutions and structures with safeguards in place to ensure our efforts to improve the lives of ordinary Canadians are effective.

For the newly designed system to be accountable, a focal point of the required *Democratic Restructuralism* is to have enterprise-wide risk management carried out by an independent CRO and their delegates staffed throughout the various departments of the federal government. Since the CRO will be reporting independently to, not just the Prime Minister of the day and their Cabinet, but all of Parliament, we will already have taken a direct step in establishing that accountability. Our duly elected MPs, representative of their communities across Canada, will be informed regularly on the issues of the day through the work of the independent RMO. The numerous committees the MPs serve on, based on their qualifications such as experience and knowledge, will receive the detailed risk reports and associated data from pertinent departments to ensure informed and sensible decisions and recommendations can be made.

Where matters of national security are not at stake, brief executive summaries concerning each relevant government department's operations should transparently be made available to the public, perhaps via a government website. Executive summaries should outline the top risks facing the department, how they are being managed, and what the residual risks remaining are in a clear and understandable fashion (one could envision a dashboard of high level information, perhaps including a rating label and colour coding so Canadians can see if there are lower or higher levels of risk meriting greater attention in their view—which would be reflected in their voting behaviour).

The bureaucracy, the numerous departments and agencies comprising the government, should be left to generally manage their affairs without interference, barring the introduction of new legislation based on informed decision-making in Parliament. This will better empower rank-and-file staff who join the civil service to perform meaningful work and serve their fellow Canadians. Only empowered front-line civil servants wanting to do the right thing can usher in a 'golden age' of the public service that we talked about earlier.

However, the Prime Minister and Cabinet must have the ability to set and influence the direction of each ministry, etc., through informed and largely transparent decision-making. For example, if certain risk reports indicate the federal payroll system is antiquated, ineffective and in need of overhaul, and that more centralized operations to consolidate its resources are needed, then the government may wish to implement a new modernization project, as in the case of the Phoenix project. Yet, it is also incumbent upon the leadership to mitigate risks where possible, such as by ensuring adequate testing and reporting is routinely conducted through the development, implementation and operational phases of such a project. The government department managing the project, which should be the same one in charge of handling the federal employee payroll, should also post routine updates concerning the project and its milestones on a government website. This would keep the public informed and able to hold the government accountable for the project's success.

Imagine if all significant projects and administrative initiatives undertaken by our government had executive updates routinely posted for Canadians to view at their leisure. That would look like real government accountability and action. And when Canadians may not have the time to educate themselves about the significant goings on in our government, be it federal, provincial or even municipal government, it should be the job of their elected officials, such as Federal MPs, provincial MPP's and local counsellors, to keep them informed. That, too, speaks to an accountable government, one that does its very best to ensure voters are not ignorant about matters of relevance to them, their families and community interests. Since most Canadians want to improve the quality of their lives and Canada's overall prosperity, they likely want to do the right thing and be informed about things that matter in this regard.

The Role and Value of the Auditor General of Canada

Of course Canadians need to also satisfy themselves that an independent RMO and CRO of the permanent federal public service are held to account. This is the job of the Office of the Auditor General of Canada (OAG): to audit federal government departments and agencies, most Crown corporations, and many other federal organizations, and to report accordingly to Parliament.[2] We also find on the OAG's government webpage that it is additionally performing the audit function for the governments of Nunavut, the Yukon, and the Northwest Territories, reporting directly to their respective legislative assemblies.

Of significance, and per the OAG website, "the 1977 Auditor General Act clarified and expanded the Auditor General's (AG) responsibilities."[3] You have likely heard of some of the AG's recent and blistering reports, such as the ones regarding the Phoenix payroll system or the CRA. Therefore, you likely would be nonplussed to learn that after the new Act was passed, that "in addition to looking at the accuracy of financial statements," the AG has the "broader mandate to examine how well the government managed its affairs."[4] From Chapter 3, we know the government can do much better.

Also of significance is how the 1977 Act maintains a Chinese wall as they say, between the role of the government and that of the AG; the dividing line being important in any organization that has decision-makers versus decision auditors. According to the OAG, "The new Act maintained the important principle that the auditor General does not comment on policy choices, but does examine how policies are implemented."[5]

Based on my experience working in the private sector, as well as the regulatory world, this is standard procedure. Senior management in business makes decisions concerning the business, such as implementing the overall strategy, financing, product or service features, etc., just as General Motors or Facebook would. The auditor, as in the case of GM or Facebook, reviews how the business policies surrounding those decisions were implemented, and whether or not they adhered to the company's own internal guidelines, policies and procedures, etc. We observed, in the case of Facebook and Cambridge Analytica, that certain privacy laws may have been violated, and likely internal and applicable company policies and procedures, if they were in place (I have not researched the matter), may have been as well. The OAG itself notes that it "is unable to respond to inquiries which do not relate to its mandate and role."[6]

To give you a flavour of the Chinese wall, here are a few examples of what the OAG will not do, which reinforces that which is the concern of government decision-makers or managers of the country versus internal auditors: "audit policy decisions, which are the prerogative of Parliament and elected officials; examine judges, lawyers or laws; . . . provide forms, reports or other publication, or other information about federal entities other than that which is contained in OAG audit reports."[7]

At this juncture of our discussion I should clarify why I believe it should be the OAG that is most suitably able to provide assurance that a newly created and functioning RMO is doing its job both efficiently and effectively as intended, rather than the sitting government's own auditors. First, you need to understand that Canada's ruling government of the day, being the Liberals headed by Prime Minister Justin Trudeau as I write this, has a team of auditors in the permanent bureaucracy, within what is known as the Treasury Board (TB).

Formation of the TB is as old as Canada itself, owing to the fact it was created in 1867 and obtained statutory powers in 1869. This is according to the official TB website, which also states the following: "The Treasury Board is responsible for accountability and ethics, financial, personnel and administrative management, comptrollership, approving regulations and most Orders-in-Council,"[8] the latter being procedural matters we need not dwell upon. What is important to focus on is that the TB is a Cabinet committee of that all too powerful Privy Council of Canada. It is also an onion we must peel.

Peeling back the onion, we learn that TB "has an administrative arm, the Secretariat, which was part of the Department of Finance until it was proclaimed a Department in 1966."[9] We need not dwell on that move either, except to note that much of what the Treasury Board Secretariat (TBS) has traditionally dealt with has had much to do with the government's own administration of its finances. It therefore stands to reason that the TBS website indicates the "Secretariat provides advice and makes recommendations to the Treasury Board committee of ministers on how the government spends money on programs and services, how it regulates and how it is managed." Even more interesting is the assertion that "the Secretariat helps ensure tax dollars are spent wisely and effectively for Canadians."[10] Still, we have to peel back the onion further to find where our government's team of auditors is located. For within the TB's TBS, there are also several other branches and sectors, such as the Office of the Chief Human Resources Officer, the Expenditure Management Sector, the Government Operations Sector, the Chief Information Office Branch, a Priorities and Planning division, the Social and Cultural Sector, Strategic Communications and Ministerial Affairs, the Regulatory Affairs Sector, the Economic Sector, International Affairs, Security and Justice Sector, the Corporate Services Sector, and a couple of other units. If you are not already lost just trying to understand the bureaucratic labyrinth known as TBS, and why it needs so many divisions, I am impressed. If you are a bit lost, you should be unsurprised to learn that there have been recent reports indicating TBS will look for potential alternative pay systems to replace Phoenix. TBS appears to have its thumb on everything.

It also houses the Office of the Comptroller General (OCG). The term Comptroller refers to a senior- or executive-manager type of accountant responsible for supervising the quality of financial reporting and accounting in an organization. The TBS website states:

> The Comptroller General of Canada is responsible for providing functional direction and assurance government wide for financial management, internal audit, investment planning, procurement [we all know how efficient that has been], project management, and the management of real property and material.[11]

Canada has had a Comptroller in one form or another since 1931, however, as is often the case in government, the Comptroller peanut has been moved around quite a bit in the organizational shell game played in Ottawa.

After numerous changes, in 2003, the OCG had been "re-established" with a "focus" targeted "on enhanced accountability." Since then, its "responsibilities include financial management and accounting policy, financial system management, internal audit, and community capacity building."[12]

The internal audit piece seems to have been part of OCG's responsibilities since 1978, when its "responsibilities" were broadened to include "financial management, program evaluation, and internal audit."[13] Therefore, if we peel the onion one more time, we now see that the regular auditing of Canada's government departments and agencies rests with the OCG's internal audit division—the OCG being just one division of a sprawling TBS that is part of TB, itself a Cabinet committee of the Queen's Privy Council of Canada—PCO. Got that?

So how often do we hear about the OCG's internal audit division uncovering major problems in our government versus the more independent OAG headline grabbing reports? Then again, how often do we hear about any scandal plagued organizations' own internal audit department taking its masters to task? I do not recall seeing any OCG internal audit reports concerning the much reviled Phoenix system, only the more independent OAG report. Obviously, by the time the OAG is involved in such issues, it is often too late to put the genie back in the bottle after wishing the mammoth boondoggles would just go away.

As you may have guessed by now, I do not put a lot of trust in the government of the day auditing itself. When I read on the TBS website that the OCG internal audit division "is a professional, independent appraisal function that provides feedback on government management practices and activities . . . promoting the overall effectiveness and efficiency of government operations and the transparency of decision making"[14]—I take it all with a grain of salt—although aspirin may be better. Apparently, "internal audit provides deputy heads with assurance as to the design and operation of the governance, risk management, and control processes in their organizations."[15]

Is that so? Is that why we have Phoenix and all the other debacles outlined in chapter 3? In his book *Irresponsible Government*, Rathgeber wrote that "what was once a powerful spending watchdog is now a mere staff agency within [TBS]" when he described the Comptroller General.[16]

I cannot help but imagine that having the OCG's internal audit unit oversee the broader operations of the government is much like having the fox guard the chicken coop. And, as to the design of our broken government, I have already assured myself through much research, that the current design is not the right one the country needs. It would be interesting to know the qualifications of all the auditors working under the OCG, as well as just how independent they really are. And if they are independent, competent and highly qualified, why do we need the OAG to duplicate the efforts in the form of yet another government auditing body? It makes no sense. Then again, as we saw earlier, we have a supposedly independent PBO duplicating the efforts of the Ministry of Finance, and quite likely, the TBS. Can you hear it friends? The death knell of a poorly designed bureaucracy desperately in need of *Democratic Restructuralism*!

The OAG is best positioned to serve as an independently designed internal audit oversight function, reporting on how the government is managing the affairs of Canadians directly to Parliament. The OAG has established a long track record of credibility in its independent reporting. Indeed, in his fall 2013 report, the Auditor General of Canada, Michael Ferguson (may God rest his good soul as he recently passed away and will be dearly missed), found some problems within TBS itself. Regarding the OAG's *Follow-Up Audit on Internal Controls over Financial Reporting*, Ferguson had this to say: "Eight years after government made it a priority to have in place effective internal controls over financial reporting, I am concerned that several large departments are still years away from knowing whether those controls are in place and working effectively."[17] So much for the fox guarding the hen house! The purpose of the follow-up audit was "to determine whether the Treasury

Board of Canada Secretariat . . . and the seven selected departments had made satisfactory progress toward addressing the two recommendations on internal controls over financial reporting in our 2011 Status Report."[18]

According to Ferguson, "With annual spending of nearly $300 billion across government, effective internal controls are a necessary part of safeguarding public assets." His sense of urgency seems palpable when he also states, "It is imperative that departments get this work done without further delay." And yet the OAG was informed by the OCG "that it does not believe it is responsible for acting on departments' timelines, including any delays." Since the OAG believes "the OCG has an important oversight role related to the completion of the work by departments," it reasonably "expected that the OCG would have taken action on those delays."[19] Given this situation, whereby as recently as 2013, several large Canadian government departments were still unable to show they have satisfactory internal controls over financial reporting, the OAG made the following recommendations to the OCG:

> We recommend that the Office of the Comptroller General of Canada should work with Aboriginal Affairs and Northern Development Canada [reconstituted organizationally as we saw in the prior chapter]; Foreign Affairs, Trade and Development Canada [now Global Affairs]; Human Resources and Skills Development Canada; Transport Canada; and Veterans Affairs Canada to see that the first full risk-based assessments of internal controls over financial reporting, the identification and the addressing of gaps and weaknesses, and the implementation of a program of ongoing monitoring, as applicable, are completed without delay.[20]

If we jump ahead and look at the OAG's March 2018 performance audit of the troubled Phoenix federal payroll system, we yet again find valuable and insightful work performed by the OAG pointing toward deficiency in TBS oversight. All Canadians aware of the Phoenix nightmare probably would have guessed by now that it is a gigantic failure as it relates to government accountability. In the words of the OAG, "The building and implementation of Phoenix was an incomprehensible failure of project management and oversight." On balance, OAG "found that Public Services and Procurement Canada failed to properly manage the Phoenix project."[21] Well, surprise, surprise! What I find to be more interesting in the OAG's report are two recommendations reflecting how TBS dropped the ball in ensuring adequate oversight of this key government project. One can only marvel at the apparent lack of OCG involvement, especially since it has an internal audit division which should have monitored the project and its necessary internal controls as well as its change management processes and policies. Consider the magnitude of these OAG recommendations as you ponder the waste associated with Phoenix or other costly projects, something we already discussed:

Recommendation. For all government-wide information technology projects, the Treasury Board of Canada Secretariat should carry out mandatory independent reviews of the project's key decisions to proceed or not, and inform the project's responsible Deputy Minister and senior executives of the reviews' conclusions.

Recommendation. For all government-wide information technology projects under its responsibility, Public Services and Procurement Canada should ensure that an effective oversight mechanism is in place, is documented, and is maintained. The mechanism should first be approved by the Treasury Board of Canada Secretariat and should include the heads of concerned departments and agencies.[22]

Just regarding these two recommendations alone, it is clear we require the kind of risk-management office outlined in this book. We need a CRO heading up a RMO that ensures effective oversight of all government operations, not only Public Services and Procurement Canada, where the dreaded Phoenix system resides. And we require our MPs to know what is going on and to be empowered to engage in meaningful debate on the issues of the day, like Phoenix, making informed decisions accordingly. Of course, Treasury Board and its master, the Privy Council Office, might not like that. That is probably why, in June 2018, in the aftermath of the OAG's scathing report on Phoenix, the head or Clerk of the PCO, Michael Wernick, stated the following at a parliamentary committee reviewing the OAG's findings: "What I take issue with is the insinuation that there is a generalized broken culture, which implies there is a generalized broken public service and I contest that."[23] As predictable, when otherwise good people might fear they are facing a personal attack on their credibility, they become participants in the blame game. They fail to recognize that they should question that something may be amiss instead of parrying a perceived attack.

In the same *ipolitics.ca* article that cited Wernick's comments above, New Democratic MP David Christopherson was quoted stating this in relation to the situation: "Do we agree that the auditor general is off the rails or do we agree that we have a huge problem made even more difficult by the top of the bureaucracy accepting there is no problem?"[24] My own view is that it is pointless to engage in the blame game, although any individual clearly associated with wrongdoing and the Phoenix project should be held accountable, as long as that may take, using independent bodies such as the OAG to conduct the required work. Canadians deserve answers. Overall however, it is obvious that we must redesign government to prevent further Phoenix-type fiascos from happening again. This means building the independent risk-management-oversight function discussed earlier. As *ipolitics.ca* reported, the Auditor General himself "told a Senate committee . . . that getting at what's wrong with the public service culture is difficult and beyond the purview of an auditor."[25] Exactly. That's why we need a nonpartisan Chief Risk Officer, not more TBS employees doing their masters' bidding!

We see more of the blame game in a late June 2018 *Hill Times* article, too, which reports that during a June 20 Senate National Finance Committee meeting, Mr. Wernick remarked, "It is 'extremely difficult' to fire anyone under a Deputy Minister level for poor performance, as they can only be terminated with 'legal test of cause' under the Public Service Employment Act." Countering that view, the national president of the Public Service Alliance of Canada said "his members are 'pissed' about [the PCO head's] comments." The president of the union also stated "If the clerk wants to start terminating federal public sector workers, maybe he should look at those responsible for Phoenix first."[26] That, although sensible, still adds more fuel or blame to the fire of confusion in Ottawa. The misunderstanding being that *someone* is not to blame so much as *something*: the poor design of our government producing wrong behaviours and results for Canada. We must demand the *Democratic Restructuralism* we need, including accountability in the architecture of better designed public institutions.

The OAG is best suited to provide the independent-internal-audit oversight over the federal government's operations. Its mandate, resources and overall capabilities should be strengthened, with those of the TBS being reviewed as to their appropriateness and effectiveness. The hodgepodge of bureaucratic organizations within TBS does appear to beg further investigation as to how they are contributing to the sanctity of Parliament specifically, and to the benefits to Canadians generally. We may require *Democratic Restructuralism* here too. Looking again toward America as an example, as we did in discerning the utility of adopting some of James Madison's wisdom concerning good design, it may even be useful to consider positioning our OAG such that it more resembles the US Government Accountability Office (GAO).

The US Government Accountability Office

It may interest you to know that the GAO "is an independent, non-partisan agency that works for Congress." The fact that it is "often called the 'congressional watchdog' "[27] illustrates the importance the US legislature places upon its activities, regardless of how even in America the embedding of enterprise risk management across government is only now taking shape. A Comptroller General also leads the GAO, whose "mission is to support the Congress in meeting its constitutional responsibilities and to help improve the performance and ensure the accountability of the federal government for the benefit of the American people." The GAO claims to "support congressional oversight" by doing such things as "auditing agency operations to determine whether federal funds are being spent efficiently and effectively; investigating allegations of illegal and improper activities; reporting on how well government programs and policies are meeting their objectives"; and even "performing policy analyses and outlining options for congressional consideration."[28] The GAO is often referred to as the supreme audit institution of the American nation as well as its watchdog.

Forgetting Donald Trump as the figurehead of modern America if you can, I can tell you that the GAO's website is very impressive. From it we cannot only glean that the Washington D.C. based organization has 3,000 employees and offices in 11 major cities across America, but that its staff are "career employees hired on the basis of their knowledge, skills, and ability." The GAO deems this as something that ensures "our independence as our agency is further safeguarded." Impressively, the "diverse staff includes economists, social scientists, accountants, public policy analysts, attorneys and computer experts as well as specialists in fields ranging from foreign policy to healthcare."[29] I found the GAO's website also to be impressive in terms of its user-friendliness and the manner in which it highlights what it calls 'key issues.'

The content available, as well as one's ability to drill down further into those key issues, reflect the GAO's credible work in the sphere of risk management.

Consequently, while I am not convinced that the GAO should also be performing a risk-management-oversight function, as that could confuse what should be distinct roles and responsibilities regardless of the degree to which they are interrelated, it has clearly demonstrated it has done some good work regarding risks facing the US. According to the GAO's website, "The key issues pages provide information about GAO's work on a range of issues facing the nation and highlight some of our most relevant reports."[30] In this regard, I found the federal issues presented, complete with easy-to-read icons that link to additional details, highly informative and well-thought-out. 'Featured issues' as of mid-June 2018 include:

> A High Risk List—programs and agencies needing continued attention; Disaster Assistance—challenges to effective government response; America's Fiscal Future—a big picture look at the nation's fiscal condition; Retirement Security—issues affecting retirement in the United States; Duplication & Cost Savings—changes that could improve efficiency or decrease costs; and Technology Assessment—analysis of critical innovations.[31]

Although climate change is not listed separately (I hope there is no political bias), this looks like something that Canadian MPs could benefit from as well as US Congress members if they had easy access to such information, with pertinent risk dashboards, etc., as outlined before. The wider public would also benefit with access to such information, suitably summarized and not containing any sensitive data posing a threat to the country. Having risk-based information available for decision-makers and voters alike is obviously one thing, facilitating its easy access is entirely another. The GAO's website proves a user-friendly and accessible database is possible, and I can envision its use in *Democratic Restructuralism* here in Canada.

If we drill down the GAO's High Risk List, just looking at one of its important issues—*Improving Federal Management of Programs That Serve Tribes and Their Members*—we find a concise and clear summary of the risk. Here is an excerpt:

> Congress recently noted through treaties, statutes, and historical relations with Indian tribes, the United States has undertaken a unique trust responsibility to protect and support Indian tribes and Indians. In light of this unique trust responsibility and concerns about the federal government in effectively administering Indian education and health care programs and mismanaging Indian energy resources, we are adding these programs as a high-risk-issue because they uniquely affect tribal nations and their members. [32]

Yes, this book is mainly about Canada and we need to turn our attention again to what is going on here and the importance of the OAG's own internal audit work. However, please note that the work of the GAO discussed briefly above reinforces the needs I outlined earlier; the need for more risk-based decision-making in our government, as well as transparency of information that is easily accessible and understood by voters. I am not sure how much the American Congress or President Trump is using GAO's key issues reports in making decisions, and if the risk-management work they do goes far enough, but I sincerely hope the US will do the right thing down there because we need to do it up here for sure.

The Defence Team We Require

At this point in our discussion on the role of internal audit, it is useful to introduce the concept of what is commonly referred to in business as the Three Lines of Defence model. It sounds like a dry and boring term, but it is absolutely crucial in terms of forcing accountability in government. That makes it a linchpin in *Democratic Restructuralism*, along with good physical design of government organizations and rightly motivated public servants. The trinity of things is always important.

In this modern and practical system of good governance, increasingly adopted in the corporate world of big business, we not only see the utility of maintaining the Chinese wall between internal audit and business decision-makers, but also one, where possible (typically in large organizations), between audit and risk management, with the latter also being a separate oversight function that resides distinctly apart from business management. In fact, the Institute of Internal Auditors (IIA) published a "Position paper" in 2013 on *The Three Lines of Defense in Effective Risk Management and Control*. Notably it considers "as the first line of defense," which OSFI does too, "operational managers." This is because they "own and manage risks."[33] Ideally, in terms of the Canadian government headquartered in Ottawa, it should be the heads of the respective departments consisting of our federal government, within the permanent bureaucracy of the federal civil service, who are the people's operational managers! And ideally, it should be our duly elected MPs who are the people's senior managers (or even Board of Directors), overseeing and guiding the work of operational managers! Of course, we know that is currently not the case, unless the sanctity of the legislature is in name only. For MPs certainly do not oversee and guide the work of the civil service effectively and efficiently, as we have tragically seen. And an over-centralized government likely does not allow its various department heads to own and manage risk!

The IIA considers the second line of defense to be "the various risk control and compliance oversight functions established by management."[34] It elaborates that "typical functions in this second line of defense include: A risk-management function (and/or committee) that facilitates and monitors the implementation of effective risk-management practices by operational management and assists risk owners in defining the target risk exposure and reporting adequate risk related information throughout the organization."[35] Well, we already discussed this in Chapter 5, including the clear necessity and benefit of implementing ERM within the federal government. We require an independent CRO to ensure in the House of Commons that the parliamentarians, the MPs who should understand and have appropriate oversight of risks, are assisted by a Risk Management Office—the RMO, that helps them understand Canada's risk exposures and routinely gives them risk-related information concerning government operations so they can perform their jobs. It is that simple.

The IIA also views a compliance function as being typically found in the second line of defense. Distinct from risk management, the purpose of the compliance function is to monitor such things "as noncompliance with applicable laws and regulations."[36] Canada already has a Privacy Commissioner, Department of Justice and, obviously, a judicial system. It is important to understand, however, that we need to distinguish between who makes the laws and who ensures the country is compliant with them and any other legally binding international agreements, such as NAFTA—if it continues to be an agreement. The IIA notes that "multiple compliance functions often exist in a single organization, with responsibility for specific types of compliance monitoring, such as health and safety, supply chain, environmental, or quality monitoring."[37] We absolutely do not want a lumbering and complicated bureaucracy, including with respect to compliance oversight. Ideally Canada would streamline the compliance function as much as possible, keeping it as practical as possible.

The idea is to strengthen compliance where necessary such as in the area of privacy legislation given issues such as those surrounding the Facebook and Cambridge Analytica scandal. That is preferable to creating an opaque black box that does not easily lend itself to transparency. In the end, we just need the compliance oversight function to ensure the government is complying with applicable laws and regulations. Certainly our government should not be collecting the banking information of all Canadians! For existing laws, any risks of noncompliance should be incorporated in the work of the RMO, as noncompliance is a risk to be understood, managed and monitored. We have had enough privacy breaches to know this is important. Routine communication should exist between the risk management and compliance functions, which should not be too unwieldy.

Within the second line of defense, the last of the three oversight functions touched upon by the IIA's position paper is "a controllership function that monitors financial risks and financial reporting issues."[38] In Canada we have the Ministry of Finance as well as the Treasury Board along with Treasury Board's Secretariat. Regarding the Ministry of Finance, it defines its role as being "primarily responsible for providing the Government of Canada with analysis and advice on the broad economic and financial affairs of Canada."[39] This appears to mainly encompass actual hands-on management of the nation's financial affairs rather than financial oversight of the Department itself, the monitoring of financial risks and reporting aspects. Therefore, we learn from the Ministry's webpages that its responsibilities entail such things as "preparing the federal budget . . .; developing tax and tariff policy and legislation; managing federal borrowing on financial markets; . . . administering major federal transfers of federal funds to the provinces and territories; developing financial sector policy . . .; [and] representing Canada in various International financial institutions and groups."[40]

Obviously the Canadian government has been busy jousting with the US Trump Administration on the NAFTA file. In the wake of the dismal

June 2018 G-7 Summit in Québec, President Trump backtracked quickly on his decision to have the US sign a joint communiqué along with other G-7 nations, disingenuously stating our Prime Minister, Trudeau, made "false statements" and that Trudeau was "very dishonest and weak."[41] There you have it again folks. The fake news and blame game seems to be around every corner we look, dividing the world continually, and preventing any possible solutions to heal it. And who could ever say Trump is a healer, when, after the Québec summit, he subsequently flies to Singapore for talks with North Korean leader Kim Jong Un—calling the vile dictator that enslaves his people a "very talented" leader. Yet one of Trump's top advisers for the G-7 Summit said our Prime Minister deserves "a special place in hell" in relation to the Québec talks and Trudeau's position for Canada.[42] The absurdity of such statements speaks to a very dark White House policy fanning potential trade wars and yet more division among the apostles of democracy. Jefferson would not be happy. That is not the New Jerusalem we want. Perhaps Trump will be cast out of the presidency, but the future remains uncertain at this time. The spiritual will of the people must prevail around the world to produce the desired design. Messages of hope must trump those of fear.

At any rate, it fell upon the Canadian Minister of foreign affairs, Chrystia Freeland, to oversee Canada's NAFTA and trade negotiations with the bombastic and disingenuous Mister Trump, rather than our Department of Finance. We see in her 2017 *Mandate Letter* signed by Trudeau that her "overarching goal will be to restore constructive Canadian leadership in the world and to promote Canada's interests and values." Specifically concerning America, her mandate is to "maintain constructive relations with the United States, Canada's closest ally and most important economic and security partner." She is tasked to "lead efforts to deepen trade and commerce between our two countries." On North American trade, she is to "strengthen trilateral North American cooperation with the United States and Mexico."[43] But enough on her job, which does not appear to directly be that of the Canadian Ministry of

Finance. More importantly, for the purposes of our discussion, a controllership or financial oversight function also does not appear to be the responsibility of the Ministry of Finance.

As discussed earlier, it is Treasury Board—TB that is supposed to be "responsible for accountability," including financial management assurance, which rests with OCG as described. However, we have seen that the OCG has been somewhat deficient in carrying out its duties. Perhaps if it focused on monitoring financial risks and financial reporting issues, especially since we saw the OAG call out the OCG on not ensuring several large departments had adequate internal controls over financial reporting, maybe we would have a better controllership/financial oversight function within the OCG. Instead, we seem to have a situation where the Government of Canada continues making colossal financial blunders in Ottawa, likely indicative of the absence of appropriate financial oversight, and supporting the OAG's findings concerning deficiencies within the OCG.

It would make good sense for the OCG's financial oversight responsibilities to be rolled into a more independently constituted Parliamentary Budget Office—PBO. We don't need that second line of defense function confusingly duplicated in each organization. Furthermore, if as its first head Kevin Page wrote in *Unaccountable*, the PBO was designed to "'kick the tires' on a business case before public money is ever spent," why not have it do just that. We observed in Chapter 5 that it was not initially set up for success. Perhaps it should be now as part of *Democratic Restructuralism* to ensure accountability of our government from a financial oversight perspective within the second line of defense. The key is oversight of work, not duplication of work.

The Liberal government under Prime Minister Justin Trudeau recently did make some changes involving the PBO. It appointed Yves Giroux as its new head in mid-June 2018 and, through changes to *The Parliament of Canada Act* that were instituted in September 2017, recognized PBO's head as an independent Officer of Parliament, reporting to Parliament via Speakers of the Senate and the House of Commons.[44] I am not sure if these changes go far enough given the concerns raised in *Unaccountable,* and I suspect we still have duplication of efforts in TBS structures which can be inefficient. There is too much power in the PMO and Privy Council, likely meaning too much power in TBS and not enough in the second lines of defense, including financial oversight. The Auditor General also should not be responsible for financial oversight, only auditing that capability as it did in the case of the OCG's shortcomings. Indeed, and as Rathgeber noted in his book *Irresponsible Government,* the Auditor General is "an after-the-fact evaluator." Therefore, in the case of the government purse for example, "the AG does not and cannot exercise control over real-time spending." Fundamentally, "only Parliament can do this."[45]

This all points to a need for a stronger second line of defense that includes independent risk, compliance, and financial oversight functions of government-wide operations. This would support decision-making in Parliament just as it supports decision-making in other large organizations. A newly established risk-management-oversight function, as outlined in Chapter 5, must focus on the nonfinancial oversight (non-internal financial control and financial reporting) risks, but all oversight functions within the trinity of the second line of defense must be coordinated to work in a spirit of effectiveness, with clearly visible independence, authority and mandates. This will eliminate any confusion. As the 2013 IIA *Position Paper* emphasized, "Duties must be coordinated carefully to assure that risks and control processes operate as intended."[46] Since Canadians want our elected officials to do what's right for everyone, this is crucial advice. The trinity of oversight functions within the second line of defense are fundamental Lego or building blocks in designing an accountable Canadian government. Maybe they should all go into a newly restored Langevin Block that also houses a museum, honouring First Peoples and of our Forefathers, so we can learn from our past instead of manipulating it. Regardless, *Democratic Restructuralism* must be our main pursuit in mending the flag and healing broken institutions that do not provide the right results.

Once elected officials are empowered to do their jobs in a properly structured government, they may find themselves thoroughly kept up to date on a variety of risk reports being generated by the RMO, depending on which committee they are assigned to, or which files they are tasked with keeping up to date on—all the while actually (rather than just looking like they are) collaborating and updating their colleagues, party heads and constituents accordingly. Empowered parliamentarians would similarly find themselves kept up to date on any compliance or financial oversight issues that may impact the country's well-being. This is how government should work when it has adopted, in practice as well as spirit, the trinity of elements within a well-ordered second line of defense. The beneficial structure of this trinity should be made lawful. But there is still one of the Three Lines of Defense remaining that we have already talked about at some length, internal audit. As they say, good things come in threes.

I already mentioned why I believe that the OAG is ideally positioned to perform the audit function in our federal government, perhaps requiring some additional resources, if need be. We now just need to clarify its role in the Three Lines of Defense model and how it should relate to the key risk-management function within the second line. The 2013 IIA *Position Paper* clarifies internal audit's purpose as the third line of defense in this manner:

> Internal Auditors provide the governing body and senior management [I call that the legislature and PMO] with comprehensive assurance based on the highest level of independence and objectivity in the organization…Internal audit provides assurance on the effectiveness of governance [think of democracy here], risk management [I call that the RMO], and internal controls [a new PBO for example],

including the manner in which the first and second lines of defense achieve risk management and control objectives.[47]

I can tell you from first-hand experience working at OSFI, which has a similar approach in its application of risk-based supervision of federally regulated financial institutions that the Three Lines of Defense model works well. Where organizations have adopted it in a sensibly practical way, the results are usually good, with business strategies and profit targets being fulfilled. For larger and more complex organizations, which obviously our federal government is (although its design is likely overly complex as well as deficient in optimal structuring), it also makes good sense for internal audit not to be involved in conducting risk-management oversight as well as its core audit function. Rather, as one blog by Paul Proctor, a vice president, distinguished analyst and the Chief of Security and Risk Management at Gartner Inc. states, "To be clear, it is management's role to address risk appropriately and audit's role to provide assurance."[48] Or as indicated by the IIA in its January 2009 Position Paper, *The Role of Internal Auditing in Enterprise-Wide Risk Management*, internal audit's "core role with regard to ERM is to provide objective assurance to the board [we can again substitute the legislature and PMO here] on the effectiveness of risk management." Apparently, "research has shown that board directors and internal auditors agree that the two most important ways that internal audits provide value to the organization are in providing objective assurance that the major business risks are being managed appropriately," plus "the risk management and internal control framework is operating effectively."[49]

In March 2012, the IIA's Practice Guide *Coordinating Risk Management and Assurance*, outlined further how internal audit should assess the adequacy of risk management in organizations, confirming whether or not they are managing risks effectively. The Practice Guide stated "in so far as internal audit will need to include the adequacy of risk management within their scope there are two dimensions to consider: whether the risk management function includes all appropriate risk areas within its remit"; and "whether the risk management function is operating effectively."[50] Of course there are some international standards and details around how to achieve this. I do not wish to get too technical, but I can tell you it is all fairly common sense. So then why should it be any different in government? Designing our government to have a strong third line of defense, the OAG, which is also tasked with overseeing the work of a newly created and independent RMO, along with appropriately reconstituted compliance and financial oversight functions, makes perfect sense.

Imagine how many problems surfaced in Chapter 3 could have been avoided? Imagine how much money could have been saved with all Three Lines of Defense reporting to Parliament and the Prime Minister on their respective oversight functions? The governing MPs and Prime Minister would be making risk-based decisions, with the opposition parties able to provide meaningful challenge in the House of Commons and in Question Period. Our privacy laws, facing so many challenges in the face of advancing technologies and issues, such as those involving the Cambridge Analytica scandal, could be meaningfully deliberated upon by parliamentarians and applicable committees. Progress could be made accordingly. The OAG, the highest level of assurance to parliamentarians, would provide comfort to them that things are working as they should. This means our MPs would be getting the right information at the right time from the RMO, the PBO and compliance function too. Decision-making for and on behalf of Canadians, by empowered MPs, would have the best possible outcomes for the nation. Could anything else be more important when it comes to government?

A strong OAG appropriately recognized as the third line of defense, along with appropriately constituted and strong second lines of defense, will drive the government accountability Canadians need and desire. This *Democratic Restructuralism* will, in turn, drive the vibrant democracy that Canada merits. We can do it. This is 'how' to do it! And doing so transparently wherever possible, as discussed, can only bring Canadians into the fullness of their collective identity and spirituality that much sooner. It could even make sense to elect the heads of the second and third lines of defense, just as we do our MPs, especially if the undemocratic Senate is abolished. Election of officials heading the oversight functions could be for terms that are somewhat longer than those served by MPs. Perhaps even those running to lead the oversight functions could belong to no specific party. I am sure we could come up with some good and workable ideas. Readers, my fellow Canadians, we are not as ignorant as a select few would have us be.

It also bears noting that the OAG should be peer reviewed by suitably advanced and similar auditing groups overseeing government operations elsewhere—like the GAO—if our American brothers and sisters opt for *Democratic Restructuralism* instead of putting up fences. The peer review will ensure that the highest line of defense, in the three lines of defense model, is providing the best and most professional defense possible. This is how best to unmuzzle the country's potential, rooting our politics more in the science of decision-making rather than the art of decision-making. The collective good of our spiritual motivations does not suggest it should be exclusive of making more informed, even scientifically based, decision-making. Both can coexist. Each has a vital role to play in the measured, thoughtful and hopeful advancement of humanity in our time.

A final and curious note on the work of the OAG . . . Currently, Canada's Commissioner of the Environment and Sustainable Development, is appointed by the Auditor General. Right now, it is "on behalf of the Auditor General" that this commissioner "provides parliamentarians with objective, independent analysis and recommendations on the federal government's efforts to protect the environment and foster sustainable development."[51] It probably makes a lot more sense for a newly established RMO to oversee, from a risk-management perspective: Canada's efforts to safeguard the environment and pursue sustainable development, if that indeed is a government objective.

We will see in the next chapter that Canada has been a bit of a laggard on the environmental file. Maybe we should be managing the risk a lot better if that is the will of Canadians and their spiritual sense of what is right. This remains to be seen given how our government is presently structured—the government having kept Canadians fairly ignorant on the subject. All things being equal, the role of the OAG on the climate file should be the same as on any other government file, to provide assurance to the legislature that the pertinent risks are being managed appropriately and effectively by the ministry concerned.

The real tragedy in our government is that so many officials are playing a role rather than performing one. Why not have elected officials and the more permanent bureaucracy perform the tasks we want them to? Every government employee should be empowered to do their job, according to well-defined roles and responsibilities and a system that drives results for the country in a straightforward, clear, transparent and accountable way. This kind of mending and healing of our broken government system, the urgent *Democratic Restructuralism* that must be ushered in without delay, is the right thing to do. It is what Canada and the world needs more of. Without exaggerating, it may be the last best hope for humanity. Individually, we cannot do it alone. Collectively we can achieve that which appears impossible on the surface. Our spirit and sense of right can and must move mountains. I hope our leaders, past, current and future alike, have the ability to listen. All will be judged based on their merits. My voice in the wilderness is a small one. My message is of invaluable importance to people everywhere. Or so I have been informed.

Chapter 8
Healing the World

Do not be conformed to this world,
but be transformed by the renewal of your mind,
that by testing you may discern what is the will of God,
what is good and acceptable and perfect.

—Romans 12:2 (ESV)

Canada, Leader of *Democratic Restructuralism*

Imagine. My son Ryan told me the other day that this is the name of the most popular song on earth, a song obviously written by John Lennon. I like the song myself, only preferring not to "imagine there's no heaven" (as the song opens with). For I can see the stars and moon at night in the midst of an enveloping darkness Dr. Martin Luther King spoke of. And I can see an obvious intelligent design that could not have arisen out of nothing. I am not going to bother Googling on the Internet if Ryan is correct or not and what the criteria used was to say that the song *Imagine* outranks any other tune in popularity. But his comment struck me. Kids have vivid imaginations themselves, and since my daughter Maya is only six and Ryan is just ten, I can attest that they have that unique sense of wonder, curiosity, innocence and creativity that, when combined, leads to a strong imagination. If only we adults could all hold on to our youthful imagination, then perhaps we could formulate better solutions for so many problems facing humanity.

Albert Einstein emphasized the global importance of imagination this way during a 1929 interview with a *Post* reporter: "Imagination is more important than knowledge. Knowledge is limited. Imagination encircles the world."[1] I think I like this famous German born physicist as much as the Frenchman, Alexi de Tocqueville. I daresay Einstein would have made a great Canadian too, one who intuitively feels the difference between what is right and what is wrong. He does not need an economist to tell him he is too incompetent to tell the difference. He would likely reply, "I believe in intuitions and inspirations. I sometimes feel that I am right. I do not know that I am . . . [but] I would have been surprised if I had been wrong."[2] Of course, Einstein, despite being a man of science, was also a man who believed in the historical existence of Jesus. He said, "No one can read the Gospels without feeling the actual presence of Jesus. His personality pulsates in every word. No myth is filled with such life."[3]

I mention this in my own book, not to be a religious fanatic, but to indicate that Einstein appears to have been moved by the words of the Gospels, which are combined in the Bible. We know the Bible, as other religious works such as the Koran, are often referred to by diverse peoples in search of wise guidance and reinforcement of their understanding of the difference between right and wrong. The vast majority of these people living in democracies are peaceful, interpreting such religious works in a positive way. It is no different than Dr. Martin Luther King and his nonviolent Baptist movement that sought more civil rights for Blacks and greater social justice. Let us then consider, regardless of any religious views or of any wrongs that have occurred in the maligned name of Christianity, Islam or other religious beliefs, that people in democracies know, as we Canadians, including our Indigenous Peoples generally do, the difference between right and wrong.

Imagine, if you can recapture that youthful quality so open to new ideas and the art of the possible, that these people also wish to make good and informed decisions that can improve the quality of their loved ones' lives, the quality of circumstances and conditions within their respective countries. Imagine such people calling for a better designed government like that of Canada's, if we demand our legislature be built to succeed rather than fail. Imagine highly informed and motivated MPs, or whatever their Democratic counterparts are labelled around the world, making the right decisions. Imagine them doing so in a transparent way such that their decisions are truly credible in the eyes of those they govern. Imagine such decisions being made around the world, *encircling* it as Einstein may have put it. Imagine the results of well-informed decision-making, the prioritizing of problems to be solved, reflective of the platform a political party ran on, which in turn was reflective of issues that a truly informed electorate cared about. Why can it not be so?

Imagine politics, not so much the art of decision-making but also the science of decision-making. Imagine risk-based government institutions working for the people and transforming democracies around the world. Imagine Canada leading a movement that pursues *Democratic Restructuralism*, leading by example. And if we let our imagination soar to the heavens, backed by the solid results achieved in mending our flag, fixing our own backyard so to speak, can we not heal the world while other nations do the same, and we all then turn toward finding solutions to common global problems? This pursuit should be the primary concern of humanity. It must be the main focus of fathers and mothers and anyone who nurtures the future.

Tocqueville opined that "in democratic countries the science of association is the mother science; the progress of all the others depends on the progress of that one."[4] We need to get the blueprints right in restructuring democracies internationally. For it is then, based on the realistic expectations of their success, that we can turn toward solving those problems that seem so impossible to solve: environmental and wildlife degradation; war; famine; poverty; disease; etc. Is it so hard to imagine? That nations blame others less and focus more on that which is responsible for most problems and wastefulness to begin with—improperly designed government with legislatures making wrong-minded decisions. It almost seems sinful. If individual countries with largely well-intended citizens can reconstitute their governments such that they make better risk-based decisions with positive outcomes, why can we not redesign our international organizations to do the same thing? Listen to your heart. You know the right thing to do. Never mind the modern-day scribes, the professors, Prime Ministers and Presidents. They have got it all wrong.

Political parties, which are still necessary as their platforms may reflect different priority issues and risks, will have to meaningfully and truthfully convince voters they should vote for them. With risk reports mainly available to the public (unless there is an immediate national security risk), as access to information must be permitted, voters will know how various government departments are managing their resources, budgets, and issues impacting service to Canadians. Such transparency will motivate government officials to keep the fake news out of their public speeches. Results, reflective of the decisions that government has made, along with the degree to which they have, if any, interfered with the workings of the general bureaucracy and its responsibilities, will be made clear for all to see. Voters will see, especially with high level routine reporting from the RMO, whether or not elected MPs have held the more permanent bureaucracy to account in how it handles its day-to-day delivery of services.

Here, in Canada, one can envision this type of new democratic design being of immense benefit. Where domestic issues and risks need to be managed effectively and efficiently, the design would be hugely advantageous. Where we exercise our right to vote in support of political candidates who also wish to address international risks, be they climate change, international or global security issues, such as the refugee crisis or terrorism, the same type of reporting and transparency should take place so voters can judge the performance of elected officials accordingly. In matters of national security, members of the independent RMO, such as the CRO, should have appropriate security clearances, along with respective legislative committees comprised of appropriate (knowledgeable, experienced, etc.) MPs, so we know security issues are being handled in a common-sense and risk-based manner. The CRO could still report to Canadians if there are matters of significant concern or material shortcomings in departmental performance (CSIS, DND, etc.) to ensure accountability.

Since, as we saw in the preceding chapter, an internal audit division also plays a crucial role in driving accountability within the federal government, that oversight function should also ensure international risks impacting Canada are being managed appropriately along with the domestic ones. If you have children, like I do, or family members or other loved ones who do, I would be so bold as to guess you share my concerns about the global issues facing humanity's future. Challenges, of one sort or another, seem to abound everywhere. Many of them appear highly complex, evolving and highly interrelated with other issues. As an example, the war in Syria has destabilized security in that part of the world (putting Russia at odds with certain Western countries, providing yet more of a seedbed for terrorist recruiting, etc.), unleashing in its mammoth destruction, mass poverty, hunger and homelessness for Syrians. The ensuing refugee crisis has placed strain and moral demands on other countries, including Canada, as well as international relief agencies. Yet just as in terms of the recently formed South American refugee caravans heading to the US border via Mexico, Lauren Markham aptly writes this in a *Globe and Mail* opinion piece: "What is certain is that migration won't stop, not if the root causes aren't tended to."[5]

The Need for Global *Democratic Restructuralism*

But here, too, the democratic world need not throw up its arms admitting defeat to some malevolent and predetermined end where there is no hope of dealing with it all and so much more. Risks need to be managed by good people willing to get out of their comfortable easy chairs. There is no need for continued ignorance amongst government leaders in the free world. There are solutions to be found in a democratic restructuring process, as articulated, that can be fruitfully adopted to improve our lives and the lives of others around the world. It is our government's responsibility to do the right thing, to lead by example. We need to do what one of America's presidents, Woodrow Wilson, implored Congress to do when bringing America into World War I—ensure the world "be made safe for democracy."

We Canadians must strive to '*Make Democracy Great Again*.' Canadians must spur others in the world to make it "safe for democracy." Ours is but a small population, but I know we can do it. There is no more time to waste. For three consecutive years in a row, millennials have warned the world and its leaders about the critical issues facing the planet. Those who took part in the *World Economic Forum's Global Shapers Survey 2017* view climate change as being the most serious issue affecting the world today (48.8 per cent of respondents chose it as their top concern).[6] These are not ignorant voters. They likely wish to be better informed by governments making informed decisions themselves. They likely want scientists to be unmuzzled and governments to be designed better such that national legislatures and international organizations around the world can actually work to manage global risks in a cooperative and solution-oriented way.

Climate Change: A Political Problem that can be Meaningfully Addressed

From a scientific perspective, the adverse impacts of climate change on humanity and our planet appear irrefutable—except perhaps to those living with a Stone Age mentality or possessing an attitude of indifference toward the environment and the younger generation who will inherit what our indifferent attitudes have wrought. For nonbelievers of climate change, consider *The Summary for Policymakers* (the summary) contained in a working group, contributing to the 2013 Intergovernmental Panel on Climate Change (IPCC). According to the summary, and without going into all the solid scientific research behind it:

> Warming of the climate system is unequivocal, and since the 1950s, many of the observed changes are unprecedented over decades to millennia. The atmosphere and ocean have warmed, the amounts of snow and ice have diminished, sea level has risen, and the concentrations of greenhouse gases have increased.[7]

Further, and again without going into too much detail here, as all of the underlying evidence can be substantiated in the reports supporting the summary: "The largest contribution to total radiative forcing [as defined in the report] is caused by the increase in the atmospheric concentration of CO_2 since 1750."[8] Moreover, "human influence on the climate system is clear. This is evident from the increasing greenhouse gas concentrations in the atmosphere, positive radiative forcing, observed warming, and understanding of the climate system."[9] Of great concern is the following statement made in the summary: "It is *extremely likely* that human influence has been the dominant cause of the observed warming since the mid-20th century."[10] From a scientific perspective, a reality check if you will, there appears to be only one way to resolve the monumental problems associated with climate change: "Limiting climate change will require substantial and sustained reductions of greenhouse gas emissions."[11] Yet, no different than other global issues, such as income inequality or poor access to adequate healthcare, climate change is a political problem more than a scientific one.

To tackle climate change head on, we must principally view it as a political problem. Thus far, it has not been perceived as a priority problem in most countries because they have yet to markedly improve the quality of life and wealth of their own citizens. They have yet to implement the risk-based decision-making structures and systems so desperately needed. And people like former US Vice President Al Gore, and so many others, while working very hard to publicly present the already massive consequences of allowing the degradation of our environment to continue, have generally avoided discussing the only plausible way to solve the monumental problem of climate change. Imagine, country after country implementing risk-based decision-making within their governments. Upon doing so, governments and people around the world, that are equipped with an understanding of the positive outcomes that come with risk-based government and improved democracy, will be more apt to apply those benefits to tackling international issues. No doubt there will be rigorous debate as legislative members around the world debate the merits of the quantitative and qualitative risk reports they receive. But it is their job to distill it down for their constituents and inform them of the risks accordingly. Imagine all of these governments transparently telling their citizens how and why certain decisions regarding the environment were made. The citizens, in turn, would hold their elected officials to account, keeping them in government if they are making what the citizenry perceive to be the best decisions for them, their children, their country, and their world. An electorate that largely knows the difference between right and wrong will honourably vote the right way, prioritizing the risks that matter to them and their children most.

Since example is usually more powerful than precept, more and more countries are likely to implement risk-based decision-making within their government institutions, thereby enabling elected officials to make the right decisions for their constituents— including with respect to environmental issues such as climate change. Once enough countries have done this, spurred on by people who generally can be counted on to do the right thing, and who have demanded it, the necessary momentum required to tackle climate change in a real and tangible way will be achieved. This will save us from ourselves as humanity now approaches the brink of disaster.

From a spiritual perspective, the words of Rev. Martin Luther King that we quoted earlier, when he addressed the serious issue of inequality between Blacks and Whites in the context of 1960s America, speak to the urgency of humanity, comprising all races, addressing climate change soon in a meaningful way. "We have been forced to a point where we are going to have to grapple with the problems that [people] have been trying to grapple with through history, but the demands didn't force them to do it. Survival demands that we grapple with them." A juxtaposition of science and spirituality, the latter factor having more to do with our knowing what is right and true, seems in order. It may be within the realm of science that facts and data comprising our tangible reality and environment appear to be most relevant. However, and no different than for the spiritually aware Lakota elder who felt "our guide was inside-not outside," it is mostly within the realm of our inner selves, our spirit and belief system, that knowing what is right resides. You may not be overly, if at all, religious. If you happen to be, though, or are spiritually aware, such as the Lakota I referred to, you know instinctively what is right and good for you, your family, your neighbours and friends, and others who may need our help around the world.

While you may be short on some specifics, you generally know what is ethical, morally right, true and loving. Catholics do not have a monopoly on spirituality versus other faiths, but the words of the current Pope, Francis, serve as one example of the kinds of spiritual thinking and insight required to solve scientific problems such as climate change. In this regard the body politic is a spiritual one. Set aside, for a moment, the Catholic Church he represents, if you can remain impartial and keep church and state separated, as they organizationally ought to be (for there are many religions we must remain respectful of), consider the spiritual wisdom and common sense Pope Francis connects with scientific fact in an environmental encyclical he wrote about three years ago. In *On Care for Our Common Home,* the Pope implores readers to grasp the realities of how humans are adversely impacting our environment and how we need to take corrective action before it is too late. Like many other religious leaders representing different faiths, like the spiritually wise Indigenous Peoples, and like morally concerned scientists attempting to do good work, all concerned about 'our common home,' he clearly knows it is right for us all to do better. "The urgent challenge to protect our common home includes a concern to bring the whole human family together to seek a sustainable and integral development,"[12] And his exhortation follows shortly after:

> I urgently appeal, then, for a new dialogue about how we are shaping the future of our planet. We need a conversation which includes everyone, since the environmental challenge we are undergoing, and its human roots, concern and affect us all.

As many of us would agree, religious or otherwise, the Pope states, "Regrettably, many efforts to seek concrete solutions to the environmental crises have proved ineffective." Therefore he logically concludes, "We require a new and universal solidarity."[13] Indeed. We will need that soon. In the fall of 2018, the IPCC issued a new and "critical 33-page Summary for Policymakers." *BBC* Environmental correspondent Matt McGrath asks, "What's the one big takeaway?" in his article "Final call to save the world from 'climate catastrophe.'

" His answer? " 'Scientists might want to write in capital letters, ACT NOW, IDIOTS, but they need to say that with facts and numbers,' said Kasia Kosonen, of Greenpeace… 'And they have.' " McGrath also reported that "this new study says that going past 1.5C [of warming] is dicing with the planet's livability." Worrisomely, the limit of 1.5 degrees Celsius of planetary warming "could be exceeded in just 12 years, in 2030." So what happens if we do not limit temperature increases to under 1.5 degrees Celsius? One example is this: "You can kiss coral reefs goodbye as the report says they would be essentially 100% wiped out at two degrees of warming."[14]

What I find unfortunate is that religious and spiritual leaders such as the Pope—and I am sure there are others—must tell governments that more needs to be done. However, given that our legislature is challenged to ensure democracy works properly, that our Indigenous Peoples have safe drinking water, and that the environment within our own borders is healthy, the situation is hardly surprising. The Pope's encyclical actually advances some unique proposals for increased "dialogue and action." They "would involve each of us as individuals, and also affect international policy."[15] I imagine the Pope and other spiritual leaders of different faiths and cultures prefer to stay out of politics and state affairs, as many of us would agree they should. But so grave are many of the global issues we face that I am not surprised in the least to hear this from the Holy Father: "We lack leadership capable of striking out on new paths and meeting the needs of the present with concern for all and without prejudice towards coming generations."[16] He bears witness to humanity's plight here.

I found it quite ironic to see that the Pope may agree with some of my own thoughts, but I am likely crossing a line of great presumption that is dangerous. I mean no offense to him or anyone else. Maybe we are just on the same wavelength, which I take to be a good thing. He does say, "If everything is related, then the health of a society's institutions has consequences for the environment and the quality of human life."[17] You already know I believe our democratic institutions are coming apart at the seams here in Canada and that we must engage in *Democratic Restructuralism*. Democracy must be strengthened, both here and around the world, so the people's voice is heard. People must be informed about the risks they face and those risks must be managed by national legislatures. In turn, well-run international organizations must reflect the will of the legislatures of their respective member states.

Pope Francis also states that "our common home is falling into serious disrepair."[18] If he forgives me for saying so, I would wager he appreciates good design. Astoundingly, given what I wrote earlier, the Pope also reasonably concludes, "Unless citizens control political power-national, regional and municipal-it will not be possible to control damage to the environment."[19] Of course! The way to get there obviously is by Canadians doing what I summarized in chapters 5 through 7. We then hopefully become an example for the rest of the world in doing what we need to do, restructuring democracy so that citizens are given back the power they need to wield, in an informed way. This is truly the way forward. Or, as the Pope puts it, using common sense much as a person of science like Albert Einstein would rather than a person of the cloth: "Decisions must be made 'based on a comparison of the risks and benefits foreseen for the various possible alternatives.' "[20]

The last I will say about the Pope's encyclical is this. He believes with flawless logic, that in tackling global environmental problems like climate change, we need appropriate systems of international governance. "What is needed in effect, is an agreement on systems of governance for the whole range of so-called 'global commons.' "[21] This makes perfect sense, but again, we cannot put the cart before the proverbial horse. First we need to clean up our own backyard. When we understand we can do just that by making representative democracy work for Canadians, then we can serve as a model for other democracies and international organizations. Once people's wishes can meaningfully be expressed by their votes in individual countries, through the effective design of democratic governments that are representative of their constituents' desires, then we can replicate that design in international organizations such as the United Nations. And there is no time to lose. Consider that "from 1998 to 2017, direct losses from all disasters totalled $2.9 trillion, of which 77 percent was due to extreme weather that is intensifying as the world warms, the U.N. Office for Disaster Risk Reduction (UNISDR) said in a report."[22]

We need to trust the wishes of the people. We need to trust that they know the difference between right and wrong, especially when they are appropriately informed by the parliamentarians or legislators they elect. Through face-to-face meetings, via websites, publicly televised debates, etc., elected officials must keep voters generally updated on the significant risks they and their nation face. An effective opposition party can challenge the government of the day. However, the opposition must be held just as accountable as the presiding government in power by an independent RMO, its governing Board comprised of regional representatives. Upon democratic countries establishing this type of structure, revitalizing and strengthening their democracies, they can send representatives to the UN who are informed as to the wishes of the people they represent. Admittedly not all countries are democracies, and most, if not all, who claim to be are not full democracies.

The United Nations: Candidate for *Democratic Restructuralism*

It has been said that only about half of the world's nations live under some form of democracy. In fact the Economist Intelligence Unit's *Democracy Index 2017* found that only 19 (of which Canada ranked sixth place along with Ireland) out of 167 countries have full democracies, representing just 4.5 per cent of the world's population. An additional 57 countries representing close to 45 per cent of the global population were deemed flawed democracies, including the US.[23] Disturbingly, "in the 2017 Democracy Index the average global score fell from 5.52 in 2016 to 5.48 (on a scale of 0 to 10)." All told:

Some 89 countries experienced a decline in their total score compared with 2016, more than three times as many as the countries that reported an improvement (27), the worst performance since 2010–11 in the aftermath of the global economic and financial crisis. [24]

This means we must safeguard our own democracy in Canada. This is our biggest challenge as all other issues impacting people can only be solved by strong democracies that make good decisions for all their constituents.

If only we had stronger legislatures around the world. If the wishes of all the people were known and voiced by the members who represent them in the United Nations, it would be a force to reckon with. If we imagine the collective membership of the United Nations as one legislature, just as capable of doing what is right as Canada's own legislature, why could it not be effective? At least it is a beginning toward trying to effect positive change. And, quite conceivably, if democracies begin to markedly improve their citizens' lives through the kind of *Democratic Restructuralism* we discussed, people in undemocratic countries may begin to see what is the right and best form of government themselves. That could easily result in the overturning of authoritarian regimes and in bolstering the number of democratic member countries in the UN. Is that so far-fetched an idea?

The United States and many other Western powers shamefully missed the opportunity to lead by example when the former Soviet Union collapsed. With an increasingly polarized society themselves, a phenomenon which continues to grow, the West was somewhat hypocritical in its claim that our way was absolutely the better way. Now, hostilities between West and East grow apace again. Iron-fisted leaders, such as Russia's Vladimir Putin, are able to maintain their powerful grip on the society they rule over, at least partially, because we have failed to lead by example. Let's not repeat our mistake again!

Government organizations are typically not visible enough with regards to their understanding and managing of dire global issues such as climate change, air and water quality, and overall environmental degradation. Even in the wake of a natural disaster, the authors of *Democracy for Realists* articulate that voters are often left wondering why their government cannot do more on the ground. "They see friends and neighbours pitching in to help immediately after the disaster. They do not understand why the government cannot do the same."[25] It is because those government representatives closest to the people, the elected parliamentarians filling the seats of the legislature, are often uninformed or too ill-informed about risks facing their constituents. This goes a long way to explaining disconnect with voters. Certainly some MPs may visit disaster sites, but many would not have a broader grasp of climate change impacts upon the nation, much less internationally. Nor would they likely know how much their constituents who elected them cared about that issue. Until such time as legislative members routinely receive the necessary information to prioritize and manage risks, such as climate change, conveying that same information to voters (so they, too, can make informed decisions regarding who to vote for), the disconnect between voters and politicians far from the ground is likely to remain. According to the World Economic Forum survey, about 78 per cent of the younger generation indicated they would be willing to alter their lifestyle to protect the environment.[26] The misalignment between government actions regarding the environment and the degree to which future generations wish to safeguard the environment is startling.

We can solve our national problems by properly redesigning our government as described earlier. Then it is time to turn toward repairing and strengthening international organizations to take on global issues of concern. The World Economic Forum also found the second and third most concerning global issues for millennials were large-scale conflicts/wars and inequality (income and discrimination), representing 38.9 per cent and 30.8 per cent of respondents' top concerns. Interestingly, government accountability and transparency/corruption ranked as the sixth largest of the top 10 global concerns for millennials in the survey.[27] Perhaps those millennials reading this book may bump that concern ahead of climate change, if they came to an understanding that most of the world's problems, be they climate change, war or inequality, have more to do with poor decision-making by ill-designed governments around the world than what they immediately appear to be on the surface. *Democratic Restructuralism* must, by necessity, be the world's top concern for all generations, including those yet to come. The antiquated organizational design issue drives the lack of accountability issue. That in turn drives the other issues of concern, all symptoms of an ailing body politic rather than the true disease itself. Wounds must be healed, the body rejuvenated. The disease eating away at democracies around the world, causing what should unify people and bind them together to come undone, must be treated.

As I mentioned previously, there is hope for humanity in tackling international issues and implementing corrective actions to solve interrelated problems. The UN needs to be reconstituted or redesigned if you will. Its members must be truly informed about the wishes of their respective citizens, whom they represent. And the organizational structure of the UN must be able to fulfil the democratic wishes of the global citizenry. The UN has done much good work since 1945 when it was founded. It provides its 193 Member States with a "forum . . . to express their views in the General Assembly, the Security Council, the Economic and Social Council, and other bodies and committees." Basically, and as noted on its website, "the Organization has become a mechanism for governments to find areas of agreement and solve problems together."[28] Whether it be disaster relief or other humanitarian aid, peacekeeping initiatives—many of which Canada has been a strong supporter of—promoting health and well-being as well as sustainable development in the wake of climate change, the UN has been the preeminent international organization doing its best. It has also been a strong supporter of democracy through a myriad of its sub organizations.

Given my interest in making democracy work better, I found all the UN initiatives to promote a system in dire need of repair, noteworthy. Apparently:

> Activities in support of democracy and governance are carried out through the United Nations Development Programme (UNDP), the United Nations Democracy Fund (UNDEF), the Department of Peacekeeping Operations (DPKO), the Department of Political Affairs (DPA), the Office of the High Commissioner for Human Rights (OHCHR), and the United Nations Entity for Gender Equality and the Empowerment of Women (UN and women), among others. [29]

I am not sure about you, but I find it pretty daunting to get a handle on all the alphabet soup of likely very good intentions. You should also note per the UN's own website that, "such activities are inseparable from the UN's work in promoting human rights, development, and peace and security." If you are still following me, this appears to include, among other examples, "assisting parliaments to enhance the checks and balances that allow democracy to thrive." It also includes "providing electoral assistance and long-term support for electoral management bodies." [30]

We certainly do not want struggling and developing nations to remain under nefarious regimes, such as fascism, communism and other undemocratic systems. We know the human and environmental destruction such infantile and morally bankrupt regimes have wrought, especially given the results of the last world wars, gulags and gas chambers included. Nevertheless, it makes more sense to promote a well-functioning democratic system that works for the people in practical terms through its deeds rather than just through high-minded words. If we are to judge the tree by its fruit, then it stands to reason we should judge the appropriateness of democratic systems by the results they bear for the citizenry. The litmus test is whether or not well-informed decisions are being made, if at all, by legislatures, and their ability to both listen to, and conversely inform, all stakeholders involved in the great undertaking known as democracy.

It is instructive to learn what the UN General Assembly has reaffirmed democracy to be. This distinguished international body perceives:

> 'Democracy is a universal value based on the freely expressed will of people to determine their political, economic, social and cultural systems and their full participation in all aspects of their lives' as previously stated in the outcome document of the World Summit in September 2005. [31]

Yet we have seen that democracy is not working that well in those countries that are supposed to be leading by example, such as Canada. The results are not ideal, both within the borders of various nation states that purport to be democratic, and internationally where global organizations have failed to reasonably and tangibly address the issues confronting humanity. For all its good intentions in the indisputably good work it has performed over 70 years of its existence, the UN itself probably needs a good dose of the *Democratic Restructuralism* we have talked about. In stating this, my intention is to in no way malign an honourable institution. The UN has been championing sustainable development, and its Intergovernmental Panel on Climate Change, which we referenced earlier in this chapter, has been doing tremendous work to raise social awareness about climate change and its negative impacts for the planet and us all. It has undertaken numerous initiatives to do the right thing. Yet despite this and the fact that it has not recognized what is needed to make existing democracies more effective, the UN has faced much criticism related to its own inadequate design.

Although a few years old, a 2015 article by Chris McGreal discussing the UN during its 70ᵗʰ year as an organization, should give us more than a little cause for concern. In *A World of Problems: the United Nations at 70*, McGreal, after noting many of the laudable good works done by the UN, had these unflattering comments to say:

> In its 70 years, the United Nations may have been hailed as the great hope for the future of mankind—but it has also been dismissed as a shameful den of dictatorships. It has infuriated with its numbing bureaucracy, its institutional cover-ups of corruption and the undemocratic politics of its Security Council. It goes to war in the name of peace but has also been a bystander through genocide. It has spent more than half a trillion dollars in 70 years. [32]

I can almost imagine such words being directed at some of the larger so-called democracies around the world. For the intellectual poverty reflected in poorly designed organizations and governments themselves is indeed manifest. It permeates democratic societies across the globe, punctuating what so desperately impedes our path forward, culminating at quite possibly the apex of our problems, the height of it all embodied in the UN. A UN whose own well-recognized flag undoubtedly needs mending.

We could envision McGreal discussing some specific Western governments when he raises these issues concerning the UN: "The organization now encompasses 17 specialized agencies, 14 funds and a Secretariat with 17 departments employing 41,000 people." Additionally, the UN "has grown so big that at times it is working against itself. Critics point to large numbers of support staff doing ill-defined jobs." [33] I do begin to wonder about the very design of this venerable organization and the behaviours this engenders amongst management ranks across the sprawling bureaucracy. I wonder about the faceless people in charge and, no different than such individuals in our own government, whether they are indeed motivated to do the right thing. It does not seem reasonable that, after 70 years, "even accounting for inflation, annual UN expenditure is 40 times higher than it was in the early 1950s." [34] I have a hunch that further research might just reveal a spate of problems and waste, but that is not within the scope of this book. Suffice to say that the UN as an institution likely needs to be restructured just like governments around the world. It advocates democracy but needs to become more democratic itself.

So when we tidy up our own backyard and send informed members to the UN who know what we want them to do, they need to find themselves in an environment that allows them to do just that. They need to be seated alongside other members of the international community at a table where global problems can be solved based on informed decision-making and the will of the people. Citing Valerie Amos, a former International development Minister from Britain, McGreal portrays the design of the UN as suffering from the same ills as bloated bureaucracies everywhere. "Many organizations have overlapping mandates. It's become an organization that's quite unwieldy in lots of respects, Lady Amos said." [35] Then, quoting Helen Clark, head of the UNDP at the time as well as a former Prime Minister of New Zealand, McGreal unveils more nonsense at the UN: " 'When I arrived, the organization was a little over a year into its first ever strategic plan' . . . Clark laughed as she said the plan she was presented with was so broad in its goals that it made no sense." [36]

Referencing David Shearer, who held senior UN roles in such challenging places as Rwanda, Iraq, and Afghanistan, we hear that "the UN was weighed down by incompetence and red tape." We learn that the UN has "built systems on top of systems on top of systems," according to Shearer. [37] We also see that wrong-minded design and motivations seem to be eating away at the UN, too, although Shearer does not put it directly so. "Getting the right people, that was the Rosetta Stone of the UN for me. Once I cracked that . . . I could use the organization how it was supposed to be used irrespective of the structure, because the structure will always protect the incompetent."[38] Like I said, we need *Democratic Restructuralism* to move forward. That it is needed in the UN as well should come as no surprise. Also of note in the 2015 McGreal article is how Ban-Ki-moon, then UN Secretary General, championed a new strategy called 'Delivering as One.' That noble initiative, ostensibly, was to have the UN working as one whole team instead of duplicating work from one agency to another. Ki-moon even saw the initiative as "the main motor of my administration and I have been engaging with all different agencies and funds and programmes so that we can 'Deliver as One.' "[39]

This may have tragically been lip service of the kind we see during our own Question Period in the House of Commons, or during media scrums in an all too powerful PMO. According to McGreal's investigative reporting, "the broader reforms never came."[40] In fact, even the head of the Chief Executives Board for Coordination, representing all UN programmes and associated programs, like the International Monetary Fund and World Bank, Adnan Amin, had this to say of the reform report, of which he was executive director: "It's led to reams of reports written in the UN, many of them impenetrable to the rest of the world because of the jargon used." The end result for Amin: "I think there's been incremental progress but I don't think we can say there's been a fundamental change in the way the UN does business."[41] That parallels what we see in our own national or provincial governments and most governments around the world. The name of the government party in power changes along with its leaders, but in name only. Such is our incremental approach, one that leads us nowhere.

Optics management ensures people are told things are changing but nothing really substantial usually does. The permanent civil service remains in place, ever whipsawed and cowed into towing a political line instead of always doing the right thing. This means the results informed governments and citizens deservedly need, instead remain elusive. Is it any wonder that

Ontarians in the most recent election, after witnessing the successive follies of the Liberals under Kathleen Wynne's government, elected Conservative Doug Ford who promised us all so much with little of those promises rooted in facts. He told voters what they wanted to hear without explaining how he would achieve positive results. In the end, and regardless of who wins the election, not a lot will change for Ontario's voters. Just like we see in the UN, which has far greater responsibilities, there is no fundamental change in the way the government does business.

We need risk-based and informed decision-making in the UN along with governments of all levels around the world. It is the right thing to do. It is the necessary thing to do. And finally, it is the spiritually aware and correct thing to do. Indigenous Peoples know this. The Pope knows it. Martin Luther King knew it and so do so many other religious and spiritually aware people across the earth. Perhaps the UN's Secretary General should have his title changed to read Chief Risk Officer. Imagine the possibilities! And not those associated with a one-world government, but a participatory legislative assembly of sovereign states voting on issues that matter to their respective constituents.

According to Amin, and in relation to the UN's reform report he was involved with: "What we have now is another multiplication of targets and goals which are an extraordinarily comprehensive assessment of what's needed to be done but there's no operational clarity around them."[42] You can almost feel the absence of risk management, including operational risk management, at the UN. Its lack of achieving better results speaks to that defect in its design, along with the wrong behaviours its ill-design is producing. I am not sure about you, but it makes perfect sense to me given this reality, when Amin questions in relation to the UN's objectives: "Who's going to do it? Who's going to monitor it? Who's accountable for it?"[43] My response as an outsider would be the Secretary General as CRO, or an independent CRO reporting directly to the head of the UN, should be doing all that. Just as an independent CRO should be ensuring Canadian MPs are receiving the necessary information from the permanent bureaucracy to do their jobs, managing issues and attendant risks with an informed perspective, so, too, should the UN's CRO ensure its members are receiving the necessary information from the UN's permanent bureaucracy (I am not sure we need its entire alphabet soup of organizations) to do their jobs. This includes addressing what millennials and other generations consider to be the greatest threats facing humanity and the planet in a meaningful way.

Apart from the number of democracies sitting at the UN table, it makes no difference if we are talking about local, regional/provincial and national governments, or the UN, good design will produce the right behaviours and the right results for our, as Pope Francis deemed it, Common Home. Save of course, for wrongly motivated people deliberately ruining the design, which we must also be on guard for, by similarly having effective governance over the UN itself. Perhaps apportioning a smaller team of representatives (we don't want unnecessary bureaucracy) from developing and advanced countries as an oversight body may help. Membership of that body, including its Chairperson, could routinely be rotated amongst nations in the spirit of equitable cooperation as well as ensuring the UN remains a risk-based and accountable organization. In a similar manner, a group of international auditors comprised of representatives from diverse countries which also only serve for a specific period of time along with the head of internal audit, could ensure that the UN is adhering to its own streamlined, effective and common sense procedures and processes. Certainly, the CRO should ensure the organizational structure of the UN is fit for purpose, that it is transparent in its operations and built for success rather than failure.

As we have seen earlier, as it concerns the sensible design of our government, the UN should have, wherever possible, a simplified structure. The structure should be reflective of its core activities so that it is more results-driven rather than driven by other motivations, be they innocently misguided or intentionally wrong-headed. It may even be useful for a newly designed organizational structure to be approved by the UN's oversight body annually, specifically outlining how it is set up sensibly to produce the results desired by its collective membership. Risks need to be prioritized according to the will of the people in each country (Democratic voting and ranking of global issues that must be addressed) and regions of the world as equitably as possible. All of this should be available for people globally to see on the UN's website, with minimum esoteric jargon, silos and general bureaucracy. It is crucial that the UN demonstrate it is a democratic and effective organization. Its representatives must reveal to all where problems for people exist, as if the world's population were only 100 souls. Then we can all identify and love our neighbours more easily, next to our maker.

An Indian ambassador to the UN, Asoke Kumar Mukerji, has been quoted as stating this: "If you look at the Secretariat of the United Nations it is dominated by industrialized economies because they are the ones who contribute the bulk of the budget and they get the bulk of . . . managerial positions." He notes the patent unfairness of it all, stating, "The G-77 is marginalized in the overall Secretariat of the United Nations."[44] Of course that all plays to the blame game being alive and well, even within what should be the best hope for humanity, the UN. For as McGreal aptly mentioned, "Western governments . . . see the UN as bloated and inefficient," while "developing countries . . . regard it as undemocratic and dominated by the rich."[45] But as you should already know by now, *someone* else is not to blame, *something* else is. That *something* is bad organizational design, which in turn breeds bad behaviour and the world's insanity of ignoring how to tackle global issues using good design, while watching out for bad apples who may usurp that good design for their own ambitious purposes.

Greater minds than my own can surely come up with the right structure. The point being if we have people wondering—Who's going to do the UN's work? Who's going to monitor it? Who's accountable for it?—well, then, we inhabitants of the earth will find ourselves achieving Einstein's definition of insanity: "Doing the same thing over and over again but expecting different results." We need more imagination. You may already know that in 2015, the same year the UN celebrated its 70th birthday, the *Paris Agreement* was concluded. It was a hopeful event for people around the world. Almost 200 countries, including Canada, agreed to reduce greenhouse gas emissions by establishing national targets. The idea was that, collectively, nations needed to stop the earth from warming up more than 2 degrees Celsius on average in relation to pre-industrial levels. As I continue writing this book, in May 2018, representatives of the almost 200 signatories to the *Paris Accord* are meeting again in Bonn, Germany, to negotiate a "rulebook" for the 2015 agreement.

According to *Reuters,* the new rules are to be in place by the end of 2018. They should, for example, outline "how to measure and account for greenhouse gas emissions and climate finance for developing nations that is meant to reach $100 billion a year by 2020."[46] We know that President Trump announced in mid-2017, and to the appall of many other countries and his fellow Americans, including many business leaders, that he intended to pull America out of the Paris agreement which his predecessor Obama had signed onto. Trump probably lacks the imagination needed to solve global problems and serve as a role model for the global community of nations. As Professor Mike Hulme, who has experience working for the Intergovernmental Panel on Climate Change, told one Australian reporter: "We can actually only deal with climate through the human imagination." Perceptively, he believes the debate around climate change must be "more political and less scientific."[47] That speaks to my own view, only that I believe the design of democracies around the world needs to be changed so we, as a well-informed and spiritually aware collective known as humanity, can make politics less the art of decision-making and more the science of decision-making.

Canada's Performance Regarding the Environment

Reuters recently reported that former Mexican foreign minister and current leader of the UN Climate Change Secretariat, Patricia Espinosa, has yet to hear what Trump wants in the 2015 climate agreement. During the May 2018 Bonn negotiations, she told Reuters that "there has not been a follow up from Washington."[48] Canada, which has yet to prove it can improve our own democracy and lead by example, once again should not cast stones in glass houses where climate change is concerned. In October 2017, in a report carried by the *CBC*, we see that "Canada is one of the biggest laggards" when it comes to dealing with climate change. That unenviable position comes "with the UN saying not only are Canada's existing targets too low, it does not yet have the policies in place to meet them."[49] When you are not managing risks and democratic outcomes well, something the UN is also plagued by, does this really come as a surprise? The *CBC* article notes Canada has committed to achieving cuts to emissions to 30 per cent below what they were in 2005, which means about 523 million tons a year." However, "it is at least the fourth time Canada has set an emission target and thus far has never met one of them."[50]

As a country we have been failing to protect our environment for some time. Ontario's Premier Doug Ford continues to place that province squarely on the path of continued failure. Mismanagement of the province by his predecessor, Kathleen Wynne, served as a precursor to this situation. Too many governments, including in our own country, remain ignorant of what is important. They are keeping voters uninformed and ignorant themselves. One's vote cannot reflect the real issues of the day, the way forward in dealing with challenges as reasonable and prudent citizens ought to. We already saw a few examples in Chapter 3 concerning how we are failing to protect Canada's national ecosystem, such as monitoring our freshwater resources and pollution levels properly in a manner that allows us to make the best decisions for Canadians and our children. The Harper government's almost declared war on the environmental file reflected what may be some of the most damaging and foolhardy decisions made by an economist (which Harper is) regarding the well-being of the nation. Admittedly, we must make good economic decisions for the country. But just seemingly kowtowing to big business and not keeping the electorate ably informed, keeping them ignorant instead, smacks of un-Canadian values. Evangelization of such a thing is questionable at best.

It smacks of the kind of misguided elitism we saw in those books written by professors of economics and other subjects who claim that voters are irrational and ignorant. Gallingly, these highbrow individuals themselves do not perceive that the government itself—its very design along with wrongly motivated individuals (many I dare say are all-knowing economists)—perpetuates most voter ignorance. Nothing much really changes after your vote. The system is set up to fail. So, too, are many other democracies increasingly turning inwards. So is the UN. We are failing the world and our future stewards, our heirs. The world cries for leadership, for risk based decision-making in government. No matter if you are a Canadian supporter of the Conservative, Liberal, or another political party, it really does not matter when they all are making too many uninformed decisions.

Writing in a chapter called *The Death of Evidence* in his 2014 book aptly called *Party of One: Stephen Harper and Canada's Radical Makeover*, award-winning journalist Michael Harris shows us just how ignorant Canada's government has been on the environmental file. We could discuss so many other files that impact our quality of life and prosperity, but I could only make this chapter so long. According to Harris, Harper's "March 2012 federal budget eliminated nearly three thousand environmental assessments, including scores of projects dealing with fossil fuels and pipelines."[51] Similarly:

> While the Harper government poured $24.6 million into
> the new Canadian International Institute for Extractive
> Industry Development at the University of British Columbia,

rare collections from the country's marine science libraries, including fifty volumes produced by the HMS *Challenger* expedition of 1872 to 1876, were being dumped in landfills.[52]

So much the better to keep people ignorant, to keep them in the dark about the value of history and information that leads to good decision-making by what should be empowered civil servants who want to do the right thing. So much the better to supplant the spirituality of Canadians knowing the difference between right and wrong with the idolatry of economic theory and a then unbridled PMO. A PMO that keeps what should be the centre of democracy, the legislature, under its tyrannical and socially polarizing control. We need to resurrect and restore the collective will of the people. It is there that goodness resides.

If you have any doubt whatsoever, consider how Harper's unprecedented attack on free speech and his, as it came to be commonly referred to, muzzling of scientists, received negative reviews even beyond our borders. Fantastically, as Harris writes, even *The Economist* magazine (which presumably Harper would look to receive favour from being an economist himself) "described the Harper government's muzzling as 'comical excess in communication control.' "[53] Of course even writers in *The Economist*, which I enjoy reading myself, are typically sensible. Harris also found that "both the *New York Times* and the prestigious British science journal *Nature* slammed Canada's government."[54] Now what I really enjoyed learning close to the middle of Harris' book was this comment: "The *Times* called Harper's suppression of federal scientists 'an attempt to guarantee ignorance.' "[55] Dear reader, I rest my case that the government itself is the cause of what appears to be voter ignorance. Voters, being my fellow Canadians for the main purpose of this book, know what is right. They have that inner spiritual guide. The design of our government IS the problem, just as the design of troubled governments elsewhere and a UN that does not generate enough positive results for the world community, for humanity's posterity, IS the problem.

Here, in Canada, the Harper government did not have a monopoly on being the cause of voter ignorance and all too often wrong-minded decision-making. We can go back in time and find other Canadian governments making bad decisions due to the flawed design of our government. But given the excess of the Harper administration specifically, he certainly could be a poster child for a poorly designed system that allows too much excess of control in an all too powerful PMO. It also bears noting that under Harper's leadership, Canada became the first nation in the world to abandon the Kyoto Protocol. Kyoto occurred before the *Paris Agreement* and committed well-off or industrialized nations to lowering their emissions by 2020, to 1990 levels. In *Party of One*, Harris also saw Canada's abandonment of Kyoto occurring "despite the scientific evidence calling for a concerted global effort to reduce carbon emissions before planetary warming becomes irreversible."[56]

Failure of Global Institutions to Manage Global Risks

As someone who has worked in the insurance industry, bearing witness to the losses sustained by Canadians dealing with extreme weather occurrences, I can appreciate it when the UN's most recent emissions gap report implores us all to do something. "The alarming number and intensity of extreme weather events in 2017, such as hurricanes, droughts and floods, adds to the urgency of early action."[57] Having also worked in the business of risk management, I can further appreciate why both the Canadian government, other governments around the world, and the UN itself, are not realistically designed to succeed on the climate or other important files that concern the greatest threats facing humanity. A June 2018 search on the UN's website for its CRO took me down a blind alley leading nowhere. It is no different when I look for a CRO within the broader Canadian government.

Granted, there does appear to be something called the Office of Internal Oversight Services (OIOS) within the UN. The OIOS has an Internal Audit Division (IAD) and my search revealed a November 2017 IAD report concerning risk management within one of the UN's key humanitarian sub-organizations. This report is entitled *Advisory review of the implementation of the Enterprise Risk Management Policy and Procedures at the United Nations High Commissioner for Refugees* (UNHCR). From it, I learned that, "in 2006, the United Nations General Assembly endorsed the adoption of Enterprise Risk Management (ERM) in the United Nations system."[58] There must have been some bureaucratic roadblocks in implementing a common sense ERM framework in the system though. It was only five years later that ERM seemed to be gaining importance as a priority, at least for the UNHCR. "In 2011, the Board of Auditors recommended that UNHCR implement ERM as a matter of urgency."[59] You would think it was an urgent matter to have ERM as an oversight function encouraging risk-based decision-making in the planet's preeminent global organization. Alas, not so.

Some two years after the Board's recommendation, or an inconceivably long seven years after the General Assembly's original endorsement, the UNHCR created an ERM unit. But even then, the IAD's 2017 advisory review stated that it was not "formally launched" in UNHCR until July 2014. And not until December 2014 were there "detailed Administrative Instructions and Procedures for Implementation."[60] The OIOS review goes on to say that UNHCR's ERM function is headed by a CRO who reports directly to the Deputy High Commissioner. It also talks about some of the methodologies UNHCR has adopted with respect to carrying out risk management and notes that OIOS conducted its review (the "advisory engagement") from March to June 2017, so just about a year before I am writing this book. However, let's get to the results of the review and see if any significant deficiencies at June 2017 existed. In this regard, the OIOS' IAD "identified 12 areas for improvement."[61] To put that into perspective, that equates to about two pages of recommendations. Immediately below are just a few highlights of the findings. I will try to avoid esoteric jargon concerning risk management. I imagine you, my readers, will definitely see a lot more realistic work needs to be done at UNHCR in terms of managing risks to facilitate better decision-making in this high profile UN organization.

Some of the observed deficiencies include (although IAD uses more polite language—*"UNHCR could consider"*):

- "Determining the roles of the Senior Management Committee and Senior Executive Team with regards to the ERM Framework and the Strategic Risk Register [means list of key risks facing UNHCR] and ensuring that they become a regular agenda item for the meeting of both these bodies";
- "Developing a dashboard report [in my experience this usually means a visual monitoring report, using say green, yellow, and red for different levels of risks and a brief overview of the status of those risks] . . . that highlights critical information and recent changes for the attention of senior management";
- "Disseminating the dashboard report . . . to all risk owners on a regular basis to inform them of risks";
- "Identifying sources of information and associated analysis needed for senior management to make informed decisions on the identification and management of strategic risks."[62]

At one point in the OIOS' IAD review this (which is often said of bureaucratic organizations I might add) is stated: OIOS acknowledges the concerns that "UNHCR is dealing with a wide range of organizational pressures and changes. The field operations particularly often feel as though they are barely able to keep pace with the various initiatives, policies and requirements developed centrally."[63] Oh how this reminds me of stereotypical government operations around the world, where there is the appearance and claim of insufficient resources, rather than an honest admission that available resources are not suitably applied to core work and services for the public good. Interestingly, the review also stated that "in the view of the OIOS, ERM is a key tool to help UNHCR deal with these various demands in an informed, risk aware and effective manner."[64] Absolutely right! However, the implementation of ERM in a correct way might likely reveal a non-results-oriented organization in need of *Democratic Restructuralism*, including the potential removal of any wrongly motivated management.

We likely need a much better designed UNHCR. That would be my guess based on the wisdom that comes with observation rather than a certain knowledge based on education. I do not need to work there to make that loaded comment. Reading the review tells me enough. If people at UNHCR cannot manage risks based on the information they are getting, they are likely set up for failure. So, too, may be the rather well-known Group of Seven (G-7) forum of advanced economies, as well as the lesser known Group of 77 (G-77) developing countries. The G-7 used to be called the G-8 from 1998 until 2014, when Russia was excluded after it annexed the Crimean portion of Ukraine. Now with Canada hosting this year's annual summit in Québec, the G-7 is comprised of our country, the US, UK, Germany, France, Japan, and Italy. All of these countries, including Canada, consider themselves to be fairly mature democracies. The EU, which is deemed a non-enumerated member of the G-7, but with its presidents of the European Council and the European commission both representing the EU at G-7 summits, is also comprised of nations considered democracies. But what has the G-7 achieved outside the UN during over 20 years of its existence?

The informal group of industrialized economies meets yearly to, as the Council on Foreign Relations (CFR) writes, "discuss issues such as global economic governance, international security, and energy policy." Yet CFR also states the G-7s' "critics note that it often lacks follow-through and excludes important emerging powers."[65] That presumably would include countries like

China, Brazil, India and others. CFR aptly notes in its backgrounder on the G-7 that its "aggregate GDP" now only "makes up nearly 50 per cent of the global economy, down from nearly 70 per cent three decades ago." And since the group does not include developing nations in their cohort, I was unsurprised to learn that it "often garnered criticism for its failure to deliver on ambitious commitments, particularly with respect to development assistance."[66]

We have seen the polarization between rich and poor continue unabated in many countries. We have seen the Syrian refugee crisis, the likes of nothing we have witnessed probably since World War II. We have seen climate change and other global issues grow in scale and importance, all while the G-7 does very little, instead of just saying the right things. One wonders why the global issues the G-7 purports to deal with are not left to a better designed and run UN which is the appropriate forum for all nations to tackle international issues. According to news reports in late May 2018, just a few weeks ahead of the June 8–9 G-7 Summit at the swanky Fairmont Le Manoir Richelieu in Québec's Charlevoix region, Canada "has budgeted $600 million to cover the costs of summit related events that are taking place throughout the year."[67] With countries such as our own not having an elected legislature that can make risk-based decisions, as woefully outlined previously, it baffles the mind to consider just what we will accomplish with our $600 million and how on earth issues have been prioritized by the G-7.

Perhaps Prime Minister Trudeau automatically knows what is important, no different than his predecessor, Stephen Harper. He views the summit as an "opportunity for seven allies to gather in a less formal, more relaxed setting . . . to talk about real issues," since "it's extremely important."[68] I do not know about you, but I would rather have a more formal process in place to ferret out the real issues for all nation states, prioritizing them by significance such that they can be resolved in a practical and positive manner. Lounging about in a relaxed fashion will not do, no matter how well-intended the photo ops are.

Even when we consider nations that are much more disadvantaged than the G-7, the G-77, we see that group also not set up for success.

The G-77 was established over 50 years ago in 1964. There were, as you may have already guessed, 77 signatories to the *Joint Declaration of the Seventy-Seven Developing Countries,* which facilitated the G-77 coming into being. Per the G-77's website, the joint declaration was issued at the end of the first session of the UN Conference on Trade and Development in Geneva. Signatories included such countries as Afghanistan, Algeria, Bolivia, Cambodia, Chad, Ethiopia, Haiti, Madagascar, Peru, Uruguay, etc. Following the initial Ministerial Meeting of the Group of 77 in Algeria in 1967, and according to the G-77's website, "a permanent institutional structure gradually developed which led to the creation of Chapters of the Group of 77"—those being "Liaison offices" in various cities across the world where UN organizations have representation. Despite the G-77 membership having grown to 134 nations and often including China in its collective pronouncements, it kept its original name "due to its historical significance."[69]

I am still wondering why more advanced and wealthier nations need their own group, just like the developing nations need to be in their own club as well. It sounds like an 'us' and 'them' thing Pink Floyd would sing about. Then again, when there are identifiable groups, it is a lot easier to cast blame, targeting them as being responsible for why things do not work as we saw earlier with advanced and developing countries alike blaming each other for the UN's lack of results. Anyway, the chief goal of the G-77 is "for the countries of the South to articulate and promote their collective economic interests and enhance their joint negotiating capacity on all major international economic issues within the United Nations system, and promote South-South cooperation for development."[70] I suppose the G7 was not really interested in that since it has its own group, or maybe it would argue it just had to tackle those issues in its own club. That is doubtful because the best way to solve problems is collectively with everyone treated respectfully at the table, regardless of wealth or status. There is so much more to being human; democracy should be for everyone.

The G-77's 1964 joint declaration in Section 1 proclaimed: "The developing countries named above recognize the United Nations Conference on Trade and Development as a significant step towards creating a new and just world economic order."[71] The G-77 also does not appear to suffer fools easily. Even over 10 years ago it was already voicing its collective concern about the way the UN was operating in terms of having proper internal controls and oversight in place to ensure it was doing the right thing. In a "statement on Behalf of the Group of 77 and China" made in October 2007 to the General Assembly, and in relation to some OIOS reports, we learn about many UN operational deficiencies. For example, we learn that "the OIOS issued 1,792 recommendations on internal control, accountability, organizational efficiency and effectiveness." We also learn the G-77 and China:

> Notes with concern serious deficiencies in internal control and the organization's exposure to serious risk of mismanagement and fraud in procurement as found out . . . The amounts involved in the reported incidents of abuse of authority and procedures are significant.[72]

This statement, made to the 62nd session of the General Assembly also "notes the OIOS' repeated concerns over the urgent need of the introduction of internal control policy including a risk-management policy in the UN Secretariat."[73] These developing countries also acknowledged another thing that struck me as being significant, serving as a marker as to where the UN was in terms of designing a means to make risk-based decisions as of 2007. In their Statement, the group "notes the ongoing work of the OIOS for developing a risk assessment methodology in accordance with international standards."[74] Well, that explains the lack of better results tackling important and global issues up until 2007. But what has been going on since then? Two recent UN reports are instructive: *Adopting an analytical framework on risk and resilience: a proposal for a more proactive, coordinated and effective United Nation's action*—prepared by a task team led by the World Food Programme (2017/6); and *Conclusions of the Thirty-Fifth Session of the High Level Committee on Management (HLCM)*—produced by the Chief Executives Board for Coordination (2018/3). The former report indicated that "the 2030 Agenda for Sustainable Development represents humanity's goals for the next 13 years," but that "there is growing concern that numerous crises will set back efforts to achieve these goals."[75] One does not need to be a rocket scientist or UN executive bureaucrat to understand that. Nor should it take such a person to comprehend that proper risk management is required for people to address global problems collectively in a solutions-oriented way.

Astonishingly, the report issued in 2017 about 10 years after the G-77 and China Statement to the 62nd session of the General Assembly, is just quite recently championing the need for an analytical framework on risk and resilience. I really do not get what the UN has been doing since 2006, when the General Assembly "endorsed the adoption" of ERM. Maybe that is why our global problems are not being adequately addressed. Never mind that the General Assembly or UN's legislature likely contains members that do not know what the priority risks are in the view of their respective nations. Back to the 2017 report: It states that "several concepts—including risk resilience and prevention—have been identified as having the potential to create an analytical framework for a more proactive, coordinated and effective approach to addressing . . . . Crises."[76] Really! That, along with the following sentence contained in the report, tells me yet again that the UN is lacking the kind of ERM framework to ensure its doing its job, enabling its members to make informed decisions: "The creation of such a framework will be critical to maintaining the universal norms and standards that the United Nations represents in this challenging period."[77] In the words of the immortal Homer Simpson . . . 'Duh'!

Are these key findings stated in the report not common sense?:

- "Risk and resilience can serve as useful framing concepts for addressing crises more proactively";
- "A risk and resilience approach needs to reflect a complex, interconnected reality";
- "The use of terms should be harmonized."[78]

There is a lot of additional detail in the 35 page report led by the World Food Programme's task team. Buried on page 23 however, is an interesting section entitled "Way Forward." It is there we read the following, which underscores the UN has a lot to do when it comes to ERM and achieving desired outcomes for all stakeholders:

> This analytical framework on risk and resilience could serve as an essential tool for supporting United Nation's system-wide efforts to achieve the 2030 Agenda. Given its emphasis on bringing together the different United Nations pillars around collective outcomes and its applicability to all types of threats, it represents an attempt to operationalize the humanitarian-development-peace-human rights nexus . . . [and it goes on].[79]

It all sounds pretty good. But where has this type of framework been for almost 75 years and how can it work if members of the General Assembly do not know what the priority risks are for their own constituents back home? If they do not have that information, along with the qualitative and quantitative data that speaks to those risks, how can they meaningfully expect to contribute to the UN's operations, and its seemingly quite new global risk-management initiatives? Does one necessarily follow the other? Meaning, we need good democratic structures domestically, in each member state, where possible, before we can have it at the UN. Only then can we really grasp the collective and international progress we are making to resolve global issues.

As for the second report, the HLCM and its conclusions issued in May 2018, we see more of the same regarding the lack of a robust and functioning ERM framework within the United Nations system. I will not go over the report in great detail. Item 20 contained within it under Section 1, "Moving from risk aversion to risk management: creating value for the UN system," paints a good overall picture:

> HLCM agreed on the need for a joint, cross-functional engagement towards system-wide harmonization of risk-management practices, including information sharing on fraudulent behaviours of implementing partners; assessments of risk appetite and risk tolerance, [etc.][80]

So there you have it: a UN composed of members from nations representing the international community, who likely do not know all the risks facing their respective countries and how voters would prioritize those risks. This problem, amplified by a UN that organizationally has yet to implement a comprehensive ERM structure, such that global risks prioritized sensibly by the legislature—the General Assembly—are well-managed with risk-based decisions being made equitably for all concerned. Oh, and let's not forget about the segregation of groups so the blame game can continue as articulated above. The UN sure looks like its flag is in need of mending. The world awaits that, and the desperately needed healing that must occur to move humanity forward.

Complicating matters is that we do not just have the G-7 and G-77, there are even more splinter groups, the G-20 and the G-24. So much the merrier. The G-20 is another forum, one comprised of finance ministers and central bank governors from 19 of the largest countries in the world along with the EU. Since the G-20 reflects, in aggregate, roughly 80 per cent of the world's GDP, as well as two-thirds of the planet's population,[81] one wonders why our Canadian Prime Minister has budgeted $600 million to host the G-7 in Québec in June 2018. What is the point? Switching gears, if you still follow me, we have the G-24. According to this group's website, it "was established in 1971 by the [G-77] as one of its chapters, and formally created in 1972."[82] The G-24's website discusses all of its objectives, much of those having to deal with assessing the International monetary situation and how that relates to the interests of the developing countries. "The G-24 has experienced instances where its nature, mission, and structure have been re-examined consistent with the evolution in world dynamics."[83] It is all pretty confusing, especially with all the offshoot groups in the UN and its alphabet soup of organizations.

If only some competent CRO could assess the risks of the UN's own organizational design, including the qualifications and insight its members bring to the table. If only that CRO could tell us if the design of the UN is fit for purpose, set up for success in a streamlined and logical way that easily lends itself to being a transparent and accountable organization. If you are not confused yet, we could spend some additional ink and time considering the World Economic Forum (WEF). In case you are unaware, the WEF was established in 1971, around the same time as the G-24. The WEF is 'committed to improving the state of the world,' just like the UN, I imagine. It "is the International Organization for Public Private Cooperation." The WEF "engages the foremost political, business and other leaders of society to shape global, regional and industry agendas."[84] You have probably heard of the elite annual meeting of the WEF in Davos, Switzerland, where all the smart and well-heeled folks go to debate the issues of the day, like climate change and the global economy.

The funny thing is, when from January 23–26, of 2018, "more than 3,000 leaders from over 100 countries" converged on Davos "to focus on finding ways to reaffirm international cooperation on crucial shared interests,"[85] these well-intended people seemed to miss the boat on the tyranny of global legislatures and how we need to democratically restructure our governments and international institutions. The 48th annual meeting of the WEF did have a good theme though, *Creating a Shared Future in a Fractured World*. However, in reading the WEF's Global Agenda for Davos, I once again saw a lot of high-sounding words and ideals, but little in the way of how nations and global institutions such as the UN can make risk-based decisions to significantly improve the quality and prosperity of everyone in a democratic way. It is no different than the G-7, G-20, G-77, G-24, and all the other organizations and groups that lack realistic solutions that come with the promise of *Democratic Restructuralism*.

On the WEF's website, I read with great interest that at Davos 2018, "Indian Prime Minister Narendra Modi listed his three most significant challenges to civilization as we know it: climate change, terrorism and the backlash against globalization."[86] Millennials, we discussed earlier, who were surveyed about their own top 10 risks, of which climate change ranked first, may also be interested in what Modi had to say. Since climate change is a visible risk to anyone with common sense, it is not something you can hide from people who see its adverse impacts and the lack of risk management, despite all the good intentions and optics management around the issue. I also found a comment made by ITUC General Secretary Sharon Burrow intriguing: "The world needs to renegotiate a new social contract and rewrite the rules."[87] Indeed, the problem is nobody is telling us how to do exactly that by adopting *Democratic Restructuralism* to make our institutions work.

Contained in the WEF's 2018 Global Agenda is an article headlined, "Governance 2.0: building a resilient model—one we can all trust." It intimates that, given the speed of technological innovations that are impacting our lives, "such as drones, blockchain, precision medicine, the Internet of all things (IoT) and artificial intelligence," these changes must be managed well. More specifically, "for the Fourth Industrial Revolution to fulfil its potential to benefit all, it must be moulded, managed and governed with agility."[88] But is adoption of more technology by government the answer? In Canada, we have suffered at the hands of the Phoenix payroll implementation fiasco along with debacles at Shared Services as outlined previously. There is no point putting a turbocharger on a car that has a wheezing engine in need of rebuilding, just as there is no point implementing technologies within government to amplify poorly designed systems and structures that do not facilitate risk-based decision-making, especially in the legislature.

Certainly IT systems need modernizing, but we need to design our institutions properly to facilitate the right democratic outcomes before implementing IT systems to amplify the benefits of a new design even more effectively (such as hosting government webpages with executive summaries outlining the priority risks the government is working on, and what is actually and measurably being done over time, for citizens to view in a transparent way, etc.). We saw in Chapter 5 that technology is not, in and of itself, the answer to our democratic woes. Technology is not the solution to the myriad of complex and dangerous global problems we face. At times, the complexity of technologies themselves and the design flaws they may come with, can actually be part of the problem. Or they can create opportunities for abuse, as in the case of all the privacy and data breaches we hear about, involving our personal banking, healthcare or other highly sensitive information.

There is also the case of the British political profiling company, Cambridge Analytica, mentioned earlier. As reported on by *Global News* in May 2018, earlier in the year, "Revelations emerged that Facebook had allowed an app developer to scrape personal data from millions of user accounts." In turn, "that developer then apparently gave that data to Cambridge Analytica." The result, to the detriment of voters, was that "the firm went on to use that personal information to target users in support of the 2016 campaign of US President Donald Trump." Topping this all off, personal information "was also allegedly used to influence the outcome of the UK's Brexit vote in favour of the camp voting to leave the EU."[89] Perhaps those allegedly using such personal data in nefarious ways believe ignorant voters are easily manipulated. Regardless, it is interesting to read in the *Global News* piece that the UK's information commissioner, Elizabeth Denham, believes Canada is trailing other countries when it comes to having appropriate privacy laws.

Denham told a UK House of Commons committee reviewing the privacy breach involving personal data of 87 million Facebook accounts and Cambridge Analytica this: "The Canadian privacy Commissioner's powers have fallen behind the rest of the world."[90] Without a systemic way of managing risks and making risk-based decisions, is it any surprise we have fallen behind? According to *Global News*, "Consecutive governments have refused to do anything to impose more stringent rules on how parties use voter data" in this country.[91] Technology certainly may be getting too far ahead of our inadequately designed government that cannot manage this and other associated IT risks.

So, when I read in the WEF's Global Agenda that, as Erik Brynjolfsoon, Director of the MIT Initiative on the Digital Economy, states, "Government agencies have to gear up for shorter turnarounds, particularly by using the data available and getting more at a faster pace,"[92] I see a huge red flag. Brynjolfsoon claims, "The technology is there; people are not pushing hard enough."[93] Maybe they should slow down instead and imagine how government organizations and institutions can be, quite simply, better designed to produce the right results. Risk-based decision-making organizations need to be built before technologies are added, to 'gear up,' for faster response times and quicker communication, both to and from constituents. One must occur before the other. I do agree with the WEF that there is a need for "dismantling unwieldy structures that hinder coordination between departments and agencies."[94] That is the place to begin, but the focus needs to be on doing so in a way that puts national legislatures, and the UN's General Assembly, as focal points for sound decision-making and transparent communication with the stakeholders—we members of humanity—involved.

The people know what the right things to do are. We just need the grand and better design that can listen to them and let them know what is going on in their government and crucial international organizations such as the UN. There is no need for continued ignorance in government and the international bodies that do not work the right way. The WEF's Global Agenda opined that "governance must build inclusion into policy and regulation." Agreed. But it also simultaneously opined this must occur "particularly in the developing economies where the focus has to be on the more basic challenges of using technologies to meet the challenges of housing congestion, poverty and inclusion, and climate change."[95] Again, my friends, technology itself is not the answer (more on that in the next chapter). *Democratic Restructuralism* and the implementation of better organizational design must come first. And that is not hard.

Let's begin anew, here in Canada, simplifying everything to better manage the risks we face and empower legislatures to do their jobs. I do not think it necessary to much further research more organizations like the EU and the UN to determine these lumbering bureaucracies likely suffer the same problems, the lack of proper structural design to facilitate the best outcomes possible based on risk-based decision-making. What a disaster for humanity. This needs to be addressed, and quickly, lest we all run out of the time we desperately need to collectively mitigate the global risks increasingly confronting us, catching us not only unprepared, but also unawares!

And yet we need to be fully aware of the risks humanity faces, lest they steal upon us, catching us all asleep, like a thief in the night robbing us of the spiritual and material prosperity we thought we had earned, but all the while let slip through our fingers. If only we had taken part. If only we had taken stock of our national and global predicament, understanding the tyranny of the legislature, the General Assembly, emanated more from that which enabled it so, rather than those who suffer under it, public citizens and civil servants alike. That we have endured such tyranny for so long emanating from something that is so desperately wrong, speaks to our strong character to withstand such an onslaught of wrong mindedness for such a prolonged period. But the ill design that forged our perilous condition does, simultaneously, give birth to a hope that things are not too late.

There is a better way forward, a more divine design if you like. We need only do that which is right. We must speak out, while the air is still breathable, against the tyranny of the legislature, and any wrongly constituted body that is set up to fail rather than succeed in the name of the people. This is the populism we need and should not shun. A non-violent movement to democratically restructure institutions that are not working for everyone; not for the Indigenous Peoples, the Blacks, the Whites, man, woman or child; not for the poor, the soul of the world one reads in Paulo Cohelo's *The Alchemist*. But the need for some form of transmutation, if not transubstantiation within the body politic of the masses, remains all the same.

We had a little discussion about Brexit earlier, but as most of you know, that is not the only issue that has plagued the EU. One could discuss at length the problems plaguing individuals in specific Euro-zone countries such as Greece and Italy and so on. It is a spider's web of interrelated issues and layer upon layer of complexity that rivals that of the 2008 financial crisis, with its own impenetrable spider's web that shrouded the crime of the century. Such situations, interrelated themselves, fuel the ongoing blame game, where unforeseen conflicts can germinate to produce even war.

Writing in July 2017 about the crisis in Greece, Simon Kuper speaks not only of a thriving blame game, but even the lack of hope amongst many Greeks themselves. On the blame side, Kuper notes how "one man explained to me that the government, in league with German and Israeli 'business lobbies,' had created a crisis to fill its pockets." Kuper writes that "Greece is the euro zone's body in the cupboard, sacrificed to save the euro." Yet he also recognizes that "many younger Athenians—who tend to be better educated—blame the crisis on older Greeks: the participants in the pre-2009 system of communal state looting."[96] Ahh . . . nothing like the blame game, which continues not only within the borders of Greece, but between many of the countries that make up the European Union. On the lack of hope side, one of the psychologists Kuper spoke with at an organization that helps migrants and poor people—Giannis Kallinikakis of Athens Solidarity Centre—had this to say: "Now people don't have hope. It's a kind of bad adaptation to the situation."[97] How could they with real wages dropping so precipitously, with the virtual implosion of civil society. A *New York Times* piece headlined "Explaining Greece's Debt Crisis," written about a year before Kuper's own piece, aptly notes how the collective decision-making power that lies with the 28 national governments forming the EU is increasingly tense, as each nation's government is "beholden to its voters and taxpayers."[98]

According to the *Times* article:

This tension has grown only more acute since the January 1999 introduction of the euro, which binds 19 nations into a single currency zone watched over by the European Central Bank but leaves budget and tax policy in the hands of each country, an arrangement that some economists believe was doomed from the start.[99]

Once again, similar to my concerns about the UN as well as democratic governments around the world, this reflects a lack of risk management. I am no expert, like so many other well-heeled and well-credentialed people claim to be, however I am ever curious, so I took a look at the EU's website. It is pretty confusing, but then I expected that. Here are some highlights of the confusion, which the website itself claims to be "a unique institutional set up."[100] See if you can follow this bureaucratic trail, all laid out nicely, if not confusingly on the EU's website: the European Council is where EU leaders periodically meet to set the broad priorities or direction of the EU. This apparently should "not be confused with" the Council of the EU because that is where government ministers from all the nations forming the EU periodically meet "to discuss comments, amend and adopt laws, and coordinate policies." It seems that the Council of the EU is fairly important because it, along with the European Parliament "is the main decision-making body of the EU."[101] Let's take a closer look at the EU's legislature, its Parliament. Remember, legislatures are the voice of the people. They represent the power of the people and should work well. We have already seen that Canada's own does not, along with that of the UN's. The EU's website claims that "the European Parliament is the heart of democracy in the European Union, representing 500 million people."[102]

The European Parliament, based in Strasbourg, France, comprises 751 Members of the European Parliament (MEPs). This sizable contingent of parliamentarians is directly elected by EU voters every five years, with the number of MEPs from each member state being mainly in proportion to each country's population, with some further rules around that. The EU's Parliament has three main roles. It, along with the Council of the EU, and based on European commission proposals, has the principal duty of passing EU laws. So it has a key legislative role, including deciding on international agreements. The parliament also has a supervisory role, such as "democratic scrutiny of all EU institutions," which sounds like a cumbersome process. Finally, it has a budgetary role, as together with the Council of the EU, it establishes the EU budget.[103] There are several other EU organizations and institutions. However If we try and fly 30,000 feet over the sizable bureaucracy, which does not seem to be working for Greeks losing hope, along with some other European countries facing an uphill battle to improve the lot of their citizens, we can raise some logical questions.

Such questions concern the European Parliament, which again as well as the Council of the EU, is the key decision-making organization for the

EU. So I ask—if the two dozen or so countries that make up the EU do not themselves have legislative bodies that facilitate risk-based decision-making by their respective elected members, how can the European Parliament's 751 MEPs be expected to? Does this explain why the EU does not appear to be working well, with so much suffering taking place in several member states? Never mind Brexit, which clearly showed most UK residents did not believe the EU was working for them. In all likelihood, the tragic circumstances that the almost disintegrating EU finds itself in has a lot to do with poor structural design. The EU does appear to carry out *impact assessments* via the European Commission. Those are conducted for "initiatives expected to have significant economic, social or environmental impacts." Moreover, they are sent to the Parliament and Council to review as they make decisions "on whether to adopt the proposed law."[104] But again, are parliamentarians really informed about what the priority risks are for their respective European countries that may adopt a new law?

Another question necessarily arises. If managing risks well and making informed decisions is more than just lawmaking, is the European Parliament really doing its job? Perhaps we have enough lawyers and need a better design to manage risks, be they Canadian, Pan European or global in nature. As we observed earlier, "budget and tax policy remains in the hands of each country," within a "single currency zone" presided over by the European Central Bank. That, coupled with the fact that each of the EU member states likely does not have strong parliaments making risk-based decisions (including Greece), with duly elected representatives both able to, and motivated to, keep their constituents informed, goes far in explaining the debacle we know as the EU. Of course, as the EU's website claims, the questionable design is "a unique institutional set-up."

We must put the power of the people, their voices, with each as valuable as the next, back in the legislature. It is right and just, and quite probably, entirely the scientific thing to do. And the transformation of our democratic institutions must be based in reality. We must beware of pernicious things done falsely under the guise of optics management, the kingdom of illusions and fake news. In her book *The Trump Card: Playing to Win in Work and Life* President Trump's daughter, Ivanka, had these character revealing thoughts to write: "Perception is more important than reality. If someone perceives something to be true, it is more important than if it is in fact true."[105] Her game-like conclusion being that "this doesn't mean you should be duplicitous or deceitful, but don't go out of your way to correct a false assumption if it plays to your advantage."[106] Unfortunately, the serious challenges facing humanity are not a game and only obvious truths will set us free from false assumptions inhibiting our collective progress. Ivanka's carefully crafted image-making, clothing lines, personal wealth, and lack of depth perception, does little to impress me. That is not a personal attack on Ivanka, only a response to her point of view. Again, all that glitters or has 'bling' is not gold or necessarily a treasure worthy of entry into heaven.

The problems associated with false perceptions are manifest. Consider the lack of success the UN experienced in attempting its right-sounding 'Delivering as One' initiative, discussed previously. This nicely worded effort never delivered the UN out of its plight, perhaps only into more confusion as we saw. Coincidentally, in Harris' book *Party of One*, we hear that when Canadian scientists attended the Polar Year Conference in Montréal in April 2012, the government decided to have them accompanied by official "minders." Harris writes: "The idea was to make sure [they] did not speak to any journalists without a set of eyes and ears from the 'Politburo'—the name some scientists privately used to refer to their departments communications operation." Ironically, Harris notes that the "derisive nickname was wickedly accurate." For "Environment Canada described its communication ideal in a 2007 media protocol that applied to all federal scientists—and which was tightened up even further by the Harper government in 2012" this way. "Just as we have 'one department, one website', we should have 'one department, one voice.' "[107]

It all sounds great on the surface, but when you probe underneath the surface and see an organizational design promoting bad outcomes, along with wrongly motivated people influencing those very outcomes, even if we presume they are well-intended, the veil shrouding government incompetence is lifted. Given just some of the publicly available information outlined in Chapter 3, it might be wise to check under the hood of all the departments and agencies of the Canadian government, and even of the provincial and other levels of government. We need to ascertain how risks are being managed, if at all.

We do have to get our hands dirty within the machinery of government. If, for example, departments and agencies are shrinking by 50 per cent or, conversely, growing by 50 per cent, that begs further assessment. Of course you would need an independent CRO and RMO, as summarized earlier to do just that. It would be the same in America, the UK, the UN or elsewhere, unless you continue to take it on faith that the government will indeed save us from itself, its incompetent design, rather than having faith that you need to do the right thing and support *Democratic Restructuralism* for yourself, your family and the future of humanity.

So many of us, be it here in Canada or elsewhere, have often found ourselves wondering why things are the way they are. Just remember this. The design of our government and international institutions are the problem. That is what is causing all the confusion and lack of progress in moving us forward. Thankfully we can fix this. Or, as John Lennon wrote in another song: *"People asking questions lost in confusion. Well I tell them there's no problem. Only solutions."*

Chapter 9
Technology's
False Promise

Design is not just what it looks like & feels like. Design is how it works.

—Steve Jobs

Many people believe technology is a panacea for much of what ails humanity. They believe technical and scientific advancements can solve many of the problems associated with our weakening democracy. They also believe automated processes within government will improve its effectiveness and efficiency, as if we are just one button away from pushing our public institutions onwards to success. The stark reality, as we will see, is that technology is not a cure-all for all that ails our institutions and democracy.

Arguably, technological innovation has benefitted people immensely in countless ways. It has created efficiencies in innumerable industries, making laborious and dull jobs good candidates for automation. Rapid advancements in healthcare and other areas of scientific inquiry, such as stem-cell research, are mindboggling. The speed and ease at which we can send messages almost instantaneously across the world, from handheld and other devices, reflects our modern age of convenience. We stream data, as if by magic. Our technical prowess notwithstanding, we have come to rely more and more on technology to make our lives more comfortable. Our reliance on wireless phones, computers and the Internet emphasizes this. The almost supernatural world of algorithms and artificial intelligence will, one day soon, perhaps predict our every want and desire as if they were somehow preordained by our maker. But how much of this is really elevating our lives and benefitting our world? Just as a coin, the promise of technological innovation has two sides.

For all its benefits, advancements in technology can result in ethical dilemmas for humanity. Whether those dilemmas revolve around medical issues (such as genetic engineering) or economic ones (such as displacement of employees and job losses within the manufacturing industry), people making decisions must consider the potential ramifications of those decisions. As well, the adoption of new technologies can result in making what should be fairly straightforward and simple processes, overly complex, even too time consuming. In the workplace, technology amplifies not only good underlying processes, procedures and assumptions, but bad ones as well. The failure of highly technical and complex 'black box' economic models during the financial crisis revealed the serious consequences of such amplification. Apart from serving as an amplifier of underlying processes and such, technology also creates new and harmful exposures for society in the form of exposing our personal information to others.

Third parties, some with criminal intent, may obtain our personal data without our consent. This can result in fraudulent activity involving our financial accounts or personal identity. It can even expose our country's assets, as well as that of private business operations in Canada, to cyberattacks and data being held hostage for ransom payments. Our trade secrets and valuable intellectual property are also increasingly at risk. So, too, is our infrastructure, much of it increasingly automated and reliant on computer systems. Consider our power generation and distribution systems for example. The effects of disruptive new technologies in our world have also created a myriad of other challenges that are not within the scope of this book to discuss, except that all of the associated risks need to be managed well by our government.

For the purposes of this chapter, it is important to note that the advantages of implementing new technologies within the operations of the federal government is fraught with peril. Firstly, there is no sense in introducing new IT systems, such as an automated payroll system like Phoenix, if they are not going to be effective, efficient, and worth the taxpayers' dollars they cost. It all reminds me of the process of ordering a cup of coffee at McDonald's in Toronto's underground path system (not in the newer McCafé's which have electronic touch screens to order food and drink from, but the other regular McDonald's outlets in the food courts). The hardworking servers in these 'regular' McDonald's will take your order, whatever it may be. They also appear to be taking orders via mobile phone for those who have planned ahead to order something rather than on the spur of the moment. Anyway, if you just want one of their great cups of coffee, you have to stand in line for quite a while during peak or very busy times. Once you have paid for you beverage, you are given a number. However, you have to stand around amidst a huge flock of people looking to pick up what they ordered. So even if you just wanted a coffee, you have to wait for your number to be called out.

You wait and you wait and you wait. Mainly you just feel sorry for the servers attempting to fill all the orders, including those of numerous customers holding their phones up by the counter and pressing for their advance mobile orders, than sorry for yourself for having to wait a bit more than seems logical. The entire process seems somewhat obtuse and confused to me, an ordinary customer. Mobile technology aside, why not have an express coffee lineup like Tim Horton's, so simple coffee orders are expedited? People would not even have to take a number as it would just be 'first come, first served' as the old adage goes. Mobile coffee orders likely would not clog the system because everyone wanting a coffee would merely show up and expeditiously get one in the express line. The poor servers handling all the chaos with the existing system would not be faced with a barrage of unhappy customers in front of them, not to mention a counter cluttered with coffee cups, with many of the orders understandably getting mixed up.

Now if you want to order that simple cup of coffee at one of the newer and fancier McCafé's, outfitted with those touch screens for ordering, it is still a game of numbers that does not always add up to greater efficiency. My personal experience is that it is just as fast, if not faster, to approach the server at the cashier and order my coffee rather than using the touch screen. I need not input how many coffees I want on the screen, or for that matter, how many milks/creams or sugar I want. The cashier does it all at lightning speed. Now, I enjoy my McDonald's coffee and am not disrespecting the chain. Tim's is OK too. The point of the discussion is to indicate that adding new technologies to a process does not necessarily speed that process up or always make it an efficient, enjoyable and hassle-free experience for those using those technologies. In government, which loves to implement new technologies and projects, along with commensurately establishing newer layers of higher paid bureaucrats to handle it all, we need to be mindful of just how much bang we are getting for our taxpayer bucks. And since Phoenix and other initiatives have cost us a heck of a lot more than such projects are worth—way more than a cup of coffee which we actually get to enjoy—maybe we should be vigilant rather than mindful!

A newly created RMO reporting independently to Parliament and the PMO, should always ensure processes, practices and procedures, are practical, coherent, transparent, and not overly complex. It should ensure that is the case in all government departments for which it needs to perform its risk assessments. The RMO must do that before ascertaining the implementation risks associated with significant IT initiatives within any of those departments. After all, one does not need a Ferrari merely to drive around the block. Therefore cost-benefit analysis is crucial in government when it comes to pursuing system upgrades and such. The need for expensive new technologies to perform government services must also be questioned by independent risk managers, by their meeting with front-line staff who are to use the new system. This is because upper management, or senior bureaucrats, may be apt to present a nice sales job when all they really want is to increase their own bonuses and responsibilities by pursuing unnecessary and costly initiatives. Refer to Chapter 6 and wrong-minded motivations to better understand the need for vigilance here.

Again, risks arising from any significant government initiatives, be they within one department or across the entire government, have to be managed well. IT risks must be managed just as any other risks, ideally with RMO staff having the specialization required to perform their independent evaluations. RMO involvement in expensive and complex government projects is crucial. It would keep our parliamentarians informed as to what is happening; whether or not projects are worthwhile; how projects are progressing upon them being approved; how project risks are being managed; and what the residual risks are for Canadians and the nation. The PBO and Compliance oversight functions would also have their respective roles to play as well, with clear lines of responsibility, including to our elected MPs. However, there is another aspect to technology that we need to consider. One that goes well beyond just managing the risks that relate to government implementation and use of technology to manage its own operations.

The Canadian government's disastrous introduction and subsequent handling of Shared Services and the Phoenix payroll system are a likely indication that it is also totally unprepared to deal with the evolving digital age and 'Internet of all things.' Those risks need to be managed with razor-sharp focus, including how the digital age is impacting the well-being of Canadians and even influencing government policy and elections, and how government runs its operations. The government would likely argue that it is doing exactly that. Certainly its updated *National Cyber Security Strategy* published in 2018, should give comfort to Canadians that our federal government is on top of things. And, in the "Foreword," the Minister of Public Safety and Emergency Preparedness Canada, Ralph Goodale, even articulates how big and costly a deal Canada's Cyber Security Strategy is. "The *Strategy's* core goals are reflected in Budget 2018's substantial investments in cyber security—totaling more than $500 million dollars over five years." Apparently, this is "the largest single investment in cyber security ever made by the Canadian government."[1]

The 35 page document, subtitled *Canada's Vision for Security and Prosperity in the Digital Age*, is fairly short on specifics in terms of how the strategy will be implemented. Broadly, "the Government's actions will evolve alongside the ground-breaking technological developments and resulting paradigm shifts that have become common in our connected world." Additionally, "cyber security action plans will supplement this Strategy" and they will "detail the specific initiatives that the federal government will undertake over time, with clear performance metrics and a commitment to report on results achieved."[2] The *Strategy* also talks about how implementation "will align with other cyber-related Government of Canada initiatives."[3] Therefore it seems, and reasonably so, that the implementation is a work in progress as action plans are developed and so forth.

Obviously, oversight of the more than half-a-billion-dollar initiative requires suitable governance, lest we end up with more costly debacles like the Phoenix compensation system. Change management will be key if there are further technological developments and paradigm shifts, as the *Strategy* seems to expect. Associated risks will need to be managed and reported on, to what should be an inviolate parliamentary legislature. However, at the end of the *Strategy* document, on page 31, we see only four short paragraphs concerning "Effective Leadership, Governance and Collaboration." There is no mention of how the risks associated with the new *National Cyber Security Strategy* will be assessed, reported on, and generally managed. We see a few general comments such as how our federal government "will streamline the way it works and collaborates with external partners and stakeholders by establishing a clear focal point for authoritative advice, guidance, and cyber incident response." Or the "government will lead, in partnership with provinces, territories, and the private sector, the development of a national plan to prevent, mitigate and respond to cyber incidents, one that ensures efficient coordination and effective action."[4]

But how will all this be successful without a risk-management-oversight body like the proposed RMO we outlined in Chapter 5, ensuring what is promised is actually done? Appropriate financial oversight would also be required in the form of a newly constituted PBO as described. So, too, would compliance oversight, given all the privacy and other laws surrounding the 'Internet of all things' and other digital technologies, in areas Canada has been lagging. It also goes without saying the Office of the Auditor General needs to be looking over the shoulders of those implementing Canada's new cyber strategy, as well as what the proposed RMO and other second lines of defence are doing to oversee that strategy. To repeat, we do not need more projects that do not have proper and independent mechanisms in place to ensure they are not financially wasteful of hard-earned taxpayer dollars and ill-managed. We have had enough of such waste already. And since such strategies are usually longer term, in stark contrast to short-term government-of-the-day thinking, we absolutely must have the eyes of all *Three Lines of Defense* on balls in play like this $500 million dollar one.

Ironically the flawed design of our government, which lacks a centralized risk-management function to collaboratively interact with all the provinces, territories, and other federal departments across the country, is also reflected in how the Internet increasingly works. I know. You are saying huh, come again? Here are the not so obvious facts. Canada, along with other nations around the world, has allowed a few big high-tech companies to become monopolies operating within their borders, without having identified, evaluated, and managed the attendant risks. The result, paradoxically being, that these monopolies are now undermining representative democracy rather than expanding it, which many people initially thought the Internet would do. In *Move Fast and Break Things*, Jonathan Taplin poignantly outlines how "the web has become critical to all of our lives as well as the world economy, and yet the decisions on how it is designed have never been voted upon by anyone." Apparently, "those decisions were made by engineers and executives at Google, Facebook, and Amazon (plus a few others) and imposed upon the public with no regulatory scrutiny."[5] Hmmm, more design problems. Look at that!

If you have any doubt the Internet is controlled by monopolies, akin to Russia's resources controlled by its oligarchs, yet, shall we say, to a more refined degree, consider the following: "Today, Google's market share is 88 percent in the United States and higher in the rest of the world." Moreover, "in 2015 Amazon's net sales revenue was $107 billion, and it now controls 65 percent of all online new book sales, whether print or digital."[6] A spinoff of this is that such monopolies are now reaping great economic rewards arising from the work created by others, such as writers and musicians who create marketable and desirable content available on the Internet. According to Taplin, "The concentration of profits in the making of art and news has made more than just artists and journalists vulnerable; it has made all those who seek to profit from the free exchange of ideas and culture vulnerable to the power of a small group of powerful patrons."[7] That is a similar predicament to that of the legislature. It, too, has been made subservient to a select group of individuals, such as those in the PMO and PCO here in Canada. And, yet, it is the legislature that must protect us from the whims of a few people controlling the monopolies that in turn control our lives.

In terms of the real economy and jobs, something of interest to all Canadians, how can we expect that leaders such as Justin Trudeau, or those at the helm of the opposition parties, really have a workable plan to help the middle class succeed? How could they when there is no risk-based plan to address all the issues arising from the job displacement caused by big tech monopolies operating in Canada? The Liberal and Conservative parties alike could not even coherently manage the risks related to the Phoenix payroll system implementation. Taplin notes that "Google and Facebook use their market power to extract monopoly rents from advertisers that are often 20 percent higher than market price," while "Amazon uses its monopsony (a market structure in which only one buyer interacts with many would-be sellers) to force authors, publishers, and booksellers to lower their prices, putting many of them out of business."[8] Originally, the Internet was thought of as a technological enabler for all kinds of small business to flourish around the world at the local level. The idea was that it would be easy to establish a presence on the web, advertise your goods and services, and prosper.

Perversely, as companies such as Google and Amazon grow to gargantuan proportions, like the giant monopolistic corporations that existed in the US just prior to the dawn of the 20th century, they increasingly control the various markets they touch in countless detrimental ways. Citing an article called *Facebook is Eating the World*, written by Columbia Journalism School's Emily Bell, Taplin illustrates how big tech firms can turn traditional business models upside down. Of course, those would include organizations that produce independent rather than fake news for the public, an essential ingredient for a successful democracy. Never mind the job-busting ramifications that high-tech monopoly disruptions are creating locally here in Canada: "I can imagine we will see news companies totally abandoning production capacity, technology capacity, and even advertising departments, and delegating it all to third-party platforms [such as Facebook] in an attempt to stay afloat."[9]

Paralleling our concerns about the increasing riches of the top one per cent relative to the rest of us, tax avoidance by elites, and the undue political influence of the super wealthy outlined earlier, we find big tech is in the thick of it. Indeed, the five largest firms in the world by market capitalization are now Apple, Alphabet (Google's parent company), Microsoft, Amazon, and

Facebook.[10] Strikingly, Taplin finds that even some of former President Obama's economic advisers agreed that "the fortunes created by the digital revolution may have done more to increase economic inequality than almost any other factor."[11] Many people might ascribe the tremendous wealth possessed by tech leaders such as Amazon's Jeff Bezos, Facebook's Mark Zuckerberg, and Microsoft's Bill Gates, etc., to their, and their company's incredible vision and innovation in the digital world. Certainly we have benefitted much from the work of these individuals and their companies. Our lives have been made easier by computers, which allow us to search an endless amount of information and data online; to store information we create; run all kinds of automated applications and systems to do things we often, and earlier, could not; to communicate faster and more efficiently by text and email; and so much more that is a book in itself.

But this misses the destructive nature of monopolies that Taplin brings to our attention. He pinpoints the problem when he explains that inequality is not simply the "inevitable by-product of technology and globalization, or even the lopsided distribution of genius," as many people, including those in the tech industry would have us believe.[12] Of course, many of us believe the high-tech disruption which results in mass and disorderly job losses in various industries is inevitable. Many of us similarly believe the increasing and uneven distribution of wealth that results from such disruption is also inevitable. And many would argue we are as powerless to do anything about this as the forlorn farmer with his horse drawn plough was, under the shadow of the tractor passing him by during the industrial revolution. Not so! It is not that simple. For as Taplin neatly summarizes, inequality "is a direct result of the fact that since the rise of the Internet, policy makers have acted as if the rules that apply to the rest of the economy do not apply to Internet monopolies."[13] Former Canadian Prime Minister Harper appears to have missed that point, both during his prior tight-fisted administration, and in his book *Right Here, Right Now*. Then again, the Liberals are not doing much about this problem either.

The absence of risk management internationally, and here in Canada, is once again the real issue though. It gives rise to an unfair playing field for leading technology companies that are displacing those of us contributing to the real economy and paying our fair share of taxes. "Taxes, antitrust regulation, intellectual property law—all are ignored in regulating the Internet industries."[14] Lack of appropriate oversight on the design and evolution of the Internet likely dwarfs the bungled IT projects mismanaged by Ottawa in importance. It is doubtfully on the radar of shallow thinking, inexperienced, self-promoting, and out of their depth leaders, especially as they cling to the old organizational ways of doing things while our nation's bonds unravel. Quoting Barry Lynn and Phillip Longman's piece entitled "Populism with a Brain," in the August 2016 issue of the *Washington Monthly*, Taplin writes: "The evidence is close to irrefutable that adoption of [a] philosophy of 'efficiency' unleashed a process of concentration that over the last generation has remade almost the entire US economy, and is now disrupting our democracy."[15] Of course the situation in the US is, to a degree, being replicated here in Canada.

Earlier we talked about all the corporations and wealthy elites not paying their fair share of taxes. In the case of big tech monopolies, tax leakage or losses for the US are instructive on the need for appropriate management and oversight of risk arising from digital age monopolies controlling and commoditizing more and more of the Internet for their purposes. For example, by 1994 Bezos had set Amazon up in Seattle, reasoning that the state was less populated, so most of his customers would come from outside Seattle and not pay sales tax.[16] The savings for Bezos? Economist Dean Baker estimated Amazon's tax-free status amounted to $20 billion in savings for its business.[17] Additionally, and exemplifying big business yet again lobbying government to do its bidding, Bezos got Republican congressman Christopher Cox and Democratic senator Ron Wyden to author the Internet Tax Freedom Act (ITFA), passed and signed by President Clinton in 1998. Although the bill allows states to impose sales tax on ecommerce, they are prohibited from imposing Internet Specific taxes. [18]

From the date the ITFA was passed up to 2015, a whopping 2,300 independent bookstores (as well as the borders chain) and 3,100 record stores closed their doors. [19] The trend of big tech monopolies paying less tax is also evident in the behaviour of Google and Facebook. Referencing *Bloomberg Businessweek* reports, Taplin finds:

> The tactics of Google and Facebook depend on 'transfer pricing', a paper transaction among corporate subsidiaries that allow for allocating income to tax havens while attributing expenses to higher-tax countries. Such income shifting costs the U.S. government as much as $60 billion in annual revenue, according to Kimberly A. Clausing, an economics professor at Reed College in Portland, Oregon. [20]

And what of other nations where big tech's tentacles reach? Taplin quotes Farhad Manjoo of the *New York Times*: "The larger Amazon gets, then, the more its rules—rather than any particular nation's—can come to be regarded as the most important regulations governing commerce." [21] Indeed. I was just reading about how a lot of cities are vying to attract Amazon's second headquarters, called HQ2, in North America, because it will create as many as 50,000 jobs and represent $5 billion of capital investments. As of late November 2017, Amazon had received 238 proposals from cities and regions in the United States, Canada and Mexico. [22] Here again it is calling the shots though. *It's HQ2 RFP (Request for Proposal)*, stipulates respondents to the proposal should "provide a summary of total incentives offered for the Project by the state/province and local community." Specifically, the summary should "provide a brief description of the incentive item, the timing of incentive payment/realization, and a calculation of the incentive amount."

And, surprise, surprise, "with respect to tax credits, please indicate whether credits are refundable, transferable, or may be carried forward for a specific period of time."[23]

Of course, and unsurprisingly, there have been some bids which go to outrageous lengths to attract Amazon's HQ2 through their incentive packages. This obviously puts the monopoly and its interests above that of the citizenry, another admission that representative democracy does not work for Susie and Frank on Main Street, just the denizens of massive wealth calling the shots. Consider the sugar-coated bid from Chicago, Illinois. According to a November 2017 *Business Insider* report, officials in that city are "prepared to let Amazon keep $1.32 billion of the personal income taxes paid by its workers annually." Apparently, while "employees would still pay the full taxes," those funds would not go toward Illinois in support of its civic infrastructure, but toward lining the pockets of Amazon.[24] This appears to be the trend in terms of polarizing society, wherein big and powerful corporations, and their chieftains, avoid paying tax and are subsidized by those common folks who actually pay their taxes. Is it any wonder the one per cent are getting richer at our expense? It is like the 2008 financial crisis. The profits were privatized but the losses were socialized. That does not sound like equitable capitalism to me, much less equitable democracy.

Citing a 2012 report from *Good Jobs First* (GJF), *Business Insider* documents that "a growing number of US States are subsidizing large companies, including Walmart, Google, Target, Sears and Boeing.[25] We all know what happened to Sears. Anyway, it is useful, as you drive down some of America's roads and across its bridges—many needing desperate repair, to remember that GJF "identified 22 personal income-tax incentive programs in 16 states that involve the diversion of about $684 million in revenues each year."[26] Our Canadian federal government needs to be on top of all the risks to our own nation, faced with predominantly American-based tech monopolies and the adverse impacts they can bring about in our day-to-day lives. Again, in the wake of the Phoenix and Shared Services fiascos, it is doubtful our government knows what it is doing. It cannot without policy decisions and laws based on a holistic risk-management process that percolates up to the highest layers of the bureaucracy.

In an opinion piece published by *ITWC* in July 2017, columnist David Crane reasons that Canada's "Competition Bureau should undertake a study of the present and future challenges emerging from the growing power of Amazon, Google, Facebook, Alibaba and others."[27] Absolutely, something should be done. And I believe a study of the risks should methodically be managed by government, by its yet to be appointed Chief Risk Officer (CRO), and yet to be established Risk Management Office (RMO)! Ideally, the CRO should not only brief the Prime Minister of the day, but also Parliament, on the risks presented to Canadians by high-tech monopolies. Parliament must make important and informed decisions surrounding digital monopolies, including any risks to our national and personal security, not just the broader economy. Those decisions should also encapsulate a solid national cyber security strategy, given all the hackers, ransomware, and state-sponsored cyber wars, etc. going on that we hear about constantly. More generally, significant high-tech monopoly risks must be thoughtfully well-managed because, as Crane questions:

> Do we really want to live in a world where a handful of monopolistic tech giants determine how we live, what we buy and what we pay, where we make our travel arrangements, how we access entertainment, what startups get access to the global platforms and on what terms, how our health is managed, and perhaps even how we vote? I don't think so.[28]

Of concern, as I write this book, the US Federal Communications Commission is looking to repeal what is commonly referred to as 'net neutrality.' Presently, as UWO's *The Gazette* notes, "Under net neutrality rules,

Internet Service Providers (ISPs) like Bell or Rogers in Canada, are required to treat all websites equally regardless of content, political leanings, or ownership." An ongoing concern is that "giving ISPs control over content access will only serve to consolidate their power more: if Bell is unhappy with a competitor they can restrict access to their website."[29] Thus far, Canada appears to have made good progress in the area of protecting net neutrality through the Canadian Radio, Television and Telecommunications Commission. Just recently in May 2018, The *Financial Post* reported on how "the House of Commons voted unanimously . . . in favour of Liberal MP John Oliver's private member's motion to support an 'open internet free from unjust discrimination and interference', and enshrine net neutrality in legislation."[30] Nice to see the House do something right! However all the risks associated with not only ISPs, but other high-tech monopolies, need to be assessed and managed in a coordinated and effective manner at the national level. Our elected officials should be briefed and do their homework accordingly, making the right decisions for Canada's future.

Europe has already been a leader in trying to reign in the high-tech monopolies and their perceived abuses. In June 2017, the European Commission (EC) levied a $2.7 billion penalty against Google for antitrust violations, not a huge amount for that firm, but enough to flag that competition matters and the potential for more fines exists. As Crane documents in his opinion piece, the EU's Competition Commissioner recognized how Google's "innovative products and services" have indeed "made a difference to our lives." However the Commissioner found that it nonetheless "abused its market dominance as a search engine by promoting its own shopping service in its search results, and demoting those of its competitors."[31] Writing about *Why Google, Facebook, and Amazon Should Worry About Europe*, Jeff Roberts also claims "the vanguard of regulatory action is Europe." According to Roberts, "Over the past years, Apple was hit by the EC with an order to pay more than $13 billion in back taxes, while Europe's top court is set to bless a decision by French authorities to hit Uber managers with criminal charges for unlicensed taxi operations."

Similarly, "Facebook has been dinged for privacy infractions related to its WhatsApp acquisition" and so on. [32]

There is also new regulation in the EU which allow citizens more control over their data. Non-compliance with the *General Data Protection Regulation* may result in whopping penalties of up to four per cent of a company's global revenues. [33] Roberts writes that "as of July, the EC was also conducting two other major investigations, including one that looks at whether contracts that oblige Android device makers to preload Google's apps are anticompetitive." Of note, and also during the summer of 2017, "the Supreme Court of Canada forced Google to delete certain search results not just in Canada but everywhere in the world." [34] All the same, and as Crane summarized in his own article, we can do better.

If we turn again to our American friends down south, we see the huge importance of reigning in monopolies throughout their colourful and instructive history. In *Move Fast and Break Things*, Taplin raises the conflict of values and ideas between such luminary figures as Thomas Jefferson, known as "the man of the people," and Alexander Hamilton, who was President George Washington's Secretary of the Treasury, "believing that capital should be free to influence politics but that politics should not be allowed to influence capital." [35] The ingenuity of his approach in discussing today's tech monopolies versus those monopolies that preceded them, is Taplin's sensible comparison of describing what goes wrong when you let big business, of any sort, pursue its own agenda at the expense of the wider public. The outcomes are generally the same, regardless of the period of history concerned.

The inimitable Thomas Jefferson was a leading proponent to have a *Bill of Rights* in the US *Constitution*, including a clause that would place "restriction against monopolies." [36] Apostles of democracy are always fair and just. Hamilton and his backers were, unsurprisingly, not in favour of such a clause. Despite Jefferson's pleas to Washington, Hamilton and his allies not only got the bill, excluding restriction of monopolies to pass through Congress early in 1791, but also without Washington's disapproval.[37] Taplin significantly concludes, "Thus the stage was set for American business to be ruled by giant corporations."[38] It was only later, toward the dawn of the 20th century, after such business moguls as J.P. Morgan and John D. Rockefeller established their own respective behemoths of companies called 'trusts,' that the US government began to explore more of what we call antitrust legislation:

> Faced with the real threat of monopoly, Congress passed the
> Sherman Act in 1890, which specified fines and imprisonment
> for anyone 'who shall monopolize, or attempt to monopolize,
> or combine or conspire with any other person or persons to
> monopolize any part of the trade or commerce among the
> several States, or with foreign nations.'[39]

What really strikes me about Taplin's research here, is not just his description of how President Theodore Roosevelt used the legislation to break up Rockefeller and Morgan's trusts, such as the former's Standard Oil Trust, but the references to Roosevelt's own unequivocal "statements on the dangers of monopoly," exerting its influence to control government.[40] Here, the iconic American President lays out what happens when society becomes polarized, when a select few play by a different set of rules, usurping representative democracy in the process:

> The great corporations which we have grown to speak of
> rather loosely at trusts are the creatures of the State, and the
> State not only has the right to control them, but it is duty
> bound to control them wherever the need of such control is
> shown . . . Corporate expenditures for political purposes . . .
> have supplied one of the principal sources of corruption in
> our political affairs.

The absence of effective State, and, especially national restraint upon unfair money-getting has tended to create a small class of enormously wealthy and economically powerful men, whose chief object is to hold and increase their power. The prime need is to change the conditions which enable the men to accumulate power which it is not for the general welfare that they should hold or exercise.[41]

Obviously, Jefferson would have agreed. He perceived the need to enshrine a variety of protective measures, including the limiting of monopolies, in a *Bill of Rights* that would preserve democracy and the rights of individuals. Here too in Canada, we have historically seen the need, paralleling that of the United States, to have a bill of rights that supports the general welfare of those living within our own democracy. Prime Minister Diefenbaker "proposed a bill of rights 'under which freedom of religion, of speech, of association . . . freedom from capricious arrest and freedom under the rule of law' would be guaranteed."[42] Viewing, at least in principle, that people were equal as Canadians, he informed the House of Commons that "his goal was to see 'an unhyphenated nation' in which citizens of many origins and religions would be regarded and treated equally."[43]

Interestingly, in the US, both Republicans and Democrats have betrayed the spirit of such forward thinking American figures as Jefferson and 'Teddy' Roosevelt. This betrayal has contributed to the growing inequality within America's borders, and arguably to a degree, that very model being copied, if not exported, around the world. This situation has created a further and dire need for *Democratic Restructuralism*. The lesson here is that the flawed design of government institutions must be re-examined—so, too, must ill-designed laws that are permitted to be passed without informed debate as to the risks to democracy. Citing Barry Lynn again, Taplin writes that former President Bill Clinton's "attitudes toward monopolization were even more favourable than those of Presidents Reagan or George H.W. Bush." By way of example, while Clinton and Gore ran in 1992 as opponents of media monopolization, Lynn found "their decision to allow the consolidation of U.S. media companies that had begun under Reagan to continue . . . cut the number of big firms from more than fifty to six."[44]

The influence big business has on government, the cronyism outlined earlier in this book, increasingly means our vote does not change things much. Bureaucracies remain in place. They are hamstrung by ministers coopted by big business. Civil servants' hands are also tied because things keep getting done the way they have for decades, with an all too powerful PMO and PCO deciding our fates instead of an informed legislature and citizenry. Decision-making is misguided and misinformed in the inhumane machinery of our government. There is no effective, transparent and unbiased mechanism within government to assess risks across the nation. Canada desperately requires a CRO and other independent oversight functions within government to rejuvenate its lost democracy, to mend its broken institutions.

Taplin quotes sociologist C. Wright Mills, whose mid-1950s book *The Power Elite*, forecasted how modern democracy would unravel in the sense that government is often influenced by big business and its interests. Those interests take precedence over the democratic needs of society overall, including the elderly, children, those with disabilities, entrepreneurs interested in opening a new small business, civil servants wanting to help make things work the way they should, the poor, and so on. For Mills, "the long-time tendency of business and government to become more intricately and deeply involved with each other has . . . reached a new point of explicitness. The two cannot now be seen clearly as two distinct worlds."[45] We have seen the implications of big business perniciously influencing the financial services sector. Large private institutions achieved regulatory capture such that an independent, healthy, and well-functioning financial-oversight system in many democracies could not take shape. Not to centre on Canada's current Finance Minister, Bill

Morneau, again, but I can only wonder about his true allegiances—whether they are to the people of Canada overall, or to those interests that may feather his personal nest.

Prior to his political career, Morneau encouraged governments to transfer Canadian workers out of more secure Defined Benefit (DB) pension plans and into riskier 'target plans,' the latter plans requiring far more actuarial services, such as those provided by Morneau-Shepell, where Morneau was Chairman and CEO.[46] Although our esteemed Finance Minister resigned as executive chairman upon being elected, he transferred his Morneau-Shepell shares to his private holding company, retaining what could be perceived as a conflict of interest. His holding company was incorporated in Alberta's lower tax jurisdiction despite Morneau being a resident of Ontario. Glaringly, as Garfield Emerson notes, "Finance Minister, [Morneau], sponsored Bill C-27—pension legislation that could directly benefit Morneau Shepell's business."[47] Incidentally, Bill C-27 supports a move toward converting certain DB pensions in Canada into the less generous targeted plans. It appears we can continue to waste billions on such projects as Phoenix, but need to target the secure pensions of hardworking Canadians.

As of late October 2017, there were reports that Morneau-Shepell shares have jumped 31 per cent since Morneau became Finance Minister.[48] And as Tom Parkin wrote for Postmedia Network, being Finance Minister, "he [Morneau] doesn't need to lobby now."[49] Emerson raises the distasteful spectre that it was only when he was "under attack," that "Mr. Morneau pledged to sell his holdings, enter into a blind trust and donate to charity the gain on his shares since he came to office."[50] Apparently, that money was estimated at $5 million. Disconcertingly for Canadians, and as Emerson, a good governance practitioner opined about Morneau, "His remedial actions confirm he controls those assets and needed to take action to address the conflict of interest allegations as minister."[51] By late November 2017, Morneau was also facing questions in the House of Commons about new revelations his father sold off about $1.5 million shares in their family-built company right before the minister announced a major 2015 tax-change. Per *CBC News*, "opposition MPs say they believe the tax news led to a dip in the stock market—including the value of Morneau Shepell shares."[52] One can only conjecture if all these bad-smelling circumstances could have been prevented by adequate risk management and compliance oversight. Our senior ministers' actions should, ideally, be vetted by independent oversight functions within government. Compliance and ethical standards should be high for MPs representing Canadians and the public trust. Only a fool would think otherwise.

Astoundingly, the dysfunctional PCO recently advised that some other ministers held certain assets indirectly. Emerson astutely writes that "the public trust in the integrity of responsible government overrules confidentiality and private interests."[53] Perhaps I am on to something when I see the PCO needs a contemporary makeover. Better yet, it needs redesigning as a good step to initiating our desperately required *Democratic Restructuralism*. After all, as Emerson argues, "Secrecy of possible conflicts of interest by members of Her Majesty's Privy Council is unacceptable."[54] Indeed, bungling and secrecy do not make for good risk management and informed decision-making, which are elements required for true democracy.

Beyond high government ministers allegedly facing conflicts of interest with their business interests, the concept of regulatory capture remains a concern in financial services regulation. In the United States, a new report by the Government Accountability Office criticized the Federal Reserve's Board of Governors for thus far failing to implement an enterprise risk-management framework. They felt that such a framework could assist the US central bank in preventing situations where regulators "adopt the mindset of the bank they are supervising, a problem known as regulatory capture." This is mentioned in an *American Banker* article, where its author cites Bloomberg News research indicating that " 'among many factors that contributed to the financial crisis of 2007–09 was weakness in federal supervision of large banks, and some analyses have identified regulatory capture as one potential cause of this weakness,' the GAO wrote in a letter to Reps. Maxine Waters, D-California, and Al Green, D-Texas, who requested the report."[55]

Clearly it is useful to design government institutions is a way that prevents, as far as possible, regulatory capture and conflicts of interest. This further underscores the need for suitable risk-management across Canada and its fraying institutions. Why mention all of this when we were discussing big-tech monopolies? As outlined in one of Taplin's chapters, entitled "Google's Regulatory Capture," "Google spends a lot of money to make sure its political influence in Washington is felt in both the executive and legislative branches of government."[56] That is something I believe we should be mindful of here in Canada, given the risks associated with any unbridled influence big business may have over our government and the workings of democracy for everyone generally. Special interest groups should not have undue leverage over majority interests. However, all interests, including that of big business, should equitably be considered by government. MPs should then be transparent in their informed decision-making about the economy, fair competition, privacy law, equality and human rights, national security and anything else that may conceivably be impacted by a monopoly such as Alphabet / Google, the largest American company by market capitalization. When voters know what information MPs are basing their decisions upon, their votes are likely to matter much more.

According to Taplin, apart from Google's Chairman, Eric Schmidt, having visited the Obama White House more than any other corporate executive in America, and its chief lobbyist, Katherine Oyama, having been an associate counsel to Vice President Joe Biden, "the list of highly placed Googlers in the federal government is truly mind-boggling."[57] For example:

- "The US chief technology officer and one of her deputies are former Google employees."

- "The acting assistant attorney general in the Justice Department's antitrust division is a former antitrust attorney at Wilson Sonsini Goodrich & Rosati, the Silicon Valley firm that represented Google."
- "The White House's chief digital officer is a former Google employee."
- "One of the top assistants to the chairman of the FCC [Federal Communications Commission] is a former Google employee and another ran a public lobbying firm funded in part by Google."
- "The director of the US Patent and Trademark Office is the former head of patents at Google."[58]

Taplin also meticulously outlines how there has been a 'revolving door' between Google and the broader American government. In terms of a few examples, there have been 53 revolving-door moves between Google and the White House, dozens of moves collectively between the US State Department, the Department of Defense, and departments involving national security and intelligence, etc.[59] Through the revolving door, generally high-ranking staff have either come from Google to the US government, or conversely, from the latter to the former. There have also been "nine moves between either Google or its outside lobbying firms and the Federal Communications Commission, which handles a growing number of regulatory matters that have a major impact on the company's bottom line."[60] Taplin believes "Google will always have a seat at the table and be able to access critical intelligence if its interests are threatened."[61] Moreover, and aside from some interesting examples, he proclaims, "My own experience in talking to legislators about Internet reform has led me to understand that Google, Amazon, and Facebook are deeply embedded in both parties, and their interests will be protected no matter who is in the White House."[62]

Canadians need to rigorously and effectively manage risks associated with non-Canadian monopolies that increasingly impact our lives. This is reflected by the regulatory capture monopolies are likely achieving in various industries, if they have not already, as well as some clear abuses that have occurred in Canada. Most of us have heard about the risks related to drug abuse, including pharmaceutical pain killers containing oxycodone that people can become addicted to, especially when there are no legal prescriptions being made for such people. Interestingly, Google has previously paid a fine of $500 million as a penalty for the amount it had profited from the advertising for illegal pharmacies on its search service, as well as the amount Canadian pharmacies had received from US customers buying illegal drugs.[63] Obviously we need to design our government institutions in a way that can methodically determine risks to our nation, whether they come from within or outside our borders. Those risks need to be prioritized accordingly. The right actions at the right time also need to be taken by the right people to mitigate applicable risks. It will only be then that we can ensure the right outcomes for Canadians. Although technology can help facilitate this process, it currently is part of the problem (one of the risks that needs to be managed as described) rather than an immediate solution.

We need to do whatever it takes to ensure the right people, with the right motivations, are in the right roles within government—including within an enterprise-wide risk-management function. The crucial RMO must inform Parliament so that meaningful debate occurs in relation to important decisions that legislators must make on our behalf. For even when we just consider the monumental risks we need to manage associated with the ever-growing big tech monopolies, we are running out of time. It is no different than climate change. Taplin's desire is that "we can build parallel structures that will benefit all creators"—ones that work to produce wealth that others have co-opted for their own profits. There is a "deadly race between politics and technology" and "the people's voice (politics) will have to win."[64] I agree. We no longer have the luxury to bungle and waste billions of dollars of taxpayers' money on a useless federal payroll system that does not work or on other failed IT initiatives such as Shared Services. There are huge issues that need to be logically addressed.

We must build the low-technology architecture to deal with today's problems, including high-tech monopolies. Principally, that starts with reorganizing the PCO to build the risk-management organizational structure that Canadians require to move forward. We will all prosper and advance by making informed decisions that distinguish between right and wrong. This will enable Canada to lead by example, in an increasingly complex world, where people are more divided than ever and are looking to blame *someone* else for their problems rather than the *something* else that is clearly responsible. The 'system' needs to be rebuilt so that it is fit for purpose in modern times. Our immediate task at hand is *Democratic Restructuralism*, not another costly and useless IT project. On everything else this depends.

CHAPTER 10
THE PATH AHEAD

If anyone, then, knows the good they ought to do and doesn't do it, it is a sin for them.

—James 4:17 (NIV)

It is about the beginning of August 2018, and I am headed for the Rocky Mountains in our almost half-century-old Volkswagen camper. My two young children, Ryan and Maya are with me, all of us catching glimpses of Canada's breadth, abundance, and sheer splendor whenever we are looking out the windows of our orange tree house on wheels. I also can imagine, if John Lennon were here in this crazy old van beside me, that he might sing a few lines—perhaps: *I'm just sitting here watching the wheels go round and round—I really love to watch them roll.* Or maybe he would tell me to sing the first line of "Watching the Wheels" before he got to his part. That probably would be suitable—*People say I'm crazy doing what I'm doing*—driving so far across the land, not knowing what awaits us on the path ahead. But that is the fun of it, especially for the kids. Life is always full of unexpected surprises. Just like Christmas. And with the recently tuned engine humming along, I just know this is going to be a great personal journey.

I also cannot help but think about all the people we are seeing both on and along the Trans-Canada Highway as we aim westward on our path to new heights. All my fellow Canadians are as wonderfully diverse in their backgrounds, talents and personalities as this country is diverse in its own natural beauty; its tough ruggedness blanketed by our makers' refinements, expressing that which defies human description. I just know my fellow Canadians are spiritually aware of the difference between what's right and what's wrong. We like to help our neighbours instead of blaming them, just like the good people of Newfoundland did after the horrific 911 attacks on America, when they welcomed 38 plane loads of people with shelter and food. Those good folks in the town of Gander knew the right thing to do without being told. And I really enjoyed watching the musical about this story called *Come From Away* in Toronto in 2018.

It is because I have faith and trust in the spirit of the Canadian people, the collective body politic, I also have confidence in what we can achieve together. Of course knowing how to do the right thing makes all the difference. Chapters 5, 6 and 7 outlined how we can correct the course of our democracy. In large brushstrokes, I summarized how we can harness the latent possibility and creativity that rests within all Canadians, transforming that source of hope into a well-designed system of government that moves us all forward. It is an example the whole world is waiting for. The path that lies ahead is by no means an easy one to traverse, especially given the existing division between nations and citizens alike. It requires us all to demand, in that nonviolent and also polite Canadian way of ours, that our political leaders begin to try and do the right thing more than they have been trying to say the right thing.

One voice can be lost among a multitude of so many others, especially when optics management and fake news sow yet more misunderstanding, division, conflict, and hopeless confusion amongst good and decent people. However, when more and more people begin to understand that our democratic system and structures are at the root of so much that ails the country, and when they know how to solve this monumental problem of the new millennium, then all those voices can affect the positive change we all need. Our shared values will coalesce into something wonderful that improves not only most of our lives, but finally enables Canada to achieve that greatness which is so long overdue. Much work will need to be done and many hearts and minds will need to be convinced of the right thing to do. However 'do' we must. We deserve it, and so does the nation whose flag has been symbolically unraveling in a heretofore aimless wind that points us down wrong roads. It is time for us to head directly towards *Democratic Restructuralism*, letting the collective spirit of Canadians fill our sails until we arrive at our correct destination.

Opponents of my view, be they past, current or future political and business elites—my detractors—will be plentiful. They will say I have written too harshly of all that is wrong with our country's government, or that I have both directly and indirectly attacked and impugned characters of good standing and repute, who themselves have attempted to do many positive things. However, it was never my intention to deny that our government does nothing good at all, and that its prior leaders and politicians never made a good decision for Canadians. This country, even today, is one of the best places on the face of the earth to live. All the same, the costs of allowing the status quo to remain, wherein our legislature is not sacrosanct in its ability to make good and informed decisions for we Canadians, is too high to endure any longer. The waste in human potential; the waste of billions of dollars of taxpayers' money going down so many black holes, like Phoenix; the waste of time in addressing our major social and environmental problems in a meaningful way—it all has to stop.

I imagine if studies were done in other democracies, not just the UN or other international organizations, to examine if their respective legislatures are making sound and risk-based decisions that rely on good information, we would also find their system of government in need of significant improvements. Do we really believe for example, and respectfully, that President Trump and the

American Congress are making the best-informed decisions reflective of the will of the good American people? The implications of the revolving door of senior government officials entering and exiting the White House remain uncertain. In the words of Lee H. Hamilton, a former US Congressman and 'distinguished scholar' at the Indiana University School of Global and International Studies, there are some big problems on Capitol Hill in Washington DC. In a March 2018 *Omaha World-Herald* article called "Congress is tanking, but does it care?" he opined as follows: "Our Congress—I'm talking about the people's body, the institution created by our founders . . . is in deep trouble. And no one seems to be offering hope." According to Hamilton, "Very few people seem to respect it, even on Capitol Hill."[1]

Citing a Pew Research Centre report, he writes, "More members of the U.S. House of Representatives are choosing not to seek re-election to that body than at any time in the past quarter-century." As one might expect, especially under the current Trump Administration, Hamilton finds that "power is shifting decisively to the president."[2] This appears to underscore the erosion of America's own supposedly inviolate legislature. Perhaps Thomas Jefferson's prophecy is coming true. It was the "tyranny of the legislature" that Jefferson perceived as "the most formidable dread at present" in his time, warning that "it will be for long years." Yet, he also warned "that of the executive will come in its turn." We wrote of this earlier, gleaning it from Tocqueville's work.

Therefore when Hamilton more recently writes that "Members of Congress over the years have delegated much of their power to other branches, especially the executive, so that they can escape accountability for tough choices,"[3] he may well be reflecting the accuracy of Jeffersonian prophecy. Remember, Tocqueville saw Jefferson as the greatest apostle of democracy, so Jefferson's warnings should be taken seriously. Hamilton finds that "congressional leaders have abandoned two centuries of precedent . . . that allowed a body representing the complexities of the entire country to arrive at policy solutions that by and large spoke to the public good."[4] This predicament or, more appropriately, this current crisis of modern American history, likely is reflected in the tragic images of young children being separated from their parents as these families try to gain entry into the US as refugees and, dare I say, illegal immigrants.

Regardless of whether you support this kind of thing are not, the caging of children forcibly removed from their parents belies a complete failure of good risk management and commensurate decision-making in Congress, as well as in the White House. On a larger scale, it speaks to a failure of the human imagination to continually ensure people are doing the right thing. Hamilton mentioned America has "got half a dozen conflicts going on around the world, armed forces in some 70 countries, incurring casualties . . . and Congress holds no hearings of any consequences to ask what's going on."[5]

Then again, with a record setting government shutdown occurring in the US, do any Americans really know what is going on? If anything, the Trump administration is only adding to the risks Americans are facing, rather than managing risks to US citizens. This is why an article published by *The Guardian*, in January 2019, is undoubtedly headlined "Forget the 'border crisis' – it is Trump's shutdown that's made us less safe." According to Michael Fuchs, "By shutting down the government, Trump has disabled America's defenses against threats to national security."[6] If you require proof, Fuchs advises that "The Federal Bureau of Investigation (FBI) has been forced to furlough roughly 5,000 people, including special agents, intelligence analysts and attorneys, according to Tom O'Connor, a special agent and president of the FBI Agents Association."[7] Perhaps Trump's skill at building towers (like the Babylonians did), qualifies him to manage risks in the absence of 5,000 FBI staff. Somehow I doubt it though. And Putin, Russia's President, may find it interesting indeed that "In all of the agencies affected by the shutdown there are [US] national security functions being hit hard, with cyber-security being one of the most vulnerable."[8]

It seems quite risky to have, "as CNBC reported, 'close to half of the employees within the Department of Homeland Security's Cybersecurity and Infrastructure Security Agency (Cisa) – which works to help secure the nation's critical infrastructure industries like banking, water, energy and nuclear… furloughed.'"[9] Fuchs' article also alludes to other risks arising from the US government shutdown, such as the "Economic strains on US government workers not being paid…"[10] He also intimates that there are huge reputation risks now facing America, as its allies grapple with the wall of confusion emanating from the shutdown. America, you require *Democratic Restructuralism* to move forward! This is likely why so many Indigenous activists gathered to march in Washington earlier in 2019, "for the first ever Indigenous Peoples March." As reported by *VOA News*, "They are seeking to bring national attention to injustices endured by Indigenous people across the globe."[11]

I wonder if John McCain, God rest his soul, feels America too has been betrayed. I will say that Americans possess a rich tradition of democracy and have long been a beacon of hope and trusted ally in the community of nations. America was already a great nation. Nevertheless, its own legislative institution, Congress, seems to be suffering from the same malaise that has beset our own Parliament here in Ottawa.

Turning to the UK and its own predicaments, consider if Brexit was in the best interest of that nation. Before you mull that over, please consider what John Crace and Chris Mullin wrote in 2017 of Westminster politics, practised in the UK and from which our own Canadian parliamentary system is derived. Crace could well be talking about Canada's own House of Commons and Question Period when he states: "Even the great set pieces of Westminster—PMQs and urgent questions to ministers—that are meant to be showcases of democracy where the government is held to account often become a procedural farce as ministers are not actually obliged to answer any questions directly."[12] Mullin, who was the Labour MP for Sunderland South for more than 20 years, had this to say of ordinary MPs in the UK.

"Most backbenchers are not so fortunate and it can be a struggle to remain relevant. As one of my more cynical colleagues once remarked, 'We come here wanting to change the world and we end up admiring the architecture.' "[13] Was Brexit then a result of ignorant voters in the UK or perhaps its own weak and ill-informed Parliament? You decide.

I will leave it up to you, after reading Chapter 8, to consider whether or not the European Union and the United Nations are being run efficiently and effectively, in the interest of its constituents, ordinary people who want their leaders to do the right thing. Am I so very wrong to suggest that we Canadians and the entire world urgently require the kind of *Democratic Restructuralism* that I have argued for? Now that you know what is so very wrong, it is up to you to do what is right. Do not listen to the Pharisees and scribes. It is up to you, your family, friends and neighbours, to push for a more divine design in our democracy. Ordinary Canadians are an innovative, resourceful, and tough people. But we are also a caring people who know, despite our imperfect nature, that healing the nation and our democratic institutions are required; perhaps what remains of the wilderness too, before it is all consumed like Sodom and Gomorrah.

It is time for us to find our collective confidence. It is time for Canadians to strike a balance between all the risks facing us that need to be addressed, be they business and economic risks or social, environmental and other risks, and our desire for mere economic wealth during our short-lived lives. Canadians are not ignorant. We can be trusted to do the right thing and vote accordingly. Now we just need our political parties to support this direction, or at least one of them to. It does not matter what each party seemingly stands for, left, centre, or right wing. Our support for any existing parties is rooted only in perception rather than grounded in any meaningful reality, such as political platforms formulated by risk-based information and what the people really want. We need a political party to commit to empowering the legislature and carrying out the *Democratic Restructuralism* required to restore and champion our waning democracy.

It could be the New Democratic Party, which has a very suitable name. Yet then it must commit to shedding its left-wing image in favour of supporting the will of all the people by strengthening democracy and rebuilding our broken institutions, such that good decisions and real leadership can take place. It could be the Liberals or Conservatives if they similarly could do the right thing which, in the case of our perception of the Conservatives, does not mean right-wing policies without grounding in common sense and the will of the people. The Greens champion tackling climate change and "evidence-based decision-making in the public interest," but could be against faith-based schools which are likely key issues for Québécois and Indigenous Peoples, along with others. As reported on by *Global News* in June 2018, "Of the four major parties vying in [the Ontario provincial election], only the Green Party of Ontario... supports defunding separate schools."[14] The Liberals like to tell everyone what they want to hear and the Conservatives like to tell as little as possible. So which party will do the right thing and redesign our government so it works as intended? Somebody or some group must step forward and get out of the comfortable easy chair of complacency. *Healing the World* depends on this and is the ultimate goal of my message. *Mending the Flag* is the precursor. It must come first even though it is not the ultimate goal.

Imagine how much we can build and achieve by becoming a beacon of light and hope for others. We are not gods. However we can do better to honour our faith, our ancestors, and our future. Imagine the example we can set for other countries, perhaps even international organizations like the UN. The world stands at a precipice, the abyss of so many poor decisions and the tyranny of the legislature staring us straight in the face—the tyranny of the executive grows apace. What will we choose to do? Mend flags and heal the world? Build strong legislatures that manage risks wisely for everyone? Build bridges and improve conditions for our children to inherit a more certain future? Or will we allow our democratic institutions to continue to fail us, our legislatures to possess more poor form than substance? Will we allow risks to continuously mount without being properly assessed and managed? Will we build more offenses than bridges, blaming others for our problems just as so many nations have done in the past? What direction will you choose? I prefer the New Jerusalem which awaits, and the kingdom of democracy as its catalyst.

We are all responsible for mending that which is broken, that something that aptly deserves blame rather than our neighbours. You now know what you ought to do. As for me, I am popping in a John Lennon CD into my old VW camper's radio set and heading down the road. I have never been down this particular road that unites Canada before, but my children are smiling broadly when they turn from looking at the mountains and wilderness, and look to me, their father, instead. We are guided by the Morning Star. We do not know what is around the next corner or behind the next rise. Somehow it does not matter, as long as I do what I said I would, and keep my promise.

If you have children, you know they must be guided correctly, down roads they have yet to take, by the wisdom and love of their parents. We would be wise to follow the wisdom of our spiritual leaders. The Pope is wise along with many other spiritual leaders. But there is also wisdom found in the ways of the Haudenosaunee, in their core Seventh Generation value. "Nations are taught to respect the world in which they live as they are borrowing from future generations." *Healing the World* also depends on this teaching for humanity's salvation. Understanding this leads to true reconciliation, to the paradise that awaits us, where *Democratic Restructuralism* within a New Jerusalem can also be found, thriving in a promised land, we all have yet to discover. Now that you have read my restorative message, the rest is up to you.

Epilogue

I understand I'm on the road
Where all that was is gone
So where to now St. Peter
Show me which road I'm on.

—Where to Now St. Peter?
(Elton John with lyrics by Bernie Taupin)

During my 2018 summer trip across Canada with my kids, my fiancé (who joined us in Alberta), and our antique VW Westfalia, we saw a lot of beautiful sites. The splendour of God's glory was magnificently visible at such places as Takakkaw Falls in British Columbia, the Bow Valley of Alberta, the abundant and richly yielding prairie lands of Saskatchewan, and the over 100 meter deep West Hawk Lake in Manitoba—great for a swim. Yet the threat of climate change, to both humanity and the earth itself, also was powerfully visible as we drove down the Trans-Canada Highway. This struck me more than the obviously majestic mountains comprising the Canadian Rockies during our sojourn in the wilderness. We bore witness to wildfires near French River and Perry Sound, Ontario. We saw their devastating and almost unstoppable force again in British Columbia, when Highway 93 through the Kootenay

Rockies was closed. And when it was opened after we bypassed it en route to the towns of Golden and Radium Hot Springs, we finally traversed it on the way back to Alberta and were astounded at the heavy smoke permeating the air, along with the incessant churn of helicopter rotors as they carried bucket after bucket of water to fight nature's wrath.

On August 8, when we headed for Calgary to overnight and meet an old friend of mine who is dean of a university department, we were similarly astounded to find that city surrounded by smoke. My old friend Jennifer said she usually could see the mountains from her home and had never seen things this bad in terms of smoke and air quality. That was no surprise considering a Regina newspaper I read during our trip indicated countries all over the world, such as Sweden, Japan, Portugal, the US, South Korea and so many more, were experiencing unprecedented heat waves. Never mind that half of California seemed to be on fire when I caught a brief glimpse of the news during one of the nights we were not camping but staying in a hotel instead. Despite all the ominous catastrophes of late, the wildfires, flooding and tornadoes that also appear to have been terrifying people, I have remained faithful to the notion that good and informed people can help avert the calamity that may face us sooner than we expect.

Since most people are good spirits, we met a lot of great and caring individuals during our journey across Canada. For instance, when our old VW sputtered and backfired as we entered Winnipeg, Manitoba, after camping in Aaron Provincial Park in Ontario, the hotel clerk at Homewood Suites kindly provided us with directions to the local VW dealership. A friendly service person there then gave us further directions to Frank's Motors, which specializes in repairing unusual rides such as ours. The VW dealership employee even called Frank's Motors ahead of time to let them know we were going to sputter our way over ASAP. We made it to Frank's on Notre Dame and they gave us a free ride back to our hotel and had Gerda ('Mystery Machine' also works), the quirky nickname given to our stout German mode of transportation, fixed by nine o'clock the next morning. Apparently the screw securing her distributor had come loose, throwing her usually impeccable timing out of whack—you gearheads know what I am talking about. The hotel gave us a free ride in their shuttle to join Gerda after she was repaired, just as they had given us one the evening before to downtown Winnipeg so we could take in some lovely sites, such as the Forks.

I can tell you that it is absolutely appropriate that drivers from Manitoba have license plates bearing the slogan *Friendly Manitoba*. My belief in that, as well as the good in most people, was reinforced the day after Frank's Motors repaired our van. By the way, Kyle is a great guy there. East of Moose Jaw, Saskatchewan, and headed for Calgary from Regina (both great cities like Winnipeg too), I lost complete engine power and found myself at the side of the Trans-Canada Highway going nowhere fast. With two small children in tow, quickly getting disappointed, the pit in my stomach grew appreciably fast. Some of you may have heard of a book called *Zen and the Art of Motorcycle Maintenance* written by Robert M. Pirsig. Well, I certainly felt I was living it outside of Moose Jaw, especially when swapping ignition coils, checking the throttle cable that joined the dual carburetors, etc. did not provide me with any clear solution to get back in the saddle and through the prairies.

They say that asking for help is a sign of strength rather than weakness. My fiancé has helped me much in that regard. So after spending about 20 fruitless minutes trying to get old Gerda's engine to turn over, and intent on picking up Donna at the Calgary Airport in the early evening, I humbly decided to pray for divine intervention while simultaneously waving my hands at any and all forms of westbound traffic like some lunatic from Ontario. Fortunately and within two minutes of my flailing about, a fellow on his trusty Harley Davidson steed stopped to assist us. His name was Leonard and, you guessed it, he was from Manitoba—Winnipeg to be precise! Within a few minutes he diagnosed that the set of ignition points in my old school distributor was not moving and found that a tiny, almost minuscule ceramic looking part, had broken in the points. That basically meant no spark was going to any of the cylinders in the engine to keep it chugging along. Yes, I had an extra set of those $14.99 points, having planned for some mechanical problems along the way. I also had the flashlight and tools Leonard used to get Gerda to fire up within 30 minutes of the engine having initially quit.

True to the slogan of *Friendly Manitoba*, Leonard insisted on not accepting any money or gifts in exchange for the fantastic and invaluable assistance he gave us on August 4 in the middle of nowhere. He just asked us to 'pay it forward' to someone else in need one day. Ironically, we actually helped a stranded motorcyclist with a flat tire in the Margaree Valley on Cape Breton Island, Nova Scotia, during a prior trip in Gerda during 2015. Individuals such as Leonard, or Zoe who we met at Camper Jam 2018 in Golden, BC, and who insisted on checking the gap was set right in our new set of points in the distributor (you guessed right, Leonard, and just ended up on the high end of the permissible range without the feeler gauge), along with the others I mentioned, remind me how most people are decent folks. And you have to give credit to all those women like Zoe who can fix their own VW Kombi ride after a fire in the engine bay or adjust a set of distributor points. That's some girl power!

I would be quite naïve to believe that there are no bad people in the world. When we were proceeding through a yield sign in downtown Canmore, Alberta, on the evening of August 7 and a car plowed into Gerda's rear end, pushing her heavy duty bumper into her original paint and crumpling her tough steel such that the left taillight was shattered into hundreds of pieces, I was quickly reminded of those who like to blame others for problems they are responsible for creating. To wit. When we got out of our van with my kids screaming and crying, the lady who hit us immediately began blaming us for obeying a yield sign and causing the accident. She never apologized or expressed concern over the sobbing children who could have been hurt (thankfully they were wearing their seatbelts and were okay). Instead she said, "I don't give a shit" and continued the blame game. After getting her license plate and firing up our own reliable VW, which incidentally has its engine in the back near where we were hit, we drove the two minutes up the road to our accommodations. One needs to be in a safe environment with the children.

The attendants at the Stoneridge Mountain Resort were wonderful, genuinely concerned about the terrified state Ryan and Maya were in. They followed up with the police for me and even came out to help assess the damage, suggesting I take photos of Gerda's bruises while they held a flashlight. The resort was a treat for the kids, a kind of reward for the family making it across Canada in our old VW camper and roughing it in the bush a few times. The behaviour of the resort attendants renewed my faith in the goodness of most people, and hopefully it has been a learning experience for my children too. I cannot say the lady who rammed our vehicle and swore at us is a bad person. I do not know her or what she is like. However, the incident served as a red flag that we should all be wary of the blame game and fake news. It may not be such a big deal regarding a fender bender where nobody involved was hurt. But imagine when people in positions of authority, such as prime ministers and presidents, engage in blaming others for major problems they have created themselves or allowed to fester.

Imagine the fake news and optics management used to beguile ordinary citizens by such people. We must be on guard to ensure that such individuals, those who play a role rather than perform it responsibly, never ascend to power or remain in positions of power if they reach such heights. The risks to us all are too great. Light must always be shed on that which is wrong so good can prevail. And it can. We are not all knowing or all seeing like our maker, whomever or whatever that force, often called God, may be. But the individual constituents of the greater body politic are largely good, desiring to exercise free will responsibly, based on personal honour like our Indigenous brothers and sisters, and fundamental laws meant to advance and support civil society and democracy, for everyone's benefit. We must not forget this. For in actively supporting the greater good, by ensuring informed and right-minded decision-making occurs within the halls of power—the government—all things can be restored. Flags can be mended, the world can be healed. This eternal truth should be heeded, observed as soon as possible by everyone, lest the fires and other devastation associated with climate change, and the folly of poor decision-making, consume and curse us all.

Grandfather,
Sacred one,
Teach us love, compassion,
and honor.
That we may heal the earth
And heal each other.

—Ojibway Prayer

Notes

Introduction

1   Justin Tang, "Canada a nation of 'distrusters,' but puts credence in journalists and runs trustworthy companies, Vancouver Sun, February 21, 2018, https://vancouversun.com/news/local-news/canada-a-nation-of-distrusters-but-puts-credence-in-journalists-and-runs-trustworthy-companies.

2   Tang, "Canada a nation of 'distrusters.'"

3   Susanna Moodie, *Roughing It in the Bush; or Life in Canada* (Toronto: McClelland & Stewart Inc., 1989): 287.

Chapter 1: Who am I?

1   History.com Editors, "Great Purge," *History*, https://www.history.com/topics/russia/great-purge.

2   Aleksandr I. Solzhenitsyn, *The Gulag Archipelago, Vol. 1: An Experiment in Literary Investigation* (New York: Harper Perennial Modern Classics, Reissue edition, 2007), 4.

3   Robert Conquest, *The Harvest of Sorrow: Soviet Collectivization and the Terror-Famine* (New York: Oxford University Press, 1986), 4.

4   Conquest, *The Harvest of Sorrow*, 3.

5   Devine Watkins, "Pope Francis recalls Ukraine Holodomor famine," *Vatican News*, November 25, 2018,

https://www.vaticannews.va/en/pope/news/2018-11/pope-francis-ukraine-holodomor-genocide.html.

6   Alexander I. Solzhenitsyn, *One Day in the Life of Ivan Denisovich*, Translated by Max Hayward and Ronald Hingley, Introduction by Max Hayward and Leopold Labedz (Toronto, New York: Bantam Books, 1981-1988), 25.

7   "USFA Mission," https://www.usarmygermany.com/Sont_USFA.htm.

8   "The Benes Decrees: A Spectre over Central Europe," *The Economist*, August 15, 2002, https://www.economist.com/europe/2002/08/15/a-spectre-over-central-europe.

9   George Putic, "How WWI Changed the Map of Europe," *Voice of America*, August 1, 2014, https://www.voanews.com/a/how-wwi-changed-the-map-of-europe/1970075.html.

10 Putic, "WWI Changed the Map."

11 Nigel Roberts, "Chernobyl: Fact and legacy," *Belarus Digest*, April 18, 2016, https://belarusdigest.com/story/chernobyl-fact-and-legacy/.

12 Mikhail Sokolov and Anastasia Kirilenko, "20 Years Ago, Russia Had Its Biggest Political Crisis Since the Bolshevik Revolution," *The Atlantic*, October 4, 2013, https://www.theatlantic.com/international/archive/2013/10/20-years-ago-russia-had-its-biggest-political-crisis-since-the-bolshevik-revolution/280237/.

13 Sokolov and Kirilenko, "20 Years Ago."

14 BBC Monitoring, "North Korea Country Profile - Overview," *BBC News*, https://www.bbc.com/news/world-asia-pacific-15258878.

15 Christian Caryl, "South Korea shows the world how democracy is done," *Washington Post*, March 10, 2017, https://www.washingtonpost.com/news/democracy-post/wp/2017/03/10/south-korea-shows-the-world-how-democracy-is-done/?utm_term=.dbb733534216.

16 Caryl, "South Korea shows the world."

17 Caryl, "South Korea shows the world."

18 "Ambassador's Greeting," *Embassy of the Republic of Korea to Canada*, http://overseas.mofa.go.kr/ca-en/wpge/m_5229/contents.do.

19 Jessica Vomiero, "Trump says he, Kim Jong Un 'fell in love' after North Korean leader wrote him 'beautiful letters,'" *Global News*, September

30, 2018, https://globalnews.ca/news/4501536/trump-kim-jong-un-fell-in-love/.

20 Brian Kenety, "Czechoslovakia: 'Island of Democracy' and refuge between the wars," *Radio Praha*, October 20, 2005, https://www.radio.cz/en/section/panorama/czechoslovakia-island-of-denocracy-and-refuge-between-the-wars.

21 Kenety, "Czechoslovakia: Island of Democracy."

22 History Online Virtual Exhibit (Long Text), "The 'Velvet Revolution,'" *Radio Prague*, http://interconnected.org/notes/2004/11/prague/mirrors/archiv.radio.cz/history/history14.html, 14 of 15.

23 Jiří Pehe, "Czechoslovakia after 25 Years: Democracy without Democrats," *Europe for Citizens*, https://eu.boell.org/sites/default/files/uploads/.../democracy_without_democrats.pdf.

24 Pehe, "Czechoslovakia after 25 Years."

25 Pehe, "Czechoslovakia after 25 Years."

26 Pehe, "Czechoslovakia after 25 Years."

27 A.J. Jacobs, *Automotive FDI in Emerging Europe: Shifting Locales in the Motor Vehicle Industry* (London: Macmillan, 2017), 165-167.

28 Daniela Lazarova, "Citing Respekt " *Radio Prague*, 1999

29 Lazarova, "Citing Respekt"

30 "Update," Crain Communications Inc., September 9, 1997

31 Michiko Kakutani, "Critics Notebook; The Writers Who Shook a Government," *New York Times*, February 8, 1990, https://www.nytimes.com/1990/02/08/books/critic-s-notebook-the-writers-who-shook-a-government.html.

32 Insurance Bureau of Canada (IBC), *Facts of the Property and Casualty Insurance Industry in Canada: 2017* (39th edition, 2017 Spring): 1, http://www.ibc.ca/ns/resources/industry-resources/insurance-fact-book.

33 *Facts of the Property and Casualty Insurance Industry in Canada: 2017*, 9.

34 IBC, *Facts of the Property and Casualty Insurance Industry in Canada: 2017*, 4.

35 Frank Holmes, "The 'Black Swan' Author Just Issued a Powerful Warning About Global Debt," *Forbes*, November 5, 2018, https://www.forbes.com/sites/greatspeculations/2018/11/05/ the-black-swan-author-just-issued-a-powerful-warning-about-global-debt/#1 1eb209f4405.

36 "The origins of the financial crisis—Crash course," *The* Economist, September 7, 2013 (from the print edition), https://elearning.unito.it/sme/pluginfile.php/.../Economist_FinancialCrisis_sept13.pdf.

37 "The Financial Crisis Inquiry Report—Final Report of the national Commission on the Causes of the Financial and Economic Crisis in the United States," *The Financial Crisis Inquiry Commission*, U.S. Government Printing Office (Washington), February 25, 2011: xi, https://www.gpo.gov/fdsys/pkg/GPO-FCIC/pdf/GPO-FCIC.pdf.

38 "Financial Crisis Inquiry Report," xv.

39 "Financial Crisis Inquiry Report," xvi

40 "Financial Crisis Inquiry report," xvi

41 "Financial Crisis Inquiry Report," xvi

42 "Financial Crisis Inquiry Report," xvii

43 "Financial Crisis Inquiry Report," xvii

44 Reporting contributed by Liz Alderman, James Kanter, Jim Yardley, Jack Ewing, Niki Kitsantonis, Suzanne Daley, Karl Russell, Andrew Higgins and Peter Eavis, "Explaining Greece's Debt Crisis," *New York Times*, June 17, 2016, https://www.nytimes.com/interactive/2016/business/international/greece-debt-crisis-euro.html.

45 Simon Kuper, "How Greeks have adjusted to the forever crisis," *Financial Times*, July 6, 2017, https://www.ft.com/content/afcdd464-6109-11e7-8814-0ac7eb84e5f1.

Chapter 2: Who are We?

1 Brooke Jeffrey, *Dismantling Canada—Stephen Harper's New Conservative Agenda* (Montreal & Kingston: McGill-Queens University Press, 2015), 327.

2 Jeffrey, *Dismantling Canada*, 328.

3 John Conway, "What is Canada? 'If our centenary celebration is to mean anything, it must be about what we are, rather than about what we are not. And this problem of our identity we have yet to solve," *The Atlantic*, November 1964 Issue, https://www.theatlantic.com/magazine/archive/1964/11/what-is-Canada/303703/.

4 Conway, "What is Canada?"

5   Guy Lawson, "Trudeau's Canada, Again—With support from President Obama and the legacy of his father on his side, Justin Trudeau sets out to redefine what it means to be Canadian," *The New York Times Magazine*, December 8, 2015, https://www.nytimes.com/2015/12/13/magazine/trudeaus-canada-again.html.

6   Aaron Wherry, "How do you screen beliefs? The troublesome task of testing for 'anti-Canadian values'," *CBC News*, September 4, 2016, https://www.cbc.ca/news/politics/wherry-leitch-values-1.3746846.

7   Wherry, "How do you screen beliefs?"

8   Wherry, "How do you screen beliefs?"

9   Conway, "What is Canada?"

10   Conway, "What is Canada?"

11   Conway, "What is Canada?"

12   Jeffrey, *Dismantling Canada*, 328.

13   Andrew Cohen, *The Unfinished Canadian, The People We Are* (Toronto: McClelland & Stewart Ltd., 2007), 4.

14   Cohen, *Unfinished Canadian*, 222.

15   John Ralston Saul, *A Fair Country: Telling Truths About Canada* (Toronto: Penguin Group—Canada, 2008), 173.

16   Saul, *A Fair Country*, 173.

17   Saul, *A Fair Country*, 174.

18   Saul, *A Fair Country*, 174.

19   Saul, *A Fair Country*, 209.

20   Saul, *A Fair Country*, 217.

21   Saul, *A Fair Country*, 222.

22   Saul, *A Fair Country*, 217.

23   Saul, *A Fair Country*, 4.

24   Saul, *A Fair Country*, 280.

25   Saul, *A Fair Country*, 280.

26   Saul, *A Fair Country*, 107.

27   Chelsea Vowel, *Indigenous Writes: A Guide to First Nations, Métis & Inuit Issues in Canada* (Winnipeg: High Water Press, 2016), 43

28   Vowel, *Indigenous Writes*, 43.

29   Vowel, *Indigenous Writes*, 120.

30   Vowel, *Indigenous Writes*, 260.

31   Vowel, *Indigenous Writes*, 261.

32   Vowel, *Indigenous Writes*, 49.

33   Truth and Reconciliation Commission of Canada website, Residential Schools, http://www.trc.ca/websites/trcinstitution/index.php?p=4.

34   Vowel, *Indigenous Writes*, 171.

35   Vowel, *Indigenous Writes*, 16.

36   Haudenosaunee Confederacy website, About Us, Confederacy's Creation, https://www.haudenosauneeconfederacy.com/confederacys-creation/.

37   Haudenosaunee Confederacy website, About Us, The League of Nations, https://www.haudenosauneeconfederacy.com/the-league-of-nations/.

38   ms Nancy (author / blogger), "First Nations Governance" Section, http://firstpeoplesvoices.com/beginning.htm#governance.

39   Nancy, "Governance."

40   Haudenosaunee Confederacy website, About Us, Who We Are, https://www.haudenosauneeconfederacy.com/who-we-are/.

41   Haudenosaunee Confederacy website, About Us, Who We Are.

42   Haudenosaunee Confederacy website, About Us, The League of Nations.

43   Haudenosaunee Confederacy website, About Us, Values, https://www.haudenosauneeconfederacy.com/values/.

44   Haudenosaunee Confederacy website, About Us, Values.

45   Nancy, "Governance."

46   Nancy, "Governance."

47   Nancy, "Governance."

48   Nancy, "Governance."

49   Nancy, "Governance."

50   ms Nancy (author / blogger), "Morality" Section, http://firstpeoplesvoices.com/morality.htm.

51   Nancy, "Morality" Section.

52   Allison Loat and Michael MacMillan, *Tragedy in the Commons: Former Members of Parliament Speak Out About Canada's Failing Democracy* (Vintage Canada Edition, 2015), 2.

53   Loat and MacMillan, *Tragedy*, 3.

54   Loat and MacMillan, *Tragedy*, 4.

55   Loat and MacMillan, *Tragedy*, 221.

56 Loat and MacMillan, *Tragedy*, 7.

57 Loat and MacMillan, *Tragedy*, 231.

58 Loat and MacMillan, *Tragedy*, 8.

59 Loat and MacMillan, *Tragedy*, 24.

60 Loat and MacMillan, *Tragedy*, 24.

61 Loat and MacMillan, *Tragedy*, 223.

62 Loat and MacMillan, *Tragedy*, 223.

63 Loat and MacMillan, *Tragedy*, 107.

64 Loat and MacMillan, *Tragedy*, 202.

65 Michael Adams, *Fire and Ice—The United States, Canada and the Myth of Converging Values* (City?? Penguin Group—Canada, 2003), 13.

66 Adams, *Fire and Ice*, 37.

67 Adams, *Fire and Ice*, 39.

68 Adams, *Fire and Ice*, 74.

69 Adams, *Fire and Ice*, 76.

70 Adams, *Fire and Ice*, 111.

71 Adams, *Fire and Ice*, 122.

72 Cohen, *Unfinished Canadian*, 162.

Chapter 3: Betrayal

1 Timothy Snyder, *On Tyranny—Twenty Lessons from the Twentieth Century* (New York: Tim Duggan Books, an imprint of the Crown Publishing Group, a division Penguin Random House LLC, 2017), 23-24.

2 Adnan R. Khan, "In Turkey, Recep Tayyip Erdogan faces a make-or-break year," *Maclean's*, December 27, 2018, https://www.macleans.ca/opinion/in-turkey-recep-tayyip-erdogan-faces-a-make-or-break-year/.

3 Khan, "In Turkey."

4 Snyder, *On Tyranny*, 24.

5 Michelle Zilio, "Phoenix pay system problems on track to cost government $2.2-billion: report," *The Globe and Mail*, July 31, 2018, https://www.theglobeandmail.com/politics/article-phoenix-pay-system-problems-on-track-to-cost-government-22-billion/.

6 Rosa Marchitelli, "Homeowner begs for leniency after BMO threatens foreclosure following Phoenix pay problems," *CBC News*, June 5, 2017,

https://www.cbc.ca/news/canada/edmonton/phoenix-pay-problems-bmo-foreclosure-1.4142184.

7   Marchitelli, "Homeowner begs."

8   Alex Ballingall, "Phoenix pay fiasco will take years, cost more than half-billion dollars to fix, auditor general says," *The Star*, November 21, 2017, https://www.thestar.com/news/canada/2017/11/21/phoenix-pay-fiasco-will-take-years-cost-more-than-half-billion-dollars-to-fix-auditor-general-says.html.

9   Ballingall, "Phoenix pay fiasco."

10 Julie Ireton, "Confusion reigns at pay centre as Phoenix deadline looms," *CBC News*, January 17, 2018, https://www.cbc.ca/news/canada/ottawa/phoenix-deadline-overpayments-confusion-pay-centre-1.4489882.

11 Ireton, "Confusion reigns."

12 Ireton, "Confusion reigns."

13 The Canadian Press, "'We have no choice': Liberals pour $142M into Phoenix pay system in hopes of fixing boondoggle," *National Post*, May 25, 2017, https://nationalpost.com/news/politics/we-have-no-choice-liberals-pour-142m-into-phoenix-pay-system-in-hopes-of-fixing-boondoggle.

14 Susan Burgess, "Phoenix fix approaching $1B as feds look at scrapping system," *CBC News*, February 27, 2018, https://www.cbc.ca/news/canada/ottawa/phoenix-eventually-replaced-federal-budget-2018-1.4554399.

15 Burgess, "Phoenix fix approaching $1B."

16 Matthew McClearn, "Unsafe to Drink," *The Globe and Mail*, February 20, 2017, https://www.theglobeandmail.com/news/water-treatment-plants-fail-on-reserves-across-canada-globe-reviewfinds/article34094364/.

17 Vowel, *Indigenous Writes*, 219.

18 CBC News Staff, "Edmonton activist calls for more research on killers of Indigenous women," *CBC News*, January 15, 2019, https://www.cbc.ca/news/canada/edmonton/muriel-stanley-venne-indigenous-killer-1.4978932.

19 CBC News Staff, "Edmonton activist calls for more."

20 CBC News Staff, "Edmonton activist calls for more."

21 CBC News Staff, "Edmonton activist calls for more."

22 Andrew Rankin, "Auditor general called out Ottawa months before Eskasoni crisis," *The Chronicle Herald*, January 21, 2019, https://www.thechronicleherald.ca/news/local/auditor-general-called-out-ottawa-months-before-eskasoni-crisis-277722/.

23 Rankin, "Auditor general called out Ottawa."

24 Rankin, "Auditor general called out Ottawa."

25 Rankin, "Auditor general called out Ottawa."

26 Laura Kane (The Canadian Press), "'You're a liar': indigenous people voice anger at Trudeau town hall in B.C.," *City News*, January 10, 2019, https://toronto.citynews.ca/2019/01/10/indigenous-people-angry-at-trudeau/.

27 Kane, "'You're a liar.'"

28 Tim Harper, "Bureaucracy blocks road to reconciliation," *Toronto Star*, November 3, 2017, A7.

29 Colin Kenny, "National Shipbuilding Strategy hobbling Atlantic and Pacific fleets," *The Guardian*, January 24, 2018, https://www.theguardian.pe.ca/opinion-canada-cant-refuel-its-own-ships-180035/.

30 Kenny, "Shipbuilding Strategy."

31 Kenny, "Shipbuilding Strategy."

32 Andrew Coyne, "Mark Norman's treatment made even more outrageous by strong whiff of politics," *National Post*, January 19, 2018, https://nationalpost.com/opinion/andrew-coyne-mark-normans-treatment-made-even-more-outrageous-by-strong-whiff-of-politics.

33 Coyne, "Mark Norman's treatment."

34 J.L. Granatstein, "If we can't defend ourselves, are we truly sovereign?," *The Globe and Mail*, January 26, 2018, https://www.theglobeandmail.com/opinion/if-we-cant-defend-ourselves-are-we-truly-sovereign/article37746320/.

35 Granatstein, "If we can't defend."

36 Andrew Coyne, "Fighter jet mess reeks of politics, deceit and cowboy economics," December 13, 2017, https://nationalpost.com/opinion/andrew-coyne-fighter-jet-mess-reeks-of-politics-deceit-and-cowboy-economics.

37 Granatstein, "If we can't defend."

38 Granatstein, "If we can't defend."

39 Granatstein, "If we can't defend."

40 Gloria Galloway, "Veteran sues Ottawa over pension-payment delays,"
    The Globe and Mail, July 4, 2017, https://www.theglobeandmail.com/
    news/politics/veteran-sues-ottawa-over-pension-payment-delays/
    article35550905/.

41 Galloway, "Veteran sues Ottawa."

42 Murray Brewster, "Ex-soldier and cancer survivor evicted during wait
    for military pension," CBC News, March 31, 2017, https://www.cbc.ca/
    news/politics/soldier-evicted-military-pension-1.3972723.

43 Brewster, "Ex-soldier and cancer survivor,"

44 David Pugliese, "Emails sink job for veterans' advocate," National Post,
    September 20, 2017, A4.

45 Pugliese, "Emails sink job."

46 Pugliese, "Emails sink job."

47 Pugliese, "Emails sink job."

48 Rob Gillies (The Associated Press), "Widow of U.S. soldier
    seeking Omar Khadr's $10.5M payout from Canada," Global
    News, July 5, 2017, http://globalnews.ca/news/3576317/
    omar-khadr-widow-of-American-soldier-afghanistan/.

49 Gillies, "Widow of U.S. soldier."

50 Gillies, "Widow of U.S. soldier."

51 Gillies, "Widow of U.S. soldier."

52 John Ibbitson, "Khadr is to Trudeau what the census was to Harper,"
    The Globe and Mail, July 19, 2017, https://www.theglobeandmail.com/
    opinion/khadr-is-to-trudeau-what-the-census-was-to-harper/
    article35736515/.

53 Gillies, "Widow of U.S. soldier."

54 Dean Beeby, "Report slams $5.6M Canadian program for Afghan
    women," CBC News, August 28, 2018, https://www.cbc.ca/news/
    politics/afghanistan-women-canada-global-affairs-banerjee-1.4800495.

55 Beby, "Report slams $5.6M Canadian program."

56 "Trudeau promises to meet with MP responsible for inviting Jaspal
    Atwal to events in India," CBC News, February 23, 2018, https://www.
    cbc.ca/news/politics/sarai-trudeau-atwal-meeting-1.4548705.

57 Candice Malcolm, "Backlog of Refugees: Government rush caused
    huge queue in private sponsorship program," news 24 hrs, 6.

58 Malcolm, "Backlog of Refugees."

59 Malcolm, "Backlog of Refugees."

60 Elizabeth Thompson, "Top CRA executives pocket $35,000 a year in performance pay," *CBC News*, January 30, 2018, https://www.cbc.ca/news/politics/taxes-cra-executives-performance-pay-1.4509390.

61 Thompson, "Top CRA executives pocket."

62 Bruce Campion-Smith, "Canada Revenue Agency unable to handle high call volumes: auditor general," *The Star (Ottawa Bureau)*, November 21, 2017, https://www.thestar.com/news/canada/2017/11/21/canada-revenue-agency-unable-to-handle-high-call-volumes-auditor-general.html.

63 Campion-Smith, "Canada Revenue Agency unable."

64 Campion-Smith, "Canada Revenue Agency unable."

65 Jason Proctor, "CRA slammed for 'reprehensible and malicious' prosecution of B.C. couple," *CBC News*, March 5, 2018, https://www.cbc.ca/news/canada/british-columbia/cra-tax-prosecution-malicious-injustice-1.4563235.

66 Proctor, "CRA slammed."

67 Proctor, "CRA slammed."

68 Proctor, "CRA slammed."

69 Dan Beeby, "Most CRA auditors polled say Canada's tax system is skewed to protect the wealthy," *CBC News*, August 17, 2018, https://www.cbc.ca/news/politics/cra-tax-avoidance-evasion-1.4787781.

70 Harvey Cashore, Dave Seglins, Kimberly Ivany, "Canada Revenue offered amnesty to wealthy KPMG clients in offshore tax 'sham,'" *CBC News*, March 8, 2016, https://www.cbc.ca/news/business/canada-revenue-kpmg-secret-amnesty-1.3479594.

71 Richard Poplak, "Export Development Canada is the Death Star in the Canadian economy," *The Globe and Mail*, March 9, 2018, https://www.theglobeandmail.com/opinion/article-export-development-canada-is-the-death-star-in-the-canadian-economy/.

72 Poplak, "Export Development Canada."

73 Poplak, "Export Development Canada."

74 Poplak, "Export Development Canada."

75 Poplak, Export Development Canada."

76 Siyabonga Hadebe, "Who benefited after KPMG 'died for the sins of others'?," *IOL*, October 15, 2018, https://www.iol.co.za/business-report/opinion/who-benefitted-after-kpmg-died-for-the-sins-of-others-17482727.

77 Ivan Semeniuk, "Troubled Waters," *The Globe and Mail*, June 12, 2017, A8-A9.

78 Semeniuk, "Troubled Waters."

79 Semeniuk, "Troubled Waters."

80 Mia Rabson, "More than 500 scientists demand improved pollution laws in Canada," *The Canadian Press*, February 12, 2018, https://www.680news.com/2018/02/12/more-than-500-scientists-demand-improved-pollution-laws-in-canada/.

81 Rabson, "More than 500 scientists."

82 Clare Hennig, "'Lied to and let down': Emotions run high in areas ravaged by B.C. wildfires," *CBC News*, August 29, 2018, https://www.cbc.ca/news/canada/british-columbia/emotions-running-hot-in-areas-ravaged-by-b-c-wildfires-1.4802263.

83 Hennig, "'Lied to and let down'."

84 Willow Smith, Karin Marley, Alison Masemann and Rosa Kim, "Is Canada one country or 13? Trudeau must end the Alberta-B.C. pipeline fight, says business leader," *CBC Radio, The Current*, February 8, 2017, https://www.cbc.ca/radio/thecurrent/the-current-for-thursday-february-8-2017-1.4524990/is-canada-one-country-or-13-trudeau-must-end-the-alberta-b-c-pipeline-fight-says-business-leader-1.4524995.

85 Smith et. al., "Is Canada one country or 13."

86 Allison McNeely and Kevin Orland, "Investors bail on landlocked Canadian oil as pipeline woes deepen," *Bloomberg News*, February 21, 2018, https://www.bnnbloomberg.ca/investors-bail-on-landlocked-canada-oil-as-pipeline-woes-deepen-1.1006080.

87 Smith et. al., "Is Canada one country or 13."

88 Francine Kopun, "Will 16,000 Sears Canada retirees see their pensions?," *Toronto Star*, January 20, 2018, https://www.thestar.com/business/2018/01/20/will-16000-sears-canada-retirees-see-their-pensions.html.

89 Kopun, "Will 16,000."

90 Kopun, "Will 16,000."

91 Kopun, "Will 16,000."

92 Kopun, "Will 16,000."

93 Kopun, "Will 16,000."

94 Les Whittington, *Spinning History: A Witness To Harper's Canada And 21ˢᵗ Century Choices* (Ottawa: Hill Time Books, 2015), 17.

95 Whittington, *Spinning History*, 17.

96 Whittington, *Spinning History*, 17.

97 Tori Weldon, "Hundreds of seasonal workers in Tracadie protest against EI changes," *CBC News*, February 12, 2018, https://www.cbc.ca/news/canada/new-brunswick/tracadie-protest-ei-1.4532004.

98 Jordan Press (The Canadian Press), "Federal analysis outlines how Liberals' extra EI benefit program topped $1.92-billion," *The Globe and Mail*, January 31, 2018, https://www.theglobe-andmail.com/report-on-business/economy/federal-analy-sis-outlines-how-liberals-extra-ei-benefit-topped-192-billion/article37801328/.

99 Press, "Federal analysis outlines how."

100 Andrew Jackson, "Why Canada needs progressive reforms in employ-ment insurance," *The Globe and Mail*, October 26, 2017, https://www.theglobeandmail.com/report-on-business/rob-commentary/why-canada-needs-progressive-reforms-in-employment-insurance/article36736240/.

101 Jackson, "Why Canada needs."

102 Jackson, "Why Canada needs."

103 Greg Weston, "EI financing agency spends millions doing nothing," *CBC News*, January 19, 2012, https://www.cbc.ca/news/politics/ei-financing-agency-spends-millions-doing-nothing-1.1137805.

104 Weston, "EI financing agency."

105 Weston, "EI financing agency."

106 Weston, "EI financing agency."

107 Weston, "EI financing agency."

108 Jackson, "Why Canada needs."

109 Jackson, Why Canada needs."

110 Simon Nixon, "Ten Years Later, Younger Workers Still Endure Costs of the Crisis," August 9, 2017, https://www.wsj.com/articles/ten-years-later-younger-workers-still-endure-costs-of-the-crisis-1502322224.

111 Trevor Dunn, "Tuition + rent + food = hard lesson for Toronto university students using food banks," *CBC News*, November 7, 2017, https://www.cbc.ca/news/canada/toronto/ryerson-campus-food-bank-1.4390357.

112 Dunn, "Tuition + rent."

113 Dunn, "Tuition + rent."

114 Staff -Canadian Press, "Liberals write off $200 million in outstanding student loans," *Global News*, February 18, 2018, https://globalnews.ca/news/4033006/liberals-write-off-student-loans/.

115 "Justin Trudeau, "On Fairness For The Middle Class," https://www.liberal.ca/realchange/justin-trudeau-on-fairness-for-the-middle-class/.

116 Daniel Tencer, "Canada's Major Cities Turning Into Islands Of Wealth, Poverty As Middle Class Disappears: Researchers," 02/06/18, https://www.huffingtonpost.ca/2018/02/06/canada-s-major-cities-turning-in-to-islands-of-wealth-poverty-as-middle-class-disappears-researchers_a_23353268/.

117 Tencer, "Canada's Major Cities."

118 Tencer, "Canada's Major Cities."

119 Tencer, "Canada's major Cities."

120 John Rieti, "Toronto Community Housing data paints 'grim' picture of future repair needs, mayor says," *CBC News*, May 23, 2017, https://www.cbc.ca/news/canada/toronto/tch-repairs-1.4128143.

121 Jennifer Pagliaro, "Law firm called in to investigate Toronto Community Housing Corp.'s HR practices," *Toronto Star*, January 29, 2018, https://www.thestar.com/news/city_hall/2018/01/29/law-firm-called-in-to-investigate-toronto-community-housing-corps-hr-practices.html.

122 Sue-Ann Levy, "Another boss exits scandal-plagued TCHC," *Toronto Sun*, April 24, 2017, https://torontosun.com/2017/04/24/tchc-boss-no-longer-with-the-agency/wcm/9f3a067a-100d-43c1-b22f-d28545431760.

123 Rieti, "Toronto Community Housing data."

124 Rieti, "Toronto Community Housing data."

125 Anna Mehler Paperny and Denny Thomas, "Canada provincial party elects new leader months before polls," *Reuters*, March 10, 2018, https://www.reuters.com/article/us-canada-politics-ontario/

canada-provincial-party-elects-new-leader-months-before-polls-idUSKCN1GN02E.

126 Levy, "Another boss exits."

127 Levy, "Another boss exits."

128 Levy, "Another boss exits."

129 Sue-Ann Levy, "TCHC board gobsmacked over ombudsman report," *Toronto Sun*, February 23, 2018, https://torontosun.com/news/local-news/levy-tchc-board-gobsmacked-over-ombudsman-report.

130 Levy, "TCHC board gobsmacked."

131 Pagliaro, "Law firm called in."

132 Matt Elliott, "Shelter Crisis is by design," *Metro News*, January 8, 2018, 3.

133 Elliott, "Shelter Crisis."

134 Elliott, "Shelter Crisis."

135 Elliott, "Shelter Crisis."

136 Lorrie Goldstein, "Wynne's Ontario? Oh are we ducked," *Toronto Sun*, June 1, 2017, https://torontosun.com/2017/05/31/wynnes-ontario-oh-are-we-ducked/wcm/ab4a0df8-cdbd-496d-a6fd-7dd011377c75.

137 Marc Montgomery, "It's the annual 'Teddy Awards': Government waste at its best (?)," *Radio Canada International*, February 19, 2018, https://www.rcinet.ca/en/2018/02/19/its-the-annual-teddy-awards-goverment-waste-at-its-best/.

138 Montgomery, "It's the annual 'Teddy Awards.'"

139 Andre Picard, "Ontario is courting a home-care fiasco," *The Globe and Mail*, March 1, 2018, https://www.theglobeandmail.com/opinion/ontario-is-courting-a-home-care-fiasco/article38175867/.

140 Picard, "Ontario is courting."

141 Picard, "Ontario is courting."

142 Picard, "Ontario is courting."

143 Picard, "Ontario is courting."

144 Bob Hepburn, "Where are the savings in Hoskins' health plan?," *Toronto Star*, March 15, 2017, https://www.thestar.com/opinion/commentary/2017/03/2015/where-are-the-savings-in-hoskins-health-plan-hepburn.html.

145 Hepburn, "Where are the savings."

146 Hepburn, "Where are the savings."

147 Darren Cargill, MD, "Bill 41, the Patients First Act, does not put patients first," *Windsor Star*, October 20, 2016, https://windsorstar.com/opinion/letters/bill-41-the-patients-first-act-does-not-put-patients-first.

148 Andre Picard, "The real health-care change we need? Strong leadership," *The Globe and Mail*, January 10, 2017, https://www.theglobeandmail.com/opinion/the-real-health-care-change-we-need-strong-leadership/article33557317/.

149 Picard, "The real health-care change."

150 Picard, "The real health-care change."

151 Cohen, *Unfinished Canadian*, 245.

152 Cohen, *Unfinished Canadian*, 188.

153 Jeffrey, *Dismantling Canada*, 289.

154 Cohen, *Unfinished Canadian*, 82-83.

155 Jeffrey, *Dismantling Canada*, 289.

156 Bacchus Barua, "Canada's health-care wait times hit new record high, again," *Maclean's*, December 7, 2017, https://www.macleans.ca/society/health/canadas-health-care-wait-times-hit-new-record-high-again/.

157 Barua, "Canada's health-care wait."

158 CIHI website, "Canadians continue to report longer wait times for care," February 16, 2017, https://www.cihi.ca/en/canadians-continue-to-report-longer-wait-times-for-care.

159 CIHI website, "Canadians continue to report."

160 Andre Picard, "The real challenge to Canada's health system is not wait times," *The Globe and Mail*, February 16, 2017, https://www.theglobeandmail.com/opinion/canada-must-address-the-problem-of-long-waits-for-medical-care/article34056251/.

161 Picard, "The real challenge."

162 Andre Picard, "Hallway medicine: Do we really need more hospital beds?," *The Globe and Mail*, November 7, 2017, https://www.theglobeandmail.com/opinion/hallway-medicine-do-we-really-need-more-hospital-beds/article36848856/.

163 Picard, "The real challenge."

164 Picard, "The real challenge."

165 Picard, "Hallway medicine."

166 Picard, "Hallway medicine."

167 Valerie Ouellet, Vik Adhopia, David McKie, "The Implant Files—'We're guinea pigs': Canada's oversight process for implanted medical devices stuns suffering patients," *CBC News*, November 26, 2018, https://www.cbc.ca/news/health/implanted-files-medical-devices-icij-1.4909196.

168 "Opioid deaths in Canada expected to hit 4,000 by end of 2017," *Canadian Press*, December 18, 2017, https://www.cbc.ca/news/health/opioid-deaths-canada-4000-projected-2017-1,4455518.

169 Staff -Canadian Press, "Opioid deaths."

170 Ibbitson, "Khadr is to Trudeau."

171 Whittington, *Spinning History*, ii (Forward).

172 Jeffrey, *Dismantling Canada*, 98.

173 Jeffrey, *Dismantling Canada*, 100.

174 CBC News Staff, "It's official – the Harper government muzzled scientists. Some say it's still happening," *CBC News*, March 23, 2018, https://www.cbc.ca/news/health/second-opinion-scientists-muzzled-1.4588913.

175 CBC News Staff, "It's official."

176 Jeffrey, *Dismantling Canada*, 149.

177 Whittington, *Spinning History*, 48.

178 Whittington, *Spinning History*, 49.

179 Whittington, *Spinning History*, 46.

180 Jeffrey, *Dismantling Canada*, 10.

181 Whittington, *Spinning History*, 46.

182 Bill Curry, "Federal budget may not win support, senator warns," *The Globe and Mail*, June 15, 2017, https://www.theglobeandmail.com/news/politics/federal-budget-may-not-win-senate-support-leader-warns/article35313166/.

183 Curry, "Federal budget."

Chapter 4: Mending the Flag

1   Andre Munro, "Populism political program or movement," *Britannica*, https://www.britannica.com/topic/populism.

2   Munro, "Populism."

3 Munro, "Populism."

4 David Molloy, "What is populism, and what does the term actually mean?," *BBC News*, March 6, 2018, https://www.bbc.com/news/world-43301423.

5 Molloy, "What is populism."

6 Heather Gautney, "On Leadership—What is Occupy Wall Street? The history of leaderless movements," *Washington Post*, October 10, 2011, https://www.washingtonpost.com/national/on-leadership/what-is-occupy-wall-street-the-history-of-leaderless-movements/2011/10/10gIQAwk-Fjal_story.html?utm_term=.2c891e34c0a8.

7 Jason Le Miere, "Rich People in America Have Too Much Money, Says the World's Second Richest Man, Warren Buffett," June 27, 2017, https://www.newsweek.com/rich-people-america-buffett-629456.

8 LaMiere, "Rich People in America."

9 Gautney, "Occupy Wall Street."

10 David Chazan, "Yellow vests call for France to hold regular referendums," December 17, 2018, https://www.telegraph.co.uk/news/2018/12/17/yellow-vests-call-france-hold-regular-referendums/.

11 Michael Levitin, "The Triumph of Occupy Wall Street," *The Atlantic*, June 10, 2015, https://www.theatlantic.com/politics/archive/2015/06/the-triumph-of-occupy-wall-street/395408/.

12 Gautney, "Occupy Wall Street."

13 Levitin, "The Triumph."

14 Tribune news services, "Measuring Occupy Wall Street's impact, 5 years later," *Chicago Tribune*, September 17, 2016, http://www.chicagotribune.com/news/nationworld/ct-occupy-wall-street-s-impact-20160917-story.html.

15 Levitin, "The Triumph."

16 Levitin, "The Triumph."

17 Justine Hunter, "A growing divide," *The Globe and Mail*, April 28, 2017, https://www.theglobeandmail.com/news/british-columbia/bcs-inequality-gap-widens-and-shapes-the-electioncampaign/article34857613/.

18 Hunter, "A growing divide."

19 Hunter, "A growing divide."

20 Hunter, "A growing divide."

21 Deborah Hardoon, "An Economy For The 99%," *OXFAM BRIEFING PAPER, JANUARY 2017*, Oxfam International (January 2017): 10.

22 Hardoon, "An Economy," 4.

23 Hardoon, "An Economy," 16.

24 Hardoon, "An Economy," 4.

25 Hardoon, "An Economy," 5.

26 Hardoon, "An Economy," 19.

27 Hardoon, "An Economy," 5.

28 Elizabeth Thompson, "Banking Industry has lobbied officials, MPs hundreds of times," *CBC News*, June 12, 2017, https://www.cbc.ca/news/politics/banks-finance-lobbying-government-1.4155703.

29 Robert Cribb and Marco Chown Oved, "Snow washing: Canada is the world's newest tax haven," *The Star*, January 25, 2017, https://projects.thestar.com/panama-papers/canada-is-the-worlds-newest-tax-haven/.

30 Cribb and Oved, "Snow washing."

31 Cribb and Oved, "Snow washing."

32 Cribb and Oved, "Snow washing."

33 Cribb and Oved, "Snow washing."

34 Cribb and Oved, "Snow washing."

35 Dean Beeby, "Canada's weak laws hobble identification of tax dodgers: document," *CBC News*, June 13, 2017, https://www.cbc.ca/news/politics/morneau-tax-havens-beneficial-ownership-uk-hammond-canada-revenue-agency-1.4157246.

36 Hardoon, "An Economy," 3.

37 Hardoon, "An Economy," 17.

38 Levon Sevunts, "More than 3,000 Canadian entities, 3 former PMs, named in Paradise Papers leak," November 6, 2017, https://www.rcinet.ca/en/2017/11/06/more-than-3000-canadian-entities-3-former-pms-named-in-paradise-papers-leak/.

39 Sevunts, More than 3,000.

40 Hardoon, "An Economy," 28.

41 Hardoon, "An Economy," 28.

42 Hardoon, "An Economy," 29.

43 Stephanie Levitz, "Poll suggests 'northern populism' brewing in Canada," *The Star*, June 25, 2017, https://www.thestar.com/news/

canada/2017/06/25/poll-suggests-northern-populism-brewing-in-canada.html.

44 Levitz, "Poll suggests."

45 Levitz, "Poll suggests."

46 Michael Swan, "Abuse and the dynamics of power," The Catholic Register, September 9, 2018, 5.

47 Sawn, "Abuse."

48 Jon Stone, "A slight increase in higher education could have kept Britain in the EU," *The Independent*, August 8, 2017, https://www.independent.co.uk/news/uk/politics/brexit-education-higher-university-study-university-leave-eu-remain-voters-educated-a7881441.html.

49 Jason Brennan, *Against Democracy* (Princeton, New Jersey: Princeton University Press, 2016), viii.

50 Brennan, *Against Democracy*, 3.

51 Brennan, *Against Democracy*, 6.

52 Brennan, *Against Democracy*, 24.

53 Brennan, *Against Democracy*, 84.

54 Brennan, *Against Democracy*, 84.

55 Brennan, *Against Democracy*, 84.

56 Brennan, *Against Democracy*, 84.

57 Brennan, *Against Democracy*, 25.

58 Bryan Caplan, *The Myth of the Rational Voter—Why Democracies Choose Bad Policies* (New Jersey: Princeton University Press, 2007), 5.

59 Caplan, *The Myth*, 2.

60 Caplan, *The Myth*, 141.

61 Caplan, *The Myth*, 79.

62 Caplan, *The Myth*, 195.

63 Caplan, *The Myth*, 64.

64 Caplan, *The Myth*, 197.

65 Brennan, *Against Democracy*, 14.

66 Brennan, *Against Democracy*, 208.

67 Brennan, *Against Democracy*, 226.

68 Brennan, *Against Democracy*, 142.

69 Brennan, *Against Democracy*, 143.

70 Brennan, *Against Democracy*, 245.

71 Brennan, *Against Democracy*, 139.

72 Brennan, *Against Democracy*, 143.

73 Brennan, *Against Democracy*, 227.

74 Caplan, *The Myth*, 5.

75 Christopher H. Achen & Larry M. Bartels, *Democracy for Realists— Why Elections Do Not Produce Responsive Government* (New Jersey: Princeton University Press, 2016), 327.

76 Achens & Bartels, *Democracy for Realists*, 116.

77 Achens & Bartels, *Democracy for Realists*, 16-17.

78 Achens & Bartels, *Democracy for Realists*, 4.

79 Achens & Bartels, *Democracy for Realists*, 264.

80 Achens & Bartels, *Democracy for Realists*, 299.

81 Achens & Bartels, *Democracy for Realists*, 139.

82 Achens & Bartels, *Democracy for Realists*, 116.

83 Achens & Bartels, *Democracy for Realists*, 299.

84 Achens & Bartels, *Democracy for Realists*, 299.

85 Achens & Bartels, *Democracy for Realists*, 299.

86 George Wolfe, "Parallel Teachings in Hinduism and Christianity," Jomar Press (1995): 1.

87 Wolfe, "Parallel Teachings," 3.

88 Wolfe, "Parallel Teachings," 4.

89 Wolfe, "Parallel Teachings," 12.

90 Wolfe, "Parallel Teachings," 16.

91 Alexis de Tocqueville, *Democracy in America,* Translated, edited and with an introduction by Harvey C. Mansfield and Delba Winthrop (London: The University of Chicago Press Ltd., 2000), xvii.

92 Tocqueville, *Democracy in America,* 145.

93 Tocqueville, *Democracy in America,* 249.

94 Tocqueville, *Democracy in America,* 249.

95 Achens & Bartels, *Democracy for Realists*, 284.

96 Achens & Bartels, *Democracy for Realists*, 301.

97 Achens & Bartels, *Democracy for Realists*, 328.

98 John Dewey, *Democracy and Education* (Mineola, New York: Dover Publications, 2004):29.

99 Dewey, *Democracy and Education*, 29.

100 Tocqueville, *Democracy in America,* 669.

101 Tocqueville, *Democracy in America,* 669.

102 Tocqueville, *Democracy in America,* 669.

103 Tocqueville, *Democracy in America,* 223.

104 Tocqueville, *Democracy in America,* 202.

105 Brennan, *Against Democracy,* 139.

106 Brennan, *Against Democracy,* 53.

107 Brennan, *Against Democracy,* 56.

108 Black Lives Matter website, What We
Believe, www.blacklivesmatter.com/about/what-we-belive/.

109 Idle No More website, The Story, http://www.idlenomore.ca/story.

110 Idle No More website, Calls For
Change, http://www.idlenomore.ca/calls_for_change.

Chapter 5: Fixing the Plumbing

1   Lex Sisney, "The 5 Classic Mistakes in Organizational Structure: Or,
How to Design Your Organization the Right Way," Excerpted from
Organizational Physics: The Science of Growing a Business, (2012-2014
Lex Sisney): 1, https://organizationalphysics.com/2012/01/09/the-5-
classic-mistakes-in-organizational-structure-or-how-to-design-your-
organization-the-right-way/.

2   Sisney, "The 5 Classic Mistakes," 1.

3   Sisney, "The 5 Classic Mistakes," 1.

4   Sisney, "The 5 Classic Mistakes," 2.

5   Sisney, "The 5 Classic Mistakes," 2.

6   Sisney, "The 5 Classic Mistakes," 2.

7   Sisney, "The 5 Classic Mistakes," 3.

8   Sisney, "The 5 Classic Mistakes," 4.

9   Sisney, "The 5 Classic Mistakes," 4.

10 Sisney, "The 5 Classic Mistakes," 4-6.

11 Cohen, *Unfinished Canadian,* 216-217.

12 Cohen, *Unfinished Canadian,* 76.

13 Cohen, *Unfinished Canadian,* 217.

14 Sisney, "The 5 Classic Mistakes," 4.

15 John Greenwood, "Canadian banks win top marks from
World Economic Forum," *Financial Post,* September 4,

2013, https://business.financialpost.com/news/fp-street/
canadian-banks-win-top-marks-from-world-economic-forum.

16 Tara Perkins, "Julie Dickson: Nobody's saviour, *ROB Magazine, The Globe and Mail*, April 17, 2009, https://www.theglobeandmail.com/
report-on-business/rob-magazine/julie-dickson-nobodys-saviour/
article4325785/.

17 Jessica Ward, "Pope Francis says no to clericalism," *mnnews today*,
October 4, 2018, https://mnnews.today/your-diocese/2018/
pope-francis-says-no-to-clericalism/.

18 International Democratic Union (IDU) website,
History, https://www.idu.org/about/history/.

19 International Democratic Union (IDU website, History.

20 Kevin Page, *Unaccountable—Truth and Lies on Parliament Hill*
(Toronto: Viking, an imprint of Penguin Canada Books, 2015), 10.

21 Page, *Unaccountable*, 14.

22 Page, *Unaccountable*, 12.

23 Page, *Unaccountable*, 15-17.

24 Raf Sanchez, "Christian sects drop their differences, and
their fists, to restore Jesus's tomb," *The Telegraph*, April
9, 2016, https://www.telegraph.co.uk/news/2016/04/09/
christian-sects-drop-their-differences-and-their-fists-to-restor/.

25 Sanchez, "Christian sects."

26 Stephen J. Harper, *Right Here, Right Now—Politics and Leadership in
the Age of Disruption* (Harper & Associates Consulting Inc., published
by Signal, a division of Random House Canada Limited, 2018), 12.

27 Harper, *Right Here, Right Now*, 2.

28 Harper, *Right Here, Right Now*, 15.

29 Harper, *Right Here, Right Now*, 55.

30 Harper, *Right Here, Right Now*, 71.

31 Harper, *Right Here, Right Now*, 87.

32 Bill Freeman, *Democracy Rising—Politics and Participation in Canada*
(Toronto: Dundurn Press, 2017), 171.

33 Freeman, *Democracy Rising*, 173.

34 Tocqueville, *Democracy in America*, 115.

35 Tocqueville, *Democracy in America*, 115.

36 Whittington, *Spinning History*, 6.

37 Elizabeth May, "On Westminster Parliamentary Democracy, Excerpted from *Turning Parliament Inside Out—Practical Ideas For Reforming Canada's Democracy*, Edited by Michael Chong, Scott Simms and Kennedy Stewart (Douglas and McIntyre, 2013 Ltd., 2017 by the authors), 17.

38 Brent Rathgeber, *Irresponsible Government—The Decline of Parliamentary Democracy in Canada* (Toronto: Dundurn Press, 2014), 20.

39 Rathgeber, *Irresponsible Government*, 96.

40 Rathgeber, *Irresponsible Government*, 33.

41 Rathgeber, *Irresponsible Government*, 44.

42 Rathgeber, *Irresponsible Government*, 97.

43 Rathgeber, *Irresponsible Government*, 99.

44 Loat and MacMillan, *Tragedy*, 197.

45 Page, *Unaccountable*, 15.

46 Page, *Unaccountable*, 90.

47 Page, *Unaccountable*, 126.

48 Page, *Unaccountable*, 128.

49 Page, *Unaccountable*, 131.

50 Page, *Unaccountable*, 132.

51 Page, *Unaccountable*, 163.

52 Page, *Unaccountable*, 7.

53 Page, *Unaccountable*, 6.

54 Page, *Unaccountable*, 175.

55 Page, *Unaccountable*, 177.

56 Page, *Unaccountable*, 181.

57 Page, *Unaccountable*, 181.

58 Page, *Unaccountable*, 181.

59 Page, *Unaccountable*, 199.

60 Page, *Unaccountable*, 56.

61 Harper, *Right Here, Right Now*, 78.

62 Harper, *Right Here, Right Now*, 77.

63 Harper, *Right Here, Right Now*, 77-78.

64 Harper, *Right Here, Right Now*, 79-80.

65 Page, *Unaccountable*, 153.

66 Department of Justice Canada, *A consolidation of The Constitution Acts 1867 to 1982, Consolidated as of January 1, 2013* (Her Majesty the Queen in Right of Canada, represented by the Minister of Public Works and Government Services, 2012): 3.

67 Justice Canada, "The Constitution Acts," 3.

68 Justice Canada, "The Constitution Acts," 3-4.

69 Justice Canada, "The Constitution Acts," 19.

70 Justice Canada, "The Constitution Acts," 26.

71 Moodie, *Roughing It in the* Bush, 268.

72 Moodie, *Roughing It in the Bush*, 11.

73 Under the direction of Ramsay Cook and Real Belanger, *Canada's Prime Ministers: MacDonald to Trudeau—Portraits from the Dictionary of Canadians Biography* (Toronto: University of Toronto Press, Universite Laval, 2007), 327.

74 Cook and Belanger, *Canada's Prime Ministers*, 372.

75 Cook and Belanger, *Canada's Prime Ministers*, 424.

76 Cook and Belanger, *Canada's Prime Ministers*, 258.

77 Justice Canada, "The Constitution Acts," 63.

78 Justice Canada, "The Constitution Acts," 64.

79 Justice Canada, "The Constitution Acts," 55.

80 Justice Canada, "The Constitution Acts," 56.

81 Government of Canada website, Privy Council Office, https://www.canada.ca/en/privy-council/corporate/mandate.html.

82 Government of Canada website, Privy Council Office.

83 Government of Canada website, Privy Council Office.

84 Government of Canada website, Privy Council Office.

85 Government of Canada website, Privy Council Office.

86 Kathryn May, "Brison says millennials will staff next 'golden age' of public service," *Ottawa Citizen*, February 15, 2016, https://ottawacitizen.com/news/national/brison-says-millenials-will-staff-next-golden-age-of-public-service.

87 May, "Brison says millennials will."

88 Government of Canada website, Privy Council Office.

89 Naomi Lakritz, "We can celebrate our future without ignoring the past," *Calgary Herald*, June 30, 2017,

https://calgaryherald.com/opinion/columnists/
lakritz-we-can-celebrate-our-future-without-ignoring-the-past.

90 Lakritz, "We can celebrate."

91 Lakritz, "We can celebrate."

92 Ruth Dantzer et al., "Risk Management for Canada and Canadians:
Report of the ADM Working Group on Risk Management," PCO
(March 2000): iv.

93 Dantzer et al., "Risk Management for Canada," iv.

94 Dantzer et al., "Risk Management for Canada," iv.

95 Dantzer et al., "Risk Management for Canada," iv.

96 Dantzer et al., "Risk Management for Canada," v.

97 Dantzer et al., "Risk Management for Canada," 11.

98 Dantzer et al., "Risk Management for Canada," 11.

99 Dantzer et al., "Risk Management for Canada," 13.

100 Government of Canada website, Treasury Board Secretariat,
Organization, https://www.canada.ca/en/treasury-board-secretariat/
corporate/risk-management.html.

101 Government of Canada website, Treasury Board
Secretariat, Framework for the Management of
Risk, https://www.tbs-sct.gc.ca/pol/doc-eng.aspx?=19422.

102 Government of Canada website, Treasury Board., Framework for the
Management of Risk.

103 Government of Canada website, Treasury Board., Framework for the
Management of Risk.

104 Government of Canada website, Treasury Board., Framework for the
Management of Risk.

105 Department of Finance Canada, *Government of
Canada Treasury Risk Management Framework*,
3, https://www.fin.gc.ca/treas/frame/tmrf08_1-eng.asp.

106 Government of Canada website, Canada and the world, Risk
Management, https://www.international.gc.ca/world-monde/fund-
ing-financement/risk_management-gestion_risques.aspx?lang=eng.

107 Government of Canada website, *Cabinet Committee
Mandate and Membership / Mandat et Composition
des Comites Du Cabinet*, January 29, 2018,
2, http://pm.gc.ca/sites/pm/files/.../cab_committee-comite.pdf.

108 Government of Canada website, Treasury Board Secretariat, Management Accountability Framework, https://www.canada.ca/en/treasury-board-secretariat/services/management-accountability-framework.html.

109 Government of Canada website, Reports of the Treasury Board of Canada Secretariat, Evaluation of the Management Accountability Framework, https://www.canada.ca/en/treasury-board-secretariat/corporate/reports/evaluation-management-accountability-framework.html.

110 Government of Canada website, Reports of the Treasury Board., Evaluation.

111 Privy Council Office, *Open and Accountable Government—2015* (Her Majesty he Queen in Right of Canada, 2015): 33., https://pm.gc.ca/eng/news/2015/11/27/open-and-accountable-government.

112 Privy Council Office, *Open and Accountable*, vii.

113 Privy Council Office, *Open and Accountable*, vii.

114 Privy Council Office, *Open and Accountable*, 7.

115 Privy Council Office, *Open and Accountable*, 69.

116 Privy Council Office, *Open and Accountable*, 70.

117 Privy Council Office, *Open and Accountable*, 54.

118 Privy Council Office, *Open and Accountable*, 8.

119 Privy Council Office, *Open and Accountable*, 33.

120 Privy Council Office, *Open and Accountable*, 34.

121 Privy Council Office, *Open and Accountable*, 43.

122 Privy Council Office, *2017-18 Departmental Plan* (Her Majesty he Queen in Right of Canada, 2017): 1., https://www.canada.ca/content/dam/pco-bcp/.../pdfs/dp-pm/dp-pm-2017-18-eng.pdf.

123 Privy Council Office, *2017-18 Departmental Plan*, 1.

124 Privy Council Office, *2017-18 Departmental Plan*, 3.

125 Privy Council Office, *2017-18 Departmental Plan*, 3.

126 Rathgeber, *Irresponsible Government*, 150.

127 Privy Council Office, *2017-18 Departmental Plan*, 3.

128 Privy Council Office, *2017-18 Departmental Plan*, 4.

129 Privy Council Office, *2017-18 Departmental Plan*, 7.

130 Privy Council Office, *2017-18 Departmental Plan*, 9.

131 Privy Council Office, *2017-18 Departmental Plan*, 25.

132 Privy Council Office, *2017-18 Departmental Plan*, 29.

133 James Bagnall, "Built to fail: Politics sabotaged Shared Services before the department got off the ground," *Ottawa Citizen*, November 11, 2016, https://ottawacitizen.com/news/national/built-to-crash-the-ugly-sputtering-beginning-of-shared-services-and-how-politics-conspired-against-it.

134 Bagnall, "Built to fail."

135 Bagnall, "Built to fail."

136 Bagnall, "Built to fail."

137 Bagnall, "Built to fail."

138 Bagnall, "Built to fail."

139 Bagnall, "Built to fail."

140 Bagnall, "Built to fail."

141 Bagnall, "Built to fail."

142 Bagnall, "Built to fail."

143 Bagnall, "Built to fail."

144 Bagnall, "Built to fail."

145 Bagnall, "Built to fail."

146 Ballingall, "Phoenix pay fiasco."

147 Kathryn May, "Jobs end for almost 1,000 public service pay advisers," *Ottawa Citizen*, October 16, 2014, https://ottawacitizen.com/news/politics/jobs-end-for-almost-1000-public-service-pay-advisers.

148 May, "Jobs end for almost 1,000."

149 Rick Gibbons, "Phoenix pay fiasco burns Miramichi and public servants alike," October 1, 2017, https://ottawasun.com/2017/10/01/phoenix-pay-fiasco-burns-miramichi-and-public-servants-alike/wcm/74e8b686-a1ae-4dd3-9ebb-bf3b0456e45.

150 Gibbons, "Phoenix pay fiasco burns."

151 Nick Faris, "Phoenix explained: Why federal civil servants aren't being paid," *National Post*, July 28, 2016, https://nationalpost.com/news/politics/phoenix-explained-why-federal-civil-servants-arent-being-paid.

152 Alex Ballingall, "Phoenix pay fiasco."

153 Alex Ballingall, "Phoenix pay fiasco."

154 Whittington, *Spinning History*, 60.

155 Andrew MacLeod et al., *Practice Guide—Coordinating Risk Management and Assurance* (The Institute of Internal Auditors, March

2012): 2., https://global.theiia.org/certification/Public_Documents/
Coordinating_Risk_Management_and_Assurance.pdf.

156 Macleod et al., *Practice Guide—Coordinating Risk management*, 1.

157 Shanon Donovan, Director, "Memorandum to the Heads of Executive
Departments and Agencies," M-16-17, Executive Office of the
President, Office of Management and Budget, Washinton, D.C., July
15, 2016, i., https://www.whitehouse.gov/sites/whitehouse.gov/files/
omb/.../2016/m-16-17.pdf.

158 Donovan, "Memorandum to the Heads." i.

159 Office of Management and Budget, Executive Office of the President
of the United States, *OMB Circular No. A-123, Management's
Responsibility for Enterprise Risk Management and Internal Control*
(Washington D.C.), 7., https://www.whitehouse.gov/sites/whitehouse.
gov/files/omb/.../2016/m-16-17.pdf.

160 Office of Management and Budget, *OMB Circular No. A-123*, 7.

161 Office of Management and Budget, *OMB Circular No. A-123*, 8.

162 Office of Management and Budget, *OMB Circular No. A-123*, 12.

163 Office of Management and Budget, *OMB Circular No. A-123*, 21.

164 Office of Management and Budget, *OMB Circular No. A-123*, 35.

165 John Palmer and Caroline Cerruti, *Is there a need to rethink the super-
visory process?* (The World Bank / BANCO DE ESPANA Eurosistema,
International Conference "Reforming Financial Regulation and
Supervision: Going Back to Basics," Madrid, June 15, 2009): 36,
http://documents.worldbank.org/curated/en/552861468054544285/
Is-there-a-need-to-rethink-the-supervisory-process.

166 Rathgeber, *Irresponsible Government*, 113.

167 Rathgeber, *Irresponsible Government*, 214.

168 Loat and MacMillan, *Tragedy*, 55.

169 Loat and MacMillan, *Tragedy*, 56.

170 Michael Harris, *Party of One—Stephen Harper and Canada's Radical
Makeover* (Toronto: Penguin, an imprint of Penguin Canada Books
Inc., a Penguin Random House Company, 2015), 310.

171 Justice Canada, "The Constitution Acts," 26.

172 Galloway, "Veteran sues Ottawa."

173 Jo-Anne Berezanski, "Comment: PM spoke of failures,
but what about change?," *Times Colonist*, September 27,

2017, https://www.timescolonist.com/opinion/op-ed/
comment-pm-spoke-of-failures-but-what-about-change-1.23033321.

174 Berezanski, "Comment: PM spoke."

175 Prime Minister Justin Trudeau, "Minister of Indigenous and Northern
Affairs Mandate Letter (November 12, 2015)," https://pm.gc.ca/eng/
minister-indigenous-and-northern-affairs-mandate-letter_2015.

176 Government of Canada website, Indigenous and Northern Affairs
Canada, https://www.canada.ca/en/indigenous-northern-affairs.html.

177 Paul Tasker, "'I worry about this': Trudeau's move to dissolve
Indigenous Affairs Department prompts concern," *CBC
News*, August 29, 2017, https://www.cbc.ca/news/politics/
trudeau-dissolve-indigenous-affairs-worried-1.4265842.

178 Tasker, "'I worry about this'."

179 Tasker, "'I worry about this'."

180 Elliott, "Shelter Crisis."

Chapter 6: Minding the Plumbers

1   Ernest Conine, "Soviet Privileged Class Is Under Fire: Perks of
Party Elite Confront Gorbachev With Dilemma," *Los Angeles Times*,
March 17, 1986, http://articles.latimes.com/1986-03-17/local/
me-22368_1_soviet-union.

2   Conine, "Soviet Privileged Class."

3   Kelly Hignett, "Power and Privilege: Elite Lifestyles in Communist
Eastern Europe," *The View East—Central and Eastern Europe, Past and
Present.*, https://thevieweast.wordpress.com/tag/privilege/.

4   Hignett, "Power and Privilege."

5   Hignett, "Power and Privilege."

6   Hignett, "Power and Privilege."

7   Hignett, "Power and Privilege."

8   Hignett, "Power and Privilege."

9   Hignett, "Power and Privilege."

10 Steven Erlanger, "Hitler, It Seems, Loved Money and Died Rich,"
The New York Times, August 8, 2002, https://wwwnytimes.
com/2002/08/08/world/hitler-it-seems-loved-money-and-died-rich.
html.

11 Lily Rothman, "Who Started the Reichstag Fire?," *Time*, February 27, 2015, http://time.com/3717003/reichstag-fire-1933/.

12 Alexander Hugh McDonald, "Tacitus—Roman Historian," *Encyclopedia Britannica*, https://www.britannica.com/biography/Tacitus-Roman-historian.

13 By Tacitus, Written 109 A.C.E., Translated by Alfred John Church and William Jackson Brodribb, *Annals*, Book XV, A.D. 62-65, http://classics.mit.edu/Tacitus/annals.11.xv.html.

14 PPBS, "The Great Fire of Rome - Background," http://www.pbs.org/wnet/secrets/great-fire-rome-background/1446/.

15 PBS, "The Great Fire."

16 Erlanger, "Hitler, It Seems."

17 Erlanger, "Hitler, It Seems."

18 Erlanger, "Hitler, It Seems."

19 Tawanda Majoni, "Zimbabwe: Grace Mugabe—The Curse Zimbabwe Needs," *NewZimbabwe.com*, November 8, 2017, https://allafrica.com/stories/201711080091.html.

20 Majoni, "Zimbabwe: Grace Mugabe."

21 Majoni, "Zimbabwe: Grace Mugabe."

22 Majoni, "Zimbabwe: Grace Mugabe."

23 Majoni, "Zimbabwe: Grace Mugabe."

24 Andrei Soldatov, "Putin Has Finally Reincarnated the KGB," *Foreign Policy*, September 21, 2016, https://foreignpolicy.com/2016/09/21/putin-has-finally-reincarnated-the-kgb-mgb-fsb-russia/.

25 Soldatov, "Putin Has Finally."

26 Soldatov, "Putin Has Finally."

27 Soldatov, "Putin Has Finally."

28 Soldatov, "Putin Has Finally."

29 Soldatov, "Putin Has Finally."

30 Soldatov, "Putin Has Finally."

31 Ingo Mannteufel, "Opinion: Vladimir Putin's great deceit," *Deutsche Welle*, March 18, 2018, https://www.dw.com/en/opinion-vladimir-putins-great-deceit/a-43032943.

32 Mannteufel, "Opinion: Vladimir Putin."

33 Mannteufel, "Opinion: Vladimir Putin."

34 Mary Hanbury and Aine sp accent ??? Cain, "Vladimir Putin may be the richest man in the world.," *Business Insider*, March 17, 2018, https://www.businessinsider.com/ how-putin-spends-his-mysterious-fortune-2017-6.

35 Hanbury and Cain, "Vladimir Putin."

36 David Marples, "Opinion: Putin not likely to soften with re-election," *Edmonton Journal*, March 27, 2018, https://edmontonjournal.com/ opinion/columnists/opinion-putin-not-likely-to-soften-with-re-election.

37 Marples, "Opinion: Putin not likely."

38 Snyder, *On Tyranny*, 13.

39 Snyder, *On Tyranny*, 24.

40 Justin Tang, "Canada a nation of 'distrusters."

41 Tom Byrnes, "The Federalists Paper #51," fd.valenciacollege.edu/file/jhelligso/federalist.pdf.

42 Byrnes, "The Federalists."

43 Byrnes, "The Federalists."

44 Pamela Newkirk, "Slavery and the contradictions of James Madison," *Washington Post*, January 5, 2018, https://www.washingtonpost. com/outlook/slavery-and-the-contradictions-of-james-madi- son/2018/01/03/3368716e-db88-11e7-b1a8-62589434a581_story. html?noredirect=on&utm_term=.73f6e22a2526.

45 Newkirk, "Slavery and the contradictions."

46 The Reverend Martin Luther King, "Martin Luther King's final speech: 'I've been to the mountaintop'—The full text," Memphis, Tenn., April 3, 1968, *ABC News*, https://abcnews.go.com/ Politics/martin-luther-kings-final-speech-ive-mountaintop-full/ story?id=18872817.

47 Byrnes, "The Federalists."

48 Byrnes, "The Federalists."

49 Byrnes, "The Federalists."

50 Byrnes, "The Federalists."

51 Byrnes, "The Federalists."

52 Tocqueville, *Democracy in America*, 151.

53 Tocqueville, *Democracy in America*, 114.

54 Tocqueville, *Democracy in America*, 119.

55   Mike De Souza, "Senior bureaucrats 'clinging' to Harper government rules and muzzling scientists, says survey," *National Observer*, February 21, 2018, https://www.nationalobserver.com/2018/02/21/news/senior-bureaucrats-clinging-harper-government-rules-and-muzzling-scientists-says.

56   De Souza, "Senior bureaucrats."

57   Rong-Gong Lin, "Trump administration tightens rules for federal scientists talking to reporters, *Los Angeles Times*, June 21, 2018, https://www.latimes.com/local/lanow/la-me-In-trump-policy-usgs-scientists-20180621-story.html.

58   Lin, "Trump administration tightens."

59   De Souza, "Senior bureaucrats."

60   Charelle Evelyn, "Harassment stats flat, mental health middling among federal employees: survey results," The *Hill Times*, April 11, 2018, https://www.hilltimes.com/2018/04/11/harassment-stats-flat-mental-health-middling-among-federal-employees-survey-results/140109.

61   Evelyn, Harassment stats flat."

62   Evelyn, Harassment stats flat."

63   Michael Petrou, "What happens when civil servants get partisan," *Maclean's*, November 11, 2015, https://www.macleans.ca/politics/ottawa/when-civil-servants-fail-to-appear-non-partisan/.

64   Dean Beeby, "Top bureaucrats met to resist partisanship imposed on public service," *CBC News*, November 2, 2015, https://www.cbc.ca/news/politics/top-bureaucrats-met-to-resist-partisanship-imposed-on-public-service-1.3294972.

65   Evelyn, Harassment stats flat."

66   Jordan Press, "What a federal ethics report reveals about how Justin Trudeau sees his job," *ipolitics.ca*, December 25, 2017, https://ipolitics.ca/2017/12/25/federal-ethics-report-reveals-justin-trudeau-sees-job/.

67   Press, "What a federal ethics."

68   Press, "What a federal ethics."

69   Press, "What a federal ethics."

70   Press, "What a federal ethics."

71   Press, "What a federal ethics."

72   Press, "What a federal ethics."

73 John Bowden, "Office that vets Trump appointees faces staff shortage, inexperience: report," *The Hill*, March 30, 2018, https://thehill.com/homenews/administration/381008-office-that-vets-trump-appointees-faces-staff-shortage-inexperience.

74 Bowden, "Office that vets."

75 NBC staff, "Trump's exit door: Everyone who's come and gone from the White House," March 13, 2018 with some updates thereafter, *NBC News*, https://www.nbcnews.com/politics/white-house/trump-s-revolving-door-everyone-who-s-come-gone-white-n856281.

76 Jonathan Bernstein, "Trump's White House Chaos Is Worsening," *Bloomberg*, November 16, 2018, https://www.bloomberg.com/opinion/articles/2018-11-16/trump-s-white-house-chaos-is-worsening.

77 Bowden, "Office that vets."

78 Bowden, "Office that vets."

79 Bowden, "Office that vets."

80 Evan Sotiropoulos, "A Reformed Senate as a Check on Prime Ministerial Power," *Canadian Parliamentary Review* (Spring 2008): 29., www.revparl.ca/31/1/31n1_08e_sotiropoulos.pdf.

81 Sotiropoulos, "A Reformed Senate," 29.

82 Sotiropoulos, "A Reformed Senate," 29.

83 Sotiropoulos, "A Reformed Senate," 29.

84 Sotiropoulos, "A Reformed Senate," 29.

85 Sotiropoulos, "A Reformed Senate," 29.

86 Sotiropoulos, "A Reformed Senate," 29.

87 Sotiropoulos, "A Reformed Senate," 30.

88 CTV News Staff, "Nigel Wright wrote personal cheque for $90K to repay Mike Duffy's expenses," *CTV News*, May 15, 2013, https://www.ctvnews.ca/politics/nigel-wright-wrote-personal-cheque-for-90k-to-repay-mike-duffy-s-expenses-1.1282538.

89 Marc Montgomery, "Canada's Senate: reputation, expense claims, oversight," *Radio Canada international*, November 16, 2018, http://www.rcinet.ca/en/2018/11/16/canadas-senate-reputation-expense-claims-oversight/.

90 Sotiropoulos, "A Reformed Senate," 30.

91 Sotiropoulos, "A Reformed Senate," 31.

92 Jeffrey, *Dismantling Canada*, 114.

93 Nick Taylor-Vaisey, "How to abolish the Senate of Canada," *Maclean's*, May 23, 2013, https://www.macleans.ca/politics/ottawa/how-to-abolish-the-senate-of-canada/.

94 The Canadian Press, "High court says no to unilateral Senate reform," *Maclean's*, April 25, 2014, https://www.macleans.ca/politics/ottawa/high-court-says-no-to-unilateral-senate-reform/.

95 Canadian Press, "High court says no."

96 Canadian Press, "High court says no."

97 Mark D. Jarvis, "Creating a High-Performing Canadian Civil Service Against a Backdrop of Disruptive Change," *Mowat Research #122* (June 2016): 1., https://mowatcentre.ca/wp-content/uploads/publications/122_creating_a_high-performing_canadian_civil_service.pdf.

98 Jarvis, "Creating a High-Performing," 1.

99 Jarvis, "Creating a High-Performing," 1-2.

100 Jarvis, "Creating a High-Performing," 3-4.

101 Loat and MacMillan, *Tragedy*, 65.

102 Loat and MacMillan, *Tragedy*, 65-66.

103 Loat and MacMillan, *Tragedy*, 68.

104 Loat and MacMillan, *Tragedy*, 75.

105 Loat and MacMillan, *Tragedy*, 80.

106 Loat and MacMillan, *Tragedy*, 85.

107 Loat and MacMillan, *Tragedy*, 85.

108 Whittington, *Spinning History*, 7.

109 Whittington, *Spinning History*, 7.

110 Rathgeber, *Irresponsible Government*, 20.

111 Rathgeber, *Irresponsible Government*, 21.

112 Rathgeber, *Irresponsible Government*, 62.

113 Rathgeber, *Irresponsible Government*, 66.

114 Rathgeber, *Irresponsible Government*, 125.

115 Rathgeber, *Irresponsible Government*, 127.

116 Rathgeber, *Irresponsible Government*, 127.

117 Freeman, *Democracy Rising*, 10.

118 Freeman, *Democracy Rising*, 10.

119 Jeffrey, *Dismantling Canada*, 82.

120 Jeffrey, *Dismantling Canada*, 10.

121 Loat and MacMillan, *Tragedy*, 125.

122 Loat and MacMillan, *Tragedy*, 125.

123 Michael Cooper, "How to Fix Question Period: Ideas for Reform," Excerpted from *Turning Parliament Inside Out—Practical Ideas For Reforming Canada's Democracy*, Edited by Michael Chong, Scott Simms and Kennedy Stewart (Douglas and McIntyre, 2013 Ltd., 2017 by the authors), 38-39.

124 Cooper, "How to Fix Question Period," 38-39.

125 Cooper, "How to Fix Question Period," 38-39.

126 Cooper, "How to Fix Question Period," 38-39.

127 Jeffrey, *Dismantling Canada*, 107.

128 Jeffrey, *Dismantling Canada*, 107.

129 May, "On Westminster Parliamentary Democracy," 33.

130 May, "On Westminster Parliamentary Democracy," 33.

131 Freeman, *Democracy Rising*, 63.

132 Whittington, *Spinning History*, 8.

133 Jeffrey, *Dismantling Canada*, 102.

134 Jason Kirby, "Public sector workers took a record number of sick days last year," *Maclean's*, January 10, 2017, https://www.macleans.ca/economy/economicanalysis/public-sector-workers-took-a-record-number-of-sick-days-last-year/.

135 Freeman, *Democracy Rising*, 63.

136 Jeffrey, *Dismantling Canada*, 121.

137 Jeffrey, *Dismantling Canada*, 82.

138 Page, *Unaccountable*, 54.

139 Whittington, *Spinning History*, 37.

140 Whittington, *Spinning History*, 22.

141 Michael Chong, "Rebalancing Power in Ottawa: Committee Reform," Excerpted from *Turning Parliament Inside Out—Practical Ideas For Reforming Canada's Democracy*, Edited by Michael Chong, Scott Simms and Kennedy Stewart (Douglas and McIntyre, 2013 Ltd., 2017 by the authors), 81.

142 Loat and MacMillan, *Tragedy*, 195.

143 Loat and MacMillan, *Tragedy*, 144.

144 Loat and MacMillan, *Tragedy*, 144-45.

145 Loat and MacMillan, *Tragedy*, 145.

146 Loat and MacMillan, *Tragedy*, 145.

147 Chong, "Rebalancing Power.," *Turning Parliament Inside Out*, 91.

148 Chong, "Rebalancing Power.," *Turning Parliament Inside Out*, 91.

149 Chong, "Rebalancing Power.," *Turning Parliament Inside Out*, 82.

150 Chong, "Rebalancing Power.," *Turning Parliament Inside Out*, 82.

151 Loat and MacMillan, *Tragedy*, 97.

152 Marie-Danielle Smith, "Liberals spent at least $4.1 million consulting Canadians on the electoral reform policy that would never be," *National Post*, February 5, 2017, https://nationalpost.com/news/politics/liberals-spent-at-least-4-1-million-consulting-canadians-on-the-electoral-reform-policy-that-would-never-be.

153 Prime Minister Justin Trudeau, "Minister of Democratic Institutions Mandate Letter (November 12, 2015)," https://pm.gc.ca/eng/archived-minister-democratic-institutions-mandate-letter.

154 Smith, "Liberals spent at least $4.1 million."

155 Smith, "Liberals spent at least $4.1 million."

156 Trudeau, "…Democratic Institutions Mandate Letter (November 12, 2015)."

157 Rachel Aiello, "Ministerial mandate changes include a renege on electoral reform, and dropped wording on promising to fulfill 'all' commitments," *The Hill Times*, February 2, 2017, https://www.hilltimes.com/2017/02/02/ministerial-mandate-changes-made-today-include-govt-breaking-electoral-reform-promise/94585.

158 Aiello, "Ministerial mandate changes."

159 Prime Minister Justin Trudeau, "Minister of Democratic Institutions Mandate Letter (February 1, 2017)," https://pm.gc.ca/eng/minister-democratic-institutions-mandate-letter.

160 Loat and MacMillan, *Tragedy*, 99.

161 Loat and MacMillan, *Tragedy*, 116.

162 Loat and MacMillan, *Tragedy*, 139.

163 Loat and MacMillan, *Tragedy*, 139.

164 Loat and MacMillan, *Tragedy*, 140.

165 Loat and MacMillan, *Tragedy*, 140.

166 TEDEd (Video created by GOOD Magazine), "If the World Were 100 People," https://ed.ted.com/featured/5rhHgDwh.

167 Jarvis, "Creating a High-Performing," 27.

168 Jarvis, "Creating a High-Performing," 28.

169 Jarvis, "Creating a High-Performing," 29.

170 Jarvis, "Creating a High-Performing," 29.

171 Tocqueville, *Democracy in America,* 298.

Chapter 7: Making it Work

1 Sisney, "The 5 Classic Mistakes," 6.

2 Government of Canada website, Office of the Auditor General of Canada, Who We Are, http://www.oag-bvg.gc.ca/internet/English/au_fs_e_370.html.

3 Government of Canada website, Office of the Auditor General., Who We Are.

4 Government of Canada website, Office of the Auditor General., Who We Are.

5 Government of Canada website, Office of the Auditor General., Who We Are.

6 Government of Canada website, Office of the Auditor General of Canada, What We Don't Do, http://www.oag-bvg.gc.ca/internet/English/au_fs_e_39450.html.

7 Government of Canada website, Office of the Auditor General of Canada, What We Don't Do.

8 Government of Canada website, Treasury Board of Canada Secretariat, About the Treasury Board of Canada, https://www.canada.ca/en/treasury-board-secretariat/corporate/about-treasury-board.html.

9 Government of Canada website, Treasury Board of Canada Secretariat, About the Treasury Board of Canada.

10 Government of Canada website, Treasury Board of Canada Secretariat, https://www.canada.ca/en/treasury-board-secretariat.html.

11 Government of Canada website, Treasury Board of Canada Secretariat, Organization, https://www.canada.ca/en/treasury-board-secretariat/corporate/organization.html.

12 Government of Canada website, Treasury Board of Canada Secretariat, Our History, https://www.canada.ca/en/treasury-board-secretariat/corporate/organization/our-history.html.

13 Government of Canada website, Treasury Board of Canada Secretariat, Our History.

14 Government of Canada website, Treasury Board of Canada Secretariat, Our Internal Audit, https://www.canada.ca/en/treasury-board-secretariat/corporate/organization/internal-audit.html.

15 Government of Canada website, Treasury Board of Canada Secretariat, Our Internal Audit.

16 Rathgeber, *Irresponsible Government*, 48.

17 Government of Canada website, Office of the Auditor General of Canada, Follow-up Audit on Internal Controls Over Financial Reporting, http://www.oag-bvg.gc.ca/internet/English/att_e_38843.html.

18 Government of Canada website, Office of the Auditor General of Canada, Follow-up Audit on Internal Controls.

19 Government of Canada website, Office of the Auditor General of Canada, Follow-up Audit on Internal Controls.

20 Government of Canada website, Office of the Auditor General of Canada, Follow-up Audit on Internal Controls.

21 Government of Canada website, Office of the Auditor General of Canada, 2018 Spring Reports of the Auditor General of Canada, Report 1—Building and Implementing the Phoenix Pay system, http://www.oag-bvg.gc.ca/internet/English/parl_oag_201805_01_e_43033.html?wbdisable=true#hd3c.

22 Government of Canada website, Office of the Auditor General of Canada, 2018 Spring Reports of the Auditor General of Canada, Report 1—Building and Implementing the Phoenix Pay system.

23 Kathryn May, "Clerk defends bureaucracy against accusations of a broken culture," *ipolitics.ca*, June 12, 2018, https://ipolitics.ca/2018/06/12/clerk-defends-bureaucracy-against-accusations-of-a-broken-culture/.

24 May, "Clerk defends bureaucracy."

25 May, "Clerk defends bureaucracy."

26 Emily Haws, "Public servants 'pissed' over PCO clerk's call to look at loosening rules to fire them," *The Hill Times*, June 27, 2018, https://www.hilltimes.com/2018/06/27/unions-fired-clerks-termination-comments-mps-split-loosening-rules/149267.

27 U.S. Government Accountability Office, About GAO, Overview, https://www.gao.gov/about/.

28 U.S. GAO, "GAO at a Glance," https://www.gao.gov/pdfs/about/gao_at_a_glance_2017_english.pdf.

29 U.S. GAO, GAO at a Glance."

30 U.S. Government Accountability Office, Key Issues, Overview, https://www.gao.gov/key_issues/overview.

31 U.S. Government Accountability Office, Key Issues, Overview.

32 U.S. Government Accountability Office, Key Issues, High Risk, Improving Federal Management of Programs that Serve Tribes and Their Members, https://www.gao.gov/highrisk/improving_federal_management_serve_tribes/why_did_study.

33 The Institute of Internal Auditors, *IIA Position Paper—The Three Lines of Defense in Effective Risk Management and Control* (The Institute of Internal Auditors, January 2013): 3., https://global.theiia.org/standards-guidance/recommended-guidance/Pages/The-Three-Lines-of-Defense-in-Effective-Risk-Management-and-Control.aspx.

34 The Institute of Internal Auditors, *IIA Position Paper—The Three Lines of Defense*, 2.

35 The Institute of Internal Auditors, *IIA Position Paper—The Three Lines of Defense*, 4.

36 The Institute of Internal Auditors, *IIA Position Paper—The Three Lines of Defense*, 4.

37 The Institute of Internal Auditors, *IIA Position Paper—The Three Lines of Defense*, 4.

38 The Institute of Internal Auditors, *IIA Position Paper—The Three Lines of Defense*, 4.

39 Government of Canada website, Department of Finance Canada, Frequently Asked Questions, https://www.fin.gc.ca/activity/faq1-eng.asp#1.

40 Government of Canada website, Department of Finance Canada, About the Department of Finance Canada, https://www.fin.gc.ca/afc/index-eng.asp.

41 Elise von Scheel, "'Special place in hell: Trump advisers blast Trudeau for comments at G7 summit," *CBC News*, June 10, 2018, https://www.cbc.ca/news/politics/white-house-adviser-kudlow-trump-trudeau-g7-summit-blame-1.4700061.

42 Katie Dangerfield, "Trudeau vs. Kim: Trump calls Canadian PM 'weak' and North Korean dictator 'talented,'" *Global News*, June 12, 2018, https://globalnews.ca/news/428614/donald-trump-justin-trudeau-kim-jong-un/.

43 Prime Minister Justin Trudeau, "Minister of Foreign Affairs Mandate Letter (February 1, 2017)," https://pm.gc.ca/eng/minister-foreign-affairs-mandate-letter.

44 News provided by the Prime Minister's Office, "The Prime Minister, Justin Trudeau, today announced the nomination of Yves Giroux as the new Parliamentary Budget Officer.," *CNW*, June 19, 2018, https://www.newswire.ca/news-releases/prime-minister-nominates-new-parliamentary-budget-officer-685930651.html.

45 Rathgeber, *Irresponsible Government*, 51.

46 The Institute of Internal Auditors, *IIA Position Paper—The Three Lines of Defense*, 1.

47 The Institute of Internal Auditors, *IIA Position Paper—The Three Lines of Defense*, 5.

48 Paul Proctor, "Memo to Internal Auditors: Stay Out of Risk Management!," *Gartner Blog Network*, April 8, 2013, https://blogs.gartner.com/paul-proctor/2013/04/08/memo-to-internal-auditors-stay-out-of-risk-management/.

49 The Institute of Internal Auditors, *IIA Position Paper—The Role of Internal Auditing in Enterprise-Wide Risk Management* (The Institute of Internal Auditors, January 2009): 3., https://na:theiia.org/about-us/about-ia/Pages/Position-Papers.aspx.

50 Macleod et al., *Practice Guide—Coordinating Risk management*, 9.

51 Government of Canada website, Office of the Auditor General of Canada, Who We Are, http://www.oag-bvg.gc.ca/internet/English/au_fs_e_370.html.

Chapter 8: Healing the World

1 Jeff Nilsson, "Albert Einstein: 'Imagination Is More Important Than Knowledge,'" *Saturday Evening Post*, March 20, 2010, https://www.saturdayeveningpost.com/2010/03/imagination-important-knowledge/.

2 Nilsson, "Albert Einstein,"

3   Nilsson, "Albert Einstein,"

4   Tocqueville, *Democracy in America,* 492.

5   Lauren Markham, "Opinion: Come Together," *The Globe and Mail,* November 3, 2018, O7.

6   Tanza Loudenback and Abby Jackson, "The 10 most critical problems in the world, according to millennials," *Business Insider,* February 26, 2018, https://www.businessinsider.com/world-economics-forum-world-biggest-problems-concerning-millennials-2016-8.

7   IPCC, "2013: Summary for Policymakers," In: *Climate Change 2013: The Physical Science Basis, Contribution of Working Group I to the Fifth Assessment Report of the Intergovernmental Panel on Climate Change* [Stocker, T.F., D. Quin, G.-K. Plattner, M. Tignor, S.K.Allen, J. Boschung, A. Nauels, Y. Xia, V. Bex and P.M. Midgley (eds.)]. Cambridge University Press, Cambridge, United kingdom and New York, NY, USA: 4, http://www.climatechange2013.org/images/report/WG1AR5_SPM_FINAL.pdf?utm_source=amp_eskimobi&utm_campaign=amp_organic&utm_medium=organic.

8   IPCC, "2013 Summary for Policymakers," 13.

9   IPCC, "2013 Summary for Policymakers," 15.

10 IPCC, "2013 Summary for Policymakers," 17.

11 IPCC, "2013 Summary for Policymakers," 19.

12 The Holy Father Francis, *Encyclical Letter LAUDATO SI': On Care for Our Common Home* (The Vatican: Libreria Editrice Vaticana / Vatican Press, 2015), 12., http://w2.vatican.va/content/dam/francesco/pdf/encyclicals/documents/papa-francesco_20150524_enciclica_laudato-si_en.pdf.

13 Holy Father Francis, *On Care for Our Common Home,* 12-13.

14 Matt McGrath, "Final call to save the world from 'climate catastrophe,'" *BBC News,* October 8, 2018, https://www.bbc.com/news/science-environment-45775309.

15 Holy Father Francis, *On Care for Our Common Home,* 14.

16 Holy Father Francis, *On Care for Our Common Home,* 39.

17 Holy Father Francis, *On Care for Our Common Home,* 106.

18 Holy Father Francis, *On Care for Our Common Home,* 44.

19 Holy Father Francis, *On Care for Our Common Home,* 131-132.

20 Holy Father Francis, *On Care for Our Common Home,* 135.

21 Holy Father Francis, *On Care for Our Common Home*, 128.

22 Michael Taylor, "Climate disasters cause global economic losses to soar—U.N.," *Reuters - Thomas Reuters Foundation*, October 10, 2018, https://www.reuters.com/article/us-global-climatechange-disaster/climate-disasters-cause-global-economic-losses-to-soar-u-n-idUSKCN-1MK16L.

23 A report by The Economist Intelligence Unit, *Democracy Index 2017 - Free Speech Under Attack* (The Economist Intelligence Unit, 2018): 3-5.

24 A report by The Economist Intelligence Unit, *Democracy Index 2017*, 2.

25 Achens & Bartels, *Democracy for Realists*, 137.

26 Loudenback and Jackson, "The 10 most critical problems."

27 Loudenback and Jackson, "The 10 most critical problems."

28 United Nations website, Overview, http://www.un.org/en/sections/about-un/overview/.

29 United Nations website, Democracy: Overview, https://www.un.org/en/sections/issues-depth/democracy/.

30 United Nations website, Democracy: Overview

31 United Nations website, Democracy: Overview

32 Chris McGreal, "A world of problems: the United Nations at 70," *The Guardian*, September 7, 2015, https://www.theguardian.com/world/2015/sep/07/what-has-the-un-achieved-united-nations.

33 McGreal, "A world of problems."

34 McGreal, "A world of problems."

35 McGreal, "A world of problems."

36 McGreal, "A world of problems."

37 McGreal, "A world of problems."

38 McGreal, "A world of problems."

39 McGreal, "A world of problems."

40 McGreal, "A world of problems."

41 McGreal, "A world of problems."

42 McGreal, "A world of problems."

43 McGreal, "A world of problems."

44 McGreal, "A world of problems."

45 McGreal, "A world of problems."

46 Alister Doyle, "'No follow up' from Trump over staying in climate pact," *Reuters*, May 9, 2018, https://www.reuters.com/article/

us-climatechange-accord-un-interview/no-follow-up-from-trump-over-staying-in-climate-pact-un-idUSKBN1IA2L5.

47 Anna Salleh, "Science can't solve climate change—better politics can, former IPCC scientist says," *ABC Science*, May 1, 2018, http://www.abc.net.au/news/science/2018-05-02/why-science-cant-solve-climate-change/9711364.

48 Doyle, "No follow up from Trump."

49 Mia Rabson (The Canadian Press), "Paris agreement targets leave 'alarming gap' to slow climate change: UN report," *CBC News*, October 31, 2017, https://www.cbc.ca/news/politics/paris-agreement-alarming-gap-climate-change-canada-no-plan-1.4381128.

50 Rabson, "Paris agreement targets."

51 Harris, *Party of One*, 153.

52 Harris, *Party of One*, 154.

53 Harris, *Party of One*, 150.

54 Harris, *Party of One*, 150.

55 Harris, *Party of One*, 150.

56 Harris, *Party of One*, 219.

57 Rabson, "Paris agreement targets."

58 Office of Internal Oversight Services (OIOS), *Report 2017/115: Advisory review of the implementation of the Enterprise Risk Management Policy and Procedures at the Office of the United Nations High Commissioner for Refugees* (November 2, 2017—Assignment No. VR2017/160/02): 1.

59 Office of Internal Oversight Services, *Report 2017/115*, 1.

60 Office of Internal Oversight Services, *Report 2017/115*, 1.

61 Office of Internal Oversight Services, *Report 2017/115*, 2.

62 Office of Internal Oversight Services, *Report 2017/115*, 3.

63 Office of Internal Oversight Services, *Report 2017/115*, 4.

64 Office of Internal Oversight Services, *Report 2017/115*, 4.

65 Zachary Laub and James McBride, "The Group of Seven (G7)," *Council on Foreign Relations*, Updated May 30, 2017, https://www.cfr.org/backgrounder/group-seven-g7.

66 Laub and McBride, "The Group."

67 Giuseppe Valiante (The Canadian Press), "Trudeau defends $600-million cost of Quebec G7 summit," *The Star*, May 24, 2018, https://

www.thestar.com/news/canada/2018/05/24/trudeau-defends-600-million-cost-of-quebec-g7-summit.html.

68 Valiante, "Trudeau defends."

69 Group of 77 (G-77) website, "Establishment," http://www.g77.org/doc/.

70 Group of 77 (G-77) website, "Aims," http://www.g77.org/doc/.

71 Group of 77 (G-77) website, "Joint Declaration of the Seventy-seven Developing Countries Made at the Conclusion of the United Nations Conference on Trade and Development (Geneva, 15 June 1964)," http://www.g77.org/doc/Joint%20Declaration.html.

72 Group of 77 (G-77) website, "Statement on Behalf of the Group of 77 and China by Mr. Imtiaz Hussain, Minister, Permanent Mission of Pakistan to the United Nations, on the Annual Report of the Office of Internal Oversight Services (A/62/281) Under Agenda Item 136: Report of the Secretary-General on the Activities of the Office of Internal Oversight Services, at the Fifth Committee During the Main Part of the 62nd Session of the General Assembly (New York, 10 October 2007)", http://www.g77.org/statement/getstatement.php?id=071010a.

73 Group of 77 (G-77) website, "Statement on Behalf of the Group of 77 and China."

74 Group of 77 (G-77) website, "Statement on Behalf of the Group of 77 and China."

75 Prepared by a task team led by the World Food Programme, *"Adopting an analytical framework on risk and resilience: a proposal for more proactive, coordinated and effective United nations action"* (Annex III—CEB/2017/6): 17., https://www.unsceb.org/CEBPublicFiles/RnR.pdf.

76 World Food Programme, *"Adopting an analytical framework on risk and resilience,"* 17.

77 World Food Programme, *"Adopting an analytical framework on risk and resilience,"* 17.

78 World Food Programme, *"Adopting an analytical framework on risk and resilience,"* 17-18.

79 World Food Programme, *"Adopting an analytical framework on risk and resilience,"* 23-24.

80 Chief Executives Board for Coordination, United Nations System, *Conclusions of the Thirty-Fifth Session of the High Level Committee on Management (HCLM)*, CEB/2018/3—29 May 2018 (Old Convent of

Santo Domingo, Valencia, 12-13 April 2018): 4., https://www.unsceb. org/CEBPublicFiles/CEB-2018-3-HLCM35-Report-FINAL_29%20 May%202018_1.pdf.

81 Laub and McBride, "The Group."

82 Intergovernmental Group of Twenty Four (G-24) website, History, https://www.g24.org/history/.

83 Intergovernmental Group of Twenty-Four (G-24) website, History.

84 World Economic Forum website, Our Mission, https://www.weforum.org/about/world-economic-forum.

85 World Economic Forum, Global Agenda, *World Economic Forum Annual Meeting 2018—Creating a Shared Future in a Fractured World* (Davos-Klosters, Switzerland, 23-26 January, 2018): 3. http://www3.weforum.org/docs/WEF_AM18_Report.pdf.

86 Ross Chainey, "What just happened? The biggest stories from Davos 2018," *World Economic Forum*, January 26, 2018, https://www. weforum.org/agenda/2018/01/davos-2018-biggest-stories/.

87 Ross Chainey, "What just happened?"

88 World Economic Forum, Global Agenda, *World Economic Forum Annual Meeting 2018*, 29.

89 Amanda Conolly, "Canada has 'fallen behind' in powers to do battle over privacy with tech giants: UK official," *Global News*, May 10, 2018, https://globalnews.ca/news/4199572/ facebook-cambridge-analytica-canadian-privacy-commissioner/.

90 Conolly, "Canada has 'fallen behind.'"

91 Conolly, "Canada has 'fallen behind.'"

92 World Economic Forum, Global Agenda, *World Economic Forum Annual Meeting 2018*, 29.

93 World Economic Forum, Global Agenda, *World Economic Forum Annual Meeting 2018*, 29.

94 World Economic Forum, Global Agenda, *World Economic Forum Annual Meeting 2018*, 29.

95 World Economic Forum, Global Agenda, *World Economic Forum Annual Meeting 2018*, 29.

96 Kuper, "How Greeks have adjusted."

97 Kuper, "How Greeks have adjusted."

98 Liz Alderman et al., "Explaining Greece's Debt Crisis."

99 Liz Alderman et al., "Explaining Greece's Debt Crisis."

100 European Union (EU) website, Institutions and bodies, https://europa.eu/european-union/about-eu/institutions-bodies_en#a-unique-institutional-set-up.

101 European Union (EU) website, Council of the European Union, Overview, https://europa.eu/european-union/about-eu/institutions-bodies/council-eu_en.

102 European Union (EU) website, European Parliament, Overview, https://europa.eu/european-union/about-eu/institutions-bodies/european-parliament_en.

103 European Union (EU) website, European Parliament, Overview.

104 European Commission website, Impact Assessments, https://ec.europa.eu/info/law/law-making-process/planning-and-proposing-law/impact-assessments_en.

105 Ivanka Trump, *The Trump Card: Playing to Win in Work and Life* (New York, NY: Touchstone, A Division of Simon & Schuster, 2009): 166.

106 Trump, *The Trump Card*, 166.

107 Harris, *Party of One*, 157.

Chapter 9: Technology's False Promise

1   Public Safety Canada, *National Cyber Security Strategy—Canada's Vision for Security and Prosperity in the Digital Age* (Her Majesty the Queen in Right of Canada, 2018): ii., https://www.publicsafety.gc.ca/cnt/rsrcs/pblctns/ntnl-cbr-scrt-strtg/index-en.aspx#section3.

2   Public Safety Canada, *National Cyber Security Strategy.*, 5.

3   Public Safety Canada, *National Cyber Security Strategy.*, 5.

4   Public Safety Canada, *National Cyber Security Strategy.*, 31.

5   Jonathan Taplin, *Move Fast and Break Things: How Facebook, Google, and Amazon Cornered Culture and Undermined Democracy* (New York: Little Brown and Company, Hachette Book Group, 2017), 4.

6   Taplin, *Move Fast and Break Things,* 6.

7   Taplin, *Move Fast and Break Things,* 11.

8   Taplin, *Move Fast and Break Things,* 21.

9   Taplin, *Move Fast and Break Things,* 167.

10 Taplin, *Move Fast and Break Things,* 8.

11 Taplin, *Move Fast and Break Things*, 8-9.

12 Taplin, *Move Fast and Break Things*, 9.

13 Taplin, *Move Fast and Break Things*, 9.

14 Taplin, *Move Fast and Break Things*, 9.

15 Taplin, *Move Fast and Break Things*, 9.

16 Taplin, *Move Fast and Break Things*, 79.

17 Taplin, *Move Fast and Break Things*, 80.

18 Taplin, *Move Fast and Break Things*, 80.

19 Taplin, *Move Fast and Break Things*, 80.

20 Taplin, *Move Fast and Break Things*, 80-81.

21 Taplin, *Move Fast and Break Things*, 82.

22 Joseph Pisani (The Associated Press), "Amazon received 238 proposals from Canada, U.S., Mexico for HQ2," *CTV News*, October 23, 2017, https://toronto.ctvnews.ca/amazon-received-238-proposals-from-Canada-u-s-mexico-for-hq2-1.3644676.

23 Amazon, *Amazon HQ2 RFP*, 6., https://images-na.ssl-images-amazon.com/images/G/01/.../RFP_3._V516043504_.pdf.

24 Leanna Garfield, "Chicago wants to give over $1 billion in taxes from workers at Amazon's new headquarters back to Amazon, *Business Insider*, November 27, 2017, https://www.businessinsider.com/amazon-headquarters-hq2-city-incentives-taxes-2017-11.

25 Garfield, "Chicago wants to give."

26 Garfield, "Chicago wants to give."

27 David Crane, "It's time for the Competition Bureau to turn its eyes on Big Tech," *IT World Canada*, July 27, 2017, https://www.itworldcanada.com/article/its-time-for-the-competition-bureau-to-turn-its-eye-on-big-tech/395188.

28 Crane, "It's time for the Competition Bureau."

29 Editorial Board, "Editorial: Canadians should be wary of a U.S. repeal of net neutrality," *The Gazette* (Western University's Student Newspaper), November 28, 2017, https://westerngazette.ca/opinion/editorial-canadians-should-be-wary-of-a-u-s-repeal/article_a882d85a-d47a-11e7-8287-87a4931709f8.html.

30 Emily Jackson, "Parliament enshrines net neutrality in broadcast, telecom laws," *Financial Post*, May

24, 2018, https://business.financialpost.com/telecom/
parliament-enshrines-net-neutrality-in-broadcast-telecom-laws.

31 Crane, "It's time for the Competition Bureau."

32 Jeff John Roberts, "Why Google, Facebook, and Amazon Should
    Worry About Europe," *Fortune*, July 20, 2017, http://fortune.
    com/2017/07/20/google-facebook-apple-europe-regulations/.

33 Roberts, "Why Google, Facebook and Amazon."

34 Roberts, "Why Google, Facebook and Amazon."

35 Taplin, *Move Fast and Break Things*, 115-116.

36 Taplin, *Move Fast and Break Things*, 113.

37 Taplin, *Move Fast and Break Things*, 114.

38 Taplin, *Move Fast and Break Things*, 114.

39 Taplin, *Move Fast and Break Things*, 115.

40 Taplin, *Move Fast and Break Things*, 115.

41 Taplin, *Move Fast and Break Things*, 115.

42 Cook and Real Belanger, *Canada's Prime Ministers*, 366.

43 Cook and Real Belanger, *Canada's Prime Ministers*, 366.

44 Taplin, *Move Fast and Break Things*, 116.

45 Taplin, *Move Fast and Break Things*, 119.

46 Tom Parkin, "Morneau Shepell, Sears and more—they've all forgotten
    about the little guy," *Toronto Sun*, October 24, 2017, https://torontosun.
    com/opinion/columnists/morneau-shepell-sears-and-more-theyve-all-
    forgotten-about-the-little-guy.

47 Garfield Emerson, "Weak governance in Ottawa is behind Bill
    Morneau's mess," *The Globe and Mail*, November 1, 2017, https://
    www.theglobeandmail.com/report-on-business/rob-commentary/
    weak-governance-in-ottawa-is-behind-bill-morneaus-mess/
    article36798541/.

48 Parkin, "Morneau Shepell, Sears and more."

49 Parkin, "Morneau Shepell, Sears and more."

50 Emerson, "Weak governance in Ottawa."

51 Emerson, "Weak governance in Ottawa."

52 Andy Blatchford, "Morneau at centre of fiery debate in
    Commons that leads to Tory MP's ejection," *CBC News*,
    December 1, 2017, https://www.cbc.ca/news/politics/
    morneau-fiery-debate-question-period-1.4427178.

53 Emerson, "Weak governance in Ottawa."

54 Emerson, "Weak governance in Ottawa."

55 Kevin Wack, "Fed faulted for failing to do more to prevent regulatory capture," *American Banker*, December 7, 2017, https://www.americanbanker.com/news/fed-faulted-for-failing-to-domore-to-prevent-regulatory-capture.

56 Taplin, *Move Fast and Break Things,* 127.

57 Taplin, *Move Fast and Break Things,* 128-129.

58 Taplin, *Move Fast and Break Things,* 129.

59 Taplin, *Move Fast and Break Things,* 130.

60 Taplin, *Move Fast and Break Things,* 130.

61 Taplin, *Move Fast and Break Things,* 130.

62 Taplin, *Move Fast and Break Things,* 131.

63 Taplin, *Move Fast and Break Things,* 133.

64 Taplin, *Move Fast and Break Things,* 282.

Chapter 10: The Path Ahead

1 Lee H. Hamilton, "Congress is tanking, but does it care?" *Omaha World-Herald*, March 16, 2018, http://www.omaha.com/opinion/lee-h-hamilton-congress-is-tanking-but-does-it-care/article_5e0ff546-a28e-56af-8c66-9d8d89b27d41.html.

2 Hamilton, "Congress is tanking."

3 Hamilton, "Congress is tanking."

4 Hamilton, "Congress is tanking."

5 Hamilton, "Congress is tanking."

6 Michael H Fuchs, "Forget the 'border crisis' – it is Trump's shutdown that's made us less safe," *The Guardian*, January 20, 2019, https://www.theguardian.com/us-news/2019/jan/20/forget-the-border-crisis-it-is-trumps-shutdown-thats-made-us-less-safe.

7 Fuchs, "Forget the 'border crisis.'

8 Fuchs, "Forget the 'border crisis.'

9 Fuchs, "Forget the 'border crisis.'

10 Fuchs, "Forget the 'border crisis.'

11 Cecily Hilleary, "Indigenous Peoples Stage Solidarity March on Washington," *VOA News*, January 18, 2019, https://voanews.com/a/

indigenous-peoples-stage-solidarity-march-onwashington-/4748635.html.

12 John Crace and Chris Mullin, "Is Westminster politics really a waste of time?," *The Guardian*, March 13, 2017, https://www.theguardian.com/politics/2017/mar/13/mhairi-black-westminster-waste-of-time.

13 Crace and Mullin, "Is Westminster politics."

14 Andrew Russell, "With up to $1.6B in savings, should Ontario defund its Catholic schools?," *Global News*, June 6, 2018, https://globalnews.ca/news/4247095/ontario-separate-schools-election/.

Made in the USA
Lexington, KY
01 September 2019